THE WINDSOR
TAPESTRY

BY THE SAME AUTHOR

Novels and Romances

SINISTER STREET
SYLVIA SCARLETT
GUY AND PAULINE

CARNIVAL
FIGURE OF EIGHT
CORAL
THE VANITY GIRL
ROGUES AND VAGABONDS

THE ALTAR STEPS
THE PARSON'S PROGRESS
THE HEAVENLY LADDER

POOR RELATIONS
APRIL FOOLS
RICH RELATIVES
BUTTERCUPS AND DAISIES
WATER ON THE BRAIN

VESTAL FIRE
EXTRAORDINARY WOMEN

EXTREMES MEET
THE THREE COURIERS

OUR STREET
THE DARKENING GREEN

THE PASSIONATE ELOPEMENT
FAIRY GOLD
THE SEVEN AGES OF WOMAN
THE OLD MEN OF THE SEA

THE FOUR WINDS OF LOVE:
  Book 1. THE EAST WIND OF
    LOVE
  Book 2. THE SOUTH WIND OF
    LOVE

History and Biography

GALLIPOLI MEMORIES
ATHENIAN MEMORIES
GREEK MEMORIES (withdrawn)

PRINCE CHARLIE
PRINCE CHARLIE AND HIS
  LADIES
CATHOLICISM AND SCOTLAND
MARATHON AND SALAMIS
PERICLES

Essays and Criticism

UNCONSIDERED TRIFLES
REAPED AND BOUND
LITERATURE IN MY TIME

Children's Stories

SANTA CLAUS IN SUMMER
TOLD
MABEL IN QUEER STREET
THE UNPLEASANT VISITORS
THE CONCEITED DOLL
THE ENCHANTED BLANKET
THE DINING-ROOM BATTLE
THE ADVENTURES OF TWO
  CHAIRS
THE ENCHANTED ISLAND
THE NAUGHTYMOBILE
THE FAIRY IN THE WINDOW-
  BOX

Verse

POEMS 1907
KENSINGTON RHYMES

Plays

THE LOST CAUSE

In preparation

THE FOUR WINDS OF LOVE:
  Book 3. THE WEST WIND OF LOVE
  Book 4. THE NORTH WIND OF LOVE

THE
WINDSOR TAPESTRY

BEING A STUDY OF THE LIFE,
HERITAGE AND ABDICATION OF
H.R.H.
THE DUKE OF WINDSOR, K.G.

by

COMPTON MACKENZIE

THE BOOK CLUB
121 CHARING CROSS ROAD
LONDON, W.C.2
1939

First published July 1938
Reprinted March 1939

MADE IN GREAT BRITAIN

PRINTED AND BOUND BY RICHARD CLAY AND COMPANY, LIMITED, BUNGAY, SUFFOLK,
FOR MESSRS. RICH AND COWAN, LIMITED, 37 BEDFORD SQUARE, LONDON W.C.I,
ON PAPER SUPPLIED BY GERALD JUDD, LIMITED

TO CLIO

WITH THE WILLINGNESS OF ONE WHO WAS
ALIVE WHEN THESE THINGS HAPPENED TO
ABIDE BY THE VERDICT OF HER COLD LIPS

AUTHOR'S NOTE

In view of the sensational statements which have appeared in various newspapers about this book, I feel it is right to give a brief account of the facts. What seemed to me the abominable treatment which H.R.H. the Duke of Windsor had received and was still receiving in spite of the complete self-effacement with which he had throughout recent events considered only what was best for the country drove me, after six months of rising indignation, to write with extreme diffidence and put my pen at his service in an attempt to restore a sense of proportion to one body of public opinion. The Duke graciously accepted my offer and I communicated to my publishers his assent. They at once agreed to release me from the contractual necessity of delivering the final two volumes of a four-volume novel (for the third volume of which I had already been paid) before embarking upon any other book. They were anxious, however, that the proposed book about the Duke of Windsor should be an authorised biography, and though I did not myself agree with them, knowing as I did how such a form would hamper any freedom of comment, I finally agreed to ask his Royal Highness if I might submit a full synopsis of the proposed biography. After reading this synopsis the Duke decided that the time was not yet ripe for such a book, and I fully appreciated the wisdom of his decision. I then went back to my original plan of writing a book which would allow me the freedom of comment I desired and avoid any attempt to paint an intimate portrait of the Duke himself. Unfortunately at this moment various rumours going round Fleet Street were gathered together by a Sunday newspaper and exploded like a set-piece at a firework display. The result was that the Duke's solicitors issued a formal statement that his Royal Highness did not intend to approve the contents of any biography.

There is probably no need for me to reaffirm here that I alone am responsible for the interpretation of various incidents, events and speeches, but in case any lingering doubt may exist in the minds of readers, I make that reaffirmation with all solemnity. I do not feel called upon yet to prejudice any action I may think necessary to take in the near future, by

commenting upon a recent sensational disclosure in another
Sunday newspaper. My provisional answer to that must be
the book itself.

Some people have thought that any attempt to present
recent history in a form which does not assume that everybody
except King Edward VIII himself was in the right must render
a disservice to their present Majesties. From such an
opinion I respectfully but emphatically dissent, and I will go
farther and assert that the readiness of certain interests to take
shelter behind a wish of their Majesties which has been
neither expressed nor implied, is a convenient, cowardly,
and fundamentally disloyal piece of self-protection. I cannot
accept the theory that a loyal admiration of his Majesty
must include an admiration of his Ministers, for whom
not he but a possibly misguided electorate is responsible. I
repudiate the notion that the monarchy exists to serve the
ambitions, the pretensions, or even the pure ideals of men
of state. The monarchy is still vital, and may it long
remain vital ! That the country has not gravely suffered from
the abdication of King Edward VIII is due to himself, to
their present Majesties, and to Queen Mary. In that conviction I have written this book. Had I fancied for one
moment that a presentation of the truth as I see it would
cause even displeasure let alone disservice to their present
Majesties I should never have contemplated the writing of
such a book. To accept the suggestion that an attempt by
a writer like myself to set recent events against the background of history will injure either the monarchical idea or
the loyalty and devotion of his people to King George VI
would demand an arrogance of which I hope I am incapable.

Some friends who had agreed with me that this book
should be written have urged that it should not be published
now ; but it has seemed to me fairer to anticipate what may
be the criticism of a decade hence by giving those who invited
such criticism an opportunity for self-justification now. My
sole aim has been to extract as much of the truth as can be
read between the lines of published facts, and I make no claim
to anything more. I readily admit that my chief concern
throughout has been to write nothing that would cause
embarrassment to the Duke and Duchess of Windsor, and
those who expect to find in these pages an elaboration or
extension of gossip may as well stop reading the book at this
point.

The task of collecting the material and putting it into shape in words within six months has been heavy, and it could not have been achieved without the invaluable help of Miss Joyce Weiner who has searched Parliamentary records, old and recent memoirs, and old and recent newspapers in the British Museum to provide the mass of material from which I was able to select what seemed significant for my contentions.

I might underestimate the strength of public opinion if I suggested that this book was written in the spirit of a minority report, but at least a minority report is a testimony to beliefs sincerely held and frankly expressed; in that spirit I have put my name to *The Windsor Tapestry*, and may God defend the right!

COMPTON MACKENZIE

June 23rd, 1938.

Cuidich an Righ

ACKNOWLEDGMENTS

THE author and publishers desire to express their sincere thanks to the following for their kind permission to quote :—To Mrs Clare Williams and Messrs Jonathan Cape for a passage from *Sophie In London*. To Mr Roger Fulford and Messrs Gerald Duckworth for a passage from *Royal Dukes*. To Messrs Grayson and Grayson for a passage from Mr W. Childe-Pemberton's *The Romance of Princess Amelia*. To Messrs Heinemann for a passage from *The Greville Diary*, edited by P. W. Wilson. To Messrs John Murray for passages from *The Letters of Queen Victoria*, edited by Lord Esher and A. C. Benson, from *The Girlhood of Queen Victoria*, edited by Lord Esher, from *Creevey's Life and Times*, edited by John Gore, and from *The Life of the Duchess of Teck*, by Sir Clement Kinloch-Cooke. To Messrs Longmans, Green and Mrs Winning Hunt for a passage from *The Love of an Uncrowned Queen* by the late Mr W. H. Wilkins, and to Messrs Longmans, Green for passages from *George, Duke of Cambridge*, by the late Canon Edgar Sheppard, and for numerous passages from the *Annual Register*. To the Oxford University Press and Sir George Young for a passage from *Poor Fred, the People's Prince*. To H.R.H. Prince Christopher of Greece and Messrs Hurst and Blackett for a passage from the *Memoirs of Prince Christopher of Greece*. To Messrs Putnam and Miss Genevieve Parkhurst for a passage from *A King In the Making*. To Mr Shane Leslie for a passage from *George IV*. To the Very Rev. C. A. Alington, D.D., the Rev. R. J. Campbell, the Rev. Alfred Thomas and Messrs Skeffington for passages from *Coronation Sermons for King Edward VIII*, edited by Dr Alington. To *The Times* for permission to quote as an appendix the article on the Prince of Wales at Oxford written by the late Sir Herbert Warren. And the author wishes to express his particular gratitude to the staff of the London Library for unfailing courtesy, consideration and help. Thanks are also due to the Soviet Embassy and the Hungarian Legation for information kindly afforded.

CONTENTS

CHAP.   PAGE

I.   EIGHTEEN NINETY-FOUR 11

II.   EIGHTEEN NINETY-FIVE 37

III. THE END OF THE NINETEENTH CENTURY . . . 56

IV.   KING EDWARD THE SEVENTH 71

V.   KING GEORGE THE FIFTH 88

VI.   MAGDALEN COLLEGE 101

VII. ROYALTY IN THE WAR. 121

VIII. THE FIRST TOURS 135

IX.   SERVICE OF ONE KIND AND ANOTHER . . . 154

X.   THE FIRST NATIONAL EMERGENCY 178

XI.   NEW WINE 195

XII. OLD BOTTLES 219

XIII. GEORGE I AND GEORGE II 234

XIV. GEORGE III 244

XV.   THE ROYAL MARRIAGES ACT 257

XVI. A ROYAL FAMILY 275

XVII. THE MARRIAGE OF QUEEN VICTORIA . . . 326

XVIII. THE DUKE OF CAMBRIDGE AND MRS FITZGEORGE . 340

XIX. THE CHURCH OF ENGLAND AND MARRIAGE . . 347

XX.   SUMMER 1936 404

XXI. AUTUMN 426

XXII. WINTER 458

XXIII. SPRING 551

APPENDIX 571

AUTHORITIES 577

CHAPTER I

On the warm and tranquil Midsummer Eve of the year 1894, or more precisely at ten o'clock on Saturday evening, June 23rd, a son was born at White Lodge, Richmond, to the Duke and Duchess of York, a grandson to the Prince and Princess of Wales, and a great-grandson to Queen Victoria, who a month ago had entered the seventy-sixth year of her life and a week ago the fifty-eighth year of her reign. Telegrams announcing the happy event were sent to Her Majesty at Windsor Castle, to the Prince of Wales at Coworth Park, Sunningdale, and to the Lord Mayor of London. The Minister of the Government present at White Lodge was the Home Secretary, Mr H. H. Asquith, Q.C., M.P., himself married hardly six weeks ago to Miss Margot Tennant, with Mr Haldane, Q.C., M.P., as his best man. At midnight the bells of Richmond and Kingston rang out joyful peals, and the news reached London in time for many clergymen to allude appropriately in their Sunday-morning sermons to the birth of a Prince, in which the simultaneous arrival of a spell of fine weather after a cold and showery month inspired much quotation of ' now is the winter of our discontent made glorious summer by this sun of York.'

That Midsummer Eve stands out in the memory of the present writer as the first fine Saturday of his first term at a public school; and it was spent in Richmond Park. No doubt he and his companion enjoyed the day like any other schoolboys of eleven, chasing the deer and the butterflies, arguing over birds, and lolling among the bracken; but what remains of it now most clearly is a dispute on the Terrace whether it was possible to see Windsor Castle upon that horizon whence Thames came winding through his valley down below. The writer swore he could. His companion swore he could not. Neither would yield to the other. That difference of opinion about Windsor Castle on the day King Edward VIII was born, which for forty years remained but one among many thousands of trivial recollections in the present writer's mind, has now come to seem an omen of divergent opinion.

The afternoon of that auspicious day was saddened by an explosion at the Albion Colliery near Pontypridd, South

Wales, in which 268 men and boys were killed. On the following evening in Lyons M. Sadi Carnot, the President of the French Republic, was mortally stabbed by an Italian anarchist as he was driving to attend a gala performance at the theatre. The President died three hours later in the Hôtel de la Préfecture amid the banging and whizzing of the fireworks intended to celebrate his visit. Two days after that 65,000 coal-miners in the South-West of Scotland came out on strike for an advance of a shilling a week on their wages, throwing 20,000 steel-workers out of employment in consequence.

We are inclined to look back to 1894 as a prosperous year of peace, as a year at the acme of what in a distracted period appears a golden age. Yet almost every week came news of anarchist intrigues in different parts of Europe, and even in Greenwich Park a French anarchist blew himself up in what was believed to be an attempt to blow up the Observatory. On the other hand, perhaps the prevalence of so much unco-ordinated violence was one result of that prosperous peace over Europe, like a fiery rash upon a surfeited body. But war was on the way in Asia. By the end of July Japan had attacked China, though the formal declaration of war by the Japanese would be postponed until two successful naval engagements had been fought. And two days after the birth of the infant Prince the British settlers in Pretoria were hooting President Krüger and cheering Sir Henry Loch, the British High Commissioner at the Cape.

There is a depth of tragic irony for us in Lord Rosebery's speech at the Guildhall Banquet that year :

" I have nothing to add to what I said of late of the deceased Emperor of Russia. . . . I think we may only now express the pious hope that that young head on whom has fallen the terrible responsibilities of that awful Crown—a Crown that involves so much of the destinies and the happiness of the human race—may not prove unequal to that burden. I think he must find some consolation in the universal tribute of regret, and even sorrow, with which his father's death has been received. And in that fact I think that we also, who try to look forward to the future of the human race, may find something to rejoice in too, because, after all, while it is a tribute to the Emperor, it was quite as much a tribute to peace.

" There is a character in English history—Lord Falkland, who was killed in the Civil Wars at the Battle of Newbury. . . . Though he was brave, he was constantly heard murmuring

among his companions : ' Peace, peace.' He could think of
nothing but an end of that war. Well, my Lord Mayor,
there are millions of Lord Falklands in Europe now. The one
passion, the one secret passion of every breast in the world . . .
the one passion of every disinterested bosom in this world is
for peace, industrial and international peace."

The Prime Minister took advantage of his text to rebuke a
growing tendency in the Press to print mischievous and misleading news as an example of which he cited an absurd report
that the Government of New Zealand " had some mind or
intention to administer Samoa."

The Times, however, confirmed the interview which had
given rise to this report, and politicians in New Zealand were
indignant with Lord Rosebery for assuming that they had not
discussed the occupation of Samoa. Samoa ? Robert Louis
Stevenson had been trying to put the case for the rebellious
natives, his blood tingling to the way they brought back to
him thoughts of clan battles long ago in Scotland. The
champion of the Samoans against German interference might
not have much esteemed even New Zealand interference;
but Stevenson died in the last month of 1894.

For Lord Rosebery, in spite of the difficult political team
he was driving, 1894 was a wonderful year. He had been
chosen by the Queen as her Prime Minister instead of Sir
William Harcourt when Mr Gladstone retired, and in June
he had led in his great horse Ladas, the favourite, as winner of
the Derby. Epsom had never heard such cheering. And
yet that famous victory weakened the Prime Minister's hold
on the electorate. Some of the votes lost by the Liberals at the
General Election next year were lost over that day at Epsom.
The National Anti-Gambling League formally invited Lord
Rosebery to choose between the Premiership and the Turf,
and all the heed he paid was to win the Derby next year with
Sir Visto, two months before the General Election.

Mr Gladstone at the age of eighty-four had retired on
March 3rd, and when Parliament was opened on March 12th
Lord Rosebery pronounced a moving panegyric on the old
man.

" Everyone can appreciate the greatness of Mr Gladstone's
character and attainments, but there is one aspect of his career
which makes his retirement especially pathetic and interesting
—I mean the long reach over which his recollection passes.
He heard the guns saluting the battle of Waterloo, he heard

some of Mr Canning's greatest speeches, he heard the Reform debate in 1831 in this House and Lord Brougham's memorable speech. He was, over half a century ago, the right-hand man of Sir Robert Peel's famous Government, and when to this coating of history which he acquired so long ago is added his own transcendent personality, one cannot, it seems to me, help being reminded of some noble river that has gathered its colours from the various soils through which it has passed, but has preserved its identity unimpaired and gathered itself in one splendid volume before it rushes into the sea."

And at the end of that year on his eighty-fifth birthday the Grand Old Man would be roused to all his ancient eloquence by the report of the Armenian massacres and would denounce the Sultan with as much vigour as he had denounced him eighteen years before in the hearing of Disraeli.

Few men have summed up in themselves a century of human history to the extent of Mr Gladstone; but that he should still be able to voice a passionate indignation six months after Queen Victoria's great-grandson was born seems less wonderful when we remember that the old woman who had opposed him so relentlessly through all that crowded century was just as vigorous as he, and that her apotheosis would not be attained until a June day three years hence. And as time is being spanned let us note that shortly after that infant Prince was born in Richmond the Princess of Wales sent a present of 106 shillings, one for every year of her life, to an old Welshwoman who was born six months after Prince Charles Edward died. And the old Duchess of Cambridge, wife of a son of George III and an aunt of Queen Victoria, had died only six years earlier in St. James's Palace, and she in babyhood might have been nursed by one who could remember the death of Queen Anne. Indeed, it is fair to say that the year 1894 was nearer to the eighteenth century than we are to-day to 1894 itself, ridiculous as such an assertion would have seemed to people then in their prime, people so acutely conscious of being *fin de siècle*, which at that date possessed all the significance we came to attach to the phrase ' post-war ' as the expression of a slightly feverish mental and moral condition.

This sense of having advanced out of mid-Victorianism had been sharpened by the production of such a play as *The Second Mrs Tanqueray* in which Mrs Patrick Campbell as Paula, trailing clouds of nicely concealed naughtiness from an ambiguous past, made the members of supposedly sophisticated audiences as nervous of looking round at their neighbours as an old maid who had been caught reading the *Decameron*. That was in 1893, and in 1894 the *Annual Register* records " protests in the press against the immorality of the Society drama " and observes that " the subject of debased womanhood, which has been for many years past freely dealt with in the French drama, has latterly invaded the English stage to a very large extent." This willingness to impugn the sexual morality of the French has been a constant feature of English opinion since the Roundheads slandered Queen Henrietta Maria. One hears of Queen Victoria listening entranced to Dr Norman MacLeod preaching in the 'seventies that the French defeat by the Prussians was a Divine punishment for their sensuality. And the fondness of the Prince of Wales for Paris was regarded by that class which congratulated itself on being the backbone of England as on a par with his fondness for horse-racing and gambling and smoking big cigars at half a crown apiece. The backbone of England ? The spleen rather, some will say, and like the spleen a menace to the health of the body when it becomes enlarged.

But the *Annual Register* could not blame France for the way Mr Bernard Shaw had " succeeded in puzzling a good many people as to the real intention of his so called ' Romantic Comedy ' *Arms and the Man* at the Avenue Theatre." It was well received by the audience on the first night, and at the end Mr Shaw was called upon for a speech. A man in the gallery booed his disapproval. " I quite agree with that gentleman," the author retorted blandly, " but what are two against a whole audience ? " However, *Arms and the Man* was still beyond the taste of any except a few *fin de siècle* audiences, and Mr J. M. Barrie came to the rescue of simpler souls with *The Professor's Love Story*, which was produced at the Comedy two nights after the birth of the new Prince, the author himself being seriously ill at the time.

Even the first volume of *The Yellow Book* which appeared in April was but tentatively decadent. The naughty 'nineties of that silly cliché of the twittering 'twenties were scarcely discernible in the first volume, even if Aubrey Beardsley did contribute a Night Piece of a lady of the town and Max Beerbohm write in defence of cosmetics to proclaim that " the Victorian era comes to its end and the day of sancta simplicitas is quite ended . . . the era of rouge is upon us." Woman would recover her strength with a " mask of paint and powder, shadowed with vermeil tinct and most trimly pencilled," Max prophesied, and vowed that artifice would defeat " the horrific pioneers of womanhood who had seized the tricycle and the typewriter with a view to the final victorious occupation of St Stephen's." But in the same volume Mr Arthur Waugh (father of Alec and Evelyn) was discussing the development of realism in the novel with an obvious belief that realism had already touched the boundary beyond which the novelist must not trespass. He might have accepted Mr George Moore's *Esther Waters* or the opening chapters of Mr Thomas Hardy's *Jude the Obscure* appearing in serial form that year under the title of *The Simpletons*, but nothing franker than such frankness. Women novelists, for instance, should leave to medical books the details of gestation. And after all with *The Prisoner of Zenda* and *The Jungle Book* the circulating libraries could afford to feel easy about the increase of realism among lady-novelists as they were still called sarcastically by the many.

Yes, apart from a few indications in art, literature, and drama of the moral decadence of the period, and apart from the New Woman it would have puzzled observers to discover a general decline from Victorian standards yet. Even the safety-bicycle, the most revolutionary social weapon since the steam-engine, had not yet seriously menaced man's ability to restrict the liberty of ordinary woman. Two years would pass before every girl's natural right would be a bicycle of her own on which she would ride out of reach of the domestic ties that had bound her since Eden. The New Woman was a bogey to the correct, but since the collapse of Mrs Bloomer's campaign for rational dress sixteen years earlier even the divided skirt was considered ' too much of a good thing ' for any except a few unsexed hoydens. In Paris women might be riding bicycles in knickerbockers and Norfolk jackets (with full sleeves of course, for fashion could not be entirely ignored even by the unsexed) and jaunty little Tyrolese hats perched upon their ample hair, but London was still too ladylike for that, and Englishwomen would not ride bicycles until they could ride them genteelly in long skirts. People were beginning to talk about the motor-car, but all except a very few as a form of conveyance which had as little chance as the flying-machine of becoming a common object of the countryside.

A Liberal Government was in power, which was still considered a sign of dangerous social unrest ; but not even its bitterest opponents could attach to it the stigma of being connected with the active anarchism that was prevalent. In the United States there had been fierce rioting over the railway-strike which had been savagely quelled, but in Great Britain the only sign of social disorder was a meeting of the unemployed on Tower Hill which setting out to march to Trafalgar Square was broken up by the police at Blackfriars. Lord Salisbury, whose domed head enclosed a museum of Conservative prejudice, warned the city portentously that industrial conflicts between capitalists and working-men like the coal strike in Scotland could only end in both having to give way to the foreigner. He also warned the country against tinkering with the Constitution and did not hesitate to say that if the movement against the Lords was real it was one which involved the safety of the Empire. The Commons could not be trusted alone. Such utterances float back to us from 1894 with an almost exquisite perfume of idiocy. Radicalism was still the enemy of Church and State, even, according to Lord Salisbury, of religion and civilisation. The Labour Party was not yet a threat to either. It was not yet considered a political party. When Mr Asquith went up to Huddersfield to rebuke that fickle constituency for returning a Conservative at a bye-election, a voice from the audience cried " Try a Labour man !", to which Mr Asquith replied that he objected to " Government by groups."

Still, Radicals, if not considered quite as bad as Anarchists, were ferocious fellows in 1894. In that year Sir William Harcourt initiated a revision of the Death Duties in his Budget, and there was talk of the House of Lords throwing out a Finance Bill that would add Death Duties of eight per cent on estates over a million pounds to the intolerable burden of an existing Income Tax of eightpence in the pound. Talk about the House of Lords throwing out the Finance Bill on top of the Irish Home Rule Bill provoked more talk about throwing out the House of Lords, and Mr Labouchere succeeded with the help of the Irish members, the Welsh Party, and the extreme Radicals in passing an amendment to the Address, praying her Majesty that the power now possessed by the House of Lords to prevent Bills from being submitted for the Royal approval should cease, and expressing the hope that her Majesty, with the advice of her Ministers, would secure the passing of that reform. He added that personally he was in favour of the total abolition of the House of Lords, but in

present circumstances a more simple plan would be to create
500 new peers, and thus to stew the existing lords in their own
juice.   Sir William Harcourt for the Government declined
to accept the amendment, and the division was taken just when
many members had paired for the dinner hour and therefore
could not vote.   By 147 against 145 the amendment was
carried, whereupon Mr Balfour from the Opposition benches
moved the adjournment " to enable the Government to
extricate themselves from the difficulty in which their defeat
had placed them."

The next day the Government had to abandon their own
Address because, said the Chancellor of the Exchequer, the
amendment of the member for Northampton was not drawn
up in a form or couched in language which the Government
were prepared to present to the Sovereign.   So the humiliated Government had to vote against their own Address when
it was put from the Chair, and after it had been negatived to
move a new Address which was agreed to.

As usual, with a Liberal Government in power, the Opposition devoted most of its energies to arguing that it had no
mandate from the country to grant Home Rule to Ireland.
It would be instructive to count the number of hours of Parliamentary business wasted between 1886 and 1914 in arguing
about Irish Home Rule, and melancholy to speculate how
much more serviceable to democracy Parliament might have
become if the first Home Rule Bill had been passed.   In
this year of 1894 Scottish Home Rule was being considered
seriously.

Lord Rosebery speaking amid loud applause at Edinburgh
said :

" I for one believe—I speak now not as a Minister but as a
man—that when we receive from Scotland that national demand
which appears to be ripening so fast, a national demand for that
local power of self-government which would cause the business
of Scotland, so long neglected in England, to be settled in
Scotland, I as a Minister shall not be standing to oppose you
in the breach, and, if I am not a Minister, as a man I shall hope
to be in the storming party."

And there was even talk of Welsh Home Rule.   The young
member for Caernarvon District, a Mr Lloyd George, in
trying to prove the existence of a distinct Welsh nationality,
remarked that an Act of Union had been passed between
England and Wales.   Sir Richard Webster asked him for the

date, and Mr Lloyd George replied, " Oh, certainly. It was passed in the reign of Henry VIII." This brought Mr Balfour up to pour ridicule on Mr Lloyd George's version of history. He had never heard of such an Act of Union and remembered that Mr Gladstone had once told the House that any distinction between England and Wales was " totally unknown to the Constitution." But perhaps Mr Lloyd George was thinking of Henry VIII's ' Act of Union,' in which it was set out that the " liberty and dominion of the Principality and country of Wales justly and righteously is and ever hath been incorporated, united, subject to, and under the imperial crown of this realm, and the people of the said dominion have, and do daily use, a speech nothing like nor consistent to the mother-tongue used in this country, and because some rude and ignorant people have made distinction and diversity between the King's subjects of this realm and the subjects of the said dominion, his Highness of his singular love, zeal, and affection desires to extirp all and singular Welsh usages and customs and bring about an amicable concord and unity."

As Mr Balfour sat down the whole House " gave way to an uncontrolled fit of laughter," for Mr Lloyd George thus early in his Parliamentary career had no retort with which to carry off one of his lapses in history or geography, but which with experience his deadly wit would always provide.

It was in 1894 that the first glimmer of the Entente was beheld, when the visits of the Prince of Wales to Russia for the funeral of the Czar Alexander III and the wedding of the new Czar Nicholas II produced a friendly feeling between the two countries, and the German attitude to this country became more sharply critical, seeming to apprehend a combination of Russia, France, and Great Britain against the Triple Alliance. Not that there was the smallest glimmer yet of any cordiality between Great Britain and France. The condemnation of Captain Alfred Dreyfus was a sign of nervousness across the Channel, and the French Press were accusing the British of impeding them in Madagascar in spite of their having been granted a free hand in Zanzibar. There was bad feeling too in the west of Africa between Great Britain and France over land they had both seized from the natives, and between Great Britain and Germany over the Cameroons. The war between China and Japan was causing anxiety about the future of various imperialisms in the Far East.

Nevertheless, in spite of distant war and over Europe the

edge of the shadows of coming events, the year 1894 undoubtedly does appear in retrospect from to-day ample and
leisurely as a stretch of fat grassland beside a sluggish river.
Ladies in full skirts, so full that *Punch* could make a joke about
a girl riding on the top of a bus whose skirt was pulled over his
knees by her neighbour in mistake for the waterproof apron
provided by the omnibus company . . . ladies in full sleeves
not yet ballooning to the extravagance of 1895 . . . ladies
with long-waisted corsets (the Swanbill was a fashionable
variety) tightly laced by young and old alike, and extremely
unbecoming when the whalebone was baffled by the adiposity
of middle-aged matrons. Fantastic indeed to the great
majority of such women must have seemed the big Tenniel
cartoon in *Punch's Almanack* depicting a Walpurgis-night
of wild women riding astride and hurdling and bicycling and
playing cricket and football, egged on by the conventionally
grim figure that symbolised female emancipation while diabolic
forms labelled Revolt and Demos swept across the sky
and Mr Punch as Faust gazed pensively down at the scene
from the Brocken. That threat of female emancipation certainly did preoccupy the commonplace minds of the year.
Mr Sydney Grundy satirised it in a play called *The New
Woman*, of which Mr Clement Scott wrote: " *The New
Woman* is the last institution [*sic*] that has aroused the ire of
the chivalrous Grundy, and started him off to battle against
what some think a very formidable social obstacle, and
others maintain to be a mere windmill that has deceived many
a Don Quixote as enthusiastic as a Grundy." The fine quality
of Mr Grundy's satire may be guessed from the dramatic
critic's remark that " the sudden exit of a lady-smoker was a
dangerous experiment, but it was so neatly and cleverly done
by Miss Gertrude Warden that there was ' no offence in 't '
whatever." It must have been Mrs Grundy who urged the
industrious playwright " to show up the ludicrous side of this,
the latest of the many new movements."

Another novelty which excited risibility was the fountain-
pen which though invented some years back was still in quotation marks and as one would expect the inspiration of much
witticism from the Bench when some poor devil of a scribbler
found himself in the talons of the Law ; but there was no
laughter yet at the motor-car, for in all England there was but
one, which a Mr Hewetson had brought over from France
where already a race had been held from Paris to Rouen, the

winner of which a steam-driven De Dion covered the eighty miles in five hours and forty minutes. Mr Hewetson and his Benz were ordered off the streets of London as a public nuisance. So he took his motor-car to Ireland where he was allowed to drive about unmolested, and it the horsiest country in Europe.

There were by 1894 few penny-farthing velocipedes still to be seen, but there were plenty of boneshakers with solid tyres, and pneumatic tyres were still enough of a novelty to earn derisive shouts from street-urchins of ' Yah, pneumatic tyres ! ' 1894 ! Top-hats and frock-coats everywhere. Half the hansom-cabbies wore top-hats, and eight thousand hansoms went on strike for a month because of the excessive terms charged by the masters—15s. and 17s. a day. The strike was brought to an end on June 11th when Mr Asquith who had acted as mediator pronounced his award, which was 12s. 3d. a day with a maximum of 16s. a day for five weeks of the year. Even a suburb like Notting Hill seemed very remote to a hansom-cabby in those days, and *Punch* had one of his elaborately manufactured jokes about the excuse one of them made for declining a fare to such an Ultima Thule. *Punch* could always score with a joke in which the notion of the ' lower classes ' daring to pretend to an interest in the cultural preserves of their betters was ridiculed. The same spirit of class-consciousness was apparent in the illustrated weeklies, for realism was not yet permitted to the camera, and the black-and-white artist knew how to make every Irishman look like a scoundrel and every Conservative Member the incarnation of noble wisdom and manly beauty.

So there were top-hats and frock-coats everywhere. Top-hats all along the Thames to watch Oxford beat Cambridge in the Boat Race on a glorious day in mid-March. Top-hats the same day at Queen's Club to see Oxford beat Cambridge at the Sports, to watch tall lantern-jawed sandy-haired Jordan win for Oxford from pink and chubby Fitzherbert in the first of those wonderful four quarter-mile races of which each great runner won two . . . to watch fair-haired Lutyens and Horan win the mile and three miles for Cambridge. Top-hats in July at Lords to watch Oxford beat Cambridge by eight wickets and C. B. Fry of Wadham make a hundred not out. And top-hats at Queen's Club even in December to see the two Universities play a tie at Rugby football of five points apiece. There were only nine first-class counties in the cricket championship, and the season on the whole was cold and wet with Brockwell of Surrey, the champion county, at the head of the averages. Cricket occupied a tremendous amount of attention and nobody dreamt that Association football would ever become the main preoccupation of the sporting world in England. Four three-quarters had finally ousted three three-quarters from Rugby football, but one London school—St Paul's—played three three-quarters and went through the Michaelmas term of 1894 without a point being scored against them by any other school team, for all that the other schools had come into line with progress.

The amateur championship of golf had been played for the first time out of Scotland two years earlier at Sandwich, and the game was beginning to take a firm hold of England. The golfing girl was already familiar, but by the man in the street golf was still considered a slightly eccentric amusement for rich men. Even Mr Balfour, the Leader of the Opposition, gained from his devotion to it a kind of distinction like that conferred by Mr Gladstone's collars or Mr Chamberlain's eyeglass and orchid or Lord Salisbury's roc's egg of a pate. It was an exciting event for the game in Worcestershire when Mr Balfour opened the new links at Broadway and declared in the hearing of the present writer that golf at Broadway was a mixture of deer-stalking, mountain-climbing, and a little golf. Whether Mr Stanley Baldwin, who was then a young man of twenty-six, played golf in Worcestershire is not recorded, but he was a member of the Worcestershire Cricket Club which was still among the minor counties. He was also advancing toward the management of the family ironworks, " a shy, thoughtful, somewhat prudish young man," according to the testimony of his eldest son, but not too shy to have got married two years earlier.

At Magdalen College, Oxford, was a suave young cleric of twenty-eight, the Reverend Cosmo Gordon Lang, Fellow and Dean of Divinity, Vicar of St Mary's and Examining Chaplain to the Bishop of Oxford. A few years earlier Mr C. G. Lang of Balliol, then President of the Union, had read the Prologue at the first performance of the Oxford University Dramatic Society. The Prologue in stilted heroics was written by a Mr George Nathaniel Curzon of All Souls and, to quote *The Times*, it was " fairly delivered by Mr C. G. Lang, made up as a doctor of divinity, though for what reason he was so attired was not apparent to the house." The play chosen was the *First Part of Henry IV*. Strange irony that the present Archbishop of Canterbury as an undergraduate should have anticipated his future dignity in a prologue to a play about a Prince and a circle of his friends who stood rebuked once upon a time. And stranger irony that this undergraduate should have become Dean of Divinity in 1894 at the very college which eighteen years on would be the Alma Mater of another Prince whose circle of friends would hear from him as Archbishop of Canterbury that they stood rebuked.

Long afterwards the Archbishop was to talk with the utmost charm of urbanity about his association with Oxford, when at a dinner-party given to his Grace just two months before the abdication of that Prince born on the Midsummer Eve of 1894 he observed to the present writer, his shrewd eyes twinkling, " Ah, yes, Magdalen ! Well, I always say of my association with Oxford that I regard Balliol as my Alma Mater to whose devoted care I can never be too grateful, and that I regard All Souls as a kind and loving wife and that I look back to my four years at Magdalen as four years spent with a most beautiful mistress, an enchanting liaison which ended in a parting without bitterness, after which I went back to my wife, who, ever kind and loving, forgave me for my infidelity." And as the Archbishop spoke those shrewd appraising eyes of his softened to a memory of his days at Magdalen, perhaps to the picture of himself in the pulpit of the University Church or perhaps to some golden afternoon in the Eights Week of 1894 when the hawthorn was in bloom along the Isis and the westering sun was shining on the scarlet blazer of the Magdalen cox and the three white lilies in his buttonhole as the crew rowed past the barges, head of the river for every one of those four years of his sojourn.

The other Primate was not yet even a theological student in 1894, but Billy Temple, a fat boy in jackets who would be thirteen in October. On that Midsummer Eve he would have been thinking about the end-of-the-term examinations at Colet Court, and to some purpose, for he came out top of the top class in Classics, Divinity, English and Mathematics. In French he was badly placed, as a future clergyman should be. He was living at Fulham Palace, for his father was then Bishop of London, and in September Temple Minor would join Temple Major at Rugby of which great school his father had been a headmaster second in renown only to Dr Arnold himself.

In 1894 Lord Hailsham, the Lord Chancellor of 1936, was a student of sugar-growing in the West Indies. His predecessor Lord Sankey had recently given up his post as a junior master at Colet Court, after being called to the Bar; but in that summer he was looking after a party of Colet Court boys in Brittany where among other holiday tasks he would preside over the reading by the present writer of the first book of Ovid's *Metamorphoses*. Sir John Simon was an undergraduate at Wadham College, Oxford. Sir Samuel Hoare was a model boy at Harrow. Mr Duff Cooper and Mr Hore-Belisha were in the nursery. The Bishop of Bradford was a House scholar at Marlborough. Mr Winston Churchill was at Sandhurst with a commission in the 4th Queen's Own Hussars before him next year. Mr Geoffrey Dawson (then Robinson), the Editor of *The Times*, was an undergraduate at Magdalen College. Mr Justice Hawke was a young barrister on the Western Circuit. The Editor of *The Church Times* was a young singer and actor. Mr Anthony Eden was three years from being born and Mr Malcolm MacDonald seven years from being born. Sir John Reith was a solemn bairn of five.

1894! Bolossy Kiralfy's great spectacle at Olympia, *Constantinople in London*: the arena filled with water and turned into a plausible reproduction of the Bosphorus. 1894. The Industrial Exhibition at Earl's Court. No sign yet of the Great Wheel, but the Chute for a novelty and Captain Boyton's Water Show. 1894. Concerts at Queen's Hall. The first performance in England of Dvořák's New World Symphony. The first performance in England of Tchaikowsky's Pathetic Symphony, and "a further interesting feature of the season was the reappearance of Messrs Grieg and Saint-Saëns, the gifted composers." 1894. Concerts at the Crystal Palace. On the Monday after that new Prince was born in Richmond *The Messiah* with Mme Albani, Miss M. Mackenzie, Mr Ben Davies, and Mr Santley as the chief soloists. 1894. The thirty-sixth series of Chamber Music 'Pops' at St James's Hall with a first performance of "two pianoforte sets lately written by Herr Brahms." 1894. Several novelties for Sir Augustus Harris's grand-opera season at Covent Garden, including Puccini's *Manon Lescaut* and Verdi's *Falstaff* first produced at Milan the previous year. Calvé in *Carmen*. Melba and Jean de Reszke in *Faust*. 1894. At the recently opened Daly's Theatre, *Twelfth Night* with Ada Rehan as Viola. Then Duse in several plays. Then Sarah Bernhardt in *La Tosca, Phèdre, La Dame Aux Camélias* and the rest of them. And Humperdinck's new opera *Hänsel und Gretel* in the autumn. What a season for a new theatre! 1894. At the Gaiety *A Gaiety Girl* with its famous *pas de quatre* gives way to *The Shop Girl* after Réjane has enchanted London for a brief season as Madame Sans-Gêne. *The Derby Winner* is the Drury Lane melodrama. *Charley's Aunt* produced in 1892 is still running at the Globe, and the *Daily Telegraph* with half a million readers proclaims everywhere on posters that it has the largest circulation in the world. The *Daily Mail* was two years away from being born to pull down that circulation, but there were nine evening newspapers of which all but three then alive are now dead.

1894! Lavender girls still cry their wares at summer's dusty end. Sweeps hidden in wicker-cages decked with boughs still go dancing and whirling down the sedate terraces of Kensington on May Day morning. Fantastic beggars fit for Dickens still haunt the streets. The muffin man's tempting bell may still be heard on foggy winter afternoons. Gipsy caravans are frequent, with befeathered brunettes in bright shawls selling brushes and brooms and slim dapper slant-eyed men sitting on the kerb to mend cane chairs. Still heard is the cry of ' Cherry Ripe ' in high summer, and the sizzle of the knife-grinder's whetstone, and the hurdy-gurdy man's melancholy tune. There is a crossing-sweeper at every other street corner. There are window-boxes full of flowers in every house. And if one listen at night from an open window on a quiet square the noise of the London traffic is like the distant boom of the Atlantic Ocean along a desolate coast.

For such a period royalty kept most of its old glamour, and that without the aid of the semi-hysterical Press adulation of to-day. Of course, even royalty sometimes behaved oddly. In the very first week of the year 1894 Princess Elizabeth of Bavaria eloped with a young officer, Baron von Siefried, and successfully hid herself with him in some Swiss fastness. However, as it was not a British princess who had eloped the British Press condescended to sympathise. The elopement according to the *Illustrated London News*

. . . caused a terrific commotion in what Jeames calls the " hupper suckles " of Bavaria, and it is not improbable that several Court chamberlains and ancient duennas have actually died of the shock.

To the world which does not live on etiquette, the runaway Princess is the most interesting figure Bavaria has produced for years. She has done marvels for that element of romance which, as a rule, is sadly lacking in royal marriages, and which makes dynasties passably human when it gets the chance. Bavaria has had a ruler who went mad about music and drowned himself, but an eloping lady is more romantic than a lunatic prince.

Contemporary references to royalty in such a strain are frequent at this date. The Liberals were in power, and that *fin de siècle* feeling had made journalists a little world-weary. Moreover, they had not completely recovered from the pleasure of being able to read stern lectures in the best Telegraphese, as superior people in 1894 called that kind of thing in newspapers, to the heir apparent, who three years earlier had been dragged into the Tranby Croft baccarat scandal.

Quoth *The Times* on June 10th 1891 :

> If the Prince of Wales is known to frequent certain circles, and to eschew others with a greater national claim upon the notice of Royalty; if he is known to pursue on his private visits a certain round of questionable pleasures into which other people, perhaps young people, are often drawn against their will from mere complaisance, the serious people—who, after all, are the backbone of England—regret and resent it.

Quoth the *Daily News :*

> The pity of it all is in the presence of the Heir to the Throne at the head of the baccarat table. . . . The Prince of Wales is bound to a pure, a simple, and a cleanly life as vigorously as if the obligation were set down in some constitutional pact. . . . Woe to the monarchy when it can no longer perform what may fairly be called its last surviving use.

Quoth the *Daily Chronicle* :

> The readiness of the Prince of Wales to dispose of himself as "a prize guest," to use Lord Coleridge's phrase, in rich but vulgar families, where his taste for the lowest type of gambling can be gratified, even at the cost of dishonouring the proudest names in the country, has profoundly shocked, we may even say disgusted, the people who may one day be asked to submit to his rule.

Quoth the *Liverpool Courier* :

> It was pure gambling in the vulgar sense. It is surely an unedifying spectacle to see the Prince of Wales, the future King of England, officiating as ' banker ' at such a gamblers' orgy—shuffling the cards for five-pound notes.

Quoth the *Nottingham Express*:

> The British Empire is humiliated, and the rest of civilisation is pointing a finger at us.

Quoth the *Dundee Advertiser*:

> The Prince of Wales is evidently not what, with such a destiny before him, he ought to be.

Hoity-toity! After these unctuous effusions of cant it is a relief to read some common sense from James Payn in the *Illustrated London News*:

> It would be extremely satisfactory if all our Royal Highnesses should, after 'office hours,' sit down with wet towels (instead of coronets) round their brows and apply themselves to the study of " the Hundred Best Books," but if the reader or I had passed our day in laying foundation-stones, and our evening in making speeches at a public-dinner, there is no knowing to what form of relaxation we might be driven. It is curious, considering the number of charitable societies, how very little charity there is in Society.

One is glad to read that the verdict was hissed in Court, and that the victorious defendants in the libel action were hooted to their carriages by the public; but reading that paragraph about the elopement of Princess Elizabeth of Bavaria one asks what would have been the comment on an elopement in the Royal Family of Great Britain. In any case there had been no lack of tragic romance in the Bavarian house without an eloping princess. There was another Bavarian Elizabeth, cousin of the mad Ludwig, who in 1894 was still wandering unattended about Europe, Empress of Austria. Slender and tall and beautiful and still youthful-seeming when over fifty, she found that solitude not in the palace she had built herself in Corfu, not in the mountains of Central Europe, but in places like the beach at Cromer where she would sit scribbling in a notebook on the sands hard by the old jetty, and if people stared too hard raise a parasol or fan against curiosity. The picture of her in the sunlight of a June day in a dust-coat of fawn-coloured silk, of her fan and her white parasol, is still vivid, though nearly fifty years have passed since the writer saw her sitting on the sands at Cromer.* Her son, the

---

* Since writing that, confirmation of the recollection has been found in Count Corti's *Elizabeth, Empress of Austria*: " From Hamburg Elizabeth went on to England, where she stayed at Cromer in Norfolk for the sea-bathing. At the end of July she wrote to her husband that she was going on a visit to the

Habsburg heir, shot himself.   Her cousin, the mad Ludwig,
drowned himself.   She used to commune with him on the
romantic Island of Roses in Lake Starnberg, and remained
except Wagner his only friend even when he had cruelly jilted
her own younger sister Sophie.   Three years after 1894
that sister, the Duchess of Alençon, would be burned to death
at a charity bazaar in Paris in a conflagration started by one
of the first films exhibited; and a year after that the Empress
Elizabeth would walk for a hundred yards with an assassin's
file in her breast to go on board the steamer at Geneva she
was taking for Montreux, none knowing she had been mortally
wounded until she fell in death.

And there had been a hint of tragic romance when the
Duke of Clarence, the elder son of the Prince of Wales,
betrothed to Princess May of Teck, died in January 1892
and the next year Princess May married his brother, then
Duke of York.   When the news of the second betrothal was
first announced popular sentiment received a shock and for
a while there was an inclination among the general public to
criticise; but popular sentiment was not proof against the
charm of the beautiful Princess May, so much more beautiful
than any of the contemporary pictures of her convey, and by
the day of the wedding in July 1893 there was nobody who
did not agree with Queen Victoria herself that it was a perfect
match.*   Probably the chief inspiration of popular criticism
had been a rumour that the Duke of York when serving in
the Navy had married morganatically in Malta a daughter of
Admiral Sir Michael Culme-Seymour.   So persistent was this
rumour that after King George V ascended the throne an
action had to be brought in 1911 to dispose of it once and
for all.

There had been a genuine morganatic romance in Princess
May's family.   In the year 1835 Duke Alexander of Würt-

Queen in the Isle of Wight, shortly after which she would be coming home;
to which he replied : ' *Edes, Szerett Letkem* [Dear, beloved soul], my infinitely
beloved angel, your dear letter made me very happy, for it was another proof
that you are fond of me, and are glad to come back to us. . . . '

" . . . At Kreuth, too, Elizabeth read Valérie [her daughter] the poems she had
written at Cromer, and her daughter was amazed at the ease and copiousness
with which Elizabeth composed verse."

* It is worth noting from Sir George Arthur's *Seven Heirs Apparent* that
" in the spring of 1893, Mr Gladstone sought an audience of the Sovereign and
voiced the popular desire—which for dynastic reasons was beginning to be
clamorous—that his [Edward VII] surviving son should marry and should
marry no other than the Princess Victoria Mary. . . . "

temberg, nephew of the Emperor, met at a ball in the Imperial Palace at Vienna a beautiful and gifted young Hungarian woman, Countess Claudine Rhédey, the daughter of László Rhédey, the last direct male descendant of an ancient Hungarian family which could trace its ancestry back to the year 1001.

The Rhédeys were related to all the great noble families of Hungary and Transylvania, and after the Reformation they had been stalwarts of Protestantism. Duke Alexander fell in love with Countess Claudine and she with him, but because, however ancient her family, she was not of royal birth she could not take his rank nor could her children count in the succession to the throne of Württemberg. So Duke Alexander married Countess Claudine morganatically on May 2nd 1835, and the Emperor a few days later created her Countess Hohenstein. There were three children. Princess Claudine the eldest did not marry. Princess Amélie the youngest married an Austrian cavalry officer, Baron Paul von Hügel. The boy became Francis, Duke of Teck, who in 1866 married Princess Mary Adelaide of Cambridge, their eldest child born at Kensington Palace on May 26th 1867 being Princess Victoria Mary Augustine Louise Olga Pauline Claudine Agnes. Then she became Princess May; then Duchess of York; then Princess of Wales; then Queen of Great Britain and Ireland; and finally Queen Mary. Her grandmother the lovely Countess came to a tragic end. On October 1st 1841 she was present on horseback with her husband Duke Alexander at a military review in Vienna. The horse bolted and threw her, and she was trampled to death by a squadron of cavalry. There is a tablet * to her memory in the church in Erdö-Szent György where she used to worship, placed there by her granddaughter Queen Mary when she first became Princess of Wales. That church has been in Roumania since the Peace of Versailles.

* TO THE MEMORY OF

COUNTESS CLAUDINE RHÉDEY,

COUNTESS HOHENSTEIN

WIFE OF H.R.H. PRINCE ALEXANDER OF WÜRTTEMBERG

DIED IN 1841.

ERECTED BY HER GRAND-DAUGHTER

VICTORIA MARY, PRINCESS OF WALES

Just before the war the writer was talking to an old Chamberlain of the Württemberg Court, who told him what an enchanting impression Princess May had made upon him when as a girl of sixteen or seventeen she used to visit the Court at Stuttgart. " She was so full of spirits always. She would hide behind a pillar at a Court ball and put out her foot to trip up some pompous functionary. Ach, it was very amusing." That would have been in 1883 or 1884. Her grandfather Duke Alexander was still alive. Did he see in his granddaughter something of his lovely bride of nearly fifty years earlier? In spite of the scepticism of journalists in 1894 there can be a good deal of romance in royal marriages.

There was a royal marriage at Coburg in 1894. The Duke of Edinburgh had succeeded in the previous year to the Duchy of Saxe-Coburg-Gotha, and on April 19th his second daughter, Princess Victoria Melita was married to the Hereditary Grand Duke Ernest-Louis of Hesse, another grandchild of Queen Victoria. The old lady who had been spending the early spring in Florence went herself to Coburg for the ceremony. So did the Prince of Wales. So did the Kaiser. So did the Empress Frederick. So did the Czarevitch. It must have been a wonderful occasion for the old Queen, surrounded by children, grandchildren, and even a great-grandchild, Princess Feodora of Meiningen who was old enough to be one of the bridesmaids. She had a special suite for herself in Schloss Ehrenberg where she found tastefully collected souvenirs of her youth including a picture of herself with the Prince of Wales aged eight, and Prince Alfred aged six holding a butterfly for his mother to admire, her arm round his neck. She and the late Duke, that clown from Coburg as Prince Alexander of Hesse called him *
when he was preparing to march with Prussia against Austria, had not agreed too well in later years ; but that April she must have looked back close on sixty years to when Uncle Leopold, the King of the Belgians, had arranged for his young nephews to visit England for the first time. She had had no doubts even then which she preferred. Albert was extremely handsome, which Ernest certainly was not, but he had a most good-natured honest and intelligent countenance. She had gone with them to see *I Puritani* at the opera, and as like herself they were excessively fond of music, they were in perfect ecstasies. Thus she had written to Uncle Leopold on May

* *Downfall of Three Dynasties*, Count Egon Corti.

23rd 1836.   She must have been thinking much of Albert now and of the days they spent at Rosenau in 1845, exploring together the haunts of his boyhood.

Wearing the ribbon of the Garter and a crown of diamonds the old Queen had watched the marriage ceremony and the departure of the seventeen-year-old bride who was wearing a dress of powder blue, the skirt and bodice embroidered with tapering sprays of rosebuds and forget-me-nots in silk, the dainty little pélerine, which was embroidered to match, having tiny shoulder-capes formed of powder-blue silk fringes. Showers of rice were thrown over the young couple, the " foremost in observing this traditional custom being the Emperor William, the Prince of Wales, and the Duke of Connaught." And on the following day the Kaiser officially announced to the Queen that another grandchild, Princess Alix of Hesse, sister of the bridegroom, was betrothed to the Czarevitch. But Coburg was crossed by malefic stars that April, for when the new Czar would interrupt the mourning for his father to wed Princess Alix in November what a doom hung over them thirty-five years away!   And the childless marriage between the Grand Duke Ernest-Louis and his Grand Duchess would be dissolved in 1901.   Four years later she would be married to the Grand Duke Cyril who in course of time and massacre would himself become the legitimist Czar.   And Ernest-Louis would also marry again in 1905 Princess Eleonore of Solms-Hohensolms, and it would be his eldest son George and his daughter-in-law Princess Cecilia of Greece who with his two eldest grandchildren would be killed in an air accident on the way to the wedding of his second son Prince Louis with the daughter of Sir Auckland Geddes.   Yes, some consequence yet hanging in the stars did bitterly begin his fearful date with that day's revels.

On the very day after the Coburg wedding some of the Radicals in the House of Commons moved a second reduction in the already reduced annuity of £10,000 granted to the Duke of Coburg on the grounds that he was no longer a British Prince. In the previous year Mr Gladstone had spoken warmly against depriving the Duke of Edinburgh of his entire annuity, and indeed when the old man handed his resignation to the Queen at Windsor Castle on March 3rd after over fifty years of public service all that the old lady said in gratitude to the man who had done most to keep her on the throne was a murmur of thanks for " a service of no

B

great merit in the matter of the Duke of Coburg." There was " not one syllable on the past." *

Sir William Harcourt on behalf of the Government again strongly opposed the motion, and " threw out a sort of half-suggestion " that the Opposition should come to the Government's rescue. Whereupon Mr Balfour " made a hearty response to this appeal." " To wrangle over every sixpence that is paid to keep up the dignity of the Crown is to show that we are, indeed what we have often been called, a nation of hucksters and shopkeepers." (*A. R.*)

But the fiercest champion of royalty that day was Lord Randolph Churchill. He became almost incoherent under emotion, and startled members by telling Mr Labouchere that if Mr Gladstone had been in the House he would have given him a good " towelling." It was some time before members grasped that Lord Randolph meant the equivalent of a beating. He spoke of the Duke of Edinburgh's services to the country over thirty years, of his farewell last year to Devonport where he had been Admiral commanding, and reminded the House that his annuity had already been cut down from £25,000 to £10,000. Owing to his devoted attention to the Navy the country was less familiar with him than with the rest of the Royal Family, but no member of it had worked harder than he.

The resolution was defeated by 298 votes to 67. Forty-two years later Lord Randolph's son would willingly have risen again in that House, which had hooted him down a few days earlier because it suspected him of conspiracy with the ex-King to override Parliament, to plead for material recognition of that ex-King's services to the country; but forty-two years later Mr Baldwin would have succumbed to the mere threat of Labour opposition, a much milder force than the Radical Opposition of 1894, and refuse even to discuss an annuity to a King who had given up his throne because he thought it was his duty to his country to do so.

The hostility that undoubtedly existed in Great Britain to the notion of paying an annuity to a Prince who was henceforth to rule in Germany owed little to republican sentiments. It was based on the old resentment against the Germanic orientation of the British Royal Family since it had been imported into the country on the death of Queen Anne. Albert had suffered from that hostility throughout his Consortship. The

* Morley's *Life of Gladstone*, iii. 513, 514.

marriages of Princess Louise to the Marquess of Lorne and of the Prince of Wales's daughter to the Duke of Fife had been welcome to the country, but the system of intermarriage by which Catholic and Protestant royalty maintained the caste without regard to the obvious signs of degeneration still prevailed, and this system was growing obnoxious to the pioneers of a new age. The innumerable minor German royalties which were hanging like Christmas-tree ornaments on the oaken family-tree of the Royal British stock irritated people. Moreover, at the back of most minds was the growing conviction that sooner or later there would have to be a struggle to the death between Britain and Germany. There was no notion yet of an alignment with France and Russia. Writers like Rudyard Kipling were still trumpeting their alarm at the Russian Bear as loudly as the Jingoes of the 'seventies. Probably the majority pictured the war as a war with all the other nations looking on. And there was a general feeling that after Prussia's treatment of Denmark, Austria, and France this new Prussianised Germany wanted a lesson. Even if she had been a German the Princess of Wales would have been greatly loved by the people of Great Britain, but her being Danish added something to her charm and beauty. And not the least element in the popularity of the Prince of Wales was a reputed dislike of some of his German relations. It was considered significant that he had been anxious to attend the funeral of the assassinated President of the French Republic in Paris, although influence was exerted to dissuade him from doing so. The Kaiser, possibly divining the direction of his uncle's inclinations, released two French officers, who in the previous year had been sentenced to long terms of imprisonment for espionage, as a practical demonstration of his sympathy with France in her bereavement. The act gave him a brief popularity in Paris.

Over in Germany there was no failure to appreciate the British attitude toward their ever-growing power. The succession of a British Prince to the throne of Coburg led a Deputy to ask in the German Parliament whether " the Federal Government deemed it consistent with the interests of the German Emperor that a Prince of the German Federation should be at the same time a subject of another State. Remarks humiliating to German national feeling had been made in the English Parliament. His Highness should renounce his British nationality, and it was unfortunate he had not done so." (*A. R.*) Count Caprivi the Chancellor in replying declared that whether or not as the son of the Prince Consort who had retained his German nationality the Duke had at any time ceased to be a German was immaterial. From the moment he became the lawful sovereign of Coburg-Gotha he recovered his German nationality. Fortunately the new Duke of Saxe-Coburg-Gotha was not called upon to declare himself under the test of war. He would die six years later without a son, and the German Duchy refused by the Duke of Connaught would pass to the posthumous son of Queen Victoria's youngest son the Duke of Albany who when war did come would, against his heart's desire, return every British decoration and fight actively for Germany.

That September the Kaiser by his rebuke of the dignitaries and nobles of East Prussia gave a demonstration of the way Germans liked to be governed.

" It has been brought home to me, to my profound regret, that my best intentions have been misunderstood and in part disputed by members of the nobility. . . . Even the word ' opposition ' has reached my ears. Gentlemen, an opposition of Prussian noblemen directed against their King is a monstrosity. . . . I, like my imperial Grandfather, hold my kingship by the grace of God." (*A. R.*)

And a month later he was declaring:

" The Army remains the only firm pillar, and therefore we must stand by it."

Then in reply to a speech by the Burgomaster of Thorn, a city in Posen which had been wrenched from the Poles at the final partition of that country, he said:

" I have learned that your Polish fellow-citizens here, unfortunately, are not behaving as might be desired and expected. I may tell them that they may reckon on my favour and interest in the same measure as the Germans only if they feel absolutely as Prussian subjects." (*A. R.*)

And Bismarck spoke against any conciliation of the Poles trodden down under the jackboot of Germany:

" Alsace will never be surrendered until the Army is lost, and just as little can Posen be given up. Not only the watch on the Rhine but the watch on the Vistula must be maintained." (*A. R.*)

In Russian Poland the inhabitants were even worse off. At the end of 1893 an order had been made forbidding the speaking of Polish in the Vilna district and closing all the

Roman Catholic churches. The peasants of Kroze in their anxiety to preserve their church from desecration occupied it and barred themselves in. Sixty-nine were killed by Cossacks; peasants of both sexes were stripped and knouted, and the women and girls outraged. In 1894 the survivors were tried for resisting the troops, and sentenced to terms of imprisonment from four months to hard labour for ten years. In 1894 there were horrible revelations of the condition of the convict prisons in Siberia, and at the funeral in Moscow of a political prisoner who had died of consumption brought on by lying on wet straw a man suddenly sprang upon a neighbouring grave and delivered an impassioned revolutionary speech the like of which had not been heard in Moscow for fifteen years. Such was the sympathy of his audience that he was able to leave the cemetery a free man.

The Czar Alexander died on October 21st, and the first month of the new Czar's reign seemed to augur a more liberal policy. He caused much enthusiasm in Petersburg when on his marriage day he drove slowly down the Nevsky Prospect without the escort of a single soldier. He also showed marked favour to the Polish deputations and recalled the existing Governor whose brutality for twelve years had been ruthless. Finally the visits of the Prince of Wales both for the funeral and the wedding kindled a friendly warmth, and Queen Victoria made the Czar Honorary Colonel of the Scots Greys. One asks why the Queen chose that particular regiment. Did she suppose the headdress of those dragoons had a Russian note?

Between the birth of the baby who was one day to be king and his christening on July 16th the Tower Bridge was opened by the Prince of Wales, and a Polar expedition left Greenhithe, financed by young Mr Alfred C. Harmsworth who after his success with *Answers* had recently bought the derelict *Evening News*. So little known generally was he that the *Annual Register* of 1894 called him Mr G. Harmsworth.

The day of the christening was wet; but Queen Victoria accompanied by the Czarevitch, Princess Alix of Hesse, and various royal relatives drove from Windsor to Richmond with an escort of the 8th Hussars. At White Lodge the Queen and her party were met by a large gathering of royalty with which were Lord Salisbury and Lord Rosebery. There were no guests from the House of Commons.

In the window of the drawing-room was a pedestal covered

with red cloth on which stood the golden bowl that was always used for the christening of royal infants born in England. The Queen and the Duchess of York were seated. The others remained standing. The baby Prince was brought in by his nurse, who handed him to Lady Eva Greville, who handed him to the Queen. From her arms Dr Benson the Archbishop of Canterbury received the baby and with the assistance of the Queen's favourite clergymen, Dr Davidson the Bishop of Rochester, Canon Dalton and Mr Carr-Glyn performed the rite of baptism, giving the Prince the names Edward Albert Christian George Andrew Patrick David. The godfathers and godmothers present were the Queen, the Prince and Princess of Wales, the Czarevitch, the Duke of Cambridge, and the Duke and Duchess of Teck. Other royalties present were proxies for the King and Queen of Denmark, the Queen of the Hellenes, the King of Württemberg, and the Duke of Saxe-Coburg and Gotha. After the ceremony the Queen took tea with the Duchess of York and later was photographed with the Prince of Wales, the Duke of York, and the baby. The other guests took tea in a marquee on the lawn. The christening-cake in a silver tray wreathed with flowers was five feet two inches in circumference decorated with the Royal arms, the arms of the Duke of York, and the arms of Edinburgh where it had been baked. On top of the cake which was two feet six inches high was a cradle of white satin and lace on which reposed a sugar crown, and against which rested crossed a little silken Royal Standard and Union Jack.

The laced-in Royal ladies; the frock-coats of the men; the preposterous furniture, which included two life-size negresses in bronze holding up trays of fruit, and a Kentia palm in a ghastly vase; the bald dome of Lord Salisbury's head; the white Dundreary whiskers of the Duke of Cambridge; those Royal cousins, the Duke of York and the Czarevitch, both so strangely alike outwardly but inwardly so different; no hint of a Rasputin in those urbane well-washed English clergymen, —and the cynosure of some thirty august personages gathered on that July day a baby not yet a month old, who will outlive them all in the warm chronicles of the human heart.

CHAPTER II

EIGHTEEN NINETY-FIVE

HOWEVER innocent of revolutionary activity, apart from outbreaks of anarchist violence, the year 1894 may seem to the present, there is no doubt that the country as a whole was uneasily aware of change in the air, and we must recognise that the result of the General Election in the summer of 1895 was fundamentally due to that malaise. At the time, the obvious explanation of the heavy defeat of the Liberals was internal dissensions within the party and the loss of Mr Gladstone's magical prestige as a leader. An examination of the total poll might declare the collapse of Liberalism more apparent than real, for it revealed that a shifting of 221,059 votes in Great Britain had been sufficient to change a Liberal majority of 43 into a Unionist majority of 152. The sum total of votes cast (including Ireland) showed an insignificant surplus of 31,688 for the Unionists, but nevertheless provided the new Government with the largest majority in the House enjoyed by any party since the first application of the Reform Bill in 1832. Yet the mood of discouragement in progressive circles was acute. The only member of the late Government who refused to be unduly depressed was Sir Henry Campbell-Bannerman. He looked at the figures and decided that if everybody had their rights the Unionist majority of 152 should be no more than a bare majority of 14.

But that mood of discouragement must have reflected a prevailing mood throughout the country which it might be flattering to call an attitude of mind. Certainly it was a sadly disheartened Liberal Party which faced the task of opposition for what was to be a whole decade. Moreover, the advanced Radicals of 1894 had been driven into a realisation that Gladstonian Liberalism was dead. The Grand Old Man had grown steadily more and more Radical all his life. Age alone set a limit to his own political growth when the arteries of most of his supporters had hardened long ago. Could he have been granted a more miraculous extension of his physical energies he would probably have discovered a way of fostering the growth of the Labour Party to achieve a perfect unanimity with advanced Radical opinion. As it was, the Labour Party developed on almost exclusively Trade Union lines and by its preoccupation with a partial democracy prepared the way for the fiasco of the General Strike of 1926 and those humiliating experiences of government in 1924 and 1929–31.

It would be extravagant to suggest that the lamentable Oscar Wilde case played any part in the collapse of Liberalism ; but it undoubtedly did a great deal to fix in the mind of the average man a profound conviction that he had been right to suspect all this much-advertised cleverness as nothing better than gilded immorality. The mood in which the electorate at Mr Baldwin's prompting would one day suspect the dynamic force of Mr Lloyd George as an influence making for general moral deterioration, and the mood in which the country not without Mr Baldwin's connivance would one day suspect the dynamic force of a King had an emotional affinity with this mood of 1895. Politicians (Radicals of course like Dilke and Parnell) who found themselves in the Divorce Court, an heir apparent who was involved in a gambling scandal, a prime minister who led in two Derby winners, and now a famous dramatist sentenced to two years' hard labour for an offence unmentionable in conversation but with that strange Victorian logic of morality printable in detail in the newspapers . . . it was time to cry a halt to anything which would even indirectly encourage these loose modern notions. Luckily for the Feminist Movement, in spite of a horde of shameless lady-novelists, none of its champions was involved in a moral disaster. Indeed, some of the leading feminists were making their voices heard on behalf of decency. Mrs Ormiston Chant had been the leader of the campaign against the living pictures at the Empire Theatre. To this was added a denunciation of the Empire Promenade, which paradoxically (if there was ever sometime a paradox in British puritanism) secured less support. In this not unexciting zest for morality the poster of a new musical comedy called *The Artist's Model* produced at Daly's Theatre was denounced as salacious. The poster represented a young woman, with bare arms, legs bare not quite so far as the knee and much less bareness of neck than was allowed in every evening *décolleté*, hiding the rest of her nudity behind a palette almost as large as herself. Of the play itself London's leading dramatic critic wrote :

> Because one or two lines of questionable character will cause a laugh in a frivolous piece, because we are all tired of jests about mothers-in-law and drink, the writer of the book seems to have assumed that a long series of jokes that would not pass in a drawing-

room ought to catch the public taste. It happened, however, that though the people in the stalls appeared to take pleasure in his not very ingenious efforts at what may be called " boulevard " humour, others in the house after a while grew sick of it and protested. . . .

Nevertheless, *The Artist's Model* was a popular success. That poster was irresistible. Early in the year Henry James's play *Guy Domville* was produced at the St James's Theatre and was the scene of an astounding display of barbarism by the audience on the first night. Poor old Henry James was brought on to take a call and was made the object of an hysterically hostile reception, presumably because of his play's lack of dramatic interest. The play certainly was dull, but what chiefly infuriated the pit and gallery was the way a young cousin of Mr Stanley Baldwin's, seated in a box, turned his back on the stage and clapped with defiant persistency at them. The behaviour of the actor-manager was nearer to a politician's sense of popular esteem than that of the young man in the box. George Alexander repudiated his author who was standing beside him in miserable bewilderment, and apologised to the audience for producing the play.

Guy Domville was succeeded after a few days' run by Oscar Wilde's play *The Importance of Being Ernest*, which was in the middle of a brilliant success when the author brought his fatal suit for criminal libel against Lord Queensberry. *The Importance of Being Ernest* was taken off after the unhappy author was sent to Reading Gaol in May. It was kept running during the case, but the theatre compromised with public opinion by obliterating the author's name from all the playbills. One had hoped that such cowardly hypocrisies were dead, but they would be flourishing forty years on.

It was with no intention of rebuking the public that *The Importance of Being Ernest* was succeeded by Henry Arthur Jones's play *The Triumph of the Philistines*, which deservedly failed. And this unlucky year at the St James's Theatre culminated in a tragi-comic episode when a Mrs Ebb-Smith committed suicide because she felt her name disgraced by Pinero's play *The Notorious Mrs Ebbsmith*. Diversified indeed are the victims of puritanism.

However, the theatrical world was cheered up in June by the bestowal of a knighthood on Henry Irving which came appropriately in the year when he produced Comyns Carr's *King Arthur* at the Lyceum. It might make a parade of fancy-dress adultery and display a wronged husband from Wardour Street, but had not Tennyson's *Idylls of the King* celebrated once upon a time the virtues of the Prince Consort? Queen Victoria went out of her way to be gracious to the actor. To him alone of those to whom she gave the accolade did she speak: " This has given me particular pleasure, Sir Henry."

It was a great moment for the stage, though even after Irving was knighted the bar against the presentation at any Court function of an actor or actress was not removed. Irving himself pointed out at a dinner that his son as a barrister had attended a levée, but that after giving up the bar for the boards he was ineligible to attend another.

After the knighting of Irving the opinion was strongly expressed that W. G. Grace who had made a thousand runs in May and the hundredth century of his career should be knighted. Instead, the *Daily Telegraph* got up a shilling testimonial to the old warrior which by the end of the year reached a hundred thousand of them. There was another cricket record broken that year when A. C. Maclaren made 424 runs against Somerset. The news of that on a golden evening in July remains the most emotionally vivid recollection the present writer keeps of 1895. It was a great summer for cricket, with five new counties for the championship. Cricket was on the threshold of its most glorious period . . . and death one might add, contemplating the mechanical imitation of a game it was to become. Indeed so early as next year Cambridge at Lords would corrupt the highest standards of the game by deliberately bowling ' no balls ' to prevent Oxford's following on.

Cycling made a great advance, and the ban on cyclists in Hyde Park was graciously removed by the Duke of Cambridge, that is they were allowed by the Ranger to disport themselves therein before ten in the morning and after seven in the evening. Battersea offered the nearest park where bicycling at fashionable hours was possible. A rumour, however, that Princess Maud of Wales had taken to cycling had to be officially contradicted. None of the Royal princesses had yet mounted a bicycle. Among the populace there was still a good deal of prejudice against lady cyclists, and one of them was fined for assaulting a lady pedestrian who had made rude remarks about her divided skirt. And there was some sensitiveness among cyclists about the dignity of their mounts. Mr Shipton, the secretary of the Cyclists' Touring Club, protested against the habit of alluding to bicycles as ' bikes ' which he stigmatised as ' unmitigated slang.'

There was other trouble over sport that year. At Henley the Leander crew, not hearing the starter's voice in the high south-west wind that was blowing, did not leave the post, and the Cornell Eight from America rowed over for that heat, to be beaten next day by Trinity Hall, Cambridge. There were accusations of unsporting conduct which were completely unjustified. And then in September Lord Dunraven who had taken over *Valkyrie III* to try to bring back the America Cup protested against the crowding of excursion steamers and refused to race, which brought the contest to a disagreeable end. These two arguments over sport would have a strange echo before the year was out.

Early in the year a photograph of Prince Edward of York in a canopied Regency cradle was published and his future subjects were informed that the infant son of the Duke and Duchess of York was " thriving exceedingly well and was entirely unaffected by the intense cold or the debates in Parliament. Both these will doubtless become in due course things with which Prince Edward will have to reckon." But who could dream that the most intense cold he would ever experience would be the sudden chill of loyalty, or with what rapidity the thermometer of a Parliamentary debate would register that chill ?

A further item of news about that little Prince was the keen delight he had displayed at the return of his grandmother, the Princess of Wales. In the week after his first birthday another photograph of him was published. He was certainly a baby with a personality, standing up and supporting himself by the seat of a cushioned chair and wearing elaborate tasselled ribbons like epaulettes. His fair hair was agreeably rumpled, his expression elvish and humorous.

Here is the legend beneath that jolly photograph, in which the fear of leaving out Albert while Queen Victoria was alive will be noted :

OUR FUTURE KING

HIS FIRST BIRTHDAY ! ONE YEAR OLD !

This royal baby, Edward Albert, was born on June 23rd 1894 and may live, as we hope, to succeed his father, King George V, his grandfather, King Albert Edward, and his great-grandmother, Queen Victoria, at a remote date in the twentieth century, when the

United Kingdom of Great Britain and Ireland shall be quite as well worth reigning over as it is now. It is to be supposed that his Royal Highness has not yet much idea of such an exaltation; but if ever an infant child showed promise of fitness to become a man worthy of high place, of dignity and conscious responsibility, this little Englishman seems likely to be the kind of person that a future generation of our countrymen will greet with respectful loyalty.

All looked well for England so far as royalty was concerned; but over in Russia the young Czar in the first month of the year took the opportunity of receiving the deputations bringing him bread and salt from all parts of his empire to declare that " he intended to protect the principle of autocracy as firmly as his father and warned those who had illusions of representative bodies not to be led away by the talk in some Zemstvos." (*A. R.*)

The hopes of democracy which had been revived by the attitude of Nicholas II on his accession faded.

One of the features of the 1895 election was the elimination of the Independent Labour Party. Even Keir Hardie was beaten, and John Burns himself barely managed to hold his seat. Nevertheless Trade Unionism as a whole increased its struggle, and those who expected to see it discredited by a set of unsuccessful strikes were disappointed. One most important democratic advance was made in 1895, which was the formation of the National Union of Women Workers, and the recognition by the Board of Trade of the right of working women to have an official labour correspondent. Miss Collet's report was a surprise, for from it transpired the fact that the number of women employed in industry had increased only by a fraction of one per cent on the figures of 1881.

With the accession of a Conservative Government to power (the Liberal Unionists under the Duke of Devonshire and Joseph Chamberlain were too far removed from Liberalism by now to make the new Government a Coalition) investments in limited liability companies showed an immense increase. It has become a British characteristic to regard a Conservative Government as a pledge of commercial security and an encouragement to commercial enterprise. This renewal of confidence nearly overstepped itself, and there was a slump in South Africa shares which produced something like a panic on the Stock Exchange. In every part of it Africa was rapidly becoming the storm-centre of the future. Slatin Pasha's escape from eleven years' captivity with the Mahdi at Omdurman reminded people that Gordon had not yet been avenged. Italy was in trouble with Abyssinia, and her military efforts were being regarded with a benevolent eye by the British Government which was anxious to discourage French ambitions in the direction of the Soudan. Uganda had been taken over most reluctantly from the British East Africa Company, and there was no Soudan or Kenya Colony of the future to make an Italian annexation of Abyssinia distasteful.

There was trouble with Belgium in the Congo Free State over the hanging of an Englishman called Stokes by a Belgian official. And the ultimate result in the future of this would be the exposure of the Belgian administration and the horrors of the rubber traffic.

But the most acute problem was the future of South Africa. The choice by Mr Joseph Chamberlain of the Colonial Office instead of the War Office to which popular expectation had assigned him was marked by the immediate invigoration of a Ministry long regarded as unworthy of an ambitious politician's notice. Mr Chamberlain made it clear within a few weeks that the Colonial Office was not going to be a quiet side-turning in the future. The French, at that time painfully sensitive to any threat of British expansion in Africa, discerned in the attention he accorded to the grievances of the Uitlanders a scheme to absorb the Transvaal and the Orange Free State in the British Empire. These absurd suspicions were treated with the contempt they deserved.

In looking back to that Unionist Government, which arrogated to itself many of the claims that a generation hence would be arrogated by the National Government, we are apt to forget that at this date Mr Chamberlain was still the renegade Radical, viewed with mistrust and jealousy by orthodox Conservatives. Queen Victoria regarded him balefully. She had never forgiven him for his association with Sir Charles Dilke in the previous decades, which carried with it the stigma of having dared to criticise the utility of the Monarchy. She need not have been perturbed. Chamberlain was *par excellence* the prosperous bourgeois. Four generations of wholesale bootmaking in London behind him, he had himself when young joined the screw-making business of an uncle by marriage in Birmingham, from which at the age of thirty-eight he could retire from active participation and, a rich man, devote himself to politics. He was a Unitarian, and as such a typical representative of Nonconformity always ready to fight the Church of England as the arch enemy. Even so late as 1894 he had retained his independence as a Liberal Unionist to vote with the Government in favour of Welsh Disestablishment.

Yet, if in domestic matters Chamberlain had always been a radical, from almost the beginning of his political career he had held strong views on the subject of a bold foreign policy and the strict guardianship of the national dignity. These he had shared with Charles Dilke. He could be called a Jingo by Lord Granville as early as 1892. In 1885 he proposed as a solution of the Irish problem a federal scheme with separate parliaments for England, Scotland, Wales, Northern and Southern Ireland with a new supreme court entrusted to decide the powers of these local legislatures, and after he left the Liberal Party over the Irish Home Rule Bill he was always more keenly alive to the needs of Ireland than many a radical who did not leave the party. The courage and self-confidence of the man were shown when after the assassination of Lord Frederick Cavendish he did his best to persuade Gladstone to send him to Ireland as Chief-Secretary. As resolute as Hercules he wanted to clear up Dublin Castle. As he grew older the federal scheme he had planned for the United Kingdom grew in his imagination to include all the Dominions and Crown Colonies. It would be fair to claim that he was the first statesman to enlarge the idea of a British Empire from the conception of a semi-accidental agglomeration or acquisition of properties all over the world amassed for the benefit of the mother country. At the same time he had the power of a great demagogue to fire so many people with his conception that without the shock administered by the conduct of the Boer War he might have succeeded in imposing his vision upon all his countrymen. He had upon his side the only poet of the day with a popular appeal, and early in the year 1896 he had in the *Daily Mail* an entirely new influence upon popular opinion. He had, moreover, the Diamond Jubilee to serve as an emotional stimulus to his conception of Imperialism. Yet within less than ten years of taking office as Colonial Secretary he was to see his great conception wrecked by the intransigeance of the Free Traders. Nobody would have more willingly admitted that the Monarchy was the outward sign of Imperial unity; but Chamberlain was a clear thinker, and it is difficult to suppose he would ever have accepted the sentimental commonplace of contemporary politicians which declares the Monarchy to be the only solid link in the chain of Empire. The domination of Unionism by Chamberlain marks the final stage in the release of the party from the spirit of the landed oligarchy. Henceforth it would be a party of hard-headed industrialists and financiers out to make money for their country and themselves which not even Mr Baldwin would be able to romanticise.

In the same year as Chamberlain became Colonial Minister and the exponent of the new imperialism the Duke of Cambridge was eliminated from the post of Commander-in-Chief, which he had held for thirty-nine years; and his retirement marks the end of something wider than a military epoch. The Duke of Cambridge had been the eldest grandchild of George III, born in Hanover in 1819 when his father the first Duke of Cambridge of this creation was Governor-General of what in 1895 could scarcely be imagined as an appanage of the Royal House of Great Britain. The unexpected death of Princess Charlotte made it necessary to provide for the succession. The Royal Princes " displayed a dutiful diligence in dismissing their respective mistresses as a preliminary to the holy estate of matrimony." The Duke of Clarence parted with Mrs Jordan by whom he had had a large family, but failed to produce an heir by Queen Adelaide. The Duke of Kent parted with Madame St Laurent with whom he had been living since 1790 and was given a daughter by the widow of the Prince of Leiningen, the Princess Victoria, two months after his younger brother the Duke of Cambridge was given a son by Princess Augusta of Hesse-Cassel. It was considered advisable for the boy, who was next to his cousin Princess Victoria in succession to the throne, to be educated in England, and in 1830 he was put under the care of King William and Queen Adelaide, a colonel in the Jäger Battalion of the Hanoverian Guards since the age of nine. On the accession of Victoria, Hanover, under the Salic Law, passed to the Duke of Cumberland, and Prince George of Cambridge took the first step in a British military career by being gazetted a brevet-colonel at the age of eighteen, after which he went to Gibraltar to learn something of soldiering with the 33rd Foot. He then became colonel of the 12th Lancers, with which regiment he served for two years in England and Ireland. It was during those years that Prince George began his liaison with Sarah Louisa Fairbrother of the Theatre Royal, Drury Lane.

How remote, even from 1895, sounds the description of him in a contemporary publication called *Actors by Gaslight*. He generally appeared in the green-room in a blue coat, with the Crown button, a white waistcoat, and black trousers " having on the first mentioned the Star of the Garter embroidered in silver, and wearing its accompanying badge, the blue ribbon and George." Prince George was anxious to marry Louisa Fairbrother, but being at this date not yet 25 such a marriage was impossible under the Royal Marriages Act of 1772 without the consent of his cousin the Queen. This consent was withheld, for Prince George was in the direct line of succession and the Queen not yet married herself. It may have been with an idea of breaking off the liaison that in April 1842 he was gazetted to the 8th Light Dragoons as lieutenant-colonel and ten days later transferred to the 17th Lancers as colonel. There were industrial disturbances in Leeds, and it was in command of this regiment that Prince George helped the magistrates to quell them in the August of that year. However, in spite of military duties the young Prince was not to be separated from the dancer, and in April 1843 he was sent out to command the troops in Corfu. In the first August he was out there his eldest son George William Adolphus was born. Prince George returned from foreign service in 1845, to be promoted Major-General and appointed to command the troops at Limerick. In 1846 his second son Adolphus Augustus Frederick was born.

On January 8th 1847, being now close on 27 years of age, Prince George married Sarah Louisa Fairbrother at St John's, Clerkenwell, being described in the Register as George Frederick Cambridge, Gent. of St Paul's, Deptford, in the Co. of Kent. Five months later a third son Augustus Charles Frederick was born.

This marriage of Prince George of Cambridge has some importance in the question whether there be or be not such an institution as morganatic marriage in this country, but this aspect of it will be discussed more conveniently later. Whatever its legality it was an extremely happy marriage. When Mrs Fitzgeorge died at her house in Queen Street on January 12th 1890 she was 74, three years older than the Duke. Queen Victoria always treated her with the greatest kindness and consideration. The eldest son was Colonel of the 20th Hussars and retired from the army in this very year 1895. It cost his father £150,000 to pay his debts and he was not mentioned in his will. The second son became Rear-Admiral Sir Adolphus Fitzgeorge, K.C.V.O., and the third son Colonel Sir Augustus Fitzgeorge, K.C.V.O., of the 11th Hussars. The elder sister of Prince George of Cambridge married the Grand Duke of Mecklenberg-Strelitz and the younger sister Princess Mary Adelaide who was fourteen years younger than himself was not married until she was 33, to the Duke of Teck.

Prince George succeeded his father as Duke of Cambridge in 1850 when an allowance of £12,000 a year was voted him by Parliament. He fought through the Crimean War where he commanded a division. At Inkerman his horse was shot under him. In 1856 he became Commander-in-Chief and his tenure of office according to Vicary Gibbs (*Complete Peerage*) was " noticeable for his steady opposition to every kind of Army Reform." It was not until the War Office Act of 1870 that the Commander-in-Chief was made subordinate to the War Minister and became one of three departmental chiefs. In 1871 the Duke was compelled to move from the Horse Guards to Pall Mall, which he resented bitterly as a blow to the rights of the Crown. The Queen resented it too, and intervened ; but she had to give way. Later the Commander-in-Chief recovered many of the powers he had lost, and in 1888 a commission was appointed to enquire into naval and military administration. This commission recommended that the office of Com-mander-in-Chief should be abolished when the Duke of Cambridge gave it up and a chief of the staff appointed instead. Campbell-Bannerman, the War Minister of the 1892 Government, disagreed with this recommendation, but thought the powers of a commander-in-chief should again be curtailed and that the Duke of Cambridge's retirement was a necessary preliminary to this. The Duke held on ; but the agitation for his retirement increased, and at last in 1895 he consulted the Queen who with great reluctance counselled retirement. So in October of this year he issued his last order, handing over the command of the army to Lord Wolseley, being then 76 years of age. Ten years earlier he had been described as " a bluff, fresh, hale, country gentle-man, with something of the vigorous healthy frankness of the English skipper, and something too, of the Prussian martinet ; industrious, punctual, rising early, seeking rest late, fond of life and its pleasures, of good dinners, good cigars, pleasant

women, of the opera, of the play." *   This is what he re-
mained until the end.   He rode in the Diamond Jubilee
Procession.   He rode at the Queen's funeral.   He visited
Germany in 1903, and at last in 1904 at the age of 85 he died,
a few weeks after the Commandership-in-Chief had at last
been abolished.   He might have been buried in St Paul's
Cathedral, but it was his wish to be buried beside his wife at
Kensal Green.   And there he lies.

It was as well for his dignity that the Duke did not cling
to the Commandership-in-Chief long enough to be involved in
the odium of administrative inefficiency that went with the
Boer War.   Lord Lansdowne, the Minister for War in the
Unionist Government, had to bear the brunt of it when the
Daily Mail started to find out what was wrong with the War
Office.

Early in 1895 a great new battleship of 14,900 tons was
launched and christened *Majestic* by Princess Louise.   Twenty
years later she would be torpedoed by a German submarine
off Cape Helles.

> Among the transports and trawlers and various craft at anchor
> we saw all that was now visible of the *Majestic* like a small green
> whale motionless upon the water.   She was subsiding rapidly, they
> said; and already in this watery sunlight she gave the illusion of slowly
> assuming to herself the nature of the waves that splashed against her
> still rigid sides.†

Later in the year another first-class battleship of 14,500 tons
was launched at Portsmouth, and christened *Prince George*
by the Duchess of York.   The second launching was blessed
with happier auguries.

In view of the reaction against modernism in 1895, a
reaction perceptible in every form conservatism can take, it is
curious that the outstanding literary and dramatic success of
the year should have been George du Maurier's *Trilby*, for
although to the present *Trilby* seems excessively sweet and
sentimental, to 1895 much of it was strong meat.   And this
success of *Trilby* first as a book and then as a play was extremely
beneficial in clearing away some of the moral atmosphere
which was oppressing 1895.   There was a moment in that
year when the double-collar reputed to have been introduced
by Oscar Wilde was nearly driven out again by the choker
against the respectability of whose parentage nobody could

* *Society in London*, 1885.   † *Gallipoli Memories*.

say a word.   The enjoyed Bohemianism of *Trilby* popularised
the soft felt hat under which the double-collar crept back into
favour.   No doubt the Englishman's head crowned with a
Trilby hat retained all its proverbial hardness where finance
was concerned, but it was impossible to feel quite so insular
and quite so superior in the matter of morals under the head-
gear of the Quartier Latin.   The tyranny of the top-hat and
the frock-coat would last for some time yet.   The bowler
for nine months of the year, and the straw hat for three would
long remain supreme.   But the vogue of the Trilby hat showed
that their appropriateness for all occasions was being threatened
with impunity, and it is not exaggeration to say that *Trilby*
struck a harder blow at the complacency of nineteenth-century
insularity than all the Yellow Asters and Dodos and Heavenly
Twins and Women Who Did and Second Mrs Tanquerays,
than Esther Waters or Tess of the D'Urbervilles or Jude the
Obscure.   *Trilby* did not affect or influence youth.   Youth,
in spite of what was seeming the invincible prejudice of their
mid-Victorian elders who ruled the roost in those last days
of the Victorian era, was going on in the way youth will.   What
Trilby did was to make older people a little less intolerant of
youth.

The political reaction of 1895 soon showed signs of a
religious reaction.   There was a strong smell of Popery in the
air, and it is significant of the fashionable attitude to read in
the ecclesiastical notes of one of the great illustrated weeklies
that incense had been entirely stamped out in the archdiocese
of Canterbury—as it was hoped to stamp out rabies with Mr
Walter Long's muzzles might have been added.   A rumour
that Princess Maud of Wales was being instructed in the
Catholic creed by Cardinal Vaughan with a view to being
married to the Prince of Naples evoked a reminder that no
Princess of Great Britain and Ireland *could* marry a Roman
Catholic.   Princess Ena of Battenberg was then a little girl of
seven.   And there had been a howl of indignation when the
Catholic Lord Mayor of London had proposed the health of
the Pope at the same time as the Queen's.   Still, if Princess
Maud could not have married a Papist in 1895 she *was*
allowed to ride a bicycle.   Bicycling was by now accepted.
There was an annual bicycle show at Olympia, and pedestrians
wrote letters to the newspapers complaining of the danger to
life and limb from scorchers.   However, there was no monthly
record of road accidents read out over the radio to show how

successfully English conservatism about the King's highway was maintaining the figures for deaths and injuries.

Incense might have been stamped out in the archdiocese of Canterbury, but it was smelling to Heaven for vengeance in many other dioceses of the country, and now that Sir William Harcourt was relieved of the strain of budgets, that long chin of his was thrust out disapprovingly at episcopal weakness in the matter of vestments and lights and illegal ornaments and Popish innovations. His liberalism was entirely political; in ecclesiastical matters he was a grim reactionary.

There had never been much peace for that party which aimed at bringing the doctrine and worship of the Church of England in closer accord with Catholic practice, and the knowledge that Lord Halifax led an even more advanced party which aimed at corporate reunion with the Church of Rome was disturbing Protestants profoundly. Lord Halifax had been a friend of the Prince of Wales since youth. Lord Halifax was a man of the saintliest private life who could be attacked for nothing except his religious activities. The Princess of Wales was reputed to indulge in High Church behaviour whenever she had an opportunity. The Prince of Wales had visited Pope Pius IX three times and not so long ago had gone out of his way to visit Pope Leo XIII. That rumour about Princess Maud ? There was no smoke without some kind of a fire. The Defender of the Faith herself was growing old. Something must be done to get the Church of England into good Protestant order before the Prince of Wales ascended the throne. That was the resolve behind the last desperate attack against Ritualism, which may be said to have been launched toward the end of 1895 when Dr Davidson, the Bishop of Winchester, newly translated from the see of Rochester, compelled the Reverend R. R. Dolling either to resign from the Winchester College Mission at St Agatha's, Landport, or to take down a small side-altar used for Masses for the dead. This is not the place to enter into the theological or ecclesiastical aspects of that episcopal ruling. The point is that Dolling was an outstanding mission worker who in ten years had transformed a Portsmouth slum into a shining example of the Christian life and that a new bishop, a favourite for the Primacy one day, was willing for the sake of strengthening episcopal authority to destroy this great work.

Dr Davidson's action so far from strengthening episcopal authority weakened it. The Anglo-Catholic party were spurred to resist it more stoutly than ever when they felt it tried to exercise itself at the expense of their religious beliefs, and the Protestant party stimulated by the success of Dr Davidson's action were urgent against what they thought was the weakness of other bishops, and began to talk of a second Public Worship Act.

The battle continued for the next three or four years until the din of ecclesiastical controversy became less blatant in the louder din of the political controversies started by the Boer War. The ultimate victory lay with the High Churchmen, and the extent of that victory only became visible when the weight of ecclesiastical opposition provided the motive force which finally compelled King Edward VIII to abdicate. That contention will be discussed more fully later in this book. For the moment it is merely necessary to note this action of Dr Davidson as crucial in the ultimate development of the situation on account of its effect on Dr Davidson himself, because it shook his self-confidence and made him for the rest of his life more anxious than even most bishops to achieve a compromise.

When Dr Benson died in 1896 the Queen wanted Davidson to be Archbishop of Canterbury, but Lord Salisbury insisted on Dr Temple. And when Temple was translated from London to Canterbury, Salisbury recommended Davidson for London, which the Queen would not hear of on the ground of her favourite's health. One may surmise that Davidson himself did not desire the diocese of London where he would have found too many difficult clergymen to deal with. On the death of Dr Creighton in 1901 Davidson was again offered London and declined it on grounds of health. Yet when he was translated to the see of Canterbury the following year he held it for twenty-six years—longer than any of his pre-decessors for four centuries. The love of compromise that distinguished Davidson as Archbishop of Canterbury, and culminated in the alternative Prayer Book which was rejected by the House of Commons, was attributed to his courtier's disposition. It is true he was a courtier. Contemptuous young Anglo-Catholic parsons used to allude to him as God's butler. But they did him an injustice. He was always haunted by the thought that he might have made a mistake in his treatment of Dolling. He had learned charity, and it was a fear of destroying what was good which made him ever afterwards sacrifice much to avoid the possibility of such

destruction.   He spoke out courageously at the time of the
General Strike, and one asks whether if he had been Archbishop of Canterbury in 1936 events would have taken the
course they did.

> This hideous demand for facilities for divorce, the extraordinary
> attitude of almost the whole episcopate to it, could never have arisen
> if we had taught plainly that marriage is a sacrament, in which God
> gives grace enabling people to live in holy love together, and therefore
> demanding from people a preparation as rigid, I need not say more
> rigid, perhaps, than the preparations needed for the reception of
> other Sacraments.*

Those words were written by Dolling in 1896.   They
represented then the opinion of an extremist in the Church
of England.   Do they still represent the opinion of an extremist, or do they now represent the orthodox belief of the
Church of England as a whole ?   We may feel sure that Dr
Lang would accept that opinion as orthodox; but would it
have been accepted by Dr Davidson ?   To that question we
shall return later.

On December 14th 1895 a second son was born to the
Duke and Duchess of York, at York Cottage, Sandringham.
It was an ill-omened date for Queen Victoria.   On December
14th 1869 the Prince Consort died.   On December 14th
1878 Queen Victoria's much-loved daughter, Princess Alice,
Grand Duchess of Hesse died.   But the date had one auspicious memory.   It was on December 14th 1871 at Sandringham that the Prince of Wales took a turn for the better in
his fight with the typhoid fever that nearly killed him, and at
Sandringham Church there is an eagle lectern presented by
his wife and inscribed, ' A thanksgiving for His mercy.
14th. Dec. 1871.'

On December 14th 1895 the Queen with almost all the
members of the Royal Family except the Duke and Duchess
of York attended a special memorial service for the Prince
Consort and Princess Alice at the Royal Mausoleum Chapel
at Frogmore, and the service was conducted by the Bishop
of Winchester to whom on the same day Dolling was writing
from Landport that he had no alternative but to resign from
St Agatha's Mission.

The announcement of the birth of the second prince was
brief enough : ' The Duchess of York on Saturday morning

* *Ten Years in a Portsmouth Slum.*

at three o'clock gave birth to a second son, at York Cottage, Sandringham. Both mother and babe are well.'

Any interest this item of news might have had was immediately forgotten on the following Tuesday when the people of Great Britain were stunned by the information that President Cleveland had addressed a message to Congress on the subject of the dispute with Venezuela over the exact boundaries of that country and British Guiana. In that message he claimed for the United States under the Monroe Doctrine of 1823 the right to settle these boundaries, and asked Congress to vote the necessary money for the cost of an inquiry. What seemed this preposterous demand by the United States following upon the "unsporting" behaviour of the Cornell crew at Henley and the crowding of the *Valkyrie III* by excursion steamers in the race for the America Cup persuaded the people of Great Britain that the United States wanted war. However, it turned out that President Cleveland wanted an election cry for the Democrats at the Presidential Election next year, the November elections having resulted in almost a clean sweep of the country by the Republicans, who had an even longer stretch of power in front of them than the Unionists

Talk of war with the United States continued for a week or ten days, and there was a financial crisis in Wall Street. The *New York World* which had disapproved of the President's message from the start cabled various representative men in England asking them to send "a word of peace". Lord Salisbury and Lord Rosebery felt unable to reply. Mr Gladstone replied: "I dare not interfere. Common sense only required. I cannot say more with advantage." Mr Redmond replied: "You ask for an expression of opinion from me, on the war crisis, as a representative of British thought. In this, as in all other matters, I can speak only as a representative of Irish opinion. If war results from the reassertion of the Monroe doctrine, Irish national sentiment will be solid on the side of America. With Home Rule rejected, Ireland can have no feeling of friendship for Great Britain."

But what seems to us now much more remarkable than anything in this crisis of long ago is that the Prince of Wales was invited to say something and found it possible to do so. All his life the Prince of Wales had been kept out of affairs foreign or domestic by the Queen. But in 1892 when Gladstone became Prime Minister he suggested that it was time the Prince of Wales was given information of the Cabinet's proceedings. The Queen objected strongly to his having all information and proposed to decide herself what news should be given to him. She disliked " the idea of national secrets being discussed over the dinner-tables of country houses." However, in the end the Queen yielded with bad grace, and Gladstone's confidential secretary was granted permission to supply the Prince with intelligence of what was going on. When the new administration was settled in, the Prince being then 54 years old was at last conceded the right to a Cabinet key to the official pouches in which private information is daily circulated among the Ministers by the Foreign Office. Perhaps it was the exhilaration of this privilege which made him feel justified in cabling to the *New York World*:

" Both I and the Duke of York earnestly trust, and cannot but believe, that the present crisis will be arranged in a manner satisfactory to both countries, and will be succeeded by the same warm feeling of friendship which has existed between them for so many years."

It will be noted that the great-grandson of George III included his son in the tactful message. Would the existing Foreign Office resent such a message from the heir presumptive ? But perhaps that is not a fair question when the heir presumptive is a little girl.

Anyway, apparently Lord Salisbury did not resent what nowadays an insolent bureaucracy might consider an infringement of the Royal rule to stand apart from controversy. Mr Gladstone dared not say more ; but the Prince of Wales dared and did.

Lord Salisbury handled the American difficulty with the coolness and perspicacity which the country expected of him as Secretary of State for Foreign Affairs, and the remotest danger of war with the United States vanished. Elsewhere the outlook was bad. The policy of isolation which Great Britain had followed for so long was regarded as a screen for selfish ambition, and the result of that isolation was evident in dealing with the Sultan over the atrocious treatment of the Armenians. It was impossible to take a firm line without involving the country in the possibility of being forced into a hostile combination of European Powers which might end even in war, and war in highly disadvantageous circumstances.

The one friendly power was Italy, but Italy could not help in any action against Turkey because such action would have violated the conditions of the Triple Alliance which bound Italy to the policy of Germany, the most influential partner of that Alliance. Germany in pursuit of trade had for two years done everything short of declaring war to oppose and thwart British policy in Africa and Asia. France was rapidly developing her Colonial Empire, and the support Italy gave to Great Britain in Northern Africa exacerbated the ill-will of France. Russia was equally hostile. In the Far East the cultivation of Japanese friendship by Great Britain stood in the way of Russian ambition. Beyond the North-West frontier of India Russia was working hard to achieve a hostile Afghanistan, and the threat of invasion from that direction was ever present in the British mind. Russian ambition to exercise a predominant influence in Balkan affairs prevented any possibility of establishing an international guarantee of good Turkish behaviour. And French support of the Russian point of view was automatic.

This was the position in international affairs when at the close of the year Dr Jameson made his raid upon the Transvaal. Mr Chamberlain might disown all knowledge of such a project, but the general belief in Europe was that the raid had been planned to bring Great Britain a step nearer to incorporating the Dutch republics of South Africa in her already vast colonial empire.

The policy of safety first which had inspired the election of a Unionist Government looked already fraught with grave dangers when 1895 came to a close. Only in the appointment of Mr Alfred Austin, a leader-writer in the *Standard*, to the poet-laureateship that had not been filled since the death of Tennyson in 1891 was the policy of safety first still clearly discernible.

That New Year's gift from Lord Salisbury to the nation did not compensate for the news of the surrender of Jameson and his raiders to a vastly superior force of Boers. And two days later the Kaiser, after consulting the Chancellor and several of his Ministers, telegraphed to President Krüger his congratulations in terms that recognised the Transvaal's independence of the suzerainty claimed by Great Britain under the Convention of 1884. He even went so far as to invite Portugal to allow German troops to be landed at Delagoa Bay for Pretoria. It was only when he found that, however jealous of Great Britain the other great Powers might be, they were not prepared to support him up to the point of war that he and the German Press backed out of their belligerent attitude and tried to explain away the Delagoa Bay business. However, from the moment that telegram was published on January 4th 1896, the proclamation of a state of war between Great Britain and Germany was written indelibly upon the minds of the majority of people in this country.

It is permissible now to regret that war did *not* break out then between the two countries. France might have taken advantage of such a war to establish herself in the Soudan, but it is incredible that she would have actively helped Germany. Without France Russia could not have moved, though no doubt she would have taken advantage of such a war to have her way in the Far East. Austria would not have stood by Germany to the possible detriment of her plans for Balkan supremacy. And Italy would certainly not have fought, because a British victory would have given her Abyssinia and a British defeat would have brought her nothing. It is highly improbable that either country could have inflicted sufficiently severe damage upon the other to claim a complete victory, and the peace by negotiation that would have followed might have ended in friendship, by establishing the fact that the only gainers from war between the two countries were their rivals. Such a war, moreover, would have cleared the air, and the air of Europe at the end of the nineteenth century badly wanted clearing.

It was in that murky atmosphere of international suspicion that on February 17th 1896 the second son of the Duke and Duchess of York was christened at Sandringham Parish Church, receiving the names Albert Frederick Arthur George.

CHAPTER III

THE END OF THE NINETEENTH CENTURY

THE little old woman who on that blazing June day of 1897 drove from Buckingham Palace to a short service outside St Paul's Cathedral and back again by way of London Bridge through Southwark and over Westminster Bridge was not a human figure to the vast majority of the spectators who thronged the route. In 1887 the enthusiastic acclamations were given to a woman whose personality had triumphed over all that once upon a time had seemed unpardonable. Her frequently tiresome behaviour, her self-indulgence and self-righteousness, and her apparent hostility to all democratic innovation had been forgotten by those old enough to remember them, and her people then took pride in her not merely as the matriarch of Europe but also as a fresh personification of the peculiar quality of England they associated with the name of her predecessor Queen Elizabeth.   To that Golden Jubilee crowd she personified moreover the triumphant zenith of the era to which she had given her name, for as yet there was hardly the faintest perceptible reaction against the infallibility of its view of human progress.   By 1897 the vast majority of the crowd which acclaimed Victoria were ignorant that there had ever been anything in her to criticise, and those able to remember earlier unpopularity were too profoundly moved by the sight of that little old woman bowing and bobbing to them from her carriage to remember it with any capacity for criticism.   She had aged so rapidly during these last three years, that little old woman.

That the contemporary observer was aware of a difference between the two jubilees is clear from the *Annual Register* of 1897:

> On the former occasion the sovereigns and princes of Europe and Asia were the most conspicuous figures in the pageant, which seemed designed to show the place occupied by Great Britain and her Queen among the nations of the Western and Eastern worlds.   This second—a more unique jubilee in the lives of monarchs—was used to show that semi-independent colonies and far-distant settlements in all parts of the globe looked up to the Sovereign of Great Britain as their Queen-Mother, whose care and protection they cheerfully and loyally acknowledged.   Thus it was that after the Empress-Queen herself the eyes and acclamations of the crowds which lined the route were directed to the colonial Premiers, the colonial troops, and the dark auxiliaries from our Asiatic and African dependencies. It was felt that between all these apparently discordant elements the Sovereign, who by the practice of public and private virtue during sixty years had made loyalty popular, was the riveting link which held them together for the common good.

When, under the leadership of Dr Temple the Archbishop of Canterbury, the mass of people gathered in front of St Paul's sang with a perfervid unanimity the National Anthem it may be suspected that the singers were offering something very nearly approaching a spontaneous act of worship to that little old woman. Time was when Disraeli, to titillate the Queen's vanity, had suggested half in joke that she should proclaim herself Empress of India, and to the immense chagrin of rival emperors the Queen had taken him at his word. Her subjects never took that title as seriously as the Queen herself; but on this June day in 1897 they accorded her from the fullness of their hearts what they esteemed the infinitely richer title of Queen-Mother.

In the speeches moving the addresses of congratulation by the two Houses of Parliament Lord Salisbury took the opportunity to deny emphatically that the Sovereign was a figurehead and insisted that such an idea indicated profound ignorance of the actual working of our institutions. "The powers of the Sovereign are great, the responsibilities are enormous." Nevertheless it was difficult to avoid a thought of that first Cecil and a reflection that the powers of the Sovereign would always depend on the extent to which they would fit in with the Cecilian conception of national power. Lord Kimberley in his speech stressed the inability of any party leader to be sufficiently impartial and the need of the Sovereign to "draw out that universal affection which acts so strongly as the cement of Empire." Note that we are already being asked to accept an emotional basis for monarchy. Mr Balfour affirmed that "no negation ever excited the passionate devotion and affectionate loyalty which the Queen has inspired in the minds of her subjects." Sir William Harcourt seemed anxious to contribute a sharper appreciation of the position of the Crown by pointing out the special note of the Queen's reign was that while Her Majesty had consented to change after change in the democratic direction, "each extension of popular right has only strengthened the monarchy and increased the confidence of the people." In other words so long as the Crown *was* a negation it would remain a precious centre-piece to adorn the constitution. It was left to Mr Dillon to introduce a touch of realism in a speech of uncomfortable eloquence which "refused in the name of Ireland to rejoice in the reign, during which her people had diminished one half, her taxation had been doubled, and forty-two Coercion Acts had been passed to deprive her of liberty. The only representatives of Ireland in the procession would be the Irish constabulary, whose occupation was to keep down Irishmen and strip off their roofs." Mr Dillon was supported by Mr Redmond who declared that

Ireland stood at the door of Britain " in poverty and sub-jection, sullen and disaffected."

The refusal of forty-four Irish members to vote for the address of congratulation on the day before her apotheosis may have fretted the Queen, until in the April of the last year of her reign she crossed to Ireland and spent three weeks in Dublin, half as long as she had spent there throughout her reign of close on sixty-three years. That gesture of an old woman within a few months of death is deeply pathetic, and not the least of its pathos is that it was made too late.

In the apotheosis of the Queen the nation was inclined to admire its own divinity at the same time. It had already been told by some statesman that its isolation was 'splendid,' but how splendid it was had not been grasped until it was told of that fourfold line of ships in the Solent seven miles long, one hundred and seventy-three of them assembled for the review without recalling a single ship on foreign service. Even the *Annual Register* had to admit that " the temptation of self-glorification under the disguise of enthusiasm for the Queen was too great to be wholly avoided."

It is a widely cherished article of the English creed that they are incapable not merely of boasting, but even of feeling the slightest inclination to boast. That fruity assertion of an immense pride under an appearance of an elaborately casual humility is a feature of Mr Baldwin in his mood of a fine old English gentleman. It was his cousin Rudyard Kipling who in *Stalky and Co.* wrote bitterly of the man who came down to the school and after making a patriotic speech waved a Union Jack to the intense mental discomfort of his audience. Perhaps it was the memory of that emotional gentleman which inspired Kipling to write as an epilogue to the Diamond Jubilee his *Recessional.* It was a tactful warning because in reminding the people of Great Britain that it was unwise to feel too self-complacent and too secure in their own might he re-minded them by implication that they still *were* the Chosen People. It was the Lord God of Hosts who was to be with them yet, Jehovah in the cocked hat and feathers of a British general. The appearance of *Recessional* in *The Times*—for which Kipling was careful to tell us in his autobiography he made no charge—was held by his admirers to justify their most extravagant praise of his gifts, and there was a new note of re-spect in contemporary reference to him. The belief that the British imperium enjoyed a Divine approbation was flattered by the revelation that the young heir of York was called David in the circle of the Royal family. The news had authority. On the card attached to the wreath from the Duchess of York for her mother's funeral it was ' David ' who shared in the tribute.

Grief for the death of the Duchess of Teck was not an engineered sorrow. She had been a woman of abounding good nature, and had come into closer contact with humble folk than any of the contemporary royalties. Moreover, she had had money worries, against which by this date other royalties seemed to the popular fancy perfectly secure ; and it was known that her financial difficulties had been made more difficult by her generosity. Her death in this year of the Diamond Jubilee reminded people sharply that the Queen was mortal. The Duchess was fourteen years younger than the Queen.

But the mortality of princes and the transience of human glory were forgotten when in 1898 with the battle of Omdurman Kitchener put an end to the Mahdi, avenged Gordon, and demonstrated to the rest of the world that the only people endowed with imperial genius were the British. The muddle poor Italy had made of her African adventure was a pathetic contrast to the professional brilliance of this campaign. The discovery of Major Marchand and the French flag at Fashoda up the Blue Nile a week later shocked the British public for a moment, but presently amused them with what was seeming a piece of froggish impudence. It might have been a suitable moment for Rudyard Kipling to repeat the warning of *Recessional*, and he was never in a better position to do so than in the autumn of 1898, for he had had the advantage of recovering from a hard fight with pneumonia in New York the previous spring when for at least a week his struggle with death had taken precedence of all news in the interest it possessed for a world-wide public. The illness of Kipling was the first big emotional stunt put across by the *Daily Mail*, and the way the *Daily Mail* compelled other newspapers to follow it was a sign of the growing power of the new halfpenny Press. Even the Kaiser cabled to New York, calling upon the poet to recover because the world could not spare him. The poet was then in a long delirium leading " an enormous force of cavalry mounted on red horses with brand-new leather saddles, under the glare of a green moon, across steppes so vast that they revealed the very curve of earth." * But in

* *Something of Myself.*

1898 Kipling was in no mood to write a poem " in the nature of a *nuzzur-wattu* (an averter of the Evil Eye)." He contented himself with advice to the United States on the white man's burden they had taken up in annexing the Philippines as the result of defeating Spain in war.

At this date imperialism was becoming so much of a gospel that when the Liberal Party was split by dissension over its future policy into two groups, neither of which was very closely related to Gladstonian Liberalism, the Liberal Imperialists managed to attach the 1884 derogatory epithet of Little Englanders to their opponents.

The death of Gladstone in May 1898 and the lying in state of the old warrior's coffin in Westminster Hall before he was buried in the Abbey were another reminder to the country that the Queen could not last much longer. Young people may not have grasped that the Liberalism of the nineteenth century was buried with Gladstone, but they did apprehend that their generation would have to hammer a new shape out of the mould of Liberalism unless they were prepared to surrender to a future in which material acquisition was to be all that counted in human progress. Wherever they looked Mammon was God. A larger experience might have suggested to them that Mammon had been successfully enshrined as the supreme deity long before the close of the nineteenth century; but it was true that the chink of gold had never before been heard with such a cataract-roar in men's ears. The Klondyke rush to stake out claims for gold was symbolical of the rush of nations to stake out their claims the world over. The United States, in expropriating Spain from the Philippines and the Spanish Main, had claimed an imperial mission. Russia, France, Germany and Great Britain were gratifying their imperial missions at the expense of Japan's imperial mission to exploit China. France was developing her empire in North Africa. Italy was hoping that an opportunity would return to gain a share of the spoil and delighted by the check Great Britain had administered to France in the Soudan. Austria was contemplating her imperial mission to control the Balkans. Russia was equally convinced of her imperial mission to do the same and had recently scored off Austria by securing the conversion of Prince Boris, the two-year-old son of Ferdinand of Bulgaria, to the Orthodox Church. As for Germany her imperial obligations everywhere were so loudly trumpeted that the people of Great Britain, unable to perceive where they could be gratified except at the expense of their own imperial obligations, settled down with a fatalistic conviction to await the moment when the two nations should come to grips in a struggle of life and death.

It is possible that, if Joseph Chamberlain had not been misled by the ease with which the Soudan had been conquered at a cost of less than two and half million pounds into fancying that the absorption of the two Dutch republics was almost as simple a matter, he might have succeeded in imparting an ideal of imperialism grand enough to convert the whole country to the realisation of it. But from the time of the Jameson Raid he was suspect, and his influence was felt by too many as that of a persuasive company promoter rather than a constitutional statesman. It is easy to be clear-sighted now and recognise in Chamberlain's conception of imperialism a path by which Great Britain might have emerged safely out of the Great War ; but he lacked the grandeur of imagination to avoid the Boer War and by surrendering to what he believed was its necessity he destroyed the idealism of the new generation, and split the conscience of the country. It is a matter for ironical reflection that the *Daily Mail* early in 1899 was advocating a plebiscite to discover what was to be the policy and who was to be the leader of the Liberal Party. With the Liberal Party in this contemptible state it is not surprising that what is called the solid majority of the country should have accorded to the Unionist Government the attributes that a generation hence were to be accorded to the National Government. The material prosperity of Great Britain in 1899 was demonstrably greater than had ever been recorded, and people congratulated themselves warmly on the correctness of their judgment in making it possible to enjoy a statesman like Salisbury in charge of Foreign Affairs, a dynamic force like Mr Joseph Chamberlain at the head of the Colonial Office, and a master of parliamentary tactics like Mr Balfour as leader of the House of Commons. Some surprise was occasioned by the appointment of Mr George Nathaniel Curzon to be Viceroy of India at the end of 1898. As Under-Secretary of State for Foreign Affairs he had upset people the previous year by apparently committing Great Britain to the cordial support of slavery in the Protectorate of Zanzibar ; but that had been quickly disowned by the Government, and no doubt if Lord Salisbury thought Mr Curzon was the right man for Viceroy he was the right man.

During 1898 and 1899 the campaign of the Evangelicals to defeat what they believed to be the Romanising elements in the national Church reached its height.   The action of Dr Davidson in driving Dolling out of St Agatha's, Landport, has already been noted, and it is to be observed that the practical sympathy of many of the Anglo-Catholic clergy with the very poor and the predominant success of 'ritualism' in slum parishes cultivated in the minds of the respectable and the secure an uneasy doubt lest all this imitation of Rome might not be hiding the menace of Socialism.   This doubt was strengthened by the promulgation of the Vatican decision about Anglican orders.   Until then the danger of these ritualistic clergymen had seemed their intention to achieve corporate reunion with Rome, an intention of which their lay spokesman Lord Halifax made no secret.   When Anglican orders were declared invalid it was not only Cardinal Vaughan who was astonished at the apparent lack of effect the declaration had on the Anglo-Catholics.   Many English Churchmen had confidently expected to see all the extremists pack up their birettas and quit the Church of which they had been such disloyal members.   When in spite of the Vatican decision they all clung to the Church of their upbringing the only feasible explanation was a natural perversity which if expressed in terms of political influence might gravely affect the future prosperity of the country.

The protagonist of the agitation to restore the Church of England to her pristine purity of doctrine, form and ceremony was a Paternoster Row bookseller called John Kensit.   This modern Tappertit, a consequential little man with a dark beard, accompanied by a consequential little wife in a black bonnet and bugle-trimmed cape, and a callow son, made a habit of protesting in the middle of 'ritualistic' services at various churches.   It was significant that the *Daily Mail*, the new power in the world of journalism, did not give Kensit more publicity than was inevitable; but the *Daily Telegraph* watching the figures of the largest circulation in the world diminishing every week decided to 'feature' the crisis in the Church of England, and in this it was supported by *The Times*.   Sir William Harcourt, aware that he was incapable of leading the Liberal Party much longer, evidently believed that he was in some way serving his political faith by testifying against the Romanisers in the Church of England and, a doughty controversialist, he was rewarded in August 1899

c

by the triumph of finally baiting the two archbishops into a formal pronouncement against the ceremonial use of incense and processional lights.

The counter-attack to Kensit's brawling in churches and what was looking like episcopal endorsement of such behaviour was led by a former member of the Society of St John the Evangelist, Father Black, who disturbed several society weddings by rising from the body of the congregation to protest against the remarriage of divorced persons against the canon law of the Church of England, and his agitation was supported by the *Church Times* which on July 15th 1898 called on the bishops to take appropriate action, and declared that the Upper House of the Convocation of Canterbury had become the " champion of laxity whereas the Lower is left to bear the burden of opposing the unrestrained desire of a society all too rapidly losing its hold on moral restraint." The bishops, however, who have always been extremely sensitive to popular opinion, could not discern any large body of support for Father Black's views and certainly none for his behaviour. So once again they lost an opportunity to lay down in clear terms what they believed to be the orthodox Anglican position in the matter of divorce and remarriage. It will be necessary later to examine more carefully how divorce appears to be regarded by the Church of England, but it is fair to observe at this point that if the Anglican bishops had shown themselves as anxious to safeguard uniformity in the matter of the remarriage of divorced persons as they showed themselves to safeguard uniformity of ritual some of the confusion in the minds of people about the marriage of the ex-King might have been obviated. A recall to religion is likely to be more effective when the fold has no gaps through which the homing sheep can slip out.

Another cause for opposing the extremist clergymen lay in the suspicion that most of them were strongly in favour of disestablishment. Feeling as they did far greater confidence in the vitality of their congregations than could be felt by their Evangelical brethren or even by that great majority of the Church of England which follows the happy, the safe and the still brightly golden mean, the Anglo-Catholic vanguard believed that endowment was not essential to the spiritual health of the clergy. Disestablishment would free the Church of England once and for all of that Erastian taint which the most fervid advocates of its true Catholicity found so difficult

to explain away.   But not a single bishop could bring himself
to believe that the exercise of his pastoral functions would not
be seriously impeded by lack of funds, for disestablishment
without disendowment was a mere dream.

In view of the widely diffused belief that the twentieth
century has been responsible for a rapid decline in the power
and influence of the Church of England the following paragraph
published in the *Illustrated London News* in the year 1898 is
instructive :

> A remarkable census has been taken in Liverpool by the *Daily
> Post*.   The results were of the usual depressing character.   In Liver-
> pool the population must be about 650,000.   The total attendance
> in the Church of England was only 22,927 in the morning and in the
> evening 33,895.   The Evangelicals are very much in the majority,
> but the High Church seems to make rather more progress.   No
> census was taken of the Nonconformist Churches.   When only one
> person out of 30 is present in the Church of England on a Sunday
> morning, churchmen of every school have something to think about
> very seriously.

What is to be noted here is the ungracious admission that
the High Church part of Anglican Liverpool was obviously
more alive than the rest, and that in a city which was particularly unfavourable to High Church notions owing to the
strength of the Orange feeling roused by the large population
of immigrant Irish.   There need be no hesitation in asserting
that the vitality of the English Church in England at the close
of the nineteenth century was given it by the devotion of its
Anglo-Catholic clergy who were practically unrepresented on
the episcopal bench at home, and it would be equally true to
assert that the comparative vigour of the Anglican Church
in the colonies was due to its freedom from the inevitable
Erastianism of the spiritual leaders of the Establishment,
among the benefits of which freedom not the smallest was a
more justly apportioned representation of the Anglo-Catholic
clergy among the episcopate.

The brawling and the bitterness became things of the past,
and the bishops seemed able to justify their efforts to achieve
a compromise by what looked like a successful demonstration
of the elasticity of the Anglican Church.   There was room
for all in that tolerant institution.   It was to be made equally
possible to deny the Resurrection or affirm Transubstantiation
provided neither the denial nor the affirmation was uttered in
so many words.   Inclusiveness was to be carried in due course

to the point of providing in 1927 an alternative Prayer Book, which was to be rejected by a curiously exclusive House of Commons, many members of which had nothing whatever to do with the Established Church; but inclusiveness was to stop short when it came to including the views on divorce held by the Supreme Governor of that Church. The elastic suddenly snapped. And this puzzled many souls outside the pale of the Anglican Church because they supposed that the Supreme Governorship had devolved from the Supreme Headship of a King whose views on divorce possessed an infrangible elasticity. Such people did not appreciate the nice balance of the compromise which allowed to King Henry VIII what it denied to his subjects and denied to King Edward VIII what it allowed to his subjects. All but two of four hundred years were required to achieve this poetic justice.

In the August of 1898 when Mr Kensit was brawling in Peterborough he who was to become in due course Supreme Governor of the Church of England was being photographed in a sailor's white top with a nautical petticoat that recalled the old salts of the early eighteenth century, photographed at Portsmouth sitting on one of the guns of H.M.S. *Crescent* of which ship his father was Captain, sitting on it as bold as Admiral Benbow with a toy spy-glass held sceptre-wise. And at Osborne that same August he was photographed again in that white top and petticoat, one of a large group of Royal relations round the Queen. He already had a sister, called Princess Victoria of York then, who was seated on her mother's knee. Prince Albert of York in white top and petticoat was standing in front of his father. Prince Edward was in the foreground leaning against one of his female cousins. Thirty-nine years later that photograph would be reproduced in a Sunday newspaper on the hundredth anniversary of Queen Victoria's accession. For the information of readers arrows with names would be superimposed pointing out who the the most important of these royalties were . . . Queen Mary, King George V, King George VI, the Princess Royal. The little figure in the foreground leaning against a female cousin was not allowed arrow or name. It was the policy of the proprietors of this Sunday paper to lead the public along the path of oblivion. By them, and it was hoped by their readers, that little white figure in the foreground was to be considered a changeling who had broken into the magic

circle of an impeccable royal tradition.   That little prince
was to be smothered not with pillows in the Tower, but by
withholding from him the pure air of publicity.

But on this sunny Osborne lawn at the end of the nineteenth
century how far away was such a mean device, how more than
ever unimaginable the touch of time !

It looked as if that expiring century, jealous of its successor,
were trying to crowd as many new inventions as possible into
the short space that remained to it.   There were rumours
of flying-machines that really flew at last ; there was a new
excitement for the bicyclist in the free-wheel.   Admirals
in battleships could communicate by wireless telegraphy
with other battleships ten and even twenty miles away.   A
convincing demonstration in a tank with a model submarine
had shown that this would soon be something more than a
model.   The turbine-engine was giving unheard-of rates of
speed at sea.   The twopenny tube was open.   The ' kinemato-
graph ' was being developed.   Bridge was threatening the
long supremacy of whist.

And in 1899 Cambridge won their first Boat Race since
what seemed, so crowded with change had been this last
decade of the nineteenth century, utterly mid-Victorian days.
The cox of the winning crew was G. A. Lloyd of Third Trinity
who a quarter of a century later would be created Lord Lloyd
of Dolobran.   Many were still riding velocipedes when last
the light-blue blades had flashed past the winning-post at
Mortlake.   Parnell was in his glory.   Golf was hardly played
in England.   Jack the Ripper was still at work.   Nobody
had seen a motor-car.   Browning and Tennyson were alive.
And Mrs Maybrick condemned to death by an already eccentric
judge in the year of the last Cambridge victory for a crime
she almost certainly never committed was still in Aylesbury
Gaol, yes, and would remain there until France and England
began to make friends.   To what an altered world would she
emerge !

And in the autumn of 1899, that year of profusion when even
runs at cricket broke all records for quantity, the Boer War !
Enough has been written about the mood in which the country
entered that war, about the mood that inspired *Punch* to publish
a cartoon of some knock-kneed old farmers tripping over
unfamiliar rifles, about the mood that made people think the
" fifty thousand horse and foot going to Table Bay " a
ridiculous superfluity of troops, about the mood which led

people into wearing Union Jack waistcoats and buttons of red or blue and khaki.   It was a mood of music-hall patriotism which will probably never be repeated.

There is one result of the Boer War however which has not been noted, and that is the secrecy which ever since it has been allowed to hang like a miasma over much of what should be public affairs.   The Unionist politicians attributed their disastrous defeat at the polls in 1906 to the freedom of criticism permitted to the new halfpenny Press during the war, and Liberal politicians when they achieved power showed that they too had learnt the lesson.   Permanent officials smarting under the criticism of the Government departments they administered concurred in the need for greater secrecy. Diplomacy, always allowed a modicum of secrecy, now wallowed in it.   Far-reaching commitments were made for the country without the country's knowing what they were.   As for the soldiers, they carried so many scars from the lash of criticism that when the Great War broke out it looked for some time as if they were more concerned to cheat the public at home of information than the enemy abroad.

From these days of Byzantine suppression one looks back in astonishment to the liberty of comment a paper like the *Daily Mail* was allowed in its youth.   When during the Great War the same paper, although submitting to silence too long, dared at last to criticise the handling of the nation's great emergency it was burnt on the Stock Exchange by the slaves of Government opinion, perhaps less from patriotic indignation than the fear the effect of the revelation of the shell-shortage might have upon the money-market.   That the health of a patient is preserved by hiding the mistakes of his doctors is a theory which permits some dubiety of opinion, and that democracy should be so naturally compared to a patient at this date is evidence of a certain anxiety about its well-being.

Admittedly Cabinet deliberations have always been held to possess the right of secrecy, in theory because a decision of the Cabinet is considered advice to the King who therefore has the right to refuse its publication.   Moreover, it was ultimately felt advisable to make assurance doubly sure by bringing the Cabinet's affairs within the Official Secrets Act.   Nobody could reasonably object to the privilege of secrecy being accorded to Cabinet deliberations so long as the issue were a live one; but there is no justification for extending a perpetual protection to the stupidities of men of state.

Lord Hardinge a few years ago pleaded for the privilege of secrecy to be attached in perpetuity to the observations of a Permanent Under-Secretary of State for Foreign Affairs, and went so far in the revelation of the ingenuous vanity of permanent officials as to argue that unless this privilege were secured no permanent official would say what he really thought in case he should one day be proved wrong. Once upon a time Cabinet ministers when they resigned stuck to their copies of Cabinet memorandums and minutes; but by 1934 the habit of quoting them in war memories by ex-Cabinet ministers had become such a menace to the reputations of their rivals that the Cabinet made a rule that all documents relating to Cabinet business must be returned by a former minister.

As Dr Ivor Jennings points out,* " If this precedent is followed, the only Cabinet minutes available for future historians, if any, will be the set kept in the Cabinet Office."

They are foxy, these politicians. So long as they were all convinced of personal immortality they did not bother about securing posterity's ignorance of their baseness or stupidity; but since more and more of them have begun to doubt the possibility of disclosures in a life to come they intend to guard the reputations they have on earth much more closely. Some of them are even optimistic enough to feel that their fair fame will outlive their bones.

Mr Lloyd George in the course of arguing for less secrecy told the House that it was always open to a minister or ex-minister to ask the King's permission to publish, but added: " As anyone who knows the Constitution will understand, that really means going to the Prime Minister."

After that we are not astonished to read in a *Sunday Times* of the autumn of 1937 that Lord and Lady Baldwin, travelling incognito, have arrived in Strasburg from Basle. The habits of royalty and secrecy evidently persist even in retirement.

How far the worship of secrecy was responsible for the course that events took in 1936 may be argued, but that it did exert a malign influence on the manner in which the delicate business of changing kings was carried through will be denied only by those interested in denying it. It was said that James II was " whistled out of three kingdoms with a song," *Lilliburlero*, and many believed that Edward VIII was whispered out of them. That there was complete freedom to criticise the servants of the State before the *Daily Mail* was

* *Cabinet Government.*

let loose upon them in the 'nineties is not suggested. Battles for freedom of speech and freedom of the printed word had resounded through the two preceding centuries. The censorship was imposed on the British drama for the protection not of morals but of official mistakes and unpopular ministers. Such a liberty of criticism as was claimed by the democracy of Athens may not be feasible to-day, alas; but obscurantism as a characteristic of government is spreading everywhere, and it is fair to say that the darkness with which the rulers of a State now surround themselves deepens in inverse ratio with the intensification of the light which is shed upon the lives of the ruled. Many lessons were learnt from the Boer War; but the most valuable lesson it taught professional rulers was the importance of being able to seal up the printing-press and gag speech, when it seemed prudent to do so, as ruthlessly as in the seventeenth century.

In the late autumn of 1900 Queen Victoria lost her grandson Prince Christian Victor of Schleswig-Holstein who died of enteric fever in South Africa. About five years earlier her son-in-law Prince Henry of Battenberg had died of fever in the Ashanti campaign. Hearts turned to a little old woman in black who had insisted on driving through London early in March that she might express to her people and give them an opportunity to express the emotion of gratitude for the good news from Africa after the black December week of 1899 and that long dark anxious January of 1900. Prince Christian Victor was not a familiar figure to the many. He had led strictly the life of a professional soldier. Still, he was a grandson of the Queen and that his name should appear on those casualty lists which then seemed so horrifyingly long was one more link forged between her and the nation. Prince Christian Victor had been an extremely popular undergraduate at Magdalen College, Oxford, in 1886–7, and incidentally a good cricketer. He was really the first of the royal family to be educated to lead the normal life of any well-bred Englishman, and when one day Mr H. P. Hansell, the tutor of the Princess of York, himself a Magdalen man of the 'eighties, would urge the claims of his old college for the Prince of Wales the memory of that great gentleman Prince Christian Victor would play a part in influencing the decision of King George.

We get a glimpse of Prince Edward a few days after the relief of Mafeking standing by his mother's side at the christening of his brother Prince Henry in Windsor Castle. The group of royalties present seems curiously different from the group which had surrounded the golden bowl in the drawing-room at White Lodge six years earlier. The Queen herself appears twenty years older. Except for Prince Albrecht of Prussia the gathering is entirely composed of the members of the intimate circle of the British Royal Family. It is symbolical of Great Britain's detachment from the rest of Europe so much accentuated by the South African War. The Prince of Wales is wearing the Star of the Garter. His bearing has much more regality than that of the genial country gentleman in a frock coat who had stood by the golden bowl at Richmond. And perhaps this awareness of being in his sixtieth year very near the Throne at last is indeed discernible in his bearing. Near he was, and the next picture of Prince Edward of York shows him in the cortège which follows the mortal remains of his great-grandmother to the Royal Mausoleum at Frogmore.

CHAPTER IV

KING EDWARD THE SEVENTH

An attempt to draw too close a comparison between King Edward VII and King Edward VIII might be rash. Considering how closely related all the Protestant royalties have been for the last two centuries their diversity as individuals is continuously remarkable. Nevertheless, there are adumbrations of his grandson in the character and career of Edward VII, and it is worth while to look back into the earlier life of that portly gentleman who on St Valentine's Day 1901 gazed with so much surprise at a disorderly irruption of members of the House of Commons into the House of Lords to stare for the first time in their lives at a King delivering the speech from the Throne—to stare at him like children outside the windows of a toy-shop.

We shall go back to August 1855 when a boy not yet full fourteen, visited with his parents the Emperor Napoleon III and the Empress Eugénie in Paris. He and France fell in love then, and never ceased to love one another. It is the fashion now to decry the part Edward VII played in the Entente Cordiale and allow him at the most a helping hand in the foreign policy of his ministers. Without Edward VII the Entente Cordiale could certainly not have been achieved when it was, and if it had not been achieved when it was it might never have been achieved at all. ' Il a je ne sais quoi qui plaît et, aux côtés de ses parents, il apparaît comme un vrai personnage de féerie.' So wrote a French exile in England. ' He has an indescribable quality of charm and, beside his parents, he looks like a real figure from fairyland.' Yet those parents found him lacking in enthusiasm and imagination and, much to their surprise " subject to fits of ill-temper which although brief were easily provoked."

In Germany two years later old Prince Metternich wrote to Guizot that the young prince charmed everybody but had ' l'air embarrassé et très triste.' No wonder. He was suffering from the Prince Consort's preposterous theories of education which included being created an unattached colonel in the army on his seventeenth birthday. For another present he received a memorandum signed by both his parents warning him of his duties as a Christian gentleman. No sooner had he been made a colonel than he was given another colonel for a governor, from whom for four years he was hardly ever parted and among whose duties was the enforcement of the parental prohibition of smoking. Colonel Bruce was with the Prince at Oxford where he had to live apart from all except two or three carefully chosen undergraduate acquaintances. He was allowed to hunt, however, and hunting became his favourite sport. He was summoned to Windsor for his eighteenth birthday and there solemnly presented with another signed memorandum warning him that he would henceforth be independent of parental authority, but reminding him that they would always be ready with advice if he asked for it. It may have been the shock of sudden freedom which made him burst into tears, for it is difficult to believe with his biographer that such emotion was caused by a " sense of his parents' solicitude for his welfare." The agreeable sentimentalisation of Victorianism which has had a recent vogue in literature should not be allowed to blind our judgment to its bleak horrors. The reaction against it came from those who had experienced it: the reaction in its favour comes from those who are safe against it for ever more.

If the shock of being granted his personal independence was

great the Prince had plenty of time to recover from what he was to find was a mere phrase without foundation in reality. The following verses from *Punch* in the issue of September 24th 1859 convey the feeling of the country about the mistakes that were being made to manufacture an Albert out of an Edward:

A PRINCE AT HIGH PRESSURE

Thou dear little Wales—sure the saddest of tales,
Is the tale of the studies with which they are cramming thee;
In thy tuckers and bibs, handed over to Gibbs,
Who for eight years with solid instruction was ramming thee.

Then to fill any nook Gibbs had chanced to o'erlook,
In those poor little brains, sick of learned palaver,
When thou'dst fain rolled in clover, they handed thee over,
To the prim pedagogic protection of Tarver.

In Edinburgh next, thy poor noddle perplext,
The gauntlet must run of each science and study;
Till the mixed streams of knowledge, turned on by the College,
Through the field of thy boy-brains run shallow and muddy.

To the South from the North—from the shores of the Forth,
Where at hands Presbyterian pure science is quaffed—
The Prince, in a trice, is whipped off to the Isis,
Where Oxford keeps springs mediæval on draught.

Dipped in grey Oxford mixture (lest that prove a fixture),
The poor lad's to be plunged in less orthodox Cam:
Where dynamics and statics, and pure mathematics,
Will be piled on his brain's awful cargo of " cram ".

Where next the boy *may* go to swell the farrago,
We haven't yet heard, but the Palace they're plotting in:
To Berlin, Jena, Bonn, he'll no doubt be passed on,
And drop in, for a finishing touch, p'raps, at Gottingen.

'Gainst indulging the passion for this high-pressure fashion
Of Prince-training, *Punch* would uplift loyal warning;
Locomotives we see, over-stoked soon may be,
Till the supersteamed boiler blows up some fine morning.

The *Great Eastern's* disaster should teach us to master
Our passion for pace, lest the mind's water-jacket
—Steam for exit fierce panting, and safety-valves wanting—
Should explode round the brain, of a sudden, and crack it.

In the summer of 1860 he was sent to Canada to accept an invitation extended to the Queen during the Crimean War. The President of the United States and the Corporation of

New York on hearing the Prince of Wales was to visit Canada extended an invitation to visit them. The notion of the Prince of Wales at the mercy of republicans disturbed his mother, but at last she consented if the visit were treated as a private one.

The Prince of Wales was accompanied by an impressive suite which included the Colonial Secretary the Duke of Newcastle and of course Colonel Bruce his governor to see he did not smoke. He made a state entry into Quebec and was so enthusiastically received by the French Canadians that strong Protestant feeling was roused in Ontario. Triumphal arches at Kingston were hung with orange ribbons and decorated with pictures of Dutch William. The Duke of . Newcastle ordered them to be taken down; but the King-stonians refused, and the royal party moved on to Toronto where they were faced with more orange ribbons and pictures of Dutch William. However, the Orangemen of Toronto were amenable and the emblems of morbid bigotry were removed. Thereupon the royal party entered Toronto in state to be warmly greeted. The tour through the United States was a great success, and when the Prince of Wales planted a chestnut beside the tomb of Washington the gesture was received with acclamation. His visit was said by the President to have " conciliated the kindness and respect of a sensitive and discriminating people."

But, when this stimulation of American and Canadian opinion was over, back the Prince was sent to Oxford with Colonel Bruce, and no sooner had he finished with Oxford than he was sent to Cambridge, still with Colonel Bruce to keep an eye on the smoking. In 1861 while at Cambridge he was called to the bar at the Middle Temple and elected a bencher of the Inn. In spite of this and in spite of having been introduced to the Princess Alexandra, then hardly seven-teen, who his father and mother and Uncle Leopold and the gloomy Stockmar had decided was one of the eligible royal young women, the discipline at Cambridge was not relaxed. At the end of November Prince Albert arrived on his usual mission of good advice, caught a chill on the journey, and died at Windsor on December 14th. The Prince of Wales was just twenty.

Four years earlier the Queen, dreading what effect on the pre-eminence of her husband the attainment of manhood by her eldest son might exert, had tried without success to secure from Parliament an enactment that the Prince Consort should have precedence in the State next to herself.   Now four years later she wrote to Uncle Leopold ten days after the death of Albert :

"And *no human power* will make me swerve from *what he* decided and wished.   I apply this particularly as regards our children—Bertie &c—for whose future he had traced everything *so* carefully.   I am *also determined* that *no one* person, may *he* be ever so good, ever so devoted among my servants—is to lead or guide or dictate to *me*."

In other words the Queen while willing to hand over to her eldest son the laying of foundation stones, the opening of bridges, and all the ceremonial chores she found so irksome, was proposing to deny the Prince of Wales any real responsibility in public affairs for close on forty years.

A tour of the Holy Land and visits to Egypt and Turkey were arranged for 1862.   Bruce, a general now, was still with him.   The British Ambassador in Constantinople reported "a certain danger in an ease of demeanour which at times challenged his dignity and in the desire for amusement." One result of the tour was to free the Prince of General Bruce who caught a fever in the marshes of the Jordan and came home to die.

When the young Prince of Wales at King Leopold's palace of Laeken had proposed to the beautiful Princess Alexandra of Denmark on September 8th 1862 he had written : " Now I will take a walk with Princess Alexandra in the garden and in three quarters of an hour I will take her into the grotto, and there I will propose, and I hope it will be to everybody's satisfaction."   The next day they visited together the field of Waterloo.

Yet in spite of this cool beginning, after his marriage with that greatly beloved Danish princess, the Prince did succeed in building up for himself a life of his own, in which the double influence of democratic and cosmopolitan tolerance exposed him to the suspicion of the Court.   In 1864 he was in trouble for visiting Garibaldi who was the guest of his friend the Duke of Sutherland.   People began to talk about his frivolity, and, though they resented the self-indulgent luxury of the Queen's mourning for Albert, the Prince's circle of friends was regarded with disapproval by the great bulk of British respectability.   Debarred from any participation in a real knowledge of State affairs the Prince not unnaturally turned to social diversion when the day's foundation stone was laid, and when there was no foundation stone to lay did not hesitate to attend a race-meeting.

And then in February 1870 came the Mordaunt divorce case. The Prince was not cited like two of his friends as a co-respondent; but Sir Charles Mordaunt accused him on the strength of his wife's confession. The Prince volunteered to go into the witness-box and denied the allegation on oath. Lady Mordaunt herself had gone mad before the case was heard which gave the law a lucrative five years of litigation before the petitioner was granted his divorce.

But although the Prince of Wales had acted with such frankness and such courage the great bulk of British respectability rolled heavily upon him and this loss of prestige coincided with a rise of republican feeling expressed by Joseph Chamberlain among others. In the following year, however, the Prince nearly died of typhoid, and as nothing so much appeals to the sporting instincts of the English as a successful recovery from a serious illness, much of his popularity returned. The Duke of Cambridge wrote to his mother, " Heaven has sent this dispensation to save us " from republicanism. Nevertheless right through the 'seventies the growth of republican sentiment was threatening the monarchy. In 1879 the heir to the throne upset the constitutional tradition by voting in the House of Lords for the Deceased Wife's Sister Bill. In 1882 he was most anxious to serve in the Egyptian campaign, but this was forbidden. It was highly creditable to the pluck and spirit of the Prince, but it was clearly undesirable he should go. Thus wrote Lord Granville to the Duke of Cambridge who had forwarded the Prince's application. No doubt his mother had objected. By 1880 he had become an intimate friend of the republican Sir Charles Dilke who as Under-Secretary kept him better informed about Foreign Affairs than had been permitted to him hitherto, and that with the warm approval of Gladstone who had already fought one or two battles on the Prince's behalf with the Queen. This friendship with Dilke led to a meeting with Gambetta which may count as the embryonic beginning of the Entente Cordiale. And it was Dilke who as President of the Local Government Board in 1884 provided him with an interest in the housing of the working-classes, on a commission to enquire into the conditions of which he served with among others Cardinal Manning and Henry Broadhurst, a Labour Member

of Parliament.   In supporting the motion the Prince made
his first and only speech in the House of Lords.   He had
" visited a few days ago two of the poorest courts in the
districts of St Pancras and Holborn, and had found the
conditions perfectly disgraceful."

So on through the years he played his part in sweetening
the atmosphere of Europe from some of its acridity.   The
older generation in England continued to regard with suspicion the lines he seemed anxious to suggest for the world's
progress.   He was disliked by the puritan element as much
for leading in to the paddock at Epsom the two great sons of
St Simon, Persimmon and Diamond Jubilee, as for paying
four visits to Popes.   He upset the etiquette of Austria
by staying with Baron Hirsch, a Jewish millionaire.   He
annoyed Bismarck by stigmatising as foolish the new passport
regulations devised to discourage Frenchmen from travelling
in Germany.   Through all the vicissitudes of international
relations he remained faithful to France.

And now nine months away from his sixtieth birthday he
was standing here in the House of Lords reading the speech
from the Throne, a Sovereign's duty which Victoria never
performed after 1861.   Indeed she had opened Parliament
only seven times in the last forty years and not at all since
1886.   Here he was, the mellow fruit of all that is most
serviceable, all that is most attractive, all that is most truly
impressive in British royalty.   The new century was not two
months old, and in the whole of Europe there was no man
better equipped to dandle that nurseling in his arms.   It was
a misfortune for the world that he did not succeed to the
throne ten years earlier.   He belonged closely enough to the
past to use his dynastic influence in the high politics of Europe
and closely enough to the present to comprehend that dynastic
influence in high politics would need severe restriction if even
dynasties themselves were to endure let alone the influence of
them upon the democracies of the twentieth century.   As a
ruler not merely of Great Britain and Ireland, but of the
British Dominions beyond the sea of which by Statute he was
declared King, he would have been in a much stronger
position to curb the dynastic exuberance of his nephew the
Kaiser.   He might have been able to give good advice to his
nephew the Czar.   However, here he was King at last : the
vital and progressive part of the nation heaved a sigh of relief.
It is difficult to convey to the present what the accession of

King Edward VII meant to young people in the first year of
this century.   Even his discarding of the name Albert seemed
a precious assurance that with it would be discarded what by
now were being regarded as the false morality, the false ideals,
and the false behaviour of the Victorian era.   In due course
what was good in that era would come into its own, but those
who had spent their first twenty years in that era were so sick
of it that some of its nourishing qualities were hardly
appreciated.

The Edwardian decade has already become a legend of
easy existence competing with many another supposedly
golden age in the chronicles of mankind; but for this the
Great War and the catastrophic repercussions of it in post-war
Europe are responsible.   Gradually through that decade the
shadow thrown by the rising glare of war was ominously
shortening as the huge red star climbed toward the zenith.
The return of the Liberals to power in 1906 flattered with
deceptive hope by preoccupying young people's minds with
visions of a domestic millennium ; but the Liberals like King
Edward VII himself came too late.   That huge Unionist
majority rotting away like a stranded whale through the first
five years of the reign had so infected the political air that the
country was unable to rise above party politics, and either
prepare for or avert the calamity drawing inexorably closer
year by year.   And the tragedy of Edward VII is that during
his decade of sovereignty the efforts he made to establish a
peaceful Europe did in the long run succeed in lining up
Europe in order of battle.   From the moment Delcassé and
Lansdowne came together to discuss the adjustment of Anglo-
French relations, and Edward VII lent the weight of his
personal charm to wooing France with a gallantry from which
age had stolen not a tittle of its accomplishment, Germany was
convinced that a plot to encircle her was afoot.   In 1908
Edward visited the Czar—the first time a British sovereign
had visited Russia.   The Czar at that date was the particular
bogey-man of the Labour Party which had not then been
faced by the Chamber of Horrors they must contemplate in
the Europe of to-day.   Three members of Parliament criticised the King's visit in the House.   The King retorted by
cancelling their invitations to his garden-party.   The Labour
Party denounced this retort " as an attempt by the Court to
influence members of Parliament."   People began to mutter
about constitutional monarchy.   The King invited the Czar

to visit him at Cowes next summer. The friends of liberty signed a protest to the Foreign Secretary; but what the friends of liberty failed to perceive was the much graver consequence than an implied sympathy with Russia's reactionary policy at home of an implied flirtation with the Franco-Russian Alliance. The friends of liberty in England were still living in the time of Garibaldi as far as foreign politics were concerned. And without any desire to criticise their idealism it may be added that they still are.

It is impossible to study the earlier life of Edward VII without being reminded continually of his grandson, and if that grandson was spared most of the horrors of that earlier education we may fairly assume that he owed a measure of gratitude to his grandfather for that relief. We know that there was a deep affection between the two. Prince Christopher of Greece has recently told a charming story of the small boy's tugging at his grandfather's sleeve while he was talking away at lunch. King Edward who was in the middle of an anecdote sternly bade him to be silent, but when he had finished turned to him with a smile and asked what he wanted to say. " It doesn't matter now, grandfather. I was going to tell you there was a slug in your salad, but you've eaten it."

The proverbial fondness of grandparents will explain that affection without attempting to link the two Edwards too closely in temperament and character. Much similarity there undoubtedly was, but there was much dissimilarity also. The only point of genuine psychological interest to the detached observer is whether the belief with which Edward VII was credited by gossip that his grandson would be the last King of England ever passed into the consciousness of the growing boy.

Throughout the reign of George V apparently well-informed talk declared the young Prince of Wales desired to withdraw from the line of succession, and when the supreme crisis occurred in 1936 that old talk was used with deadly effect in prejudicing opinion against Edward VIII. There is no evidence available to lend the slightest justification for such talk after his accession. On the contrary all the evidence we do possess gives the lie to it.

No doubt it was with the approbation of his grandfather that Prince Edward of Wales was sent to Osborne as a naval cadet and thence for the completion of his early naval training to pass on to Dartmouth and serve as a midshipman aboard the *Hindustan.* The Prince of Wales, his father, had had a naval education, and to him it must have seemed the ideal early training for youth. The tradition had been started when George II sent his grandson Prince Edward of Wales to sea as a midshipman in 1758, at the age of nineteen with an instruction to Lord Howe that he was to act respecting him just as if he had not any such person on board the ship. "He came, not only without bed and linen of any, almost of every kind, but I paid also for his Uniform clothes, which I provided for him with all other necessaries, at Portsmouth." Thus Admiral Earl Howe wrote to Admiral Sir Roger Curtis. However, if Prince Edward of Wales started at the bottom he soon reached the top. After eleven months' experience at sea in the *Essex* he was made Captain of the *Phoenix,* a 44-gun frigate. A year later he was created Duke of York and Albany, and in 1762 at the age of twenty-three he hoisted his Flag as a Rear-Admiral. Five years later he died. The same tradition was carried on by Prince William, afterwards Duke of Clarence and St Andrews and finally King William IV. He was only thirteen when in Portsmouth harbour he came aboard the *Prince George* the 98-gun flagship of the Honourable Robert Digby, Rear-Admiral of the Blue. There is a portrait of him by Benjamin West at this date, a red-faced boy, robed as a Knight of the Thistle with a conical head and beautiful hands, one long slim finger of which is pointing to a terrestrial globe. Prince William with a Bible in his chest given him by King George III, and plenty of dry bedding was accompanied by the Reverend Henry Majendie who with the rank of honorary midshipman was to act as his classical tutor, and with that auspicious start become in due course a bishop. Prince William's shipmates asked him by what name he was rated on the ship's books.

"I am entered as Prince William Henry," the future King of England replied, "but my father's name is Guelph and therefore, if you please, you may call me William Guelph, for I am nothing more than a sailor like yourselves."

There was no doubt about the thoroughness of Prince William's nautical training. He was not promoted third lieutenant for close on six years after several voyages and serving his gun when Rodney beat Langara off Cape St Vincent in 1780. At twenty-one he was Captain of the frigate *Pegasus.* Nelson counted him "in his professional line superior to nearly two-thirds of the list." On the other hand one of the officers in the *Pegasus* thought he "was deficient in almost all the qualities necessary for a person in high command."

We are reminded of Prince William when we hear of Prince Edward of Wales telling a fellow-cadet at Osborne that his name was "just Edward, that's all." His nickname was Sardines, the origin of which, so puzzling to his biographer Mr Bolitho, may be guessed without severely taxing the mind as a schoolboy antithesis to Wales. And the new cadet was not a massive boy.

There was presumably never any intention that Prince Edward should take up the Navy seriously as a career like his father before him and his great-uncle the Duke of Edinburgh. The Navy might be the Senior Service, but it was not the traditional service for a prince in the direct line of the succession. That being the case it is permissible to speculate whether Eton might not have been a wiser choice. Better cradles for the deep than Osborne and Dartmouth cannot be imagined; but their education is concentrated upon one object and one object only, which is the turning out of a British naval officer. Such an education severely restricts the prospect before the growing boy. It may be retorted that the prospect before Prince Edward would have been severely restricted wherever he found himself as a boy. Only his own death or a most improbable revolution could prevent his becoming King of Great Britain and Ireland, King of the British Dominions beyond the sea, and Emperor of India. That is true, but the particular restriction which Osborne and Dartmouth impose upon the prospect is imposed in order to secure professional efficiency in a career where lack of it may lose a great ship or the lives of men. The alertness of a naval officer can never be relaxed whether it be war or peace. To the father of Prince Edward who but for the death of his brother the Duke of Clarence might have expected to enjoy a long career as a professional sailor no better education than what he had received in the old *Britannia* can have suggested itself. He was over thirty before as Captain of H.M.S. *Crescent* he paid off his crew. He was as genuinely a sailor prince as Prince Louis of Battenberg. To him his time in the *Britannia* had taught the value of the discipline considered necessary to give a man the right to command others and the ability to use that right in strict accord with the standards of an officer and a gentleman. He, however, had had the gratification of putting that early training to the test of practical experience. He had found how well it worked in the gunroom, in the wardroom, and in the captain's cabin. His son was never to be allowed to carry its lessons beyond the gunroom, and even there but for a voyage of a few weeks. He hated leaving the Navy to go to Oxford. And it was an unnecessary strain upon his enthusiasm for the position he was called upon to confront to remove him from the Navy just when the preliminary grind of Osborne and Dartmouth was beginning to be worth while.

The paradox of a naval education is that while it lays upon its subjects responsibilities that seem unduly heavy for their tender years it often contrives to retard unduly their mental development and discourage initiative. Few can have failed to observe the enduring youthfulness of the naval officer as one of his attractions. This is due to the close corporate life of shipboard and the discouragement of individual judgment except when it is required to obey and carry out orders with professional efficiency. If a boat has to be launched it must be launched without a mistake; but it must not be launched without the order to launch it. We sometimes forget in pondering the glorious career of Nelson that he was the least typical of British admirals, and how heavily throughout that glorious career of his he paid for his unwillingness to conform. Prince William got on capitally with Nelson, but when Nelson was recalled from the West Indies he did not like his successor. So, with an independence he had learnt from Nelson, he took his ship the *Pegasus* from Antigua to Halifax. This roused the Government at home, and he was ordered to spend the winter in Quebec as a punishment for his disobedience. To these orders he paid no attention, but sailed his frigate across the Atlantic in the middle of winter to Plymouth. Here he was ordered to remain in disgrace, but he made love to the daughter of a local merchant, and King George, his father, hearing of his behaviour, thought it wiser to give him another frigate. "William was ever violent when controlled," he wrote to Lord Hood.

However, whether the slightly cramping effect of Osborne and Dartmouth on somebody who is not intended for a professional sailor was any more cramping than education at Eton or Winchester would have been in the position of Prince Edward of Wales is questionable. The problem of adjusting the education of a future monarch to the changing conditions of the twentieth century must have been an exceedingly tough one.   Still, it frets the sympathetic imagination to reflect upon the bitter disappointment of his removal from the Navy.

When Edward VII succeeded he was able to give outward expression to the new conception of the Throne which had been incubated by the imperialism of the last quarter of the nineteenth century.   He liked pomps.   And the country wanted pomps.   The longing was expressed by Elgar in his *Pomp and Circumstance* which was first performed at Queen's Hall in the autumn of 1901.   That march was to be the national anthem of Edward's reign.   People were growing a little tired of having their imperial obligations dinned into their ears by Kipling, always, as it seemed, with an exaggerated emphasis on the superiority of the Colonies over the Mother Country.   The English have ever been genuinely ready to acknowledge the superiority to themselves of the Scots, the Irish, the Welsh, the Australians, the Canadians, the New Zealanders and the South Africans at a public entertainment, but they have cherished in their hearts a conviction, for which they are much to be respected, that elsewhere they are fundamentally superior to the whole of the rest put together.   They were willing to allow in public that not they but all the other parts of the Empire had won the late war ; but they did not really believe it, and why indeed should they ?   When on receiving news of the Rhodes Bequest the *Daily Mail* declared that it was expected the advent of Rhodes scholars would transform Oxford from a provincial university into an imperial university, Oxford was more ready to think that the intention of Cecil Rhodes was not so much to civilise Oxford as to give his scholars an opportunity of being civilised by Oxford.   And the high opinion Oxford had of itself, which the combined influence of Cecil Rhodes, Lord Nuffield, and female undergraduates has not even yet completely shattered, was matched by the high opinion London had of itself as the hub and helm of the British Empire.   Of King Edward's similar belief Londoners were left in no doubt when they saw Buckingham Palace being cleaned up and refaced.   There was to be an end of those withdrawals to Windsor or Osborne or Balmoral.   Oh, yes, a week now and then with the Sandringham partridges and pheasants, and if it had to be, two or three weeks with the stags and grouse at Balmoral, and of course a trip to the 'Continong' from time to time.   That's what any Londoner would do if he could afford it.   Anybody liked to

get away from London for a bit, but nobody wanted to go
and *live* anywhere else.

> Give my regards to Leicester Square,
> 　Dear Piccadilly and Mayfair,
> Mention me to the folk round there,
> 　They'll understand.
> Speak of me to the boys you greet,
> Tell them in Bond Street soon we'll meet,
> 　Remember me kindly to Regent Street,
> And give them my love in the Strand.

It was in Edward VII's all-too-brief reign that people were
singing that kind of song about London :

> Take me back to London town
> 　Where the folk are kind to me.
> Trafalgar Square, oh, ain't it grand !
> 　Oxford Street, the dear old Strand.

A feeble enough jingle of words when put down in cold print,
but when those choruses were sung by an audience at the
Canterbury or the Tivoli or the Holborn Empire they said
much more to the hearts of Londoners than anything Kipling
could say.

London was never so much itself as in that first decade of
the twentieth century when the old world was dissolving into
the new with a leisurely grace the impatient war destroyed so
swiftly that perhaps we attribute to it a leisurely grace it did
not really possess, marking only the swiftness with which it
was destroyed. When Edward VII came to the throne motor-
cars were still a subject for jest. When he died the lingering
hansom-cabs were a subject for sentimental pity.

Those drawing-rooms at Buckingham Palace. At night
now, not the afternoon ceremonies of Queen Victoria's day.
The state-coaches of the great families. *Did* they ever drive
as a matter of course beside Green Park ? Or are they something remembered from a childish picture-book ? The black-
and-yellow liveries of the three Devonshire footmen standing
up behind with their tall sticks and powder and tricorne hats ?
The wine-coloured liveries of the three Portland footmen
with their cocked hats ? They seem now like the footmen
in the doorway of Alice in Wonderland's Duchess. Yes,
King Edward liked pomps, and he took an immense pleasure
in the scrupulous correctness of his pomps. He must have
inherited that from his grandfather the Duke of Kent who
was rendered inarticulate with rage by the sight of a button

out of place. No wonder he looked with pained amazement at the disorderly irruption of those members of the House of Commons to hear him read his speech from the Throne in the House of Lords. Yet it was an omen. The last two years of his reign would be spent amid the strife of the two Houses over Mr Lloyd George's Finance Bill.

Perhaps only by a Londoner can the full rich flavour of Edward VII's reign be appreciated. Recent biographers of Edward VIII who have essayed to evoke the peculiar aura of his grandfather's reign appear as awkward as smokers accustomed to inhaling cigarettes with a plump Partaga of the finest crop in perfect condition. True, the clumsy tight-lipped performance cannot completely disguise the aroma for others, but one feels with a contemptuous pity how small is their own pleasure in that aroma.

There was something symbolic in that Coronation postponed from June to August. It was as if the great city desired to make him hers in that month when in her reputed desolation she was most essentially herself. Of late years London in August has not been much different from London in any other month. London herself has not been able to preserve all the integrity of her character in this remorselessly egalitarian epoch. She like most of her inhabitants has been reduced to the lowest common denominator of cities. But in 1902 a Coronation in August was as astonishing as a minuet of Louis Quinze ghosts in the gardens of Versailles. And the abrupt silence which succeeded that August pageantry remains as impressive in the memory as the silence of that May morning when people woke to the news that the King was dead. His loss was felt nowhere so sharply as in London. There was a peculiar poignancy for London in looking back to eight years earlier and remembering that in August he had again been well enough to be crowned. Now the fell sergeant allowed no escape to August from his arrest, and never was a London August so desolate. There was no time he would have chosen more reluctantly to die than at the beginning of a London season, he, with his exquisite tact, his consummate sense of fitness.

Let those who in the altered London of to-day suppose that enshrinement in the hearts of Londoners was of comparatively little importance to a King with so many titles to far-flung rule remember that in 1901 London was still not merely the commercial nerve-centre of the Empire as now but also the deciding factor in public opinion. The London mob which had made and unmade, deposed and restored the kings of the past, was still predominant, if with the extension of the amenities of material progress it could no longer be called a mob. A London hostile to Edward VII would have meant in a comparatively short time a hostile British Empire. It was not until the advent of wireless coupled with the speeding up of newspaper distribution secured a simultaneous public opinion independent of London's lead that the power of the mighty city as anything except a commercial influence waned into extinction. London would have kept Edward VIII against a whole Cabinet of Baldwins, against a whole Parliament of Baldwins; but London opinion no longer counted as a decisive factor, and the London mob which drove out James II, which brought back Charles II, which made Charles Edward's march on Derby a wasted effort, which imposed the Reformation on the rest of the country, which even hooted Queen Victoria once upon a time, the London mob, that mighty expression of human passion, political prejudice, and practical common sense, was reduced to a few young people in Trilby hats and Burberry coats carrying posters on which was inscribed 'We Want Edward.' They had no more effect in 1936 than down-at-heel sandwich-men distributing leaflets to advertise a vegetarian restaurant. And yet even they, when they booed outside 10 Downing Street in the fog and rain, were enough to blanch the cheeks of the Cabinet ministers emerging.

It may be held extravagant to claim that no monarch within living memory has done quite so much for the stability of the throne as Edward VII in that brief reign of his. Yet the claim appears less extravagant when we regard the positive rather than the negative contribution he made to the prestige of the monarchy. Without Gladstone the reign of Victoria might have ended in a republic. And nobody realised this better than her eldest son. Without Albert she would never have achieved that matriarchal sublimity which became her strength. Without Disraeli she would never have added to the crown those intangible jewels that flashed with the grandeur and domination of her Empire. Without her eldest son royalty might have faded into too remote and too mystical an abstraction. We are still under the spell of the letters and journals which reveal how much everybody had to endure from her egocentricity, and in reading them we are so much fascinated by the relentlessness of its self-indulgence that we forget what it might have cost the country if it had been allowed all the self-indulgence it so greedily, so voraciously demanded. No doubt it was good for the minds of her ministers to be kept spinning all the time, but it was fortunate for the dynasty that she had such well-turned tops to whip.

There was added to Queen Victoria's advantages the fact that she was preceded by William IV. The mistaken view of William IV as a peppery genial old retired admiral, a royal nonentity who lacked royal dignity, has become accepted as posterity's judgment upon him. It is well to bear in mind that he was faced by the tremendous problem of the Reform Bill and the rejection of it by the House of Lords, and when we bear that in mind to bear in mind also that he refused to let himself be deterred from his own belief in the justice and necessity of democratic reform even by the man he admired most, the Duke of Wellington. He refused to create the peers to outvote the die-hards ; but when Wellington failed to form a ministry and Grey returned to office it was William IV's circular letter to the Tory peers which secured the passing of the Reform Bill. Moreover, his assessment of foreign affairs was singularly acute, and there is documentary evidence of the correctness of his constitutional principles in the " Statement of His Majesty's general proceedings, and of the principles by which he was guided from the period of his accession 1830, to that of the recent changes in the administration, 14 Jan. 1835," which he drew up for Sir Robert Peel.

There is not the same danger of underestimating Edward VII's handling of what threatened to be a real constitutional crisis between the Lords and the Commons. We know that if it had been necessary he would have created, much against his own prejudice, the peers required to outvote the opponents of the Finance Bill, and we may speculate on the extent to which he would have been able to intervene in the deplorable progress of the Unionist agitation against Irish Home Rule which has ultimately all but lost Ireland to the Crown. Whether George V could have handled the intransigeance of Ulster and what was the equivalent of a threatened mutiny by his military officers at the Curragh will remain a speculation for ever, because the crisis was solved by the larger issues of the European War.

King Edward VII recognised long before the war that monarchy would have to work hard for its living if it was to survive far into the new century, and it was he who was called upon to perform the difficult operation of adapting it to the changed outlook of political mankind. As a youth he had watched Blondin performing on a tight-rope over the Niagara rapids, and the spectacle had somewhat alarmed him. Yet he was to achieve much more remarkable feats of equilibrium performing on the tight-rope of monarchy above the rapids of democracy's irresistible Niagara.

If Edward VII had succeeded to the throne at the same age as his grandson the year would have been 1881. That was the year he was such friends with Charles Dilke and the two of them were planning an Entente Cordiale. The difference it might have made in Europe if . . . but such an ' if ' is too melancholy a reminder of another ' if ' that awaits the speculation of historians in 1956, when the normal course of mortality shall leave only the tombs of those chiefly responsible for that broken conditional to hear it mooted.

CHAPTER V

KING GEORGE THE FIFTH

THE sharpest prescience would have hesitated to foretell in the year of his accession the position King George V would live to gain in the esteem and affection of his subjects. Candour requires it to be recorded that the first impression of the new reign on London was a foreboding that it would initiate a reaction into a modified form of Victorianism, the memory of which lay too heavily on the minds of the younger generation for the prospect to be regarded with enthusiasm. In noting the contrast the Edwardian Court had presented to its predecessor it was hardly apprehended how little Courts were likely to count in this new world of the twentieth century and what a much heavier burden of personal deportment was to be laid on the King himself. Edward VII had had a few years in which, while the country was reaching a full awareness of the fact that the nineteenth century was over and past, he could adapt the monarchy to face the new conditions that would come with such a rush when they came.

The most important constitutional change directly due to Edward VII's initiative was the addition of the official status

to the practice of the premiership. This had been decided
upon while Mr Balfour was still in power, but he preferred
the alteration to be held over for his successor. So when
Sir Henry Campbell-Bannerman became Prime Minister a
Royal Warrant accorded him precedence as such after the
Archbishop of York. The new status did not debar
the Prime Minister from holding another Cabinet
office.

It is tempting to ascribe this change to Edward VII's
anxiety for greater freedom to develop the business of reigning
and relief from the least temptation to govern, but that is
unwarranted conjecture. Yet he had had so long to ponder
over the business of monarchy that it is reasonable to attribute
to him a measure of deliberate forethought in suggesting this
new constitutional position for the Prime Minister. What will
be the final judgment of democracy upon this change it is
still too soon to guess, even after a generation's experience of
it. The ultimate implications of this formal recognition of
the Prime Minister as such seem to have escaped constitutional
historians. Dr Ivor Jennings for instance in *Cabinet Government* denies that the office of Prime Minister is known to the
law. That may be true, but the letters patent of 1905 conferring precedence upon the Prime Minister as such surely
effect something more than a " casual recognition of a constitutional situation." The fact that the Chequers Estate
Act 1918 refers to " the person holding the office popularly
known as Prime Minister " was by then arguably an error in
legal phraseology.

Whether known to law or not, the office of Prime Minister
is becoming a threat to the Constitution if the Constitution is
to remain an expression of democratic sovereignty. A curb
must be imposed on the autocratic tendencies of premiers, which
become more and more plainly discernible as the original
practice of the premiership fades into the haze of the past.
It will be necessary later to examine with the closest attention
this disquieting acquisition by a minister of a power most
inadequately controlled by a parliament the paralysis of whose
functions by a combination of elaborate procedure with
unmanageable excess of business promotes an ever-increasingly
subservient delegation of its functions to a Cabinet; and
when we pause to reflect on the influence a premier may exert
upon the ambitions of individual members of that Cabinet to
succeed him, sinister is the word, with all the suggestive

implications of such an epithet, with which we are compelled
to qualify that power.

George V was lucky to find Mr Asquith as this new
Grand Vizier * squatting cross-legged across the Constitution.
Therefore the Oriental potentialities of the office in the hands
of a man who should delight to explore them remained undis-
covered ; for Mr Asquith was graced at once with a scrupulous
loyalty toward his colleagues, with a lawyer's veneration for
the Constitution agreeably coloured by the gratitude all lawyers
should feel to the author if not of their being at least of their
continuing to be, and finally with that profound respect for
the truth which strengthens a man against the lust for
universal approbation.

The General Election in the autumn of 1910 gave the
verdict of the people on the rash action of the Lords in rejecting
the Finance Bill of 1909. They surrendered at discretion,
and the Unionist Party sought for its revenge in the defeat
of Irish Home Rule.

People in London continued to murmur that the new
régime was dull ; but presently a group of poets brought out
the first volume of what they called Georgian poetry, and
young intellectualism displayed the winsome self-consciousness
of children newly breeched and eager to run about in the
playground of a new era. The cerements of the Victorian
era had served them for the long-clothes of intellectual babyhood. Meanwhile, the godfather of this new era must have
been asking himself what he was going to make of the business
of kingship. It was clear that it could not exist indefinitely
on the pomp and circumstance of royalty. The Georgians
were turning against Elgar as the Edwardians had turned
against Kipling. His father had safely crossed the tight-rope
and nothing was going to induce him to attempt to re-cross
it. It was his job to remain on what was still terra firma and
walk as carefully on that as if he were on his father's tight-
rope. What could he do to enhance the prestige of the
monarchy ? Housing ? His father had taken an interest in
housing all his life, but he had never been able to persuade his
ministers to take an interest in that problem. The only
housing with which a King was supposed to concern himself
was that of himself, for which he was voted an annual allowance.
£18,000 a year his father had had to maintain the royal

---

* Mr Gladstone on one occasion explicitly denied that the Prime Minister
was a Grand Vizier. That was still true in his day.

palaces, and it was not a farthing too much. This business of travelling round Europe and giving the foreign papers something to speculate about? But his father had been brought up in that old dynastic world, in that small world of major and minor royalties always quarrelling among themselves like less exalted families. Besides, the way the larger world was going, dynastic amenities no longer meant a great deal to its security. He certainly could effect no more than his father in that direction, and it was highly improbable he could effect as much. And he disliked foreign parts. An Englishman could be of greater use in England, and what was more enjoy himself better there. After all, why should he *do* anything? People did not want him to do anything. They wanted him to *be* something. That was his job. To be an Englishman. To sum up in himself what Englishmen thought an Englishman ought to be. George III had done it. To be sure, the effort prolonged over a reign of sixty years had at last driven him incurably mad; but what people remembered about George III was his success at making an Englishman out of a German. It was much easier for his great-great-grandson to be an Englishman: for him there was nothing in England that was not better than anywhere else in the world. Yet in being what an Englishman thought an Englishman ought to be he must take care to remain Every Englishman. He must add to his task the business of persuading Every Englishman that if he were King of England he would be what George V was. Set a good example in fact. One seems to hear from over seventy years ago an echo of Queen Victoria's recorded determination ' I will be good.'

There was much to help George V in his domestic life, the careful impression of which on the minds of his people was effected without wearying them by too sedulous and too blatant a prominence in the Press. It was not easy to succeed Queen Alexandra, who from the day she arrived at the Bricklayers' Arms Station in 1863 had been the best-loved woman in the country. Yet the new Queen was able to convince the country in a very short time that Queen Victoria's early devotion to her had shown the profundity of her judgment. This was most unmistakably a Queen, and the imagination of the people welded her and King George into a single personality in a way they had never welded Queen Alexandra and King Edward. That combination, once it had been given time to make itself felt, proved irresistible. Not only was King George Every Englishman, Queen Mary was Every Englishwoman, and when to that was added a family that was Every English Family the degree to which the King was occupied in governing his country became relatively of no account. Yet at first, it must be repeated, the general effect of this representation of ordinary family life played under the fierce light which is supposed to beat upon a throne but is usually tempered by screens of newspapers seemed a little dull.

Those who, remembering the Silver Jubilee, question that assertion are reminded on the authority of the *Annual Register* recording the Coronation on June 22nd 1911 that " the crowd was at no time greater than that at the Coronation of King Edward VII. The frequent extra trains from the suburbs were far from full; it was unexpectedly easy to get away after the procession had passed ". And it is to be remembered that the Coronation of King Edward VII had been postponed from May to August.

The Coronation of King George V came at a time when aeroplanes were as rare as motor-cars in 1895, and regarded with even greater suspicion by everybody. On May 21st the French War Minister had been killed, and the Prime Minister seriously injured when watching the start of the Paris-Madrid race they were struck by an aeroplane trying to avoid a group of cavalry. Parliament hastily passed a law empowering the Home Secretary (Mr Winston Churchill) to prohibit aeroplanes from passing over certain areas to be defined by him, under penalties eventually reduced to six months' imprisonment and £200 fine, the trial to take place before a court of summary jurisdiction. Introduced on May 25th the measure became law on June 2nd, and shortly afterwards the Home Secretary prohibited flights over London during the Coronation period, as well as over Norwich and Windsor Castle during the King's projected visits. King George disliked and distrusted aeroplanes as much as Every Englishman disliked and distrusted them at that date.

Prior to the Coronation, on White Rose Day, June 10th, the Prince of Wales had been invested with the Order of the Garter at Windsor, and a service revived for the first time since the eighteenth century was held in St George's Chapel. On the afternoon of that day he watched a cricket-match, at Cumberland Lodge in Windsor Great Park, between Charterhouse and a team of veterans captained by Prince Albert of

Schleswig-Holstein, a brother of Prince Christian Victor.
The veterans won, and W. G. Grace was presented to the
Prince of Wales who sat talking with him for a long time.

A week later a procession of 40,000 Women Suffragists
marched in a great column four miles long from Westminster
to the Albert Hall where £103,000 was raised for the cause.
" The only adverse criticism on it was that it was pageantry
rather than politics." Thus the *Annual Register*, a strange
carping five days before the Coronation. It would presumably have ceased to be pageantry and turned back into politics
if the Women Suffragists had pulled down the Coronation
decorations on the route.

It was the question of the House of Lords not Women's
Suffrage which was to the fore at the moment, and with the
House of Lords busy docking clauses from the Parliament
Bill which had been passed by the Commons to dock the power
of the Lords tempers were bad all round in spite of the Coronation festivities. The Coronation itself had been held on
what, looking back at 1911, seems to have the been only
moderately cool day throughout that blazing summer. And
Germany, perhaps supposing that Great Britain was too much
occupied with the political crisis and the Coronation festivities
to pay inconvenient attention to her behaviour, or perhaps
misled by the cordial reception the Kaiser had been given at
the unveiling of the Queen Victoria Memorial outside Buckingham Palace on May 16th, suddenly sent the *Panther* to
Agadir and demanded compensation from France in West
Africa for what looked like her proposed partition of Morocco
with Spain. The King in his speech at the memorial ceremony had laid particular stress on the presence of the Kaiser
and on " the strong and living ties of kinship and friendship "
between the two sovereigns and the two thrones.

The news of the German cruiser's arrival at Agadir reached
the House of Commons dramatically enough toward the close
of a somewhat acrimonious debate on the Declaration of
London, the Bill to ratify it being read for the second time
by 301 to 231 amid Opposition shouts of ' Traitors ! '

It was a few days after this that the Prince of Wales received
his formal Investiture at Caernarvon Castle. He had accompanied his father and mother to what had been an extremely
cordial reception in Ireland where at this date the hope of
receiving Home Rule at last was greener than it had been
since the Union, and it was under the happiest auspices that

he reached his Principality to be the central figure of a function that was profoundly moving in what may be called the sentimental recognition at once of Welsh nationhood and Welsh democracy. He preceded the King and Queen from Holyhead to Caernarvon and was received at the water-gate of the Castle by the constable, Mr Lloyd George. Earlier in the year a committee of the Privy Council had reported adversely against the petition from various Welsh bodies to introduce the Red Dragon of Wales into the Royal Standard and the coinage, and at a Council held at Buckingham Palace the King had approved of this report.

Care was taken now to salve the injured feelings of Welsh nationality by flying the Red Dragon from the Castle, and in the replies which the Prince of Wales delivered to various addresses he was provided by Mr Lloyd George with a few sentences in Welsh. Moreover, at the religious service two Nonconformist ministers officiated with the Welsh bishops, and a revivalist hymn was sung in Welsh.

The ceremony of the Investiture was held on a platform between the Black Tower and the Granary Tower, in the course of which the Prince was invested by his father with the Mantle, Sword, Coronet, Ring, and Rod. He then did homage to the King and took his seat on the third throne. It was the duty of the Home Secretary to read the Letters Patent, and on a dark December day six months more than a quarter of a century hence that Home Secretary, Mr Winston Churchill, would recall most poignantly to the House of Commons this bright summer's day when a young Prince a week or so after his seventeenth birthday, entered formally upon the task before him.

After fluttering for a moment in a butterfly's deep-damasked wings before the public eye and by that brief appearance charming people to forget the political crisis and the Moroccan crisis and even the heat of the fiercest summer since 1868, the Prince of Wales was gazetted on July 31st as a midshipman to H.M.S. *Hindustan* and sailed two days later to complete his training.

At home his father was having an even more arduous course of training as what Lord Rosebery in the exciting debate on the Parliament Bill called a " young and inexperienced King."

When one reads over the debates in the Lords and the Commons during those weeks immediately after the Coronation it is hard to believe that they were spoken so comparatively short a while ago, so prehistoric sound the sentiments expressed and the phrases in which they were delivered.

In so far as they revolved as much round the exercise of the Royal Prerogative as the power of the House of Lords to reject or amend the Parliament, it is of interest to note the contempt some of the Peers were prepared to show for the Royal Prerogative when their own privileges were in danger of being lost.

When the Liberal Government resigned in 1910 and asked for the verdict of the country on the right of the House of Lords to reject a Finance Bill sent up from the Commons, the General Elections returned 274 Liberal and 41 Labour Members against 272 Unionists and Liberal-Unionists. The balance of power was held by the 82 Irish Nationalists; but the verdict of the country was clearly against the House of Lords.

On July 20th 1911 the Prime Minister sent the following letter to the Leader of the Opposition:

10 *Downing Street.*

DEAR MR. BALFOUR,

I think it is courteous and right, before any public decisions are announced, to let you know how we regard the political situation.

When the Parliament Bill in the form which it has now assumed returns to the House of Commons we shall be compelled to ask that House to disagree with the Lords' amendments.

In the circumstances, should the necessity arise, the Government will advise the King to exercise his prerogative to secure the passing into law of the Bill in substantially the same form in which it left the House of Commons, and his Majesty has been pleased to signify that he will consider it his duty to accept and act on that advice.

Yours sincerely,

H. H. ASQUITH.

It was known that if the Lords refused to heed this warning there would have to be a creation of enough peers to outvote the Opposition; but nevertheless the Unionist Peers, Members of Parliament, and Press were divided about surrender.

The King put off his visit to Goodwood on July 24th and

D

saw Mr Balfour and Lord Lansdowne, and later on the Prime
Minister at Buckingham Palace.   On that day the House of
Commons met to deal with the amendments sent down from
the House of Lords.   Mr Asquith on entering the House was
greeted with yells of ' Traitor ! ' by the Opposition, and when
he rose to speak he was howled down with more yells of
' Traitor ! ', Lord Hugh Cecil " taking a prominent part in
the disturbance " (*A. R.*).   Sir Edward Carson then moved
the adjournment of the debate, to which the Speaker replied
that there was no debate as yet, and urged the right of free
discussion.   Thereupon Mr Asquith rose again to begin his
speech, to the accompaniment of catcalls, derisive inter-
ruptions, and shouts of ' Leave the King out ! ' and ' Who
killed the King ? '   At last he declined " to degrade himself
further by pressing his arguments on the Opposition," and
curtly stated that unless the House of Lords returned the Bill
with reasonable amendments the exercise of the Royal prerogative would be invoked.   Mr Balfour in replying taunted
the Government with trampling on the Constitution and
dragging the Crown in the dust at the decree of the
Nationalists.

Sir Edward Grey then moved the adjournment, and on
Mr F. E. Smith's rising to oppose the motion he was shouted
down.   There was a hullaballoo for five minutes when the
Speaker adjourned the House in view of the " grave disorder."   Perhaps it should be mentioned that during these
days the thermometer varied between 95° and 97° F. Englishmen who are intolerant of nations more at the mercy of the
sun than themselves will note what might be the effect of
excessive sun upon their own phlegmatic dignity.

At this moment it abruptly dawned on everybody that the
situation in foreign affairs was acutely critical, and it was
discovered that the King's postponement of his Goodwood
visit might have been as much on account of the crisis over
Morocco as of that over the Constitution.   Sir Edward Grey
had an audience of him on July 25th.   A Cabinet Council
was held that afternoon.   And next day the 26th (observe
these fateful July dates) the Atlantic Fleet was ordered to
Portsmouth, instead of proceeding to Norwegian waters.   On
July 21st Mr Lloyd George at a City banquet in the Mansion
House had given a public warning that Great Britain was not
prepared for peace at any price, and that speech did more to
frighten Germany off than any diplomatic conversations.   On

July 27th Sir Edward Grey was able to announce to the House of Commons that the British Government had made it clear to the German Government that unless it reached a satisfactory arrangement with France Great Britain would have to take an active part in the discussion under the terms of the Algeciras Treaty and the Anglo-French agreement.

After this excursion into reality Parliament returned to the Constitutional crisis. A vote of censure was moved by Mr Balfour on August 7th. Ministers had " done a great wrong to the King and his office . . . had corrupted the fountain of honour at its source . . . the Prerogative of the Crown had been so grossly misused that the existing condition of things could not be allowed to last."

Mr Asquith proposed with his Majesty's express leave to disclose communications hitherto treated as confidential, and read out the statement made to the King on November 17th 1910 before his Majesty's ministers took the responsibility of advising dissolution, in which it was made clear that if the policy of the Government should be approved by an adequate majority they held the King's consent to exercise his Constitutional powers, which might involve the prerogative of creating Peers, if needed, to secure that effect should be given to the decision of the country. His Majesty had discussed the matter in all its bearings and had felt he had no alternative but to accept the advice of the Government.

The vote of censure was rejected in the House of Commons by 365 to 246, and Mr Asquith was as loudly cheered outside the House as in it. The House of Lords after indulging in the barren pleasure of passing a Vote of Censure on the Government by 282 to 68 had presently to decide whether they would support brave words with equally brave action when the Parliament Bill was sent back to them shorn of all their amendments. In the event discretion proved to be the better part of valour by 131 to 114, and the motion that the House do not insist on the amendment was carried. Dr Lang, the Archbishop of York, " should, reluctantly, vote for the Government; there were times when ' he that ruleth his spirit is better than he that taketh a city.' " No doubt the bogey of Disestablishment and Disendowment provided something like a strait waistcoat for his spirit. And all he and his fellow-Primate and the eleven bishops who voted with him secured in the way of thanks was to be called " an ignoble band of clerical traitors," by Mr Garvin in next Sunday's

Observer. On the same day as the House of Lords fell like noble Romans upon their swords the House of Commons voted themselves £400 a year each. The temperature rose to 100° F. in the shade at Greenwich, the highest ever recorded in England.

But the sun had not finished with England yet. Labour unrest was intensifying. The seamen's strike had been victorious in July. In Manchester engineering 'strikes in sympathy' had been started, and this was the first time the country had heard of such co-operation. The London dockers struck on August 1st and no sooner was this strike on the verge of settlement than the carmen came out. The railwaymen were turning restless. The dockers were called out in Liverpool. There was rioting in the city. Troops were asked for and two men were killed by Hussars escorting rioters in prison vans. Bluejackets were landed to protect the Mersey docks. There was rioting in Glasgow and Cardiff. The railwaymen came out in spite of desperate efforts by the Government to negotiate a settlement, supported by a special prayer authorised by the Archbishop of Canterbury for use in parish churches. There was considerable disturbance, and in Llanelly the troops fired on a crowd, killing two men and wounding many others. Mr Winston Churchill was criticised for his aggressiveness as Home Secretary and seemed defiantly proud of having acted with vigour and determination in a crisis.

And a crisis it was, how much of a crisis began to transpire only in November. It seemed that in August and again in September the country had been on the verge of war with Germany. Mr Lloyd George's speech at the Mansion House was now recognised as a substitute for an ultimatum, in spite of its not having received the formal authorisation of a collectively responsible Cabinet.

In September the British North Sea Fleet had been cleared for action. The German Fleet manœuvring in Norwegian waters had been watched by British destroyers. A plan for Anglo-French co-operation had been worked out and an Expeditionary Force was to be sent across the Channel. Mr Lloyd George and Mr Winston Churchill had persuaded the Cabinet to agree to this; but the Navy would not give any support to such a plan, and that was why Mr McKenna, the First Lord of the Admiralty, had changed places with Mr Churchill, who was going to ginger up the Navy after gingering up the police at the Home Office.   Dr Max Schultz, a German subject, was sentenced at Exeter Assizes to 21 months imprisonment for espionage.   Mr Max Schultz,* a British subject, was sentenced at Leipzig to seven years' imprisonment for espionage.   It was high time for Sir Edward Grey to muzzle the dogs of war, and this he proceeded to do in the House of Commons on November 27th.   Yet at the end of the debate on Foreign Policy, the only thing of which the country had a clear impression was that the Glasgow iron merchant Mr Bonar Law, the newly elected Leader of the Unionist Party, had no desire to embarrass the Government in their handling of foreign affairs.

How near the country was to war with Germany in that blazing summer of 1911 will never be known now.   The discretion of Germany was probably the deciding factor for peace.   It was on the eleventh of that November that the King and Queen loudly cheered by the crowds drove from Buckingham Palace to Victoria whence by special train they proceeded to Portsmouth to embark on the *Medina*, the P. and O. liner which, escorted by four cruisers, would take them to Bombay to celebrate " the solemnity of the Coronation " at the Delhi Durbar.   About a fortnight earlier the Prince of Wales had landed from his training cruise in H.M.S. *Hindustan* and returned to Dartmouth.   If war had come that summer . . .

King George V must have felt an ineffable relief when the *Medina* moved westward through the mist and rain of the Channel among the great battleships that accompanied her for a part of the way.   The strain of this year had been almost continuous.   It had begun as early as January when a certain Edward F. Mylius had been prosecuted for publishing a libel concerning the King in a paper called the *Liberator* printed in English in Paris for the advancement of republican doctrines.   Mylius asserted that in 1890 when the King was a midshipman in the Mediterranean fleet he had secretly married a daughter of the Commander-in-Chief, Admiral Sir Michael Culme-Seymour.   This had twice been contradicted the previous year, in a speech by the Dean of Norwich in July and in a letter to *Reynolds' Newspaper* from one of the King's private secretaries, Sir Arthur Bigge, on October 30th.   Now with the seizure at Newhaven of copies of the *Liberator* intended for distribution in England Mylius was arrested and tried before the Lord Chief Justice and a

* This is not a misprint

special jury. Sir Michael Culme-Seymour gave evidence that his wife and two daughters first came out to Malta in 1893, that his younger daughter, Laura Grace, died unmarried in 1895 without ever having spoken to the King, and that his other daughter Mrs Trevelyan Napier had not met the King between 1879, when she was eight years old, and 1898. Mrs Napier and her three brothers confirmed this in the witness-box. It was proved that the King had not been in Malta between 1888 and 1901, and that the registers of the island showed no record of such a marriage. Mylius, who was not represented by counsel, argued that the King ought to have appeared in court as a witness and made affidavits, failing which the case should be dismissed. On this objection's being overruled he refused to say any more. He was found guilty and sentenced to twelve months' imprisonment. When sentence had been passed the Attorney-General read a statement signed by the King that he was never married except to the Queen, and never went through the ceremony of marriage except with the Queen, and that he would have given evidence in person to this effect if he had not been advised by the Law officers of the Crown that it would be unconstitutional for him to do so.

And so this rumour which had persisted for so many years was finally disposed of. One detects now in King George's statement a note of regret that he was debarred constitutionally from giving the lie to the silly tale in person, but that is after an experience of his reign and a recognition of the directness and the sincerity which he was to hand on to his eldest son. At the time most people would never have supposed that he was really anxious to appear in the witness-box of a court of law.

And then after the strain of the Coronation, with that question whether it had been as successful as it ought to have been which haunts every display of royalty, had come all that fuss about the Prerogative under the brazen sky of an exhausting summer. King George must have been rendered slightly anxious about the demands the future might exact from that Prerogative. It looked as if it might be difficult to keep the Crown clear of the increasing bitterness of party politics. A young and inexperienced King? Was forty-six so young? It is tempting to fancy that it was while the *Medina* was sailing on her way to India that George V, surrounded by the bluejackets and naval officers whom he understood so well and hearing night and day the old familiar sea-sounds, decided that whatever politicians might say the most powerful Prerogative left to a King of England was to express in himself the best of an ordinary Englishman.

It is improbable that King George was familiar with the words of Charles James Fox in his brief history of the early part of the reign of James II, but with what sincerity he might have echoed them, sailing down the Red Sea where the Turkish lights extinguished for the war with Italy had been relit in his honour.

" How vain, then, how idle, how presumptuous is the opinion that laws can do everything! And how weak and pernicious the maxim founded upon it, that measures, not men, are to be attended to ! "

CHAPTER VI

MAGDALEN COLLEGE

In February 1912 it was announced that the Prince of Wales would matriculate at Magdalen College, Oxford. The greater part of the interval before going up to the University in October was spent in France with the Marquis de Bréteuil either at the Château of his host or exploring the Riviera. His visit made a most favourable impression in France where it was accepted as an earnest of the intention of Great Britain to stand by the Entente in the trouble ahead. The rapidity with which war came when it did finally come should not deceive posterity into supposing that a sense of impending doom did not hang heavily over Europe in those last years before the war. The madness which took possession of the Unionist Party after the rabies of that sun-smitten summer of 1911 is evidence by itself of the gods' determination to destroy. Of that determination all sensitive minds were aware and, what was so bitter, hopelessly aware.

If there had been any left alive in France with long enough memories the likeness between the young Prince of Wales and his grandfather when he was a young Prince of Wales could not have failed to strike them. They would have recognised the same shyness, the same hint of sadness, and the same charm of *féerie*. The cause of some of that sadness

was to be sought in the decision to cut short his naval career
and send him to Oxford.   His tutor, Mr Hansell, told Miss
Genevieve Parkhurst (*A King in the Making*) that " although
the visit to France was fruitful in its intellectual results and
that it did, in a way, help to take the boy's mind from the sea,
it did not make him forget it entirely."

It was no longer necessary for a prince to try to heal old
wounds or sweeten old animosities with his personal intervention.   By now France had made up her mind that friendship with England was essential to her future as a nation, and
the mere presence on her soil of that prince was enough to
offer her a new pledge of such a friendship.   The Prince was
to pay a visit to Germany the following year, but from the
moment France was chosen as the first foreign country
in which to air to the world his young manhood the world
knew what that gesture stood for.

When the Prince of Wales took up residence at Oxford in
October 1912 he was given a considerable measure of freedom.   He was accompanied, it is true, by Major the Hon.
William Cadogan, his Equerry, who had rooms in College,
and by his tutor Mr H. P. Hansell who was an old Magdalen
man.   Two or three undergraduates, sons of friends of the
King and Queen, came up to Magdalen at the same time,
but it is not recorded that those supposedly suitable friends
took up more of his attention than other members of the
College.   He was granted the privilege of asking to lunch
anybody whose company he favoured.   There was nothing
in his residence at Magdalen to recall the absurdity of his
grandfather's nominal undergraduate life at Christ Church,
Oxford, and Trinity College, Cambridge, over fifty years
before.   Even if such an anachronism had been contemplated
it could not have long withstood the effect of a perfectly
normal education at Osborne and Dartmouth.

Magdalen in 1912 was very much what Magdalen had
been in the year the Prince was born, though some of the
rigidly exclusive tradition of the College had been loosened.
It was once said that if a member of any other college were
asked what college he would have chosen after his own
everybody would choose Magdalen.   This compliment was
accepted by Magdalen men as a natural tribute to the self-
evident truth of the statement that the University of Oxford
was composed of Magdalen and a number of other colleges.
Magdalen men welcomed guests from other colleges and

to a certain extent visited other colleges ; but for a long time it was considered to cast a suspicion upon a Magdalen man's appreciation of the inestimable privilege of being a Magdalen man if he became a member of any club outside his college gates, always excepting Vincent's and the Grid. There was an equal distrust of the Bullingdon and the Union. Prince Christian Victor when up in 1886–87 declined election to the Bullingdon. In 1904 a Magdalen man was elected President of the Union, less it was believed for his own achievements on the playing-fields of politics than out of astonishment at the novelty of such a candidature. However, this excessive demand upon self-sufficiency which had been rigorously maintained during the last decade of the nineteenth century had been much relaxed during the first decade of the twentieth century, and by 1912 Magdalen men were able to feel it was not a mark of eccentricity to share in the general life of the University.

This self-sufficiency and exclusiveness had had a tendency to break the College itself up into self-sufficient and exclusive cliques, and as a device to break up these cliques breakfast was instituted in the Junior Common Room and forbidden to be served in rooms. In old days it was the custom of the second-year men in College to invite the freshmen to breakfast in batches and at this critical meal to pass judgment upon their likelihood to become acquisitions to the College. Failure to pass this difficult social test was felt to impose an unfair handi-cap on the newcomer, and that was another reason for the J.C.R. breakfast, which before the war was an unique in-stitution in the College life of Oxford. Breakfast was served at any time between eight and ten so that there was no undue formality, and the blushing freshman might any morning have the overwhelming honour of being invited to pass the toast to a blue and be nodded to thereafter by the great man in the quad.

Nor was breakfast the only device to intensify the conception that if a man was worthy to come to Magdalen at all he ought to be worthy of associating with everybody in the College. Every Sunday night after dinner in Hall dessert with the accompaniment of port, burgundy and claret was taken at the two long tables set at right angles to one another in the J.C.R., the walls of which were hung with photographic reminders of the glorious achievements of Magdalen in sport. This dessert which involved a great deal of drinking of healths

was followed by what was called an ' after,' the institution of
which legend ascribed to Oscar Wilde. Four or five people
wrote their names down at the beginning of each term as
giving the ' after ' on a certain date, and the ' after ' consisted
of a smoking-concert in as large a room as could be secured,
for the whisky and lemon-squash drunk, the cigars and
cigarettes smoked, and the glasses smashed at which the
week's hosts cheerfully paid. An ' after ' cost roughly
about £20. The evening came to an end at a quarter to
twelve with the singing of the Magdalen song, which has
apparently vanished since the war from human memory.
The man chosen to sing the song was chosen for his prowess
on the river or his popularity in the College which somehow
rarely seemed to coincide with a resonant voice. Each
verse was followed by a rousing chorus.

> Let the spirit of the past,
> Like a mantle round us cast,
> Be our heritage and glory set before us,
> And we'll raise and raise again
> The victorious refrain
> Of ' Magdalena Floreat ' in chorus.

And before that a good deal about the ' scarlet and lilies '
(the racing colours of the Eight) and ' being true black and
white (the college colours) all our days.' The words lack
the authentic note of the greatest English poetry, but they
had a dithyrambic inspiration for youth and it is sad they are
now no longer sung.   But in 1912 the Prince of Wales would
have heard that chorus rolled out and may have joined in it
with many who would remember it in the mud of Flanders
and die like the song itself.

A much more important feature of Magdalen life than either
the ' afters ' or the Junior Common Room was the steward
of the J.C.R., Richard Gunstone. Gunner, as he was
always called, had come to the College as J.C.R. boy before
Edward VII was an undergraduate, and by 1912 he would
have been over seventy. He had a florid clean-shaven face,
with a small dumpling of a nose and a pair of benignant intensely blue eyes, and the gentle voice one so often hears in
the very deaf, for by now he was very deaf indeed, in spite of
which his capacity for sharing intimately in the life of the
College was undiminished.   Gunner had his office underneath
the J.C.R.—a small room at the foot of the steep stone staircase which led up to it out of Cloisters, with a smaller room

leading out of it that served as a store cupboard from which the orders of the day were supplied, and to which Gunner always retired to make a cup of lemon-squash or open a bottle of whisky. The office itself was not luxuriously furnished, and the accommodation was small. There was a window-seat with a view of the College kitchens, a square table, and a couple of Windsor chairs. Over the fireplace was a gilt mirror stuck round with the fixture cards of the University and the College, with notices of grinds and musical clubs and debating societies, and all the printed petty news of Oxford. A few photographs of winning crews, a bookcase with stores of College stationery, a Chippendale sideboard on which stood a glass-topped case of priced cigars, and a drawerful of Gunner's relics completed the furniture. The wall-paper of oily texture was of that indefinite brownish yellow one finds in the rooms of old-fashioned solicitors.

Yet the office itself, haunted though it was by the accumulated personalities of every generation at Magdalen, would scarcely have possessed the magical effect of fusion it did possess, had not all these personalities endured in a perpetual present through the conservative force of Gunner himself. He seemed to all these young men that came within the fragrance of his charm to be as much an intrinsic part of the College as Addison's Walk. The bearded President, the dry-voiced dons, the deer-park, the elms, the ancient doors and traceries, the lawns and narrow entries, the groining and the lattices, the very tower itself, were all subordinate in the estimation of the undergraduates to Gunner. He knew the inner history of every rag ; he comprehended why each man was popular or unpopular or merely ignored ; he was a treasure-house of wise counsel and kindly advice ; he held the keys of every heart. Something there was in him of the old family butler, a little more of the yeoman farmer, a trace of the head gamekeeper, a suspicion of the trainer of horses ; but all these elements were blended to produce the effect of someone wise and saintly and simple who would trouble himself to heal the lightest wounds and could rouse with a look or a gesture undying affection. This tutelary spirit haunted chiefly the corner behind the fireplace and the window, sitting on a high stool at an old-fashioned high sloping desk on which the big black leather-bound ledger of the current year was always spread open. On the shelves above were the account books of bygone years going back to the 'seventies, the names of every undergraduate of the College entered therein in Gunner's calligraphy and everything they had ordered, from a pound of biscuits to a dozen bottles of burgundy.

It was the habit after Hall to adjourn to Gunner's office for coffee which was set ready in serried cups on the table in the middle of the little room. What a jam it was! The men were packed like socks in a hosier's shop. It was almost impossible to lift the cup to one's lips. And the chatter!

Nevertheless the freedom of Gunner's at coffee-time was not for everybody. No freshman would have ventured to enter it until, supported by one or two fellows at the end of his third term, he and they would squeeze in and stand as inconspicuously as possible close to the door, trying to detect all the while in the glances of their seniors an expression of pained astonishment at such audacity. Gunner's had all the quality of the most exclusive club, and yet it was not a club. It was any man's right to take his coffee in Gunner's, but that man had to decide for himself when the position he had attained in the life of the College entitled him to take advantage of such a privilege. It was a superlative test of democracy because the challenge had to be made by the individual. He had to back his own nerve, his own sense of proportion, in a word his own personality. When Gunner's was empty in the morning or the afternoon the freshman could go in and listen to the old man's stories about the past and perhaps obtain from the old man a shrewd judgment upon one or other of his contemporaries; but he would never have ventured to ask Gunner if he thought the moment was ripe for him to take coffee in his office after Hall. That he must decide for himself with the help of some of his friends equally perplexed. Of course, this custom bore hardly on what Gunner himself used to call the ' quiet men ', in which he included of his charity, which was almost infinite, not merely the genuine scholarly recluse, but the man who withdrew from the communal life of the College either through what is known in current cant as an ' inferiority complex ' or out of a kind of inverted snobbery.

People were less tolerant before the war, and conformity was exacted much more strictly then. Magdalen was a democracy, but like a Greek democracy it was jealous of the privileges of citizenship, and the Magdalen man had to bear the conventional marks of such or expect to find himself ignored.

Biographers of King Edward VIII, paraphrasing one another in the way of biographers, have stressed the democratic character of Magdalen; but none of them has come near to grasping the peculiar quality of that democracy,* and consequently they have ascribed to royal graciousness to all sorts and conditions of men what was more truly royal acquiescence in the Magdalen theory of a collegiate unity. Every year when freshmen with handles to their names came up to Magdalen these handles were affixed to the names painted on the boards in the entrance of each quadrangle staircase. The first order a Magdalen freshman with a handle gave was to have his handle obliterated whether he was a duke or a mere honourable. At Christ Church the handles were retained. That custom marked one difference in the point of view of the two colleges in the days before the war.

A feature of the Magdalen tradition was the lively sense of continuity it enshrined. Gunner himself was the link between the generations of the past and present life of the College, and he communicated that security of changelessness which enabled the old Magdalen man revisiting it to be not just a former member of the College, but as much a vital part of it himself as the whole swarm of contemporary undergraduates buzzing in the little room that was the amber in which the ephemeral flies of a few all too brief terms could be immortally preserved in the semblance of their fugitive life.

In Gunner's benevolent form the very spirit of the College was incarnate. His memory was invincible. Neither name nor face was ever forgotten. Some old Magdalen man would

---

* Miss Parkhurst in *A King in the Making* has made a brave but unsuccessful effort to explain 'Gunner's', and it may be suspected that Mr Bolitho's equally unsuccessful effort to grasp the peculiar quality of the Magdalen idea has been due to his relying upon Miss Parkhurst. The following paragraph is a notable example of the danger of a little learning :

"He met the undergraduates freely in the junior common room, a sort of club-room, known as the [*sic*] 'Gunners' room, an abbreviation for the old steward Gunstone who used to run this room and which is a gathering place for the lower classmen. It began almost with the beginnings of the college and was then a place where the students who were the sons of commoners could foregather for good times, the sons of the nobility having their own rendezvous. With the growth of democracy, it too was changed into a place for all undergraduates, whether they were from the public schools, or provincial grammar schools, Rhode [*sic*] scholars, sons of tradesmen, or the landed gentry or the nobility." (*A King in the Making.*)

be made a bishop or the governor of a province or an ambassador, and Gunner would be asked what he was like. "Oh, he was very rowdy. He was one of the wildest men we ever had. We'll look up his J.C.R. account." And down from the shelf would come some ledger of the late 'seventies. "Here we are. John William Smith. November 5th. He had twelve bottles of champagne that night, and didn't they all get tipsy! Smith went to pull the Dean out of his bed, and it was a wonder he escaped being sent down. His friends had to put *him* to bed that night. But he was a very nice fellow. Very popular with the other men. He rowed bow in the Eight. I often used to tell him he drank too much for a rowing-man." "Well, they've just made this chap Smith Ambassador to Ruritania, Gunner," somebody would shout. "Have they? I expect he'll do well. I don't suppose he drinks so much nowadays," Gunner would chuckle with that laugh of his that was like the gurgle of decanted wine, making his drab little office seem the heart of the world's wit as well as of the world's wisdom.

And when this ripe old room was empty how pleasant it was to sit and listen to Gunner's ripe old stories, how amazingly important seemed the trivial gossip of the College in this historic atmosphere; how much time was apparently wasted here between eight and ten at night, and what a thrill it always was to come into College about half-past nine of a murky evening and stroll round Cloisters to see if there was anybody in Gunner's. Yet it could not really be accounted a waste of time to sit and slowly mature in Gunner's; and sometimes about half-past nine the old man would be alone, the fire would be dying down and, during the half-hour that remained of his duty, one could peel a large apple very slowly and extract from him more of the essence of social history than could be gained from a term's reading of the great historians.

When the King and Queen came to visit the Prince of Wales at Magdalen, Gunstone received them in his office and was much taken by the homeliness of King George, for whom he did his two great tricks—one the drawing of a banana down into a decanter by lighting paper and creating a vacuum, the other a complicated business of kneeling on the hearthrug and holding the tongs to one's ears with a string attached telephone-wise to the shovel which was held by Gunner, who would bend over and strike on it Magdalen chimes with the poker.

"Did you really do the banana trick for the King, Gunner?"
"Oh yes, he liked that. And he liked Magdalen chimes too.
He was very homely. I thought he was a capital fellow. He
got a good hold of the tongs. But the Queen was more
interested in the cigars. She couldn't make out what the
figures meant in the cigar tray. 'Why, Ma'am,' I told her,
'those are the prices of the different brands.' 'Good gracious,
Mr Gunstone,' she said, 'I never knew before that cigars
had different prices. I thought all cigars were the same price.'
Fancy her thinking that. I must say I was very surprised.
She can't know much about smoking. But the King was
very homely. He looked at the Prince's J.C.R. account,
and he asked what the three-halfpence was for I had entered
every day. 'Oh, that's his apple,' I told the King. 'What?'
said the King, laughing, "does he still eat his apple every
morning? He's always done that.' 'Yes,' I said, 'every
morning regularly. And you ought to speak to him about the
way he will start peeling it as soon as he comes out of the
J.C.R. He'll slip on the stone stairs one of these days and
give his head a nasty bump, and perhaps cut himself with his
penknife. I've spoken to him about it myself several times,
but he won't listen to me. He'll pay more attention to you.'"

This story of the three-halfpenny apple, already related
in print by the present writer, has been twisted almost out
of recognition by biographers of Edward VIII, each paraphrasing the last, to demonstrate the habit of meticulous
accountancy he was supposed to owe to the counsel of his
mother. Would that this little story were the only story that
has been twisted almost out of recognition!

A portrait of Gunner drawn by the present writer in an
early novel of his evoked from Mr H. P. Hansell, two years
after he had ceased to reside at Magdalen College as the
tutor of the Prince of Wales, the following letter which
testifies to the comparatively unchanged character of Magdalen
during 1912 to 1914. It was written on the twenty-second
birthday of the Prince of Wales, himself at that time with Lord
Cavan's Fourteenth Army Corps preparing for the Battle
of the Somme:

Buckingham Palace
June 23rd, 1916

DEAR SIR,
Having resided at Magdalen College from 1882 to 1885
and again from 1912 to 1914 I read your 2nd volume of

Sinister Street with the greatest interest and delight. I am sending you a copy of the reproduction of Seymour Lucas's drawing of the dear old man, which is exhibited in this year's Academy. It is to be hung in ' Gunner's '. I could not help wishing that it had been reproduced as a frontispiece of your book.

With many thanks for much pleasure at a sad time.

Yours faithfully,

HENRY P. HANSELL

The stories about the Prince's sojourn at Magdalen are numerous and often pointless, but three have a certain significance and have not hitherto appeared in print. The first relates that when he went up to Oxford he did not like riding, but that Major Cadogan insisted on the importance of mastering the art of horsemanship. So his Equerry used to wait for the Prince on the outskirts of Oxford with a spare mount and the Prince would ride out on a bicycle to meet him. Then after the lesson, sometimes having been photographed on horseback as well, he would dismount and ride back to Oxford on his bicycle. By the end of his time at Oxford, however, he was hunting regularly. That physical courage which has been the most constant feature of his House from George I onwards even his bitterest enemies will allow him to the full.

The second story relates that the publication of a photograph showing the Prince of Wales being charged off the ball in a football match with the Magdalen Second Eleven caused a certain amount of anxiety in high quarters about the dignity of the heir apparent. That in the end he was not forbidden to play football was a landmark in the progressively democratic character of the British monarchy. It is one thing for a King's son to conform to the hierarchy of seniority in the Royal Navy and behave like any junior officer. It is altogether another thing for him to be reduced to the common level of the most typically plebeian game in Great Britain. Fortunately the Prince's tutor was able to assure a certain august personage that Association football was held in high esteem at Magdalen, and that the heir apparent's dignity was rather enhanced than lowered by his performance at it.

A third story relates that during the first year he was up at Oxford the Prince took advantage of the permission accorded to lunch with whom he liked either in his own rooms or in other people's, to lunch most often with what

Gunner called one of the very quiet men, a poor scholar of no apparent importance in the fashionable life of the college.

" X—— is his great friend. He sees more of him than anybody, and I'm very glad of it because he's a very nice fellow, but very quiet. Hardly any of the men in College know him by sight."

One of the biographers has repeated a legend that the Prince of Wales was secured for Magdalen from Christ Church, "royalty's traditional haunt," through the "gyratory abasements" of the President, Sir Herbert Warren. As stated already, the man chiefly responsible for the Prince's going to Magdalen was his tutor H. P. Hansell, and Christ Church could claim only Edward VII when Prince of Wales, whereas Magdalen could claim a much earlier Prince of Wales in the elder son of James I. Prince Henry Frederick matriculated at Magdalen in August 1605 when he was eleven and a half. In the following year when he was not yet thirteen De la Boderie, the French Ambassador, wrote on October 31st, 1606 :

" None of his pleasures savour the least of a child. He is a particular lover of horses and what belongs to them, but is not fond of hunting ; and when he goes to it it is rather for the pleasure of galloping than that which the dogs give him. He plays willing enough at tennis, and at another Scots diversion very like mall [golf no doubt] ; but this always with persons older than himself as if he despised those of his own age. He studies two hours, and employs the rest of his time in tossing the pike, or leaping, or shooting with the bow, or throwing the bar, or vaulting, or some other exercise of that kind ; and he is never idle. . . . He is already feared by those who have the management of affairs, and specially the Earl of Salisbury, who appears to be greatly apprehensive of the Prince's ascendant ; as the prince, on the other hand, shows little esteem for his lordship."

This Prince of Wales declined all suggestions of brides chosen for him by others, and at the age of eighteen he was planning to go to Germany and choose a wife for himself when typhoid fever, believed at the time to be poison, carried him off to the intense grief of the whole nation. " The lamentation made for him was so general, as men, women, and children partook of it."

Apart from his much more precocious development, and that it was death not abdication which befell, how much there is in that Magdalen Prince of Wales three centuries earlier to foreshadow his successor.

Although Warren was not primarily responsible for the decision to send the Prince of Wales to Magdalen his name is so intimately bound up with the renown of the College of which he was President from 1886 until 1928 that some attention must be paid to his personality. The last President but one of Magdalen, Dr Routh, whom Gunstone could remember, had belonged so much to the eighteenth century that he was wearing a wig in 1854 when he died in his hundredth year. Routh was succeeded by Bulley who lived to be ninety. So that of Warren's two predecessors one was born in 1755, the other in 1796. Magdalen had already ceased to be a close corporation of Fellows and Demys in the time of Bulley, but when T. H. Warren of Balliol was elected a fellow in 1877 he was the main influence in developing the College to play a richer part in University life, and when at the exceptionally early age of thirty-two he was elected President he lived for the glory of the College.

Warren in his respect for worldly success may be considered a typical product of Balliol under the Mastership of Benjamin Jowett. In Warren's case that respect for worldly success was accorded as much to those who had inherited it as to those who had earned it or were likely to earn it. This gave him the reputation he had of being an arch-snob, and extravagant anecdotes of his exploits in the way of deference to rank were as numerous as the Spoonerisms of the Warden of New College. He was the son of a Bristol business man and a Welshwoman. To the former he owed his practical ability, to the latter the imaginative colour which enabled him to accept himself seriously as a descendant of William de Warenne and decorate his drawing-room with blazonries of this mythical ancestry. When a man is capable without the slightest justification of believing himself to be descended from a Norman paladin he is likely to have an exaggerated respect for the titles of his own contemporaries. In appearance he was a burly man with a very dark beard before it whitened and what seemed, accentuated by a prominent set of teeth, an insincere and somewhat chilly smile which did much less than justice to his kindness, tempered though that kindness too often was by the claims of worldly success. Owing to Warren's failure to attract to the College that combination of brains with social advantages which Balliol ever since the days of Jowett had found so easy, he was inclined to regard his scholars as valuable members of the College only in so far as they were likely to secure firsts in the Schools.

Brilliance which was not entirely preoccupied with academic success he discouraged unless it was accompanied by prowess in sport or social eminence, which could happen but rarely. He wrote a certain amount of undistinguished verse, and in 1911 was elected without the slightest justification to the University Chair of Poetry. For his fulfilment of that position Oxford owed him nothing; for his practical work in various University posts from Vice-Chancellor downwards Oxford owes him much.

His President said * of the Prince of Wales that " bookish he will never be : not a ' Beauclerk,' still less a ' British Solomon.' Kings, perhaps fortunately, seldom are this last. This is not to be desired, but he will not want for power of ready and forcible presentation, either in speech or writing." The qualifications are typical of Warren's deference to expediency. He had essentially the mind which in bishops and politicians we applaud as conciliatory, but in lesser men sometimes denounce as time-serving. In spite of his early scholastic achievements both at Clifton and at Balliol Warren was *par excellence* the cautious second-rater whose many virtues and talents were never sufficiently recognised because only in snobbery did he achieve an authentic pre-eminence. Yet a reading of his ' report ' on the Prince in *The Times* which is printed as an appendix will suggest that Warren had obtained a fairly deep insight into the Prince's character, and it may be doubted if any other Head of a college would have penetrated more deeply. In any case no criticism of what was essentially a harmless and romantic snobbery should be allowed to deprive him of the chief credit for the renown his Presidency secured for the College he served with all his heart. The freshmen might laugh at him when year in year out he gave the same address to them gathered in Hall and always wound up by adjuring them to keep the white lilies of Magdalen unspotted, but they would not have been a week in residence before they would all be feeling acutely conscious of the superiority of Magdalen over any other college in the University and filled with a passion for Magdalen to excel at everything except learning, which the great majority of

* *The Times*, November 18th 1914.

them would have been surprised to hear there could ever be the least question of not despising.

And even as the freshmen of Magdalen used to laugh at their President so we now laugh at the young men before the war for extending a similar romantic idealisation to the business of fighting for their country. It is impossible to doubt that if the moment come the young men of to-day will turn to the business of fighting for their country with not less despatch than their predecessors, and if now the poems of Rupert Brooke may embarrass them like a love-letter read by one who loves not, those poems will seem much less merely romantic then. The exaltation of the mind which created them was akin with the mood in which Raleigh penned his sublime apostrophe to death, and the spirit in which men like Rupert Brooke set forth was fired with an ardour and urgency of adventure which had been wanting since the days of Elizabeth. Some of the effect the outbreak of war had on an Oxford college may be gathered from a letter of Gunstone's written in the middle of 1915:

"A service in the College Chapel in commemoration of all of ours who have fallen in the war. . . . It was a very solemn affair. I could not sleep that night for thinking of all those fine young fellows I had parted from only a short time before. Over thirty names read out, and since then many have to be added to the list. . . . Mr Benecke is the only Don up, the place is deserted. Only 30 undergrads out of our usual 150 came up last term. It will be worse in October. . . . Day after day I find Magdalen men in the list of killed and wounded."

Enclosed with the letter was what was probably the first and last poem the old man ever wrote:

Magdalen College,
Oxford.

DESERTED

No sound across the Cloistered quad
As daylight fades away,
No laughter borne upon the air,
No light with cheerful ray.

Where are the sounds of long ago
That echoed through these halls?
Naught but silence now is found
Among the old grey walls.

> The heavy doors look sinister,
>   Deserted is the stair,
> Stilled are the steps for evermore
>   That used to enter there.

On the back of this half-sheet of college notepaper the old man had written the names of forty Magdalen men already killed, a dozen of them contemporaries of him to whom the letter had been sent.   And this was only the first year of war. By the same mail arrived a list of Oxford men serving with the forces.   Christ Church and New College were first with 780 each.   Magdalen came next with 670.   But the first two colleges could draw on an average every year of 300 undergraduates in residence, Magdalen on no more than 160, so that proportionately Magdalen was far ahead of any other Oxford college.   670 men serving in August 1915 meant that practically every Magdalen man up during the last twenty years was in the Navy or in the Army.

Gunstone himself had retired from his stewardship of the Junior Common Room when the Prince of Wales left with the rest to seek active service.   He had promised Hansell not to retire until the Prince went down.   Little had the dear old man dreamed that his retirement would be spent in collecting every scrap of information he could glean from the newspapers about the careers of men for whom such a career was the last they had been expecting when they had shaken hands with him at the end of the summer term in 1914, and come out for the last time from his little office to see the lawn in the middle of Cloisters glowing green in the June sunshine, they who expected to be drinking their coffee after Hall in Gunner's again next October.   There may have been nothing heroic in the readiness of those young men of 1914 and 1915 to volunteer.   There may have been nothing behind their impulse except a desire to do the right thing, comparable in kind yet not in degree to the impulse which would prevent their wearing a black tie with tails or brown boots with a top-hat.   However, since none of them considered himself a hero and since none of them made a book about his sufferings, they are owed by the living at least as much respect as they pay to the debunkers of war who were lucky enough to live to debunk it.   Peace will never be secured by denying honour, virtue, and renown to those who fought in the last war, and war if it comes again will be so much the more intolerable because humanity will have failed to avert it by the appealing methods of the advertisement strip.

It was from such a Magdalen that the Prince of Wales set out like so many of his contemporaries and seniors to get out into the very middle of the war at the earliest moment possible. He had been a corporal in the Officers' Training Corps at Oxford, but naturally his first hope was to rejoin the Navy. The Admiralty declined the responsibility. Such caution in the early days of the war is intelligible enough, but not therefore less deplorable, whether we regard the effect on the country or on the Prince himself. What dead-sea fruit all those years of training must have seemed, what a sterile pretence, what a puppet laid away in cotton-wool he would have been thinking himself! Who dies if England live? What humbug it would have sounded!

However, he was allowed to be gazetted to the first battalion of the Grenadier Guards, and in training with them at Warley hope of getting out to the Front rose again. It was no doubt absurd of these young men before the war to pine to be in the thick of it, but they suffered from an incurable romantic perversity, and we who have said good-bye to all that may humbly remember that so many thousands of them said good-bye to life itself.

The training with the Guards continued, but the likelihood of getting out to France was seeming more and more remote. Mr Asquith in *Memories and Reflections* noted:

> *October 15th*, 1914. I went to see the King this morning. . . . He is much exercised about the Prince of Wales, who is eating his heart out to go to the Front, his battalion of Grenadiers being already gone without him. It is proposed that French should take him on his staff.

One day in that autumn of 1914 the Prince of Wales, a guardee ensign, tackled Lord Kitchener in the War Office. Now that was an act of courage for a young Grenadier even if he was the heir apparent. Lord Carson once told the present writer that the members of the Cabinet were so frightened of Kitchener that none of them would ever dare ask him a question. The project of the Suvla Landing was being discussed, and in their perplexity the members of the Cabinet begged Carson to beard the lion in his den. Lion is not the great cat to choose for a comparison. Kitchener

was a tiger with cold unblinking steel-blue eyes more frighten-
ing than any tiger's, and when asked an awkward question
like a tiger disturbed in his jungle lair.

Carson, with that swart bulk of chin out-thrust, put the
question.

" Can you not tell us, Mr Secretary for War, what
chance the proposed new landing at Suvla has of being
successful ? "

The tiger (Clemenceau was but a mangy old tiger-cat
beside Kitchener) moved his head, the eyes unblinking.

" How the devil do I know ? I haven't been there,
have I ? "

And the Cabinet had to accept this as an answer. Not
even Carson ventured to ask another question, though Carson
was a brave man. And out in Gallipoli Sir Ian Hamilton,
who if called upon to do so would have charged the Turkish
lines alone, used to shudder at the notion of arguing with
Kitchener even by cable.

> A General laying down the law to a Field Marshal is as obnoxious
> to military " form " as a vacuum was once supposed to be to the
> sentiments of nature. The child who teaches its grandmother to
> suck eggs, commits a venial fault in comparison. So I have had to
> convey my precepts insensibly to Milord K——, to convey them in
> homœopathic doses of parable.

Thus Sir Ian Hamilton in his Diary, and whether Prince
of Wales or not a subaltern arguing with a Field Marshal
was in imagination beyond any conceivable obnoxiousness to
military form.

But the Prince of Wales was set on getting out to France,
and he had the courage to argue with Lord Kitchener in the
War Office itself.

" What does it matter if I am killed ? " he asked. " I
have four brothers."

So early in life was he prepared to " let them down ". He
was actually ready to abdicate from life.

But Kitchener did not say :

" This is grievous news, Sir." He said, " If I were sure
you would be killed I do not know if I should be right to
restrain you. What I cannot allow is the chance, which
always exists until we have a settled line, of the enemy's
taking you prisoner."

No doubt the capture of the Prince of Wales would have

been an immense encouragement to Germany. Nevertheless, the refusal of that permission to go to France was perhaps the first real lesson he had of what may be the bitterness of kingship. George I at Neuhaüsel and Neerwinden, George II at Oudenarde and Dettingen, George III preparing to command in person the troops mustered to resist Napoleon's invasion, poor George IV telling stories of his behaviour at Waterloo which, little enough of merit though anybody will allow him, may after all have been an expression of his desire to be there, William IV fighting his gun off Cape St Vincent, Queen Victoria driving out to be shot at again so that the miscreant could be apprehended, Edward VII completely unconcerned by the attempt on his life in Brussels—they were all brave, the princes of that House.

Yet if we take the courage of the Prince of Wales for granted as the inherited quality of a long ancestry of courage, we must read with emotion the letter * Sir Dighton Probyn wrote to Sir George Arthur when the line was considered settled after the first Battle of Ypres.

"I saw the dear . . . Prince of Wales yesterday. He came to wish me good-bye—and it really was delightful to see the change that had come over him since he had last been in this room. On the last occasion he really *cried* with sorrow at the idea of 'being disgraced,' and he said he was not being allowed to go to the war. Yesterday his face beamed with joy. Do let Lord Kitchener know this."

And to plane away any hint of bias let us hasten to record that Mr Stanley Baldwin was not a whit less anxious to serve his country than the Prince of Wales. In 1924 when he was Prime Minister he revealed how much. He had seen the first volunteers of Kitchener's Army ". . . and, as I saw them, I wished that I was with them. I wanted to do service for my country, and the chance came to me. I was offered service in the Government and, to my delight, in an unpaid post. I felt, 'well, now I can pull my weight!' I learned at that time to put myself in the background; I regarded myself as dedicated to the service of my country."

In June 1915 Mr Baldwin served on a committee to examine the problem of enemy aliens. In August 1915 he added his signature to those of thirty-nine other Members of Parliament

* Quoted by Mr Bolitho in his *Edward VIII.*

at the foot of a letter asking Mr Asquith to receive a deputa-
tion to bring before him the view that " only by the early
adoption of a measure of compulsory service can the war be
brought to a successful termination." And in December
1915 he served on a committee appointed to examine the best
way of raising money for the war from the ' working classes.'
He was finally recommended by Lord Beaverbrook or Sir
J. C. C. Davidson to Mr Bonar Law as his Parliamentary
Private Secretary in the new Government. " I admit,"
says Lord Beaverbrook in his *Politicians and the Press*, " I
did not foresee in any way the remarkable talents he was
going to develop. He seemed simply a sound steady man
who could be absolutely depended upon by his Parliamentary
Chief."

In January 1917 Mr Baldwin became a Junior Lord of
the Treasury (unpaid) and was soon promoted to be joint
Financial Secretary to the Treasury (still unpaid) a post
which he retained until 1921.

On June 23rd 1919, the Prince of Wales's twenty-fifth
birthday, the following letter appeared in *The Times*:

RICHESSE OBLIGE

A PATRIOTIC DUTY

SIR,—

It is now a truism to say that in August 1914 the nation was face
to face with the greatest crisis in her history. She was saved by the
free-will offerings of her people. The best of her men rushed to
the Colours; the best of her women left their homes to spend and be
spent; the best of her older men worked as they had never worked
before, to a common end, and with a sense of unity and fellowship
as new as it was exhilarating. It may be that in four and a half
years the ideals of many became dim, but the spiritual impetus of
those early days carried the country through to the end.

To-day, on the eve of peace we are faced with another crisis, less
obvious, but none the less searching. The whole country is exhausted.
By a natural reaction, not unlike that which led to the excesses of the
Restoration after the reign of the Puritans, all classes are in danger of
being submerged by a wave of extravagance and materialism. It is
so easy to live on borrowed money ; so difficult to realise that you are
doing so.

It is so easy to play ; so hard to learn that you cannot play for long without work.   A fool's paradise is only the ante-room to a fool's hell.

How can the nation be made to understand the gravity of the financial situation ; that love of country is better than love of money ?

This can only be done by example, and the wealthy classes have to-day an opportunity of service which can never recur.

They know the danger of the present debt; they know the weight of it in the years to come.   They know the practical difficulties of a statutory capital levy.   Let them impose upon themselves, each as he is able, a voluntary levy.   It should be possible to pay to the Exchequer within twelve months such a sum as would save the taxpayer fifty millions a year.

I have been considering that matter for nearly two years, but my mind moves slowly ; I dislike publicity, and I hoped that someone else might lead the way.   I have made as accurate an estimate as I am able of the value of my own estate and have arrived at a total of about £580,000.   I have decided to realise twenty per cent of that amount, or say, £120,000 of the New War Loan, and present it to the Government for cancellation.

I give this portion of my estate as a thank-offering, in the firm conviction that never again shall we have such a chance of giving our country that form of help which is so vital at the present time.

Yours etc.,
"F. S. T."

It never struck even Mr Austen Chamberlain who became Chancellor of the Exchequer in the new Government elected a month after the Armistice that the initials " F. S. T." stood for his own Financial Secretary to the Treasury. And it is melancholy indeed to have to add that so few other rich men followed Mr Baldwin's example that instead of the fifty million pounds it was to save the taxpayer the sum total of their patriotic disgorgement did not save the taxpayer the interest on half a million.   The story of Mr Baldwin's generosity to the taxpayer did not become generally known for several years.   No doubt the giver had hoped it would remain a secret for ever, but as Portia says, ' How far that little candle throws his beams !   So shines a good deed in a naughty world,' and many will recognise in the anonymity of this munificent gesture another illustration of Mr Baldwin's paradisial innocence.   He was himself more emotionally impressed by the romance of that unpaid Government post in the days when he was ' doing his bit.'   At Leeds in 1925 he proclaimed :

" I had the opportunity of giving my services to the country without any feeling that it was necessary to be remunerated for them. There is nothing singular in that. There must have been millions of men who felt as I did. I have never said or believed that that service which I had the opportunity of rendering was one whit higher or better than any other."

The admission in that last sentence would console the Prince of Wales for what *he* always called ' the insignificant part he played in the war': console perhaps even the dead. But one grows embarrassed by Mr Baldwin's depreciation of himself, and hears with some relief that in 1921 he was made President of the Board of Trade. The new post carried a salary of £2000 a year, and that even for a man who still had £460,000 of his fortune left was something.

CHAPTER VII

ROYALTY IN THE WAR

A SUMMARY of the Prince of Wales's experience during the first months of the war may be read in an extract from a despatch of the Field-marshal Commander-in-Chief of the British Army in the Field dated at General Headquarters on April 5th, 1915:

> His Royal Highness the Prince of Wales is the bearer of this despatch.
> His Royal Highness continues to make most satisfactory progress. During the Battle of Neuve Chapelle he acted on my General Staff as a Liaison Officer. Reports from the General Officers Commanding Corps and Divisions to which he has been attached agree in commending the thoroughness in which he performs any work entrusted to him.
>
> I have myself been very favourably impressed by the quickness with which His Royal Highness has acquired knowledge of the various branches of the service and the deep interest he has always displayed in the comfort and welfare of the men.
> His visits to the troops, both in the field and in hospitals, have been greatly appreciated by all ranks. His Royal Highness did duty for a time in the trenches, with the Battalion to which he belongs.

No doubt the Prince of Wales would have preferred to spend the whole time with the men of his platoon whether they were in the front line of trenches or not.   Equally no doubt all that could be done to keep him away from the front line was done, and his efforts to dodge the surveillance of generals have become legends.   Such legends need not be recapitulated.   His courage is unassailable.

As was mentioned above he himself was wont to refer afterwards in public speeches to the 'insignificant part he played in the war.'   One may reflect that however insignificant he may have considered it he never forgot through all the years afterwards his comradeship with those who had fought.   It was left for a clerical gentleman in Paris on the nineteenth anniversary of the Armistice to let him know that such comradeship had become an embarrassment if it was to involve his association with the living in their tribute to the dead.   The soil of Flanders, the dust of Gallipoli, the sand of Mesopotamia, nay the very waters of the seven seas would rise in the pulpit to protest against such a *faux pas* in the sight of Almighty God.   Such was the implication of that clerical embarrassment.

The award to royal infants of a Field-marshal's baton on which to cut their teeth has now become a custom of the past. The Prince had to wait two years before he was gazetted Captain.   There would be no criticism of a Prince of Wales who had ordered his Army forward to the butchery of a Verdun ; but he was familiar with every part of the Western Front.   In 1916 he went out to Egypt and the Soudan.   In 1917 he visited King Victor Emmanuel on the Italian Front. It is greatly to be regretted that he never saw Gallipoli.   Not, let it hastily be added, because his position at that date was strong enough for him to have exerted the slightest influence on the attitude at home toward the project of opening the Dardanelles, and certainly none on that of G.H.Q. in France. That inside view of Gallipoli would have been of value to the Prince himself, because it would have revealed to him, perhaps on the very day he came of age, what might ensue from one bold spirit's attempt to overcome the opposition of the many when such opposition was being deliberately fostered by the prejudice or jealousy or caution or crassness reflecting a powerful oligarchy.   A few months more than twenty-one years later Mr Winston Churchill, speaking under great emotion, would tell the House of Commons that what had been done, or left undone, belonged to history, and that to history, so far as he was concerned, it should be left. None had a better right to trust in history than he, who had lived to see his project to force the Dardanelles, assailed once as wild and costly folly, accepted as a commonplace of prudent strategy.

However, the Prince of Wales did not reach Gallipoli, and therefore speculation whether his mind would have responded to the lesson it offered is beside the point. What is not beside the point is to remind contemporary readers that the most damning evidence of the determination of a prejudiced Cabinet, a jealous High Command in France, a cautious Admiralty, and a crass public opinion to regard the Dardanelles Expedition as a side-show was the failure to send the Prince of Wales to Gallipoli in the early summer of 1915. The Mediterranean Expeditionary Force was a microcosm of the British Empire, and a more representative microcosm than the much larger force on the Western Front in 1915.

Anxious biographers, historians, and commentators searching to find excuses for what they have ventured to call King Edward VIII's eccentric behaviour have discovered in the war-time experience of the Prince of Wales those first unsettling concomitants of his life which were to lead ultimately to his desiring to settle down with the woman he loved. They point out that even during the war he was all over the place. It has been observed above that no doubt the Prince would have preferred to remain in the front line with the men of his own platoon ; but even the conditions of front-line life in France and Flanders lacked some of the humdrum quality of a secluded rural existence. Indeed, it is not extravagant to suggest that an existence which leaves a young man as agreeably surprised to find himself alive after another day as a centenarian to find himself alive after another year is every bit as unsettling as serving as a liaison officer to one General after another Commanding Corps or Division, as visiting King Victor Emmanuel on the Italian Front, or as studying the defences of the Suez Canal. War itself is a sufficiently violent unsettlement of all human nature without looking for the particular aspects of it which are likely to upset one individual more than another.

It does not detract a millimetre from King George's moral

stature to point out that the task of deportment for a middle-aged man during the war was a comparatively easy one, provided he had no temptation to sentimentalise or desire to dramatise his inactivity. That was impossible for King George, because nobody had a heavier weight of responsibility and nobody was more fully occupied than he was. Moreover, he could feel reasonably sure that his people, even the stupidest of them, would appreciate that fact. He visited the wounded at home; he crossed the Channel several times and showed himself to his troops in the field; he was up at Scapa Flow with the Grand Fleet; he gave the nation a shock by being thrown with his horse falling on top of him; he allowed it to be made known that for the duration of the war no alcoholic liquor would be served at his table. He spared the blushes of his subjects by refraining from indulging in that suggestion of mutual back-smacking which was such an offensive feature of the Kaiser's association of himself and the German people with the favour of the Almighty. In fact throughout the years of war his personality slowly but ever more surely impressed itself upon the minds of his subjects as that of one who summed up most perfectly in the thoroughness of his actions and the modesty of his demeanour the popular conception of the man who, as the current phrase of that meiosis so dear to the English had it, was ' doing his bit.'

But the spectacle of the unfailing ability of King George V to adapt his behaviour to his people's ideal of a modern constitutional monarch, to provide neither more nor less than the amount of jam deemed necessary to flavour and lighten that huge, heavy roly-poly pudding of bourgeois sentiment, must not be allowed to obscure the gravity of the crisis that the progress of the war was seeming to the existence of royalty or the urgency of the question that progress was compelling every royal personage to ask himself. It would involve no exaggeration to assert that for the larger number of European royalties, major and minor, belligerent and neutral, the result of the war was regarded exclusively from the standpoint of its effect on their own position in the future. In this respect the British Royal Family were fortunate in being able to enjoy from a contemplation of the past some assurance that, provided they adapted themselves to the popular belief in their utility and the popular notion of how that utility should be demon-strated, they could rely with the utmost confidence on the pro-

found affection of the British people for the monarchical
institution—an affection which has survived the blow to
Kingship dealt when Mary, Queen of Scots, was tried and
executed for treason to a Queen of England whom a quarter
of her subjects believed to be a bastard and usurper; the
second blow to kingship dealt when Charles I was tried and
executed for treason to his own subjects; and the final blow
to kingship which was dealt when James II and VII was
abdicated and the legitimist line excluded from the succession;
such an affection, however cruel sometimes, must be held
cruel only to be kind to monarchy.

Nevertheless, whatever confidence might be placed in that
affection for the institution of monarchy, King George with
the inestimably valuable help of his Consort, left nothing undone not merely to relieve any possibility of straining that
affection by even so much as being a few seconds late for a
ceremony, but also by the gradual assumption of a patriarchal
dignity and authority to give a living force to the new aspect
of the monarchy as the symbol of British unity the world over.
It will be necessary in due course to examine more closely this
new conception of the monarch.   For the present it is enough
to observe King George was careful during the war to weld
for monarchy foundations strong enough to support the
colossus it was proposed not by him but by his advisers
to erect upon those foundations.   King George had the
advantage of ruling over an Empire old enough to see a
rebellious offshoot grow into a tree as mighty as itself.   He
was absolved from the disagreeable task of seeming to be
extolling his own grandeur by extolling the grandeur of his
people.   The Kaiser in demanding for Germany a place in
the sun always appeared to be demanding it for himself.
Even his own Imperial claims were suspect, and in their
hearts the majority of the German peoples regarded him as a
pinchbeck Barbarossa, a Charlemagne of shreds and patches.
What veneration was still accorded to the name Emperor was
accorded to the old Habsburg whose death for years had been
awaited as the signal for a European conflagration, that conflagration the kindling of which was precipitated by a spark
from Serajevo.   Once upon a time England had supported
Austria and Prussia to help herself wrest from France all she
could of the world outside Europe.   Now she was helping
France to retain her position in Europe in order to secure the

retention of what they had both amassed outside Europe. And France was a republic.

A hint of King George's doubt about the future of royalty may be detected in his remark to Walter Hines Page, the American Ambassador : " Knowing the difficulties of a limited monarch, I thank heaven I am spared being an absolute one." Certainly he was made sharply aware at the beginning of the war of the country's feeling about the German royalty from whose stock he had sprung when a vulgar agitation succeeded in driving Prince Louis of Battenberg from the Admiralty. King George himself had never associated himself prominently with his royal German relatives. He was as completely English in temperament, outlook, tastes, behaviour and speech as John Bull himself. Yet the hysteria of war seemed capable of anything. The shortage of shells was attributed to the fact that General von Donop was Master of the Ordnance. Sir Eyre Crowe, the Assistant Permanent Under-Secretary for Foreign Affairs, incurred vulgar suspicion when it was learnt he had a German wife and a German mother. Lord Haldane was driven from public life because he had once admitted that Germany was his spiritual home. Even Mr Asquith himself could be easily manœuvred out of office because the public remembered that Mrs Asquith had sent flowers and fruit to German officers interned at Donington Hall. The hysterical belief in pro-Germanism in high places reached its height in 1918 with the trial of Mr Pemberton-Billing, M.P., at the Central Criminal Court on a charge of publishing a false and defamatory libel on Miss Maud Allan.

To quote the *Annual Register* :

The action arose from an indecent paragraph in an insignificant journal conducted by Mr Pemberton-Billing, M.P., with the object, as he practically boasted, of forcing exposures by means of libel. In this particular instance the primary object of his attack was Miss Maud Allan and her performance of Oscar Wilde's play " Salome ". But the case very soon developed into a whole series of promiscuous innuendoes, in which pro-Germanism was united with every sort of unnatural vice, against many thousands of English men and women, including Mr Justice Darling himself, who was the Judge in this case. The bone of contention—the estimate of " Salome " as a play—was overshadowed by the mysterious German " Black Book " mentioned by several witnesses, including Mrs Villiers-Stuart, as a sinister compilation of names in this country likely to be useful to the Germans.

The jury's verdict was in favour of Mr Billing. But it may be of interest to note that three months later Mrs Villiers-Stuart was sentenced for bigamy to nine months' imprisonment without hard labour.

What is of considerably greater interest to note is that the " Black Book " was a list of possible purchasers of a well-known make of German automobile issued as a guide to its travelling salesmen before the war, and that this harmless commercial document inspired scenes at the Old Bailey unprecedented in a British Court of Justice. Mr Justice Darling was less able to preserve order or keep the evidence relevant than the King of Hearts in *Alice in Wonderland*. It is depressing to have to record now that some of the blowflies of rumour which were buzzing round London in 1918 are still alive and still dropping their foul eggs in the brains of fanatical dunces and madmen. The trial was pandemonium, *but* the jury found for the defendant. Twelve good men and true believed the farrago of filthy nonsense which turned the court into a cesspit. Those twelve good men and true represented public opinion under the inflence of rumour. The *Annual Register* attributed the morbid interest in what *The Times* called a scandalous trial to the " effect of the air raids, the food situation, the inconveniences of travelling, and the general atmosphere created by the war." It must be argued, however, that the fundamental cause was the susceptibility of the human mind to the degradation of rumour when rumour's blazing torch is kindled at the secret fire of base passions fed by ignorance. Eighteen years after this revelation of the depths of credulity to which English men and women are capable of sinking under the strain of unusual excitement, rumour would once more kindle her torch at that secret fire and consume the reputation of a King.

With evidence of what rumour could effect in times of peace by crediting him with a morganatic wife and now with fresh evidence throughout the war of the alarming power of it in every direction, George V could not but preoccupy himself with a possible suspicion of pro-Germanism being directed against himself. With the spread of insanity in public opinion his declaration at the unveiling of Queen Victoria's memorial about the strong and living ties of kinship and friendship between himself and the Kaiser might be raked up. In June 1917 he announced that the Princes of his family

E

who were his subjects and bore German names and titles should relinquish these titles and adopt British surnames.   Accordingly the Duke of Teck became Marquess of Cambridge, his brother Prince Alexander of Teck Earl of Athlone, Prince Louis of Battenberg Marquess of Milford Haven, and Prince Alexander of Battenberg Marquess of Carisbrooke.   Cambridge was to be the family name of the first two peerages, Mountbatten of the other two.   When the second Duke of Cambridge wedded Louisa Fairbrother as George Frederick Cambridge, Gent. at St John's Clerkenwell how little he thought he was anticipating his great-nephews by seventy years.   And who, three centuries hence, if titles last and the House endure, will associate Mountbatten with a little place in Hesse dragged from obscurity to provide Countess Julia Hauke with a title as the morganatic wife of Prince Alexander of Hesse, herself the daughter of a Polish general and the granddaughter of Salome Schweppenhaüser whose father was a German pastor ?   The new Lord Carisbrooke took a step still further away from that ancestry by marrying Lady Irene Denison a month after he ceased to be a Battenberg.

This absorption of the two morganatic titles of Teck and Battenberg into the English peerage was followed by the King's abandonment of all German titles for himself and his family, and the issue of a proclamation that his House and Family should henceforth be known as the House and Family of Windsor.   Hanover and Brunswick, Saxe-Coburg-Gotha, and even the tremendous names of Guelph and Wettin themselves rolled out of existence by that old castle beside the Thames ! Geologists assert that the Thames was once a tributary of the Rhine when the North Sea was land.   That the House of Windsor was once an offshoot of Guelphdom already seems just such another antediluvian fact.   Still, at the time the change was made, although the Czar had been deposed, Germany was bubbling with petty royalties and there was no sign yet of their all being absorbed into the person of an Austrian painter.

The dissociation of the British Royal House and Family from its German connections so firmly effected by King George V with the enthusiastic approval of his peoples, however gratifying it might be to them, was regarded by the German royalties as a betrayal of the Blood.   A long process of inbreeding, much intensified during the eighteenth and nineteenth centuries, had evolved from the Protestant rulers of petty German states what we now recognise as the type of royalty.   We can

leave out of account the Catholic royal strain which has played
no part in English history since slandered saintly Mary of
Modena

The popular Monarchy in which the King was the
father of his people ruling by Divine right had made
excessive demands on royal humanity, and in the end what
shreds of it were left clinging to James II vanished when he
was jockeyed off the throne and out of the succession by the
Whig oligarchy.   In the new monarchy which took its place
the monarch ceased to be the father of his people ruling
by Divine right and became the expression of the political
party in power reigning by " popular " consent.   That was
why for five generations the Prince of Wales as a matter of
course became the expression of the political party not in
power.   It was the Reform Bill followed by the accession of
Queen Victoria which broke up this tradition of government.
For the next hundred years the new power of Parliament,
which seemed so alarming to the landed oligarchy of the time,
would be slowly and steadily undermined by the executive
until it reached the position we are in to-day when, although
the King's head be still on the coins, the King's justice still
nominally administered, and the King's ministers still liable to
dismissal, the King himself is an expression of perfect behaviour,
to which has been added a successful presentation of him to
the Dominions as a kind of diluted Mikado.   The present
writer is not desirous to argue whether such a state of affairs
makes for good or ill.   He is merely concerned to point out
the accentuation of the ideal status of kingship and the diminu-
tion of the real status.   We are faced with the paradox that
adverse criticism of the monarchy is a more heinous offence
than adverse criticism of the king.

How much the executive dreaded any action that might
seem to suggest their indifference to the benefit of monarchical
institutions was often evident during the war, and the continual
interference of the British Government with French anti-
monarchical projects was always attributed by the French to
the directly exerted influence of King George.   That was a
misapprehension of the facts : but it is true that certain officials
of the Foreign Office concealed their own dislike of shaking the
stability of monarchical institutions by allowing it to be
attributed to royal intervention.   It is also true that King
George did not hesitate to express adverse criticism of his own
diplomats who *en poste* failed to offer their resignations when

royal relatives of his own had to be admonished in the interest of the international situation. The conduct of affairs in Russia, in Spain, and in Greece was undoubtedly hampered by royal sentiment; and because the French saw relatives of King George on so many thrones he was blamed for what they believed was the excessive consideration accorded to their occupants. The French objected to the freedom enjoyed by royal correspondence, and made no bones about denouncing this freedom as the most fruitful source of intelligence to the enemy. The family is the unit of French life and that the royal family of Europe was not bound together by ties much closer than the ties of the countries over which they ruled was to the French mind incredible. It was not until the deposition of the Czar that the British Government agreed to the deposition of King Constantine of Greece, and that was only because public opinion in Great Britain was growing so impatient of what it thought was the undue indulgence allowed him that it was feared it might react against the esteem and affection for the British monarchy.

The royal family of Greece was an epitome of the royal family of Europe. The King himself was a nephew of Queen Alexandra and a first cousin of King George. The Queen was a sister of the Kaiser and also a first cousin of King George. Prince Nicolas was married to the Grand Duchess Helen Vladimirovna who was a first cousin of the Czar. Prince Andrew was married to Princess Alice, a daughter of Prince Louis of Battenberg.

Public opinion attributed King Constantine's apparently pro-German attitude to the influence of his wife. In this public opinion was wrong. That attitude was due entirely to his respect for what he believed was the invincible military strength of Germany. As an example of the insolence with which this belief imbued the Greek General Staff may be cited the visit to Lord Kitchener in November 1915 of General Dousmanis, the Chief of Staff, and his Assistant Colonel Metaxas (the present Dictator) who both arrived at the British Legation flaunting their German decorations. That belief in Germany's invincibility being strong enough to survive Lord Kitchener's personal exposition of the Allied position in November 1915, it was unlikely that a visit from the late Mr W. B. Harris would have the slightest influence. Yet it had been seriously believed that Mr Harris's ' way ' with royalty would exert an effect. Harris was the *Times* corre-

spondent in Morocco, who had entertained various Princes and
Princesses at his famously beautiful house near Tangiers.   His
theory about royalties was that they must be amused like
children and that if one knew how to amuse them according to
their taste any favour would be granted, in this case the favour
of entering the war on the side of the Entente.   He was like
that eighteenth-century courtier who divided the human race
into whites, blacks, and royalties.   Harris believed that the
circumstances of their upbringing and education and the
effect of their sheltered dependent lives kept them from ever
really growing up, and his success with them was the success
which a servant always has with the children.   He was even
prouder of his way with royalties than of his way with Moorish
dignitaries.   He chattered with gusto of a trick with bread
and butter with which he had convulsed many royal tea-tables.
The King was in his counting-house counting out his money
and the Queen was in the parlour eating bread and honey as
one listened to Harris's tales of royalty.   One observed in
him who was not a professional courtier the mannerisms and
gestures which had marked the professional Edwardian courtier.
The resemblance to an upper servant recurred.   It was like
sitting in the housekeeper's room and hearing tit-bits about
the gentry.   One recalled how when staying in one of the
royal establishments the valets addressed one another by their
masters' titles and took their precedence belowstairs.   Flunkeydom is in a state of decay nowadays whether it be the flunkeydom of the great house or the higher flunkeydom of the court
officials.   That grand absurdity of manner is no longer easily
to be found.   And that very decay of flunkeydom may indicate
a fundamental change in royalty itself.   Still, even nowadays,
the courtier, if he may have lost the grand manner of flunkeydom, has preserved the baser traits associated with his condition from an immemorial past.   The behaviour of some
courtiers during December 1936 will always occupy a distinguished place in the annals of menial treachery.

After the failure of Mr Harris to lure King Constantine to
war by humorous sallies and tricks with bread and butter the
British Government reverted to the more conventional paths
of diplomacy, not, it has to be admitted, with any more success
than Mr Harris with his bread and butter.   If Venizelos had
immediately gone all out for a republic with French backing
the situation that arose in Athens in 1916 might easily have
been precipitated a year earlier.   But Venizelos did not want

a republic. At that date he was as firm a believer in the institution of monarchy as the British Government. What he
wanted was to eliminate King Constantine and replace him
with another monarch. His private hope was Prince Arthur
of Connaught. However, even if such a shuffle had been
possible to arrange with the royal family of Europe, it was
prohibited by the self-denying ordinance which the three
guarantor powers of the Greek constitution had entered into
not to put one of their own princes on the throne. Those
powers were Great Britain, France and Russia.

At last in June 1917 King Constantine was deposed and
exiled; the present King George II, then Duke of Sparta, was
excluded from the succession; and the throne was given to his
younger brother who reigned for three years as King Alexander.
It was the hope of Venizelos that the young King—he was
twenty-four when he ascended the throne—would wed an
English princess; but Alexander loved Mademoiselle Aspasia
Manos, a daughter of Colonel Manos, the ex-King's Master of
the Horse. Lovely as fabled Helen and tall as Hera, her
cheeks the burnt rose of an old vase, she added to outward
beauty an eloquence ennobled by sincerity, graced by wit, and
fired by passion. "Suddenly she stopped in the glittering
dust of the half-made Athenian street beneath the full blue
velvet sky of afternoon and, raising her arm above her head,
denounced the proposal of the Entente to cede Cavalla to the
Bulgarians, declaimed against the iniquitous hypocrisy of great
nations, and called down vengeance upon the enemies of her
country." Among the last she counted the great Cretan, and
when Alexander desired to make her his queen Venizelos
refused to empower such a marriage. By that refusal he
believed himself to be expressing the general wish of the
Hellenes. So Alexander wedded Aspasia morganatically,
and in 1919 he died from the bite of a monkey, leaving an
infant daughter. How far Venizelos was wise, how far foolish
in preventing Aspasia Manos from being Queen of the
Hellenes that monkey's bite has made a question for ever
unanswerable. The great mass of the Greek people believed
that the monkey's bite was a sign of Heaven's disapproval
of the deposition of Constantine. He was restored to the
throne by popular vote, only to be exiled again two years later.
The French Government wished to forbid his return; but
the British Government with the support of Italy preferred to
compromise, and in the end the three Governments issued a

declaration that King Constantine would not be recognised and that the subsidies which Greece had been receiving from them would be withdrawn.   Finally, Great Britain abandoned Greece to the treachery of France and Italy and the vengeance of Turkey, and put the blame on Mr Lloyd George who almost alone among British statesmen seemed to appreciate that the Mediterranean held a problem for the future of Europe and Asia.

King Constantine was sacrificed, and if any suspicion lingered of Great Britain's superstitious veneration for monarchy it was made abundantly clear that there was no element of super-stition in it, but that monarchy was regarded merely as a convenient abstraction.   If such an assertion seem intemperate let it be noted that, before the Greek plebiscite to decide on the restoration, the Great Powers issued a pro-clamation that the recall of King Constantine would create an unfavourable situation between Greece and themselves.

When it *might* have been serviceable to depose King Constantine the British Government blocked the way.   When it *was* serviceable to depose him the British Government ac-quiesced.   When it *would* have been serviceable to support openly his restoration the British Government accepted a verbal compromise which left him and his unhappy country in the air.   When both crashed, and in the agony of the Asia Minor disaster the convicted authors of it were court-martialled and shot, the British Government, which shared with France and Italy a major responsibility for that disaster, profoundly shocked by the revolutionary notion that an administration could be held capitally responsible for injury to the State, withdrew His Britannic Majesty's diplomatic representative from Athens.   Two years earlier ex-Colonel Malone M.P. had asked at the Albert Hall what were a few Churchills or Curzons on lamp-posts compared to the massacre of thousands of human beings.   That question earned him six months in gaol.

The years passed.   Greece without a king was perpetually convulsed by political dissensions ; but it was significantly not until a menacing situation developed between Great Britain and Italy that the Government of this country, realising too late the strategic mistake of that surrender to Italy of Rhodes and the Dodecanese, warmly supported a fresh restoration of King George II, with an eye on Corfu and Crete and Mitylene, the vital importance of which to sea power in the Mediterranean had been revealed by the late war.   Monarchy in Greece became a shuttlecock.   No doubt, it could be argued that the Greek dynasty owed its existence as such to the need for installing a commissionaire outside an establishment in a rowdy thoroughfare, and the choice by the Great Powers of a suitable candidate for the post.   Such an argument but adds weight to the suspicion that the Great hidden Powers which rule a country like our own are not less inimical to popular kingship than the Great open Powers which attempt to control the course of European events, and that in the words of Disraeli " as the power of the Crown diminished, the privileges of the people have disappeared ; till at length the sceptre has become a pageant, and its subject has degenerated into a serf."

The treatment of monarchy in Greece has been discussed at some length because it is the only monarchy in Europe which during the last twenty years has experienced a comparable series of reverses and triumphs and ultimately survives with what at the moment of writing appears a prospect of stability.   Its vicissitudes are the outstanding example in Europe of the spell the magic of kingship can cast upon a people which by character and temperament might have seemed the most naturally republican in the world.   It may appear an impertinence to suggest that so small a country can offer a lesson to the far-flung British Empire ; but there is a lesson, and it is that a statesman, even as great a statesman as Venizelos, cannot afford to break that spell without imperilling the sanctity of the ground it guards.   When we come to examine the statesmanship of Earl Baldwin it may be possible to exonerate him from all blame for the course of certain events.   Meanwhile, on that bright horizon of British monarchy there yet lingers a cloud of black smoke from the funnels of that ship whose helm he once directed.   He has handed the wheel to another, but most of his old crew are still serving and the black smoke is still defiling that bright horizon.   That ship should not be fuelled with the reputation of a king, for it is the ship of State.

But remote, how immeasurably remote from such a stokehole fed with slander, lie, and innuendo by the dark shapes of malice, envy and morbid lewdness and the pale dirty forms of expediency and fear, is the reputation of the young Prince of Wales during those years of war.   The stories now are all of his enchanting revelation of a simple boyish heart beneath a royal tunic.   He plays football with the Tommies in the mud of Flanders.   He asks for a light for his cigarette and shudders not at the horny hand which offers it.   He thinks being killed is great sport.   That story had but a brief currency.   Like the poor chap in Gallipoli whose pal was blown to pieces beside him, the country which had thought the war ' funny at first ' all too soon found it was ' very serious really.'   The Prince of Wales would have enough of that infallible royal tact to agree with the country.

Yet, behind all those tales of journalists who forbidden by the censor to reveal that war was inhuman consoled their readers by revealing that the Prince of Wales was not, there do emerge the first faint outlines of the man whose humanity was one day to stand in no need of any journalist's hackwork to demonstrate it.   And now all they can find to say of the effect of the war on that Prince of Wales was how much it unsettled him.   No doubt it did.   And it unsettled others who like him must look back across the estranging gulf of war to the Magdalen elms and lawns, yes, and many many another more who across the same estranging gulf must look back to fetid slums and the asphalt playgrounds of the poor.   It is a decency on which the mind dwells with relief that here and there some of those men who came back from the war with the Prince of Wales sent him a word of fellowship across the more estranging gulf of abdication.

CHAPTER VIII

THE FIRST TOURS

THE Prince of Wales remained with the troops until after Christmas 1918.   Whatever he could give of good fellow-ship he gave.   Then he came back to play a more arduous part in peace than, never for lack of trying, he had been allowed to play in war.   It is pleasant to find that the first public appearance after his return home the *Annual Register* of 1919 records is of his presence at the National Sporting Club on March 31st to watch the immortal Jimmy Wilde defeat the American, Joe Linch.   More significant, how-ever, though not recorded in the *Annual Register*, is that the thousands outside Buckingham Palace on Peace Night were not content with the appearance of the King and Queen. They wanted the Prince of Wales and would not disperse until he came out on the balcony and said a few words.   He had already caught the imagination of London.   He was the symbol of the new world that was to rise from the ashes of war, the expression of that new spirit which was so critical already of the new Government elected in December 1918 that at every bye-election since the Coalition-Unionist candidates were finding turnovers of ten thousand votes and more against them.

When Mr Hector Bolitho's biography of King Edward VIII appeared serially in a magazine called *Leisure* in the middle of the King's brief reign he wrote of this return from the War :

> The Prince of Wales added new forces to his inheritance during the years in France. . . . He was moulded by deeper experience of life than any of his ancestors had enjoyed. . . . His power was to lie in the sympathy with which he understood his own troubled generation. For himself, his standards were as rigid as those of his father.   But his experience made him understand the young in a *new* way, through the gentleness of his judgments.

When Mr Hector Bolitho's biography of Edward VIII appeared in volume form *after* the King's brief reign, those words vanished.

Instead we read :

> From the time of his return to England the Prince of Wales chose an independent way.   It led him far from the traditions of his father's Court.   He resented the old order . . . as independence increased, he was almost stubborn in his habit of turning his back upon the conventions of polite society.

A few pages further on Mr Bolitho wrote in his serial :

> The newspapers . . . called him Galahad.   He was not made dizzy by this praise . . . indeed, it has been said that he hated the signs of his popularity and sought more and more to escape from compliments and cheers.

But when King Edward VIII had become the Duke of Windsor and the book appeared, Mr Bolitho in his volume wrote :

> The newspapers . . . called him Galahad.   *At first* he was not made dizzy by this praise.   He tried to escape from the flattery and cheers. . . . Although the Prince did all that was asked of him, his modesty was slowly shaken. . . . His slimmest platitude was printed in big letters

in the newspapers.   It is little wonder that he fell into the harmless
conceit which afterwards grew dangerously, so that it destroyed his
self-judgment and made him over-assured; which made him lose all
capacity of knowing the difference between wild popularity and calm
esteem

On his return from the war the Prince of Wales was
allowed an establishment of his own, and York House in
the confines of St James's Palace soon became the focal point
of that part of the younger generation which was still able to
believe that Jerusalem could be built in England's green and
pleasant land without previously destroying every vestige of
the old order.   The numbers of such optimistic conservatives
among the succeeding generation would be greatly diminished,
but that was not the fault of the Prince of Wales.   Within
the severely restricted field of his political activity he did all
that was possible to express the spirit of that younger generation which had been tried by four and a half years of war,
so many of the well-graced leaders of which were dead.
Mr Bolitho (in his book, not in the previous serialisation
of it) proclaims that the standards of the Prince of Wales
" were distressing to his father and to older prelates and
statesmen " but admits that " they seemed to be in harmony
with the aims of the mass of younger people."

Mr Bolitho himself had been lucky enough to escape those
years of war.   He was away in New Zealand when in 1916
he became eighteen years old.   At the age of twenty-two he
was attached to the suite of the Prince of Wales in his native
land and made his entrance into literature by writing a book
With the Prince in New Zealand.   We must presume it was
then he acquired that authoritative knowledge of those
weaknesses of his future King on which one day he would
with such judicious candour expatiate after that King had
relinquished the throne; and, seeking an excuse for Mr
Bolitho as he with always so superb a condescension seeks
excuses for his King's failings, let us remember that the
common cry of curs yelped encouragement.   But let us
return to that shell-shocked generation with whose aims
the Prince of Wales seemed in harmony.

And now a large claim will be made, a claim so large that
to the great majority of contemporary readers it may appear
but grandiose as some forgotten architectural folly.   That
claim is that the deciding emotional factor which prevented
revolution during the decade which succeeded the Peace of

Versailles was the captivation of the popular fancy by the personality of the Prince of Wales.   Prelates and older statesmen, good King George himself, might be distressed by the standards of the post-war world, but their distress would have been completely ineffectual.   Old men's tears could not water into fertility that desert made under the name of peace.   The popular mind became gradually filled with a green-decked image of hope.   The Prince of Wales had learnt from his war experience what poor humanity desired. It soon became evident that he intended to discover in peace the most practical steps toward the attainment of poor humanity's desires.   And from the start his personal attitude was discernible.   How far in those days his own plans, his own aspirations, his own emotions were thwarted until that ultimate frustration of December 1936 cannot yet be related in detail.   *Noblesse oblige*.   Consideration for the feelings of others is the final courtesy we exact from princes.   For years he fired his bullets at the sandbags of bureaucracy, bullet after bullet buried in that deadweight of administrative inertia, until at last disarmed by love they found him powerless to fire another shot.   Then raising their lum hats cautiously above the parapet of sandbags, the grand old champions of Safety First crept into the open, where they hastily covered themselves behind a fresh barricade heaped from the impermeable suet of bourgeois sentiment.

Nevertheless, those bullets fired by the Prince of Wales, which now that he is gone we are being taught to believe were the extravagant pastime of a vain and ill-adjusted mind, kept an immense body of restive opinion patient.   This figure of seemingly inexhaustible vitality whom common pity moved and common joy made mirthful was restoring to his country the old conception of kingship.   Here was a leader for the time ahead, and a leader who wanted to march at the head of his men.   In those days, before Europe had broken out into that erysipelas of dictatorship which made fascism a word of dread to the workers, the leadership of a Prince of Wales was not fraught with the political implications that would one day be used with such vicious effect against the leadership of a King.   So, during that decade, the country was more and more inclining to faith in the might of his protectorship when he should be King.   Once again the King's justice, not the Executive's justice.   Once again the King's money, not the Bank of England's notes.   Once again

the King in Parliament, not the King in the waistcoat pocket
of the Prime Minister. Thus dreamed perhaps a mere
handful of idealists, but what encouraged them to dream
was the spectacle of the Prince of Wales day by day winning
the confidence of the whole Empire by the vitalising magic
of personality. Could his grandfather have done that if he
had not been thwarted by Queen Victoria? No, not even
he. Alas, what those idealists forgot was that the modern
executive of a world state was something a great deal more
formidable even than Queen Victoria. Still, the power of
the people if implemented by the right man in the right
place? It would be overwhelming. To be sure there were
whispers up above about the unconventional princeliness of
the Prince. They did not dare, however, to imperil his
popularity by open criticism. They had to think of the
stability of that throne whose rocking would have pitched
them sprawling from their own seats. So they bided their
time.

That is not intended to suggest a conspiracy. Political
conspiracy in this country nowadays does not extend beyond
the conspiracy of politicians to drive one prime minister out
of office and substitute another. It may be observed in passing that the need for such conspiracies is a sign of the
unhealthy growth of the prime minister's power during this
century.

No, there was no conspiracy. What the ruling class did
during those years when the popularity of the Prince of
Wales was at its height was to take advantage of it to strengthen
the sentimental ties with the Dominions and Colonies and to
use it at home to appease what was called industrial discontent, a cynical name for a discontent that was due to lack
of industry. There were always whispered complaints of
the Prince's refusal to conform to the approved standards of
royal progresses; but these whispers were never frozen in
print until after King Edward VIII ascended the throne.
When the Prince of Wales danced all the evening with the
daughter of a local shopkeeper he was Prince Charming
choosing a Cinderella: it was only after his abdication that
such a slight upon Cinderella's sisters in official circles became
bad form. Even most of those who recognised and praised
ungrudgingly his services to the State as Prince of Wales
were misled by the hysteria of propaganda against him into
believing that he had cracked under the strain of kingship.

They did not perceive that it was the official view of kingship which had cracked under the strain of his personality.

In the words of Lord Baldwin in his tribute to Lord Jellicoe: " It is that God-given gift of personality which is a form of manifestation of genius and is inexplicable, for it cannot be taught by book-learning, it cannot be acquired merely by a desire to obtain it. A man has it or he has not."

That personality, matured by the diverse experience of men during the war, in a position subordinate as a prince to senior officers and as an individual to circumstance, was to receive its first real test when he left England on August 5th 1919 bound for Canada in the battle-cruiser *Renown*. On the same day the King conferred the Order of Merit on Mr Lloyd George in recognition of his pre-eminent services " both in carrying the war to a victorious end and in securing an honourable peace." If Mr Lloyd George had supposed that laurels made a comfortable mattress he was not long in being undeceived. In fact on the very day the Order of Merit was conferred upon him he was faced by the prospect of a general strike, and it was not encouraging to know that nearly half the policemen in Liverpool had come out already. On that day, too, a police barrack in Ireland was entered by armed men who bound the police with ropes and seized a quantity of arms and ammunition. And on August 5th 1919 how far was Mr Lloyd George from guessing that the shamrock would grow greener among his own withered laurels !

The feeling throughout the country that a higher minimum wage able to meet the rise in prices had become a necessity was reflected in the House of Commons where a Bill was introduced to raise the salaries of several ministers from £2000 a year to £5000. Now that the war was over the voices of a few members were allowed a hearing in criticism of the wild prodigality to which the periodical voting of immense votes of credit with patriotic silence and promptitude had habituated the executive. Mr Bonar Law implored the House to accept the Government's assurance that the increase of salary was required not in the interest of ministers but solely in the interest of the State. The fall in the value of money and rise in prices made this increase imperative. This was exactly what 26,000 bakers out on strike had just pointed out ; but there was no threat of a ministerial strike, and the Bill received a majority. Then came the question of rewarding the admirals and generals, and there was some opposition to the

£585,000 proposed. However, Mr Lloyd George pointed out that the common soldiers and sailors were drawing a hundred millions a year in pensions by comparison with which £585,000 did not seem excessive. The justice of the proportionate expenditure is perhaps not immediately perceptible; but the grants were endorsed by a large majority.

On August 12th the Prince of Wales landed at St John's, Newfoundland. In the first speech of his tour he said that this loyal and ancient colony like other States of the Empire had " to watch over the welfare of its people and to see that every class and every section enjoys in just measure the fruits of its increasing wealth."

These words may have been written for him. He had not yet acquired that later facility for making his own speeches. At the time he may not have comprehended what such words involved if they were to become deeds. What can be affirmed with certainty is that the constant enunciation of such sentiments gradually exasperated him with the abyss between speech and action.

A week later at home the Profiteering Bill would become law. This measure, which by its title seems to blow such a sonorous bugle outside the gates of those grown rich by war, was directed against the small retailers and did not touch the real profiteers of war. They stuck to their gains as stoutly as those who fought stuck to their guns. Mr Baldwin had intimated two months back that if all would follow his example and return to the country a fair proportion of their fortunes his £120,000 would mount up to twelve hundred millions. His calculation was too excessively optimistic by all but half a million pounds. Every class and every section were not yet to enjoy in just measure the fruits of the Empire's increasing wealth.

The Prince of Wales was met at St John's by the Duke of Devonshire, the Governor-General of Canada. His grandfather had been accompanied by the Duke of Newcastle on his Canadian tour close on sixty years before. Those two eighteenth-century dukedoms provide the only point of similarity between the two royal progresses.

It was the Prince of Wales's task to demonstrate to the people of Canada the vitality of the Mother Country. He demonstrated it by the vitality of himself. Few more gruelling feats have been accomplished than he accomplished in those ten weeks. Fifty towns were visited between the Atlantic and the Pacific coasts. In every one of them he had to leave the impression that hugely as he had enjoyed every moment of his tour the highlight of it was that particular town. Thousands of people had to be shaken by the hand until both his own hands were bruised into limpness, and every handshake had to convey the impression that it was his most cordial response. He had to speak in French at Montreal and be careful of not arousing the jealousy of Toronto. He had to plant a Union Jack on the Heights of Abraham and avoid offence to Quebec. He had to be dressed up as an Indian chief. He had to win the hearts of the West by his horsemanship. With the knowledge of serious labour troubles during the previous months he had to propitiate Labour, and in propitiating Labour he had to be careful not to alarm Capital. He had to travel hundreds of miles and lie down every night wondering if he had left anything unsaid or anything undone that day which would have helped the success of the task he had been set, that task he fulfilled by doing so much more than had ever been expected of him. And it all sounded so easy to those at home who read in the papers about his triumphant progress or saw bits of it on the films. After all, he *was* the Prince of Wales. Training on top of inheritance made it simple to be a cynosure. Who could not do as much and as well if he had happened to be born into the purple? Gradually, however, in justice to popular imagination, it did dawn on his father's subjects that he was playing the part of a Prince of Wales more vigorously, more thoroughly, and more effectively than any previous holder of the title for centuries. Only a Prince of Wales who was discarded in advance by England could stand the comparison. This modern Prince of Wales knew how to capture the hearts of an Empire as completely as Charles Edward caught the hearts of his Highlandmen.

Energy, courage, compassion, and sincerity: these were the outstanding qualities of the two princes. Both reached full maturity somewhat later than the average man. Neither cared for books as much as for people. Both possessed the defects of their great qualities: restlessness, obstinacy, ready emotion, and impatience of convention, none of which is a noxious defect. Both set out with ardour to achieve much: both were frustrated less by the limitations of their own characters than by the limitations of others. And here the comparison ceases.

On September 15th at Calgary the Prince of Wales said: "Nothing can set Canada back, except the failure of different classes and communities to look at the wider interests of the Dominion as well as to their own immediate needs." On September 18th at the City Temple Mr Lloyd George appealed " for a brotherhood in the building of a new Britain which should be a monument to the heroism of the dead."

Mr Lloyd George had been longer at the job of uttering pious rhetorical aspirations: he was probably not at all surprised when the response to his latest was a national railway strike lasting ten days. On October 14th, when the Prince was on his way eastward back to Montreal, the Church Congress met for the first time since the outbreak of war. Many had considered that failure to meet earlier a convenient evasion of responsibility. The proceedings were notable for little except pious rhetorical aspirations. A hint of freedom for the Church from the thraldom of Parliament brought a protest that though the Church's relation with Parliament had some disadvantages they were slight compared with the advantages such a relation gave of comprehensiveness and freedom in the Church. And it would have been so easy to take a firm and consistent position in regard to divorce if only the Church had not feared the financial results of cutting clear of Parliament. However, perhaps that clinging to Parliament had nothing to do with financial prudence: perhaps, like that hibernation of the Congress during the war, it was a convenient way of evading responsibility.

At the end of October " in response to an increasing desire that Parliamentary Government should return to the normal working " the Government reverted to a Peace Cabinet. At the same time it was " pressed upon the Prime Minister privately that the time had come for him to resume regular attendance at the House of Commons." Mr Lloyd George admitted there was something in such a request, and agreed to attend once a week at question time. Later he hoped to be able to attend twice a week. Note how the office of Prime Minister is escaping from parliamentary control to identify itself with the executive instead of the legislature. It was being attempted to convert an emergency of war into a custom of peace.

On November 4th the Prince of Wales, addressing at Toronto the largest audience of his tour, set out the conception of the British Empire.

" The Dominions are no longer colonies; they are sister-nations of the British nation. . . . I regard myself as belonging to Great Britain and to Canada in exactly the same way. This also means that when I go down to the United States next week, I shall regard myself as going there not only as an Englishman, and as a Britisher, but also as a Canadian, and as a representative of the whole Empire."

This avowal was made in full sincerity, and it would be from British Canada, whose chief city is Toronto, that the first bitter opposition to his proposed marriage would be manifested. In the future such an avowal flushed with the enthusiasm of that wonderful tour would react against him.

The Prince kept the Two Minutes' Silence of that first anniversary of the armistice in the station at Baltimore. That night he made his first speech in the United States at a Washington banquet. His future wife was at that time living in Washington. He did not meet her; but he fell in love with America.

Aware though he might have been that a great deal of the success of his Canadian tour was owed to his own ability to sustain the part of Prince of Wales in the way the people wanted, he knew that his position as Heir Apparent added something to the best he could give of himself. Everybody was prepared to think him marvellous. In the United States, if there may have been some glamour of royalty about him, it was a glamour which aroused more curiosity than veneration. As Prince of Wales he was given a good break; but it was as a man that he took full advantage of it. He won the affection of America at the time by his response to that delirious welcome of New York. What is more he did not return to England and sneer at the hospitality he had received. He looked back to it with gratitude as an offering of affection not of snobbishness. There is a vulgar error among the English that Americans are more snobbish than themselves, and a quaint notion that because the American Colonies once kicked out a British king the citizens of the United States have been kicking themselves ever since. The welcome to the Prince of Wales was attributed by people at home to a repressed passion for crowns and coronets. They approved of the enthusiasm in Canada. That was shown to *the* Prince of Wales as the Heir Apparent to the Throne of the British Empire. But the enthusiasm of the United States was for *a* Prince of Wales. Could they but have realised what deadly criticism any Englishman, and particularly any well-bred Englishman, may expect from the average American unless he can escape from the impedimenta of his country and caste!

While the great battle-cruiser *Renown* was bringing the Prince of Wales home across the Atlantic—on November 25th to be exact—the new Bishopric of Bradford was founded by an Order in Council. Dr. Blunt was not the first Bishop. He was at this date Vicar of St Werburgh's, Derby, unconscious of the powder-monkey's part destiny had prepared for him. And while *Renown* was still on the Atlantic Lady Astor won a bye-election at Plymouth—the first woman to sit in the House of Commons, and an American at that! The *Mayflower* was back in the port from which she started on September 1st, 1620, all but nine months of three hundred years ago.

On December 1st *Renown* arrived at Portsmouth. The Prince had a great welcome from the people of London in spite of very bad weather, and a dinner in honour of his return was given at Buckingham Palace that night, at which the King proposing his health expressed his satisfaction with the way he had carried out the two very important missions entrusted to him.

On December 18th the Prince of Wales was welcomed back to the City of London with a banquet at the Mansion House. In his speech he gave an outline of the Imperial— or what he preferred to call the Commonwealth—idea. But his peroration was the best part of that speech.

" A year has passed since the Armistice, and in many parts of the world millions of people are still torn by conflict, haggard with want, and almost broken by despair. . . . What is our duty now? It is to show the world that we can work at our social, economic, and industrial problems with a general fairness and sympathy, striving wholeheartedly towards one goal. That goal is happier conditions of life, to ensure that every man and every woman in the country may enjoy the just proceeds of their labour, and that every child born into the country may have a sporting chance."

That goal may have sounded attainable then. He was to learn a little more painfully with every year that passed what a maze of vested interests, departmental jealousies, and political expediencies were interposed between him and that goal.

On March 16th 1920 the Prince of Wales embarked again on *Renown* for Australia and New Zealand. In February he had been made a Freeman of Windsor. The first port of call was the Barbados where he was able to assure the inhabitants that the rumour of the island's forthcoming sale to the United States was unfounded. And then on through the Panama Canal and up to San Diego in California. Then Honolulu and Fiji. And on April 26th Auckland.

The progress through New Zealand was a repetition of the Canadian tour except that the scenery was different and that the people were more English. Neither difference lessened the tax upon the Prince's energy.

Mr Bolitho who was with him testifies to it:

"And behind all this marvellous noise of happiness" . . . One must break off to note that this marvellous noise included that of thousands of people incessantly singing *God Bless the Prince of Wales*, gramophones in cottages playing *God Save the King*, and even the cheers of prisoners allowed to sit on the high walls of their gaols . . . "and behind all this marvellous noise of happiness he carried the burden of days of strain. One incident shows, as much as any, how his inner spirit remained calm through it all." And then Mr Bolitho relates a story about the Prince's anxiety for his servant's hand which had been hurt in closing the door of his car. In spite of meeting hosts of officials all day, addressing five separate gatherings, and reaching his night's lodging fit for nothing but rest he saw that his man's hand was properly bandaged before he went to bed.

When King Edward had left the country that incident in the serial which showed the calmness of his inner spirit showed in the book "that his natural kindliness was not yet soured within him."

"Those who lived near to the Prince" . . . near, mark you, near . . . "were able to observe the changes which experience was bringing him." And so from this favoured critic one hears in the book of the Prince's self-deception about the value of his travels, of his superficial photographic view of human nature, of transient and disconnected knowledge, of his inability to know men's hearts. Just as well, we may interject. And so, Mr Bolitho continues, "this speed of living was . . . to contribute to his unhappiness when the test of his character came, in the winter of 1936." It may be granted at once that such criticism of a reigning monarch might have been dangerous, but if some of the prudence of the serial had been allowed to influence the book we should have found it a praiseworthy timidity.

While the Prince of Wales was obtaining his "superficial" knowledge of Australasia the Government at home was not displaying too profound a knowledge of Ireland. The murder of the Lord Mayor of Cork was followed by a verdict of wilful murder from the coroner's jury against David Lloyd George and others. And matters were going from bad to worse all the time. On May 16th Joan of Arc was canonised in St Peter's, Rome. But this did not seem to remind the English that they had sometimes made mistakes or suggest a wiser attitude toward Ireland. What was happening to Mr Lloyd George? Had the Babel of Versailles dimmed his own national consciousness? Could he no longer hear the west wind blowing? Or did he really believe he was another Welsh Tudor? It was a grim coincidence he should choose one of that name to command his mongrel Black-and-Tan police.

The Prince of Wales reached Melbourne at the end of May. The tour of Australia was to be the most exhausting progress of all. Moreover, owing to a certain amount of republican talk it was particularly necessary that the Heir Apparent should be a personal success. It is reasonable to accept the sincerity of the words above the arch on the wharf built for him to walk under on leaving Melbourne in *Renown*. Those words were, "Australia is proud of you."

We read in Mr Bolitho's book (not in the serial) that "on the surface, King George and Queen Mary had every reason for being proud." But in the course of the paragraph we are led to suppose that in their hearts they regarded these tours as a mistake and likely to hurt the development of their son's character. Fathers, regal and commoner, will always distrust the resounding success particularly of an eldest son; mothers, regal or commoner, that of an eldest daughter. The natural jealousy of the father is nothing for adverse comment, but it must be regarded as universal. So far is royalty not exempt from that human weakness that on the contrary it is rather more prone to it than the rest of mankind; royalty, and artists of every sort creative and interpretative.

The Prince of Wales was making a good job of his tour; but he was not behaving as his father had behaved before him on those Colonial tours as they were called then. It certainly taxes the fancy to picture King George as Duke of Cornwall and York passing under an arch of flower-dropping lassies at Bendigo or accepting a suit of yellow silk pyjamas from the girls of Ballarat.   If one may so put it, King George had all the talents, but none of the genius of royalty.   If his son may have lacked some of the talents he had the genius of it beyond any except a dozen princes in the history of man.   God knows the present writer would not do that Prince a disservice by suggesting fresh cause for complaint in calling him a genius ! He recognises that genius is synonymous in the minds of the commonplace with instability and eccentricity.   He merely invites his readers to picture King George receiving a suit of yellow silk pyjamas from those girls of Ballarat who had each contributed to them a single stitch.   No doubt the authorities would never have allowed those zealous young women to subject him to such a test of royal graciousness.   That they did not interfere with the present to King George's eldest son proves their belief in his ability to fulfil in himself every young woman's dream of a fairy Prince of Wales.   Perhaps it *was* turning the Prince of Wales into a film-star, but in a film-star epoch it was extremely fortunate for the British dynasty that it was able to produce a Prince of humble dreams to conquer humble hearts during that wild post-war decade.   Anyway, whether with or without the approval of King George, his energy and charm and common humanity were used for the benefit of his country which expressed its gratitude by not voting him even the pension of a worthy civil servant who sticks to his stool until he is superannuated.

Day in day out through June, July, and August the Prince toured Australia with a brief holiday beyond the Blue Mountains at the end of that ordeal for his energy.   On August 27th he reached Samoa homeward bound.

Mr Bolitho in his serial gave us a romantic picture of the Prince pondering over Robert Louis Stevenson's story: " his escape from the old world and his peace in the new, the difference between the pomp and anxiety of his life in England and the peace, after life, of this burial on a mountain top." " How sympathetically one understands," Mr Bolitho adds in an exhalation of good nature, " if ever he was tempted during these spells of quiet to wish for escape."   Mr Bolitho's understanding and sympathy were so perfect that he deleted the whole of this meditation from the book when King Edward was gone. In the book the Prince just walked back to the ship without any of Mr Bolitho's beautiful prose in his mind. It is difficult to withhold a tribute of admiration for the thoroughness of the *volte face* : it has the gymnastic, nay, the acrobatic precision of a perfect somersault. But let us see what his publishers claim for it.

> This book, planned and begun in different circumstances, possesses an importance not attaching to any biography of any English King which has been written within living memory. Mr Bolitho has long been engaged on this biography for which he had been granted exceptional facilities. He was attached to the Duke of Windsor when he made his tour of New Zealand as Prince of Wales, and during his researches into the history of earlier generations of the English Royal Family, the author was able to gain first-hand recollections of the Duke's boyhood and early manhood. He has, in a sense, grown up with his subject; he has a special admiration and sympathy for the ex-King.

" I hope you will consider what is spoke comes from my love," Mr Bolitho might plead with Iago.

From Samoa the Prince sailed on across the Pacific to Honolulu. From Honolulu by way of Acapulco, Colon, Trinidad, British Guiana, Grenada, and Dominica he came home, reaching Portsmouth on October 11th after an absence of seven months.

During that absence the situation in Ireland had grown steadily worse, not the least exacerbating factor being the appointment of the Canadian Sir Hamar Greenwood as Chief Secretary. However, in spite of the slow martyrdom of the Lord Mayor of Cork who had succeeded the previous one murdered by masked agents ; in spite of the Duke of Northumberland's discovery that the fight for Irish freedom was being financed by Russia ; in spite of the British Government's suggestion that the *Daily Herald* was being financed by Russia, which stung the *Daily Herald* into calling the British Government " a notorious liar " ; in spite of Sir Hamar Greenwood's official denial that the British Government had authorised the Black-and-Tan atrocities ; in spite of the beginning of a coal strike ; in spite of the unemployed riots in Whitehall ; and in spite of the passage of the Matrimonial Causes Bill which allowed a wife to divorce her husband for adultery without cruelty, the Church Congress met at Southend in a mood of rosy optimism. The Bishop of Chelmsford, the President, may have been responsible for this by assuring the Congress that " in the history of the world there had never been a Treaty of Peace so impregnated with the teaching of the Sermon on the Mount as that signed last year." Dr Inge, in the discussion that followed, spoke against " the fatuous policy of trying to get Germany permanently crippled," not however in obedience to any precept uttered by the Saviour of mankind, but because such a policy " would drive Germany into an alliance with the Military Government of Russia."

Fear of Russia was to dominate the imagination of England during that decade of the 'twenties. Fear of England obsessed Russia not less completely. And the Intelligence Services of both countries were as happy as schoolboys with all the money they wanted to manufacture the bogeys with which their Governments scared one another and the general public. Mr Baldwin was a particular master of these Guy Fawkes tactics. He made the flesh of the electorate creep, with a richer unctuousness of horrification than had been heard since the Fat Boy frightened Mrs Wardle with the tale of what he had seen in the arbour at Dingley Dell.*

The Prince of Wales was disappointed when he came back from that Australian tour to find how difficult it was to turn the minds of his countrymen at home toward the Dominions overseas. In the speech he made at Oxford on February 8th 1921, on receiving an honorary degree, he said that the topic of the Dominions and Crown Colonies was a favourite one of his, and one about which he was rather apt to be long-winded. That Oxford speech is interesting because it escapes from conventional rhetoric and shows the ability an intensive experience of speech-making during his tours had given him to express something of his own personality in the words he spoke. Probably he had held forth to statesmen, and probably the King had managed to suggest, in that gruff downright way of his, that his eldest son supposed he knew more about public affairs than he had any right to suppose. Whether it would have been possible to turn the Prince's tours to practical account cannot be argued here. All that can be affirmed is that Imperial affairs occupied a backseat in the public mind. We have read a good deal lately about the disappointment of our high hopes of him : we have heard less about the disappointment of some of his high hopes of us.

* Since these words were written the evidence at the trial of many prominent followers of Trotsky in March 1938 has made it clear that the Russian Bear stood in greater danger from the claws and teeth of the British Lion than the Lion from the hug of the Bear.

One other point in that Oxford speech may be noticed: "There is a period which is now commonly known as ' pre-war '. Well, Oxford is the last ' pre-war ' thing that I can remember."

The steep stone stairway down into Cloisters from the Magdalen J.C.R. . . . Gunner's little room. . . . Gunner's stories . . . and the scarlet and lilies on the river . . . and the black-and-white shirt of the soccer eleven . . . and voices of men now dead shouting across the quad in front of the President's lodgings, the voices of men shouting where now stood the memorial to their yielded youth . . . and the deer-park . . . and the dappled shade of Addison's Walk . . . and the leaves drifting down Longwall under the pale blue October sky . . . and the High on a sunny morning at May's end . . . and that leisurely ample well-graced under-graduate life before the war. " There is a saying about Oxford, ' Know you her secret none can utter.' We all of us know that secret, and though we cannot put it into words, few of us can ever forget it." It may be extravagant to endow these words of his with any peculiar poignancy. They may be no more than a polite rhetorical cliché of the moment, no more than one of those slim platitudes for which Mr Bolitho deprecates too much attention. And yet, when we consider the seven years in bondage to publicity the Prince had spent since he went down in June 1914, must we deny to a prince what we allow to a poet? We do know that, after a period of unsettlement caused by removal from the Navy, he was happy at Oxford, and it was the last pre-war thing he remembered.

And now we must turn back once more to Mr Bolitho, not with any desire to scrape off what little gilt is left upon that tarnished weathercock of a narrative, but because tarnished though it may be, the vane swings true to the veering wind of public opinion and so plays its part in history.

In the serial :

> His address to the Royal National Lifeboat Institution . . . can still be read with interest. It had the shape and repose of a well-written essay, and it is still lively with information . . . it was common sense which gave the spirit to his speeches, and his sincerity and humour gave them power

From the book the shape and repose of the well-written essay have vanished, and only the liveliness of information remains. Common sense has departed too, and with it power,

and though sincerity and humour are allowed to stay, the most
" effective " part of his oratory is " his engaging smile."
In the serial :

> There was another problem which went *even* deeper with the Prince
> than his interest in the trade and life of the Empire.   His compassion
> made him turn again and again to the returned soldiers. . . . His
> balanced judgment and dislike for self-pity made him turn to the
> problems of the living as much as to the veneration of the dead.

In the book ' even ' with a subtlety of depreciation dis-
appears from in front of ' deeper ', in order to give his ex-
subjects a hint of shallowness denied to his subjects.   The
' compassion ' of a reigning monarch becomes the ' natural
anxiety ' of a Duke of Windsor.   After that we are not surprised to find that ' balanced judgment and dislike for self-
pity ' are no longer among his qualities.   Instead we read
that " lacking a focus for his natural affections, he developed
what might be described as an obsession about those in want."
It was an obsession he shared with silly women like the Little
Sisters of the Poor.   And so much was he at the mercy of this
idiotic obsession about those in want that " he did not consider
them in relation to other classes, which was necessary from
the point of view of the State.   He could not tread quietly or
work cautiously, which was the true and helpful way with the
poor."
Yet, although these words have been added to detract from
the value of the service which that Prince of Wales gave to the
poor, many of us will be grateful to Mr Bolitho for his addition.
In the serial:

> It must always be a matter for wonder that his character kept its
> shape during those years when he was not allowed either the unin-
> terrupted influence of his parents or the steadying certainty of life in
> his own home.

But wonder or not, his character survived in the serial.   It
only began to deteriorate in Mr Bolitho's book.   There we
read instead:

> The tragedy of these restless years increases as the story of King
> Edward is unfolded.   It seems to lead on, with growing tempo, to
> the state of mind in which he signed his abdication. .   . For most
> British people the estrangement of King Edward came suddenly
> during the dark month of 1936, but for his mother it began years
> before . . . when he should have remained with his parents to

grow more and more into the strength of their family example. The theme bears reiteration, for it is like a mournful chorus in a Greek tragedy warning us of the destruction with which the story ends.

Mr Bolitho could only have made those remarks about a man of twenty-seven a little more ridiculous by lamenting that he was not tied to the apron-strings of the two Archbishops as well. So far, the only evidence of deterioration has been the anxiety of the Prince of Wales to do something at once for those in want, and an intelligible impatience of official inertia. Therefore to the uninformed public all this talk about warning of destruction suggests follies and even vices to which the Prince was known to be liable and against which he required careful guarding. Let the detractors of King Edward have the courage to say in so many words of what they accuse him. Then they can be answered. We who know that a campaign to kill his reputation has been deliberately encouraged demand definite accusations which we will meet. We cannot assail rumours in print because by doing so we give them more material shape. We cannot appeal to sentiment now : we might as well burn sticks of lavender in a sewer. Those who believe that the use of such a word unduly exaggerates the state of affairs should read the anonymous letters the present writer has received from all over the world since his intention to write this book was made public. And let this be noted. Every letter of abuse has been anonymous. Not one of these pimps to scandal, even in farthest Australia, has had the courage to put his name or his address. Such lily-livered rats may lurk in their sewer, but the stench from their lurking-place is the fouler for that. And let it be noted that the many who have written from all over the world to applaud the present writer's intention have signed their names.

Mr Bolitho treads as quietly and works as cautiously at his task of denigration as he would have liked the Prince of Wales to handle the problem of the poor. We are left with the impression that from the time he sailed to Canada on that first tour his end was from his behaviour a foregone conclusion to those who like Mr Bolitho had " in a sense grown up with his subject." Strange metamorphoses are recorded of humanity, but none so strange of literature as this metamorphosis of a toothless serial into a sharp-fanged book.

CHAPTER IX

SERVICE OF ONE KIND AND ANOTHER

On June 22nd 1921 King George and Queen Mary crossed to open the new Parliament of Northern Ireland, and in his speech the King appealed to all Irishmen " to stretch out the hand of forbearance and conciliation, to forgive and to forget, and to join in making for the land which they loved a new era of peace, contentment, and goodwill. Two days later Mr Lloyd George invited Mr de Valera and Sir James Craig to a conference in London " to explore to the utmost the possibility of a settlement." On July 11th a Truce was agreed upon.

It is not known yet whether the King's words exerted any direct effect on the position ; but it is unlikely. The British Government could not face the moral condemnation of the rest of the world much longer. General Smuts probably had more influence in changing its heart than the King, but it has been stated that Mr Lloyd George drafted the King's speech. The preliminary exchanges between him and Mr de Valera went all in favour of Mr de Valera, and finally on October 10th a conference was held in Downing Street between representatives of Sinn Fein and the British Government, the Government of Northern Ireland standing aside for the present. A few days later, the Pope telegraphed to the King his prayer that " an end might be brought to the age-long dissension between England and Ireland." The King telegraphed back his hope of " a new era of peace and happiness for his people." Thereupon Mr de Valera telegraphed to the Pope his " confidence that the ambiguities in the reply sent in the name of King George would not mislead the Pope into believing that the people of Ireland owed allegiance to the British King," and continued with an unmistakable affirmation of the independence of the Irish people. However, as this telegram had been despatched without reference to the nine delegates in London the conference was not broken off.

It is generally believed in Great Britain that Mr de Valera's successive steps to repudiate Irish allegiance to the King were intended as a personal slight to the monarch. This is to misunderstand him. Mr de Valera could not be blind to the gradual establishment of the monarchy as the only link between the various nations of the British Commonwealth of Nations, and his repudiation of allegiance to the Throne is from his point of view a logical necessity if Eire is to preserve her right of secession from the British Commonwealth.   He will not accept what he can argue is a novel view of the position of the monarchy, and he has never been prepared to commit his country to a state in which secession could be called rebellion.   The loyalty of what is known as Northern Ireland to the Crown must not be over-estimated.   In 1912 fanatics were openly arguing that the Kaiser should be invited to come over like Dutch William and save them from Home Rule and the Pope.   If this statement is sounding fantastic reference is invited to the *Annual Register* of 1912 where it is recorded that this suggestion was printed in leaflets circulated at many Orange meetings.   And nowhere was the propaganda against King Edward VIII fiercer or fouler than in Northern Ireland, where they got it into their heads that he was unduly sympathetic with Popery and ready to abolish the partition.   How far the dark and secret elements of the Government of Northern Ireland working in collaboration with the dark and secret elements of the National Government in Great Britain were responsible for propaganda which was circulating assiduously as far back as April 1936 may never be discovered now, for this kind of plot avoids the damning evidence of paper and ink.   The exposure which the Report of the Council of Civil Liberties gave in 1936 of the terror established by the Government of Northern Ireland under the Civil Authorities (Special Powers) Act of 1922 does not prejudice the political student in favour of that Government's scrupulousness.

Given a free hand to tackle the Irish problem when he returned from Canada at the end of 1919, the Prince of Wales might have found a solution.   The Government preferred the Auxiliaries, the Black-and-Tans, and Sir Hamar Greenwood.

On October 26th of that parched exasperating year of 1921 when only a week earlier the thermometer had still marked 76° in the shade the Prince of Wales sailed for India in the *Renown*.   It was agreed that his visit would have a beneficial political influence.   A dispassionate examination of the tour leaves an impression that he was able to do very little.   Whenever he had an opportunity of displaying personal courage he never failed to take advantage of it; but his whole progress was inevitably fenced in by anxious officialdom.   Rioting in one part of Bombay while in another part he was making a conventional speech in which nothing of himself can be traced. Empty streets in Allahabad. Empty streets in Lucknow. Rioting in Madras. Gilded elephants, jewels and peacock-plumes, pageantry and sport with the Indian princes.

It was a more successful business in Mr Bolitho's serial than in his book.

In the serial :

> Turn also from the rights and wrongs of British rule in India, and search only into the story of the Prince's conquest.

But in the book :

> Search into the story of the effect upon the Prince himself.

In the serial *The Englishman* was right in describing him as " the greatest ambassador of his time " and it was not exaggeration to say " he did more to establish the relations between the masses of India and the Crown on a solid basis of personal contact in four months than edicts could have done in a generation."

In the book the rightness of the description is cut out, and *The Englishman* must have been exaggerating after all, for " it was not exaggeration " is deleted.

No doubt like *The Englishman* the Prime Minister was exaggerating when on January 20th 1922 he telegraphed the Cabinet's thanks to the Prince :

" My colleagues and I wish gratefully to express to Your Royal Highness on behalf of the British people our warm appreciation of the spirit in which you have entered upon and are fulfilling your high undertaking and our pleasure in the deep impression that you have made.

" From unofficial no less than official sources, in all parts of India which you have visited, convincing tributes have reached us of the respect and affection which you have inspired. We know that you have reached the real heart of India, and that there as everywhere, your personality will leave an unfading memory. Your fortunes and your happiness are so dear to every nation of the Empire that India touches us all when she shows her heart to you. Every incident of your progress is watched with interest here.

" We rejoice in the splendid hospitality of the Indian Princes, in the enthusiasm of Indians of every class, in the great greeting of Indian children, in every spontaneous tribute you receive, and we look forward more than ever before to the welcome home which we shall give you from yet another great Imperial mission successfully discharged."

Some words of Mr Bolitho in the serial supply what might be an enthusiastic footnote to that telegram :

> If this is true, it is not enough to suppose that this power came to him only because he was the Prince of Wales.   He could have set the tide of Indian affairs back a hundred years if he had not made his appeal in the strength of his own goodness of character and fearless honesty.   He was slowly seeing the changes which the new era demanded.

But in the book the enthusiasm has evaporated :

> If this is true it was because of his good nature and because of his democratic manner that the Prince succeeded.   His easy address, which would have been impossible in a permanent official or Viceroy, was engaging in an illustrious visitor who passed quickly by.

In the serial :

> His grandfather had referred to the British people as his *subjects* when he spoke to them.   His father, in the autumn of his life, was to talk to them as his *people*.   The Prince's thoughts and aims were forming, more and more securely during these years of travel, and it was to be noted, even when he became King, that he still called his people his *fellow-men*.

But in the book :

> King Edward VII had referred to the British people as his *subjects* and King George spoke of his *people*.   King Edward VIII stepped down still further and usually addressed his *fellow-men*.

Observe the subtle omission of " the autumn of his life ". That is to remove any possible suspicion that the Prince of Wales may have played an important part in changing the key of kingship.   After this Mr Bolitho's book goes on to contrast the Prince's " gayer rewards of popularity " with the " great bulwark of respect " for King George.   The Prince " mistook the gay accident of popularity for calm esteem," and his " self-confidence flourished accordingly."

We have already granted that Mr Bolitho could not write so freely of a reigning monarch, but he was not bound to write what he considered flattery.   He could have related the bald facts and supplemented them later when he could criticise with impunity.

From Calcutta the Prince went to Burma, from Burma to

Madras, and up to Delhi, leaving Karachi in the middle of March and sailing down to Ceylon. From Ceylon he went to Singapore where he received a great ovation; from Singapore to Japan where he stayed nearly a month in the beauty and blossom of the Spring. Then he travelled through Malaya and reached Plymouth on June 20th 1922, three days before his twenty-eighth birthday.

A good deal had happened at home while he was away. The Irish Free State had been constituted. The Geddes axe had been raised. The independence of Egypt had been proclaimed. M. Briand had allowed himself to be photographed while taking a lesson in golf from Mr Lloyd George at Cannes, and fell from power a few days later never to regain it. German indemnities looked as far off being paid as ever. M. Poincaré had become Premier and Foreign Minister of France. The ghastly massacre of the Greek refugees in Smyrna had followed the defeat of their army in Asia Minor. Italy had seized the opportunity of the Greek collapse to repudiate the arrangement about the Dodecanese, and the British Government weakened by intrigue at home and Franco-Italian encouragement of Turkey, had been able to do no more than protest. From now on Rhodes would be a threat to British interests in the Mediterranean. Constantine had been driven from the throne and replaced by the Crown Prince as a figurehead King. Princess Mary had been married to Lord Lascelles in Westminster Abbey. Sir Henry Wilson had retired from the General Staff to become a member of Parliament, Mr Horatio Bottomley had been expelled from Parliament to serve a sentence of seven years' penal servitude, and Sir Basil Thomson had retired from Scotland Yard to write books. Mr Montagu, the Secretary of State for India, without consulting his colleagues had published a communication from the Government of India to him urging among other things the evacuation of Constantinople and the restoration of Smyrna to Turkey. Mr Montagu had then resigned from the Cabinet.

In defending his action in a speech at Cambridge, Mr Montagu said he had been accused of outraging the doctrine of collective Cabinet responsibility. The Prime Minister had demanded the price, which it was in the power of every genius to demand, and that price had been complete disappearance of Cabinet responsibility; but he had now brought out this doctrine at a convenient moment and made his late colleague the victim of his new creed. The country had been governed by a dictator. Cabinet responsibility was a joke.

That had been in March. In June Sir Donald Maclean moved a reduction of £100 on the item for the Cabinet Secretariat. He expressed apprehension at the way in which the power of the Prime Minister was being repeatedly increased, and contended that it was not in the interests of the nation that more power should pass into his hands. Mr Lloyd George in his reply " made light of the criticisms which saw in the Secretariat a new means of developing a system of personal Government to usurp the functions of departments, and to enable the Prime Minister to override the decisions of old and established departments." (*A. R.*)

When King Edward VII suggested that the Prime Minister as such, without regard to any other office he held, should have precedence after the Archbishop of York he had not foreseen that the effect of a great war might be to leave that Prime Minister with a technical precedence after the Archbishop of York but an actual precedence immediately after God. All through that year discontent with the Coalition Government grew, and that discontent was concentrated on the personality of Mr Lloyd George. Other people were beginning to see themselves walking immediately after the Archbishop of York on ceremonial occasions.

On October 20th at the end of his speech at the Guildhall when the Prince of Wales had told the City about his experiences in India and the Far East he concluded :

" May I now say how grateful I am to the Prime Minister, Mr Lloyd George, for the words in which he has proposed the toast of my health, and I regard it as a great compliment that so distinguished a public servant has found time amid the storms and stress of the last few days, to join us at the Guildhall this afternoon. We welcome him here, as he too, perhaps, may welcome a brief moment's respite to the calmer atmosphere of this historic hall, whose walls have echoed the voices of so many of England's famous statesmen, and whose foundations have stood firm through centuries of political crisis, and still stand firm as England stands firm to-day."

In every speech of the Prince of Wales in which he has occasion to reply to a toast given by Mr Lloyd George there is a noticeable warmth of friendship, and one of the ' ifs ' of

F

history will be 'if' Mr Lloyd George instead of Mr Baldwin had gone on this very date in an October fourteen years in the future to see the King at Fort Belvedere . .

But behind the "storms and stress of the last few days" alluded to in the Prince's speech was the figure of Mr Baldwin himself, and his activities must now be examined.

Mr Baldwin had had the opportunity of observing the methods by which Mr Asquith had been ousted from the Prime Ministership in 1916, and in the course of his observation he may have noted the skill with which Mr Lloyd George had outmanœuvred first Sir Edward Carson and then Mr Bonar Law to obtain the Prime Ministership for himself. The ultimate verdict of history will be that the conspiracy was justified by the result; but that has often been history's verdict on conspiracies.

When Mr Bonar Law's health broke down in the opening of 1921 and he left the Coalition Government Mr Baldwin entered the Cabinet as President of the Board of Trade. He was considered a safe man, and he held an impregnable Conservative seat at Bewdley.   By the Spring of 1922 there was much criticism of the Coalition which was an expression of the resentment that the Conservative Party felt at being fettered to Mr Lloyd George.   They had accepted his leadership as a patriotic duty in war-time, but saw no reason why the horrors of war should be unduly prolonged in peace.   Mr Baldwin was nobly conscious of the ingratitude they were showing, and in March he rose in the House of Commons to declare: "There are a large number of Tories here to-day who would never have been here if they had not had the Lloyd George 'token' in 1918.   It sits badly on these men to indulge in captious criticism of the Prime Minister."

However, during the next few months the attacks upon the Coalition Government from every quarter were intensified, and Mr Baldwin may have asked himself if the Lloyd George 'token' or 'coupon' would be quite as valuable at the next election which must be held in 1923 at the latest. We have heard from Mr Baldwin's own lips the passionate relief with which after two and a half years he was at last given the chance to serve his country in an unpaid job, and knowing this desire of his for self-immolation we can appreciate how deeply he would have felt the election of any Government which did not offer him an opportunity of continuing to serve his country.   It is important when we come

later to consider his actions in 1936 never to lose sight of
Mr Baldwin's complete disinterestedness, for the purity of
which we have his own reiterated assurances.   In April 1936
he would be reminding an audience of his Bewdley constituents that never once had he seen in Worcestershire the
pageant of the damson and apple blossom since 1914, and yet
" some people may tell you that Prime Ministers make no
sacrifices."

As the months of 1922 went by Mr Baldwin became so
worried about Mr Lloyd George's future that he looked round
more and more anxiously for a sign from the Conservative
leaders of the Coalition that they appreciated what a Jonah
Mr Lloyd George was in the Party ship.   Yet none of them
seemed eager to throw him overboard.   At last, according to
Lord Ronaldshay in *The Life of Lord Curzon*, Mr Baldwin,
Sir Arthur Griffith-Boscawen, the Minister for Agriculture,
and Lord Peel, the Minister of Transport, " approached Lord
Curzon with a request that they might meet together at his
house to discuss their action as occasion might require, and
they gave him definite assurances that, from this time onward,
they were prepared to associate themselves with him and to
join him in resigning if the necessity arose."

We are reminded of the scene in Brutus's orchard when
the conspirators approach him to discuss the action required
to remove Julius Cæsar, and indeed there is a Shakespearean
touch about Lord Curzon's reflection : " When a group of
Cabinet Ministers begin to meet separately and to discuss
independent action, the death-tick is audible in the rafters."

Some obscurity still attaches to the preliminary plotting,
which is after all not to be wondered at.   We shall never be
perfectly sure whether Darnley was blown up or strangled,
nor who was privy to the deed.   Conspiracies are not cross-
word puzzles.   Lord Ronaldshay quotes a letter from Sir
Arthur Griffith-Boscawen to Lord Curzon on October 2nd
that he was " greatly alarmed at the . . . terrible risks of
war which some of our friends appeared prepared to take and
their distrust of diplomatic methods " and says that he was
acting on behalf of Mr Baldwin.   On the other hand, Lord
Beaverbrook in his *Politicians and the Press* says that Mr
Baldwin was still supporting the policy of most of the members
of the Cabinet in holding on at Chanak, and at the same time
soothing Mr Bonar Law's fear of war.   Superficially it may
look as if Mr Baldwin was running with the hare and hunting

with the hounds, but this is contrary to our idea of Mr Baldwin's character, and we must presume that either Sir Arthur Griffith-Boscawen or Lord Beaverbrook was jumping to conclusions. Lord Beaverbrook had visited Constantinople in September, with the encouragement of Mr Lloyd George, and had returned with a formidable account of Turkish intentions. With this he frightened Mr Bonar Law, who wrote to *The Times*. The letter was published on October 7th and it advocated withdrawal from any attempts to implement the peace settlement in Europe or Asia unless the French accorded us as much support in the Near East as they expected from us on the Rhine. Mr Bonar Law had been an enemy of strong action in the Near East since the days of the Gallipoli Expedition, for the ultimate failure of which he must stand arraigned at the bar of history as one of the individuals most heavily loaded with guilt.

Mr Bonar Law's letter may have influenced the French policy, for Lord Curzon succeeded in obtaining French support, and the Turks accepted negotiation. Nevertheless, the Press attacks on the Coalition continued, and Mr Austen Chamberlain, the leader of the Unionist Party, called a meeting at his house of the other Unionist Ministers in the Coalition to discuss the advisability of an election. This was on October 12th. At this conference Mr Baldwin seconded by Sir Arthur Griffith-Boscawen urged the senior ministers to throw over Mr Lloyd George and purify the Party of any taint of Liberalism.

Mr Baldwin had announced his bold intention to Mrs Baldwin in words that echo across time like Roland's horn at Roncesvalles. He had hurried back without her from Aix-les-Bains, and when she arrived in London he told her that he was distressed to oppose his senior colleagues and risk having to resign from the Cabinet.* " I could do nothing else. I'm going out of politics for good. We shall have the long holiday that we have promised ourselves for so long. We'll go to the South of France for two or three months."

He might have taken the opportunity to visit that Worcestershire whose beauties of nature and cultivation had been so long denied him by his own self-sacrifice. The damsons and apples would not have been in blossom at this season, but the mangel-wurzels were ripe for clumping.

* *Stanley Baldwin* (Adam Gowans Whyte).

" Then," he went on, " I shall go into business again, though I don't know exactly who will give me a job."

> This was the noblest Roman of them all;
> All the conspirators save only he
> Did that they did in envy of great Cæsar;
> He only, in a general honest thought
> And common good to all, made one of them.

Mr Austen Chamberlain summoned a meeting of Coalition-Unionist Members of Parliament for October 19th at the Carlton Club.   He would ask for a vote of confidence in the Government and in himself as leader of the Party, and further for a motion to dissolve Parliament immediately and go to the country once again as a Coalition.

The conspirators had a busy week, and it may be noted that Sir Samuel Hoare's house was used as a rendezvous. We shall hear of Sir Samuel Hoare again.   Of Lord Curzon's behaviour during this week it is difficult to find an explanation that is not more consonant with vaulting ambition than with the strictest code of honour, but he had been dead over ten years in 1936 and his motive need not detain us.   In any case he came down at the last fence.

The real problem was Bonar Law's attitude.   If he spoke against the Coalition the Coalition would be smashed, and urged by Lord Beaverbrook Mr Bonar Law consented to slay it.   However, it fell to Mr Baldwin to move the motion that the Conservative Party should fight the election with its own leader and its own programme, and therefore he has been credited since with being the bold St George who slew the Dragon of Wales; but, loth though one may be to deprive a man of the glory of a disinterested action, it must be asserted that it was the speech of Mr Bonar Law not Mr Baldwin's which overthrew Mr Lloyd George.

Curiously enough the crowd outside the Carlton shouted ' Judas ! ' at Lord Birkenhead as he walked up the steps of the Club,* and that because he was rightly believed to be loyal to Mr Lloyd George in this crisis.   Perhaps Mr Baldwin reminded himself that he owed that first chance to serve his country in an unpaid job to Mr Bonar Law's offer to him of the post of his Parliamentary Private Secretary in 1917, and persuaded himself that in spite of his public tribute to Mr Lloyd George as recently as last March he was really

* *Stanley Baldwin : Man or Miracle?* (Bechhofer Roberts).

under a slighter obligation of loyalty to him than to Mr Bonar Law. At any rate, in his speech, he made no bones about attacking Mr Lloyd George.

"As I am going to speak for a very short time, I will not beat about the bush, but will come right to the root of the whole difficulty, which is the position of the Prime Minister. The Prime Minister was described this morning in *The Times*, in the words of a distinguished aristocrat, as a 'live wire.' He was described to me and others in more stately language by Lord Birkenhead as a dynamic force, and I accept those words. He *is* a dynamic force, and it is from that that our troubles, in my opinion, arise. A dynamic force is a very terrible thing. It may crush you, but is not necessarily right. It is owing to that dynamic force and to that remarkable personality that the Liberal Party, to which he formerly belonged, has been smashed to pieces; and it is my firm conviction that, in time, the same thing will happen to our Party.

"I do not propose to elaborate, in an assembly like this, the dangers and the perils of that happening. We have already seen, during our association with him in the last four years, a section of our Party hopelessly alienated. I think that, if the present association continues, and if this meeting agrees that it should be continued, you will see some more breaking up; and I believe the process must go on inevitably until the old Conservative Party is smashed to atoms and lost in ruins.

"I would like to give you just one illustration to show what I mean by the disintegrating influence of a dynamic force. Take Mr Chamberlain and myself: Mr Chamberlain's services to the State are infinitely greater than any that I have been able to render, but we are both men who are, or who try to be, actuated by principle in our conduct, giving all we can to the service of the State. We are men who, I think, have exactly the same view on the political problems of the day. We are men who, I believe—and certainly on my side—have esteem and, perhaps, I may add affection for each other. [*His Majesty, as Prince of Wales, has honoured me for many years with a friendship which I value, and I know that he would agree with me that it was not only a friendship but, between man and man, a friendship of affection.*] But the result of this dynamic force is that we stand here to-day, he prepared to go into the wilderness if he should be compelled to forsake the Prime Minister,

and I prepared to go into the wilderness if I should be compelled to stay with the Prime Minister.   If that is the effect
of that tremendous personality on two men occupying the
position that we do, and related to each other politically in the
way that Mr Chamberlain and I are, that process must go on
throughout the Party.   It was for that reason that I took the
stand I did and put forward the views that I did."

   And all this delivered with a sincerity too meticulous to split
even an infinitive let alone a party : all this delivered with
that careful fumbling for the phrase which showed he had had
but little time to compose a speech for delivering that day, so
he must tell what he had to tell truthfully, sincerely, and
plainly, with no attempt to dress up or to adorn.   True he did
not use that preamble on October 19th 1922.   He had not at
that date achieved the mastery of his later manner ; but now
that his voice is familiar over the microphone hardly a reader
will not appreciate the tenderness with which he announced his
desertion of Mr Lloyd George and his reluctance to drive Mr
Chamberlain into the wilderness.   He would display the same
tenderness when he was confronted by another dynamic force
in 1936.

   It is amusing to note that at the Church Congress which
opened at Sheffield on October 10th Dr Inge " expressed
doubts as to whether sudden conversion was a normal experience at all, and said it was certain suggestion played a very
important part in the matter."   On the other hand the Archbishop of York (Dr Lang) " took the view that conversion was
a natural process."   And as Mr Baldwin would fairly soon
take precedence immediately after the Archbishop it was
lucky he agreed with him, for his own conversion, from
believing in March that captious criticism of the man who
put him in the Cabinet did not sit well on him to believing
in October that, even if it cost him a long holiday in the South
of France, captious criticism sat on him better than his own
clothes, might have puzzled a psychologist.   But perhaps
suggestion did play a very important part.   Perhaps suggestion made Mr Baldwin wonder how long Mr Bonar Law
would stand the wear and tear of the Prime Minister's Office,
and what plums (not from Worcestershire orchards) might
reward the junior members of the Coalition Cabinet if the
senior members should quixotically decide to stick to Mr
Lloyd George by refusing to take office without him ; perhaps
suggestion even went so far as to implant a doubt whether

a peer like Lord Curzon, in spite of his willingness, indeed his anxiety to be free of Mr Lloyd George, stood a real chance of ever becoming Prime Minister.   Perhaps suggestion went so far as to . . . but such speculations belong to the theological scepticism of a Dr Inge.   Mr Baldwin *was* converted. How is of less importance.   In 1937 he would remind a gathering of youth at the Albert Hall that the young men shall see visions, and the old men shall dream dreams.   In 1922 he was fifty-five, just the right middle age to do both.

The meeting at the Carlton Club decided by 187 votes to 87 to smash the Coalition, and three hours later Mr Chamberlain communicated the result to Mr Lloyd George, who at once resigned and advised the King to send for Mr Bonar Law.   Therefore when the Prince of Wales responded to his toast the next day at the Guildhall he was no longer Prime Minister.   This adds a fresh warmth to the words of the Prince.

The next day Mr Lloyd George defended the late Government up at Leeds and " referred to the lack of brains among the revolting Conservatives."   He regretted that Mr Bonar Law had put himself in the position, as a horseman, of not holding the reins but of holding on by the tail.

Two days later Lord Curzon proposed and Mr Baldwin seconded the election of Mr Bonar Law as Leader of the Unionist Party.   He was a mortally sick man.

Mr. Baldwin's horror of dynamic force was not in much danger of being excited by the new Cabinet.   Lloyd George, Austen Chamberlain, Balfour, Birkenhead, Winston Churchill all gone, and to compensate for them the electorate were offered Sir Philip Lloyd-Graeme (Cunliffe-Lister), Sir Samuel Hoare, Sir Thomas Inskip, Sir William Joynson-Hicks, and Mr Baldwin himself.   However, the electorate, prominent among which were masses of women voting early, evidently dreaded dynamic force as much as Mr Baldwin and this Government was returned.

The Prince of Wales had come back from the Indian tour with what seemed a passion for horses.   It was ascribed by gossip to a friendship he had accorded to Major E. D. Metcalfe who had been his A.D.C. in the East.   This friendship roused jealousy, and one heard complaints about the Prince's fondness for new friends.   The answer is that Major Metcalfe was best man at the Duke of Windsor's wedding in 1937. Jealousy covers a multitude of slanders.

In the late autumn of 1922 the Prince took a toss hunting and damaged an ankle.   This meant the cancellation of one or two engagements and inspired the first moans about the Heir Apparent's taking unnecessary risks.   Why did he not get married ?   The marriage in April 1923 to Count Calvi di Bergolo of Princess Yolanda of Italy, with whom rumour had obstinately coupled the name of the Prince of Wales regardless of the constitutional bar to marriage with a Catholic princess, allowed the King and Queen to pay an official visit to Rome in early May without being credited with matrimonial intentions on behalf of their son ; but his marriage became an unfailing source of speculation after the wedding of the Duke of York and Lady Elizabeth Bowes-Lyon on April 26th.   This seemed in public opinion to be clear evidence that the careful isolation of the Blood Royal for a couple of centuries was to be finally abandoned.   There was no need to be looking around now for Princess Yolandas.   The future Queen might be sought somewhere in Great Britain.   So why did not the Prince of Wales get married ?   All sorts of fantastic theories might be heard in scandal's most authoritative accents.

In the general collapse after the war of so much of what would have been eligible royalty the Prince of Wales might feel himself absolved from the duty of marrying into the Blood Royal, and with this sense of freedom from an obligation the sense of freedom for his own choice was intensified.   Whatever sympathy his well-wishers may feel for him that sympathy would be immeasurably deepened if they knew the truth.   It is not the object of this book to probe into the personal life of the Prince during these years.   It is enough to remind readers of his words in that farewell broadcast.   " And he [the new King] has one matchless blessing, enjoyed by so many of you, and not bestowed on me, a happy home with his wife and children."   One virtue of which the most ruthless slander has failed to strip the Duke of Windsor is his sincerity.   Those words could not have been spoken by a man who had not for a long time ardently desired to be happily married.

Much praise has been written of her present Majesty, and perhaps some of those who have been sickened by the rapidity with which adulation of his ex-Majesty has changed to disparagement will henceforth doubt the conviction of writers who extol the virtues and graces of royalty.   That is the penalty they must pay for the behaviour of blacklegs to truth.   However, the wriggles of a few turncoats do not impose nudism on their colleagues, and it would be a piece of self-conscious pusillanimity in the present writer if he did not take advantage of recording her marriage to the Duke of York to record at the same time what a rich gift that April day bestowed upon his country. He would have to travel far back into the past of that country to discover the bride's prototype, as far as to that first James of Scotland who was held a prisoner in England for eighteen years and came north again with Jane Beaufort as his Queen. And James married Jane in St Mary's, Southwark, all but one year of five full centuries before the Duke of York married Lady Elizabeth Bowes-Lyon in Westminster Abbey.

She has a simplicity and directness of manner and speech which perfectly express the simplicity and directness of a mind that has regarded without fear the responsibility of the most exalted position a woman can hold in the world of to-day ; and withal there is about her such a sweet gravity of demeanour as forbids at once the fancy that her imagination had not been preoccupied by the responsibility of what she was undertaking. Intelligence is eagerly attributed to royalty by courtiers, but in the case of the Queen it is an intelligence which could shape itself before she passed into that royal state wherein the external appurtenances are so anxiously guarded that contact with reality becomes impossible. She is most unmistakably a Queen. Even when Duchess of York that mysterious effluence of the ages flowed around her, but the treasure of her youth's freedom gleamed through that effluence with such a singular beauty that none who had been privileged to behold it could ever forget the emotion of the experience. Those words are written in awareness of how feebly the writer has contrived to net in words his impression of a great lady, but they are written from his heart and with that poor excuse for such insipidity of eloquence he turns regretfully from one of the figures on this thronged tapestry whose motives cannot be questioned and to whose beautiful integrity of purpose and character all must bow. And it does not yet seem to have dawned on this country that when King Edward VIII in his agony of purpose scribbled on that pencilled note, of which Mr Baldwin made such dramatic use—*Duke of York. He and the King have always been on the best of terms as brothers, and the King is confident that the Duke deserves and will receive the support of the whole Empire,* he was giving to the country the best advice he knew, for which advice he has not yet received a particle of credit.

Less than a week after King George returned from Italy to the rigours of that cold and wet summer of 1923 Mr Bonar Law was ordered by his doctors to give up work and on May 20th he placed his resignation in the hands of the King. Without a change in the Government it was not the custom for a retiring Prime Minister to recommend his successor. When Gladstone resigned Lord Rosebery was Queen Victoria's personal choice. Everybody, including Lord Curzon himself, expected Lord Curzon would be asked to form a Ministry. To Curzon's consternation, so tremendous that he burst into tears on being informed of the King's decision, Mr Baldwin was invited instead and accepted. The spirit in which he did so we may hear in his own words.

Speaking to his constituents he said :

" I am just one of yourselves, who has been called to special work for the country at this time. I never sought the office. I never planned out or schemed in my life. I have but one idea, which was an idea that I inherited, and it was the idea of service—service to the people of this country. My father lived in that belief all his life, and behind him members of my family, in an obviously more restricted way, practised the same thing."

May one interrupt this serenade to service for a few moments to observe that the Prince of Wales opening the International Air Conference, opening the new anatomy, biology and physics departments at Guy's Hospital, opening the Triennial Congress of the International Surgical Society, dedicating the Monument of British gratitude to the Belgian People in Brussels, addressing the guests at the Royal Caledonian Schools dinner, addressing the Honourable Society of Cymmrodorion and the American Universities Union and the Pictorial Posters and Advertising Exhibition at the Royal Academy and the Newspaper Press Fund Diamond Jubilee and the London Society of Medicine, touring the West Riding and making speeches at Rotherham, Bradford, York and Leeds, presiding at the celebrations of the eight-hundredth anniversary of St Bartholemew's Hospital, touring Northumberland and making speeches at Alnwick, Morpeth, Newcastle-upon-Tyne and Gosforth, presiding at the dinner of the British Empire Service League, celebrating the centenary of the Royal Asiatic Society, touring Nottinghamshire and making speeches at Worksop, Mansfield, Nottingham and East Retford, touring North Wales and addressing the Borough Council, the University College, the Infirmary, and the National Library of Aberystwyth, the County Council and the Borough Council of Caernarvon, and the Merioneth County Council at Dolgelly besides making speeches at Colwyn Bay, Denbigh, Ruthin, Mold and Wrexham, proposing the toast of the Dominions and India at the Overseas League, speaking to the Child Emigration Society and the British Institute of International Affairs, and proposing at the dinner of the Royal Navy Club the toast of " The Work of the Fleet in all Theatres of the Great War culminating in the Surrender of the German Fleet on the 21st November 1918 ; also to the memory of Lord Hawke and all who were with him at Quiberon Bay on the 20th November 1759," may one interrupt that serenade in Worcestershire to observe that the Prince of Wales's performance of these tasks among many others in 1923 was also due to an inherited idea of service to the people of this country ?   Yet in not one of these speeches of which we have the printed record does the Prince of Wales say a word about his service.   But perhaps he was less humble than Mr Baldwin, who must now be allowed to continue.

" It is a tradition ; it is in our bones ; and we have to do it. That service seemed to lead one by way of business [*which was grateful*] and the County Council into Parliament [*after the difficult feat of losing Kidderminster to the Liberals by being offered a seat at Bewdley that was conservatively speaking foolproof*], and it has led one through various strange paths to where one is ; but the ideal remains the same, because all my life I believed from my heart the words of Browning : ' All service ranks the same with God.'   It makes very little difference whether a man is driving a tramcar or sweeping streets or being Prime Minister, if he only brings to that service everything that is in him and performs it for the sake of mankind."

And lest any should suspect an assumed humility in those sentiments let it be recorded that when some journalists gathered outside 11 Downing Street offered their congratulations to the new Prime Minister Mr Baldwin replied gravely : " I need your prayers rather than your congratulations."

It is permissible to suppose that King George was impressed by Mr Baldwin's humility under the load of greatness he thrust upon him, for he himself was a humble man.   Moreover, Mr Baldwin would have been personally much more agreeable to him than Lord Curzon.   It is equally permissible to suppose that Mr Baldwin's ability to present himself to the public as a man in the street who had suddenly found himself Prime Minister with as much astonishment as a man in the street might suddenly find himself rich because he had guessed the results of ten football matches did give the public a genuine confidence in the grandeur of their country.   Mr Baldwin never made the mistake of suggesting that he was clever. What he relied upon was the purity of his motives and the rugged worth of his character which he always suggested he shared with his audience.   He had another superlatively useful gift.   He could always stand up like a man and own himself in the wrong, and what was more contrive to suggest to his listeners that he was protecting the men who had caused him to go wrong.   He could always succeed in making those who refused to accept him at his own valuation appear morally inferior to himself.

When the Coalition was displaced *The Times* expected "a cessation of that interference with the proper function of the Foreign Office which was so unfortunate a feature of the Lloyd George system." Yet after Mr Baldwin became Prime Minister he took advantage of returning through Paris from his annual holiday at Aix-les-Bains, which he always preferred to Droitwich as a solvent of rheumatism, to have a heart-to-heart talk with M. Poincaré, over the head of his Foreign Minister, Lord Curzon, about the difficulties of the Ruhr situation.   After the talk a communiqué was issued to the public stating that the two Premiers had found that there was no divergence between them in purpose or principle in regard to the reparations question.   And this after an exchange of notes between the two countries during the previous month in which their respective attitudes had appeared incompatible and irreconcilable.   One or other of the Premiers must have given way, and the French Press were sure it was Mr Baldwin.   They were so pleased that they compared his visit to the visit of King Edward VII in 1903 which had laid the foundation of the Entente.   In England "it was confidently expected in well-informed quarters that Mr Baldwin would take an early opportunity of putting the interview in its true perspective.   This expectation was not realised," says the *Annual Register*.   To the journalists waiting for him at

Dover he would say nothing except that he had had a very bad crossing. He was not going to repeat that disastrous indiscretion of the Press interview he gave at Southampton on his return from the Debt negotiations in America. However, a few days later, he addressed the students of the Philip Stott Social College at Northampton, and to this curiously inappropriate audience he said:

" It was my good fortune in an interview which I had last week with the President of the Council in Paris to help, as I believe, to restore that atmosphere of confidence between France and ourselves which had for some time been lost. No more and no less ! "

It was expected that he would say more at the opening of the Imperial Conference on October 1st, but Mr Baldwin did not refer to the Paris communiqué, and nobody to this day has ever found out what did happen in Paris. It was known that M. Poincaré had kissed Mr Baldwin good-bye at parting. That was all. And the general feeling was that M. Poincaré's cordiality was like the smile on the face of the tiger after eating the young lady of Niger.

"I think Baldwin has gone mad," Lord Birkenhead wrote to Mr Austen Chamberlain at this date. " He simply takes one jump in the dark, looks round; and then takes another."

The next jump was a General Election in November because it was his " only course as an honest man." He wanted to find out if the country would try Protection as a remedy. Mr Baldwin discovered that the country did not want Protection, and this surprised him because Admiral Sir Reginald Hall, the Chief Agent of the Unionist Central Office, had said that it did, and the Admiral had been in charge of Naval Intelligence during the war.

The Prince of Wales came back in October from a stay of a few weeks on the ranch he had bought in Alberta. Mr Lloyd George had also been out in Canada. Early in November Lady Louise Mountbatten was married to the Crown Prince of Sweden, and a week or so later Princess Maud was married to Lord Carnegie. When *would* the Prince of Wales get married ?

In summing up the year the *Annual Register* said:

Cabinet responsibility to Parliament, which had been practically non-existent under Mr Lloyd George, was re-established . . .; and Mr Baldwin as Premier showed himself a genuine constitutionalist, utterly averse to governing either behind the back or over the head of Parliament. . . . On the whole it may be said that the House of Commons in 1923 recovered the place in the counsels of the nation which it had held not merely before the Coalition of 1915 but before the " secret diplomacy " of 1906, and played a greater part than for many years previously in determining the national policy both at home and abroad.

It may be true that Mr Baldwin did not succeed in directing the foreign policy of the nation behind the back of Parliament; but if he could have swallowed M. Poincaré instead of being swallowed by him it is difficult to believe that any scruples of constitutionalism would have deterred him from making further experiments in such heart-to-heart talks over the state of Europe, even if they should include being kissed by the moustachio'd premiers of a dozen countries. ' All service ranks the same with God.'

The election at the close of 1923 brought the Labour Party into office for the first time, but only with the help of the Liberals. It was clear they could do little. Nevertheless, Mr Ramsay MacDonald, whose late partnership with Mr Baldwin was to destroy his effectiveness as a party leader and his reputation as a statesman, did manage in the few months of office he was granted, to clear up some of the confusion into which the foreign policy of the country had been flung through the competing ambitions and cross intrigues of individual politicians. He was wise enough to join the office of Secretary of State for Foreign Affairs to that of Prime Minister, and on February 1st 1924 a note was despatched to Moscow stating that Britain " recognised the Union of Socialist Soviet Republics as the *de jure* rulers of those territories of the old Russian Empire which acknowledged their authority." Mr Baldwin thought " the Government had been unduly precipitate in recognising the Russian Soviet," and warned it against the dangerous characteristics of that body. Probably dynamic force was among them.

The nervousness over the result of establishing diplomatic relations with Russia was repeated in the nervousness over the Prince of Wales's riding. He took one or two tosses early in the year, and on March 15th his horse fell on him at a point-to-point race at Buxton. In the House of Commons a member asked the Speaker to remonstrate with the Heir to the Throne against exposing himself to unnecessary risks. To this the Speaker replied archaically: " I have no tongue to speak save as the House shall direct me." The matter was then dropped in Parliament, but some of the newspapers took it up, and pressure was brought to bear on the Prince to give up steeplechasing. His job was to display an interest in the British Empire Exhibition at Wembley, not go careering about the country over fences. It was rumoured that the King had given his eldest son one of those jobations in the style of Queen Victoria to her eldest son; but it is not recorded whether the shoe of Mr Baldwin's advice was applied to the wheels of the Prince's wilfulness. Anyway he had to cut down the exuberance of his personal amusement, and being a young man who gave his whole heart to anything, duty or diversion, he was depressed accordingly. The Prince did not count himself a Latinist. Otherwise he might have quoted from Tacitus, *ingrata quae tuta, ex temeritate spes.* Safety brings discouragement, rashness hope.

The Labour Government endured until October, when the Liberals decided that the audition had lasted long enough and voted with the Conservatives to turn them out. It was the suicide of Liberalism.

On the eve of dissolution the Duke of Northumberland presiding over the annual conference of the National Unionist Association at Newcastle turned to Mr Baldwin and asked for a " call to arms ". Roland's horn was stopped up. The most stirring tucket Mr Baldwin could blow was a dreary " disquisition on the importance of a settled and contented Germany as the most effective barrier of Western civilisation against Bolshevism." However, five days before the country went to the polls the country received a call to arms from the *Daily Mail* in the shape of a communication sent the previous evening to M. Rakowsky, the Soviet Chargé d'Affaires in London, about an alleged letter from Zinovieff, head of the Third International at Moscow, to the Communist Party in Great Britain. A copy of the letter was attached and was characterised by the Foreign Office Note as " containing instructions to British subjects to ask for the violent over- throw of existing institutions in this country, and for the subversion of His Majesty's forces as a means to that end."

M. Rakowsky said the letter was a clumsy forgery, which is the accepted opinion now; but Mr MacDonald in an effort to stand by the permanent officials managed to make the country think the letter was genuine, and all the thanks he got for his chivalry was abuse from the conservative members for slighting poor civil servants who could not speak for themselves. The mystery of the Zinovieff letter has never been completely cleared up. Mr J. D. Gregory who signed the communication, a copy of which fell into the hands of the *Daily Mail*, resigned three years later from the Foreign Office after an indiscretion over inside information which was used by friends to gamble on the see-saw of the franc. Stalin has put Zinovieff beyond answering any more questions in this world.* The committee of investigation set up by the new Cabinet decided the letter was genuine, but the only evidence of its genuineness they could have received must have been supplied by the Secret Service, which destroys its value. Probably the letter had been forged to use as propaganda against the Russian Agreement. It transpired three years later that the *Daily Mail* had secured their copy from an independent source, but the intervention of the Foreign Office was never satisfactorily explained. Anyway it did its work. Old women looked under their beds every night for bombs after that letter, which could be described in the words of Bob Acres' servant for his master's challenge to Ensign Beverley :

> By the mass ! it don't look like another letter ! It is, as I may say, a designing and malicious-looking letter; and I warrant smells of gunpowder like a soldier's pouch ! Oons ! I wouldn't swear it mayn't go off !

Yet Mr Baldwin, who could never have suspected that the Zinovieff letter might be a forgery deliberately published when it was to discredit the Labour Party, was astonished at the enthusiasm which greeted him in South-East Lancashire during the last days before the election. In his modesty he did not grasp that he was as welcome as a fire-extinguisher in a combustible world.

Some attention has been paid to this business of the Zinovieff letter because it is an indication of the lengths to which otherwise honourable men will go when they believe their country is in danger. It is an indication, too, how easily this country can be unbalanced by the hysteria of mass credulity.

* And since writing that, shut up Rakowsky for twenty years.

Before that Guy Fawkes election, the Prince of Wales had left Southampton in the *Berengaria* on August 23rd for a visit to the United States and Canada. There was criticism of the second United States visit He was overdoing this democratic royalty business. Even Americans themselves complained he had got in with the wrong set. All this talk about dancing till six in the morning and playing the ukulele . . . why couldn't he get married and settle down? After all, he was thirty and an heir apparent unmarried at thirty was all wrong. The ranch in Alberta was another matter. Freedom and easiness there were Empire products. But not in the United States. It was making kingship cheap for those Yankees. They should never have been allowed to come into the war at all. What had been the result? A burden of millions a year to the British taxpayer in order to repay a loan which had all been spent in buying American goods. The next thing we should hear was that the Prince of Wales was going to marry an American. It might be time he settled down, but it must not be with an American woman. Anyway, the younger generation was going to the dogs. It was time the whole country settled down. Thank God, Stanley Baldwin was back at the helm. The next thing would be that the Prince of Wales would be going Bolshie. Still, it couldn't be denied he was good for trade, and as long as he kept inside the Empire one mustn't grumble too much at him. But he ought to be married. A man should really be thinking seriously of settling down when he reaches thirty.

However, in March 1925 the Prince left Portsmouth in the *Repulse* to visit Africa and South America and the rumours in well-informed circles about the second visit to the United States died down. From the time he reached the Gold Coast until he left Cape Town for Montevideo at the beginning of August it was an exhausting business. Moreover, there were special difficulties in South Africa owing to a less enthusiastic feeling for the Union Jack there than in other parts of the Empire. It is not easy to affirm with any assurance that the Prince's visit effected a great deal. All one can say is that it was not his fault if it did not. The ease with which the British Government was able to secure from the Dominions approval of the particular line it was taking in 1936 against the King's marriage has created a doubt of the Dominions' ability to think clearly or feel strongly about anything except trade.   So long as the Prince was a good salesman he was useful.   When he showed signs of being as much interested in social reform as in commerce he was less useful.   If it is as easy to shift from the throne what we are asked to believe is the only link that binds together the British Commonwealth of nations as to shift an ornament from a mantelpiece, it is no more a cause for Imperial self-approbation than the failure of the mantelpiece to collapse when the ornament is shifted. No Dominion, except possibly Eire and she counts herself a mother country, stands to gain anything at the moment from secession.   All that every Dominion asks is immediately granted, and almost the whole burden of defending those Dominions is borne by the British taxpayer.   And that with an Empire extending over a quarter of the globe's surface a small island off the west of Europe should have had even one perfectly healthy person incapable of being employed during these years of reconstruction will be regarded by historians of the far future with amazement.   Perhaps they will decide that after the war of 1914–18 this country, unable to make up its mind whether it wanted to administer the Commonwealth or the League of Nations, ultimately failed to administer either.

King Edward VIII was certainly one of those dangerous dynamic forces of which Mr Baldwin in homely speech expressed such a dread to the Carlton Club on October 19th 1922.   The opportunity came to turn that dynamic force against itself, but in taking advantage of that opportunity that itch of self-justification which always frets the surface of English character had to be smeared with an ointment, and the ointment used was the moral failure of the King.   This was rubbed in so prodigally that though the itch has been allayed the ointment is still glistening.   The result is that for the present the whole Empire is debarred from the services of the Duke of Windsor, and no sooner is that realised than the itch begins again, which necessitates the application of a fresh ointment, made up this time of the theory that the Duke's services are no longer valuable in any case.   When his prestige was greatest we have had to make the greatest efforts to lower it.   What a heavy cloud of disillusionment hung over the insignificant paragraph that announced the Duke of Windsor had put up his Alberta ranch for sale !

The narrative of these Empire tours has deliberately been

shorn of picturesque detail, deliberately washed of colour.
All the speeches and the banquets, all the glittering recep-
tions, the innumerable addresses of perspiring mayors, the
obsequious officials, the rallies of boy scouts, the massed choirs
of children white and black, the bunting and the roses, the
flags, the firing, the cheers and music, the singing crowds,
plumes, pageantry, gilded elephants, guards of honour, the
triumphal arches of wattle or palm, the perfumes of a thousand
strange flowers, the battlefields of the Transvaal, the Union
Jack planted on the heights of Abraham where Wolfe died,
the trade winds and the grey Atlantic, the Southern Cross
rising and the Great Bear setting, all that mighty Empire to
which he gave such ardent service reduced to one sentence:
This Ranch for Sale.

The last of those four imperial tours ended at St Helena,
where the Prince planted an olive-tree beside the empty grave
of Napoleon. He might have planted olive-trees all over
Europe; but a constitutional king must not be his own
gardener. He leaves gardening to his ministers.

CHAPTER X

THE FIRST NATIONAL EMERGENCY

THE visit to St Helena did not bring the tour to an end.
From there the *Repulse* steamed westward across the Atlantic
to Montevideo. People at home were a little puzzled by
this extension of the African tour to South America. They
were unaware that a larger volume of British capital was invested in South America than in almost any part of the Empire
except India. They thought it was a capital notion for the
Prince of Wales to sell British goods to the Argentine, but
they knew that in return the Argentine Republic would
expect to sell Argentine goods to Britain, and they wondered
what effect this would have on the Dominion trade. It was
difficult for the newspapers at home to explain the commercial importance of the Argentine without running the risk
of putting a doubt into the heads of the people at home
whether Britain was getting as much out of the Empire as

the Empire was getting out of Britain.   The present writer is not equipped to argue the economic pros and cons of this question.   He must be content to record that presumably the Government at home viewed the Prince's visit with benevolence, and that the Prince himself registered in the Argentine perhaps the greatest personal triumph of his career. One must have followed in his steps somewhere across those oceans to appreciate that power of his to weld peoples in a common enthusiasm.   The genius of his vitality burned like the flame of a solderer's lamp.

At Montevideo on August 14th 1925 the Prince of Wales said :

" In the realm of Statecraft Uruguay appears to have devoted much thought and labour to the universal problem of providing the greatest happiness for the greatest number. In matters relating to labour, the administration of justice, suffrage, relief for old age, and kindred questions her laws and practices have reached an advanced stage.   The recent revision of the Constitution and the new electoral law mark another step in the direction of making the people's voice effective in determining the destinies of the country."

These words may be considered no more than the conventional compliment of the polite visitor.   Yet it is difficult to believe that the Prince's advisers would have encouraged him to offer such a testimonial to the most advanced democratic Government in the New World unless the evidence of its success spoke for itself.   We can be certain that the profoundest effect of the South American visit on the Prince himself was to confirm his determination to do everything he could to secure to his own future realm " the greatest happiness for the greatest number."   His democratic ambitions were to receive a shattering lesson at home.

The material is not yet available for the historian to write authoritatively of the state of affairs between the Prince and his father in that autumn of 1925.   It was widely believed and has been stated in print that there were disagreements and that the Prince went so far as to threaten to renounce his right to the Throne and take up his permanent residence in Canada unless he were allowed more personal initiative and afforded more official help in his projects for social reform. Such ambitions were by no means grateful to a Government which had already made up its mind to break the political menace of Trade Unionism for a long time to come.

There might never be a better opportunity. The leaders of the Labour Party looked incapable either of far-sighted strategy or skilful tactics. The Liberals were no more than the sediment of a great party. It was vital to prevent the dangerous possibility of Mr Lloyd George's being accepted as a leader of the Labour Party, a position for which he was obviously angling with rich bait. The election at the end of 1924 had given the Conservatives the largest majority in their history. The Zinovieff letter had provided the material to paint Labour even redder than it had already been painted. And at the head of the Government was the ideal man to work the confidence-trick on a grand scale. When in October 1925 the Prince of Wales returned from the African and South American tour the Government's plans for war at home were being prepared, and the way in which the industrial crisis arose is so suggestive of the methods by which the " constitutional crisis " arose that the attention of the reader is invited to Mr Baldwin's behaviour in the industrial crisis as a sidelight which may illuminate the other. Let it be noted that the subjunctive mood is used.

The play started in 1925 when Mr Macquisten, the Conservative Member for Argyll, who had drawn March in the ballot for private members' Bills, gave notice of his intention to bring in a Bill amending the law of 1913 that allowed trade unions to impose on their members a levy for political purposes which the individual unionist could avoid only by ' contracting out '. In other words he was forced to notify his political sympathies. Mr Macquisten's Bill proposed to abolish this compulsory levy, which he argued injured the Conservative working-man, that noble savage whose primeval innocence was in danger from the corrupting influence of agitators.

The Government appointed a Cabinet Committee to enquire into the working of the political levy and to advise them what Government support should be accorded to this Bill. It was believed that whether with or without that support the Bill could be carried. On March 5th—the day before the second reading—Mr Baldwin made a speech at Birmingham appealing for peace in industry, which wound up:

" England!   Steady!   Look   where   you   are   going !
Human hands were given us to clasp, and not to be raised
against one another in fratricidal strife ! "

It seems incredible now when reading this dismal piece of
rhetorical claptrap that the whole country was once upon a time
affected by it ; but the country was affected, and Mr Baldwin
himself has deemed it worthy of preservation in one of the
volumes of his collected speeches.

The next day Mr Baldwin himself moved an amendment to
Mr Macquisten's Bill " that this House while approving the
principle of political liberty embodied in the Bill, is of opinion
that a measure of such far-reaching importance should not
be introduced as a private member's Bill."

" For two years past," he said, " in the face of great difficulties, perhaps greater than many were aware of, I have
striven to consolidate and to breathe a living force into my
great Party.   How did we get here ?   It was not by promising
to bring this Bill in ; it was because, rightly or wrongly, we
succeeded in creating an impression throughout the country
that we stood for stable government and for peace in the
country between all classes of the community.   Those were
the principles on which we fought ; those were the principles
on which we won ; and our victory was not won entirely by
the votes of our own Party, splendidly as they fought.   I
should think that [*with the help of the Zinovieff letter*] the
number of Liberals who voted for us ran into six figures, and
I should think that we probably polled more Labour votes
than the other side [*a blank cheque on probability this*].   We
offer the country to-day this : we, at any rate, are not going
to fire the first shot [*so nations bent on war have promised many
times*].   We stand for peace . . . we want to create an
atmosphere, a new atmosphere in a new Parliament for a new
age, in which the people can come together.   We therefore
deliberately abandon what we have laid our hands to.   We
know we may be called cowards for doing it.   We know we
may be told that we have gone back on our principles.   But
we believe we know what at this moment the country wants,
and we believe it is for us in our strength to do what no other
Party can do at this moment, and to say that we at any rate
stand for peace."

Such noble sentiments had not been heard since Joseph
Surface, and the Labour Party lapped them up like Sir Peter
Teazle.   Mr Thomas called the Government's attitude a

" very difficult and very bold step." Mr Henderson spoke of his party's " intense satisfaction." And when the proposer and seconder withdrew the Bill, Mr Baldwin could sit back and reflect on the ease with which he had led the Labour Party up the Garden of Eden.

Mr. Baldwin's speech that day may be read in full elsewhere, and it should be read, but it is not fair to let it pass here without extracting another revelation of his own generosity. He had been talking of the good old days of Baldwins when a wicked coal strike threw a thousand men in the foundry out of work, through no fault of their own.

" I confess that that event set me thinking very hard. It seemed to me at that time a monstrous injustice to these men, because I looked upon them as my own family, and it hit me very hard—I would not have mentioned this, only it got into the Press two or three years ago—and I made an allowance to them, not a large one, but something, for six weeks to carry them along, because I felt that they were being so unfairly treated."

The fashion for public men to weep in the House of Commons had not set in at this date, but many a hard-headed employer of Labour must have wiped away a furtive tear and wished he could give his own charity such a testimonial. The political stage was heaped with bouquets, of which one of the most fragrant was offered by Mr Thomas when he bore witness at Cardiff to Mr Baldwin's goodwill twenty years ago in fighting for recognition of the Railwaymen's Union by the Great Western of which he was a director.

In spite of Mr Baldwin's sentiments on behalf of industrial peace he made no practical effort to adjust the trouble that threatened in the mining industry, but went on rocking himself to and fro on his own admired cadences. The best he could produce in the way of a solution was to say at the end of June when replying to a vote of censure:

" I think it would be useful if the House itself would examine and consider, as the Government are proposing to do, whether any form of subsidy may be possible to give . . . that stimulus and lift in the region of these industries which seem at the moment beaten down into a position of hopelessness."

He was eagerly asked if he was referring to the mining

industry, but refused to commit himself.   In the words of
Mr D. C. Somervell,* one of his blindest admirers :

It was, it seems, an unpremeditated rumination of a rambling mind,
the sort of thinking aloud which should be indulged in only by persons
whose thoughts do not matter.

It is remarkable that whenever Lord Baldwin's admirers
are confronted with a difficult fence in his speeches or actions
they go round it by imputing to him a slowness of wit akin
to cretinism with which his bitterest critics would never dream
of charging him.

At the last moment in July, when faced with the prospect
of a strike by the Railway and Transport Unions in sympathy
with the lock-out in the mines, he put up a subsidy which cost
the country twenty-four million pounds and when the subsidy
was withdrawn left industry where it was when it was offered :
but with this difference, the Government was now ready to
fight the Triple Alliance of the three Unions.   It had not
been ready in July.

There were many who believed that Mr Baldwin had wasted
the taxpayers' money for a stupid gesture.   There was even
a strong feeling among his own party that he should be
removed from the leadership.   His noble sentiments were
merely encouraging the Socialists.   Perhaps they were.
Perhaps they were intended to encourage them.   In his
Rectorial Address on *Truth and Politics* to the University of
Edinburgh in the autumn of this very year Mr Baldwin said :
" Machiavelli's conception of mankind has not been dispelled
or disproved. . . . He is in all our hearts."

Yet if there had been one man in the Labour Party with
an eye for human motive in that autumn and winter of
1925–26 the Prime Minister could have been hoist with his
own petard.

In that October after giving the subsidy he was already
substituting threats for sentiment, so successfully were the
Government's plans maturing.   He foreshadowed more
drastic official action.   The Government would employ all
the power which the law gave it to put down sedition.   The
Government would do its utmost to secure industrial peace ;
but if its efforts failed, its first duty would be to maintain
law and order, and its own duty to assure the maintenance of
essential public services.

* *The Reign of King George V.*

A few days later twelve prominent Communists were arrested in London and Glasgow on a charge of sedition under the Mutiny Act of 1797, the first use of such a law for a century. A few days after this a *Daily Herald* van was wrecked and 8000 copies of the paper destroyed by five Fascists, who at his date were an insignificant and a purely comic organisation. The Public Prosecutor withdrew the charge of larceny and substituted a breach of peace which was treated by the magistrate as a negligible offence. The Home Secretary when questioned in the House said he " had given orders three or four weeks previously that equal justice should be meted out to all parties." This is perhaps the frankest admission ever made that the judicature of this country now acts when required at the bidding of the executive. The Home Secretary at this date was Sir William Joynson-Hicks who throughout the period of national emergency bobs in and out like Joey the clown with his red-hot poker in the old-fashioned harlequinade.

Mr Baldwin's appointment of such a man to the Home Office at this time provides an outstanding instance of his political skill. To the public Joynson-Hicks appeared as a buffoon. They laughed at his indiscretions, his petty injustices, his cap-and-bells puritanism. If some tragedy on a grand scale were the outcome of the national emergency Mr Baldwin could be carried pick-a-back out of any responsibility for it by this Yorick of the executive. And what was more he would still be able to get himself believed a stupid man.

The accused Communists after a trial lasting eight days were all found guilty of conspiring to publish seditious libels. Five (including Mr Harry Pollitt) were sentenced to twelve months' imprisonment; the other seven were invited by Mr Justice Swift to leave the Communist Party, and on their refusal were sentenced to six months' imprisonment. On the evidence offered the sentences were an attempt at genteel terrorism, and the Home Secretary, that suburban Rhadamanthus, made a pitiable exhibition of himself when Mr Ramsay MacDonald moved a vote of censure in the House, expounding the majesty of the Law and apologising for his own seditious language in the cause of Ulster thirteen years ago, doubling indeed the parts of Pooh-Bah and Ko-Ko in this Parliamentary comic opera. The vote of censure was defeated, of course, but it gave the Liberal Party an opportunity to earn a little more contempt by abstaining from voting on a motion that in its essence was a declaration of the right of speech to freedom. A few days later the Government had to make the humiliating admission that the story circulated during the war about the boiling down of corpses for fats had been deliberately invented as war propaganda against the Germans. It was an awkward moment to be compelled to expose unscrupulous methods of propaganda in high places, even if they had been patriotically employed against the Germans.

Hardly more than a month after the Prince of Wales returned from South America, Queen Alexandra died on that snowy twentieth of November. For the fifteen years since she became Queen Dowager she had devoted herself entirely to charity. Few women can have been so deeply loved by an adopted country as she was. We who loved her thank God she was spared knowledge of the treatment that was to be accorded to her favourite grandchild whose affection for her lightened something of the grief for the loss of her eldest son the Duke of Clarence, from which, however, she never really recovered. The laudation of royalty has a bitter tang for us who learnt how little it was worth after December 10th 1936; but all that has been written to celebrate the incomparable sweetness of that disposition, the generosity of that heart, and the outward grace and beauty of that person could not be contaminated by flattery, so easy and so grateful was the tribute of praise the highest and the humblest desired in all truth and regard to pay that exquisite Queen.

It is not proposed to examine at length the curious efforts made by Mr Baldwin and the Government to bring together the miners and the owners; but it will be apparent to any reasonably acute student of politics who follows carefully the course of affairs from the time the subsidy was offered until it was withdrawn that the Government desired to precipitate the General Strike for which they had not been ready when it was threatened in July 1925 but for which by the Spring of 1926 they were completely ready.

On May 1st a Royal Proclamation was issued declaring that, in virtue of the threatened cessation of work in coal-mines, a state of emergency existed such as was contemplated in the Emergency Powers Act of 1920. On the afternoon of that day the General Council of the Trade Union Congress ordered a general strike to begin at midnight on Monday,

May 3rd, if the miners' notices had not been withdrawn. Negotiations, however, were still carried on with a committee of the Cabinet, and on Sunday, May 2nd, Lord Birkenhead drafted a formula which gave the leaders of the Trade Union Congress an opportunity to call off the General Strike without being humiliated. The delegates retired according to some accounts to another room : in other accounts they left 10 Downing Street to discuss the possibility of accepting Lord Birkenhead's formula which was :

" We, the Trade Union Congress, would urge the miners to authorise us to enter upon discussion, with the understanding that they and we accept the report of the Samuel Commission as a basis of settlement, and we approach it with the knowledge that it may involve some reduction in wages."

While the delegates were either out of the room or out of the house word came that some compositors of the *Daily Mail* had refused to set up in type certain phrases which they considered insulting to the workers. Mr Baldwin sent a letter to the delegates informing them it had come to his knowledge that strike notices had already been sent out, that certain overt acts of insubordination had already been committed, and that negotiations could not be resumed until the strike notices had been unconditionally withdrawn. The delegates hurried back to expostulate, but were told that the Prime Minister had gone to bed.

In the House on the next afternoon, the General Strike being due to begin at midnight, Mr Baldwin said :

" I shall be told among other things, ' This is the end of all your dreamy, visionary speeches about peace and all that kind of thing.' Let me say this. I have worked for two years to the utmost of my ability in one direction. I have failed so far. Everything that I care for is being smashed to bits at this moment. That does not take away from me either my faith or my courage. We may in this House to-day be full of strife. Before long the angel of peace, with healing in his wings, will be among us again ; and when he comes let us be there to meet him. [*But Mr Baldwin had not been there to meet the delegates last night.*]

" I shall pick up the bits. I shall begin again. I may not see what I have dreamed of in my lifetime, but I know that the seed I have tried to plant in men's hearts these two years is germinating [*until Mr Baldwin sat down with all his weight on the seedlings*]. I know it is germinating in the hearts and minds of men, and that it is in that direction, and in that direction alone, that we shall pass after much suffering, through deep waters and through storms, to that better land for which we hope."

He did not add that he had abundance of oil to pour over the side of the Ship of State on her anxious course, with the help of which he hoped to calm the waves. Mr Baldwin's behaviour on that fatal Sunday night has been abused as mere stupidity, as the sudden pugnacity of a weak man, or as the result of letting his own cooler and saner judgment be over-ridden by reactionary extremists like Lord Birkenhead and Mr Winston Churchill; but nobody, at any rate in print, has suggested that he jumped at the excuse offered by the unauthorised printers' strike to let the General Strike go on, and make his grand experiment. Long ago, we have it on the authority of Rudyard Kipling,* an Epping Forest farmer, who must have been a judge of character, had laid it down that a certain pair of boys " did each other no good." Those boys were the poet and his cousin Master Stanley Baldwin. " Yet the worst I can remember," Rudyard Kipling says, " was our self-sacrificing war against a wasps' nest. . . . We defeated the enemy unscathed." Note how early that pride in making sacrifices began, and note also that Master Stanley and Master Rudyard were themselves unhurt. One asks if the farmer's dictum was inspired by the stings he and others had received from the wasps Master Stanley and Master Rudyard had stirred up.

Presumptuous though it would be to pretend a knowledge of Mr Baldwin's dreams in Downing Street that night, it is perhaps a permissible if extravagant flight of fancy to suppose that he figured in every one of them as the saviour of his country, a slow-voiced, heavy-gaited, pipe-smoking Roger de Coverley, who had stirred up a wasps' nest in an ecstasy of self-sacrifice.

Nobody in the country gave such an impression of heroic magnanimity as Mr Baldwin during that General Strike. Hear him over the radio:

" I am a man of peace. I am longing and working and praying for peace [*but who slammed his bedroom door on the delegates?*]. But I will not surrender the safety and security

* *Something of Myself.*

of the British Constitution. You placed me in power eighteen months ago by the largest majority accorded to any Party for many, many years. Have I done anything to forfeit that confidence? Can't you trust me to ensure a square deal for both parties, to secure even justice between man and man?"

He would revert to that 'trust me' patter, which is dangerous patter for a politician on account of its association with the confidence-trick, in a broadcast before the Election of 1929.

"You trusted me once. Won't you trust me again?"

But the electorate in spite of that nauseating song 'Stanley Boy' which was the Marseillaise of the Safety First election refused to trust him, and some years passed before Mr Baldwin recovered the trust of the public by handling the ex-King's Abdication on somewhat similar lines to his handling of the General Strike.

When the Abdication was on the horizon Mr Baldwin had a stout ally in the Archbishop of Canterbury, but when the General Strike had been precipitated he had not quite so stout an ally in Dr Lang's predecessor. Dr Davidson " issued an appeal to the Government in which he deprecated the turning of the strike into a political issue and called on the Government to procure a simultaneous cessation of the lock-out and the strike." (A. R.) The Government, however, had the support of Cardinal Bourne. Cardinal Manning would not have bowed so low.

Not merely did the Government refuse to listen to Dr Davidson's appeal, but they forbade the broadcasting of it. The Government in December 1936 would be less chary of an Archbishop's broadcast. The Liberals showed themselves subservient to the mood of the indignant middle classes, and Sir John Simon rose in the House to lay down the proposition that a general strike was illegal, which was soon found to be bad law but good propaganda, and the Government used it to support them in the esteem of the country. Yet the country grew so suspicious of the way the General Strike had been brought about that Mr Baldwin went to the microphone again to protest his messianic vocation. So the General Strike came to an end. Mr Baldwin received the ovation he deserved for a successful demonstration of peace in our time. The King joined in with a message from Buckingham Palace to forgive and forget. Mr Baldwin hurried back to the microphone. He had discovered the perfect medium for his oratory. In this broadcast " he called upon employers to act with generosity and on workers to put their whole hearts loyally into their work "; but he dodged making any definite promise to the representatives of the workers to secure them against victimisation. He had involved the country in a loss of at least thirty million pounds on top of the subsidy. He was now to involve them in a loss twenty times as great because in his anxiety to be recognised as a man who saved the country from what might have been the horrors of a General Strike less gentlemanly than the one he had defeated with such emotional success, he forgot that the situation in the coal-fields was now worse than ever.

Fascinating though it would be to unravel in detail the intricate cat's-cradle of half-hearted negotiations in which Mr Baldwin put his political conscience to sleep during those critical months the bittersweet pleasure must be foregone. An occasional glimpse at that moral siesta must suffice.

On June 12th the Prime Minister was blowing his own cornet, with the familiar tremolo stopping, at a large Unionist rally in Wiltshire. Instead of telling the country what he and the Government were doing to bring the coal lock-out to an end he went rambling back to the General Strike. True to his incorrigible sentimentality he discovered a golden age of trade unionism when it was " a genuine product of the British democratic spirit " before it was corrupted by the " alien and foreign heresy " of class warfare and the pursuit of political power. This had made a general strike sooner or later inevitable. " If it had not come in my time," he declared, " it would have come in that of my successor." Hark to the lullaby he is humming to his conscience, as he goes on to claim that the old constitutional attitude of keeping promises made collectively is being largely abandoned, though he does not add in favour of breaking promises made individually over the microphone. But as we listen to that lullaby, " *If it had not come in my time it would have come in that of my successor*," we hear another lullaby crooned to a Prime Minister's conscience ten years hence: " *I am convinced that where I have failed no one could have succeeded*."

By what monstrous arrogance of the mind did Mr Baldwin

discover in himself so infinitesimal a portion of human fallibility ?   He, the head of the Government, on any evidence available, had made the experiment of precipitating a General Strike costing millions, merely on the strength of his own opinion that a General Strike was sooner or later inevitable. The duty imposed upon him by the responsible post he had judged himself fit to hold was to avert that strike.   He plunged the country into that strike as many a blind and wilful statesman before him has plunged his country into war.   He dared to speak of the General Strike as if it were a Flood and he a Divinely instructed Noah.   It was meet he had that day an audience of Wiltshire moonrakers, for to a mind so confused between the calamities caused by natural forces and the calamities precipitated by human folly the moon's reflection in a pond might plausibly have presented itself as a cheese.   And it will be with the memory of his speech that June day in Wiltshire that we shall be examining another speech, made not to moonrakers but to the House of Commons, in a melancholy December ten years hence.

On that June day to him the " great lesson of the strike was that the British people was not going to throw over Parliament to set up divine right either of the capitalist or the trade unionist, and they were not going to bow to a dictatorship of either."

Three days later Mr Baldwin prostrated himself before capital by announcing to the House that he should almost immediately " lay before it a measure for suspending the Seven-Hours Day Act.   By a skilful use of quotations from the Coal Commission's Report he tried to make it appear that the step was taken in the interests of the miners themselves." Thus the *Annual Register* of 1926.

This announcement exacerbated the situation in the coal-fields.   On July 28th Sir Arthur Steel-Maitland, the Minister of Labour, moved the second reading of the Eight-Hours Day Bill and naïvely announced that as the miners would not agree to a reduction of wages the Government had been driven to propose a lengthening of the working-day.   Mr Walsh, a miners' member, asked Mr Baldwin how he could reconcile this measure with his professed desire not to lower the standard of life of the working-classes, and Mr Wheatley suggested that the Prime Minister's reputation for political honesty had been greatly exaggerated.   Mr Ramsay Mac-Donald, however, dissociated himself from the personal attacks

on Mr Baldwin.   The heat of the debate was no doubt cooled
for Mr MacDonald by the shadow of coming events still five
years away.

The Eight-Hours Bill was passed on July 1st, and before
going on with the history of the coal strike it is worth while
reminding readers that Sir Austen Chamberlain had to
explain to the House why Abyssinia had recently appealed
to the League of Nations for protection against the designs
of Italy and Great Britain.   It appeared that as the price for
Italian support of Britain in the dispute with Turkey over
Mosul he had made an arrangement with Signor Mussolini
for mutual recognition of spheres of influence in Abyssinia,
and granted Italy " exclusive right " to certain concessions.
This had roused French suspicions that Britain and Italy were
diddling her over the tripartite arrangement of 1906.   So
Sir Austen Chamberlain explained to the House that the
Italo-British agreement contained no threat to the integrity
or independence of Abyssinia.   By " exclusive right " Great
Britain had meant " exclusive " only as against her own
concessionaries.   He welcomed the opportunity Abyssinia's
protest to the League had afforded to demonstrate the innocence of British policy.   Sir Austen Chamberlain had already
acquired from his leader a certain agility at the game of
Puss-in-the-corner.

But we must return to the coal stoppage.

Alarmed by the situation into which the country was drifting
while the Government was coiled up in the inertia of a boa
constrictor gorged with the poor ass of a general strike it had
swallowed, various citizens of goodwill endeavoured to bring
about a settlement.   Among such were the Society of Friends
and the Industrial Christian Fellowship, an undenominational
body which included leaders of the Anglican Church and the
Free Churches.   This latter body drafted a memorandum
which was accepted by the Miners' Executive as a correct
statement of the terms on which they would advise the men
to resume work.   It was an eminently fair proposal, and
Dr Kempthorne, the Bishop of Lichfield, who in his pre-
episcopal days had had a long experience of parochial work
in the industrial areas of the north, forwarded a copy of the
memorandum to the Prime Minister.   In the words of the
Annual Register " Mr Baldwin now repeated his House of
Commons performance of furtively holding out a hand and
hastily withdrawing it before it could be grasped."   In other

G

words he made a series of speeches, each contradicting what had been said in the last, and winding up at Norwich by laying down that "masters and men should settle the dispute by themselves, and the less the Government interfered the better."

Snubbed at an interview with the Prime Minister, the Bishop of Lichfield and his colleagues published their memorandum; but all the thanks they received was to be jeered at by Cabinet Ministers, Press and public as busybodies meddling in matters they did not understand, and it need scarcely be added that other ecclesiastics with more respect for the Government and the capitalists hastily disowned them.

Mr Lloyd George tried to argue with Mr Baldwin; but it was useless, and when the Prime Minister was reminded that at the beginning of the trouble he had said the parties would never reach agreement if left to themselves he replied that that remark had been made three months ago and since then they had been through a bitter experience from which he hoped they had learnt something.

So the situation grew worse daily, and on July 30th the Home Secretary's red-hot poker was again in evidence. The state of emergency was to be proclaimed for another month. Sir William Joynson-Hicks' Jack-in-the-box mind was enjoying its extra-judicial authority, though he was compelled to admit, a little regretfully it seemed, that there had been remarkably few prosecutions under the Regulations.

On August 4th Parliament was adjourned for three months with the provision that it could be summoned in three weeks if the stoppage lasted as long.

Two days later Mr Baldwin sent a message to the United States which was published in the American Press just before a Labour delegation arrived to appeal for subscriptions to relieve the misery of the miners and their dependents. In this message he asserted that there was no severe distress among them, and not even malnutrition among the children much less starvation. To this he added a defence of the British Government's conduct and the usual justification of himself. Mr MacDonald thought it beneath his dignity to reply in the American Press, but Mr Lloyd George, caring neither for his own nor the Prime Minister's dignity, drubbed him soundly. Let the people of South Wales who are said to have turned against the Duke of Windsor for a

broken promise after his visit to the distressed areas on the
eve of his abdication remind themselves of the bread Mr
Baldwin contrived with such dignity to deny them and
their children ten years previously.

We are not surprised to hear that, soon after this message
to the American Press to divert a display of practical sympathy
with the miners and their dependents into an expression of
admiring sympathy with himself, Mr Baldwin, " acting on
medical advice, quitted London for his usual summer holiday
at Aix-les-Bains." He left Mr Winston Churchill behind in
charge of the coal situation, and Mr Churchill nearly pulled
off an agreement; but though he carried with him the Coal
Committee he was outvoted by the rest of the Cabinet who
preferred to wait until Mr Baldwin returned from his holiday on September 15th. As was to be expected he at once
surrendered unreservedly to the owners. So on the wretched
business dragged; but that did not depress Mr Baldwin.
Addressing the Annual Conference of the Unionist Party at
Scarborough on October 7th he was braced by the fine air
into proclaiming that his " efforts to bring about a better
spirit in industry had not been wasted." Since Mr Pecksniff
forgave everybody at the end of *Martin Chuzzlewit* no comparable instance of impenetrable human complacency has
been recorded in fact or fiction.

At the end of October the Home Secretary satisfied the
House that the Emergency Regulations must be continued;
but it was a curious comment on the moral superiority of the
legislature over the few poor devils of starving miners who had
tried to intimidate blacklegs that most of the sitting was taken
up with the discussion of its own sobriety. Dr Salter, a
Labour Member, had recently informed a temperance meeting
that he had seen " members of Parliament of all parties drunk
in the House, not on one, but on many occasions." A
Unionist member moved that this speech was " a gross libel
on the members of the House, and a grave breach of its
privileges." Dr Salter, however, refused to retract or withdraw his accusations, and during the discussion Mr Baldwin
testified to the " great improvement which had taken place
in the drinking habits of the House within his own experience." A few Labour members were in favour of
inviting Dr Salter to name the drunken gentlemen before a
Committee of Privileges; but Mr Lloyd George tactfully
pointed out the inadvisability of such a step, and the House

contented itself with passing a unanimous motion in favour of its own sobriety. All parties were learning from Mr Baldwin the falsity of the old adage that self-praise is no recommendation.

Almost to the close of that drenching November, the wettest for seventy-eight years, the miners kept up their fight, but it was a losing fight and men were being starved into work in ever increasing numbers. At the Lord Mayor's Banquet in the Guildhall on November 9th Mr Baldwin " characterised the General Strike as a stain on the annals of England, and the coal stoppage as another monument to human folly which had plunged the country into vast losses, and would leave behind a heritage of bitter memories of wasted strife and suffering." Of his own share in the responsibility for both he did not boast, but cheered up the well-fed guests by assuring them " he did not hold with those who prophesied the early decline of England."

On November 15th the House of Commons approved making broadcasting a Government enterprise. It was the least they could do for a method of communication which had served them so well in this critical year and made the Prime Minister's voice as welcome a sound in every home as the singing of the kettle on the hob. Controversy was to be prohibited. The Prime Minister's self-praise was not held to be controversial.

By the beginning of December the coal strike was broken. The miners went back to work on the terms offered by the owners in July after the Eight-Hours Act, which meant that they were much better in some districts than in others.

The coal stoppage cost the country hundreds of millions of pounds. It was the most calamitous industrial dispute Great Britain had ever experienced. Apart from the loss to the export trade the damage to internal commerce was huge. The misery it cost to so many thousands of men, women and children is hardest to forgive. The trade unions of Russia subscribed nearly a million pounds to the Miners' Federation for relief, but the United States, thanks to Mr Baldwin's advice, contributed only a few thousand pounds. The country showed its opinion of the Government by giving Labour much increased support at three by-elections held at the end of the struggle. At Smethwick Sir Oswald Mosley who had flung over the Government for Labour was returned with a quadrupled majority in spite of feverish efforts by

his late colleagues to prevent the renegade's return. Mr
Baldwin was not impressed by Mr MacDonald's invitation
to " ask the verdict of the country " and receive " the
doom which the Government's actions merited."   He read
the Labour Party an avuncular lecture on the danger of
listening to extremists and declined Mr MacDonald's challenge
to go to the country " save in good time."   It was close on
Christmas, that Christmas of which Mr Baldwin has spoken
with such nostalgia over the microphone.   The miners'
cupboards might be bare, but he would have one of his rare
chances to visit the old home in Worcestershire.   He would
have a well-deserved but brief holiday from the cares of a
Prime Minister who had sacrificed all except a few days
at Christmas to his country.

It must have been a heartening experience for the Prince
of Wales, that year of 1926.   No wonder he began to interest
himself in flying.   Yet not only in flying.   Early in the
stoppage he sent ten pounds to the Miners' Relief Fund with
a message expressing the hope that the struggle would not end
in the humiliation of either party.   That message was much
resented by those who believed that the workers deserved and
required humiliation.   There was talk of a Prince of Wales
who had ' gone Bolshie '.   Politicians, permanent officials and
courtiers began to wonder if this young man would be quite
as malleable as they hoped to their theories of kingship.

On April 21st 1926 was born Princess Elizabeth Alexandra
Mary of York.   The event is recorded in the *Annual Register*,
but the birth of the infant princess was not considered
important enough to be given an entry in the index.

CHAPTER XI

NEW WINE

THE exhaustion that succeeded the fever of 1926 vouchsafed to Mr Baldwin a measure of the industrial peace on
which his heart was set, and he felt justified in leaving the
country at the end of July to accompany the Prince of Wales
and Prince George to Canada where the sixtieth anniversary
of Canada's status as a Dominion was being celebrated.   He
was back home a month later.

The Prince of Wales, with every difficulty put in his way, was trying to give the country a lead in aviation, and perhaps it is still insufficiently appreciated how much his example meant in the way of overcoming some of the general distrust in Great Britain of flying. That distrust persists. People listen with equanimity to the announcement over the radio of a steadily maintained monthly death-roll of round about five hundred and some fifteen thousand injured in road accidents, but still the average man or woman believes it is more dangerous to fly in an aeroplane than to drive in a motor-car. No doubt the belief that a flying accident must almost certainly be fatal plays a part in this timidity, but it does reflect unfavourably on the ancient renown of an audacious and adventurous nation. The Prince's habit of flying as a matter of course was a valuable spur to laggard initiative. Yet he was continually being exasperated by the suggestion of his foolhardiness. King George himself had an acute prejudice against flying, and although one did not expect a man of his age to become an enthusiast he should have appreciated the obvious fact that unless the younger genera-tion of royalty took to travelling by air as a matter of course the country would continue to regard the business as un-warranted recklessness.

In September 1928 the Prince of Wales and the Duke of Gloucester went to East Africa. On November 12th Dr Davidson, the Archbishop of Canterbury, was succeeded by Dr Cosmo Gordon Lang, to whose Primacy of York Dr Temple was translated from the see of Manchester. On November 21st the public was alarmed by the first bulletin announcing the illness of King George V. That day beyond Kwakuchinga the Prince killed his first lion. Most of his sport in East Africa had been with a cine-camera. One seldom detects in chronicles of the Prince's career the sports-man's ardour to take life, which is quoted as another example of his wrong-headed attitude toward normal behaviour.

Six days later the Prince received news of his father's illness, and hurried to Dar-es-Salaam. Here he was kept waiting three days for the destroyer *Enterprise* in which he sailed on December 2nd, reaching London on the evening of December 11th. The King was better, but his condition remained critical until the end of the year.

Enterprise was steaming at thirty knots and nearing Aden when the new Archbishop of Canterbury was being enthroned.

On the same day six Councillors of State were nominated for the purpose of summoning the Privy Council and for the transaction of other business on behalf of His Majesty. They were the Queen, the Prince of Wales, the Duke of York, the Archbishop of Canterbury, the Lord Chancellor, and the Prime Minister.

It was after the nomination of those Councillors of State that the rumour began to run of the King's dour battle for life inspired by anxiety at the prospect of the Prince of Wales's succession to the Throne while the affairs of the country were still in so critical a state. What would happen if a Labour Government came into power? The way things were going after the Arcos fiasco in the Spring and the apparent inability of Mr Baldwin to do anything more than sit on his stern and slide as slowly as possibly downhill, a Labour Government was beginning to look alarmingly probable in the near future. So in circles where well-fed rumour moves the pessimism about the future was black. The rest of the country, ignorant of the Prince's disbelief in the doctrine of Safety First, thought only about the King's illness in terms of a well-beloved figure in danger. They listened over the radio to the news of his fight and prayed for his victory over death; but, innocent souls, they did not guess that he was fighting to save them from the rule of one not competent to rule them wisely.

Meanwhile, the distress in the mining areas was increasing day by day, especially in South Wales and Northumbria. As early as April the Lord Mayor of London had opened a fund for the distressed miners, but by November 1st it had reached only £90,000, a sum utterly inadequate for the need. On December 3rd Mr Baldwin assured Parliament that the Government were always thinking about the distressed miners, and that they did not see any need to make a special grant. On December 5th a Conference of Mayors from all over England and Wales met at the Mansion House to consider measures for relief. Mr Neville Chamberlain, the Minister of Health, informed the Conference by letter that the unemployment of a large number of miners must be considered permanent, and that the only solution was the migration of the unemployed to other places either in England or abroad. That letter supplied a bitter footnote to the Government's handling of the industrial situation in 1926.

Pressure on the Government was renewed, and on December 17th Mr Baldwin announced they were prepared to make a grant of £155,000 to the Lord Mayor's Fund, £100,000 to help emigration, and £20,000 for distressed mining areas in Scotland. At the same time he insisted that it was a good thing for the work of relief to be left mainly to private charity, and reminded the House of Commons that in the scripture charity was identified with love. This gave Mr MacDonald an opportunity to remind the Prime Minister of a Persian proverb which defined charity as " a virtue that is required to overtake neglect and indolence."

Soon after this, the Prince of Wales who had assumed the Presidency of the Lord Mayor's Fund, made a broadcast appeal at Christmas, and drew in money a great deal more rapidly than Mr Baldwin's citation of scripture. Moreover, hearing complaints that the work of relief was proving slower than the growth of the Fund, the Prince paid a sudden visit to the distressed areas of Northumbria, where he criticised the administration forcibly, and disconcerted mine-owners and officials. Soon after he returned to London the work of relief moved on faster. And that had been a genuine surprise visit. It had not been an arranged demonstration of poverty only too glad to be poor for the sake of a royal smile. What is more, the nation as a whole recognised the earnestness of the Prince's intention. The country warmed to him. The country was glad King George had recovered and hoped he would live a long time yet; but the country had no doubts about his successor.

In May Mr Baldwin came to the microphone and after reminding people they had trusted him once asked if they would not trust him again. To the trumpet call of ' Stanley Boy ' and the war-cry ' Safety First ! ' the Conservatives charged. For a standard they had a personal letter from Mr Baldwin addressed from Downing Street and carrying the Prime Minister's seal, which was censured as an abuse of his official status, begging the country to vote for stability. The charge was not a success. 130 Conservatives were unseated.

The new Labour Government did not get a chance of doing much, because it could always be defeated by a combined Conservative and Liberal vote, with the result that the safety-first germ infected them. In any case the new Government lacked first-class men.

History may discover in those closing years of the third decade of the nineteenth century the last desperate efforts of

Europe to build a new world out of the débris of the war and, should a greater catastrophe supervene, may assign the major blame for it to English conservatism, which under the guise of prudence, opposed an inert sponge to absorb the wine of enthusiasm. On the other hand, should that greater catastrophe be averted, history may accord the supreme credit for such an achievement to that very conservatism. We who write with that future still unresolved are the slaves of our own prejudice, and should that prejudice incline us to believe in the first of the alternatives we enjoy an advantage which is rare in controversy of preferring to be proved wrong than right.

The resignation of Lord Cecil from the Government on August 27th 1927 may be counted a crucial date in the future. It was only after much hesitation that the Cabinet allowed the letter in which his reasons were set forth to be published. In effect that letter impeached the British Government for its failure to make " an advance in the direction of security, arbitration, and disarmament " and by implication to cast upon it the major responsibility for blocking the way to peace. His letter was answered by Mr Baldwin in a speech that suggested he was more anxiously concerned with the pulse of the British electorate than with the palpitating heart of Western humanity.

That autumn the Prince of Wales addressing the great muster of ex-Service men in the Albert Hall on Armistice night urged them " by their every action, their everyday conversation, and even their very thoughts to seek peace, and ensue it." Some will consider such words the lip-service to peace as familiar in the mouths of politicians as quacking in the mouths of ducks. Such sceptics are reminded of the speech King Edward VIII made to his Brigade of Guards in that only summer of his reign. It would be wiser to believe that within the severe restrictions of his position the Prince of Wales was trying to direct public opinion to support men like Lord Cecil of whose sincerity and indifference to personal prestige there was no doubt. However, from the moment the country acquiesced in the resignation of Lord Cecil it was disagreeably obvious to unsentimental observers that what Mr Baldwin would one day refer to as ' a wave of pacifism ' would spend its force prematurely. We are now in 1938 faced with the spectacle of insane rearmament. The hysteria of peace has become the hysteria of war.　Yet there is no example of any words from the Prince of Wales to encourage that reaction.

In 1929 the publication in England of Remarque's *All Quiet on the Western Front* served as a sharp stimulus to the peace drive, and it became all too clear that the public mind which was susceptible to such an influence was capable of being swayed just as irrationally in the opposite direction.　A desire for peace which was primarily directed by fear lacked all moral value; a surrender to war could be launched by fear even more easily.　The pacifist movement culminated in a series of resolutions, begun in the Oxford Union and copied by every other University throughout Great Britain, affirming that the various student bodies would not in any circumstances fight for King and Country.　It is always an ungrateful task to chill the warmth of youthful idealism; but those resolutions must be condemned, because they failed to affirm the larger idealism which would have assured youth elsewhere that British youth was aware how much less altruistic the pacific example of their country to the rest of the world was rendered by the comfortable consciousness that it already had enough territory to make aggression no longer a temptation.　Great Britain's moral sway over the League of Nations could be justified only by an abundant sacrifice of what she had acquired in the past, and if she was indisposed to make such sacrifices it would have been more honest to follow the lead of much-abused newspaper-proprietors like Lord Rothermere and Lord Beaverbrook and influence the British Commonwealth to withdraw with herself from the League and concentrate upon the economic and moral unity of the Commonwealth.

There were many ardent pacifists who believed that the greatest threat to peace lay in the ultimately irreconcilable ambitions of great combines and who, contemplating the comparative tranquillity and prosperity of the Scandinavian states and inspired by the example of Ireland, desired to break up the whole of Britain into its component parts and thus, as they believed, compel the British Commonwealth to achieve significant form by obtaining that definition of which the amorphous preamble to the Statute of Westminster would in 1931 so cruelly reveal the lack.　Such a practical recognition of the rights of small nations might, it was imagined, offer an inducement in the future for nations like Norway and Denmark to enter into a voluntary association with the

British Commonwealth. It was felt that the Westminster Parliament was no longer representative and that in any event its power was always being further circumscribed by the power of the Cabinet, which in turn was too subservient to the authority of the Prime Minister. Added to this was a growing distrust of the practically uncontrollable power with which the vast growth of the civil service was providing the executive and, most serious of all, the evidence of the increasing subordination of the judicature to the executive.

In October 1928 the country was astonished to hear that the Prime Minister had scraped home for the Rectorship of Glasgow University by only sixty votes from Mr Cunninghame Graham, the nominee of the Scottish Nationalists, with Sir Herbert Samuel, the Liberal nominee, a bad third and Mr Arthur Henderson of Labour an even worse fourth. This is not the place to relate the negotiations behind the scenes by which the established political parties tried to make use of this new and unsuspected force to assist their own aggrandisement. It is enough to say it was fully recognised that if the Nationalist movement in Scotland were not checked that movement would certainly extend to Wales and perhaps even to Northumbria, which was suffering intensely from the Government's handling of the industrial situation.

Three years later in October 1931 the Scottish Nationalist candidate defeated Sir Robert Horne, Professor Gilbert Murray, Mr Tom Johnstone, and Sir Oswald Mosley. He had the advantage of receiving the votes of the Distributist Party which were decisive in the result.

The distributists have never threatened the equanimity of established political parties, and it is unlikely that they ever will in this country. They represent an attempt to give a means of practical expression to the economic and cultural needs of the individual, and in doing so to resist with equal fervour the enslavement of man by communism, totalitarianism, and capitalism. Much of distributist doctrine is informed by the Catholic theory of human duties and aspirations, and as an idealistic political philosophy it is unassailable. It demands, however, of human nature the good will that human nature after nearly two thousand years of Christianity has failed to achieve, and it is exposed to criticism on account of its lack of a feasible plan to overcome all the difficulties which the age of machinery has added to the task of preserving the small economic unit. A country like Portugal or Ireland can rely largely on distributism for its economic doctrine, but even as it depends for its effect on the destruction of Big Business it depends for being put into effect on the break up of large international combines. It is as much fundamentally anti-imperialistic as anti-communist. Hence it is vulnerable on both flanks. The theory of Social Credit offers what Distributism offers and something more, and the care that is taken to make it sound a fool's paradise suggests that its growth is seriously alarming the money monopoly. Moreover, social credit can point to a victory in Alberta, Canada, and what is possible in Alberta is not unimaginable elsewhere. Social credit is also more feared by communism than any other theory of economics if one may judge by the attention awarded by communist writers to demonstrating its absurdity.

When Sir Oswald Mosley was defeated in the Glasgow Rectorial Election he had recently resigned from the Labour Government to form what was then called the New Party. With him among others were associated Mr John Strachey, now one of the most effective voices of communism, and Mr Harold Nicolson, now (*facilis descensus!*) a National Labour M.P. Sir Oswald Mosley's creation of the New Party was due to the exasperation with inertia and complacency which drove him out of the Conservative Party, only to find after holding office in the Labour Government of 1929 the same inertia and complacency there in dealing with the problem of unemployment. The New Party became the British Union of Fascists and naturally suffered in consequence from the skilful use various interested centres of propaganda were making to create odium against Italy over the Abyssinian business. To 'Fascists', noting the success of Hitler, Sir Oswald Mosley has now added 'National Socialists' on his badge, and by making use of anti-Semitic agitation has finally become identified with Hitlerism.

There was a moment when Sir Oswald Mosley looked like possessing a chance of making real headway, but his anti-Semitic propaganda, while it brought him apparent success with the groundlings, did him no good, and what seemed his willingness to encourage a loutish violence copied from the knockabout tragedians of Germany finished him off with the great majority of Britons. It may be too late to recover his lost ground, and that is a pity because he is a great orator; he had the makings of a popular leader.

We are left with the communists, and it is undeniable that as things are now communism presents to ardent youth a more potent attraction than any other political creed. In the first place they can deny Utopia as their spiritual home and point to Russia. The minds of every intelligent man and woman, and with particular insistency of every intelligent young man and young woman, are now haunted by the problem of why in a world richer in the sum total of its material wealth than ever before in the history of mankind poverty and misery should be allowed to continue. The urgency of that problem has been sharpened by the ever more steadily diffused doubt whether this may not be the only world which mankind will experience. Loss of faith can only be accepted with equanimity by the dullard in mind and body. If faith in man's immortality be lost ardour of mind will seek to replace it with faith in man's immortal purpose on this earth, his brief abiding-place. Only in communism can such ardour of mind find a faith which is perpetually refreshed by what it believes in Russia to be evidence of the miracle it has wrought. How far such minds are being misled is beside the point. What all middle-aged people must face is that at this moment the spirit of a crusade (and with what bitter irony does a Christian believer write that word!) is animating more and more young people every day. That crusade aims to destroy human misery and want, and youth will ally itself with whatever political theory seems to offer the speediest road to wage that crusade with success. What old and middle-aged people must ponder is that youth all the world over is confronted by their future in a world which the old and middle-aged are only concerned to see last out their time.

Circumstances have much helped the advancement of communism during the last decade. The great *terra incognita* of Russia still endures to give the lie to those who prophesied the experiment was doomed to fail within a short space of time. The whole of the official British attitude from 1917 to 1929 was based on that belief. Consequently it was hoped that by harrying communists in this country they would be kept from spreading their doctrines, and that with the collapse of the Russian experiment they would vanish. At the same time it was paradoxically feared that the Labour Party might at any moment turn red as rapidly as a lobster in a kettle of boiling water. Hence such devices as the Zinovieff letter. By degrees common sense asserted itself sufficiently to apprehend that the greatest barrier to the spread of communism in this country was not the Conservative Party but the Labour Party. Then came the Italian–Abyssinian business, which allowed non-Catholic Christians of various denominations to establish the basis of an entente with communism, and on top of that came the Spanish business which solidified that entente. The admission of communists to the Popular Front may end in democracy's being swallowed by communism or in communism's being swallowed by democracy. It would take a major prophet to forecast that result.

But this begins to savour of political discussion, and that was not the reason for mentioning these movements which during the latter part of the second decade of the twentieth century made, in various degrees of intensity and extent, an ever more insistent appeal to the youth of the nation as a way of tearing up the patchwork quilt their elders were sewing for what might prove to be the shroud of Europe. It was merely desired to call attention to the atmosphere of desperate experiment provoked by the inertia of the statesmen responsible for rebuilding Europe after the war. A bold gesture by Great Britain such as was imagined by Lord Cecil might have saved the situation and secured disarmament; but that gesture was not made, and a Germany embittered by the failure of the victors to honour the avowed intentions of peace turned to Hitler in a final effort to recover its vitality as a nation.

The communist secure in a positive material creed declares the condition of Europe to be evidence that the death agony of capitalism has begun. The Catholic equally secure in a positive creed which transcends materialism declares the condition of Europe to be the logical result of turning aside from the way of life God Himself indicated when He was Man. Other creeds are not worth considering against these two because all other creeds either compromise in the hope of acquiring a measure of universality or are content with self-sufficiency. It is clear for instance that the Nazi faith of Germany cannot possess either a pragmatic utility or an absolute truth except for Germans.

Communism has already been faced by a major heresy in totalitarianism which is to communism as menacing as the Protestant Reformation was to Catholicism. Both when set against Catholicism are seen to be different aspects of the worship of humanity instead of God. And what, it may be asked, has all this to do with the Prince of Wales in the third decade of the twentieth century? Are we to believe that his mind was greatly preoccupied with distributism or social credit or the political evolution of Sir Oswald Mosley?

No, but what we are to believe is that he, occupying already a position of unique authority and within a few years of attaining the most exalted position of any in this perplexed world of to-day, was Every Young Man, and that when the moment came for him to be faced with the alternative of sacrificing his integrity as an individual to preserve his integrity as an institution or the contrary, all over the world for one brief instant those called extremists and revolutionaries shook hands in a unanimous desire that he should confound the politics of the inert mass. He was in fact the symbol of something much greater than the British Commonwealth of Nations : he was the symbol of life.

There was in him some quality potent enough to extract the essential unity of the many mutually contradictory cures for a sick world, and that unity was the greater vitality all these extremists, revolutionaries, cranks—call them what you will—possessed above the normal man. They recognised his vitality, clasped hands for a moment in agreement, and returned again to their divergences ; but that fugitive unanimity was a pledge that the fellowship of man was ultimately attainable.

It may be granted that without the prestige of his position the Prince of Wales might never have been a mundane figure. But is such a postulate worth consideration? He cannot be detached from his position and judged accordingly. What captured the imagination was a Prince of Wales who had come to life. It was the miracle of a Galatea emerging from the rigid sculpture of royalty. " He was another Stuart at last," said the writer to a famous English statesman after that King was gone. " A Stuart? He was a Plantagenet ! " was the answering ejaculation. He was certainly flowing outside the conventional stream of the Blood Royal. It will be wiser perhaps to regard him as the proto-type of some king in the future than to discover in him a link with the past.

Anyway, it does not matter. Only to God is a man what he is : to other men he is what they suppose him to be. If

a Canadian with bright teeth and a voice like crisp toast
could produce Buchmanism, if a house-painter with a Charlie
Chaplin moustache and a rag-doll uniform could restore the
confidence of Germany, if a Staffordshire baronet of ancient
lineage could persuade young suburban Englishmen to behave
like a boy-scout's dream of being grown up, if many stranger
miracles of personality than that could be wrought, why
should not this prince of elfland lead Europe to peace ?

Back in 1894 Lord Rosebery, speaking at the Guildhall
Banquet, had declared that the one secret passion in every
breast was for industrial and international peace. If it was
a passion then, what word has force enough to describe the
intensity of the longing now ? Nobody could have explained
Great Britain to the rest of Europe so well as the Prince of
Wales in those years when the last stand was being made
against rearmament ; but no advantage was taken of that
unique personality. He went out again to the Argentine in
1931 to make the British Empire Exhibition as much of a
success as it could be in the trade depression. He visited
other South American countries. At home he worked as
hard as ever to help business. He took a personal interest
in the Duchy of Cornwall's estates in Kensington and in the
Duchy itself. He was a faithful supporter of 'Tubby'
Clayton and Toc H. And continuously he was preoccupied
with the future of the poor.

According to Mr Bolitho " he became increasingly stubborn and conceited over his popularity. Every incident of
fifteen years of his life had contributed to the weakness of
self-centredness, and his fantastic vanity over his own capacity
was a matter for disappointment."

That kind of statement can only be rebutted by stories of
official incompetence, neglect, jealousy, laziness and dis-
loyalty ; but these cannot be told, and so ' things standing
thus unknown ' writers are free to wound the Prince's
name with impunity provided they avoid the statement
of facts which can be categorically denied.

The legend of Fort Belvedere during those last years of
the reign of King George V is like some legend in Suetonius
of a dead Cæsar's retreat. Fort Belvedere itself had been
built by George II as a protection against Prince Charles
Edward. Strange irony that its silent rusted guns should in
the end menace the reputation of the only Prince of that
House who as a figure of romance threatened the supremacy

of Charles Edward. In 1929 the Prince of Wales adapted this disused stronghold in Windsor Great Park to his own taste for modernity. It was a similar impulse which made his grandfather express his conception of modern life in the purchase and development of Sandringham, or if it comes to that, which made Queen Victoria express her conception of modern life in the purchase and development of Balmoral. One of the most ridiculous topics for ill-considered censure of King Edward VIII was his preference for the place that expressed something of his own personality over places that expressed the personalities of other people. The burden of royalty is sufficiently heavy without adding to it the necessity of carrying the architectural burdens of one's predecessors.

The trouble over Fort Belvedere was that the Prince of Wales seemed to prefer gardening and golf and jigsaw puzzles and dancing to the gramophone and even darts to shooting driven grouse or pheasants, fishing salmon or stalking deer. A more serious trouble was that he seemed to prefer the company which shared his personal amusements to the conventional company of the English and Scottish country-house which enjoyed the pleasures of sport they offered. This company was cosmopolitan—" that raffish group that now lords it over London society, that mongrel pack of (mainly) immigrant aliens, naturalised or otherwise, the Invaders, the most heartless and dissolute of the pleasure-loving ultra-rich, the hardest and most hated people in England." Thus a critic in his war-paint of blue British woad described the society preferred by the Prince of Wales, and when such words are apparently endorsed by the Archbishop of Canterbury over the microphone, it is small wonder that the bulk of respectable opinion in this country should get an exaggerated notion of the private life of the Prince of Wales. We must not be scornful of such misdirected opinion. We must remember that such opinion was living in a continuous state of hungry credulity, which the gossip-writer and the strip-advertiser had fed to their own profit long before the Archbishop of Canterbury flung that great gobbet of unleavened scandal into its gaping maw. It will be more useful to examine that broadcast pastoral when we have found our way out of the labyrinth of episcopal inconsistencies in the journey we must make in due course in an attempt to discover what exactly are the doctrine and practice of the Anglican Church in regard to marriage. We shall then be in a better position to estimate how much justification there was for what the man in the street fancied was an abuse of fair play. The general opinion now is that the Archbishop flung his crozier at a man who was down and that his crozier proved a boomerang. Others fancy that the inextinguishable candle which Master Ridley and Master Latimer lighted at Oxford has been abruptly snuffed out by an Archbishop of Canterbury and that the snuffed wick is making a most unpleasant smell. It may be possible to modify such an anti-clerical opinion. That remains to be seen.

What can be stated now is that most of the disapproval of the Prince's circle of friends was founded on a misapprehension of the significance of externals. The comments of the Press on the baccarat scandal at Tranby Croft quoted in an earlier chapter strike us as comic nearly fifty years later. That this should be the effect argues either a progressive deterioration of morals over the years that have passed or the gradual achievement of a truer sense of proportion. And it is more likely to be the latter. Morals have been going to pieces for so long in the view of the older generation that there can be no room for further deterioration. The Christian who takes pride in the reasonableness of his creed can remind himself that it is God's prerogative to judge the sinner, man's to judge only the sin. Hence it is certainly premature and probably unwise to suspect our sisters of fornication because they varnish their nails, and not less premature and certainly still more unwise to suspect a prince of debauchery because, following the custom of the time, he likes jazz, drinks cocktails, and enjoys lying in the sun on the Lido or the Riviera. It is pathetic that in what purports to be a stimulating book a writer should be driven to administer such bromides as these. He begs forgiveness of the minority, and entreats the majority to consider the possibility that people who to simpler ways appear bad are usually no worse than the outwardly respectable, and very often a good deal better. It is also painful to remind the majority that another pledge to the Christian of the reasonableness of his creed is the curious lack of respect his Saviour showed toward the respectable. Indeed, He was rebuked for the company He kept by distinguished . . . well, perhaps ecclesiastics is not quite the word. The Bishop of Bradford wished that King Edward VIII " gave more positive signs of his awareness " of the need of God's grace. Courage, sincerity, compassion : are these exclusively pagan virtues ? Dr Blunt is a theologian. He knows the answer. Dr Blunt will not take it amiss if we apply to him his own words " and ask you to commend him to God's grace, which he will so abundantly need, as we all need it [for the Bishop is a man like ourselves] if he is to do his duty faithfully."

The reason for this request is that in England in December 1936 the Bishop denied that his address to the Bradford Diocesan Conference had been inspired by rumours about the King's desire to marry Mrs Simpson, but declared it had been written six weeks before and had no reference when delivered except to the King's lack of churchmanship ; but from Quebec in August 1937 the Bishop was reported by Reuter to have admitted that he had deliberately said what he did to his Diocesan Conference. " I took the risk because of the danger that silence [about the Mrs Simpson affair] was doing to the Crown and the Empire." Communists, according to him, were handing round cuttings from American papers to Bradford mill-hands and repeating current gossip.

When we have examined some episcopal speeches in the House of Lords about divorce we shall hesitate to believe bishops incapable of the most extreme casuistry ; but no casuistry has yet been refined which will exonerate the Bishop of Bradford, if he was correctly reported, from confusion of mind on one side of the Atlantic or the other. And if the Bishop was incorrectly reported and if there was no need to commend him to God's grace we can place to the poor little account of our own good deeds one work of supererogation.

And now back to that graceless Prince of Wales at Fort Belvedere whose respect for the truth was such an embarrassment to everybody. If the present writer were as credulous as Suetonius he could not hope to titillate his readers with stories comparable to the stories Suetonius retailed of Tiberius at Capri, stories which scholars have demonstrated to be completely devoid of truth after they had enjoyed an unimpeached credibility for centuries. He must content himself with recording that every one of those rebuked friends whom he has had the privilege of meeting personally struck him as delightful people. And one fact he remarked, which was that all of them spoke with the profoundest respect of the man who had honoured them with his friendship. They recognised his liability suddenly to turn ' royal ', but all had the grace—no, we must not say grace—all had the generosity to admit that these cold reminders of his rank were usually caused by their own tactlessness. Even that excessively human Prince of Wales was not always proof against the selective breeding of a thousand years. In short this reputedly " raffish group lording it over London society " in the words of the critic quoted above impressed a man of middle-age who has travelled widely, met many kinds of men and women, contemplated humanity from solitude, enjoyed a diversity of adventures, and written some fifty books as a civilised and intelligent society whose sophistication was on a level with that of the Horace who has consoled Lord Baldwin for the isolation of a Prime Minister's life. And in that category of pleasure-seekers they must be left with their rumbas and tangos and undignified Latin volatility, with their clock-golf and swimming-pools and hard tennis-courts and all the other hideous expressions of contemporary frivolity, with their cocktail-cabinets and jazz records and enjoyment of good food and all the other evidence of twentieth-century debauchery. Surely there is a danger not merely of making mountains out of molehills thrown up by busy burrowers in the darkness of scandal, but even of making mountains out of golf-tees.

The present writer's first meeting with that Prince, who had just come down to earth from the azure of a June sky, evoked a memory which prompted his pen a few pages back to write 'a prince of elfland', the pen expressing the memory without conscious manipulation. For the moment he was tempted to strike out the words, fearing they would convey a sentimentality that was not intended, and then recognising that his pen knew better than he, he left them. A prince of elfland? Sojourning here until he found that for which he was searching? Not yet found, and as the years passed, receding ever farther from all hope of finding it? In his lithe gait as he entered the room expectation, in his eyes a strange fixity of purpose, and a moment later across them a cloud, from which they seemed to emerge focused now upon the obvious and the ordinary as they had been focused for how many intolerable repetitions. It may have been no more than a trick played by shyness, and yet . . . and yet why should that first look lasting no longer than two or three steps across a room haunt and preoccupy the memory with so sharp a sense of remoteness from the humdrum of this mortal life? And who that once upon a time had marked such a look would not rejoice when it found that which it was seeking ?

But if the intrusion of fantasy like this be rejected as unwarrantable there is still left the magical influence of that personality upon our time, and we who beneath its spell believe that his worldly defeat was a spiritual triumph shall count ourselves happy in eternity to have lived in this witching hour of history. We on earth now cannot write with the knowledge of the future, nor even if we possessed that knowledge could we use it ; but at least we have lived in the midst of these events ; and with all its freedom of eloquence, all its richness of knowledge, all its power of judgment the future will be envying us, as we have envied the dead centuries the lovers and the heroes that they lapped. And in this chromium-plated age we have jousted at Aspramont and Montalban, have seen the Argive ships beached along the Trojan shore, have heard King Mark's hunting-horn, have known what Dante knew of love and dreamed what Shakespeare dreamed of princely chronicles : it is no light thing.

In Belgium after the war the Prince of Wales once visited a hospital wherein lay twenty-eight men torn to pieces in battle. Twenty-seven he greeted in turn. And then they told him that was all. But he, remembering that there were twenty-eight, asked to see the twenty-eighth. They explained that this case was too ghastly a wreck of humanity. He was no more than a breathing lump of ruined flesh. None knew even his nationality. The Prince demanded to see him, and against what was left of that face he put his cheek.

Says Sir Almeric Fitzroy in his *Memoirs* : " Surely an act of compassion entitled to live in history with Sir Philip Sydney and the cup of water on the field of Zutphen. He who can so bear himself in the dread presence of extreme misery must have a genius for pity."

We remember the story of the Untouchables at Delhi, story after story of his direct contact with the poor at home whom he visited, of so many many instances of spontaneous gestures of that love on which the whole of Christianity rests and without which Christianity would crash by denying its God. Yet he failed to give positive signs of his awareness of the need of God's grace. So they said once upon a time of the Samaritans, but it was a Levite who passed by on the other side. But so many of these gestures of compassion were made under the emotion of the moment. Probably the same charge could be levelled against the compassion of God's little poor man of Assisi.   But he did not realise that in dealing with poverty one must move slowly and cautiously. There is much to be learnt from the Sermon on the Mount, but nowhere that safety first is the true inspiration of charity.

So we think of the Prince of Wales through those years after the war, for ever anxious to achieve something to make the poor comfortable and the wretched happy, for ever demanding a display of practical gratitude to the men who had given to their country's service all they had to give, for ever working at the task to which he had been called not by choice but by inheritance, and for ever finding his plans thwarted and frustrated by tired men with sluggish arteries. And because he declined to spend his leisure and take his pleasure with the same conventional minds he was criticised for his lack of dignity, sneered at for his exaggerated notions of his own ability and popularity, and slandered for enjoying the amusements of the age into which he was born.   He did not delight in taking the lives of animals.   To some this seemed a deplorable insensitiveness to the natural behaviour of aristocracy ; to others it seemed a welcome sign that killing animals for sport was coming to be less an infallible sign of aristocracy than a relic of the time when the pastimes of leisure were more narrowly circumscribed.   That is one of the inevitable evolutions of manners which the next fifty years will effect, and the Prince of Wales was drawing near to the sentiment of the majority in this regard.   Balmoral bored him, which was taken as an affront to Scotland ; but it is useful to observe that Balmoral and Balmorality are an expression of a nineteenth-century Scotland by which many Scots are as profoundly bored as he was.   No man would have responded more warmly to the West than he if fortune had taken him the road another Prince once trod.   Anyway, he was the first of his name that could wear a kilt as if it were not a costumier's compliment of the season.   Allusion has been made to his suddenly turning ' royal ', and this was often held against him when he was Prince of Wales.   He was accused of being too familiar one moment and then turning suddenly on people he fancied were presuming upon his familiarity. A little imagination would help in judging those apparent inconsistencies of behaviour.

To take an example known to the writer.   On several occasions the Prince went up to Oxford for a day or two in

after years. Once on entering the Junior Common Room at
Magdalen he bade everybody be seated, telling them he was a
Magdalen man and did not wish to be treated ceremoniously
but as a member of the College.   The next time he went into
the J.C.R. nobody stirred, and he asked sharply if that was the
way to treat the heir to the Throne.   It sounds inconsistent.
But surely the instinct of those undergraduates should have led
them to pay him the courtesy of rising and allow him to put
them at their ease a second time.   If Gunner had still been
in his little room he would have offered those young men a
word of good counsel.   The Prince might have desired
wildly to be taken for granted, but his position was eternally
forbidding it.   The struggle in his mind between these two
compulsions was persistent, and unless the force of them be
grasped now it will be impossible to grasp the final struggle
of December 1936.   Steeplechasing, squash-racquets, violent
exercise, dancing, even flying all represent the efforts of a
mind wrestling with the irreconcilable dualism of character and
status.   One may speculate that if he could have kindled official
enthusiasm for his own hopes and plans for the under-dog that
mental struggle might have been adjusted.   Instead, those
hopes and plans were thwarted in every direction, and it became
increasingly obvious to him that in succeeding to the most
high and mighty throne on earth he would be placed upon a
resplendent pedestal as a mechanical toy of which his Ministers
kept the key, and that the measure of his success as a Sovereign
would be the regularity with which his royal mechanism
answered to their winding.

There is a hint of exasperation with official complacency in
a speech the Prince of Wales made on May 12th 1931 to the
Manchester Chamber of Commerce soon after his return from
the second South American tour.   On the previous day,
when in the House of Commons the vote for the Department
of Overseas Trade had been discussed it had been pointed out
that the reports of Trade Missions which had visited South
America, Egypt, and the Far East all called attention to the
same lesson—" that the prices of British goods were too high
and that British merchants did not sufficiently consult the
requirements of those whom they desired for their customers."
(*A. R.*)   What was not discussed in the House was the handi-
cap imposed on British exports by the return to the gold
standard, or what amounted to a heavy duty on them levied in
the interest of the banks.

It might be rash to assume that the Prince of Wales was aware how tightly the prosperity of the whole country was being bound up with the prosperity of banking. What he did realise after his last visit to South America was the gloomy prospect that faced British trade unless it woke up. He pointed out in the course of a speech which lasted nearly an hour that British manufacturers were adhering too closely to tradition and failing to adjust themselves to the changes of the times. " He advised them, in order to compete with foreign prices, to sacrifice some of the high finish and solidity they have been accustomed to give, without, of course, lowering their standard of mechanical efficiency and usefulness. He urged the heads of businesses to pay more frequent visits abroad, and criticised the British as being sadly behind the Americans in the matter of advertising." (*A. R.*)

That speech a few sentences of which have been excavated from the *Annual Register* was not the speech of a conventional heir apparent, and the prospect of being ruled by such a man was alarming to many. The influence of the Crown was still potent, and instead of being used as a brake on modernity it was apparently going to be used as a spur. It is not desired to argue here whether the Prince of Wales was giving good or bad advice. The point to be made is that he was a naturally revolutionary spirit with positive opinions of his own he was willing to express and anxious to practise. Like all revolutionary spirits, he had to suffer the imputation of extravagant behaviour from those incapable of understanding the standards which the revolutionary spirit takes for granted. Those who argued that it was his business as heir to the throne to acquire the sober and solid qualities of his father forgot that they had taken advantage of other qualities when it suited them and that they were inviting the Prince of Wales to achieve a metamorphosis of himself into another being. If at this date elder statesmen and prelates were despairing of the prospect of King Edward VIII as successor to King George V it was their duty to take the risk of shocking the country now by publishing their apprehensions ; but they were too jealous of their own position to accept that risk. It is necessary to go further. *If* King George V was so completely convinced of his eldest son's unsuitability for kingship as we are now invited to suppose, it was his duty to take time by the forelock and secure his renunciation of the Throne in favour of his present Majesty. May it not be juster to the memory of

King George V (pending the verdict of history in possession
of documents to which we have no access and from which we
could not quote in any case) to assume that he recognised the
magic his eldest son exerted over the less contented side of
his realm and equally his dread lest any attempted change in
the succession might react against the stability of the Throne ?

When in August 1931 the Bank of England succumbed to
the nervous alarm of finding itself in the position of one of its
own wretched clients called upon to pay off an overdraft, an
overdraft, moreover, which had been incurred by injudicious
gambling, there was no hesitation in begging the King to help
the situation, which was represented as the approach of national
bankruptcy.   Probably the Labour Government was making
a muddle of matters : the mutual contradictions and recrimina-
tions in which its members indulged are no testimonial to the
competency of that Government.   Even now it is impossible
to get at the exact truth, but the salient fact seems to be that
the English banks had tried to obtain from the French and
American banks the necessary credit to enable them to tide
over their difficulty of getting in money owed to them by
Germany where they had lent vast sums at what, to put it
coldly and realistically, was the danger of imperilling the
financial stability of their own country.

On August 9th 1931 the Old Lady of Threadneedle Street
flung herself on her back in the traditional style of hysterical
matrons, drummed with her legs on the pavement, and howled
for Mr Ramsay MacDonald to come down from Lossiemouth
and restore her.   Mr MacDonald drenched the old lady with
sal volatile from the Economy Committee, but to no purpose.
When the Cabinet met, the opinion was expressed that the
hysterics were being prolonged with the intention behind
most female hysterics of having her own way.   It was even
suggested, though of course not in so many words, that the
Old Lady of Threadneedle Street had been carrying on
with Mr Baldwin and Sir Herbert Samuel as well as Mr
MacDonald, and that as a result she bore in her womb
the embryo of a three-headed bulldog whose name—National
Government—had already been chosen.   And the Cabinet
resented Mr MacDonald's attempt to saddle them with
the responsibility of procuring an abortion by doing what
the Old Lady wanted.   In the end the King travelled up
to London from Balmoral by the night train on Saturday
August 22nd and according to popular gossip let loose so

much admiral's language at Mr MacDonald that he frightened him into accepting the paternity of the National Government, of which the Old Lady of Threadneedle Street was safely delivered on August 25th. The alacrity with which Mr Baldwin entered one of those destructive Coalition Governments he had so much deprecated in 1922 is a remarkable instance of his self-sacrificing patriotism, and the modesty with which he consented to serve under Mr MacDonald is an equally remarkable instance of his political skill. What the National Government wanted now was a nurse : when the time came for it to be handed over to a governess he would not refuse the situation for all the blossom in Worcestershire. Besides, he had been having a difficult time with Lord Rothermere and Lord Beaverbrook whom in June of the previous year he had accused of trying "to dictate, to domineer and blackmail "; to which in the following March he had added that the editor of the *Daily Mail* was a liar and a cad.

But even as Lord President of the Council in the new Cabinet he was sacrificing a great deal. A month after the General Election to save the pound he was telling an audience at Aberdeen that he was "a countryman bred and born, exiled in London for many years but counting the days when I can lay down my burden [*that phrase should be noted*] and go back to the country."

A queer election, that election to save the pound, when bedridden old folk were wheeled to the polls and when Sir Herbert Samuel, a member of the Cabinet, was opposed by a Protectionist at Darwen. 'I did not know the Tories intended to shoot their prisoners,' he observed.

Soon after the General Election the pound went off the gold standard without uttering a chink, to the great advantage of everybody including the banks ; but no doubt by that time the banks had made their arrangements. There was a general display of economy. The King forwent £50,000 from his Civil List, and the Prince of Wales gave up £10,000 from the revenue of the Duchy of Cornwall.

It was in the fateful year 1931 that on June 10th, White Rose Day, the twentieth anniversary of his investiture as a Knight of the Garter, the Prince of Wales first met, at a party given by Mrs Benjamin Thaw, Mr and Mrs Ernest Simpson. In nine more days Mrs Simpson would be thirty-five, in thirteen days the Prince would be thirty-seven. She had been presented at Court earlier in the evening. Her husband was a native of

New York, of British parentage. From Harvard he had enlisted in the Coldstream Guards early in 1918 and had become an ensign six months later. When the war was over he returned to Harvard, took his degree, and had for some years been a business man in London. He and Mrs Simpson had been married in 1928. She was the posthumous child of Teakle Wallis Warfield, a Marylander, after whom she was called Wallis. Her mother had been a Virginian, a Miss Alice Montague. On both sides she came of old landowning Colonial stock, and before that of ancient English stock. In November 1916 at the age of twenty she had married at Pensacola in Florida Lieutenant E. Winfield Spencer, of the Aviation Corps of the United States Navy. Like so many war marriages it proved a mistake, and on December 10th 1927 at Warrenton in Virginia Mrs Spencer was granted a divorce on the grounds of her husband's desertion. There had been an attempt to mend the marriage when Mrs Spencer had gone to to join her husband in Shanghai where he was stationed.

It is significant that when the friendship between the Prince of Wales and Mrs Simpson was first gossiped about in the comparatively small circle of those people in London who know or believe they know what is going on, such gossip was unanimous in judging that the friendship was one entirely for the good of the Prince. He was not so restless. She had encouraged him to take a keen practical interest in his garden at Fort Belvedere. To put it in a word that friendship had made him a happy man. The general note in fact was cordial approval, and it was *not* regarded as a love-affair.

So without anticipating the course of this association, the divulgement of which would be timed with such skill and employed with such deadly effect against these two friends, justice and reason alike demand that we should assent to the proposition laid down in the motto of the Most Noble Order of the Garter : *Honi soit qui mal y pense.* Shamed be he who thinks evil of it. Here was a woman who was at once debonair housewife and domestic worldling, a woman of wit and humour and charm, of high spirits and infinite vitality, a woman by all disinterested testimony frank, loyal, and sincere, a woman clear-cut as a gem, and with only as much hardness as any woman worthy of being greatly loved must possess if she is to sustain the integrity of love against hard circumstance. Here was a prince who could have chosen for one expression of love from so many women, *tot milia formosarum,* but who by any pitiable little scrap of honest evidence in that pigs'-swill of scandal never once contemplated an easy and dishonourable way out of a situation that has turned so many millions of men to meanness, cruelty, and cowardice, since Adam set his first despicable example of feeble excuse. We are told now that King George's last days were darkened by anxiety over his son's friendship with Mrs Simpson. Yet Prince Christopher of Greece has recently revealed that she was a guest at the reception at Buckingham Palace on the evening before the wedding of the Duke of Kent and Princess Marina. She was presented to him there by the Prince of Wales himself. And he adds :

" The Prince of Wales scarcely left her side all that evening, despite the fact that some of the most beautiful women in Europe were doing their best to attract his attention. He appeared never even to notice them. He was in love as it is given to men and women to love only once in a lifetime."

Would it not be honest to admit that, if the unwavering devotion of the Prince of Wales to Mrs Simpson was beginning to cause anxiety, such anxiety was allayed by the comforting reflection that she was a married woman ; and that if that divorce of 1937 had been granted in 1933 the Royal Marriages Act could have been and no doubt would have been used to prevent the Prince of Wales from marrying her ? Let that be remembered, and let it be remembered at the same time that the whole behaviour of that Prince when he became King gives the lie to every base suggestion of an easy and accommodating standard of morality.

Thanks to the remarks of the Archbishop of Canterbury about the King's friends there is a widespread belief that the woman he gave up a throne to marry was one of a raffish set. That is false. On the contrary her influence strengthened all the approved virtues of domesticity. The courage of the man himself under the fearful ordeal of that black December should be enough to convince others of the worth of what he was fighting for. The present writer is acquainted with the capacity of episcopal credulity in regard to the Duchess of Windsor, and his knowledge of such credulity has left him perplexed by the difficulty certain Anglican divines experience in believing the fundamental truths of the Christian faith. The handicap under which any writer must suffer in challenging the fantastic lies in circulation about the Duke and Duchess is obvious. And so the present writer must be content to asseverate that he has been able to apply completely destructive criticism and demonstrate the utter absurdity of every single story for the truth of which the sponsors of it have ventured to lay before him the evidence. That being so, he cannot be expected to pay more respectful heed to rumours that lack even as much substantiation as the preposterous material he has already pulled to pieces. The pity is that so many worthy prelates and lesser dignitaries should have allowed their intelligible anxiety to demonstrate the vitality of Anglicanism to impugn their common sense. The broadcast of the Archbishop of Canterbury dropped like manna at the feet of infidels, but like a brick on the heads of his fellow-Christians.

Fort Belvedere is deserted now, and it is surely an excess of caution which allows it to fall into decay as well. We know that the prospect of the Duke's return to it horrifies many people whose consciences are haunted by words said and things done in the recent past. Nevertheless, it is painful for many other people to read * of the red flags rusting in the holes of the miniature golf-course, of the dead leaves on the surface of the swimming-pool, of weeds between the flagstones of the terraces, of a handful of darts lying on the window-sill of one room, and of the names of the flowers and shrubs obliterated by the weather from the wooden pegs, some of which may have been written by those two who gardened there.

CHAPTER XII

OLD BOTTLES

ONE of the first jobs of the newly elected National Government of 1931 was to draft the Statute of Westminster which was an attempt to " put into legal form the resolutions adopted by the Imperial Conferences of 1926 and 1930 for determining the relations between the constituent parts of the British Commonwealth of Nations." (*A. R.*)

The fateful part of this Statute, which at the time " the Government . . . considered entirely superfluous " (*A. R.*), was the cloudy preamble setting out that :

* *Sunday Dispatch*, January 16th 1938.

. . . Inasmuch as the Crown is the symbol of the free association of the members of the British Commonwealth of Nations, and as they are united by a common allegiance to the Crown, it would be in accord with the established Constitutional position of all the members of the Commonwealth in relation to one another that any alteration in the law touching the Succession to the Throne or the Royal Style and Titles shall hereafter require the assent as well of the Parliaments of all the Dominions as of the Parliament of the United Kingdom.

We shall not pause now to discuss whether or not a legally unjustifiable use was made of this Statute exactly five years after it was passed. For the moment, it will be enough to note that among the few who criticised the Statute was Mr Winston Churchill, not it may be added on account of any possibly injurious use to which it might lend itself against the status of the monarch, but because it might be used by the Irish Free State to dishonour the treaty of 1922 and because it would complicate the future of India.

Yet now as we read his protest made on that November day " against this final breach with the pre-war conceptions of Empire . . . needlessly obliterating old famous landmarks and signposts which, although archaic, had historical importance and value," we cannot but feel he stands there in the House in the dark and disquieting shadow of a November still five years away.

At the opening of 1932 the country was still in a state of highly oxygenated economy, of which the Government took advantage to ask income-tax payers to be prompt. In the moving words of the *Annual Register*:

> From the first day of the year there was a veritable rush to the income-tax offices, which were literally besieged by persons anxious to settle their account and so help the nation in its emergency. Many persons in order to raise the money required sold securities or postponed other payments almost equally urgent. The results to the Treasury were highly satisfactory.

It is an ungrateful task to remind those who in January 1932 sold their securities and involved themselves in debt that there was no emergency which could be held to warrant such a sacrifice either of themselves or their neighbours. That appeal to pay promptly was indeed as impudent a piece of propaganda on behalf of its own virtue as ever a Government has made, savouring rather of the methods of the advertiser of a patent medicine than of a responsible executive; but that does not detract from the merit of the amiable, if credulous, response.   It served, however, to impress once again on the minds of many members of that Government the ease with which the public could be herded into a sheepfold of opinion. That lesson would not be forgotten when the time came to flatter the morality and the magnanimity of the people at the expense of their King.

On January 19th 1932 the Prince of Wales, at a moment when there was some friction between Great Britain and the Argentine over economic divergences, addressed the Argentine Chamber of Commerce in London and stressed the need of strengthening the cultural ties between the two countries.   He mentioned that the University of Buenos Aires had formed a committee for Anglo-Argentine cultural relations and appealed for funds to found two scholarships at Oxford for students from Buenos Aires.   Later in the year these two scholarships were instituted as the result of this appeal, on the lines of the Rhodes scholarships and bearing the name of the Prince of Wales.

The National Government plodded along upon its weary way.   In June 1933 a world Economic Conference representing sixty-six States was held in London.   It was opened by King George, who in the course of his speech remarked that this was the first time any Sovereign had presided at the opening of a conference of all the nations of the world. It was a justifiable expression of pride, but when we remember those great œcumenical councils of the putative Dark Ages and how much more they contributed to the advancement of human thought and the guidance of human action than this World Economic Conference of 1933 the occasion appears more unusual than significant.   It was not a good omen for the success of the gathering that it should meet in the Geological Museum, South Kensington, and in due course it broke up without effecting anything.   The petrified monsters of that ancient economic world were playing idly with their own coprolites.   No specimen of blue argillaceous limestone on view in the museum could offer so rich an exhibition of fossils as that world conference, to which Panama alone of reputedly civilised States invited sent no delegate.

The Argentine Mission which reached this country in the same year, to discuss the future of Anglo-Argentine trade relations, was more successful and ended in a Trade Agreement. Before the Mission left the Vice-President of the Republic Dr Julio Roca had paid a tribute to the personal influence of the

Prince of Wales in creating the atmosphere of amity from which practical results might be expected. And when the Mission arrived in London it was the Prince who greeted them.

In January 1934 the Prince of Wales broadcast a review of the progress made by the voluntary movement for relieving unemployment, which two years earlier he had inaugurated in a speech at the Albert Hall. He pointed out that the occupational centres were creating a feeling of good fellowship, but he wanted these centres developed into proper clubs " with facilities for educational, recreational, and social activities." He did not want them confined to the unemployed, thereby trying to counteract the growth of the unhappy notion that unemployment had to be considered a permanent feature of the time. He recognised the danger of creating a Fifth Estate by surrendering to such a belief. Once again, at the risk of fatiguing by reiteration, the sanity of his attitude in regard to unemployment must be emphasised.

On May 6th, a day of azure weather which brought back a memory of the weather that used to grace the occasions of Queen Victoria, the Silver Jubilee of King George's reign was celebrated with a spontaneity and warmth of affection beyond the power of the most adulatory pen to exaggerate. The old King stood in the imagination of his people like an oak-tree which had survived as stormy a quarter of a century as history had known. He might have seemed dull in 1910 when young people were too near the protracted reign of his grandmother to desire any reminder of it, but these young people were now fifty years old themselves and had been granted a middle-age denied to how many thousands of their contemporaries. They beheld in King George a reminder of their own youth before the war. Yes, he was the oak-tree on top of what had been a well-loved hill in youth, and though the slopes of the hill were now built over the tree still stood in a quiet space of green at the top. He had not done a great deal in any direction of which the ordinary man's knowledge could be cognisant, but with dignity and devotion he had done everything expected by the ordinary man of a modern king. And there was something to add to that. His Christmas broadcasts had brought him into every home of his realm. That he would say the very words which would touch the hearts of his people was to be expected, but what made the real effect was the way he said them. His voice in every tone and modulation was exactly what his people thought a King's voice ought to be,

and when to that was added a timbre of a homely roughness
the success was complete.   There was nothing ' la-di-da '
about the King's voice, and the radio public was inclined to
suspect every voice in advance of being ' la-di-da '.   Mr
Baldwin's voice had not been ' la-di-da ', but there was always
a cynical minority which suspected the sincerity of Mr
Baldwin's masterly assumption of the ordinary man who had
woken up one morning to find himself Prime Minister   There
was always an odious minority which believed that Mr Baldwin
had aimed to be Prime Minister, enjoyed being Prime Minister,
and longed to go on being Prime Minister.   That dismal and
ill-minded minority classed Mr Baldwin's own conception of
himself as Prime Minister with such mythical expressions of
sentiment as Santa Claus.   There was nothing of Santa Claus
about King George on those Christmas afternoons when he
sat by himself and spoke to the Empire.   And there was no
minority to question his utter sincerity.

The first real warmth of affection had been kindled earlier
by his illness in December 1928.   That had brought home to
his people how much too easily they had taken him for granted
and what a loss his death would be.   And when after his
illness he had refused to consider going abroad for his con-
valescence, but had given to Bognor the right to add Regis to
its name, that had endeared him all the more.   Even Queen
Victoria had supposed that the Riviera was advisable in winter.

So what a greeting they gave him on that blue May day and
all those other days when he drove with Queen Mary through
various districts of London !   And one had not to be more than
middle-aged to remember the wedding of the Duke of York
to the beautiful Princess May on that sunny July day in 1893
and the drive from the Chapel Royal to Liverpool Street
Station for the honeymoon at Sandringham.

But all our admiration of King George and Queen Mary
should not tempt us into contrasting the love and the esteem
they enjoyed with the love and the esteem given to the Prince
of Wales.   His task had been infinitely more difficult; it
would have been more difficult in any case, but his determination at twenty expressed to Queen Alexandra never in any
circumstances to marry a woman unless he loved her gave
the poignant stamp of truth to that last broadcast utterance of
his about the inestimable blessing he had been denied.   It
would be impertinent to attempt the least elaboration of the part
Queen Mary played in King George's renown;   but perhaps

H

a personal reminiscence may be intruded which may give a
picture to the reader.   It was in Guernsey—a blazing breath-
less summer day in 1921.   The ceremony of the seigneurs'
homage to the Duke of Normandy had just been performed in
St George's Hall.   The King in undress half-white naval
uniform was standing on the platform among pots of hydran-
geas and in adjusting his glasses he dropped the paper from
which he was about to read his reply.   He was on the point of
bending down to pick the paper up when with the most
superbly regal gesture that can be fancied the Queen swept
her own copy of the speech in front of him, and stood in an
equally superb regal attitude motionless as a statue while the
King read from the paper held before him.   That action and
attitude of hers may stand as symbolic of the help and support
she gave him throughout their reign.

Mr Bolitho suggests that " the impression made by King
George in the closing year of his life . . . brought an eclipse
to the popularity of the Prince of Wales."   This is surely a
most contentious statement, and if it were true would cast
an unpleasant reflection on the loyalty and imagination of
the English.   According to Mr Bolitho, " the Prince's own
changed character was in part to blame for the rift which
grew between him and his father's people."   Where is the
evidence for the growth of such a rift until the lute was
picked up by the Archbishop of Canterbury and brought
down with a crash on Britannia's head ?   Mr Bolitho goes on
to argue that " the post-war period was tired of the standards
it had invented for itself," and leaves us to deduce from his
observation that the post-war period was tired of the Prince
of Wales.   He presumably was to be treated as any other
ex-Service man who had outlived his utility.   A respect for
some of those English qualities which were discerned in King
George forbids the present writer to believe the nation capable
of such flaccid ingratitude.   And what was this change in
the Prince's character ?   It certainly was not obvious to the
majority.   Perhaps as he was growing older he was growing
more impatient of criticism from people older than himself
who persisted in regarding him as still in his twenties.   Perhaps it *was* difficult to realise, as Mr Baldwin would next
year invite the House to remember, that he was not a boy,
although he looked so young.   Nevertheless, it is permissible
to speculate that the country at large fully appreciated the
fact that in 1935 the Prince was forty-one, and it is certain

that the country expected from his accession to the Throne a
vitality of progressive effort of which with all his great qualities
King George was by reason of his age and health no longer
capable.   It was disappointment, not fulfilled expectation,
which roused that parrots' scream and baboons' chatter:
' He let us down '.

The stimulation of the country by the resounding success
of the Silver Jubilee indicated to the doctors of the electorate
that it was advisable to take advantage of the mood by holding
an election as soon as it was decently possible.   In the
glowing words of the *Annual Register*:

> The outstanding feature of the campaign was undoubtedly the
> personal popularity of Mr Baldwin, which was enhanced by every
> speech he made.   It was not that he said anything very new or
> striking, but he managed to convey the impression that he was a man
> to be trusted in the present emergency [*sic !*], that the causes which
> the average Englishman had most at heart—peace, security, orderly
> progress, democracy—were safer in his hands than they would be
> in any other.   Of all the figures on the political stage he alone was
> habitually thought of by the general public as a national and not
> merely a party leader; and not without reason, for in his political
> character he exhibited a unique combination of Conservative, Liberal,
> and Socialist traits, and it was he who gave the tone to the whole of
> the Government.

So this pantechnicon of political opinion rumbled back
into power with 385 Conservatives, 32 National Liberals,
and 8 National Labour members.   The second and third
heads of this parliamentary Cerberus were hardly more than
cysts.

A notable contribution which the new Government made
to progress and prosperity was revealed by Mr Baldwin
soon after the new House of Commons assembled, when in
answer to Opposition criticism he boasted that " representations made by himself and others " had induced " a firm of
tinplate manufacturers which in the summer had announced
its intention of removing from South Wales to Lincolnshire "
to stay in South Wales.

This brilliant feat of persuasiveness was not repeated when
there was a question of inducing Italy to remove from
Abyssinia.

On December 6th 1935 Sir Samuel Hoare on his way to
skate in Switzerland for his health stopped in Paris over
the week-end and before leaving on Monday December 9th

for his holiday he had concluded an agreement with M. Laval, the French Premier and Foreign Minister, by which a set of proposals were to be laid before Signor Mussolini and the Negus as a basis for peace negotiations. Large slices of Abyssinia were to be handed over to Italy and Italy was to be given economic control over another large slice. Sir Samuel then went on to cut figures of eight on the Swiss ice, in the course of which he fell and hurt his nose. Meanwhile, the Paris Press, on the principle that the sooner perfidious Albion is committed the better, had published versions of the proposed terms on the morning Sir Samuel left Paris. The British Cabinet met and after considerable discussion, in the course of which it was rumoured that Mr Eden had threatened to resign, approved the proposals. The next day in the House, answering Mr Attlee the Leader of the Opposition, the Prime Minister said that as the suggested basis for peace had not been laid before Italy and Abyssinia it would be premature to make a statement on the subject at present. " I have seldom spoken with greater regret," he added portentously, " for my lips are not yet unsealed. Were these troubles over, I would make a case and I guarantee that not a man would go into the Lobby against us." He did not quote the ghost of Hamlet's father:

> But that I am forbid
> To tell the secrets of my prison-house,
> I could a tale unfold whose lightest word
> Would harrow up thy soul.

But no doubt he was successful in making each particular hair of the Members to stand on end, like quills upon the fretful porpentine.

Next day, however, all the anti-Italian papers howled ' shame! ' at such a betrayal of the League of Nations and denounced Sir Samuel Hoare's attempt to pour the oil that was to have been used for ' sanctions ' on the stormy waves of the European situation. Mr Baldwin realised that the sedulous propaganda against Italy had done its work. The country was against the proposals. On December 12th Mr Eden hurried to Geneva to assure the startled representatives of the League that the proposals were " neither definite nor sacrosanct." Some of the effect of this was spoilt by the revelation that the Foreign Office had telegraphed to the British Minister in Addis Ababa urging him to use his utmost influence to induce the Emperor to give " careful and favourable consideration " to the proposals, which included a refusal to let the Abyssinians construct a railway through their corridor to the sea.

Sir Samuel Hoare, in spite of his damaged nose, returned to England on December 16th; but the country was in a fever of indignation, and Mr Baldwin, exhaling the tepid fires of Safety First like a lazy and good-natured dragon prodded into vigilance for the golden apples of Threadneedle Street he was supposed to be guarding, told Sir Samuel he intended to throw over the proposals and inform the House accordingly on December 19th. On this Sir Samuel Hoare resigned.

The debate in the Commons was packed, and there were many distinguished visitors including the Prince of Wales. Sir Samuel Hoare, being now a private member, was allowed to make his statement before the Opposition moved its resolution, which the Government fearing for its majority announced would be regarded as a vote of censure, and was hard put to find an amendment its followers could accept without plunging the country into another election only six weeks after such a brilliant success at the polls. However, an amendment was successfully evolved.

Sir Samuel Hoare made a speech which curiously antici- pated the speech that Mr Neville Chamberlain, when Prime Minister, would make in February 1938, after Mr Eden's unhappy (and one may still pray not too disastrous) tenure of the post of Foreign Secretary came to an end with his resignation. It was a speech informed with common sense, and it pointed out the meaninglessness of the phrase ' collec- tive security ' when applied to a collection which left one nation—Great Britain—to translate the words into action. It was his belief that there was a grave risk of war and he did not think he should have acted wisely in refusing to do everything possible to avoid that risk. When Sir Samuel had finished there were tears in his eyes and he left the House—the little boy that Santa Claus forgot. This embarrassing habit of lachrymosity has become a feature of a public man's exit from one scene of his career before he enters smiling to play another: the films may be responsible, or possibly it has been the strain of Cabinet life with Mr Baldwin. It was noticeable that Mr Eden after a comparatively bracing year with Mr Chamberlain succeeded in relinquishing the post of Foreign Secretary without tears; but perhaps he was sustained by the consciousness of rectitude and the flattery of the Labour Members.

Mr Attlee's speech for the motion was a feeble affair which fell between the stools of party advantage and bellicose sentimentality.

Mr Baldwin's speech in reply was the collapse of a Humpty Dumpty from the fence on which he had been sitting, and it was to take not the King's horses and the King's men to put him together again, but the King himself next December.

This December the Prince of Wales, cupping a hand behind an ear, was leaning perilously over the Gallery to hear Mr Baldwin's views on friendship.

The Prime Minister began by begging the sympathy of the House for himself on account of his personal affection for Sir Samuel. (' *I would ask the House, which I know will not be without sympathy for me in my position to-day . . .*' *Can the Prince of Wales hear those words from a year away in his ear as he leans over ?*) And then he went on to proclaim that he was going to speak with perfect frankness (*with no attempt to dress up or to adorn*).

" I will pass over the question of the Leader of the Opposition, ' Was it fair to send him to Paris to negotiate ? ' Is it fair very often in politics to expect Ministers to discharge their duties, as they are expected to do, when they are very tired and worn out ? It happens to all of us. It happens to every one in the high places of this world, and we neither ask for nor expect quarter. [*Yes, they're noble fellows, up there in the Himalaya of politics. But was Sir Samuel as ill as all that ? He was not too tired to go skating and fall on his nose.*]

" When my right honourable friend went to have those conversations, there was an absence of liaison—on which I am going to say a word—during that Sunday. [*What was the telephone doing at* 10 *Downing Street or Chequers ? Throughout that rambling speech he said not another word about that absence of liaison. So perhaps both telephones were out of order. Perhaps the Foreign Office telephone was out of order.*] We were not aware until it was accomplished, that an agreement had been come to. [*How could anybody be aware something had happened until it had happened ? It's a pluperfect impossibility.*] It was not until breakfast-time on Monday morning that I received a letter from my right honourable friend urging that the Cabinet might endorse what he had done, as he believed it to be a necessary piece of work at the moment. Almost immediately afterwards, and before we had had time to study the documents, the leakage took place. [*That morning before Sir Samuel left for Switzerland. What persuaded him that the leakage was unimportant ?*] I will say nothing about that, but this was our position. We were summoned [*By whom ? Mr Baldwin presumably. He was the foreman-plumber. This anxiety to share the blame with his colleagues makes him vague with his pronouns.*] We were summoned to consider whether we could endorse the action of our colleague, or whether we would repudiate it. . . . Here, although we were all responsible [*collective Cabinet security*] the chief responsibility was mine, as it must be, and I decided at once that I must support the colleague who was not present to give his reasons. . . . In nine times out of ten, our instinct is to stand by a colleague who is absent. [*Yes, they certainly are noble fellows, but this collective security on behalf of a colleague might impose a severe strain on the collective security of the country. Such loyalty explains numerous otherwise inexplicable imbecilities of Governments.*]

"I can quite see, looking back, that I ought at any cost to have fetched back my colleague from Switzerland. I see that, and I acknowledge it frankly. If I thought of it, I dismissed it in a moment because I knew how necessary rest was for him . . . you may say that it was an act of weakness on my part. It certainly was an error of judgment. It certainly was an error with which we were all concerned [*the other boys were there too, teacher*] but for which I am chiefly responsible."

Then after a parenthesis about the fatal modern notion that speed is essential to diplomatic plumbing he at last revealed to the House why he and his colleagues after having approved the agreement threw it down the drain they had just mended.

"I was not expecting that deeper feeling which was manifested by many of my honourable friends and friends in many parts of the country on what I may call the ground of conscience and honour. [' *I did tell His Majesty once that I might be a remnant of the old Victorians, but that my worst enemy could not say of me that I did not know what the reaction of the English people would be to any particular course of action.*'] The moment I am confronted with that, I know that something has happened that has appealed to the deepest feelings of my countrymen, that some note has been struck that brings back from them a response from the depths."

So with his finger once again safely on the pulse of the electorate, which he had temerariously relaxed to feel the pulse of Sir Samuel Hoare, Mr Baldwin decided that the negotiations must be dropped.

" If there arose a storm when I knew I was in the right, I would let it break on me and I would either survive it or break," he cried, and then dropping his voice ' to the extreme peril of the Prince of Wales, who was straining over the Gallery to hear him,' wrote a reporter who was present, Mr Baldwin murmured solemnly :

" But if I felt after examination of myself that there was in that storm something which showed me that, however unconsciously, I had done something that was not wise or right, then I would bow."

And then in case there should be any lingering suspicion in the mind of the House that in bowing he was taking all the blame for a *bêtise* which had disgusted the whole world, Mr Baldwin added quickly that never again, while he was Prime Minister, would he allow a Foreign Secretary to go abroad and conduct negotiations.

We have already quoted some glowing words about Mr Baldwin from p. 91 of the *Annual Register* of 1935. On p. 109 of the same volume we read :

> Sir Samuel Hoare, though he had failed to convince the House, had won its respect and sympathy by his manly and able defence. His reputation at the end of his speech stood perhaps higher than ever before. . . . The Prime Minister, on the other hand, by his abject confession of error, had done nothing to retrieve himself from the discredit which his conduct during the past week had brought upon him. His speech was generally regarded as wholly ineffective, and the opinion was freely expressed that his days as leader of the Conservative party were numbered.

That pantechnicon of political opinion is already in danger of being ditched ; but the lithe figure who on that December night has been leaning over the Gallery of the House of Commons cupping with his hand an attentive ear will provide it on another December night with an opportunity to avoid the ditch and rumble safely into the stable of retirement.

And so we reach 1936. On January 17th it was announced that the King had a cold. At five minutes before midnight of Monday January 20th the old oak-tree fell. On Tuesday

morning King Edward accompanied by the Duke of York
flew from Sandringham to see the Prime Minister.   That
night Mr Baldwin delivered to the nation over the radio his
late master's panegyric given with all Mr Baldwin's mastery
of homely emotion.

One sentence may be extracted.   He has been voicing
the sympathy of the Empire with Queen Mary:

" If she were not suffering to-day, he would be, and she
is bearing what might have been his sorrow for him ; and I
cannot help feeling that with a King, knowing how lonely
the high places of the world are, and knowing that he has
no one but his wife with whom he might have really intimate
converse—I tremble to think what it might have been for
him had he been alone in his awful task with no voice by
him to cheer, to comfort, and to encourage."

Apart from a faint suggestion that he beholds himself on
the same level as the King and the repetition of a phrase
which he had used a month ago to excuse Sir Samuel Hoare
for being very tired and worn out, there can be nothing but
praise for the observation.   But the Prime Minister's sensitiveness to a King's loneliness in his awful task was not
touched by King Edward's question about the possibility of
having a wife who would not have the position of Queen,
and when he was told that this was impossible (we shall
examine later the potentialities) ' he behaved as a great
gentleman ; he said no more about it.'   This tribute to the
King's breeding would impress us more profoundly if we
could discover that after the King had left the country and
Mr Baldwin had been received into the chivalry of Windsor
the new Knight of the Garter had behaved as a great gentleman, not by keeping silence but by speaking out over the
radio and denouncing that campaign to kill a King's wounded
name.   Indeed, as one ponders that silence of Lord Baldwin
one begins to consider it even less estimable than the Archbishop of Canterbury's speech.

Mr Bolitho says of his Grace's welcome to the new King,
' There was little hope and no enthusiasm from the venerable
prelate who had been King George's friend. . . . He did
not bend his conscience to the occasion with fine phrases, and
his reception . . . was cold and dark with presentiment.'
Yet at the Dinner of the Worshipful Company of Stationers
and Newspaper Makers as recently as November 1934 the
venerable prelate had bent his conscience to a most courtier-

like speech in proposing the health of the Master, the Prince of Wales. It was at this dinner that the Prince said :

" Restriction of any kind in regard to a genuine expression of opinion, however extreme, is, I am glad to say, entirely contrary to our belief and to our traditions. We should be thankful that in this country we enjoy freedom of opinion, freedom of discussion in our books as well as in our speech, and that we can point with pride to a free Press."

It is to be feared that this estimate of the contemporary freedom that books or Press enjoy was unduly generous ; but at least the direction of the Prince's own beliefs was apparent. And those beliefs would be severely tested not so long after this dinner.

The alleged hurry over the funeral of King George was given publicity at a luncheon by Sir Gerald Wollaston, Garter King of Arms, when the Duke of Windsor was on his honeymoon. It drew from the Duke the only protest he ever permitted himself against that campaign. 'What a rotten story !' It transpired that King George was buried on January 29th because Queen Mary had wished it.

It is useful to turn to Mr Bolitho for what was seemingly the official view of the new reign.

> When he attended his first Council meeting at St James's Palace, the Ministers and leaders who were there were comfortably [*sic!*] pleased by his dignity and his apparent wish to do what was right. It did not seem possible that he could have his tongue in his cheek as he renewed his promises before them. It was not in his nature to deceive other men, but it was a sad fault in his nature that he was able to deceive himself. . . . Many people within the circle of the Court and Government had thought that abdication was already in the King's mind.

Another rotten story ! And that was the official mood against which he had to contend for almost a year. Yet his words to the Privy Council are as simple and as obviously sincere as words can be :

" When my father stood here twenty-six years ago he declared that one of the objects of his life would be to uphold constitutional government. In this I am determined to follow in my father's footsteps and to work as he did throughout his life for the happiness and welfare of all classes of my subjects.

" I place my reliance upon the loyalty and affection of my people throughout the Empire and upon the wisdom of their

Parliaments to support me in this heavy task, and I pray
that God will guide me to perform it."

Mr Bolitho is so willing to be helpful at the opening of
King Edward's reign that he resumes the old Bolitho manner
of respectful awe at the smallest evidence of Royalty's common
nature with the rest of mankind.

> One afternoon he walked in Oxford, recapturing old pictures of
> his days at Magdalen, and he went to the porter, without fuss, and
> asked, " May I use the telephone ? . . ." Those who loved him
> recognised his true nature in these incidents, and hope became high
> again.

It was on March 1st, St David's Day, that King Edward
first spoke directly to his people, and in the closing words of
that broadcast he made crystal clear the spirit of the reign he
then hoped would be a happy reign :

" I am better known to you as the Prince of Wales, as a
man who, during the war and since, has had the opportunity
of getting to know the people of nearly every country of the
world under all conditions and circumstances.   And although
I now speak to you as the King, I am still that same man
who has that experience and whose constant effort it will be
to continue to promote the well-being of his fellow-men."

The present writer well remembers the elation with which
he heard those words uttered exactly two years ago at the
moment of penning this sentence.   He has played them
over again now upon a gramophone-record.   And a ghost
of the old elation has floated past his chair hearing those
words uttered in that grave staccato, the timbre not yet
carrying all the homely roughness of his father's voice but
still here and there marked with traces of it.   The ghost
floats away: the elation dies down to a memory.   And in
the gloom which succeeds that elation recaptured for a minute
the writer can take a measure of comfort from the thought
that never for one instant did he doubt the integrity of that
King's resolve and never for an instant esteem him culpable
to God or man of the dereliction of his duty.

And in that spirit of confidence he leaves for a while the
central figure of this tapestry not yet fully woven, to attempt
to find a pattern in the complicated warp and woof of circumstance, ecclesiastical observance, constitutional, law, royal
usages and manners in the past from which Edward VIII
stepped out of kingship into common humanity.

CHAPTER XIII

GEORGE I AND GEORGE II

CONSTITUTIONAL historians have come to a gentleman's agreement that the Act of Settlement, which decided that on the death of Queen Anne the Crown should pass to the Electress Sophia and her Protestant descendants, did not establish the elective character of the English Crown. A deliberate avoidance of the shallows of legal casuistry and the moral overfalls they so often cause in stormy weather does not commit the present writer to renouncing his Jacobite conviction that the Act of Settlement completed the destructive process against kingship which began with the execution of Mary, Queen of Scots, was carried on by the execution of Charles I, and was taken a step further by the fictitious presumption of James II's abdication at the inglorious Revolution. The Act of Settlement may not establish the elective character of the English Crown as a general principle, but it certainly provides a precedent for which in any particular emergency the English Crown may be considered elective, and to the mind which refuses to regard compromise as a philosophic absolute it must appear as a distinction without a difference. Perhaps the following extract from Mr Harold Temperley's account of the Revolution and Revolution Settlement in Great Britain from the *Cambridge Modern History* will serve as well as any to illustrate that illogical English conception of the Constitution for which Lord Baldwin has expressed his admiration :

> Expediency had rendered it needful to alter the succession, and to make the Crown elective, *pro hac vice*, but the case was not intended to form a precedent. In this, as in every other instance, the Revolution Settlement rested upon compromise rather than upon the general principles, which, however, the particular occasion went far towards establishing in each case.

The result of that particular occasion was the substitution of a new king at the expense of over sixty royal personages with a better right to the throne, outside election, than the Elector of Hanover, and with the introduction of that dynasty, the introduction of a set of moral standards hitherto unknown in the country over which they were called upon to rule.

When George I came over from Hanover and ascended the throne in 1714 he left behind him in the gloomy lodge of Ahlden a divorced wife who had been imprisoned there for twenty years.   He had visited England as early as 1681 with the idea of marrying the Princess Anne, but he had been called back suddenly to marry his sixteen-year-old cousin, Sophia Dorothea of Zell.   The bright prospect of being able to unite the two principalities of Hanover and Zell into which the house of Brunswick-Lüneburg had been split was more attractive to his parents than the foggy outlines of a future in England.   Duke George William of Zell had married his mistress, Eléonore d'Olbreuse, a French Huguenot from Poitiers, and his daughter, Sophia Dorothea, had been legitimised.   For years, Duke Ernest Augustus, his younger brother and his wife Sophia, the proud grand-daughter of James I, had resented the influence of the hated ' French-woman '; but at last Sophia put her pride in her pocket and decided that her eldest son George Louis should marry for the sake of unity and the possibility of thereby creating an influential Electorate.   To this ambition the unhappy child was sacrificed.   At first, the young princess swore that nothing should persuade her to marry her detestable cousin ; not even if she were dragged to the very altar.   When she was presented to the loutish and surly young Electoral Prince she fainted.

She was a beautiful creature—

a brunette with large velvety eyes, regular features, brilliant com-plexion and rose-bud mouth. Her figure was perfectly proportioned; she had an exquisite neck and bust and slender little hands and feet . . . she had the Frenchwoman's dislike of anything coarse or unrefined . . . her dancing was perfect. . . . She was a skilled musician, and could express herself gracefully in writing. Her conversation was sprightly, she was full of wit and repartee. . . . She had the Frenchwoman's emotional temperament; she was easily depressed and easily elated and was capable of strong and unceasing passion. But her instincts were always generous and she was absolutely free from meanness in word or deed. *

This girl was handed over to her disgusting cousin, George Louis, with a handsome dowry of which she could not touch a thaler for herself and was sold as ruthlessly as any Cir-cassian slave.   Her unfortunate mother made one stipulation and one stipulation only, which was that George Louis should send away his mistress, Madame Bussche.   This demand was argued over for some time as unreasonable, but in the

* W. H. Wilkins, *The Love of an Uncrowned Queen.*

end the Duchess Eléonore had her way. The betrothal was accomplished. The marriage contract was signed.

When the Duchess Sophia, who had arranged the whole lamentable business, reached home she wrote to the Duchess of Orleans, " Ernest Augustus always had a queer head and how such an idea could have entered it passes all my understanding. However, one hundred thousand thalers a year is a goodly sum to pocket, without speaking of a pretty wife, who will find a match in my son, George Louis, the most pig-headed stubborn boy who ever lived, and who has round his brains such a thick crust that I defy any man or woman ever to discover what is in them. He does not care much for the match itself, but one hundred thousand thalers a year have tempted him as they would have tempted anybody else."

This horrible and unnatural wedding was celebrated in the private chapel of the Castle of Zell on November 21st 1682. There were two children—George Augustus, afterwards George II, King of Great Britain, and Sophia Dorothea, afterwards Queen of Prussia. George I treated his wife with complete brutality during the few years they lived together, surrounding himself with those ghastly German mistresses for whom his appetite, even in old age, was never exhausted. There was the Countess of Darlington, who, from her bulk, was called the " Elephant and Castle ", and of whose " enormous figure " Horace Walpole remembered being terrified as a boy. " The fierce black eyes, large and rolling, between two lofty arched eyebrows, two acres of cheeks spread with crimson, an ocean of neck that overflowed and was not distinguished from the lower part of her body, and no part restrained by stays." And there was her rival, the Duchess of Kendal, " head of the extraordinary seraglio, whose elongated figure attenuated almost to emaciation " earned her the nickname of the Maypole, and who " was complaisant enough to allow the King to extend his favours to younger rivals." Sir Philip Francis says of these ladies that honours were given them " to reward their merits in their respective departments, and to encourage the surrender of prudery in younger and handsomer subjects."

We are still ignorant, except through vague legends, of what exactly happened on that dark night in Hanover when the handsome Count Königsmarck vanished for ever from mortal eyes, but, in spite of her passionate defenders, we are driven to presume that the unhappy young princess was convicted of infidelity, bitter though it be to use such a word, to her detestable consort. Her children were taken from her. She was divorced in December 1694 and kept a close prisoner in the lodge of Ahlden and its marshy demesne for thirty-three years. The fancy is haunted by that picture of her driving about at night in a coach with coal-black horses decked with funereal plumes. It was not known for certain that Königsmarck had been murdered, until after the death of George I. The new King, on his first journey to Hanover, ordered some alterations in the Palace and the skeleton of Königsmarck was discovered under the floor of the Elector's dressing-room. George II never forgave his father for the treatment of his mother and he had intended, if she had outlived George I, to bring her over to England and declare her Queen Dowager ; but Sophie Dorothea, from whose out-raged womb sprang the two royal families that a couple of centuries later, would lead one half of the world in war against the other, died before her son could indulge his piety. She was released from her misery on November 3rd 1726. Shortly before her death she was seized with a kind of brain fever, following still another wrong done to her by that implacable husband, and she wrote a letter which she gave under seal to be delivered by a confidential attendant to George I. Then delirium seized her and, after some days of railing against her ruined and tormented life, she died.

The King had always been nervous about the prospect of his wife's death because a French fortune-teller had warned him that he would not survive her a year. At the time, it was generally believed that this prophecy had been inspired by the Duke and Duchess of Zell, who were afraid that the Duchess of Kendal might persuade him to " remove entirely the obstacle to her conscientious union with their son-in-law." Horace Walpole declared " George gave such credit to the denunciation, that, on the eve of his last departure, he took leave of his son and the Princess of Wales with tears, telling them he should never see them any more ; it was certainly his own approaching fate that melted him, not the thought of quitting for ever two persons he had hated." A doubt has been thrown on this story by historians anxious to make the best of George I, on the grounds that Horace Walpole was ignorant that the King had already divorced Sophia Dorothea ; but was Walpole ignorant of this ? It was common gossip, not only that George had divorced his wife, but that he had

been married to the Duchess of Kendal by Lancelot Black-
burne, Archbishop of York. A word about this prelate in
passing. He started a prosperous career soon after his
ordination by going out to the West Indies on secret service
and later served as chaplain on a buccaneering ship. He
was a jovial cleric, but his life was so notoriously loose that
he was commonly credited with being the father out of wedlock of a distinguished archdeacon of the same name and of a
bishop of Norwich. In neither case was the affiliation justified, but that it could be believed is evidence of the licentious
renown in which his character was held by contemporaries.
Indeed his preferment from the see of Exeter to the primacy
of York in 1724 was generally attributed to his complaisance
in the matter of his royal master's alleged marriage to the
Duchess of Kendal.

On the day that he received news of his wife's death George
attended a performance at the Haymarket Theatre, and
for night after night he tried to smother his superstitious
fears by attending the playhouses which normally he disliked.
All the while his hatred of his wife was not relaxed against her
in death, and he refused for seven months to allow her to be
buried where she had wished at Zell. Finally he consented
to this in May 1727, and a few weeks later set out for Hanover
with the Duchess of Kendal. He reached Delden on the Dutch
frontier of Germany at midnight on June 9th, stopped here at
the inn to change horses and ate a glutton's meal, which concluded with a quantity of melons, strawberries and oranges.
Just before he started again for Hanover, having left the
Duchess behind at Delden, a man thrust into his hand the
letter Sophia Dorothea had written before her last illness.
In this letter, she summoned him to appear within a year and
a day before the Judgment Seat of God and there to answer
for the many injuries she had received from him. Soon after
he read that missive he had a seizure. Before he lost consciousness he kept groaning, " To Osnabrück, to Osnabrück ",
and at ten o'clock that night he was carried into the little
room at Osnabrück where he was born. Here he was laid
fully clothed on a bed, and the doctors worked upon his
apoplexy ; but neither plasters nor Spanish flies, warm irons
nor cupping availed. At forty minutes after midnight on
Wednesday, June 12th, the death rattle was heard and the
soul of George I went to keep that fearful tryst. For a long
time after death his tongue hung far out of his bluish mouth,

and in broadsheets it was widely circulated that the Devil had caught him by the throat at last.

The Duchess of Kendal, who had encouraged the King's superstition for many years, firmly believed that, in the shape of a raven, he visited her that morning. Back in England, as soon as George II heard the news of his father's death, he produced two pictures of his dead mother which he had kept hidden all these years and of which he hung one in the Queen's dressing-room and one in their bed-chamber. Presently the Archbishop of Canterbury arrived with George I's will, which George II at once pocketed. It was presumably burnt afterwards.

The precedent thus set for the relations betweeen the monarch and the heir apparent in the new dynasty was carried on in varying degrees of bitterness, not merely in the next reign but in every succeeding reign where there was an heir apparent. Not in every case was the disagreement due to the question of marriage ; but so many disagreements in this Royal Family, whether with the heir apparent or other members of it, male and female, were caused by the question of marriage that it is hardly hyperbole to add that the iniquitous and un-natural marriage of George I seemed to have launched a set of avenging furies, who, however much their savage hold might be toned down by eighteenth-century classicism, always re-main unmistakably furies. And if it be a permitted extrava-gance of the fancy to discern shapes haunting the corridors and staircases of Windsor and Kew, of Kensington, Hampton Court and St James's it is not less permissible to discern avenging shapes from the time of Henry VIII haunting every episcopal palace in the land.

George II's eldest son, Frederick Louis, had been brought up at Herrenhausen in Hanover and it had always been understood that he should marry his cousin, Princess Wilhel-mina of Prussia. George I had looked favourably on this marriage, but it had been violently opposed by the Prince of Wales who mortally hated Wilhelmina's father, Frederick William, King of Prussia, and had once challenged him to a duel. Although Prince Frederick had never seen his cousin, he had managed, at the age of twenty-one, to fall romantically in love with the idea of marrying her, and it was known that George I's last journey to Hanover had been intended to include arrangements for the marriage of his two grandchildren.

A year went by, and when George II took no steps either

to arrange the match or to bring his eldest son to England, Frederick made up his mind to marry his cousin Wilhelmina without consulting anyone else. He sent a secret envoy to Berlin, who got into touch with the Queen of Prussia and found her delighted at the prospect of bringing off the match on which she had set her heart long ago. Foolishly, however, she communicated her young nephew's plan to the English envoy at the Court of Berlin. He reluctantly had to inform the Queen that she had made a mistake in confiding in him because he would have to let his Royal master know what was being proposed. Both George II and Queen Caroline were furious and, although they had kept their eldest son out of England for fourteen years against the advice of their ministers, they now sent a Colonel Lorne (or de Launay) to fetch him from Hanover to London at once. Prince Frederick was giving a ball at the time; but Colonel Lorne was peremptory, and they left Hanover that night. In Berlin the news created consternation. The Queen took to her bed, Princess Wilhelmina fainted, and the King thrashed both her and her brother, afterwards Frederick the Great.

Over in England, George II, who had been voted an extra £100,000 on his Civil List thanks to Walpole's policy of bribing even royalty to suit his own ends, refused to make his son, the Prince of Wales, the same allowance of £100,000 he had received from his father. The young Prince was soon hampered by debt, and although he had been cherishing his romantic passion for Wilhelmina, he succumbed to the temptation of the old Duchess of Marlborough who proposed he should marry her granddaughter Lady Diana Spencer, with a dowry of £100,000. The marriage was to be celebrated secretly by her private chaplain at a lodge in Windsor Park. Somehow or other Sir Robert Walpole found out about it and, believing that such a marriage would too greatly benefit the Tory Party, he exercised his influence as Prime Minister to stop it. Frederick's heart turned back to Wilhelmina. He pressed his father to raise his allowance and let him serve in the campaign on the Rhine. This was refused. He pressed to be given a wife. It was 1734, and he was twenty-seven years of age. The following year George II visited Hanover, and while he was there met the Princess Augusta of Saxe-Gotha, who he thought would be a suitable daughter-in-law. When, on his return to London, the Prince of Wales again applied for his £100,000, a separate establishment, and a wife, King George and Queen Caroline in consultation decided it would be cheaper to get their son married and thus earn the extra allowance he would be voted by Parliament than to pay his debts themselves. Five privy councillors were despatched to the Court of Saxe-Gotha. This done, they told the Prince of Wales whom he was to marry. Poor Frederick in despair sent for the Prussian Minister at St James's and asked him to beg the help of the King of Prussia and the hand of Wilhelmina; but the letter which Baron Borck sent to Berlin was intercepted by Walpole who communicated its contents to the King. Probably in any case the King of Prussia would have declined the match with the son of his hated brother-in-law. In the end, the Prince's desperate need for money compelled him to agree to marry Augusta and accept an allowance of £50,000, which was far below what he required to maintain his establishment in the style expected of him.

Augusta was only seventeen and arrived at Greenwich in the royal yacht, carrying a doll. In April 1736 they were married in the Chapel of St James, whence after the ceremony the whole company escorted them to their bedchamber.

> The Bride was undressed by the Princesses; and being in Bed in a rich undress, his Majesty came into the Room, and the Prince following soon after in a Night-gown of Silver Stuff, and Cap of the finest lace, the Quality were admitted to see the Bride and Bridegroom sitting up in the Bed, surrounded by all the Royal Family.

Thus the account in the *Gentleman's Magazine* of that month and year.

The popularity of the Prince of Wales was growing all the time, and his popularity was an important asset to the House of Hanover in counteracting the dazzling reports of that other Prince of Wales over the water. It would be tedious to recount the endless disputes over money between the Prince and his parents which culminated in a motion brought before both Houses of Parliament. The Prince's supporters were defeated by only thirty votes in the House of Commons. From that time onwards, until his death in 1751, he and his father and mother were hardly on speaking terms.

Frederick, Prince of Wales, has suffered heavily at the hands of contemporary chroniclers. The most vivid account of the Court of George II during that critical decade of the seventeen thirties is to be found in Lord Hervey's Memoirs, so vivid that we can almost smell the wax of the guttering candles and hear the flip of the cards at the quadrille and commerce tables. The story of the birth of the Prince of Wales's eldest child, when the Princess of Wales was taken in travail at Hampton Court and hurried into a coach by her husband so that the infant might be born at St James's away from the atmosphere of his parents' hate, is horrifying in its details. Not less horrifying is the narrative of the death of Queen Caroline, who, stronger-minded and coarser than any queen except Elizabeth, was yet too sensitive to reveal the source of her malady as a rupture. Hervey and the Prince of Wales had quarrelled over something, and Hervey pursued him with the bitterness of what one may suspect was not a quarrel over a woman as is suggested, but over Hervey's hurt pathic vanity—Hervey, who lives for ever as Pope's

> Amphibious thing! that acting either part,
> The trifling head or the corrupted heart,
> Fop at the toilet, flatterer at the board,
> Now trips a lady, and now struts a lord.

Until the publication of the Egmont Diaries we had been dependent for another impression of Frederick in the diary of Bubb Dodington which is the dull work of a rich careerist. There is a mystery in the relationship between the Prince and his parents which we can now never hope to fathom. It is easy to understand his father's hatred for him, but his mother's hatred for " Fretz "—expressed as we have it in the very words she spoke—is baffling. Queen Caroline can be called a great woman. Sir Robert Walpole entirely depended on her support for what, if the substitution of the House of Hanover for the House of Stuart be accepted as advantageous, must be regarded as equal to the piece of Cecilian statesmanship which secured Elizabeth on the throne of England. Caroline was a woman who faced the facts of masculine weakness, with an honesty and equanimity that are hardly to be matched in the history of womanhood. That ex-buccaneer the jolly old Archbishop of York told her " he was glad to find that Her Majesty was so sensible a woman as to like her husband to divert himself." This diversion was mistresses. Why she, with all her qualities of head and heart, spurned her eldest son to give all her maternal affection to his savage brother Cumberland is incomprehensible. It is a maniacal hatred, and we lack the full knowledge of her youth and the first years of her married life that might explain it. A complete inability to speak the truth or to be aware that he was lying was charged against Frederick. We may assume that he did often lie, but when we regard his upbringing the blame for this seems to rest rather with his parents than himself. He was reproached for his fickleness and his readiness to sacrifice everything for a cheap and easy popularity. But here again, such facts as we have from unprejudiced observers contradict his enemies. He was supported by statesmen like Bolingbroke and Pulteney, who, granted that they were out of favour with the political power in the ascendant, seem to have genuinely believed in the good qualities that might have served Frederick if he had succeeded to the throne. He unquestionably had held the affection of the London mob and in those days that meant he was as near to being a democratic prince as was attainable. He was accused by his enemies of being a coward, but we hear of him distinguishing himself at a fire, and we know that he was as anxious as any other member of his House for active service in war. It was said that he supported the Italian opera only to annoy his father who supported Handel, but modernity may have prompted him to do this as much as hostility to his father.

It would be ridiculous to suggest even a shadow of a possible comparison between him and his great-great-great-grandson; yet he does display an infinitely faint adumbration of the kind of influence that a later Prince of Wales would exert over the country. We do see in Frederick evidence that time is moving on. His prime was spent in years which, whatever they contributed to the material greatness of the country, displayed the very worst of that country's potentialities for evil, and somehow with all his follies and instability he moves through that dark gin-sodden London of falling jerry-built houses, of brutal crime and still more brutal punishment, of religious deadness and moral degradation, of prostituted literature and corrupt politics, as through the glimmering dawn of a brighter future, and it is not rash to prophesy that two hundred years from now posterity will discern a similar glimmer of a still brighter future round the path of him who was lately Prince of Wales. Perhaps this glimmer always clings to heirs apparent. It was of Frederick Prince of Wales and Mr Pope that Horace Walpole related this brief duologue. 'Mr Pope, you don't love princes.' 'Sir, I beg your pardon.' 'Well, you don't love kings then!' 'Sir, I own I love the lion best before his claws are grown.'

Postscript

It was only after this chapter was finished that the writer of it had an opportunity to read Sir George Young's just published story of Frederick, which he calls *Poor Fred : The People's Prince*. So completely did it bear out the theory put forward rather tentatively here that it was hard to resist the temptation to rewrite this account of Frederick with greater elaboration. However, it seemed better to advise every reader whose interest in this forgotten Prince of Wales had been stirred to lose no time in reading Sir George Young's book for himself. He will find in it some extremely nutritious political thought and much entertaining social history. One extract is irresistible :

> This [*i.e.* that Christmas Day in 1736 when it was believed that George II might have been drowned] was the turning-point of the Prince's life. The dice of death were to fall in such a way that on this occasion only was he to have the opportunity of building an England and an Empire that would have altered the history of the world. . . . A ruler of different character would have seen his time come, would have seized it in time, and time would have assured him success. Possibly a ruler who is too democratic to be a dictator when democracy demands it, who is too constitutional to be unconstitutional in defence of the Constitution, and who thereby deprives himself of the highest place in history, therefore deserves the lowest. It is a nice point in political casuistry which need not concern us—though it quite possibly will.

CHAPTER XIV

GEORGE III

The sixty years of King George's reign have been fused into a precious ingot of British glory, which is nursed in Clio's ample lap as proudly as that other great ingot of the Victorian reign it almost rivals. In contemplating so rich a

weight of solid achievement we are too apt to overlook the
truly fantastic figure of the man himself as he passes from a
frozen monarchical symbol into that unhealthy hothouse of
what is fondly believed to be the quintessence of English
domesticity, to emerge from it in a royal madness the like of
which had not been known since Lear wandered by the edge
of Dover cliff dressed with flowers. This fugleman of
modern political experiment has been reduced to a pop-eyed,
decollated profile on a silver shilling. The true significance
of his pervasive influence, an influence, if one include the
whole length of his reign, possibly as profound as Queen
Victoria's, has been lost sight of by the majority. Every
biography of George III turns into one of those eighteenth-
century mezzotints in which the humanity of the chief figure
cannot compete with backgrounds of military and naval
panoply, of colours, drums and muskets, and the cannonade of three-deckers in action; or it melts into a pastoral
landscape as remote from actuality as those golden ruins of
Claude or Poussin bathed in a benignancy of eternal mellow
sunlight. It is altogether outside the scope of this work to
attempt a full-length portrait of this complicated and uncanny
personality, so ridiculously libelled by the half-contemptu-
ous, half-affectionate epithet of Farmer George; and the
partiality of lighting up one aspect of his character at the
cost of leaving in undeserved dimness so many others is fully
appreciated. The contrast between the pure domestic life
which George III led with his wife Charlotte of Mecklenburg-
Strelitz and the marital habits of three generations of his
House told increasingly in his favour with the many, particularly after he was dead. But before that marriage, soon
after his accession, he had fallen in love with Lady Sarah
Lennox, the youngest daughter of the Duke of Richmond,
and had been observed to ride many a morning along the
Kensington Road from which the object of his affections was
to be seen making hay in the broad meadow before Holland
House. Gradually a legend was evolved of his having sacrificed love to duty. That he sacrificed love may be true: that
it was upon the altar of duty there is no evidence.

George II had known Lady Sarah as a child, and, according
to her son Henry Napier's *Memoir of Lady Sarah's Early Life*,
when he heard of her return to the house of her eldest sister
Lady Holland he had insisted although so young that she
should be brought to Court, and on her appearance in the

midst of the circle had begun to joke and play with her as if she had been a child of five years old. She had naturally coloured up and had shrunk from this unexpected familiarity upon which the King had turned abruptly from her, and had exclaimed in a gruff voice, " Pooh, she's grown quite stupid." So untoward a compliment, says Napier, finished his poor mother's distress, and it was at this very moment that the young Prince, afterwards George III, was struck with admiration and pity, feelings that ripened into an attachment, which, as Napier had been told, never left the King, even in his most unsettled moments until the day of his death.

When George III was in the first year of his reign, Lady Sarah was a lovely girl of fifteen. Lord Holland in his *Memoir on the Events attending the Death of George II and the Accession of George III* wrote of his young sister-in-law that her beauty was not easily described, otherwise than by saying that she had the finest complexion, most beautiful hair, and prettiest person that ever was seen, with a sprightly and fine air, a pretty mouth and remarkably fine teeth and excess of bloom for her cheeks, little eyes,—but this was not describing her, for her great beauty was a peculiarity of countenance, that made her at the same time different from and prettier than any other girl he had ever seen. The King, then Prince of Wales, had always talked to her with looks of pleasure and admiration ; and as the crown had neither lessened her beauty nor his sense of it, this had still continued, and his niece Lady Susan Strangways, who was ever with her, had come in for her share in the discourse.

Lady Sarah and Lady Susan driving in a little chaise together used to meet the King on his morning rides ; and once it was said that " wanting to speak to him, she went dressed like a servant-maid, and stood amongst the crowd in the Guard Room, to say a few words to him as he passed by." * The King was giving broad hints to Lady Susan that Lady Sarah would make his postponed coronation " a much finer sight," and at last urged her to tell Lady Sarah all that he was saying about her.

And then something went wrong.

It seems that Lady Sarah hurt the King's pride by a flirtation with Lord Newbottle, who was described by Lord Holland as a vain and insignificant puppy, lively and not ugly, who had made love to all the girls, but was much in love

* *The Grenville Papers.*

with Lady Caroline Russell, the Duke of Bedford's daughter. Lady Sarah had tried to get him from her, and had been so pleased with her success that she had grown too much pleased with his Lordship. It had really been a commerce of vanity, not of love on either side.

The influences at Court hostile to the intellectual and political predominance of the Foxes were brought to bear heavily against the possibility of a match between Lady Sarah and the King. Most bitter of all were the Princess Dowager of Wales and Lord Bute. They had their own plans for the Royal future. The most was made of the flirtation, and when Lady Sarah, who meanwhile had broken her leg out riding, should next come to Court it was hoped that the King would show his resentment. Lord Holland remarked that it had hurt him and Lord Albemarle to see so much ridiculous German pride as had appeared in the sensible English Duke of Cumberland * on this occasion. They might think a white Princess of Brunswick, Anspach or Saxe-Gotha superior to the daughter of the Duke of Richmond and it suited their interest and understanding. But he could not forgive that his friend the Duke of Cumberland should think so, nor could he see without wonder such a triumph of silly prejudice over manly sense and reason. He however was (as Lord Holland believed he might be) " easy upon that head by then, and had no apprehensions of so great a degradation of his family."

Yet in spite of the flirtation and in spite of all the mischief that had been made of it when Lady Sarah came to St James's for the King's birthday party on the 4th of June he seemed as much enamoured as ever. Horace Walpole wrote to Lady Ailesbury : " *The birthday exceeded the splendour of Haroun Alraschid and the Arabian Nights . . . do you remember where a prince has eight statues of diamonds, which he overlooks because he fancies he wants a ninth, and to his great surprise, the ninth proves to be pure flesh and blood ? . . . Somehow or other, Lady Sarah is the ninth statue ; and you will allow has better white and red than if she was made of pearls and rubies.*"

And Lord Holland had written that the King had no eyes but for her and had hardly talked to anybody else . . . all eyes had been fixed on them.

The Court was on tenterhooks. A Lady Barrington famed for her beautifully shaped back caught hold of Lady Sarah one

---

* The hero of Culloden.

day as they were entering the Presence Chamber together and said, " Do, my dear Lady Sarah, let me take the lead and go in before you this once, for you will never have another opportunity of seeing my beautiful back."

The King was certainly still deep in love. Lord Holland noted that Her Ladyship, with modesty very natural to her, and yet with looks as unaffected, had returned the fondness of his eyes and gallantry of his discourse as much as ever he could wish. He was in love with her, and it was no less certain she loved him ; and if she now ever thought of Newbattle [*sic*] it was to vex and hate herself for the foolish transaction he had before related. It would be impossible to write down so much discourse as the King had held with her, nor was that so remarkable as the *language de yeux*. Among other things, he had desired his sister to dance ' Betty Blue,' a dance, he said to Lady Sarah, that she was acquainted with. He was very fond of it because it was taught him by a lady, looking very significantly. She really did not know who he meant. A very pretty lady, said the King, who came from Ireland November was a twelvemonth. She then knew, but did not pretend to know. He was talking to her then, said he, and she had taught it to him at the ball on " Twelve night." Indeed, said Lady Sarah, she did not remember it. The King repeated that might be, she taught it him at the ball on Twelve Night and indeed, he had a very good memory for whatever related to that lady. He had got a pretty new country dance of his own for the late King's birthday if he had lived to it and he named it " the 25th of February " (which was Lady Sarah's birthday). She coloured, and " in this *pretty* way did those two lovers entertain one another and the eyes of the whole ball room for an hour." He stopped very remarkably as he was going and turned and spoke again and again as if he could not force himself from her. On Sunday, June 7th, he looked out of sorts and melancholy, said nothing to her but what he might have said to any other young lady, looked languishing and as if he loved her, talked a great while to her, and with great favour and civility to Lady Caroline and Lady Susan, but " there were not those ardent looks of fondness, nor any particular expressions to Lady Sarah. The ladies say he has been tutor'd."

And that tutoring was the end of Lady Sarah's likelihood of becoming Queen. Many years later Queen Victoria would decide in conversation with Lord Melbourne that the King was " *détourné* by her levity over Lord Newbottle." No doubt that unfortunate attempt to cut out Lady Caroline

Russell played its part as an emotional stimulus to be finished with Lady Sarah. The real inspiration of the King's behaviour, however, was fear of the Whig bondage which had lasted since James II was abdicated, and to break which George had been brought up to believe was his royal task. Marriage with Lady Sarah would have kept him in thraldom to the Whig oligarchy. The young King was ambitious to exercise the Royal Prerogative, and only if duty be held synonymous with ambition can he be said to have sacrificed love to duty in turning away from Lady Sarah.

It is one of history's most fascinating ' ifs ' to speculate what would have happened if, instead of marrying one of what Charles II used to call those " foggy " German princesses, George had wedded the great-granddaughter of Charles II himself.

Nervously that marriage with Princess Charlotte of Mecklenburg-Strelitz was arranged, nervously and secretly, the reason for which, Queen Victoria notes in her journal, " Lord Melbourne said was on account of keeping it from Mr Fox on account of Lady Sarah Lennox." Lady Sarah felt piqued, but could write sincerely to her dearest Susan, " *My disappointment did not affect my spirits above an hour or two, I believe. I did not cry, I assure you, which I believe you will, as I know you were more set upon it than I was. The thing I am most angry at is looking like a fool.*" That letter was written in July 1761.

At the end of August, Princess Charlotte, escorted by the Duchess of Hamilton, the Duchess of Ancaster, and the Countess of Effingham, left Cuxhaven for Harwich. It was blowy Bartlemy-tide weather, and the voyage took ten days during which the peeresses in waiting lay prostrate with sea-sickness, while, above the creaking of the timbers and the whistling of the shrouds, the ugly little Princess of sixteen played *Rule Britannia* on a harpsichord and *God Save the King* on a guitar, mingling with both Luther's hymns. She then consoled the seasick ladies by assuring them that God had not singled her out for nothing. Charlotte was right. The country of her adoption was to have sixty years of her.

Just before the royal coach reached St James's about half-past three in the afternoon, one of the ladies said to the other, looking at her watch, that they would hardly have time to dress for the wedding. " Wedding ! " the Queen exclaimed. " Yes, Madam, it is to be at twelve." Whereupon Charlotte fainted ; but Lady Effingham who had a bottle of lavender-water threw it in her face and brought her round just as the coach stopped at the garden-gate of St James's Palace.   Here George was waiting surrounded by his Court, and the young Queen (already married by proxy, so anxious were the Bute party to make it a certainty) found a crimson cushion laid for her to make obeisance.   She prepared to prostrate herself before some " hideous black old Duke ", but the King caught her in his arms.   And from this moment, the Queen used to relate, she never knew real sorrow until his illness.   It is questionable, however, whether Queen Charlotte was capable of experiencing deep sorrow.

Lady Sarah's grief for the broken match had been confused with grief for a dead squirrel, and presently both had been tempered by adopting a " little hedgehog that she saved from destruction in the field."   She had enjoyed, too, the pleasure of snubbing the King the first time she had met him after the announcement of the Mecklenburg match and of treating his sister the Princess Augusta " *de haut en bas* ". In August she was writing to " Dear Pussy " (Lady Susan) to tell her she had been invited to be a bridesmaid and had accepted.   She had already decided to be a trainbearer if invited, because that would be " *the best way to see the Coronation*."

Lady Caroline Russell and Lady Susan Fox-Strangways were also among the ten bridesmaids, but Lady Sarah " *was by far the chief angel*," Walpole wrote.   " *Nothing ever looked so charming*."   The poor little Queen's " *Violet velvet mantua and ermine were so heavy that the spectators knew as much of her upper half as the King himself*," Walpole wrote again. The King appeared " mentally absent " and never took his eyes off Lady Sarah throughout the ceremony.   He only showed signs of emotion when the Archbishop of Canterbury reading the marriage-service came to the words—' And as Thou didst send Thy blessing upon Abraham and Sarah to their great comfort, so vouchsafe to send Thy blessing upon these Thy servants.'   At the Drawing-Room next day the old Jacobite Earl of Westmorland, who had been persuaded to make his first appearance at Court since the Hanoverian Succession and was purblind, mistook Lady Sarah for the Queen, " plumped down on his knees, and took her hand to kiss !   She drew back startled, and deeply colouring exclaimed, ' I am not the Queen, Sir.' "   ' Oh, he always loved Pretenders,' George Selwyn laughed, when he heard of this blunder.

The following June Lady Sarah married Sir Charles Bunbury.

" At this very time H.M. was very very ill," Lord Holland noted. " It might well have, but it had no relation to his ill usage of that sweet girl and worse of himself in her regard."

The young King in fact was suffering from his first fit of insanity after his accession. It took the shape this time of a melancholia without delusions. He and the Queen were both victims of the eternal hungry plotting of that " witch of Endor " Augusta, Princess Dowager of Wales, whose unpopularity in the country was acute. She had already been suspected of poisoning her husband ' Poor Fred '. George and Charlotte were practically secluded from all except their own society at this time. On August 12th of that sad year 1762 the future King George IV was born, to be loved by his mother but by the time he was seven hated with a lunatic hate by his father.

Lady Sarah's first marriage was not too happy. Later she married George Napier and was the mother of the historian of the Peninsular War, dying blind at the age of eighty-two in 1826 six years after the King who always remembered her with regret. Many many years later he was attending at the theatre a performance by Mrs Pope who in face and manner was very like Lady Sarah. The King fell into a reverie, oblivious of the Queen's presence. ' She is like Lady Sarah still ! ' he was heard to murmur to himself with a deep sigh.

George III was sharply criticised at the time for his lack of frankness and courage over Lady Sarah, and it was only the adulatory historians of later days who built up that sentimental legend of a sacrifice of private happiness to the public weal.

" *It's quite dark, and I have no time to call for candles,*" Lady Sarah had written at the end of that letter to Lady Susan in which she had confided in her friend how little anything except her pride was hurt by the King's jilting of her. Lady Susan herself would marry two years later William O'Brien, a handsome young actor. ' *A cruel blow,*' Walpole would write in aristocratic dismay, ' *and a melancholy affair for Lord Ilchester.*' But dark though it was, that July night nearly two centuries ago, Lady Sarah's mouth keeps for us a magic of live colour beyond any crimson Reynolds knew, and Lady Sarah's little eyes still flash across that darkness, and not a phrase of those artless letters of a fifteen-year-old girl but is written with last night's ink and lighted with modern electricity.

And as from her letters this vivid figure of girlhood hay-making in meadows which in the overbuilt London of to-day are still as green as once they were in that fine fled summer of long ago comes to life, we wonder what miseries may not have sprung from George III's cowardice and duplicity and foolish royal pride in wedding " *Miss Charlotte of Mecklenburgh* [*sic*] " and denying himself the gratification of what one day an Archbishop of Canterbury would call " a craving for private happiness "; what miseries and heartaches to the numerous royal but human beings that were the result of his impeccably decorous domestic life with Queen Charlotte.

But Lady Sarah Lennox is not the only reputed love of George III's early life. There is the strange story of Hannah Lightfoot, which may provide a key to unlock the behaviour of George III in jilting Lady Sarah and his motives for forcing upon the country the Royal Marriages Bill of 1772. The Fair Quakeress was born in 1730, the daughter of Matthew Lightfoot, a shoemaker of Execution Dock, Wapping. On the death of her father in 1732 or 1733, Hannah was adopted by one of her mother's brothers, Henry Wheeler, who kept a linen-draper's shop at the corner of St James's Market, not far from where nowadays Jermyn Street runs into Regent Street. According to legend the young Prince used to notice her as the royal family passed in chairs attended by yeomen of the guard on the way from Leicester Fields to the Opera or St James's.

What is sure is that on December 11th 1753 Hannah Lightfoot married a certain Isaac Axford, at Keith's Chapel, Curzon Street, where until the Marriage Act of the same year marriages could be performed by virtue of a licence on a crown stamp and a guinea certificate. This marriage was believed to have been arranged by the Princess Dowager to keep the young Prince of Wales (he was only fifteen and a half!) out of mischief. Whether that was so or not, it is certain that very soon after her marriage, Hannah disappeared and her supposed husband remarried in 1759, so that pre-sumably this marriage with Axford was never valid. By 1760 it had become a vulgar belief that the young Prince had married Hannah Lightfoot and had three children by her. Huish writing while George III was still alive says:

" His [George's] affections appeared to be fixed too firmly to be weakened or destroyed by human art or invention ; and no doubt existed of the intention of His Majesty to remove those State forms which proved such formidable obstacles to the consummation of his union with the daughter of a subject. . . . Great as might have been the existing prejudice at the time to a union of our sovereign with a native, it is certain that the clamour raised against it proceeded more from family pride and political intrigue than from any actual objection to the individual who had so completely enchained the affections of our sovereign. The alarm was industriously spread throughout the country of the danger to which it was exposed from a spurious offspring of the sovereign ; the extent of his amour was investigated in the most inquisitorial manner, the circumstance of his being the father was bruited abroad as corroborative of the pressing need of an immediate union with some foreign princess. . . ."

It is clear that the last part of this paragraph does not refer to Lady Sarah Lennox, and if as seems probable it refers to a child or children by Hannah Lightfoot advantage of the popular rumour may have been taken to force upon the King the urgency of marriage with a German princess. He may have been told that marriage with Lady Sarah would not silence tongues and that the succession might even be disputed.

What might have been used against the King became apparent only in 1866. In that year, a Mrs Ryves petitioned the Court of Probate and Divorce to declare that Henry Frederick, Duke of Cumberland, and her grandmother Olive Wilmot were lawfully married and that her mother, Olive Wilmot Serres, was her legitimate daughter. A quantity of documents were produced, all of which, except two or three, were declared by the leading handwriting expert of the day to be genuine, and among them were what the Court was startled to read as two certificates, signed by the Rev. James Wilmot, and witnessed by Lord Chatham and J. Dunning * purporting to declare that on April 17th 1759 Wilmot married George, Prince of Wales, to Hannah Lightfoot. Other documents supporting these were signed George P. and George Guelph, and the handwriting was declared genuine by the expert. Mrs Ryves, the petitioner, a woman seventy years old, with-

* Became Solicitor-General, and later Lord Ashburton.

stood for three days a searching examination by the Attorney-General, Sir Roundell Palmer ; but, in the end, as might have been expected, the jury found against her.   Nevertheless, nobody who reads through the whole of that case can help wondering why if these documents were in the words of the Lord Chief Baron ' indecent,' and in the words of the Lord Chief Justice, ' treasonable,' Mrs Ryves was treated with such extraordinary leniency.   The documents themselves were impounded, but Mrs Ryves herself walked out of Court, without even an admonition from the learned judges ; and at the conclusion of the case, her counsel affirmed on his honour as a gentleman that he believed in the genuineness of the documents, for which avowal he was rebuked by the Court for violating legal etiquette.

As recently as 1910 Miss Mary Pendered, who made a careful analysis of the Hannah Lightfoot legend, was refused permission by the authorities to examine these documents " in the interests of research ".   These documents having been declared forgeries, it is surely reasonable that they should be available to competent historians.   Whatever may be thought of the documents purporting to establish the marriage of George III and Hannah Lightfoot, it is difficult to refuse all credit to the possibility of a marriage between the Rev. J. Wilmot's daughter Olive and the Duke of Cumberland in 1770. By the way, James Wilmot himself as a Fellow of Trinity College, Oxford, had to keep his own marriage secret, having, it was alleged, married a sister of Count Poniatowski who was afterwards King of Poland, a friend of his at Oxford.   William Beckford believed in the Hannah Lightfoot marriage and he, a friend of the Pitts, testified in print that Wilmot was on intimate terms with Lord Chatham and that the Pitt family accepted the genuineness of the story.   He believed Wilmot to be the original Junius, and the evidence for such an identification is not to be despised.   Now if Wilmot did marry his unacknowledged daughter Olive or Olivia to the Duke of Cumberland * in 1770, then the marriage in the following year of the Duke with Mrs Horton, the daughter of Lord Irnham and sister of the fire-eating Colonel Luttrell, was bigamous, and if George III, knowing of the Wilmot marriage, threatened to expose his brother, and if Mrs Horton, to whom Cumberland was said to have revealed the secret of the

---

* Henry Frederick, brother of George III. The hero of Culloden was now dead.

King's marriage, threatened him with exposure, the agitation of George III which led to his forcing through the Royal Marriages Bill in 1772 is more easily understood than it can be at present.   He had shown definite signs of aberration in 1762, and it is not beyond possibility that in an earlier moment of aberration he did marry Hannah Lightfoot.   The seclusion in which he was kept by his mother and the unhealthy atmosphere of Leicester House, all the more unhealthy because it was concealed by the perfume of a frigid and unnatural morality, must have had a most deleterious effect on a temperament that was certainly not less amorous than those of the rest of his family.   Students conversant with the various delusions of George III's bouts of madness throughout his life will find it easy to believe him capable of any folly in youth.

In 1770 the King had had to find £13,000 to pay Lord Grosvenor's damages and costs in a criminal conversation case against his brother Cumberland, the scabrous details of which were published to the world.

On September 7th of that year the following suggestive paragraph appeared in the *Public Advertiser* :

> The defence of H.R.H. (Henry Frederick, Duke of Cumberland), so often advertised as written by an M.P., is quite a catchpenny, the writer being Col. L—ll, who is no member at all. We are told that his defence will speedily be followed by a new publication, entitled *The Letters of an Elder Brother to a Fair Quaker*, which will entirely retrieve the Literary Fame of an illustrious family, which has been lately endangered by a hasty and incorrect writer belonging to it.

The King may by now have heard rumours of his brother's marriage with Olive Wilmot, and in 1771 he knew for certain that the scapegrace had married Mrs Horton, " a young widow of twenty-four, extremely pretty, not handsome, very well made, with the most amorous eyes in the world, and eyelashes a yard long, coquette beyond measure, artful as Cleopatra, and completely mistress of all her passions and projects. Indeed, eyelashes three-quarters of a yard shorter would have served to conquer such a head as she has turned." *

The Duchess of Cumberland kept her charm for Wraxall, who, writing of her in 1786, when she was forty, says :

> Her personal charms fully justified the duke's passion. No woman of her time performed the honours of her own drawing-room with

---

* Walpole.

I

more affability, ease and dignity. The King held her in great alienation, because he believed that she lent herself to facilitate or to gratify
the Prince of Wales' inclinations on some points beyond the limits of
propriety.

Completely mistress of her passions and her projects ? If
that mad marriage did take place and if she knew the secret
of it, it would account even better for the King's alienation.
George III's reception of the news of his brother's marriage was
strange. Apparently, the Duke took him out in the garden
and gave him a letter which he asked him to read at once.
Having done so the King called his brother a fool and a block-
head, and declared that this woman " could be nothing and
never should be anything," after which violent explosion he bade
Cumberland go abroad. Now, Mrs Horton may have been
a gay widow, but she was the daughter of a peer and the
sister of a man who had fought the obnoxious Wilkes ; and,
unless we presume that the King was taking up a dog-in-the-
manger attitude over his own weakness in being dissuaded from
marriage with Lady Sarah Lennox, there was really no call for
all this agitation. Cumberland had caused a grave scandal by
the exposure of his morals and manners in the Grosvenor
suit, and almost as much by the revelation of his illiteracy.
One letter of his read out in Court convulsed the audience :
" I *got* to supper about nine o'clock, but I could not eat, and so
got to bed about ten." That, Walpole considered, was the
letter of a cabin boy. *Tempora mutantur !*
Surely the marriage of such a profligate dunce to a woman
of rank and fashion and wit like Mrs Horton should have been
welcome if there was no just cause or impediment. The more
one ponders it, the more one inclines to believe that the Royal
Marriages Bill was the result of a determination in George
III's mind that he would guard the Royal family for the future
against its own imprudence, not perhaps forgetting even his
own, rather than an outburst of spleen on account of a younger
brother's marriage with a commoner at a date when the
succession might be considered safely provided for. The
conviction that there was a more compelling reason grows in
strength. It is worth noting an assertion of the *Historical
Fragment* of 1824 :

Queen Caroline [wife of George IV], at this time, laboured under
a very curious, and to me, very unaccountable delusion, and she fancied
herself neither a wife nor a queen. She believed his present Majesty

to have been actually married to Mrs Fitzherbert, and she as fully believed that his late Majesty was married to Miss Hannah Lightfoot, a beautiful Quakeress, previous to his marriage to Queen Charlotte, that a ceremony of marriage was a second time solemnised at Kew (under the colour of an evening's entertainment) after the death of Miss Lightfoot, and as that lady did not die until after the birth of the present King, and H.R.H. the Duke of York, her Majesty really considered the present Duke of Clarence heir to the throne.

If Queen Caroline's delusions were not unaccountable, the ponderous remark of the Lord Chief Justice in the Ryves case that it was nothing less than a claim to the throne loses force, because Queen Victoria was not descended from either of the two elder children of Queen Charlotte. It is with the possibility of a heavier weight upon that overstrained mind than the marriage of the Duke of Cumberland to a dashing Derbyshire widow that we must read the King's message to Lord North after the first debate on the Royal Marriages Bill:

I do expect every nerve to be strained to carry the Bill through both Houses with a becoming firmness, for it is not a question that immediately relates to Administration, but personally to myself, therefore I have a right to expect a hearty support from everyone in my service and shall remember Defaulters.

Queen's House, Feb. 26th, 1772
3 minutes past 11 p.m.

CHAPTER XV

THE ROYAL MARRIAGES ACT

Yet before we attend the debates in the two Houses upon the Royal Marriages Bill one more royal marriage must be mentioned. In 1766 Caroline Matilda, the youngest and prettiest and cleverest of King George III's sisters, had been married to the degenerate young King of Denmark Christian VII. She was only fifteen years and three months old, for she was a posthumous child of Frederick, Prince of Wales. "*The poor Queen of Denmark* [a lady wrote to a friend] *is gone out alone into the wide world . . . it is worse than dying. . . . They have just been telling me how bitterly she cried in the coach, as far as anybody saw her.*" Sir Joshua Reynolds who painted her portrait before she left complained he could do justice neither to his sitter nor himself because she was weeping all the time.   The marriage was approved of in England as " adding security to the Protestant religion," but the rest of her story is like one of Webster's tragedies of blood, madness, and horror.   She bore a son to the unspeakable Christian whom to compare to the young Caligula was no exaggeration.   In the background were two dowager queens, one of whom, Juliana, cherished ambitions for a second son of her own.   Christian went travelling in London and Paris.   In London the little King, " as diminutive as if he were out of a kernel in the Fairy Tales," strutted " like a cock-sparrow, or like the late King (George II)," Walpole wrote.   He was much fêted and flattered, but spent his nights " disguised as a common sailor, in the stews and pot-houses of St Giles."   On his way home to Denmark he brought back from near Hamburg a handsome young doctor called Struensee.   He was consulted by the Queen—it was said by some for a disease with which her husband had infected her—and the consultation led to a friendship which developed into a passionate intrigue.   The madness of the King grew.   Struensee acquired dictatorial power.   Then on a January night in 1772, the Dowager Juliana being the mover, Struensee and his chief supporter were seized in a Palace coup after a masked ball.

The Queen with her six-months-old daughter was imprisoned in a castle by the sea near Elsinore.   Struensee was tried, confessed under torture to the guilt of his relations with the Queen, and was executed after being mutilated.   It was feared that the conspirators intended to try the Queen for her life, but Keith, the British Minister at Copenhagen, moved energetically and the Danish capital was threatened with a British squadron.   The young Queen barely yet twenty was deprived of her infant daughter, and went to live in exile at Zell where she died of an inflammation of the throat in 1775 at the age of twenty-three.   She was buried close to where the unhappy Sophia Dorothea had been buried fifty years before. ' Elle est si blonde,' complained the little madman who was her great-granddaughter's husband.   He hated Caroline Matilda for that fairness.

Worry, to which may be assumed was added remorse, about her daughter's fate hastened the end of the Princess Dowager who, on February 8th 1772 died in London of a cancer in the breast, borne with immense courage.

Two days after George III sent that message to Lord

North about the Royal Marriages Bill, the same lady who had written of the departure from England in tears of that sister who so much resembled him wrote to another friend :

> " *I have very little intelligence to send you from Denmark, as there is a profound silence at St James's on that subject . . . the unhappy young Queen is imprisoned in a castle dashed by the waves. I am persuaded you would think it an alleviation of her misfortunes, if I could tell you it is the very castle once haunted by Hamlet's ghost.*"

The misery of Caroline Matilda was providing a fashionable Gothic thrill ; but with her in our thoughts as we read the preamble to the Royal Marriages Bill which Mansfield, Thurlow, and Wedderburn had drawn up between them, it is difficult to forgive George III for daring to claim a fatherly right as King to the care of his relations.

The King's message to both Houses relative to marriages of the Royal Family was sent down on February 20th. It was as follows :

" His Majesty being desirous, from paternal affection to his own family, and anxious concern for the future welfare of his people, and the honour and dignity of his crown, that the right of approving all marriages in the Royal Family (which ever has belonged to the kings of this realm as a matter of public concern) may be made effectual, recommends to both Houses of Parliament to take into their serious consideration whether it may not be wise and expedient to supply the defect of the laws now in being ; and, by some provision, more effectually to guard the descendants of his late majesty King George the second (other than the issue of princesses who have married or may hereafter marry into foreign families) from marrying without the approbation of his Majesty, his heirs or successors, first had and obtained."

That same day Charles James Fox resigned from his post as Junior Lord of the Admiralty. This defection alarmed Lord North as much as the threatened defections of Mr Eden were believed to alarm Mr Baldwin throughout his manipulation of public affairs, a manipulation which, in some of its outward characteristics, curiously recalls those of his eighteenth-century predecessor.

The number of years during which Lord North had sat in the House of Commons, and his constant habit of taking a part in its debates, had furnished him with a thorough knowledge of the weaknesses of human nature, which no living statesman was more dexterous in turning to his own advantage. He possessed also a complete acquaintance with the rules and constitution of the House of Commons. As its leader, no one ever enjoyed in a happier degree the art of parrying a direct question with an indirect answer. If it happened to be expedient to stave off a troublesome debate, he could keep the House amused for hours. Sometimes on these occasions, he was pathetic, sometimes humorous, sometimes he affected to be confidential. In the art of bewildering, and at the same time of entertaining, he was unsurpassed. To his audience his language had all the appearance of being concise and his arguments of being unanswerable and yet, on cooler consideration, not one person perhaps, of those who had gone away delighted with his eloquence, could recall that the Prime Minister had thrown a single additional ray of light upon the subject under discussion, or had supported his arguments by a single additional fact.*

As we read this we have to look again at the opening sentence to confirm that it really is Lord North who is being described and not Mr Baldwin, and it may be added that throughout the debates upon the Royal Marriages Bill the King was sending Lord North scribbled notes, with which perhaps he fumbled as effectively as years hence his successor would fumble with a scribbled note. Fox's reasons for resigning from the Ministry were, according to a letter he wrote to Lord Ossory, very complicated, but he goes on to state definitely: " I should not have resigned at this moment merely on account of my complaints against Lord North, if I had not determined to vote against this Royal Family Bill, which, in place, I should be ashamed to do.

Yet a contemporary newspaper sneered :

C[harles] F[ox] resembles a Pickpocket at a Fire, who makes a great Bustle and exclaims loudly against the Negligence of one Person who occasioned the misfortune and only watches for fit Opportunity to steal something.

Horace Walpole noted in his Journals that " Lord North and the Ministers were ridiculously alarmed, and so much terrified by the defection of Mr Fox and the disapprobation of others, that they obtained a modification of the Act, and brought it in the next day with an alteration, exempting Princes from positive prohibition of marriage after twenty-five years of age, and enabling them, after leaving a declaration for a year before the Privy Council to marry, unless Parliament make an objection."

* *Life and Reign of George III* (Jesse).

Here is the text of the Royal Marriages Bill as it was presented by the Earl of Rochford to the House of Lords on February 21st 1772:

" An Act for the better regulating the future Marriages of the Royal Family.

" Most Gracious Sovereign,

Whereas your Majesty, from your paternal affection to your own family, and from your royal concern for the future welfare of your people, and the honour and dignity of your crown, was graciously pleased to recommend to your parliament to take it into their serious consideration whether it might not be wise and expedient to supply the defect of the laws now in being, and by some new provisions, more effectually to guard the descendants of his late Majesty, King George the 2nd (other than the issue of princesses who have married, or may hereafter marry into foreign families) from marrying without the approbation of your Majesty, your heirs or successors, first had and obtained:

" We have taken this weighty matter into our serious consideration, and being sensible that marriages in the royal family are of the highest importance to the state, and that therefore the kings of this realm have ever been entrusted with the care and approbation thereof; and being thoroughly convinced of the wisdom and expediency of what your Majesty has thought fit to recommend upon this occasion:

" We, your Majesty's most dutiful and loyal subjects, the Lords spiritual and temporal, and Commons in this present parliament assembled, do humbly beseech your Majesty that it may be enacted; and be it enacted by the King's most excellent Majesty, by and with the advice and consent of the Lords spiritual and temporal and Commons, in this present parliament assembled, and by the authority of the same, that no descendant of the body of his late Majesty King George the second, being the grandchildren and presumptive heirs of the reigning king, male and female (other than the issue of princesses who have married, or may hereafter marry, into foreign families) shall be capable of contracting matrimony, without previous consent of his Majesty, his heirs or successors, signified under his or their seal manual, and declared in council (which consent, the better to preserve the memory thereof, is hereby directed to be set out in the licence and register of marriage, and to be entered in the books of the privy council) and that every marriage or matrimonial contract, of any such descendant, without such consent first had and obtained, shall be null and void, to all intents and purposes whatsoever.

" Provided always, and be it enacted by the authority aforesaid, that in any case such descendant of the body of his late majesty King George the second, being above the age of 25 years, shall persist in his or her resolution, to contract a marriage, disapproved of, or dissented from by the King, his heirs or successors, that then such descendants, upon giving notice to the King's privy council, which notice is hereby directed to be entered in the books thereof, may at any time, from the expiration of twelve calendar months after such notice given to the privy council aforesaid, contract such marriage : and his or her marriage, with the person before proposed and rejected, may be duly solemnised, and shall be good, without the previous consent of his Majesty, his heirs or successors, as if this Act had never been made, unless both Houses of Parliament shall, before the expiration of twelve months, expressly declare their disapprobation of such intended marriage.

" And be it further enacted by the authority aforesaid, that every person who shall knowingly or wilfully, presume to solemnise, or to assist, or be present at, the celebration of any marriage with any such descendant, or at his, or her, making any matrimonial contract, without such consent as aforesaid, first had and obtained, except in the cases above-mentioned ; shall be duly convicted thereof, incur and suffer the pains and penalties ordained and provided for by the statute of provisions and praemunire, made in the sixteenth year of the reign of Richard the second."

On February 26th, the Bill was read a second time in the Lords, and debates centred round questions to the Judges whether the King *was* entrusted by law with the care and approbation of the marriage of the descendants of his late Majesty King George II, other than his present Majesty's own children. Such procedure slow as a procession of indeterminate clouds did not please the King who wrote from Queen's House, the embryo of Buckingham Palace :

Lord North—I cannot say the management of the Debate in the House of Lords has edified me. I hope there will be a meeting to-morrow to settle the mode of proceeding on Friday.

The next day he sent another stinger to Lord North :

Your having seen Lord Mansfield will I hope enable you to give good advice to the Lords this evening for the management of to-morrow's Debate.

On Friday February 28th the Judges, Mr Baron Smythe speaking, delivered an unanimous opinion that the care and approbation of the King's children and grandchildren, and of the presumptive heir to the Crown, do belong to this realm ; but they were unable to find precisely determined to what other branches of the Royal Family such care and approbation extended. Then the House went into Committee to debate whether more questions should be put to the Judges ; but, to the advantage of their reputation and dignity, what Fox called " the glorious uncertainty of the law " was by vote of the House not further tested.

It was on Monday March 2nd that the first enacting Clause of the Bill was read to the House in Committee.

The Marquis of Rockingham lamented the precipitation with which this Bill was driven on. He thought it went too far in giving the King the care and approbation of marriage over all the descendants of George II. In an eloquent but perhaps exaggerated estimate of Royal fertility, he thought those descendants might amount to many thousands.

The Lord Chancellor,* who had had a share in drawing the Bill, was prepared to defend every clause, every sentence, every syllable, and every letter in it. He would accept no amendment from the noble Marquis who had just spoken or from any other noble Lord. If any inconvenience arose from this Bill Parliament would take care to remedy it a hundred years hence. He agreed that all power might be abused, but it was better to risk that than not to give power. " It is not against religion to annul marriages, for you have done so in the Marriage Act and in the Act for preventing lunatics from marrying. The Royal Family are not in those Acts, and therefore this Bill ought to pass." And with a refreshing credulity which recalls the Age of Faith, the Lord Chancellor concluded, " the King cannot make a bad use of this power, because Parliament would punish any minister who advised the King ill."

" The Episcopal Bench," says Sir G. O. Trevelyan in *The*

* Lord Thurlow.

Early History of Charles James Fox, " supplied a casuist who had the nerve to descant volubly and minutely upon those features in the controversy which such laymen as Sandwich and Weymouth avoided as indelicate." The Bishop of Oxford had feared for the moral danger of preventing members of the Royal Family marrying from inclination; but Warburton, the Bishop of Gloucester, suggested they could enjoy themselves without marriage. Now that he had the Bishop's sanction, said a noble Earl, he would drive with his chariot and liveries to places whither he had hitherto been in the habit of going incognito.

Lord Camden, being ill of the gout like so many noble lords, could not stay long in the House and could not fight the Bill inch by inch and therefore begged leave to state the whole of his objections then. He admitted the necessity of the Bill to guard the King's honour against misalliances; he recognised that all things were essential to Kings and that even their very robes and ornaments were not ceremonies. But the " descendants of George II " created too extensive a line. The Royal blood was the reverse of a great river. It was one great source at first, but the farther it went the more it spread itself until at last it was divided into an infinity of parts. It would be dreadful if the powers of wardship should extend so far: he knew a man that had the blood royal of England in his veins that was an alehouse keeper. If the Bill was restrained to his Majesty's life he would have consented to ten times as much as was now required, but other kings might be bad men and Parliament could never do otherwise than agree with a king on such an occasion. To differ with him would be such an affront to a king that if he was in Parliament at such a time he would rather agree to what he did not like than put such an affront. " Lay all other restraints and terrors on the royal marriage; make it necessary to have the banns published in St James's Chapel; lay heavy penalties on the offending party; banish him forever from Court; incapacitate him if you will from ever sitting in Parliament but do not annul a marriage between persons of age."

However, Lord Rockingham's amendment was rejected, and on the following day, Tuesday March 3rd, the Bill was passed in the House of Lords after a long debate by ninety votes to twenty-six.

Fourteen of the dissentient lords, headed by the Earl of Radnor, signed a protest of great length and force in the journals of the House, and six other dissentient lords signed another. In *The Parliamentary History* printed by Hansard in 1803, the final clause of the Radnor protest reads as follows:

> And because the Bill is essentially wanting in its avowed purpose, in having provided no guard against the greater evil, the improper marriages of the princes on the throne.

In the *Annual Register* of 1772, the final clause of the Radnor protest is amplified:

> Notwithstanding the harshness and cruelty of the Bill, it is in several instances extremely defective in providing for its own purpose, but essentially so in its having provided no remedy, at any age, against the improvident marriage of the King reigning, the marriage of all others the most important for the public.

This last contention bears reiteration, and it is commended to the notice of the former Solicitor-General for Australia, Sir Robert Garran, who, on December 4th 1936, declared that the Royal Marriages Act " was passed at the instance of George III, who had a quarrel with his brothers for marrying subjects: and its wording as it does, requiring the consent of the King, may at first sight be thought not to refer to the marriage of the King himself. But the King is a descendant of George II, and thus clearly within the terms of the Act : and the consent required is not merely the personal consent of the King, but his consent signified under the Great Seal, and declared in Council."

With that opinion Sir Robert Garran misled a continent, and a continent that was one of his Majesty's Dominions.

Queen Victoria was herself preoccupied with the Royal Marriages Act in 1838 when she and Lord Melbourne were manœuvring for position in the matter of dealing with her own marriage, that marriage over which he and she outwitted one another in the end. In the Journal of October 6th 1838 we read:

> I asked the Chancellor if *any one* of the Royal Family when of age could marry anybody without my leave? He replied " *Certainly not.*" I turned to Lord Melbourne and told him he was quite right. Spoke of it being rather severe. I said fortunately there was no law which gave the Sovereign the power to *make* any of them *marry by force.* Lord M. said there was no such power ; though people often forced their daughters to marry, by their influence, and he knew

many girls would obey, if their Parents told them it was for their best and for their happiness. Said I liked best to judge for oneself in such matters.

The next day, Wednesday March 4th, the Bill was brought down from the Lords by Lord Chief Baron Parker and Mr Baron Smythe, when the Opposition tried to hold matters up by moving that the Bill should be printed, which, after a debate, was lost. On Monday March 9th it was ordered for a second reading. No strangers were admitted to the House of Commons, and though several peers applied to be admitted to the Gallery, the door was kept locked. The debate was long and violent, and every kind of argument was brought up by the Opposition in criticism of the " cruelty, the tyranny and the injustice of this unconnected, inconsistent Bill." At half-past one in the morning, Sir William Meredith moved that, as several members had retired from fatigue, the House should adjourn, but the adjournment was negatived.

Colonel Isaac Barré then rose to speak. The Colonel was the member for Chipping Wycombe, a son of a French refugee from Rochelle who had settled in Dublin and prospered as a merchant. He had graduated at Trinity College, had served with Wolfe in Canada, and had been at the hero's side when he fell at Quebec. As an Opposition orator his invective dismayed the Government. The King hated him next to Wilkes and steadily obstructed his promotion in the Army. His figure was massive and swarthy, and a bullet, lodged loosely in his cheek, had given ' a savage glare to his eyes '.

The Colonel seemed less sure than the Lord Chancellor of Parliament's willingness to punish ministers. " The spirit of administration and the ductility of this House have for some years been as such," he said, " that I should not be surprised to see the majority of the House, if ordered by a certain noble personage whom I have in my eye, attempt to come hither upon their heads," and we can fancy the way that savage glare was directed against Lord North. It is cause for deep regret that there was no loose bullet in the cheek of any honourable members in December 1936.

After making Lord North squirm for a few more phrases, the honourable and gallant member continued, " I therefore congratulate the abettors of the Bill upon the prospect of the fine harvest which lies before them. The Crown will certainly show its gratitude for so great an accession of prerogative.

What though this violent Act tears away the brightest jewel in his Majesty's diadem, the affection of the people, and in its place substitutes fear and jealousy? Such a consideration is in these days of no moment. ' Oderint dum metuant ' seems now to be the favourite maxim inculcated by those whom the king delighteth to honour. Having sapped the foundations of the Constitution, having in their own opinion imposed the yoke, and riveted the chains of the people, they would, in order to make everything sure and solid, reduce every branch, every individual of the Royal Family to the same abject state of servitude. . . .

" But is this plan calculated for making the royal line entirely subservient and obsequious to the sovereign, and for producing that despotic calm, at which they aim? On the contrary, it will prove the source of endless dissentions and quarrels as well among the Royal Family as among the people. Do you imagine that any man arrived at the age of maturity, much less a spirited young prince, will submit with patience to the loss of his rights as a man, to that power enjoyed by the meanest subject, to the right of disposing of himself in marriage, when he has arrived at the legal age of maturity, at the common years of discretion, which entitle all but idiots and lunatics to chuse a helpmate for them, as their own fancy directs. Is it the intention of this Bill to make us insinuate that our Royal Family are but idiots or lunatics? . . .

" Sir, you need not smile. Princes, like other mortals, must be rocked in their cradles, and have their rattles and hobby horses. However much deified upon the throne, they were once but boys. I wish they did not frequently continue so, and prove themselves not only less than men, but more mischievous than unlucky boys. Had this Bill been calculated for confining their freaks and sallies within bounds, its object would be rational because, as the influence of the Crown is now so much extended, they are of all others most to be dreaded. You may give them what epithets you please ; you may call them God's vice-regents and vicars-general upon earth. Names will not alter the nature of things. They will not prove less tyrannical and despotic. Nay, the higher you exalt them, the more they will trample upon their subjects. When this is the state of the case, why should I wonder that you have chosen this dark and midnight hour for so black and atrocious a deed? This is the murderous season of the night, and you have with propriety pitched upon it, for giving a vital stab to liberty, and for effecting a purpose much more hellish than gunpowder-treason. Kings, Lords and Commons may soon be replaced, all blown up in the air; but a lost Constitution who can restore? Men are the offspring of a single generation; but a system of wise laws is the work of ages."

It was three o'clock when the Colonel sat down; but the Ministry still resisted a division, and in the end the Opposition walked out. Good fortune once upon a time allowed the present writer to inhabit a little house in Westminster, to which on such arduous occasions Lord North was wont to retire and enjoy the company and refreshment of a discreet housekeeper. The little house has been pulled down now to make way for a pallid elephantiasis of heaven-affronting offices, and gone is that lovely ceiling from which plaster plaques of Pope, Handel, Garrick and Reynolds representing the four arts, would have looked down upon the Prime Minister when he wrote his account of that long and violent debate before he sent it round to his Majesty across St James's Park in the darkness of that March morning.

The King replied at 8 o'clock a.m. from the Queen's House:

Lord North—Nothing can be more pleasant than Your Account of the Debate. I am desirous of knowing more of it, therefore I wish You would call here at any time that suits You this Evening.

" Lord North," commented a current newspaper, " is like a School-Boy who has had a hard Task imposed upon him. Though he continually counts his Lesson he cannot get it by Heart; he is in continual Dread of black Monday, and to prevent the Lash heartily wishes his Master would rusticate him."

Lord Baldwin too ever sighed for rustication.

Later on that day (March 11th), the House went into Committee and debated until midnight. The most remarkable speech was made by Lord Folkestone, son of Lord Radnor whose name had headed the protest of the dissentient Lords. It was a speech worthy of the Liberalism of that great family of Pleydell-Bouverie, whose motto was *Patria cara, carior libertas.*

" Mr Speaker, I cannot possibly give my assent to this motion, nor can I content myself with giving a silent negative. The question seems to be simply this, whether we shall enter upon the alteration and improvement of a Bill, which, in my opinion, cannot be so altered, that it ought to pass. It is built upon such false principles, and contains so many exceptionable positions, that I think it ought to be immediately rejected. It is introduced with a preamble highly inadmissible, a preamble which claims a new, unheard of prerogative, a right to the care and approbation of the marriages of the Royal Family as ancient and acknowledged. A claim, Sir, founded on the Opinion of the Judges in 1717, which, I beg leave to say, is a very bad foundation, because it was extra-judicial at the time when it was given, and is unsupported by the authority of the present Judges. After the free, and, I think, deserved criticisms, that have been made upon this *grand opinion*, as it is called, it will not, I hope, appear presumptuous in me to express my doubts of its authority ; and I shall do so, for this simple reason, because I conceive a right without a remedy, which, in this instance, if it means anything, must mean a right of directing a marriage without means of forcing a compliance ; a right of prohibiting a marriage without means of punishing disobedience, is, in law, as in common sense, a non-existent ; and that there is no such remedy I infer, because the Judges who gave this opinion, as well as those who have defended their claim here, have produced no one positive proof of it, and those oblique ones which they have produced may all be reduced to one or other of these causes : either an apprehension of imprisonment, which, however illegal, the crown formerly exercised at pleasure, or the vanity of having the king a party to their marriage settlement. I infer it likewise from the conduct of ministers upon this present occasion ; the marriage of the Duke of Cumberland, who, if there be such a prerogative as is contended, must out of mere consistency have it enforced against him, since it is thought so flagrant as to occasion this Bill. . . .

" Sir, if we compare the notorious occasion of introducing this Bill . . . with another part of the preamble, we shall find a doctrine, which I cannot help thinking the representative of the people, that people, whom I think obliquely insulted by the words, will unitedly oppose, we shall find it is the opinion of the minister speaking in His Majesty's message, that an alliance of a subject with a branch of the Royal Family is dishonourable to the Crown. Sir, I will speak to that point presently, but I must say a few words as to the partiality that has introduced this Bill. Sir, report says that the King's other brother is married to a private person, and if it describes her rightly, to one more exceptionable, in point of birth, than the Duchess of Cumberland. The point I allude to is so evident, that as I would not wantonly offend anyone, I purposely omit it. . . ."

We must interrupt Lord Folkestone's admirable speech to explain this allusion, which was to the reputed marriage of the King's second brother the Duke of Gloucester to the Dowager Lady Waldegrave. This had taken place as long ago as 1766 when the Duke was twenty-three. It was common gossip:

> Whole groups were attentive while Lane talked so clever,
> And Waldegrave's fair widow looked buxom as ever;
> Full many a lover who longed to accost her,
> Was kept at a distance by Humphrey of Gloster.

But although no doubt the King had strong suspicions, his brother did not make suspicion certainty until his wife's pregnancy in the summer of the year 1772 made it imperative to make a formal announcement to the King in December.

The lady in question was the widow of Lord Waldegrave whom she had married in 1759 when she was twenty-four and he was " as old again as she, and of no agreeable figure; but for character and credit the first match in England." He had been one of George III's governors in his minority and the principal influence against the ideas of his mother and Lord Bute. Lady Waldegrave gave her husband three daughters and, since the death of Lady Coventry, was " allowed the handsomest woman in England." " She was the favourite sitter of Sir Joshua Reynolds, by whom her portrait was seven times eagerly and carefully painted in every stage of her beauty; and when in our time, the papers of the great artist were brought to light, a lock of golden brown hair, marked as hers, was discovered in a recess of his pocket-book." Her character was not less beautiful.

She was one of the four natural daughters of Sir Edward Walpole (Horace's brother) and Mrs Clements, a Durham milliner, and when she married the Duke of Gloucester, was thirty-one years old. The letter which she wrote to her father when her pregnancy made further concealment impossible deserves to be rescued from dusty book-shelves:

St Leonards, 19 May, 1772.

My Dear and ever Honoured Sir,

You cannot easily imagine how much every past affliction
has been increased to me by my not being at liberty to make
you quite easy. The duty to a husband being superior to
that we owe a father I hope will plead my pardon, and that
instead of blaming my past reserve, you will think it com-
mendable. When the Duke of Gloucester married me
(which was in September 1766) I promised him, upon no
consideration in the world to own it, *even to you*, without his
permission, which permission I never had till yesterday,
when he arrived here in much better health and looks—
better than I ever saw him—yet, as you may suppose,
much hurt by all that passed in his absence ; so much so that
I have had great difficulty to prevail on him to let things as
much as possible remain as they are. To secure my
character, without injuring his, is the utmost of my wishes,
and I dare say that you and all my relations will agree with
me that I shall be much happier to be called Lady Waldegrave and respected as the Duchess of Gloucester than to
feel myself the cause of his leading such a life as his brother
the Duke of Cumberland does, in order for me to be called
your royal highness. I am prepared for the sort of abuse
the newspapers will be full of. Very few will believe that
a woman will refuse to be called princess if it is in her
power.

To have the power is my pride, and not using it in some
measure pays the debt I owe the Duke for the honour he
has done me. All that I wish of my relations is that they
will show the world that they are satisfied with my conduct,
yet *seem* to disguise the reason. If ever I am unfortunate
enough to be called Duchess of Gloucester there is an end of
almost all the comforts which I now enjoy, which if things
go on as they are, *are many*.

Sir Edward sent this letter to his brother Horace, whose
social caution had kept him on tenterhooks during the rumours
of the marriage, to the malicious delight of his friends. Two
years before Gilly Williams was writing to George Selwyn :
"*The Duke of Gloucester has professed a passion for the Dowager
Waldegrave. He is never from her elbow. This flatters Horry
Walpole not a little, though he pretends to dislike it.*"

Horace now declared this letter of his niece was a better letter than any he had written or could write. It could be wished that the social caution of to-day might be shamed as easily by an attitude of mind which shamed even the social caution of Horry Walpole once upon a time.

Although the announcement of the " highly disgraceful step " kept the King awake several nights at the notion of being defeated by the pride and vanity of this unwelcome sister-in-law, in a few years' time he had sufficiently recovered from the marriage to give his own daughter Princess Mary in marriage to that royal changeling born in 1773, and moreover to give advice about the education of their daughter, the Princess Sophia of Gloucester, for whom he recommended as governess a Miss Dee of Taplow. In spite of what should have been the kindly link of two clandestine marriages, it is recorded that the royal brothers and their duchesses were on the worst of terms, " the Cumberlands circulating stories about the Gloucesters."

And now we must listen to a few more extracts from that great speech of Lord Folkestone's :

" I assert that the interests of posterity are evidently neglected by this Bill, and it is with peculiar pleasure I quote in support of this assertion the authority of two of those ten Judges, who concurred throughout the year 1717, and whom I produce on this principle only, that the favourable testimony of an opponent is most favourable. Judge Powys says, ' the education of a prince concerns the public much more than his marriage, which concerns private life only,' and Mr Baron Fortescue, the reporter himself, says ' an ill chosen match will be most to the prince that marries, and will little affect the State, so long as the prince is steady and adheres to the Constitution. . . .' "

Lord Folkestone continued : " The other parts of the Bill are little less questionable. It gives a discretionary power to the king for the time being, of approving or disapproving all, or any of the marriages that may be proposed by all, or any of the royal family, till 25 years of age absolutely, so that the king is not only declared by this Bill fully able, wise and sufficient at eighteen to chuse a proper marriage for himself when the inconveniences of an improper one must be doubly inconvenient, but is authorised to put an uncontroulable negative upon any or all of the marriages proposed by any, or all of the royal Family till 25, the inconveniences of whose improper marriage must be comparatively trifling and insignificant. I would speak as delicately as possible, but I will not limit myself, when I think delicacy will be prejudicial. The partiality of the present reigning family against the heir-apparent has been notorious; it is beyond denial certain. But if it were not, it is a very supposable case, and as such I take it. Let us then suppose some future king takes exception to his eldest son, whether upon good or bad reasons is immaterial, in consequence of this he prevents his marriage. He has a second or third son, who is a favourite, and he consents to his marriage; this younger son has children, who stand in a great probability of succeeding to the Crown, on account of the restraint upon the Prince of Wales. I shall be told this restraint lasts, only till 25; I wish it may then cease. The power of restraining is then transferred to the Parliament. Now, not to speak disrespectfully, or even suppose the ductility of modern Parliaments; figure to yourself, Sir, some future one under the influence of the Crown, and to give my argument greater scope, let it not be unconstitutional influence, but such as arises from a series of popular acts, by which we will suppose he has ingratiated himself with his subjects, indeed so much as to be, I will say, improperly beloved by them. Will a Parliament at such a time, if at any, fail to disapprove of a choice known to be disapproved of by the sovereign, and which by the direction of this Bill, cannot but be known to be so?"

What Lord Folkestone's remarkable vision of the future failed to embrace was a Parliament so ductile to a Prime Minister as to deny itself even the courage of affirming by a vote its objection to the marriage of a future king, a Parliament as ductile, indeed, as a row of scrawny chickens with their beaks pressed to the chalk line of Mr Baldwin's rustic eloquence.

Said that current newspaper from which we have quoted: "Lord Folkestone is a Dealer in old Rags and forgotten Remnants, the Revolution and the Rights of the Subject."

If they were rags and remnants in 1772 they are now in 1938 scarcely as substantial as frayed ends of cotton.

Yet, in spite of every effort of oratory, which included some fierce and brilliant speeches by Fox, in one of which he asked if the dignity of the Crown depended upon the marriages of the Royal Family, the Bill was passed. At the last moment, an attempt was made to restrict it to the reign of George III, and this amendment was defeated by a narrow majority of eighteen, which might have been no more than six if twelve minority voters had not been locked out. The King was delighted. At 6 p.m. on March 24th, he wrote:

Lord North—the finding you have so early this day finished the Royal Marriages Bill gives so much satisfaction, and I shall at all times with pleasure reflect the Spirit and Zeal you have shown in conducting it through the different stages.

Other people were less pleased. On March 24th the leader of the *Public Advertiser* ran as follows:

. . . Mr Sawbridge in particular said it was "a Bill to gratify the 'Rancour of a Monster,' and the Malice of a 'Man.'" No gentleman in the administration defended the Bill, but trusted to the Book of Numbers. . . . Sir Joseph Mawbey moved to correct the titles of the Act, and to make it co-extensive with its contents by adding these words "AN ACT FOR ENLARGING AND EXTENDING THE PRE-ROGATIVE OF THE CROWN, AND FOR THE ENCOURAGEMENT OF ADULTERY AND FORNICATION, UNDER THE PRETENCE OF" regulating the marriages of the Royal Family; but this was objected to and the later words continue to form the title.

The Royal Marriage Bill has now passed our most faithful Commons, in unlimited Extent it was drawn by Lord Mansfield, so that every Descendant of our now more-than-ever-to-be-lamented Sovereign George the Second is in Vassalage and Slavery and the kings of this limited Monarchy are erected into Family Tyrants, to trample upon the laws of Nature and Religion. One Resource of comfort still remains—the Reflexion that the arbitrary acts of a despotic House were all repealed by his beneficent son King Edward VI.

The Royal Marriage Bill has been passed to the Expence of two British Baronies, five Irish ditto, one Advancement from ditto to an Irish Earldom, one Blue Ribbon, three Red ones, the Baronetage, three Reversionary Patent Places, Twenty Five Thousand Pounds in occasional Gratuities, besides innumerable promises of Lottery Tickets. In so very interesting and constitutional a Light is this Bill seen by our worthy representatives.

But the Town had the last word and wrote its own epitaph on the Bill:

> Quoth Dick to Tom, "This Act appears
>   Absurd as I'm alive:
> To take the Crown at eighteen years
>   The wife at twenty-five,
> The mystery how shall we explain,
>   For sure as Dowdeswell said,
> 'Thus early if they're fit to reign,
>   They must be fit to wed?'"
> Quoth Tom to Dick, "Thou art a fool,
>   And little knowest of life,
> Alas! 'tis easier far to rule
>   A kingdom than a wife."

CHAPTER XVI

A ROYAL FAMILY

I.

The Prince of Wales, afterwards George IV

THE moral glory of George III has ever been considered the perfection of his domestic life with Queen Charlotte and the fifteen princes and princesses they brought into the world. It is time that an imaginative historian examined very closely the foundations on which that legend has been erected, for it is straining a reasonable assent to axioms like the influence of heredity, the benefit of judicious education, and the power of pious example when we discover that of the thirteen children who reached full maturity only one managed to achieve an unexceptionable domestic happiness for himself or even to offer a specious appearance of it to others. Probability demands that the blame should be justly apportioned between parents and children. Virtue, as Hamlet told Ophelia, could not so inoculate their old stock, but they should relish of it. We can no longer accept even those notorious uncles of Queen Victoria as sinning more than they were sinned against. In spite of such ardent witnesses to the perfection of that domestic interior as Madame D'Arblay, Mrs Delany, and Mrs Pependiek, in spite of the carefully disseminated eulogistic gossip of the Court ladies and royal governesses, the historian capable of examining it with the revolutionary curiosity of a Freud and the crystallising acumen of a Stendhal may discover that it was but a stage setting of which the backcloth was a view of the terrace at Windsor and the audience an assembly of credulous burghers watching the daily scene of the Royal Family jigging before it like marionettes. Old Mrs Delany, when staying with the Dowager Duchess of Portland at Bulstrode Park, wrote on the 12th of August 1778 :

> The royal family, ten in all, came at 12 o'clock. The king drove the queen in an open chaise. The Prince of Wales and Prince Frederick rode on horseback all with proper attendants, but no guards. Princess Royal and Lady Weymouth in a post-chaise ; Princess Augusta, Princess Elizabeth, Prince Adolphus, about seven years old, and Lady Charlotte Finch in a coach ; Prince William, Prince Edward, Duke of Montagu and Bishop of Lichfield,

in a coach; another coach full of attendant gentlemen.   These, with
all their attendants in rank and file, made a splendid figure as they
drove through the park and round the court, up to the house.   The
day was as brilliant as could be wished, the 12th of August, the Prince
of Wales's birthday.   The queen was in a hat, and an Italian night-
gown of purple lutestring, trimmed with silver gauze.   She is grace-
ful and genteel.   The dignity and sweetness of her manner, the perfect
propriety of every thing she says or does, satisfies everybody she honours
with her distinction, so much, that beauty is by no means wanting to
make her perfectly agreeable, and though age, and long retirement
from court, made me feel timid on my being called to make my
appearance, I soon found myself perfectly at ease; for the king's
condescension and good humour took off all awe but what one must
have for so respectable a character, severely tried by his enemies at
home, as well as abroad. . .

It seems sacrilegious, nay blasphemous, to declare the
faintest scepticism in the presence of such devout raptures.

Breakfast was offered; all prepared in a long gallery, that runs the
length of the great apartments, a suite of eight rooms and three
closets.   The king and all his royal children, and the rest of the train,
chose to go to the gallery, where the well-furnished tables were set;
one with tea, coffee, and chocolate; another with their proper accom-
paniments of eatables, rolls, cakes etc; another table with fruits and
ices in the utmost perfection, which with a magical touch had succeeded a cold repast.   The queen remained in the drawing-room.   I
stood at the back of her chair, which, happening to be one of my
working, gave the queen an opportunity of saying many flattering and
obliging things.   The Duchess Dowager of Portland brought her
majesty a dish of tea on a waiter, with biscuits, which was what she
chose.   After she had drunk her tea, she would not return the cup to
the duchess, but got up and would carry it into the gallery herself, and
was much pleased to see with what elegance everything was prepared.
No servants but those out of livery made their appearance. . . .
I said I was particularly happy at that time to pay my duty to her
majesty, as it gave me an opportunity of seeing so many of the royal
family, which age and obscurity had deprived me of.   " Oh ! but,"
said her majesty, " you have not seen *all* my children yet."   Upon
which the king came up and asked what we were talking about, which
was repeated, when the king said to the queen—" You may put Mrs
Delany into the way of doing that, by naming a day for her to drink
tea at Windsor Castle.". .

The Duchess of Portland and Mrs Delany were in such haste
to accept this gracious invitation that they went the very next
evening, reaching Windsor at seven.

At eight the king came into the room with so much cheerfulness and
good humour, that it is impossible to feel any painful restriction.   It

was the hour of the king and queen, and eleven of the Princes and Princesses, walking on the terrace.   They apologised for going, but said the crowd expected them but they left Lady Weymouth and the Bishop of Lichfield to entertain us in their absence.   We sat in the bay-window, well pleased with our companions, and the brilliant show on the terrace, on which we looked; the band of music playing all the time under the window. . .

These scenes of domestic bliss are recurrent in the letters and journals of the time and, as we study the life of this royal vivarium, we gradually apprehend that the falsification or human emotion we had always attributed to Queen Victoria's influence had started fifty years before Queen Victoria was born.

Here, for instance, is the way the new Georgianism could handle Dr Cornwallis, the Archbishop of Canterbury:

MY GOOD LORD PRELATE,
        I could not delay giving you the notification of the grief and concern with which my breast was affected at receiving authentic information that *routs* made their way into your Palace.   At the same time, I must signify to you my sentiments on this subject, which hold those levities and vain dissipations as utterly inexpedient, if not unlawful, to pass in a residence for many centuries devoted to divine studies, religious retirement, and the extensive exercise of charity and benevolence.   I add, in a place where so many of your predecessors have led their lives in such sanctity as has thrown lustre on the pure religion they professed and adorned.

From the dissatisfaction with which you must perceive I hold these improprieties—not to speak in harsher terms— and on still more pious principles, I trust you will suppress them immediately, so that I may not have occasion to show any further marks of my displeasure, or to interpose in a different manner.

May God take your Grace into his Almighty protection,
I remain, my Lord Primate,
Your gracious friend,
G.R.

In fairness to the present Archbishop of Canterbury readers must be informed that it was not his predecessor's own craving for private happiness but his gay wife's love of pleasure which provoked a scandal celibacy would doubtless have avoided, and caused his friends to stand rebuked.   There is fortunately no evidence that Archbishop Cornwallis ever disgraced the episcopal violet by treading a minuet at Lambeth.

It was on the fourth of June 1781 that George Selwyn noted how " one coach came by after another, each stuffed with royal children, like a cornucopia with fruit and flowers." And we who have been so long accustomed to reading of George III's tragic disillusionment over the behaviour of his children when fledged and flown from the august rookery, have taken it as much for granted as everybody took King Lear's tragic disillusionment for granted until Tolstoi drove a critical troika through that tragedy and demonstrated how completely King Lear deserved all that happened to him.   The many examples of selfish behaviour which preceded that tragic disillusionment are, except for the major folly of the Royal Marriages Act, beyond the scope of his book.

The first effect of the Act would be on the heir apparent. In 1783 the Prince of Wales came of age, and the Rockingham Ministry, which included Charles James Fox, proposed to vote him £100,000 a year on the Civil List.   This at once aroused the hostility not only of a king to an heir apparent but also of a father who was morbidly enjoying the dependence of all his children upon himself.   He could not forgo the indulgence of his patriarchal greed ; and greed it certainly was, for the fifteenth of his children was born in this very year, and he could look forward to at least another twenty-five years' tyranny over grown-up daughters if not over sons.   So George III opposed the grant of £100,000 a year to the Prince of Wales and offered to provide £50,000 himself, thus repeating to the very sum George II's behaviour to his own father, poor Frederick.   Naturally, there were plenty to trade on the Prince's expectations ; and, although it might be rash to surmise that he would have kept clear of debt, the first impetus to run into debt was provided by a paternal self-indulgence which was presented to his subjects as a piece of patriotic altruism.   The long struggle between George III and his eldest son had begun ; and marriage as usual was considered by the rest of the world to be an easy solution of all difficulties.

In May 1785 Lord Malmesbury invited the Prince to consider this solution as one that would be welcomed by his friends, who were now in Opposition and most anxious to help him out of his financial loss. Here is the very conversation as it was recorded in Lord Malmesbury's Diaries:

Lord Malmesbury May I suggest, Sir, the idea of your marrying? It would, I should think, be most agreeable to the King; and, I am certain, most grateful to the nation.

The Prince (with vehemence) I never will marry! My resolution is taken on the subject. I have settled it with Frederick. No! I will never marry.

Lord Malmesbury Give me leave, Sir, to say most respectfully that you cannot have really come to such a resolution. You *must* marry, Sir. You owe it to the country, to the King, to yourself.

The Prince I owe nothing to the King. Frederick will marry, and the Crown will descend to his children; and, as for myself, I do not see how it affects me.

Lord Malmesbury Till you are married, Sir, and have children, you have no solid hold on the affections of the people, even while you are Prince of Wales. But if you come to the throne a bachelor, and his royal highness the Duke of York is married, and has sons to succeed you, your situation when King will be more painful than it is at this moment. Our own history furnishes strong examples of the truth of what I say.

Was this vehemence of the young Prince the vehemence of a devoted celibate? On the contrary, it was the vehemence of a young man who had fallen in love with the only woman he would ever love truly throughout all the splendour and misery of his twisted life. Mrs Fitzherbert was the youngest daughter of a Catholic squire in Hampshire, Walter Smythe. She had been married at nineteen, first to Edward Weld of Lulworth and after his death to Thomas Fitzherbert of Swynnerton, being left a widow for the second time in 1781 with a jointure of £2000 a year. Since then after a sojourn abroad she had been living in a delicious house on Richmond Hill where in the summer of 1784 the Prince met her and fell madly in love. She, connected by blood and marriage with many of the old Catholic families of England, was for a long time fearful of causing a grave scandal, and when we consider that materially she had everything to lose by the connection we need not hesitate to believe that she, now a woman of twenty-eight, fell deeply in love with the young prince. She refused a secret marriage, but at last succumbing to threats of suicide and scenes of painful emotion she was prevailed upon to give him her promise after he had actually wounded himself. This promise she took back, and in an attempt to escape from an unhappy and untenable situation withdrew to Holland to the despair of the Prince who proposed to follow her. This was forbidden by George III, who may or may not have understood the real reason of his son's desire to economise by living abroad for awhile. Mrs Fitzherbert remained abroad for a year, but finally surrendered to the Prince's importunity expressed in letters that ran to thirty or forty pages. On December 21st 1785 in her own drawing-room in Park Street they were married by a clergyman of the Church of England, in the presence of her brother and uncle.

By the Act of Settlement the marriage would have excluded the Prince of Wales from the throne because she was a Catholic, but by the Royal Marriages Act, the consent of the King not having been obtained, the marriage was legally null and void. Poor King George! If he had not forced that Act upon the legislature, he could have gratified a hatred of his eldest son, which began when the latter was a boy of seven, by seeing the throne pass to the Duke of York of whom he believed himself to be so fond.

Mrs Fitzherbert has been sneered at for having been supposed to say that the marriage was all nonsense and that she was becoming no more than the Prince's mistress; such sneers fail to appreciate the Catholic and sacramental view of marriage. While the gossip of the town was speculating whether or not she and the Prince were married, she regularly and openly attended to her religious duties, and it is a tribute to those hated Catholics dreaming of emancipation that even the gossip of the town accepted this fulfilment of her faith's obligations as evidence of her marriage. In the very month in which she was married, the Duke of Rutland was told that " H.R.H. had never been so sedate and rational." Some of the Prince's friends, however, had heard with dismay the rumour of the projected marriage, and Charles Fox, ten days before it was accomplished, wrote to remonstrate:

". . . I was told just before I left town yesterday that Mrs Fitzherbert was arrived, and if I had heard only this I should have felt most unfeigned joy at an event which I knew would contribute so much to Your Royal Highness's satisfaction; but I was told at the same time that from a variety of circumstances, which had been observed and put together, there was reason to suppose you were going to take the very desperate step (pardon the expression) of marrying her at this moment. If such an idea be really in

your mind, and it is not too late, for God's sake let me call
your attention to some considerations, which my attachment
to your Royal Highness, and the real concern that I take
in whatever relates to your interest, have suggested to me,
and which may possibly have the more weight with you when
you perceive that Mrs Fitzherbert is equally interested in
most of them with yourself.   In the first place, you are
aware that marriage with a Catholic throws the prince contracting such a marriage out of the succession of the crown.
If there be no doubt about her previous conversion, consider
the circumstances in which *you* stand : the King not feeling
for you as a father ought ; the Duke of York professedly
his favourite, and likely to be married to the King's wishes ;
the nation full of its old prejudices against Catholics, and
justly dreading all disputes about succession.   In all these
circumstances your enemies might take such advantages of
any doubts of this nature as I shudder to think of, and
though your generosity might think no sacrifice too great
to be made to a person whom you love so entirely, consider
what her reflections might be in such an event, and how
impossible it would be for her ever to forgive herself.   I
have stated this danger upon the supposition that the
marriage could be a real one, but your Royal Highness
knows as well as I that according to the present laws of the
country, it cannot, and I need not point out to your good
sense what a source of uneasiness it must be to you, to her,
and above all, to the nation, to have it a matter of dispute
and discussion whether the Prince of Wales is not married.
If there should be children from the marriage, I need not
say how much the uneasiness as well of yourselves as of the
nation must be exaggerated.   If anything could add to the
weight of these considerations, it is the impossibility of
remedying the mischiefs I have alluded to.   For, if your
Royal Highness should think proper, when you are twenty-
five years old, to notify to Parliament your intention to
marry (by which means alone a *legal* marriage can be
contracted), in what manner can it be notified ?   If the
previous marriage is notified or owned, will it not be said
that you have set at defiance the laws of your country, and
that you have now come to Parliament for a sanction to
what you have already done in contempt of it ?   If there are
children, will it not be said that we must look for future
applications to legitimate them, and consequently be liable

to disputes for the succession between the eldest son—and the eldest son after the legal marriage ? And will not the entire annulling of the whole marriage be suggested as the most secure way of preventing all disputes ? It will be said that a woman who has lived with you as your wife without being so, is not fit to be Queen of England : and thus the very thing that is done for the sake of her reputation will be used against it ; and what would make this worse would be that the marriage being known (though not officially communicated to Parliament) it would be impossible to deny the assertion. In the meantime, a mock marriage (for it can be no other) is neither honourable for any of the parties, nor, with respect to your Royal Highness, even safe. This appears so clear to me that, if I were Mrs Fitzherbert's father or brother, I would advise her not by any means to agree to it, *and to prefer any other species of connection with you to one leading to such misery and mischief.*

"It is high time I should finish this very long, and, perhaps your Highness will think, ill-timed letter ; but, such as it is, it is dictated by pure zeal and an attachment to your Royal Highness. With respect to Mrs Fitzherbert, she is a person with whom I have scarcely the honour of being acquainted, but I hear from everybody that her character is irreproachable, and her manners most amiable. Your Royal Highness knows too, that I have not in my mind the same objection to intermarriages with princes and subjects that many have.* But under the present circumstances, a marriage at present appears to me to be the most desperate measure that their worse enemies could have suggested."

To this letter the Prince replied from Carlton House at 2 o'clock in the morning of December 11th 1785 :

DEAR CHARLES,
          Your letter of last night afforded me more satisfaction than I can find words to express, as it is an additional proof to me, wh I assure you I did not want of yr having that true regard and affection for me wh it is not only ye wish but ye ambition of my life to merit. Make yourself easy, my dear friend ; believe me the world will now soon be convinced that there not only is, but never was any

* No doubt Fox had told the Prince about the way George III had behaved to his aunt Lady Sarah Lennox twenty years before.

ground for these reports, wh of late have been so male-volently circulated. I have not seen you since the apostacy of Eden.* I think it ought to have that same effect upon all our friends that it has upon me ; I mean the linking us closer to each other ; and I believe you will easily believe these to be my sentiments, for you are perfectly well acquainted with my ways of thinking upon these sort of subjects. When I say my ways of thinking, I think I had better say my old maxim, wh I ever intend to adhere to ; I mean that of swimming or sinking with my friends. I have not time to add much more, except just to say that I believe I shall meet you at dinner at Bushey on Thursday, and to desire you to believe me at all times, my dear Charles,

Most affectionately yours,
GEORGE P.

It is easy to blame the Prince of Wales for deceiving his best friend, but it is not less easy to recognise with charity the immensity of the problem by which the Prince was faced if he were to gratify his craving for private happiness without dishonouring the woman in whom it was enshrined.

Except for not giving up her religious duties, Mrs Fitz-herbert's own discretion was absolute ; but the consideration with which the Prince treated her in public and demanded that she should be treated confirmed the general opinion that there had been a marriage. Lord Lothian,† writing to the Duke of Rutland in March 1786, believed there had been a marriage and added he was very sorry for it " because it does infinite mischief, particularly among the trading and lower sort of people, and if true must ruin him in every light." So even in those days a tale of true love was bad for business.

But the Prince himself was happy. In his youth " his home had been unhappy, and his parents unsympathetic ; then he was thrown upon the town without any home life at all. But this beautiful and gracious woman, with her purity of purpose and unobtrusive goodness, made a home for him such as he had never known before. Though the Prince of Wales's public life belonged to the nation, his home life was his

---

* William Eden, afterwards first Baron Auckland, had just deserted the Whigs and accepted office under Pitt. By a curious anticipation of another of his name his work for the future was rather that of a diplomatist than of a statesman and he was employed on special missions in negotiating treaties on the Continent.

† This was the gentleman who as Lord Newbottle had helped to ruin Lady Sarah's chance of becoming Queen.

own.   He had the right to ask that it should be kept sacred, and none should grudge him the quiet hours he spent under the roof of the woman he loved, and who believed herself bound to him by the holiest ties.''

These words of W. H. Wilkins express with an imaginative lively charity a point of view about a man whom historians have vied with one another to abuse with little imagination and no charity.   They are commended to the attention of the present.

But in spite of private happiness, the bill for doing up Carlton House had to be paid, and in 1787 the Prince's friends moved in the House an appeal to his Majesty to relieve the Prince's financial distress.   It was a dangerous motion because the Whigs relied much on Nonconformist opinion, and Mrs Fitzherbert was only a little less obnoxious to Nonconformist opinion as a Papist mistress than she would have been as a Papist wife.   The Tories tried by dark threats to frighten the Opposition from persevering.   Mr Pitt was much concerned that, with infinite reluctance, he should be driven to the disclosure of circumstances which he would otherwise think it his duty to conceal.   This answer to Alderman Newnham who had introduced the motion caused a sensation in the House.   Several Whig members rose to deprecate the motion and urge the Prince's friends to withdraw.   Mr Fox was not in the House.   Mr Sheridan was.   He had written *The School for Scandal*, and he was not prepared for Mr Pitt to play Mr Snake.   He called his bluff, and when, later in the evening, the question was reopened, Mr Pitt made one of those equivocal disclaimers so familiar in the mouths of Prime Ministers.   The disclosure he might have thought it his duty to conceal referred merely to the pecuniary embarrassments of the Prince of Wales.   At the next debate Fox came to the House and gave a denial of the Prince's marriage so vehement, so explicit, and so defiant that people really did begin to believe there might never have been a marriage, and indeed it remained a subject of historical controversy until the publication of the documents connected with it in the early part of this century.

The King and Pitt, satisfied by this public repudiation of the marriage, came to financial terms with the Prince ; but he himself had the difficult task of winning the forgiveness of the woman who had sacrificed everything for him and who felt she should have been spared such public ignominy.   The Prince put all the blame on Fox, which caused a breach between them that lasted over a year and made his best friend abhorrent to the woman he loved.   In an endeavour to make amends, he asked Sheridan to say something in the House which would soften the denial of the marriage, an extremely delicate task which the great dramatist carried through in a speech that would have done credit to one of his own stage characters but did not satisfy Mrs Fitzherbert.   For some time, she refused to see the Prince, and once again he threatened suicide.   The town declared his behaviour was driving his father mad, but it was not observed that the madness of his father's behaviour might drive his son mad as well.   In the end, Mrs Fitzherbert, as she always did, forgave the Prince because she loved him.   Both the Cumberlands and the Gloucesters went out of their way to show their sympathy. So did many of the great Whig ladies.   So too did the great Catholic families.   The Archbishop of Canterbury thought it was all " very odd.   The lady is more received than ever she was and stands more forward."   But Archbishop Cornwallis was dead, and Archbishop Moore lacked a worldly, rout-loving wife to lighten the fog over Lambeth.   He was busy promoting the Sunday-School movement and " dispensing his patronage with somewhat more than due regard for the interests of his own family."

In 1788 the King went mad, and the Government prepared to oppose the Regency for the Prince of Wales.   Fox was abroad, but hurried back for the fray.   In spite of his denial of the marriage the rumour of its truth was still current.   No Popery was still the war-cry.   Pitt was called upon by addresses from towns all over the country to save them from the menace.   The Prime Minister knew that the more he could restrict the Prince's powers the more grateful it would be to popular opinion.

On February 7th 1789, when the Regency Bill was in Committee, the following Clause fell to be debated :

" Provided also, and be it enacted by the authority aforesaid, that if his said Royal Highness George Augustus Frederick *shall at any time marry a Papist* ; then, and in every case, all the powers and authorities vested in his said Royal Highness, by virtue of the Act shall cease and terminate."

To this Rolle, the bulldog Tory squire from Devon who had forced from Fox his denial of the Prince's marriage, rose to move as an amendment, to insert after the words *shall at any time marry a Papist*, the following : *or shall at any time be proved to be married, in fact, or in law, to a Papist.*

Fox had been forewarned of Rolle's intention to move this amendment and press him to repeat his denial of the marriage, and had deliberately kept away from the House.

Mr Rolle said : " That he meant nothing personal or disrespectful, nothing injurious to the feelings of any individual. He spoke from the regard he had to the principles of the Constitution which were the bulwarks of our freedom, and out of veneration for the House of Brunswick, and the wish to secure the Protestant succession in that House, because that succession would secure our liberties . . . if any person would step forward and confirm the declaration solemnly made by the right hon. gentleman [Mr Fox] in that House two years ago, he would be satisfied . . . but as doubts and scruples had nevertheless been still entertained without doors, he wished them to be effectually silenced, and that the question might be set at rest for ever."

Lord Belgrave attacked Mr Rolle for casting doubts on Fox's declaration that there was no truth in the report that " an indissoluble union had taken place with a very amiable and respectable character, whose religious opinions differed from the religious opinions of the Established Church of this country."

Mr Pitt could not accept the amendment and did not wish to advert to anything that had formerly passed in the House.

The Attorney-General said :

" The House could not legislate on rumours, and with regard to the particular rumour in question, he knew of nothing that could warrant him to believe it to have any foundation."

For the information of the Committee the clause of the Royal Marriages Act (12 George III) was read.   The clause provides that, previous to the marriage of the descendants of George II taking place *lawfully*, His Majesty's (George III) consent to such a marriage must be obtained, and signified under his own sign manual, which consent must have the sanction of the Great Seal, and that all marriages contracted without the royal consent being so formally signified, were declared to be *null and void*, and of no effect whatever.

But Mr Rolle was not to be intimidated by the Attorney-General's exposition of the law.   He had heard it to be the opinion of some of the first lawyers in the country that nothing contained in the Act just referred to altered or affected the clause in the Act of William and Mary which enacted that any heir of the Crown who married a Papist forfeited his right of the Crown.

Mr Rolle was now severely criticised by various members of the Opposition for questioning the validity of an Act of Parliament regularly passed, and it was argued that the excluding clause of the Act of Settlement had no bearing on a subsequent Act which made a marriage of any of the Royal Family without the King's consent null and void. The rumours about the marriage of the Prince of Wales were false, libellous and calumniatory.

Then Mr Dundas (Treasurer of the Navy) said:

" When he heard that a recent Act of Parliament was the only reply fit to be given to questions of the deepest importance, he could not admit that a matter of such magnitude should rest on such a point, nor would he agree that the effect of the Act of Settlement was virtually done away by a posterior Act, which did not specifically repeat the clause. . . . So to say was surely paying a bad compliment to the Prince of Wales, and resting his cause on a weak and loose foundation. He was ready to say that he disbelieved the rumour for other and he conceived better reasons. He lamented a thousand and a thousand times the absence of the right hon. gentleman (Mr Fox), who had made the declaration two sessions ago which had decided his (Mr Dundas's opinion) at the time, and since continued to preserve it fixed and unmoved . . . and therefore he was ready to say he did not give the *smallest* credit to the rumour which had been so often referred to in the course of debate. The hon. gentleman on the other side (Mr Grey) seemed anxious to provoke a discussion on the whole subject; he, for one should feel no delicacy in the world, but for a single consideration, and that was because two persons must necessarily be made the objects of the discussion. With regard to one of the high and respectable personages alluded to (the Prince of Wales) he certainly should feel but little difficulty, although no man felt more respect for that exalted personage than himself; but with regard to the other amiable character (Mrs Fitzherbert) he confessed that when the Sex came into question in that House, he knew not how to agitate a subject of such delicacy. He therefore wished at all times, to shut the door upon such discussions."

To this Mr Grey replied: " That so far from feeling regret

K

for the manner in which he had delivered his sentiments, he was happy at having delivered his opinion, since it had drawn from the two right hon. gentlemen (Mr Pitt and Mr Dundas) express declarations they neither of them believed the reports so often alluded to in the course of the debate. . . . With reference to the absence of Mr Fox, he assured the Committee that it was due to the character of his right hon. friend to declare that no consideration of health, or any other circumstance, would have prevented his attendance in his place if he had not, at the moment been fully satisfied that what he had asserted on the former occasion was *strictly true*. Had the case been otherwise, his right hon. friend would have been present *even at the risk of his life*."

The amendment was then negatived, without a division.

(*Parliamentary History*, Vol. 26. 1786–88.)

The loyalty with which the Prince's friends stuck to him over what amounted to a serious attempt to exclude him from the succession and the danger to which, by that denial of a marriage they must have known had taken place, they exposed their political reputations should perhaps suggest to prejudiced historians that the Regent may have possessed virtues to be weighed against the vices and follies for which he has been so vigorously and (being dead) so boldly condemned. However, there is no intention to set up a defence now. The point to be noted for future reference is that Rolle voiced clearly a legal suspicion that the Royal Marriages Act was not as invulnerable as it ought to be. If a marriage like this was automatically null and void, how could that excluding clause in the Act of Settlement affect it?

It will serve no useful purpose to discuss the marriage of the Prince of Wales with his cousin the Princess Caroline of Brunswick: it was brought about solely by the ruthless financial blackmail his father used. The Prince separated from Mrs Fitzherbert in May 1794. In April 1795 he married Princess Caroline, requiring repeated glasses of brandy to face the ordeal. A year later he separated from the Princess of Wales, and in June 1796 he tried to return to Mrs Fitzherbert. Up to and after the marriage, she had behaved impeccably. She avoided the Prince, refused to answer his letters, and attended no public or private entertainments at which he was present for three years after he was separated from his legal wife. At last in 1799, she half promised to rejoin the Prince, and then immediately afterwards drew back. From Windsor Castle he wrote her a passionate letter, reminding her of her marriage vows, declaring he could no longer endure the misery of the last five years, and swearing that if she would not be reconciled he would, whatever the consequences, publicly declare his marriage. "*Think not,*" he wrote, "*that prayer or any advice whatever, will make me delay my purpose, or forswear my oath. Thank God, my witnesses are living. . . .*" The force of that last ejaculation we shall learn in the history of another royal marriage.

The astonishing thing was that nearly all the members of the Royal Family were united in begging Mrs Fitzherbert to return to the Prince. All his brothers except Prince Ernest, and even his two sisters, Princess Augusta and Princess Mary, declared it was her duty to do so; most astonishing of all, Queen Charlotte herself sent private assurances of her countenance and support. It is clear from this that the whole of the family except the periodically lunatic father recognised the value of Mrs Fitzherbert's moral influence. At last, worn out by this barrage of royal entreaty, she wrote to the Prince that she would ask Rome what her position was. Father Nassau, the priest at the Warwick Street Chapel where she worshipped, went to Rome and returned with the decision of the Pope that according to the law of the Church she was the wife of the Prince of Wales, and that if she were satisfied of the sincerity of his penitence she was free to rejoin her husband. In June 1800 the Prince and Mrs Fitzherbert were formally reconciled, and for eight years they lived together in happiness, Mrs Fitzherbert remaining on terms of intimate friendship with the whole of the Royal Family, except the King and Prince Ernest, who was now Duke of Cumberland. No wonder the *Encyclopædia Britannica* calls this a morganatic marriage.

Time was passing. Mrs Fitzherbert was over fifty. All might have continued well if Lady Hertford had not tried to make her play gooseberry for her own intrigue with the Prince; but the final parting was not far off. Anti-Catholic feeling was growing stronger all the time throughout the country, and perhaps when the Prince became Regent he grew nervous of the effect on the stability of the Throne. His temporary interest in Lady Hertford no doubt facilitated the step he was about to take. To inaugurate the Regency he gave a fête, to which Mrs Fitzherbert was invited, but at the same time informed there would be no place for her at the Regent's table. She went to Carlton House and asked him if this were true.

" You know, Madam, you have no place."

" None, Sir," she replied, " but such as you choose to give me."

Next day, she wrote :

" Much as it has ever been my wish during a period of nearly thirty years to save you from every embarrassment in my power, yet there are situations when one ought not entirely to forget what is due to oneself. You, Sir, are not aware in your anxiety to fill your table with persons only of the highest rank, that, by excluding her who addresses you merely for want of those titles that others possess, you are excluding the person who is not unjustly suspected by the world of possessing in silence unassumed and un-sustained a Rank given her by yourself above that of any other woman present. Having never forfeited my title to Y.R.H.'s public as well as private consideration, by any act of my life, to what could this etiquette be for the first time imputed ? No one, my dear Sir, has proved themselves thro' life less solicitous than myself. But I cannot be indifferent to the fair, honourable appearance of considera-tion from you, which I have hitherto possessed and which I feel I deserve, and for which reason I can never submit to appear in your house in any place or situation but in that where you yourself placed me many years ago."*

The character of George IV has been the cockshy of so many playboys of abuse that we can spare him another missile, but even the most charitable interpreter must find this gesture of his hard to translate into an excusable form, and it is impossible, under the recent events that oppress our memories, to refrain from comparing George IV to his detriment with another Prince who when faced by the problem of treating a woman like an honourable man showed himself so brave, so frank, so faithful and so true.

For the next seventeen years Mrs Fitzherbert lived in strict retirement. When George IV was dying, she hoped for a summons to his bedside. Perhaps his attendants, fearing the emotional effect of her presence, withheld any commu-nication. Yet the King asked for her several times, and he

---

* Quoted by Shane Leslie in his biography of George IV.

died with a miniature of her round his neck that went down with him into the tomb.

After the King's death, Mrs Fitzherbert left London and went to live at Brighton, so intimately associated with bygone days of happiness with that dead George.   There she received kind messages from William IV, who requested to see all the documents establishing her position and character.   Dear King William was moved to tears by their perusal and, longing to do something kind for her, offered to make her a duchess. She replied that she preferred to keep the name Mrs Fitzherbert which she had never disgraced.   So then King William, whose character the deeper one dips into it the sweeter it proves like some fat old-fashioned red rose, insisted on her servants wearing the Royal livery and allowed her to put on widow's weeds.   She died in the year 1837 at the age of eighty-one.   The documents she showed to William IV now rest in the Royal archives at Windsor.

Our final comment shall be taken from *The Croker Papers*:

> One reason why Mrs Fitzherbert may like this place is that she is treated as queen, at least of Brighton.   They don't quite *Highness* her in her domestic circle, but they MADAM her prodigiously, and stand up longer for arrival than for ordinary folks, and, in short, go as near to acknowledging her for *princess* as they can, without actually giving her the title.   When she dines out she expects to be led out to dinner before princesses—mighty foolish all this. . . .

Mighty foolish indeed, but it is not much to hold against an old woman who had loved so truly and so long.

II.

The Duke of York

Frederick, Duke of York and Albany, the second son of George III, was born almost a year after his elder brother, to whom he was always devoted and by whom he was always loved, and this is a tribute to both princes, so much was Frederick his father's favourite.   In 1790 he married Princess Frederica of Prussia, niece of Frederick the Great and great-granddaughter of the unhappy Sophia Dorothea of Zell. The match caused an outburst of enthusiasm which no doubt reflected the public's opinion of the mysterious celibacy of the Prince of Wales. Here was an authentically royal bride. The tradesmen were quick to take advantage of the popular marriage. Even Princess Frederica slippers were on sale everywhere. The marriage itself was less successful than its reception; in fact it was over in less than a year. For the next thirty years the Duchess lived with her dogs and her parish duties at Oatlands Park near Weybridge. Farington has an amusing entry in his Diary on September 25th 1806 about the Duchess of York. " She has walked in Kensington Gardens without a servant arm in arm with Culling Smith, whose wife Lady Anne Smith has a situation in Her establishment. She has also walked with 20 others. The D. spoke to K.12 months ago abt. Her manner of going on and of a Divorce. King reminded Him of His own infidelity in that respect and said He would only bring trouble upon Himself."

The Duke and Duchess never openly quarrelled; but three years before that bit of gossip the Duke had set up house with Mrs Clarke in Gloucester Place. This witty and attractive wanton had risen from the obscurity of Ball and Pin Alley, Chancery Lane, to be the leading *demi-mondaine* of London. In the end, the Duke was involved in a grave scandal over her traffic in army commissions. Later she left England for France, and a daughter, not by the Duke of York, was said to be the ancestress of George and Gerald Du Maurier.

All the stories we hear of the Duke of York reveal him as brave, generous, and affable. He was not a success as a General commanding in the field, but he was a capable Commander-in-Chief, apart from that unfortunate business over Mrs Clarke's sale of commissions which was made the worst of largely through the jealousy of his brother the Duke of Kent who hoped for his job. The British Army owed him much. He was, indeed, not unworthy of his column, so typical of the more Germanic aspects of England and rising with such a wealth of warning near the German Embassy. He has been much reproached for the support he gave his elder brother against George III; but that ' ingratitude ' may tell as much against the child-devouring egotism of his father as himself.

III.

The Duke of Clarence, afterwards William IV

William, Duke of Clarence and St Andrew's, born in 1765, was as genial a royal figure as may be found in all English history. Perhaps Nelson exaggerated his merits as a naval officer, but Nelson's judgment cannot be entirely ignored. It costs a pang not to linger for a while over many enchanting stories of William from the time he was a midshipman to the time he was a king. As a young man he was continually falling in love with jolly girls in every port, and his father was continually calling on the Admiralty to rescue him from what he considered unsuitable marriages for the Blood by sending William to a new ship in a new port. At last, baffled in his longing to lead what would certainly have been a model of fecund domestic life, he settled down in 1790 with Mrs Jordan at Bushey " and brought up his ten children with very tender affection; with them and for them he seemed entirely to live."

After William parted from Mrs Jordan he made half a dozen attempts to marry English heiresses and two or three to secure foreign royalties. At last, in 1817, the death of the Regent's daughter, Princess Charlotte, made it imperative for the succession to be secured. So William and two of his brothers found approved German princesses. The Duke of Clarence married Princess Adelaide of Saxe-Meiningen and the wedding was celebrated at Kew on the same day as that of his younger brother the Duke of Kent to the widowed Coburg Princess of Leiningen. William was then fifty-three, and his young wife only twenty-six. Two daughters were born to them, one of whom lived but a few hours, and the other, Princess Elizabeth, a few months. The Duchess of Clarence was a woman of great beauty of character and a simple piety much more truly Evangelical than Queen Charlotte's. Her behaviour toward the successfully reared daughter of the brother-in-law with whom she had been simultaneously married was an example of Christian charity and even of forbearance.

William IV had a hatred of sham and show and spent only £30,000 on the Coronation where George IV had spent a quarter of a million. Indeed he tried to avoid a Coronation altogether, and when at last he was persuaded he stipulated that none of the bishops should kiss him.   The Court officials found him disgracefully intolerant of ceremony, and his passion for continuing the life he had led as Duke of Clarence and walking about like a private citizen horrified those whose only *raison d'être* was to keep the royal mummies dusted and the wax models of kingship steady on their pedestals.   Five days after attending the nocturnal funeral of George IV in a purple cloak as chief mourner and embarrassing the politely lugubrious congregation by nodding to various acquaintances and shaking hands with others as the coffin passed, he reviewed the Guards and, never having donned military uniform in his life, managed to get the spurs half-way up his legs.   After the ceremony he changed into mufti to take a stroll in St James's Street, where he met a friend.   Presently the members of White's heard a commotion in the street, and looked out to see King William and Mr Watson-Taylor arm-in-arm being swept along the street by an enthusiastic crowd, and then his Majesty being kissed on the cheek by a woman of the town. The loyalists sallied forth to rescue their sovereign from such base familiarity, and escorted him still hanging on Watson-Taylor's arm into St James's Palace.

"Oh, never mind all this," said King William beaming. "When I have walked about a few times, they will get used to it and take no notice."

The only person that genial monarch really hated was the Duchess of Kent, and his one passionate hope was to live till the Princess Victoria came of age in order to deprive his sister-in-law of the Regency.   He succeeded, but by a margin of less than a month.

IV.

The Princess Royal, afterwards Princess of Württemberg

If the sons of George III were cheated out of a normal domestic life by their father, the effect of the *patria potestas* on his daughters was even more disastrous.   They were all as much devoted to him as he to them, but they were naturally preoccupied with the subject of marriage, and the King used to 'howl' when it was mentioned.   The eldest, Princess Charlotte, was born in 1766, and in 1797, at the age of thirty-one she, by then Princess Royal, could stand

it no longer and negotiated a marriage for herself.   The happy
bridegroom was Frederick, Prince of Württemberg, a
widower " whose fat gives him an appearance like deformity :
His Shape is not that of fat men in common.   The Princess
Royal seems much pleased.   The Bishop of Norwich thought
her low yesterday at Court, and observed that she sighed. . . .
Each of them was agreeably disappointed in finding the other
of better appearance than they expected." *
Madame d'Arblay wrote to a friend :

> " A private letter from Windsor tells me the Prince of
> Württemberg has much pleased in the Royal House, by his
> manners and address upon his interview, but that poor
> Princess Royal was almost dead with terror, and agitation,
> and affright, at the first meeting.   She could not utter a
> word.   The Queen was obliged to speak her answers.
> The Prince said he hoped this first would be the last dis-
> turbance his presence would ever occasion her.   She then
> tried to recover, and so far conquered her tumult as to
> attempt joining in a general discourse from time to time.
> He paid his court successfully, I am told, to the sisters,
> who all determine to like him ; and the Princess Royal is
> quite revived in her spirits again, now this tremendous
> opening sight is over."

The Prince had incurred suspicion over the death of his
first wife, and George III, thinking he would be unable to
clear himself, had consented to his becoming a suitor for the
Princess Royal's hand.   Unfortunately for exigent fathership,
the obese Prince cleared himself of every charge, and the King
had to submit to lose his eldest daughter.   Madame d'Arblay
records in another letter some amusing news of the wedding
from Princess Augusta, and adds a comment of her own
which explains why the Princess Royal accepted the fat
widower :

> " When I told her I had heard that Her Royal Highness
> the bride had never looked so lovely, she confirmed the
> praise warmly, but laughingly added, ' 'Twas the Queen
> dressed her !   You know what a figure she used to make of
> herself, with her odd manner of dressing herself ; but
> mamma said, ' Now really, Princess Royal, this one time is
> the last, and I cannot suffer you to make such a quiz of

* Farington's Diary.

yourself; so I will really have you dressed properly. . . .'
"The word *quiz*, you may depend, was never the
Queen's. . . . The Royal Family is persuaded this estimable Princess is happy . . . she was here in utter sub-
jection, for which she had neither spirits now inclination
. . . her style of life was not adapted to the royalty of her
nature, any more than of her birth; and though she only
wished for power to do good and confer favours, she thought
herself out of her place in not possessing it."

The Princess Royal died without children in 1828.

The Duke of Kent

Edward, Duke of Kent and Strathearn, was born a year
after the Princess Royal. His youth with Baron Wangenheim
as a governor recalls slightly the experience of his grandson
Edward VII. Prince Edward's establishment in Geneva
was costing £6000 a year when he was twenty years old; but
the Prince himself was allowed only 31/6 a week for pocket-
money, and the Baron intercepted his letters to his father
asking for more. At last he could stand it no longer and
escaping from Geneva in 1789 reached London where
his two elder brothers looked after him at Carlton House,
to the rage of George III, who ordered Prince Edward off to
Gibraltar as Colonel of the Royal Fusiliers. Later he was
sent to Canada where for his brutal discipline he was extremely unpopular with the men under his command. One
deserter was ordered 999 lashes. Another was condemned to
death and marched in grave clothes behind his coffin two
miles to the gallows, Prince Edward riding at the head of the
obsequies and the band playing Dead Marches. Arrived at
the foot of the gallows, the Prince declared himself as the son
of the condemned man's sovereign, but not as his colonel,
able to exercise the Royal prerogative of mercy, and the
wretched man was reprieved. In this story of the Duke of
Kent we recognise that unpleasant gloating over pain and
ignominy of which his daughter was sometimes capable.
She was much perturbed to hear soldiers were no longer to be
flogged.

In Quebec the Duke of Kent took as his mistress a French Canadian of good family who was to live with him for twenty-seven years. He was upset when the death of the Princess Charlotte made it necessary for him to marry. To Mr Creevey he wrote, " *She is of very good family and has never been an actress, and I am the first and only person who has ever lived with her.*" Indeed, the whole liaison possesses a faint adumbration of Victorianism, for he and ' Madame ' disapproved of gentlemen's getting drunk and neither of them would play cards on Sunday. The Duke had hoped to provide a respectable independence for Madame de St Laurent when he was forced to leave her—" a certain number of servants and a carriage was essential "—but Madame de St Laurent* herself decided it was time to think of a more important future than any with which the Duke could provide her and she spent the rest of her life in a convent.

The Duke of Kent married the Princess of Leiningen, daughter of the late Duke of Saxe-Coburg and widow of the Prince of Leiningen by whom she had two children. Her brother Leopold, afterwards King of the Belgians, had been the husband of the dead Princess Charlotte, the daughter of George IV. The Duchess was not an extremely attractive personality, but she managed to produce the Princess Alexandrina Victoria within less than a year after marriage, and so she cannot be ignored. The Duke, in debt to the last, mostly owing to his extravagance over new houses, died at Sidmouth when his little daughter was a year old. His wife outlived him for nearly forty years, consoled by the loyalty of Sir John Conroy.

VI.

Princess Augusta

Princess Augusta was born in 1768. She was a great favourite of Madame d'Arblay, who says she had a " gaiety, a charm about her, that is quite resistless ; and much of true, genuine, and very original humour." She was never married though she was believed to have cherished a *tendresse* for the

* A novel has just been published about some alleged children of this liaison. There was none.

handsome and snobbish Court Physician, Sir Henry Halford. Their intimate correspondence was handed over to Queen Victoria. The following scene related by Miss Burney brings so vividly before us the emotional preoccupations of those poor princesses, captives to their father's disordered egotism, that it is worth quoting in full as a revelation of life at Windsor. Mr Turbulent was Charles de Guiffandière, the French master at Windsor. The Princess was nineteen at the time of this entry in Madame d'Arblay's Diary:

With all the various humours in which I had already seen Mr Turbulent, he gave me this evening a surprise, by his behaviour to one of the Princesses, nearly the same that I had experienced from him myself. The Princess Augusta came, during coffee, for a knotting shuttle of the Queen's. While she was speaking to me, he stood behind and exclaimed, *à demi voix*, as if to himself, " *Comme elle est jolie ce soir, son Altesse Royale !* " And then seeing her blush extremely, he clasped his hands, in high pretended confusion, and hiding his head, called out, " *Que ferai-je ?* The Princess has heard me ! "

" Pray, Mr Turbulent," cried she, hastily, " what play are you to read to-night ? "

" You shall choose, ma'am; either *La Coquette corrigée*, or——" (he named another I have forgotten).

" Oh, no ! " cried she, " that last is shocking ! don't let me hear that ! "

" I understand you, ma'am. You fix, then, upon *La Coquette* ? *La Coquette* is your Royal Highness's taste ? "

" No, indeed, I am sure I did not say that."

" Yes, ma'am, by implication. And certainly, therefore, I will read it, to please your Royal Highness ! "

" No, pray don't; for I like none of them ! "

" None of them, ma'am ? "

" No, none;—no *French plays* at all ! "

And away she was running, with a droll air, that acknowledged she had said something to provoke him.

" This is a declaration, ma'am, I must beg you to explain ! " cried he, gliding adroitly between the Princess and the door, and shutting it with his back.

" No, no, I can't explain it; so pray, Mr Turbulent, do open the door."

" Not for the world, ma'am, with such a stain uncleared upon your Royal Highness's taste and feeling ! "

She told him positively she could not stay, and begged him to let her pass instantly.

But he would hear her no more than he had heard me, protesting that he was too much shocked for her, to suffer her to depart without clearing her own credit !

He conquered at last, and thus forced to speak, she turned round to us and said, " Well—if I must, then—I will appeal to these ladies, who understand such things far better than I do, and ask them if it is not true about these French plays, that they are all so like one to another, that to hear them in this manner every night is enough to tire one ? "

" Pray, then, madam," cried he, " if French plays have the misfortune to displease you, what *National* plays have the honour of your preference ? "

I saw he meant something that she understood better than me, for she blushed again, and called out, " Pray open the door at once ! I can stay no longer; do let me go, Mr Turbulent."

" Not till you have answered that question, ma'am ! what *Country* has plays to your Royal Highness's taste ? "

" Miss Burney," cried she impatiently, yet laughing, " pray do you take him away !—Pull him ! "

He bowed to me very invitingly for the office; but I frankly answered her, " Indeed, ma'am, I dare not undertake him ! I cannot manage him at all."

" The *Country !* the *Country !* Princess Augusta ! name the happy *Country !* " was all she could gain.

" *Order* him away, Miss Burney," cried she, " 'tis your room: order him away from the door."

" Name it, ma'am, name it ! " exclaimed he; " name but the *chosen nation.*"

And then, fixing her with the most provoking eyes, " *Est-ce la Danemarc ?* " he cried.

She coloured violently, and quite angry with him, called out, " Mr Turbulent, how can you be such a fool ! "

And now I found . . . the Prince Royal of Denmark was in his meaning, and in her understanding.

He bowed to the ground, in gratitude for the term *fool*, but added with pretended submission to her will, " Very well, ma'am, *s'il ne faut lire que les comédies Danoises.*"

" Do let me go ! " cried she, seriously; and then he made way with a profound bow as she passed, saying, " Very well, ma'am, *La Coquette*, then ? Your Royal Highness chooses *La Coquette corrigée ?* "

" *Corrigée ?* That never was done ! " cried she, with all her sweet good humour, the moment she got out; and off she ran, like lightning, to the Queen's apartments.

What say you to Mr Turbulent now ?

For my part I was greatly surprised. I had not imagined any man, but the King or Prince of Wales, had ever ventured at a *badinage* of this sort with any of the Princesses; nor do I suppose any other man ever did. Mr. Turbulent is so great a favourite with all the Royal Family, that he safely ventures upon whatever he pleases, and doubtless they find, in his courage and his rodomontading, a novelty extremely amusing to them, or they would not fail to bring about a change.

Poor Princess Augusta ! In her case George III triumphed completely. To her frustrated emotional life it was a great excitement when her brother the Duke of Cumberland came back from the wars, one side of his face shot away at Tournai. To Queen Charlotte said her daughter Augusta, " How lucky it is that Ernest has just come back so seasonably with that wound in his face. I should have been shocked else not to have had one bit of glory among ourselves." It is a remark Jane Austen might have invented for one of her immortals. No wonder George IV never travelled without a complete set of the works of that sublime woman.

Princess Augusta died unwed in 1840.

VII.

Princess Elizabeth, afterwards Landgravine of Hesse-Homburg

Princess Elizabeth was born in 1770. A rumour ran that she contrived a secret marriage for herself in early youth with a Mr Ramus, one of the Pages, by whom she had children ; but " the circumstances were unromantic " (Childe Pemberton). Elizabeth was the confidante of her youngest sister Amelia in her pathetic romance, but afterwards behaved badly to her, and treated her with some unkindness during her last illness. At the age of forty-nine, just before her father was released from that last dark decade of madness, she married the Landgrave of Hesse-Homburg, " a monster of a man—a vulgar-looking German corporal, whose breath and hide is a compound between tobacco and garlick. He has about £300 per annum." His Serene Highness had " a snout buried in hair " and so little control over his body as to be sick in the carriage in which he drove off on his honeymoon, so sick that he had to be put up on the box. However, late though it came, when at last she was regularly married, a latent goodness stunted by that crowded unnatural family life revealed itself, and she is remembered at Homburg for her charity. She died in the same year as her sister Augusta.

VIII.

The Duke of Cumberland, afterwards King of Hanover

Ernest, Duke of Cumberland and Teviotdale, was born in 1771. This tall sinister Prince, lacking any of the geniality of his brothers (the Duke of Kent could unbend out of uniform) was unjustly suspected of two murders, one being that of his own valet, and suspected of enormities even worse than murder. He came as near to the English conception of the Devil as any human being has succeeded in coming. He was a good soldier, a man of such personal strength that, after losing his left eye and being severely wounded in the right arm on May 10th 1794, on December 10th of the same year in the sortie from Nimeguen, he lifted a French dragoon clean off his horse and rode back with him into the English camp. He was a cruel disciplinarian and took it out of that regiment of light dragoons which nearly sixty years before had so exasperated the first Duke of Cumberland by refusing under Cope to face the claymore at Prestonpans. He was not less brutal in politics where he was the hammer of the Whigs and the scourge of the Catholics.

In 1814 the Duke decided to marry and—to the intense annoyance of his mother—he chose her own niece Frederica who, after the death of her first husband, one of the Prussian princes, had been betrothed to Queen Charlotte's youngest son, the Duke of Cambridge, and had jilted him for the Prince of Solms-Braunfels. She had sons by both husbands, and she and her three sisters were all famous for their lightness of heart, loveliness of face, and looseness of morals. That Queen Charlotte's brother, the Duke of Mecklenburg-Strelitz, produced them is extraordinary.

Queen Charlotte was furious at the proposed marriage of this merry widow of thirty-seven and wrote nervously to her brother :

"MY DEAR BROTHER :
          . . . As I have reason to believe that paternal advice will have a salutary influence on your daughter I think I may confide to you what will be essential for the princess on her arrival here. The usages of this country being so different from what they are on the Continent, in every respect, I fear that my son may not be sufficiently attentive to them. As this is for you alone, I confide to you that it is not the fashion here to receive morning visits from gentlemen, to which she will be exposed, by the circumstance of the Duke being a Colonel of a regiment, unless he himself introduces them to her : she should also be very circumspect in the choice of ladies with whom she

shall associate, which will be so much the more necessary as the Duke has acquaintance among our sex, who, although not actually of bad conduct, might, however, become injurious to her in point of policy. I have found that the advice of the dear King ' of being uniformly polite to everyone, of doing nothing in the spirit of party, and of adhering closely to his family,' has been my surest guidance during my long residence here : and I think I cannot do better than to transmit those sentiments to you, dear brother and friend, as father to my niece and future daughter-in-law, which you will make use of in such a manner as you shall judge proper.

I have sent by the messenger six pounds of tea and two cheese ; eat the latter to my health : and in drinking the tea, remember a sister, whose attachment to you will not cease but with death.

Sir, my dearest brother,

Your very affectionate sister and faithful friend,

CHARLOTTE.*

However, in spite of this letter Queen Charlotte never did receive the Duchess of Cumberland, and even a Tory House of Commons refused to grant the Duke an increase of income on his marriage. When Queen Victoria ascended the throne, the Salic Law gave the Kingdom of Hanover to the Duke. For another fourteen years he ruled his Kingdom with that defiance of democracy which had made him so much feared and hated in England. The Hanoverians liked it.

IX.

The Duke of Sussex

Augustus, Duke of Sussex, was born in 1773. He, who all his life was to support the cause of progress, showed signs of Liberal convictions as early as seven years old when he was locked in the nursery and sent supperless to bed by his father for having been detected sporting the election colours of Admiral Keppel. Luckily for himself he was so delicate as a boy that he spent most of his time abroad with a governor. In 1792, at the age of nineteen, he was in Rome, where he met the Countess of Dunmore with her two daughters Virginia

* Quoted by Roger Fulford in *Royal Dukes*.

and Augusta. The Earl was away administering the Bahamas. Lady Augusta Murray was an attractive young woman whose portrait by Romney shows the deeply cleft chin of a sensuous temperament and full shapely lips that do not belie the chin. She was a year or so older than Prince Augustus, who wrote of her some time later :

> " The well-known accomplishments of my wife caught my peculiar attention. After four months' intimacy, by which I got more particularly acquainted with all her endearing qualities, I offered her my hand unknown to her family, being certain beforehand of the objections Lady Dunmore would have made me had she been informed of my intentions. The candour and generosity my wife showed on this occasion, by refusing the proposal and showing me the personal disadvantages I should draw on myself, instead of checking my endeavours, served only to add fuel to a passion which already no earthly power could make me resign."

The old story. The fact that he could *not* marry her made marriage more imperative than ever. How imperative we may judge by the following document which Augustus presented to Augusta :

> " As this paper is to contain the mutual promise of marriage between Augustus Frederick and Augusta Murray, our mutual names must be put here by us both, and *kept in my possession.* It is a promise *neither* of us can break, *and is made before God our Creator, and all merciful Father.*"

It then proceeds to the following declaration :

> " *On my knees before God our Creator*, I, Augustus Frederick, promise thee, Augusta Murray, *and swear upon the Bible, as I hope for salvation in the world to come*, that I will take thee, Augusta Murray, for my WIFE, *for better, for worse, for richer, for poorer, in sickness and in health, to love and to cherish, till death us do part, to love but thee only, and none other ; and may God forget ME if I ever forget THEE ! The Lord's name be praised ! So bless me ; so bless me, O God !* And with my handwriting do I, Augustus Frederick, this sign, March 21st 1793 at Rome, and put my SEAL to it and my NAME.
>
> (*Signed*) AUGUSTUS FREDERICK."

In Rome there was an Anglican clergyman called Gunn, whom Augustus persuaded to defy the penalties under a Praemunire to celebrate a royal marriage without the King's consent. Perhaps Mr Gunn thought Rome was the city in Europe where a Praemunire might be most safely defied. If Mr Gunn should find second thoughts were best, Augustus was ready to tell him that his honour was involved. To this suggestion, Augusta replied:

" Then my treasure, you say you will talk of honour to him. There is no honour in the case; if there is, I will not marry you. I love you, and I have reason to hope and believe you love me; but honour in the sense you take it is out of the question. I cannot bear to owe my happiness to anything but affection; and all promises, though sacred in our eyes and those of Heaven, shall not oblige you to do anything towards me that can in the least prejudice your future interests. As for honour, with the meaning Mr Gunn will annex to it, I am ashamed to fancy it; he will imagine I have been your mistress, and that humanity, commonly termed honour, now induces you to pity me, and so veil my follies with an honourable marriage. My own beloved Prince, forgive me if I am warm upon this. I wish you to feel that you owe me nothing; and whatever I owe you, I wish to owe to your love and to your good opinion, but to no other principle. Tell Mr Gunn, my own Augustus, that you love me, that you are resolved to marry me, that you have pledged your sacred word; tell him if you please, that upon the Bible you have sworn it, that I have done the same, and nothing shall ever divide us; but don't let him imagine that I have been vile. Do this my only love, but pray take care of the character of your wife, of your

AUGUSTA."

The faint air of Lydia Languish that clings to this epistle should not make us smile too broadly. Augustus was extremely good-looking; Augusta was genuinely in love. Augustus, moved by the exquisite femininity of such sentiments, wrote back:

" Do, my dearest Augusta, trust me; I will never abuse the confidence you put in me, and more and more will I endeavour to deserve it. I only wait for your orders to speak to Mr Gunn ; say only that you wish me to do it, and I will hasten to get a positive answer. See, my soul, it only depends on *you* to speak ; *thy* Augustus thou wilt find at all times ready to serve *you*. He thinks, he dreams of nothing but to make thee happy. Can he not succeed in this, all his hopes are gone ; life will be nothing to him ; he will pass the days in one constant melancholy, wishing them soon to conclude, and finding every one longer than the other. Indeed, my Augusta, that cannot be the case ; my solemn oath is given, and that can never be recalled. I am yours, my soul, ever yours."

Whether Augusta still held back or whether it was Mr Gunn we do not know, but ten days later on April 4th 1793 the Prince wrote again in the strain of his eldest brother in parallel circumstances, that eldest brother of whom in youth he was a sort of aquatint :

" Will you allow me to come to you this evening ? It is my only hope. O, let me come, and we will send for Mr Gunn : Everything but this is hateful to me. More than forty-eight hours have I passed without the smallest nourishment. O, let me live not so ! Death is certainly better than this ; which, if in forty-eight hours has not taken place, must follow ; for, by all that is holy, till when I am married, I will eat nothing ; and if I am not to be married, the promise shall die with me ! I am resolute. Nothing in the world shall alter my determination. If Gunn will not marry me, I will die . . . I will be conducted by you in everything ; but I must be married or die. I would rather see none of my family than be deprived of you. You alone can make me ; you alone shall this evening. I will sooner drop than give you up. Good God, how I feel ! and my love to be doubted sincere and warm. The Lord knows the truth of it ; and as I say, if in forty-eight hours I am not married I am no more. O, Augusta, my soul, let us try ; let me come ; I am capable of everything ; I fear nothing, and Mr Gunn, seeing our resolution, will agree. I am half dead. Good God, what will become of me ? I shall go mad, most undoubtedly."

To this appeal, Lady Augusta yielded and wrote in reply :

" My treasure, my dearest life and love, how can I refuse you ? And yet I dare not trust to the happiness

your letter promises me.   You shall come if you wish it;
you shall do as you like; my whole soul rejoices in the
assurances of your love, and to your exertions.   My
mother has ordered her carriage at past seven, and will not,
I fear, be out before the half-hour after.   To be yours
to-night seems a dream that I cannot make out.   The
whole day have I been plunged in misery, and now to awake
to joy is a felicity that is beyond my ideas of bliss.   I
doubt its success ; but do as you will ; I am what you will ;
your will must be mine ; and no will can ever be dearer
to me, more mine, than that of my Augustus, my lover,
my all."

They were married by Mr Gunn that night without witnesses, but the marriage contract was endorsed in the Prince's
own handwriting.   In winter, the married couple returned
to England ; and here, fearing that the marriage abroad might
be invalidated, but with a curious disregard of what might
have been supposed would be its automatic invalidation by
the Royal Marriages Act, Mr Augustus Frederick and Miss
Augusta Murray were married all over again at St George's,
Hanover Square, nobody protesting any just cause or impediment when the banns were called.   A few days more than
nine months later, a son was born in Essex.   Somehow the
secret leaked out, and the Prince left England in January,
three days after the child was born.   A week later, the Court
officials broke the news to the King, who ordered the marriage
to be annulled.

The decree was announced by the Dean of Arches on
July 14th 1791.   This law-suit, said Prince Augustus, " was
begun immediately after my departure from England and conducted with great inhumanity, as it is not only not sanctioned
by the laws of our country but even in defiance of them.   *My
wife* was prosecuted the second day after she was brought to
bed, and perfectly defenceless, for her husband was absent."

It should be borne in mind that Lady Augusta Murray
belonged to an offshoot from the proud house of Atholl.   Her
grandfather had fought at Prestonpans, Falkirk, and Culloden
on what many in their hearts still considered the right side.
Apart from the inbred stock of minor German royalty Lady
Augusta's genuine royal blood was as plentiful as her husband's.

In September of this year, with a forged passport she
managed to evade the order of the King to detain her in

England, and joined her husband in Berlin where they lived together for six years. The eternal question of money, which was the ruin of all those princes' natures owing to their father's use of the purse-strings to strangle their good impulses, led Augustus to send his wife back to England in the year 1800, in the hope of obtaining his Parliamentary grant. When this did not materialise he came over to England himself to live with his wife in Mayfair. Chronic asthma drove him abroad for the rest of the winter, and at the beginning of 1801, he left for Lisbon. From on board ship he wrote to say he had heard Brownsea Island off the coast of Dorset was to let at a rent of £250 a year, and that the climate there should be mild enough to make wintering abroad unnecessary in the future. To his little son he wrote a birthday letter addressed to " Prince Augustus Frederick." In August of that year a daughter was born, Emma Augusta. It was now that the Dukedom of Sussex with a grant of £12,000 a year was offered to him, doubtless on condition that he would separate from his wife. This he did, allowing her £4000 a year.

Lady Augusta proved less patient under such a separation than Mrs Fitzherbert. She insisted on calling herself the Duchess of Sussex and used the Royal Arms. Farington notes in his Diary of August 1804 :

> Lady Augusta Murray has a very singular shaped face. The Lower part from the Nose falling as if shaved off. Her sister still more plain. I thought them coarse and confident-looking women. She has entered Herself in the subscription book at Ramsgate *Duchess of Sussex*. We saw Her Son, a fair boy of 11 or 12 years of age seemingly, and very like the Royal family. Lady Hamilton is grown prodigiously large and exposed her fat shoulders and breast manifestly.

Sic transit ! Thus pass two of Romney's beautiful ladies.

In 1806 the Duke brought an injunction to stop his wife's pretensions. Three years later, he applied to have Lord Moira appointed guardian of his children and to remove them from his wife's custody because she was bringing them up as a prince and a princess. Lady Augusta appealed to the Lord Chancellor, but he confirmed the decision of the Court. She was now known as Countess d'Ameland. When the children were taken to live with their father they were known as Augustus d'Este and Emma Augusta Maria d'Este, the name being taken from Italian ancestors common to both their parents.

The young Augustus entered the army and became a full Colonel in 1838. In 1830 he was created by William IV a Knight Commander of the Hanoverian and Guelphic order, granted a pension of £500 a year out of the Civil List, and appointed Deputy-Ranger of Hyde Park and St James's Park. He died in 1848. His sister, Emma Augusta, married in 1845 as his second wife Sir Thomas Wilde, who became Lord Truro a year later, and was Lord Chancellor in 1850.

In spite of William IV's obvious attempt to make matters pleasant all round Sir Augustus d'Este, shortly after the death of his mother in 1830 filed a bill in Chancery, submitting that he was entitled to examine witnesses to prove the marriage of his father the Duke of Sussex, to establish the validity of the marriage, and to perpetuate the testimony of the witnesses, Mr Gunn, who had performed the marriage, being now over eighty years of age. The arguments put forward by learned counsel will be mentioned later when the subject of morganatic marriage is being examined. Meanwhile, we have to note that the reason for Sir Augustus d'Este's attempt to establish legitimacy was caused by his father's marriage to Lady Cecilia Buggin, with whom the Duke of Sussex had been friendly for some years. Mr Creevey noted on October 6th 1827:

> Old Sussex comes here on Monday and Ciss Buggin too. Was there ever such a low-lived concern? And Brougham comes to meet them, so they will have it their own way in politics.

However, the Duke did not venture to make another marriage until the death of Lady Augusta Murray, Countess d'Ameland, in 1830.

Lady Cecilia Buggin née Gore was the daughter of the Earl of Arran by his third wife, and the widow of a Sir George Buggin who had been something in the City. She was on the shady side of forty when her marriage took place in St George's, Hanover Square, the very church in which the Duke had married Lady Augusta Murray. No application was made to the Privy Council under the requisitions of the Royal Marriages Act, but no steps were taken by William IV to annul it. At the same time, no steps were taken by the Duke of Sussex to have his second wife's position regularised. The marriage was announced by the arrival of the Duke and Lady Cecilia Buggin in the same carriage at a party. They did not, however, live together, the Duke remaining officially

in Kensington Palace and Lady Cecilia in a house on the
north side of Hyde Park.   Of one of their appearances at a
party, the observant Creevey recorded on March 11th 1832:

> Of course Ciss was there, and every inch a Princess.   Suss:
> handed her out and she sat next him, and it was very amusing to see
> how distinctly she showed herself to be his wife, and the mistress of
> the house. . . .

By 1834 the name Buggin was proving too severe a strain
on whatever romance was attached to this middle-aged couple
and by Royal licence on March 2nd 1834 Lady Cecilia
dropped Buggin to assume her mother's maiden name of
Underwood.   It may have been a more romantic step, but it
did not prove more practical.   In November 1838 Creevey
was writing:

> Everything within and without the Guildhall, and throughout the
> whole day went off to everybody's unqualified satisfaction: always
> excepting one occurrence, and which is really most provoking—that
> old goose Sussex would not have his *Gosling* Ciss invited to the banquet:
> he wanted blank admissions for two ladies (her and Lady Gore) but
> the city authorities said " No.   The Queen shall have no one to
> meet her at dinner who will not give their names," and to that they
> stuck after much fighting. . . . I have no patience with those idiots
> *Ciss* and *Suss* for getting into such a mess and upon such an occasion as
> dear little Vic's day of trial and triumph.

In 1840, what—if he had been asked—genial and good
King William would probably have granted for nothing the
young Queen Victoria granted in the interest of a bargain in
Royal etiquette.   As the eldest surviving son of George III
in England, the Duke of Sussex took precedence immediately
after his niece, and the Queen wanted this place for her
husband Prince Albert.   The first two months of 1840
caused heart-burnings.   Lord Melbourne was positive,
according to the Queen's Journal, *none* of the Royal Family
could marry without the Sovereign's leave but was less positive
about the cause of the Royal Marriages Act, " which, he
believed, was due to the Duke of Cumberland's marriage with
a Mrs Luttrell, which was very much disliked."   Lord
Melbourne here exhibits the characteristic woolliness of the
species prime minister.   The next entry of the Queen's is
dated February 6th 1840, " I told Lord Melbourne there
would be a great bit of work I feared about the Duke of
Sussex and Lady C, for he had insinuated without mentioning

the exact thing, to ask Lord Melbourne to ask me something that he had very near at heart. ' Oh, that'll never do,' Lord Melbourne said."

However, between them, Melbourne and Victoria seem to have found a way out of the difficulty because on the not inappropriate date of April 1st 1840, *The Times* announced, " It appears by the Gazette of last night that Lady Cecilia Underwood has been created Duchess of Inverness." This was followed on April 3rd by the publication of a letter in those portentous columns :

" Sir,—May I beg you will inform me whether the Duchess of Inverness (late Cecilia Underwood) is now to be publicly acknowledged as the wife of the Duke of Sussex ? If so, why is she not to be the Duchess of Sussex ? If not, why has she been so cheated ? If this marriage is acknowledged, surely it will be an act of Justice to Sir Augustus d'Este and his sister to restore them to their proper station in society by repealing the Act of Parliament which invalidated the marriage of their amiable mother Lady Augusta Murray with the Duke of Sussex."

The anonymous writer of this letter signs himself A TRUE CONSERVATIVE AND A LOVER OF JUSTICE, and it should be noted that politics were now entering into it because the Duke of Sussex was the darling of the Whigs, thanks to his genuinely democratic tastes and sympathies. The letter was followed up in *The Times* of April 13th 1840 by an article, replying to one that had appeared in the *Dublin Evening Mail* of the 8th of April in which the details of the d'Este case were recalled and the Duke was castigated for his conduct in not securing the recognition of Lady Augusta Murray as his wife. *The Times* " handed over its contemporary to the judgment of the public."

It is obvious from what we have now or heretofore written on the subject that we can have no desire to wound the feelings of the Royal Duke, or to censure the proceedings now in progress for the public recognition of his second marriage. What we have said and still continue to say, is this—that if it be just and expedient to legalise the wedlock with all its consequences between the Royal Duke and Lady Cecilia Underwood, justice and expediency equally warrant the giving of the Royal and legal sanction to the marriage of his Royal Highness with Lady Augusta Murray; and that the former cannot be done,

and the other left undone, without a cruelty and injustice which we
trust the Royal Duke is incapable of recommending, and which we
hope the Queen will neither adopt nor tolerate, and which we are quite
certain would be indignantly resented by every man of honour in the
Empire.

This unmistakable recognition of morganatic marriage is
commended to the attention of the present Editor.

The choice of the Duchess of Inverness for a title was
inept because the Duke of Sussex's own second title was Earl
of Inverness and if he had desired to visit Scotland as a Scots-
man, which his portrait by Beechey in full Highland dress
seems to show might have been his will, he and his wife
would have appeared as the Earl and Duchess of Inverness.
It would have been more logical to anticipate the recent
precedent of refusing to grant her the prefix H.R.H. but
allowing her the same title as her husband. Yet that would
not have solved the problem of precedence. The refusal of
the prefix H.R.H. to the Duchess of Windsor has created sad
confusion among the experts of rank. Even Burke and
Debrett, hitherto as affectionate brothers as Tweedledum and
Tweedledee, have met like them to have a battle. H.R.H. the
Duke of Windsor is likely to prove less amenable to the com-
promises of chivalry than his great-great-uncle, the Duke of
Sussex. The latter would come smiling to a reception, with
the Duchess of Inverness hanging on his arm; but when the
Queen entered, she had to be left half-way down the room
and her husband would go and sit at the Queen's table. On
one occasion at Lansdowne House, the Queen did allow the
Duchess to sit at her table, but only on the express condition
that she took her place as the junior duchess. In less exalted
circles the Duchess of Inverness was treated as Royalty. She
was curtsied to and visitors were expected to write their
names in her book instead of leaving cards. In 1843 death
freed the Duke of Sussex from the vexation of precedence.
This extract from a letter of the Queen Dowager Adelaide to
Queen Victoria indicates a generous if perhaps illogical point
of view:

22nd April, 1843.

MY DEAREST NIECE,

I am just come back and feel very anxious to
know how you are, and beg at the same time to offer you
my most affectionate condolence on the melancholy event

which has taken again another member of our family from us.

. . . I have been with the poor Duchess of Inverness on my way to town and found her as composed as possible under the sad circumstances, and full of gratitude to you and all the family for all the kindness which she had received. I pity her very much. It must be her comfort to have made the last years of the Duke's life happy, and to have been his comfort to the last moment.

I wish you good-night, dearest Niece, and beg you to give my best love to dear Albert, and to believe me most devotedly your most affectionate aunt,

ADELAIDE.

And the obituary notices are worth pondering by readers of to-day. *The Times* was generous:

. . . These courtly virtues, which may seem easy of imitation, but which imply no small surrender of private comfort and indulgence, were, more than any political bias, calculated to endear him to the British people. But their regard for him was cemented by ties more strong than these. He had identified himself by marriage with them,— he had made himself one of them,—he had overstept the barriers of an absurd, impolitic and indefensible, but most stringent enactment to unite his fortunes with those of a British subject; he braved the resentment of the Crown; he risked the hereditary dignities of the Succession, in order to enjoy the blessing of domestic peace with the daughter of a British peer. It was this honest tribute to the natural supremacy of man's best and purest affections—this noble contempt for the paltry etiquette of Royal alliances—this constitutional vindication of a civil right—in opposition to a parliamentary prohibition,— which earned for him the sympathetic favour which generally greeted him wherever he went.

And if we affirm that, on this account, if on no other, he amply deserved his popularity. The Royal Marriages Act is an insult to the commonality, to the peerage, to the majesty of this realm. It has perpetuated a consobrinal continuity of intermarriages, which can only ensure moral and physical evils. It was reasonable, therefore, that a Prince of the Blood, who had the courage to break a stupid law, for the sake of common sense and common feeling should receive the grateful homage of a people who pride themselves upon the robustness of their intellect and the power of their natural affection.

From the provincial papers, which were now beginning to be a political force, the following extract from the *Worcester Herald* may be noted:

A law than which nothing viler is to be found in any code of legislation, placed the Duke in a most painful position as regards the tenderest
and dearest relations of human life; and it is humiliating to think that
the Church, degraded by being made the instrument in the case of most
unchristian cruelty, was called upon to separate those whom God hath
joined, not for delict on the part of either the husband or of his unhappy
and amiable wife, but to obey the mistaken and fearfully erroneous
dictates of man.   That unnatural, unrighteous and truly Eastern Act
still disgraces our statutes.   Its destruction would come most gracefully from our amiable Queen, and be a worthy offering to the *manes*
of her much loved uncle.

Lord Baldwin's grandfather George might have read those
words in the *Worcester Herald* that same evening, and perhaps
thanked Heaven that the Baldwins were Methodists.

Here is a picture of the semi-royal widow from the *Memoirs
of Mary Adelaide, Duchess of Teck*:

> After settling down for the winter at Kew, the Duchess seldom
> drove to town in the evening, except to attend a theatre, or to dine
> with the Duke of Cambridge or the Duchess of Gloucester and
> occasionally with the Duchess of Inverness, who still lived at Kensing-
> ton Palace, and was quite a personage in London society.   She was
> small of stature, old-fashioned in dress, and quaint rather than dis-
> tinguished in appearance, but her kindness of heart and general
> *bonhomie* secured for her a large circle of friends and acquaintants.
> The furniture of her apartments, and all her surroundings, were
> reminiscent of days gone by.   She was most hospitable—in fact, no
> visitor ever left her presence without hearing the words, " Come and
> dine."   Her entertainments were void of ostentation, but she was
> always careful to observe the respect due to rank, and whenever the
> Duchess of Cambridge and Princess Mary dined with her, a gentleman
> was deputed to receive them at the entrance; and as they passed down
> the long corridor which led to the reception-room, the footmen,
> drawn up on either side, and wearing semi-royal liveries and nankin
> tights, bowed low.   The small dining-room, fitted up as a tent,
> lacked ventilation—some of the Duchess's guests called it stuffy—but
> the dining-room used on great occasions was large and very convenient.

The Duchess of Inverness survived her husband for thirty
years, did not die indeed until Mr Baldwin, who is now our
leading authority on morganatic marriages, was a little boy of
six, his mind filled with Jacobite romance by his Mac-
Donald mother, in a household which found it difficult to
stand up when the band played *God Save the Queen*.   The
preposterous state of affairs in which the Duchess and her
husband were involved was perpetuated on their common

tomb in Kensal Green. Many a passer-by must have been puzzled by the inscription:

In Memory Of
H.R.H.
AUGUSTUS FREDERICK, DUKE OF SUSSEX
Sixth Son of His Majesty King George The Third.
Born 27th January, 1773.
Died 22nd April, 1843.

In Memory Of
CECILIA LETITIA, DUCHESS OF INVERNESS
Wife of H.R.H. Duke of Sussex
Died 1st August, 1873.

X.

The Duke of Cambridge

Adolphus, Duke of Cambridge, born in 1774, was jilted early in his life by the Princess who afterwards took his brother the Duke of Cumberland as her third husband. At the age of forty-three, when Princess Charlotte died, he was still canonically as well as officially unmarried, and, what may by now be seeming peculiar, had neither a morganatic wife nor a mistress. Forthwith, he proposed for the hand of his cousin, Princess Augusta of Hesse-Cassel to whom he was married on June 1st 1817. This charming, good and generous woman was the grandmother of Queen Mary, and died not five years before that granddaughter was married to the Duke of York. The domestic life of the Duke of Cambridge was too happy for this chronicle of frustrated emotion; but if the Duke himself escaped from the effects of the Royal Marriages Act, his son did not, and further attention will be paid to his story.

XI.

Princess Mary, afterwards Duchess of Gloucester and Edinburgh

Princess Mary was born in 1776. In the words of her youngest sister, she was " Mamma's tool," and she seems to have been used all her life as the family confidante, even although she was sometimes a chatterbox at the expense of her loyalty. Queen Victoria was devoted to her aunt in her old age and felt her death acutely.

In 1816 at the age of forty, when George III was safely mad, Princess Mary married her cousin, the Duke of Gloucester, the son of that frowned-upon marriage in the early years of the reign. ' Silly Billy,' as he was nicknamed, was slightly wanting, and did not always treat his wife too well. He once locked her up in a room and kept her for a while on bread and water. Nevertheless she had been fond of her cousin for twenty years and lost her youth waiting for permission to marry him. An extract out of a letter from Lady Albinia Cumberland to her daughter may amuse :

> " Well, the wedding is over : Dear P^{ss} Mary looked most lovely and *Angelic really* . . . very modest and was quite overcome. . . . After the ceremony, the Regent and the Duke of C. saluted her, and I don't think the Duke of Gloucester did. She then went to the Queen and sisters and was quite overcome, was obliged to sit down, nearly fainted but soon recovered and exerted herself to the utmost. . . . The heat of the rooms, the number of the coaches and the heat of the night was awful. . . . The Duke of Gloucester kissed Miss Dee [*the governess George III had chosen for his sister*] and many more . . . but I did not *see* him go to his new sisters. I suppose he did . . . think of going twenty-six miles late at night after all the agitation she has undergone. . . . The Duke of Gloucester kissed the Regent and the Duke of Cambridge. . . . I am glad it is all over for I thought it very disagreeable and a very long ceremony."

The Duchess of Gloucester died in 1857 without children, surviving her husband 23 years. She was buried at Windsor.

XII.

Princess Sophia

Princess Sophia, the most beautiful (with the lustrous prominent eyes of hysteria) of those six beautiful girls was born in 1777, and her history is shrouded by tragedy's darkest cloak. The accepted version of the story is that Princess Sophia fell in love with a General Garth, an equerry of the King's, thirty-two years older than herself, to whom she was secretly married at Ilsington near Dorchester. According to Greville, " he was a hideous old devil with a great claret mark on his face "; but this Greville did not consider any reason for doubting her being in love with General Garth, " for women fall in love with anything—and opportunity and the accidents of the passions are of more importance than any positive merits of mind or of body. The Princesses were secluded from the world, mixing with few people, their passions boiling over and ready to fall into the hands of the first man whose circumstances availed him to get at them."

On the other hand Miss Burney writing in her diary in 1789 says : " I was sorry to lose Major Garth, who seems a man of real worth, religious principles, and unaffected honour, with a strong share of wit and a great deal of literature." He had gone out to Jamaica on service, but by 1801, the fatal year, he was back in the Royal household.

On one occasion the Princess Sophia was ill and moved from the Lower Lodge at Windsor to a bedroom in the Upper Lodge where the King and Queen were staying with their suite. The bedroom chosen for her was immediately over General Garth's. Nine months later, the Princess bore an infant son. It was reported that George III, who was intermittently mad at the time, was kept in ignorance of what was happening by telling him that his daughter was dropsical and had been cured by roast beef, which the King was in the habit of relating afterwards to people as a very extraordinary fact.

The son grew up to become Captain Garth, and was alleged to have been told by General Garth on his death-bed that his real father was not himself but the Princess's brother, the Duke of Cumberland. Whatever the truth may be, the unhappy

Princess Sophia suffered to the end of her life. She lived alone in Kensington and, to add to her loneliness, went totally blind. Her chief pleasure was to finger and talk about a little collection of curios she had made in youth. From time to time, servants were instructed that no one was to enter her apartments for a whole day, and on these days she was visited by her son. Princess Sophia died in 1848 and was buried in Kensal Green. Beneath her name on her solitary tomb are inscribed the words " *Come unto me all ye that labour and are heavy laden and I will give you rest.*"

Princess Mary Adelaide, afterwards Duchess of Teck, wrote: " Thank God, my poor dear Aunt Sophia . . . died without a sigh with Mama's hand in her own. . . . I doubt not she is now reaping that reward in Heaven to which the patience and sweet temper with which she bore her suffering, and her generosity and kindness to every one entitled her."

XIII and XIV.

Prince Octavius and Prince Alfred

The elder was born in 1779 and the younger in 1780. Both died in early youth.

Prince Alfred, the younger, endured terrible pain before he died at two years of age of what sounds like cerebral meningitis. The King was extremely upset and wrote to the Bishop of Worcester, " *I sometimes think it unkind to wish his recovery had been effected . . . and perhaps end thus at a more mature age.*" Certainly the little Prince was spared that cursed unnatural life his father would have done his best to ensure for him. Prince Alfred was the Queen's favourite and so King George was able to be comparatively philosophic. " Had it been Octavius I should have died too," he said.

Nine months later, the four-year-old Prince Octavius did die. Lady Charlotte Finch, the governess of the Royal children, related that, when she had to wake the King in the night on account of the illness of any of her charges, she used to be surprised by his not coming immediately to the room.

At last she discovered that, before the King left his own room, he used to pray first for the recovery of his child and then for the resignation and support of himself. It was only later on in his madness that he was granted by the Almighty at a personal interview the privilege of raising people from the dead.

Three months after the death of Octavius in 1783, the fifteenth and youngest child Princess Amelia was born.

XV.

Princess Amelia

The story of George III's fifteen children, which had touched the deeps of tragedy with the ill-starred Sophia, comes to an end with the gentle pathos of Princess Amelia, whose tale of thwarted love might have been laid away in Mrs Gaskell's lavender. She was always delicate, and we hear of physicians going down to Windsor to attend a knee for ' scrophula ', which sounds like tuberculosis. All agreed she was an enchanting child, and the crowd that used to travel down from London to watch that domestic scene played upon the terrace of Windsor Castle was doubled in numbers by the prospect of getting a peep at " the little Princess, just turned three years old, in a robe-coat covered with fine muslin, a dressed close cap, white gloves and a fan." Thus Miss Burney, writing in 1786. The little Princess " walked on alone at first, highly delighted in the Parade, and turning from side to side to see everybody as she passed."

For the first five years of Princess Amelia's life the King was fairly sane, but in 1788 he suddenly embraced all his family in church one day, and a few weeks later went completely mad. His youngest daughter was sent for to calm him. Whereupon he got hold of her and vowed nobody should ever take her from him again. The following year he recovered his reason, and Amelia had the pleasure of watching the transparencies in the windows of the Castle that were added to the general illuminations in honour of the happy event.

In spite of her delicacy the youngest Princess matured quickly and by fourteen was said to have looked seventeen. But she was not confirmed for another three years, of which spiritual event the King wrote to the Bishop of Worcester that the Archbishop of Canterbury "*seemed much pleased in the preparatory conversation he had with her at her being well grounded in our holy religion and the serious task she has taken upon herself.*"

In the autumn which followed that melancholy year 1801 of Sophia's misfortune and the King's recurrent insanity Princess Amelia stayed on, after the rest of the Royal Family had left Weymouth, in the care of Miss Gomme who had been one of the sub-governesses for over twenty years. Riding had been declared good for the Princess's health, and the King's equerry who attended her daily rides was General Charles FitzRoy, a son of Lord Southampton, and a handsome man twenty-two years older than she. When they returned to Windsor the rides continued, and after a year Miss Gomme confided in Princess Mary her fear lest an intimacy might have sprung up. Princess Mary confided this fear to Miss Goldsworthy, another sub-governess, and as 'Gooly' was so deaf that everything had to be shouted at her, Amelia's secret became everybody's.

In 1803 Miss Gomme, goaded by Amelia's reproaches, said she should have to inform the Queen, whereupon Amelia anticipated Miss Gomme by writing to her mother about the business. The Queen wrote a long letter back to impress on her youngest daughter that she must not quarrel with Miss Gomme, whose name she spells Gumm or Gum, but never Gomme. The correspondence continued for some time without any mention of General FitzRoy, Queen Charlotte being only concerned that the King should hear nothing of the matter. An indignant correspondence was also carried on between Princess Amelia and Princess Mary. It should be understood that all these royal correspondents were living in Windsor Castle at the time, and that in conversation the matter was never mentioned. Queen Charlotte decided that the rides with FitzRoy should go on in case by their discontinuance the King should be worried. She was also urging her daughter in letters not to tell her brothers anything of the business. Actually the Prince of Wales was in the full confidence of his youngest sister and very sympathetic. So too was the Duke of York; but the Duke of Cumberland was

L

harsh, and the Duke of Kent double-faced. The other brothers were away. Amelia was fretting herself into serious illness, and by the end of 1803 she was already preparing for death. She wrote to FitzRoy:

> "*It is my last dying and only wish that to you, my beloved Charles FitzRoy, my best friend and everything, and who nothing but my unfortunate position parts me from—as I feel assuredly I am the chosen of your heart as you are of mine—I leave you everything I have. . . .*"

1804 was a bad year. The King was making family life intolerable, sacking all the Queen's servants and talking for hours at a stretch. "The Queen was ill and cross; the Princesses low, depressed, and quite sinking under it," noted Malmesbury. The Prince of Wales reported that his father was even saying "the most improper things in the presence of his daughters," Greville noted.

However, in 1805 George III was normal again and plotting to get his little granddaughter the Princess Charlotte away from the Prince of Wales. The trouble was that now his youngest daughter was grown up he was hungering to have more children around him. Charlotte came to Windsor six years later and was not a great success at fifteen. "She hates her 'Granny' as she calls the Queen—loves nobody here except Princess Mary and Sophia, goes swaggering about, and she twangs hands with all the men, is in awe of no one, and glories in her independent way of thinking. Her passion is Horses—that and mathematics are the only amusements she has." Thus Lady Albinia Cumberland. And if Princess Charlotte had not died there would have been no Victoria. It is an awe-inspiring reflection. Charlotte was a diverting hoyden. She once pulled off a bishop's wig. However, the King failed to get hold of her in 1805.

At this time Amelia was writing to FitzRoy as his affianced wife and anticipating the time when she should be twenty-five and able to put her case for marriage before the Privy Council under the terms of the Royal Marriages Act. She was even signing her letters to him "*Ever your own, very own, A. F. R.*", or at other times "*Your affectionate and devoted wife and darling.*"

The Duke of Sussex wrote a kindly letter to his youngest sister entreating her to be prudent; but in October 1807

Miss Gomme and Miss Goldsworthy, who had been abused in anonymous letters for encouraging the intimacy between Amelia and FitzRoy, became " outrageous " and accused the Queen of being the arch-encourager.   Rather late in the day, the Queen now wrote to advise her dear Amelia " *to subdue at once every Passion from the beginning, and to consider the impropriety of indulging any impression which must make you miserable, and bring a disgrace to yourself and a misery to all who love you.*"

Poor Amelia felt driven to elope, but was dissuaded by her new friend Mrs Villiers on account of the shock it would be to the King's mind.   Mrs Villiers also found that FitzRoy some years before had lent Amelia £5000, " for both she and her sisters had been horribly cheated when they first had their allowances from the country, and she had incurred great debts."   FitzRoy wanted the money to be considered a gift, but Mrs Villiers urged repayment.   " She agreed to do so by instalments of £500 per quarter.   These payments passed through many hands for the few remaining quarters of her life."

Amelia now tried to gratify her own thwarted maternity by taking an interest in little Emma Augusta d'Este and the young Fitzclarences.   Presently both her mother and all her brothers and sisters, except the Prince of Wales, seem to have turned against her.   It is welcome to be able to record that Amelia believed that she had in him, " not only a brother, but a father and a friend."

At last, on August 7th 1808, she became twenty-five years old, and her confidante Mrs Villiers was writing to her brother Lord Boringdon to get hold of the Royal Marriages Act. " *We don't know where to get hold of it.   It was made about the year 1771 or 2 or thereabouts.*"

Perhaps if FitzRoy had taken his courage in his hands and asked Amelia to elope with him now all might yet have been well, but one suspects that this lover who was now forty-seven was too cautious.   There was no elopement, and Princess Amelia fell into a decline.   In the summer of 1809 she seemed to get better and was anxiously waiting for an answer from the Privy Council ; but was her request ever formally put before the Privy Council ?   One fancies not.

In 1810 Amelia's health grew much worse.   The Princess of Wales, who of course was not received at Windsor, was going about saying FitzRoy and Amelia were married, which set afoot a strange rumour that the reason why the Royal Family objected to the marriage was that FitzRoy himself was a natural son of George III.   Later on the rumour was elaborated into a preposterous tale that the King's final madness was caused by his discovery of the marriage between half-brother and half-sister.   It is almost certain that there never was a marriage, and that those signatures " A. F. R." and Amelia's allusions to herself in letters as FitzRoy's wife were but the expressions of a passionate longing for the time when she could so sign herself.   It is an old device to console heartsick lovers.

In August 1810 the unhappy Princess was attacked by erysipelas.   She sank rapidly, and the King, now nearly blind, was in despair, keeping the physicians three hours at a stretch answering enquiries about his daughter's health and spending much time discussing with her his hope of her Salvation.

Princess Augusta and Princess Mary arranged for secret visits from FitzRoy to the invalid, who was too weak to bear even the sound of a pianoforte (and the pianoforte was not yet a very resonant instrument) played in the next room. To compensate her for the loss of the music she had so much loved Princess Augusta " gave her a bird which sang very sweetly, and had a very soft note, and she took pleasure in listening to it." *

At one o'clock in the afternoon of All Souls' Day 1810 Princess Amelia died tranquilly.   Her last words were to her sister Mary:

" Tell Charles I die blessing him."

The King, to whom she had given a ring she had had specially made for him, broke down utterly and presently passed into the madness which lasted for the remaining ten years of his life.   Almost his final act of sanity was the choice of his youngest daughter's burial anthem.

> I had a dove and the sweet dove died;
> And I have thought it died of grieving:
> O, what could it grieve for ?   Its feet were tied
> With a silken thread of my hand's own weaving.

So Keats would write " to some music as it was playing " nine years later, an echo perhaps of the music that poor old mad king was for ever playing to himself.

* Miss Knight's *Autobiography.*

On November 13th the funeral took place at night, like all royal obsequies at that date, the way to St George's Chapel being lined by the Staffordshire Militia with torches.

When the will of the late Princess was opened it was found she had left all she had, except a few personal trinkets to her family, to Lieutenant-General the Honourable Charles Fitz-Roy. This did not please the Royal Family, and in the end by a trick the residuary legatee was persuaded to give up all his rights. The Prince of Wales sent him the sardonyx snuff-box which had been left to himself by his sister in her will. FitzRoy declined to accept the snuff-box, and the final touch of irony was that even the balance of the £5000 which FitzRoy had lent to Princess Amelia was never repaid. In 1816 FitzRoy married a Mrs Savage and died in 1831 in his seventieth year.

The King was comforted over the death of his youngest daughter by " a happy delusion that she was in Hanover, not only alive and well, but endowed with the gifts of perpetual youth and health."

A few months after her death Lady Albinia Cumberland wrote to her daughter about the King:

". . . the mind is the same—constantly talking, laughing, sometimes singing. His conversation for now a fortnight was with those that are dead—particularly Prince Octavius whom he doted on. He formed a plan of his marriage. . . . He could only be persuaded to dress in white, which was by wearing a towel, bed-gown and drawers—no stockings and only gaiters. All his ideas were on Purity. He would only drink water or milk and would not eat. Sometimes he thought himself in Heaven and that it was the day of Judgment, and spoke for all the wicked. . . . He appears always happy, except when it is necessary to oppose him in his wishes—then his rage is excessive. . . . Poor things! how I do pity them! But no one so much as Princess Sophia. She is quite broken-hearted! "

In the year 1786 a German lady Sophie de la Roche gave an account in her diary for Tuesday September 19th of an audience Queen Charlotte granted her:

At eight o'clock, during prayers and afterwards in the ante-chamber, the thought struck me that I had beheld their Majesties and the princesses humbly prostrate before God, and now I saw them full of

magnanimity towards me.   I was fully aware of the honour done to
me, for I was not unacquainted with the laws for the ordering of
humanity as introduced by an all-wise Deity to mankind, though I
clearly felt my heart incline before their virtue.   Rather Fate has
granted them the highest position in a great monarchy, and this
distinction made by Providence in itself merits the highest esteem
from the community; I, however, admired rather the moral onus
they had imposed upon themselves.   As my first impression of the
queen was gained from a picture of her and two of her children,
bearing the inscription, " Good queen, good mother," this impression
was revived and accompanied by the tenderest of emotions as I beheld
her surrounded by the four princesses.

The King, a most distinguished and handsome man, listened with
kind attention while I spoke with his worthy consort, and addressed me
very graciously, adding, however, that as " an authoress they should
not speak to me in German."   I replied that " I rejoiced for my
Fatherland that their majesties still loved its language."   Thereupon
he laid his hand upon his breast with fine manly frankness, saying,
" Oh, my heart will never forget that it pulses with German blood.
All my children speak German."

At that moment the princesses approached.   Her eldest Highness,
a really lovely princess; Princess Augusta, lively and attractive; the
two youngest ones very innocent and sweet.   They all addressed me
in German; are all kindly disposed, and their beauty proves that they
are children born of purest love. . . .   Some thoughts from two poets of
whom I am very fond occurred to me; and with Jacobi in his prologue
to *Elysium* I spoke the words:

> She smiles at thee—of queens the very best,
> Of innocence the priestess blest !

These thoughts were most compelling as I beheld her there encircled
by her children, her piety and culture fitting her for great motherly
devotion.

The King recalled Thomson's poem on *Liberty*.   I fancied I would
rather have seen him King of England than of any other realm.

In spite of our knowing from Fanny Burney's Diary that
the Queen was extremely annoyed at the way this audience
had been secured by Madame de la Roche through the " in-
delicacy " of another lady of the Court Queen Charlotte was
such a mistress of simulation and dissimulation that she was
able to send the gushing foreigner away in a rapture, and that
is significant when we consider how firmly the legend of the
purity and beauty and truth of that Georgian manifestation of
Windsor domesticity persists to this day.   The subsequent
behaviour of the Princes does not assail it ; such a falling away
is reprobated as the ingratitude of unnatural sons toward the

best of parents.   They live on, two or three of those Princes, to oppress Queen Victoria with their disgraceful avuncular existence.   We behold them vanish at the touch of her wand like pantomime demons, and swiftly again the Victorian legend of Windsor domesticity begins a fresh cycle.

Here are two contemporary comments on that morbid family life created by George III, to set off against Madame de la Roche's sentimental view of it.   The first is from Lady Charlotte Campbell, in a reminiscence of the Princess of Wales expressing to herself her dislike of Greville:

> . . . I could forgive him for anything he said of myself, because I have good broad shoulders; but he calls my daughter [Charlotte] an abandon'd little thing, and, damn me [she often swears that oath], if he ever shall meet her at this house again.   The case vas, you see, that Mr Greville abuse all the royal family to her, vich vas a great impertinence, as I should say, and she, poor little ting, vanted to excuse dem; so, ven Mr Greville, in his wisdom, said it was a pity the duke should have his mistress here, vare the princesse vas, she answered, Oh, lord upon us, vat would you have; de dukes cannot marry, dey must love somebody; but she is a young ting, and not prepared for such matters."

And the second is from a leader in *The Times* upon the death of Queen Charlotte in 1818:

> Were it safe to found a judgment, on the recent dispersion of the princes of the blood royal, and of some of the princesses, we might, however reluctantly, conclude that Her Majesty had not altogether succeeded in attaching to her the hearts of her children.   The Duke of Cumberland is out of the question.   The inflexible, though well-meant, determination of the Queen to stigmatise her niece, by shutting the doors of the royal palace against her, may excuse strong feelings of estrangement or resentment, on the part of the Duchess or of her husband; but that the Dukes of Clarence, Kent, and Cambridge at the same time should have quitted, as if by signal, their parent's death-bed, is a circumstance which in lower life would have at least astonished the community.   The departure of Princess Elizabeth, the Queen's favourite daughter, who married and took leave of her in the midst of that illness which it was pronounced would shortly bring her to the grave, may perhaps have been owing to the injunction of Her Majesty. The Duke of Gloucester stands in a more remote degree of relationship: Prince Leopold more distant still; but they all quitted the scene of suffering at a period when its fatal termination could not be doubted.

The ugly little princess who nearly sixty years earlier had played *God Save the King* on her guitar to the seasick duchesses in the North Sea was buried on December 2nd with solemn nocturnal pomp of sable plumes and velvet mourning-cloaks and torches. The King himself was blind and mad. Her lovely rival of long ago Lady Sarah was blind. Throughout that history of outraged nature, smothered passion, broken hearts, perjured vows, of wives repudiated, mistresses discarded, and children wronged not one example is there of a bishop's intervening to denounce the sins against the sacrament of marriage which were being encouraged by the Royal Marriages Act. Not one bishop ventured to rebuke George III for his pride before that pride was terribly abased. The laxity, scepticism, and cynical indifference of the clergy do not invalidate the doctrines and discipline they are ordained to expound ; but the memory of their predecessors' cowardice and neglect should be ever present in the minds of the Anglican bishops of to-day, and if thereby they are rendered contrite and humble their spiritual influence may yet be felt.

CHAPTER XVII

THE MARRIAGE OF QUEEN VICTORIA

WE have already noted a letter from the Princess Victoria of Kent to her uncle the King of the Belgians, written on the eve of her seventeenth birthday in which she gives him her opinion that one of her young cousins, Prince Albert, is " extremely handsome " and that Ernest " certainly is not ", though " he has a most good-natured, honest, and intelligent countenance." No more damning description of a young man than that of Ernest could be penned by a girl of seventeen. A fortnight later, she was writing to thank her beloved uncle " for the prospect of *great* happiness " he had contributed to give her " in the person of dear Albert." " Allow me then, my dearest uncle, to tell you how delighted I am with him, and how much I like him in every way. He possesses every quality that could be desired to render me perfectly happy "; and, to leave no doubt in Uncle Leopold's mind, she gushed on for a few more sentences about her joy in Albert and her desire that her uncle should have a special care for his health.

We can feel fairly confident King Leopold was satisfied that his nephew Albert had made an impression on the girlish fancy of his niece. Leopold as the husband of Princess Charlotte had had experience of a royal maiden, and as the expected consort of a future Queen of England he was in a position to offer the best of advice and provide the best of training for a young nephew who might be luckier than himself. So far as his own ambition would allow him Leopold had loved that young princess who with her child had been killed by the incompetence of a couple of English doctors. His own ambition had now been gratified by becoming King of the Belgians and husband of the Princess Louise-Marie, daughter of King Louis-Philippe. To be sure the father of Louis-Philippe was believed not to be the Duke of Orléans, the contemptible Égalité, but a Tuscan *guardia* called Chiappini, whose son had been exchanged for the daughter that would lose Égalité his Bourbon wife's inheritance. However, Louis-Philippe, supposititious or not, had married the daughter of a Naples Bourbon and an Austrian Archduchess. So there was plenty of authentic Bourbon-Habsburg blood for the Belgian dynasty Leopold was founding. Still, he never completely recovered from his disappointment at not becoming Prince Consort of the Queen of England, and there is no doubt the prospect of a match between his niece and nephew afforded him the warmest vicarious satisfaction. There was a story being whispered round Europe that Albert was not the son of his brother Ernest-Anthony, the Duke of Coburg; but Louise, who as heiress added Gotha to the Coburg Duchy, was not divorced until 1826, five years after Albert was born, and there is no evidence beyond rumour of his irregular paternity. His mother after her divorce married again and died in 1831. To her husband Graf von Pölzig she bequeathed a substantial annuity on condition that he should never be parted from her embalmed body. Pölzig married again, but continued to travel round with the body of the dead Duchess until one day it was lost on a journey. Luckily for him the annuity was still paid, and that reminder of his former felicity was therefore unmourned. A tale like this should help posterity to judge Albert's extreme prudery with sympathy. It might prejudice any boy of twelve against sexual indulgence to know that the embalmed body of his dead divorced mother was travelling round Europe as a condition of her second husband's income.

It has become an *idée fixe* with the biographers of Queen

Victoria's youth that those expressions of her interest in Albert
are to be discounted as the expression of a sister's love for a
brother and, according to Lytton Strachey, as an expression
of it inspired and even dictated by her governess Baroness
Lehzen.   Strachey talks of them as having happened " years
ago, when she was a mere child,"—a careless treatment of
dates.   To Strachey's emotionally incomplete mind Victoria's
girlish fancy for her handsome young cousin was less
comprehensible than the loves of the triangles might have
been.   It is easier to believe that Victoria fell in love with
Albert at their first meeting and resolved then that he should be
her future husband.   What probably did happen during the
first two years of her reign was that her mind was enchantingly
occupied with the pleasure of being Queen and with the
ability to put people in their places, whether it was her mother
or dear Queen Adelaide or her aunt the Duchess of Cambridge
or the unfortunate Lady Flora Hastings.   On top of that,
she was no doubt fascinated by an agreeable intimacy with a
man of the world like Lord Melbourne—a man so much of
the world, be it remembered, that he had been co-respondent
in two divorce cases and had had for a wife the most notoriously
complicated piece of female emotion the century had produced,
a wife who had won the heart of the difficult Lord Byron
himself.   In shouting after the Queen " Mrs Melbourne ",
the London mob overstepped the mark, but to any man who
knew how to play the part of *cavaliere servente*, whether it was
Lord Melbourne or Lord Beaconsfield or John Brown, the
Queen could provide a wealth of response.   It was a shock
to find with the publication of her letters and journals that a
woman believed to be inhuman was, in fact, human ; but it is
better that she should remain human than to follow the present
fashion of trying to make her superhuman.

On January 2nd 1837, in writing to thank her uncle for an
account of some ball in Brussels, Victoria tells him that the
last ball *she* was at was one which came to an end at half-past
three in the morning by her dancing a country dance with
Albert.   And then—mark the girlish cunning of the little
princess—her uncle is to tell both the young gentlemen that she
often thinks of that night, which since she had danced more
often with Albert at that ball than she had with Ernest was a
discreet message for the young gentleman to whom she wanted
it to be given.   It must be insisted that the chief reason why
Queen Victoria had such confidence in Uncle Leopold's

views about her marriage was his own marriage to that daughter of George IV who by dying with her infant son in childbirth made necessary that hasty mating of three middle-aged dukes, from whose tontine of begettings she and that cousin Prince George of Cambridge, two months older than herself but sprung from a junior father, were the survivors.   No doubt the Cambridges had thought their George would make an admirable husband for Victoria.   The young Queen had other ideas.   Dear old King William had thought one of the princes of Orange would make an admirable husband for her. Victoria had other ideas even then, and the strength of these ideas was reinforced by Leopold, who had himself cut out a Prince of Orange as husband for Princess Charlotte and had no desire now to see the moral aggrandisement of his rival in Holland.   When Leopold failed to secure the throne of Greece, he decided to live in England and, what is more, to go through with a morganatic marriage with the actress Caroline Bauer.* After he was elected King of the Belgians in 1831 and had the perpetual neutrality of his country guaranteed by the great Powers, he settled down to ripen into the Nestor of Europe. But he stuck to his £50,000 annuity from England and was determined to marry his nephew to his niece.

So on Boxing Day 1837 we find that niece aged eighteen and a half arranging with this rococo Nestor how the nephew is to be educated.   He reports progress.   Studies at Bonn will be over by the beginning of May.   The time from May till the beginning of August might be used in another visit to England if his niece approved.   A *séjour* at Coburg would *not* be of much use.   Perhaps three months with Uncle Mensdorff would give him time for some manly accomplishments but to make him enter the Service would *not* do at all.   Victoria must not be worried about Albert's imbibing political principles. Prague was not a town where politics were at all agitated, and in any case no one in three months could make him imbibe political principles.   Would his niece communicate with him after she had turned over in her mind what he had written? No answer to that letter remains, but we can conclude that the young Queen did not advise a visit from Albert to England between May and August.   She preferred to run the risk of his imbibing political principles at Prague.   The fact of the matter was her mind was delightfully taken up just now with

* She was a cousin of the impeccable Stockmar, who himself encouraged the clandestine marriage which took place at a house in Regent's Park in 1829.

the pleasure and profit of long talks with Lord Melbourne. Naturally, there was no question of anything in the nature of a *tendresse* for her Prime Minister, but there was plenty of time to settle down and she did not want to spoil the enjoyment of her new position by making Lord Melbourne jealous of her interest in a young man, especially as that young man had first to be drilled and moulded into a suitable husband for herself, that self she held in such immeasurable esteem.

In February 1838 the Queen's journal seems to suggest that there was an inclination on her part to sound Lord Melbourne on the subject of marriage, for she told him that Uncle Leopold had been " amazingly frightened when the Prince of Orange came over with his sons as he had always imagined that the late King had some intentions about " a marriage between her and one of the young Dutch princes. On this Lord Melbourne told Victoria that King William certainly had entertained such intentions and that he had had to tell him the connection with Holland was not politically desirable.   The King had always been afraid of a marriage the Duchess of Kent had in view and wanted to forestall her. Then, the young Queen notes, Lord Melbourne had told him he had better be sure first " if the Parties themselves liked it . . . of which, Lord Melbourne said, the King never seemed sensible : at which I laughed."

Was ever a more significant laugn recorded in a journal ? It is as richly charged with meaning as Lord Burleigh's famous nod in the play.   We shall be paying respectful homage to that laugh if we say it expressed Victoria's reflection how easy it was to deceive a man so wise in the ways of the world and of women as Lord Melbourne, a contempt for her old uncle King William, a triumphant recognition of the superiority of her own matchmaking wit to her mother's, a chuckle at the secret correspondence that was being carried on between her and Uncle Leopold, and a delicious trill of elation at how much one of the parties was well on the way to liking it and the other party being drilled by Uncle Leopold to justify that liking.

Lord Melbourne went on to say that the Prince of Orange had asked him if he or the Government had any objection to such a connection and Lord Melbourne had said none, personally, " no more than to any other Prince in Europe," and surely as he said that, he must have looked up quickly from under those shaggy eyebrows of his to invite a confidence. The confidence was not forthcoming.   The Queen merely noted in her journal that night that " it was all very curious and interesting for me to hear." By mid-April, however, the campaign between the allies for the education of Albert was in full swing. Campaign is not an inappropriate word. Victoria had fixed upon Baron Stockmar as " commissary-general," in order to give " *unité de l'action et de l'ensemble* " : such *unité de l'action et de l'ensemble* as would not be repeated until another April exactly eighty years later, when it was given to Marshal Foch.

Prague was apparently ruled out as a suitable background to a vacation. The young gentleman returned to Bonn and remained there until the end of August.

" On one thing you can rely that *it is my great anxiety* to see Albert a *very good and distinguished young man*, and *no pains will be thought too much on my part if this end can be obtained. . . .*"

Thus wrote King Leopold underlining heavily.

On October 6th 1838 came that conversation already noted between Melbourne and the Queen to let her Prime Minister know, in case he had any lingering doubts in the matter, that she liked best to judge for herself in these questions.

In April 1839 it looked as if Lord Melbourne were discouraging the Coburg match : " cousins are not very good things " and " those Coburgs are not popular abroad." Apparently it was to reassure him that the Queen declared her " feeling was quite against ever marrying." Melbourne agreed that it was a very serious thing both as regards its political effect and her own happiness. On this she praised Albert to him and reminded him that he was younger than herself,* presumably with the notion of suggesting how much this would facilitate his ductility. As the conversation continued, very tactfully on Lord Melbourne's part, he let the Queen know that a foreigner might not be popular in the country. At this hint of opposition the Queen observed that " marrying a subject was making yourself so much their equal, it brought you so in contact with the whole family," and immediately Melbourne, scenting opposition, agreed. Then the Queen asked why she need marry at all for three or four years. " I was so accustomed to having my own way, that I thought it was 10–1, that I shouldn't agree with anyone.

* Three months.

Lord M. said, ' Oh, but you would have it still,' " and the Queen adds in brackets ' my own way ', as if she or anyone else could ever need such an elucidation.   It is amusing to notice her laying the odds.   That must have been Lord M.'s bad example.   Devout Victorians may be grateful he did not teach her to swear, for he used much strong language.

Now enters female duplicity.   On July 12th the Queen opened the ball by expressing a fear that too many of her relations had come over that year, and when Melbourne told her " there had been no remarks made about it ", she sighed becomingly and told him how tiresome it was that her cousins Ernest and Albert were coming over.   She really had no great wish to see Albert, because the whole subject of marriage was " an odious one ", but, though there was no engagement between them, " the young man was aware of the possibility of such a union ", and it was not right to keep him on.   Lord Melbourne suggested she should make *them* distinctly understand nothing could be done for a year, whereupon female duplicity replied how disagreeable it was for her to see *him*. " It's very disagreeable," Lord Melbourne agreed, and perhaps the twinkle was quenched by those shaggy eyebrows.   The Queen begged her Prime Minister to say nothing about the marriage to anyone else.   Indeed, she almost anticipated the very words of her great-grandson ninety-seven years later, " You and I must settle this between us.   I won't have anyone interfering."

Three days later the Queen wrote to ask Uncle Leopold if Albert were aware of his family's wish relative to herself: a strange question from one who but three days before had told Melbourne that the young man was aware of such a possibility.   Her second question is more like that of a client who, threatened with a breach of promise suit, writes to his lawyer.   She wanted to know if Albert perfectly understood there was no engagement between them.   " Engagement " was heavily underlined.   And Uncle Leopold was to tell Uncle Ernest (the Duke of Saxe-Coburg) that even if she found she liked Albert he must be prepared to wait for three years if necessary.   It is the next paragraph in this letter which has misled historians into asserting that at the first meeting, just before her seventeenth birthday, she liked Albert only as a friend, a cousin, a brother, but no more. What Victoria said was that if she found, on meeting him again, that she only liked him platonically—which, in her own words, " was not likely "—she was anxious to be acquitted of any breach of promise, for she had never given one.   In a word, it is clear she had intended to marry Albert from the first time she met him, but was protecting herself in case he did not live up to her expectations during this crucial coming visit, by stipulating that he was to be dismissed without a grievance.

On August 6th the Queen's journal records that Lord Melbourne admitted with a laugh—after some hesitation—that he did not like the connection very much.   It was then he received a warning from those prominent light-blue eyes. *Much* as the Queen loved her country and *all* that she was ready to do for its good, she still thought her own " liking was one of the principal things."   In fact, she seems to have had a disgraceful and unbishoply ' craving for private happiness,' which, it may be added, she was often able to gratify. There was further discussion about marrying subjects, which was abruptly concluded by the Queen's murmuring she had heard Albert was very handsome.

On September 25th she wrote to Uncle Leopold that he was to keep the cousins in Brussels in order that they should not arrive at Windsor until Thursday the 3rd, and " if possible, *early.*"   The reason for this was that a number of her ministers were coming to Windsor to stay from Monday to Thursday " on affairs of great importance," and on account of gossip she did not want them to be there when the cousins arrived ; but the ministers were to be cleared out of Windsor early on Thursday morning and there was to be no time wasted after their departure.   Meanwhile, sweet and twenty concludes, " a day or two at Brussels will do these young gentlemen good, and they can be fitted out there for their visit."

On October 1st We were not amused, and as a result We were writing severely to Uncle Leopold that the *rétard* of these young people put Us rather out.   The Queen had received a letter from Albert yesterday to say he and his brother could not leave Brussels before the 8th.   " I think they don't exhibit much *empressement* to come here, which rather shocks me," she commented.

On October 10th the cousins arrived and she received them at half-past seven.   She found them " grown and changed and embellished," and Albert, whom she beheld with some emotion, " *beautiful* ".   The next day she was admiring " Albert's mouth with delicate moustachios, and slight but very slight whiskers." His figure too was beautiful, " broad in the shoulders and a fine waist." Five quadrilles were danced, two of them with dearest Albert, and apparently in spirit all the others, for she noted what a pleasure it was to look at Albert when he galloped and valsed with " that beautiful figure of his."

To Uncle Leopold she wrote of Albert's beauty and fascination and of her delight in their (*sic*) companionship. And she tells him that as she writes these words, " they are playing symphonies of Haydn under me."

On October 13th the Queen may have been humming to herself the Surprise Symphony when in her next talk with Lord Melbourne she admitted that seeing her cousins again had changed her opinion about marriage a good deal and that she must decide soon, which was difficult.

" Another week," suggested Lord Melbourne. " Certainly, a very fine young man and very good-looking."

The Queen readily agreed to this opinion, but added praise of her own for Albert's amiability and good temper, so necessary because she had such a bad temper. Then, in a burst of frankness, she confessed the advantage of beauty. Lord Melbourne had already told her beauty was not to be despised, but earlier on, when she was misleading him, she had pretended to esteem it of no account. Even now, lest he should suspect her of Mother Eve's failings, she reminded him how religious her cousins were.

" That strong Protestant feeling is a good thing in this country," Lord Melbourne agreed, " if it isn't intolerant."

That evening the Prime Minister wrote to Lord John Russell from Windsor Castle :

" What I mentioned to you the other day is exactly taking the course which I expected, and which I then traced out to you. A very strong impression is evidently made, and as much was said to me to-day as is sufficient to prove that the mind is, indeed, made up and will be declared shortly. I think, myself, that it is time this should be effected, and I do not know that anything better could be done. He seems a very agreeable young man—he is certainly a very good-looking one—and as to character, that we must always take our chance of. Supposing it to be decided, what would you say with respect to time ? Delay in such matters is always objectionable. It would, of course, be, in every point of view, and for every purpose necessary to have a Parliament."

The next day the Queen declared that the Mind was made up.

" You have ? " exclaimed Lord Melbourne, contriving to appear much surprised.

After this, with great skill the Queen managed to throw on her Prime Minister the immodesty of being the one to suggest a quick wedding.   Then they talked of how the proposal should be made, over which she and Lord Melbourne had many a laugh—in spite of his having been the co-respondent in two divorce cases.

That evening Victoria wrote to Uncle Leopold of her happiness and of the way she had consulted Lord Melbourne about the whole affair, which, as we have seen, was no more than the way she had decided to tell him she was determined to marry Albert.   She was also delighted to let her uncle know that she should be getting married at the beginning of February : she had been much delighted, too, by Ernest's pleasure, which she explained was due to his adoration of dearest Albert.   There is, of course, another explanation.

Leopold wrote back from Wiesbaden on October 24th his *Nunc dimittis*, and the Queen in her reply told him that as " *Parliament* had nothing whatever to say regarding the marriage approving or disapproving in a manner which might affect it, it was proposed to assemble all the Privy Councillors in November when the cousins had left and announce to them her intention."   The letter concluded with a message from Lord Melbourne to King Leopold, " That he can have no other object than that which he considers best to secure my happiness, which is closely connected with the well-being of the country."

Lord Melbourne had certainly a larger humanity than Mr Baldwin, and some of us may think a larger wisdom, even those of us who may be prejudiced by the complacency with which that twenty-year-old Queen takes so much for granted the identification of her country's well-being with her own craving for private happiness.

A letter from the Queen to her uncle the Duke of Sussex is typical of those she sent to all her English royal relatives :

My dear Uncle,
           The affection which you have shown me makes me

feel certain that you will take interest in an event which so nearly concerns the future happiness of my life; I cannot, therefore, delay any longer to inform you of my intended marriage with my cousin Albert, the merits of whose character are so well known by all who are acquainted with him, that I need say no more than that I feel as assured of my own happiness as I can of anything in this world.

As it is not to be publicly known, I beg you not to mention it except to our own Family.

I hope you are well and enjoying yourself. Believe me always your affectionate Niece

VICTORIA R.

On November 18th, five days before the announcement of her forthcoming marriage was made to the Privy Council, a letter was sent by the Queen to Lord Melbourne, giving him an account of the visit of the Cambridges. She notes that they " were all very kind and civil,"—George, like the Coburg cousins, " grown ", but unlike them, " not embellished ". Amusingly, the Queen drops into the first person when she records Prince George's pleasure at being clear of her. She also mentions that the Duchess of Gloucester " was suffering so much from the necessity of keeping the secret." So the Duchess of Gloucester still found it difficult to keep a secret even thirty years after poor Princess Amelia was in her grave.

The history of the Queen's marriage—from the day she first met Albert to the day she proposed to him—may be summed up in Greville's comment:

> The Queen settled everything about her marriage herself, and without consulting Melbourne at all on the subject, not even communicating to him her intentions. The reports were already rife while he was in ignorance, and at last he spoke to her, told her he could not be ignorant of the reports nor could she; that he did not presume to enquire what her intentions were, but that it was his duty to tell her that if she had any it was necessary that her ministers should be apprised of them. She said she had nothing to tell him, and about a fortnight afterwards she informed him that the whole thing was settled.

In a biased article in the *Daily Telegraph* of December 5th 1936, Dr Ivor Jennings, an expert on the Constitution, had to admit the right of reigning sovereigns to choose their consort without consulting any minister, and added:

" It might be that if a young and inexperienced Queen could decide for herself, a King of mature age and long experience of the duties of the office (even if new to the Throne) could do likewise. The circumstances are, however, different. . . . Queen Alexandra and Queen Mary bore their share of the burden of public service, thus placed by the monarchs upon themselves. The wife of any king in the future will be expected to play the same part."

What this amounts to saying is that there are more foundation-stones to lay nowadays, more bridges and bazaars to declare open, more ships to name, more nurses and girl-guides to inspect, more wearisome ceremonies of every kind to attend graciously and becomingly.

Whatever explanation there may be of Melbourne's attitude, nobody can be blind to the fact that she outmanœuvred him. We might have expected as much from Lord Melbourne, who had been dragged into the Norton separation proceedings so blatantly that Dickens parodied the evidence against him in Mr Sergeant Buzfuz's speech in Bardell *v.* Pickwick. Probably the British Public is right in its instinct to distrust the political capacity of a man who has been a co-respondent. He is rejected by the world on the grounds of morality, but the real reason for rejecting him is expediency. Such a statesman can be caught napping, as Lord Melbourne was caught napping by Queen Victoria. We may surmise too that he was a little in love with her himself. Yes, that charming and susceptible man of the world was undoubtedly caught napping. It must be remembered that rumours of this intended marriage were prevalent throughout 1838 and, though the Whigs were amenable, the Tories bitterly resented it.

In December 1838 *The Times* was writing :

> There is no foreigner who sets his foot in England less welcome to the people generally or looked at with more distrust and alienation than Leopold, the Brummagem King of Belgium, who is nothing better than a provisional prefect of France, on whose ruler his marriage has made him doubly dependent.

A month later the *Sun*, a Whig paper, stated positively that the Queen was going to marry Prince Albert. Next day, *The Times* asked if somebody had not been hoaxing the *Sun*, and Melbourne's paper, the *Morning Chronicle*, authoritatively contradicted the *Sun*. In August 1839 the *Morning Post* announced the marriage again, and one suspects that some of these announcements may have been inspired from Brussels as a test of public opinion. However, on November 25th, when at last the marriage was undeniable, *The Times* thundered:

> On Saturday the Privy Council, according to precedent, assembled for the purpose of receiving the Sovereign's gracious communication of her intended marriage. According to precedent, the summons was a general one, and it might have been expected that some regard to the same precedent would also have been preserved in the Royal declaration. . . .
>
> For the most part, with the alterations necessary to suit the circumstances, the precedent of King George III has been followed in the declaration of Queen Victoria, but in this declaration HER MAJESTY'S MINISTERS have omitted *one passage*, and that is the passage which carries the PLEDGE FOR THE PROTESTANT RELIGION.
>
> Do we infer from this omission that our Sovereign is unfriendly, or even indifferent to the religion of her family, and people? We allow no suspicion of such a nature to have a moment's place in our minds. Do we conclude that the Prince to whom she is about to unite herself is regardless of the Protestant faith? All testimonies concur to establish a contrary persuasion. Queen VICTORIA and Prince ALBERT are as little open to any suspicion of anti-Protestant bias even as her MAJESTY'S grandfather himself.

Apart from the desire to make party capital, *The Times* was suspicious of the way one or two of the Coburg princes had accepted Catholicism as a velvet lining for their crowns, though this was not true of Leopold.

> In the case of 1761 [*The Times* continued] the Sovereign was a male, and, therefore, unlikely to be swayed in the momentous question of religion by the female partner of his throne; the case of 1839 is that of a Sovereign whose sex does not preclude the probability that conjugal affection may have considerable weight in a matter of such importance. It may be, and we have no doubt it is, the perfect truth, that the influence of the Prince now selected is not likely to be exerted in any way unfavourable to the Protestant faith; but was it not then due to him, as well as to the people, *to let that truth be stated?*

But in a long article published on the Queen's wedding-day, February 10th 1840, *The Times* surpassed itself. After much criticism of the unpopularity and untrustworthiness of the House of Saxe-Coburg, the best of a bad job was made by thus summing up the good that Prince Albert might effect:

> He has the means of so directing and so assisting her future footsteps as to retrieve for HER MAJESTY much of what (we speak with frankness but with all respect) she has forfeited in the hearts of the most

loyal, enlightened and virtuous of her subjects, through her unhappy bias towards persons and principles which are hourly undermining the deep foundations of her throne.

We have said that it devolves upon Prince Albert to counteract a host of " evil " influences, and to aid his Royal Consort in repairing " many very grievous errors " into which selfish and treacherous counsellors have betrayed her, and which her constant separation (continued by them) from all but one section or coterie of her subjects has served to render extremely difficult of correction.

QUEEN VICTORIA has scarcely been permitted to see the general aspect of the British aristocracy, or to become acquainted with their sentiments, their characters or their manners.   The petty, artificial world, framed and got up for her deception, is no more capable of suggesting to her mind the vast moral and social creation beyond its narrow boundaries, than one or two leaves of a *hortus siccus* can exemplify the productions of a noble forest, or a varied and inimitable landscape.   Let any honest impartial eye take a survey of the Court of Queen Victoria—that Court which a mercenary and profligate, a contemned and odious Administration has, for its vile purposes, surrounded her—and then answer us whether her new consort will find there a faithful sample of the dignity and character of this realm ?

Are the heads of the nation to be discovered at the Queen of England's court ?   Has the worth or wisdom or eminence of the nation any access to the society of the Sovereign ?   Have the clergy of England, or any of them—have their representatives,—bishops, priests or deacons, the opportunity of communicating personally with the temporal head of the Church of England ?   Are they or any of them, ever seated at the Royal table, or received into the Royal presence or favoured with the Royal smile ?   No, such associations comport not with the policy of her Ministers.   The ear of the Sovereign is whispered from the choicest of her subjects—the palace doors are locked inexorably against all but a certain clique.   In so far as on *them* depends, the confidential advisers of HER MAJESTY have laboured to make their Sovereign the QUEEN of a frivolous, factious and worthless coterie, to the amazement and alarm of the Ministers of all the Courts of Europe.   *Is this as it ought to be ?*

Clearly it was the duty of Dr Howley, the Archbishop of Canterbury, to let the Queen's friends know that they stood rebuked, even although in 1820 as Bishop of London he had laid it down " that the King could do no wrong either morally or physically." This prelate was a sterling example of reactionary opinion. In 1829 he had led the opposition to Catholic Emancipation. In 1831 he had opposed the Reform Bill at first, but, with that exquisite episcopal sensitiveness to the way of the wind, had not opposed the third reading. In 1833 he had successfully moved the rejection of the Jewish Civil Disabilities Bill. In 1839 he had denounced Lord John

Russell's education scheme. Yes, he would have been an admirable adviser at Windsor.

And surely we may say of that savage *Times* attack of a hundred years ago " *autres temps, autres mœurs.*" We are not impressed by the debauchery of a Court in which the twenty-year-old Queen was dancing country dances at half-past three in the morning or playing battledore and shuttlecock with her Prime Minister as late as eleven at night. It is conceivable that 2036 will decide that jazzing at Fort Belvedere to gramophone records, or drinking a cocktail before dinner, or even planting rhododendrons with the help of an American lady were less noxious diversions than *The Times* of 1937 presumably supposed them to be. Or, perhaps not. Perhaps, instead of writing ' *autres temps, autres mœurs,*' we should write, ' *plus ça change, plus c'est la même chose.*'

CHAPTER XVIII

THE DUKE OF CAMBRIDGE AND MRS FITZGEORGE

THE story of the marriage of the Duke of Cambridge with Louisa Fairbrother has already been related, but in view of the bearing that marriage has on the question of morganatic marriage in this country, it may be as well to amplify some of the details, all of which reflect great credit on the Duke of Cambridge himself, and as much cannot be said of the details of those other royal marriages under the English rose.

On February 26th 1840, that is to say sixteen days after she was married, Greville notes that the Queen gave a dance at Buckingham Palace, adding in brackets (". . . for they are always dancing or doing nothing ") without asking Prince George of Cambridge to it and recorded this as a trifling example of the " state and animus of the Court."

In November 1842 Greville, who occupied the confidential post of Clerk to the Privy Council, noted that he had been busy trying to think of a way to stifle scandalous stories which had gone all over the world about Prince George of Cambridge and Lady Augusta Somerset. It was said that he had got her with child and that the Queen had been exercising her right under the Royal Marriages Act to forbid his making an honest woman of her. Apparently, the only foundation for the story then being circulated freely in both British and continental newspapers was that while her father the Duke of Beaufort was abroad, Lady Augusta had had a light flirtation with the Prince during the past year at Kew, a flirtation, one is glad to read of a hundred years ago, " such as is continually going on without any serious result between half the youths and girls in London."

The result of Greville's cogitations was that he on behalf of the Duke of Beaufort, and Lord Adolphus Fitzclarence (why did he not send the Reverend Lord Augustus Fitzclarence, the Rector of Mapledurham ?) on behalf of Prince George, went to the editorial office of *The Times* and asked them to put in a formal contradiction of the story. But, as Greville adds, " there is such a disposition to believe such stories and such reluctance to renounce a belief once entertained, that even the contradiction in *The Times* will not secure the lady against the calumny for the rest of her life," and then he notes that, although Lady Augusta never was with child, she was inclined to behave with very little prudence, delicacy or reserve, but adds of the Prince, " Fortunately he is a very timid, unenterprising youth, not unwilling to amuse himself, but by no means inclined to incur any serious risks, as he has abundantly shown on other occasions. His vanity prompts him to make love to the ladies whom he meets in his country quarters, and as princes are scarce, his blood royal generally finds easy access to rural and provincial beauties, but when he finds these affairs growing serious and the objects of his admiration evince an embarrassing alacrity to meet his flame with corresponding ardour, I am told that he usually gets alarmed and backs out with much more prudence than gallantry."

These comments by Greville possess an amusing fatuity for us because in that very month of November 1842 this timid and unenterprising youth was already on such intimate terms with Miss Sarah Louisa Fairbrother of the Theatre Royal, Drury Lane, that on August 27th 1843 she would present him with his eldest son, George William Adolphus. This coming event, however, was still a close secret.

In February 1843, that grand woman the Duchess of Cambridge arrived at Windsor Castle with Lady Augusta Somerset. The Duchess of Kent, the Queen's mother, had championed the fair name of Lady Flora Hastings under a similar accusation of pregnancy, which turned out to be an incurable disease of which the unfortunate lady of the Court died, and this had been one of the episodes which made the second year of the Queen's reign so unpopular.

According to Greville, the visit of the Duchess of Cambridge and Lady Augusta passed off without open unpleasantness; but soon afterwards the Duchess of Gloucester visited Windsor, and to her the Queen held forth in a rage, vowed that the story about Lady Augusta was true and that the Duchess of Cambridge had behaved abominably in bringing her to Windsor to avoid the scandal. 'Mamma's tool' of a long ago Windsor girlhood, enchanted by the prospect of being deedy, asked if the Queen wanted her to tell the Duchess of Cambridge what she had said. When the Queen issued her royal command in the affirmative, the Duchess grew a little nervous and asked that a written note of authority might be given her. So a note was delivered.

The Duke and Duchess were furious, and the Duke wrote to ask her Majesty if she supposed they would bring Lady Augusta to Windsor or allow her to stay at Kew with their own daughter * unless she were innocent of the charge. The Duke declared he was as much bound to protect her as if he were her own father. This letter was answered by Prince Albert who wrote that as " Prince George had given his word of honour that the story was untrue, *he supposed* they *must* believe *that it was so*." Naturally, this reply did not satisfy the Duke of Cambridge, nor the Duke of Beaufort who by this time had been informed of what had happened. The angry father wrote to Sir Robert Peel and demanded an audience of the Queen. The Prime Minister argued he would gain nothing by such an audience, because the Queen would merely bow him out as she had bowed out Lord Hastings. However, the Duke of Cambridge insisted that Peel should communicate with the Queen and at last, after a great many pourparlers and much negotiation amongst them all, Peel wrote to the Duke of Beaufort or the Duke of Cambridge or both to say the Queen was now entirely satisfied and begged there might be no further discussion on the subject. Greville observed that the whole business was not very creditable to the Queen and her husband, especially after the Flora Hastings affair, but " between the prudery of

* Princess Augusta, not their younger daughter Princess Mary Adelaide, afterwards Duchess of Teck.

Albert and her love of gossip, and exceeding arrogance and heartlessness, this *tracasserie* arose."

It has been noted in an earlier chapter that efforts were made during these years to keep the young Prince George of Cambridge out of mischief by preoccupying him with military matters and even moving him out to Corfu, but it was all to no purpose. In 1846 his second son Adolphus Augustus Frederick was born, and in 1847 his third son Augustus Charles Frederick was born, six months after he had married Louisa Fairbrother at St John's, Clerkenwell.

St John's, Clerkenwell, where on January 8th 1847 George Frederick Cambridge, bachelor, gentleman, of St Paul's, Deptford in the County of Kent, married Sarah Louisa, ninth child and fifth daughter of Robert Fairbrother, theatrical printer, is the little eighteenth-century church off the Clerkenwell Road in which the annual chapter of the Order of St John of Jerusalem is held. From its gallery hang the banners of H.M. the King, and of the Kings of Belgium, Norway, Denmark, and Sweden. In the vestry is displayed a photostat of the entry of the Duke of Cambridge's marriage; but the verger was rather taken aback when somebody enquired for the entry of this marriage, because most visitors to the church are ignorant of its existence and it is a little *bonne bouche* that he keeps for them after they have looked at the knightly banners. This intelligent and enthusiastic verger, however, could not add much to what is known about the marriage. He believed that suspicion did not arise until after the arrival of the Duke's wife in the Crimea to nurse him, and that Queen Victoria would not recognise the marriage which was " morganic." However, the marriage earned fame for the Vicar who married the pair—a Mr Hughes, whose photograph hangs near the framed copy of the marriage entry. In a French book that had been written about the Duke, of which no trace can be found, the verger said it was mentioned that when royalty entered a room where the Duke and his wife were sitting and she started to rise, he would say " Sit down, Louisa, sit down! "

Canon Edgar Sheppard, father of a more famous son, wrote an official memoir of the Duke of Cambridge, but he recorded little of his married life and the circumstances of the marriage.

As early as when he was twenty years old, the Duke of Cambridge in letters made it as clear as the young Prince of

Wales made it at the same age to Queen Alexandra that he would marry only a woman he could love. " He was ready and eager to devote to the service of his country unselfishly and unsparingly all his energies and all his abilities, but he claimed that his private life was his own, to be disposed of as he thought proper," and, let it be remembered, that when Prince George of Cambridge married Louisa Fairbrother he was within four or five degrees of the throne. Repeated persuasion was used to make him marry some Royal princess, but he was adamant. " The marriage was, of course, morganatic. . . . Mrs Fitzgeorge, as she became on her marriage, took up her residence in Queen Street, Mayfair." Canon Sheppard then publishes some extracts from the Duke's private diary when Mrs Fitzgeorge was dying :

> Christmas Eve. 1889. To Queen Street, and distributed my little Christmas presents. All seemed pleased, and nobody more than dearest Louisa, but we missed her dear presence when the little gifts were laid out in the dining-room.
> Christmas Day. To me, this year more than ever this season is a sad one for many reasons, and I have lost almost all interest in the cheerfulness and brightness with which this day was surrounded in bygone days. We missed dearest Louisa sadly at our quiet little festive board.

Mrs Fitzgeorge was failing rapidly as 1889 passed into 1890. However, on the anniversary of their wedding-day, January 8th, " which " the Duke writes " we have kept always together," she rallied slightly and three days later she was able to take Communion.

> At ten o'clock [wrote the Duke] went to meet the Sub-Dean Mr Sheppard in Queen Street. Dearest Louisa appeared stronger and better and was able to keep her dear eyes open, which she could not do the last few days She was quite herself and most keenly attentive during the celebration, and seemed none the worse for it. To me this service has been an immense satisfaction, and I do thank God for his great mercy in enabling her to take it before passing away from amongst us.

On the next day, January 12th 1890, she died.

> Sunday, Jan. 12th—My beloved wife breathed her last calmly, peacefully, softly at about 4 of this morning. We had been expecting this painful event all through the night, but lungs and heart were so sound that they continued to perform their function until strength gave way under the weakness caused by the absence of all nourishment which could no longer be taken in the unconscious state she was in All her children as well as myself, the nurse, dear Rowley, and the

female servants were surrounding the death-bed, a peaceful gathering of devotedly mourning and affectionate hearts. Mr Sheppard, the Sub-Dean, recited the prayers for the dying. May the Almighty have mercy on her dear Soul and give us strength and me in particular to bear up against the overwhelming loss we have sustained. After coming home, at once wrote to Ponsonby and the Prince of Wales asking the former to announce it to the Queen, which he kindly did, and later on I received a most affectionate message from Her Majesty, which I highly appreciate, and which would have been such a joy to my beloved one had she known the fact. The Prince of Wales called on me to express his sympathy and sorrow at my heavy affliction. I had some hours' rest and then went to Queen Street where dear Mr Sheppard gave a short touching service at the death-bed side. My beloved one lay lovely in death still amongst us. Her countenance was beautiful, quite young to look at, though 74 in actual age. The sorrow of my heart has this consolation that my beloved wife is now in peace and rest after her terrible and very prolonged sufferings, and God will be merciful to her Soul. She was good and kind and affectionate and true and tenderhearted, and my little home of 50 years * with my beloved Louisa is now come to an end. .

17th January. The loneliness of my position becomes more marked to me at every hour of the day. It is a terrible blow, which even now I hardly have realised. Public opinion all most respectful to her memory, and sympathetic to me in my sorrow. . .

Public opinion was, indeed, respectful and sympathetic. *The Times* wrote in a sedate little obituary on January 14th:

We regret to announce the death on Sunday, at the age of 74, of Mrs Fitzgeorge, wife of H.R.H. the Duke of Cambridge. Mrs Fitzgeorge, before her marriage, was a Miss Fairbrother and in her early days was known as an accomplished actress [but only in pantomime, *The Times* omits to add]. The circumstances of her domestic life call for no long notice, but it should be said that she always lived on the most affectionate terms with her husband and that during his illness after the battle of Inkerman, she went to the Crimea to nurse him. Several of her sons follow his Royal Highness's profession. It is stated that in the course of Mrs Fitzgeorge's long and painful illness the Queen has sent to make frequent inquiries at her residence in Queen Street, Mayfair.

---

* If the Duke is not using a round number, and he is always meticulous about dates, that puts the beginning of the liaison with Louisa Fairbrother in 1839 or 1840—probably in 1840 after he reached the age of twenty-one. So at the time he was accused by Victoria and Albert of an intrigue with Lady Augusta Somerset he was already semi-domesticated. It is possible that the Augusta Somerset story was another attempt to break up his intimacy with Louisa Fairbrother, and it was no doubt to assist in this and also avoid further unpleasant repercussions of the story that he was sent out on military duty to Corfu in 1843.

The Queen's interest in Mrs Fitzgeorge is re-asserted in the notices of the Duke's own death in 1904, but from his remark in the Diary one infers that these marks of royal consideration had not been frequent.

There is nothing, however, which would lead one to believe that the outspoken remarks in *Reynolds' News* on the death of Mrs Fitzgeorge are anything except an expression of republican sentiment.   That paper put it:

> In the eyes of the law therefore, she was only a concubine, although I have no doubt from the reports which one has heard concerning her, she was a much more worthy woman, and a much abler, than nine-tenths of the females who prance in Court circles.   The Queen would not receive Mrs Fitzgeorge at Court, but that was no disgrace to the dead lady, who was a much larger hearted woman than Victoria herself.

The funeral of Mrs Fitzgeorge certainly caught the public interest and most of the newspapers devoted a good deal of space to it.   Crowds of people lined the carriage-way that mild day in January and would have crowded the chapel twenty times over had not the guardians of Kensal Green cemetery restrained them.   At 6 Queen Street hundreds of people gathered and waited for a couple of hours before the massive oak coffin was carried out of the house.   On it was inscribed, " Louisa Fitzgeorge, the beloved wife of H.R.H. the Duke of Cambridge."   There were wreaths from the Duke himself and from their sons and daughters, from the Duke and Duchess of Teck, Mrs Fitzgeorge's brother and sister-in-law, and so many from friends and colleagues that the hearse seemed to be a moving mass of flowers drawn by four coal-black horses.   Apart from the chief mourners who followed it were the Queen's equerry, Colonel du Plat, and the Duke of Teck (the Duchess was ill at the time), and among the crowd who waited at the cemetery was Lord Wolseley.

The service was read by that faithful friend Canon Sheppard, and the Duke was much affected.   He walked alone to the grave in the short stage made by the hearse from the chapel, leaning heavily upon his stick.   So anxious were the spectators to see him that in no " intentional or disorderly way " they were massed upon the tombs around and strayed amongst the mourners.   For hours afterwards they filed in detachments to look upon the lilies, hyacinths, violets, roses and azaleas by which the grave was hidden.

The Duke's mausoleum is still be to seen in Kensal Green next to the family tomb of General Sir John Aitchison. It is not far from the spot where lie the Duke of Sussex and his morganatic wife.

At St John's, Clerkenwell, it is clearly remembered that King Edward once sent for the marriage register in which appears the entry of the Duke's marriage. Sir Almeric Fitzroy, who, like Greville, was Clerk to the Privy Council, records in his Memoirs that when the King examined it, he said, " There are three errors in this. In the first place, the Duke never signed himself as George Cambridge—one was his name and the other his title; and, in the second place, he never was at Dartford in his life; and thirdly, his father's names are given inaccurately."

King Edward does *not* seem to have shown in this what Sir Almeric Fitzroy refers to as his " extraordinary precision in matters of personal detail." The answer to the first observation is self-evident; to the second that the entry says ' Deptford ' not ' Dartford ', and research by the church authorities has proved that Louisa had a sister living at Deptford, whose address was probably used; and to the third that the name of his father is not given.

Miss Sidney Fairbrother, a kinswoman of the present writer, told him that there had been a trunkful of letters from Queen Victoria and various royal personages to Mrs Fitz-george, but that these had been destroyed. All that Miss Fairbrother possesses is an engraving of her relative as Robin Hood in a Drury Lane burlesque.

CHAPTER XIX

THE CHURCH OF ENGLAND AND MARRIAGE

It is desired at the outset of this investigation into the attitude of the Anglican Church toward marriage, divorce, and the remarriage of divorced persons to disclaim any inten-tion of trying to impugn the true Catholicity of that Church. Such Catholicity has been the subject of controversy for close on four hundred years, but it is not a controversy for these pages, and Roman Catholics who follow this investigation are asked to bear this in mind, and to bear in mind at the same time that the most vital body of Anglican opinion, reduced though it may have been sometimes for years at a stretch to the opinion of an infinitesimal minority, has always believed in the true Catholicity of the Church of England. It would be neither pertinent nor decent, and would moreover serve no useful purpose, to criticise such a belief, and if such criticism may seem to be obtruding itself Anglicans are asked to accept an assurance that it is directed entirely at the form in which that belief has sometimes been expressed whether by word, action, or implication, never at the belief itself. The first postulate to be demanded will be an admission that the *occasion* of the Church of England as we recognise to-day what is called the Church of England on the first page of the Book of Common Prayer was the desire of Henry VIII to marry Anne Boleyn. This leaves out all discussion of the *causes* which made such an occasion possible. They will be estimated according to the prejudices of the theologian and the historian, and do not concern us.

Allusion is commonly made to the divorce of Henry VIII. This term is not strictly accurate. There was no divorce in the Western Church. What Henry sought was the annulment of his marriage with Catherine of Aragon on the ground that it was never a valid marriage because she had been for four months the wife of his dying brother Arthur. Even if that marriage had been consummated, it was believed that marriage with a deceased brother's wife, although contrary to the law of the Church, could be allowed by a papal dispensation. However, the marriage was certainly not consummated. Prince Arthur was hardly fifteen and Catherine herself not yet sixteen when it took place at St Paul's in November 1501. The following April Catherine was left a virgin widow, and not long afterwards when Henry VII lost his wife proposals were actually made that he should wed his daughter-in-law, to the horror of Catherine's mother Isabella. Finally Catherine was betrothed to Arthur's younger brother Henry in 1503 when that Prince was twelve years old. They were married in June 1509, seven weeks after Henry VIII's accession to the throne, and they were crowned together a fortnight later.

The bull of dispensation granted for this marriage by Pope Julius II in 1503 provided for the possibility of consummation and every objection in the future was guarded against. Moreover, a few months later a papal brief was issued confirming the bull of dispensation. The numerous stillbirths of this marriage may probably be attributed to Henry's infection by syphilis, and the scruples about the validity of the marriage his lack of a male heir caused at last were doubtless encouraged by his displeasure in a wife six years older who was ageing more rapidly than himself in the Spanish fashion. As early as 1524 Henry was talking about annulment, but it was not until he became infatuated with Anne, the younger sister of his former mistress Mary Boleyn, that he took practical measures and in 1526 asked Pope Clement VII to declare his marriage with Catherine null and void. The request was refused. The long battle between the Pope and the King began. In 1529 Henry discovered that Wolsey had broken the statute of Praemunire * by exercising the legatine authority which the Pope at Henry's own request had conferred upon him. That meant all his property was forfeit to the Crown. Wolsey submitted; but he anticipated the block by dying on his way to the Tower.

The ingenious Henry and his lawyers now discovered that the whole of the clergy of England were guilty of a Praemunire by having obeyed the legatine authority of Wolsey. An information was filed against them in the King's Bench, and in January 1531 the Convocation of Canterbury met to sue for pardon. This was granted in return for a fine of £100,000 and assent to the formula of royal supremacy.

" We acknowledge His Majesty to be the singular protector, only and supreme lord, and, so far as the law of Christ will allow, supreme head of the Church of England and Clergy."

Those are the terms in which the great surrender was made.

The Convocation of York followed suit, paying £18,000 and after an argument about the formula subscribing to it. Thereupon Acts of Parliament were passed granting formal

---

* The second Statute of Praemunire passed in 1393 enacted that the right of presentation to church benefices belonged to the King's Court, the illegality of any juridical interference by Rome, and the forfeiture of all lands, goods and chattels against all who abetted any attempt by Rome to override the authority of the King's Court. Under Elizabeth refusal of the oath of supremacy was made a breach of the Statute. As we have seen in the time of George III all those who assisted at a royal marriage without the King's permission were liable to a writ of Praemunire. To-day the Dean and Chapter of a cathedral who should find that the guidance of the Holy Spirit had led them to elect any Bishop except the one notified as the choice of the Sovereign might be deprived of their stocks and shares, their furniture and their clothes.

pardon to the clergy and the laity of England for their offence.

The King was now armed to deal more aggressively with the Pope, and in 1532 the death of old Warham, the Archbishop of Canterbury, enabled Henry to appoint as his successor Thomas Cranmer, the pliable cleric he needed. At the beginning of 1533 Henry was privately married to Anne Boleyn. Two or three months later Convocation was summoned to declare the validity of the marriage of Arthur and Catherine and to deny the power of the Pope to grant a dispensation for marriage with the widow of a deceased brother.

On May 29th Cranmer sitting as president of the archiepiscopal court at Dunstable set aside the marriage with Catherine as null and void, and declared the marriage with Anne Boleyn valid. The Pope gave his judgment a few months later in a contrary sense. *Roma locuta est: causa finita est.* From that time onward a series of enactments made the breach with Rome complete.

We need not follow Cranmer through the subsequent annulments he obtained for the marriages of Anne Boleyn and Anne of Cleves. He was dough in Henry's hands. However, after the death of his royal master the Archbishop made an effort to clear his conscience to his own satisfaction, and with the help of expert advice from Geneva, the sickly precocity of Edward VI, and the greed of the Protector he led the movement to bring the Church of England into line with continental Protestantism, the last thing Henry VIII would have tolerated, even although the trend of continental Protestantism was in favour of destroying the indissoluble bond of holy matrimony.

It was natural that the Protestant Reformers should desire to loosen the rigidity of any institution the sacrosanct character of which tended to uphold the claims of ecclesiastical authority to supreme jurisdiction. It was to this end that the sacramental theory of marriage was rejected.

There are two Sacraments ordained of Christ our Lord in the Gospel, that is to say, Baptism, and the Supper of the Lord.

Those five commonly called Sacraments, that is to say, Confirmation, Penance, Orders, Matrimony, and Extreme Unction, are not to be counted for Sacraments of the Gospel, being such as have grown partly of the corrupt following of the Apostles, partly are states of life allowed in the Scriptures; but yet have not like nature of Sacraments with Baptism and the Lord's Supper, for they have not any visible sign or ceremony ordained of God.

Thus the Twenty-fifth of the Thirty-Nine Articles " agreed upon by the Archbishops and Bishops of both Provinces, and the whole Clergy in the Convocation holden at London in the year 1562, for the avoiding of Diversities of Opinions and for the establishing of Consent touching true Religion." *

In the report of the Commission appointed by Henry VIII and carried on by Edward VI (*Reformatio Legum Ecclesiasticarum*) of which Cranmer was the presiding spirit and the chief drafter, the separation from bed and board of the old Canon Law was abolished, and absolute divorce for adultery, desertion, cruelty, for the absence of the husband over a period of years, and even for extreme incompatibility was substituted. Divorce was withheld from parties guilty of adultery and penalties imposed, but remarriage was granted to the innocent party. The Commission's Report was not carried into effect owing to the death of Edward VI and the accession of Mary.

Although there is little doubt that the Report was the expression of a practice that was growing frequent but was not yet enacted into law, it is generally assumed that the case of the Marquis of Northampton was a solitary exception. Northampton was a brother of Catherine Parr, and as soon as his terrifying brother-in-law was dead he obtained a *separatio a mensa et thoro* from his wife Anne, daughter of Bourchier, Earl of Essex, and even before the proceedings were finished married Elizabeth Brook, a daughter of Lord Cobham. This was too much even for public morals during the Protectorate and Northampton had to separate from his new wife while an Act of Parliament was passed bastardising the children of his first wife. In 1552 another Act of Parliament established the legality of his second marriage. One of the first Acts in Mary's reign repealed the 1552 Act; but Northampton did not marry again until the second marchioness was dead. To the case of a man so conspicuous as Northampton

---

* This statement in the Prayer Book is not strictly accurate. Queen Elizabeth struck out Article XXIX and added a clause to Article XX. The Articles were committed to Convocation in 1571, when Article XXIX was restored, and the Queen's addition to Article XX retained in the English version but struck out of the Latin version, and as both the English and Latin versions were declared authoritative and official a bad pot-hole was left in the *Via Media* of salvation.

M

no doubt care was taken to give every advantage of legality and when the whirligig of time brought revenge every disadvantage of illegality.   Howard in his *History of Matrimonial Institutions* says " there is strong evidence that from about 1548 to 1602, except for the short period of Mary's reign . . . new marriages were freely contracted after obtaining divorce from unfaithful partners.*

At last in 1602 a second remarriage of Hercules Fuljambe after obtaining separations from the beds and boards of two wives was declared invalid by the Star Chamber.   That such action was necessary is of itself evidence of the growth of the habit of remarriage after being granted separation from bed and board by an Ecclesiastical Court.   Further, and this is more important, it is evidence that the long struggle to purge the Church of England of Presbyterianism and continental Protestantism was inclining toward success, though the struggle would be renewed with increasing bitterness and sustained almost throughout the seventeenth century, until after what some might call a Pyrrhic victory the Church of England would relapse exhausted into the latitudinarianism and indifference of the eighteenth century from which it would be rescued by the Oxford Movement and imbued with whatever definite character it enjoys to-day.

In 1603 the Convocation of Canterbury framed the *Constitutions and Canons Ecclesiastical* which in 1604 received the sanction of the Crown.   Two years later York in the words of the Reverend J. V. Bullard, Proctor of the Convocation, was " practically forced to agree.   But York Convocation (in the Lower House) has more than once . . . repudiated any desire to raise this difficulty."

Mr Bullard dedicates his annotated reprint: " To my father and uncle the only laymen I have known who, not being ecclesiastical lawyers, possessed copies and were acquainted with the contents of the Canons of 1603–4."

The reverend and learned Proctor quotes Lingard (*History of England*) on the reaction of the legislature :

---

* An attempt has been made in Dibdin and Chadwyck Healy's *English Church Law and Divorce* to traverse this statement, and the authority of these learned ecclesiastical lawyers has been quoted as decisive by the Report of the Joint Committees of the Convocations on *The Church and Marriage*.   A careful study of the work in question has not suggested the slightest justification for qualifying Howard's assertion.   Indeed, a close perusal of *English Church Law and Divorce* has but served to heighten the sense of confusion and inconsistency about marriage and divorce prevailing in the sixteenth century.

It was contended that the clergy had no power to create offences which should subject the delinquent to the *civil punishment* consequent on the sentence of excommunication: and in the next session of Parliament a Bill passed the Commons declaring that no Canon or Constitution ecclesiastical made within the last ten years or to be made thereafter, should be of force to impeach or hurt any person in his life liberty lands or goods, unless it were first confirmed by an Act of the legislature. The Bishops united in opposing this Bill as derogatory to the authority of the Convocation and of the King the head of the Church.   Several conferences took place between the two houses: but the Parliament was dissolved before the third reading, and the decision of the question fell to the judges in Westminster Hall, who have often declared that though the Canons of 1604 bind the clergy by whom they were framed they have no power to bind the people as long as they want the approbation of the legislature.

And on this Mr Bullard comments:

The popular misunderstanding of the judges is to the effect that nothing contained in the 1603–4 Canons is binding on the laity.   But the 1603–4 Canons were in many respects only restatements of old Canons *which had the approbation of the legislature.*   Such Canons were, and are, binding on the laity even though the 1604 Canons added new penalties not approved by the legislature and therefore not enforceable so far as those new penalties are concerned.

If that contention be sound, surely the laity of the Church of England have reason to ask which of the Canons are binding on them and which are not.

Canon 107 for instance declares:

In all sentences for Divorce, Bond to be taken for not marrying during each other's Life.

In all sentences pronounced only for divorce and separation *a thoro et mensa*, there shall be a caution and restraint inserted in the act of the said sentence, that the parties so separated shall live chastely and continently; neither shall they, during each other's life, contract matrimony with any other person.   And, for the better observation of this last clause, the said sentence of divorce shall not be pronounced until the party or parties requiring the same have given good and sufficient caution and security into the court, that they will not in any way break or transgress the said restraint or prohibition.

This Canon is the rock on which the opponents of the remarriage of divorced persons is based; but it is followed immediately by Canon 108 which declares:

The Penalty for Judges offending in the premises.

And if any Judge, giving sentence of divorce or separation, shall not fully keep and observe the premises, he shall be, by the Archbishop of the province, or by the Bishop of the diocese, suspended from the exercise of his office for the space of a whole year; and the sentence of separation, so given contrary to the form aforesaid, shall be held void to all intents and purposes of the law as if it had not at all been given or pronounced.

Now it is certain that this Canon has been rendered obsolete by the removal of matrimonial jurisdiction from the ecclesiastical courts to civil courts, so why should the laity suppose that Canon 107 is not equally obsolete?

But there is another observation to be made. The Canons were originally framed in Latin, and nobody knows who is responsible for the accepted English translation which as Mr Bullard points out is often quite inaccurate. The inaccuracy in Canons 105–108 is productive of some ambiguity.

Canon 105 is headed:

No Sentence for *Divorce* to be given upon the sole Confession of the Parties.

Here the Latin gives us: "*Pro conjugio dirimendo*" for divorce; and later in this Canon we get "divorce and nullities of matrimony" to translate "*divortiorum et nullitatis matrimonii.*" So far clear enough.

Canon 106 is headed:

No Sentence for *Divorce* to be given but in open Court.

But the Latin says: "*divortii et separationis,*" and thus makes a distinction familiar enough to us nowadays between divorce and separation from bed and board.

However, later in Canon 106 we get "*separatio a thoro et mensa,*" or "for annulling of pretended matrimony." Divorce is not mentioned.

In Canon 107, the crucial one for the justification of refusal to remarry divorced persons, we find that the Latin heading "*Separatis, eorum altero superstite, nova copula interdicta*" is translated "In all sentences for Divorce, Bond to be taken for not marrying during each other's Life."

But the Latin literally translated says: "A new tie is forbidden to *separated* parties, either of them being alive."

Furthermore in this Canon the Latin explicitly refers to "*separationem thori et mensae,*" and again to "*sententia separationis,*" whereas the English inserts "*divorce and* separation," and on the second occasion translates ' *separatio* ' as ' divorce.' That this cannot be explained away by a looseness of translation which considers ' *divortium* ' and ' *separatio* ' interchangeable is suggested by Canon 108, for here we have both in English and Latin an apparently express statement that divorce and separation are not the same : " *Sententiam separationis, seu divortii.*" True, it might be maintained that ' *seu* ' is used with the sense ' *seu potius,*' thus making ' *separatio* ' and ' *divortium* ' identical, but such an ambiguity is unusual in ecclesiastical Latin.

It is crystal clear that Canon 107 forbids the remarriage of separated parties, but it is by no means so clear that the Latin and authoritative version forbids the remarriage of divorced parties. It may be suspected that the Puritans succeeded in retaining the possibility of distinction with a view to their avowed object of loosening the bonds of matrimony, the attack on which at present was confined to the use of the ring in the form of solemnisation. That such a trick was not beyond those worthy Divines is shown by the retention of Elizabeth's addition to Article XX in the English and the excision of it in the Latin.

However, although Canon 107 is always fired off with appropriate solemnity in the battle over the marriage law of the Church of England, it is imprudent to rely on a collection of weapons so many of which are recognised as obsolete by the gunners of controversy, indeed as dangerously obsolete. Anglican apologists prefer to rely on the words of that form of solemnisation to prove that the Church of England is committed to the doctrine of the indissolubility of matrimony. It may be granted at once that both the parties in phrases of singular poignancy and beauty take a solemn vow before the Minister to cleave to one another as long as they live and that the Minister (described on this occasion as a Priest) joins their hands, with the words ' Those whom God hath joined together let no man put asunder '; and it may be granted that the apparent intention of such a solemnisation of matrimony is to bless and confirm a sacramental union between the man and the woman. Yet knowledge of the circumstances in which the Book of Common Prayer was put together induces a doubt whether all the compilers were animated by the same spirit. In the Roman rite the vows are unnecessary, because it is plainly called ' The Rite of Celebrating the Sacrament of Matrimony,' and the parties

have already been taught in the catechism that matrimony
is indissoluble, being a Sacrament they confer upon themselves
by the Grace of God, and that the Priest's part is that of a
formal witness to the solemnisation, with authority to give
it the Church's blessing. The vows made in the Anglican
Rite by the parties must logically be held to exclude ' *separatio* '
if they are to be accepted as final and binding.

> " *I take thee to my wedded wife [or husband], to have and*
> *to hold from this day forward, for better for worse, for richer*
> *for poorer, in sickness and in health, to love and to cherish,*
> *till death us do part, according to God's holy ordinance ; and*
> *thereto I plight thee my troth.*"

It is sad to reflect that those moving cadences may have
been penned by Cranmer himself, who at the same time in
the *Reformatio Legum* was planning another blow at the
indissolubility of matrimony. Similarly, the declaration of
the priest, ' Those whom God hath joined together let no
man put asunder,' is nullified by any acceptance in the
future of the right of an ecclesiastical court to grant ' *separatio*
a mensa et thoro,' and cannot therefore be recognised as
more than a pious ejaculation testifying to an ideal. Once
the vows of the parties have been broken and the declaration
of the priest has been mocked by the acceptance of judicial
separation nothing remains in the English marriage service
itself which affirms the impossibility of remarriage.

That ejaculation of the priest and those solemn vows provide a tempting argument to use with uninformed laymen
who are always impressed by it ; but it is putting the marriage
service on the same level as a solemn vow to abstain from
alcohol. Such a vow does not mark the individual who
takes it with the indelibility of total abstinence. The breaking of such a vow is a sin, but a priest could absolve a man
from such a vow. A priest cannot unmarry a man who
has been validly married. The Church cannot do it. It is
a popular superstition that annulment of matrimony on the
ground that there was an impediment which made it an invalid
sacrament is as frequent in the Roman Catholic Church as
divorce outside it. The figures show about fifty annulments
every year, which are not many for over 340,000,000 Catholics
—more than half the professing Christians throughout the
world. It is surprising that even those Anglican theologians
who now accept matrimony as a sacrament should be content

to sustain the teaching of the Church of England about matrimony by citing the Anglican marriage service. They know perfectly well the doctrinal pit into which such a line of reasoning will precipitate them.

Perhaps this is a suitable point at which to present the point of view of orthodox Anglo-Catholicism. The name of the present writer's correspondent is not given, but it is a name which would carry weight. He had been asked to give an approved explanation of what seemed the ambiguous sacramental teaching of Article XXV:

" In reply to your question, I really do not think that Article XXV can be taken to bear the construction which you place upon it.

" As you know, the word ' Sacrament ' has had a number of different meanings attached to it at different times. If you had asked St Peter on the Day of Pentecost how many sacraments Christ had ordained in His Church, he simply would not have known what you were talking about! Early Christian writers apply the word ' Sacrament ' to all sorts of things. St Hilary calls *Holy Scripture* a ' sacrament,' he also speaks of *prayer* as a sacrament, and alludes to ' the sacrament of *fasting*.' St Augustine speaks of ' the Sacrament of the *Creed* ' and ' the Sacrament of the *Lord's Prayer*,' while St Jerome calls *Martyrdom* a sacrament. Gradually the term came to be confined to ' an outward and visible sign of an inward and spiritual grace,' but Peter Lombard was the first to formulise the number as *seven*.

" The compilers of the XXXIX Articles sought to emphasise the distinction between the two Sacraments of Baptism and the Lord's Supper (which they call ' Sacraments of the Gospel ') and the other five, on the ground that the latter ' have not any visible sign or ceremony *ordained of God*.' In this sense the Catechism defines a Sacrament as an ' outward visible sign . . . *ordained by Christ Himself*,' as the means by which we are to receive the ' inward spiritual grace ' which the sign signifies. In this strict sense the Catechism asserts that there are only two Sacraments ' generally ' (*i.e.*, universally) ' necessary to salvation,' but neither the Catechism nor the Articles ' definitely deny ' that ' those five commonly called Sacraments ' are means of grace, but merely assert that they have not 'the same nature of Sacraments' with the other two, on account of the outward sign *not having been specifically ordained by Christ.*

"But although these two great Sacraments are severed off from the other five . . . so far from denying them to be Sacraments, the writers of all the formularies acknowledge or imply that they are in some sense 'Sacraments'. The Homilies *directly call Marriage a Sacrament*; and of Orders they say, 'neither it, nor any *other* Sacrament else be *such* Sacraments as Baptism and Communion are'. So that we have two of the five expressly called 'Sacraments,' besides the allusion to 'other Sacraments.' The Article could not say that the five have not '*like* nature of Sacraments with Baptism and the Lord's Supper,' unless the writers meant that they were in some sense 'Sacraments.' And the difference assigned (which is further remarkable) does not relate to the inward grace but to the outward form. . . . In the same way the Homilies expressly say that 'absolution' has the inward grace, 'forgiveness of sins,' only 'not by express word of the New Testament, annexed and tied to the visible sign, which is imposition of hands.' (Bishop Forbes on the XXXIX Articles, p. 451.)

"I hope you do not consider all this as 'casuistry.' The fact is that the Articles are highly technical theological statements, and if the 'average conventional Anglican' approaches them without any theological training whatever, he is not likely to understand them."

We may agree at once with our correspondent that "the word 'sacrament' has had a number of different meanings attached to it at different times." But what we have to ask ourselves is whether in the year the Forty-two Articles— reduced in the Prayer Book of Elizabeth to the present number of Thirty-nine—were compiled there was the slightest ambiguity left in what the Catholic Church and the Orthodox Church of the East taught about the seven sacraments. And the answer is that there was none. What the Reformers attempted in Article XXV was to reduce five of the seven sacraments to sacramentals.

The sacramentals do not produce sanctifying grace *ex opere operato*, by virtue of the rite or substance employed, and this constitutes their essential difference from the sacraments   The Church is unable to increase or reduce the number of sacraments as they were instituted by Christ, but the sacramentals do not possess this dignity and privilege (*Catholic Encyclopædia*).

The Church might decide to-morrow to abolish the blessing of candles, ashes, palms, the rosary, and holy water; but the Church could not abolish the Sacrament of Matrimony. Yet the Church has never taught that all the sacraments were equal in dignity and necessity, and has always accorded to the Eucharist the first in dignity " because it contains Christ in person, whilst in the other sacraments grace is confirmed by an instrumental virtue derived from Christ " (St Thomas Aquinas).

The Anglican Catechism, which until a new catechism is produced must be supposed to contain all the doctrine of the Anglican Church necessary to perfect instruction in the fundamentals of the faith of an Anglican, states positively that Christ has ordained two sacraments only, as generally necessary to salvation, Baptism and the Supper of the Lord. From this Anglo-Catholics argue that because the other five sacraments are not explicitly denied their existence is implied and recognised.

But if this be so surely it can only be held to be so by something like a *suppressio veri*. Moreover, it is not accurate to say that the Eucharist is generally necessary to salvation if in such a statement it be linked with Baptism. In that sense only Baptism is generally necessary. The statement of the Anglican Catechism would deprive of salvation a newly baptized infant that has not made its first communion, which is absurd. And even if we allow that the Anglican Catechism by not explicitly denying that " those five commonly called Sacraments " are sacraments accepts them as such, we are once again in difficulties with Article XXV which does explicitly state that they are " such as have grown partly of the corrupt following of the Apostles, partly are states of life allowed in the Scriptures." It is true that in the famous Tract 90 of the Oxford Movement Newman managed to swallow the Thirty-nine Articles; but the obstinate theological indigestion the effort caused him drove him finally for relief to Rome.

The Homilies are left, and to the Homilies, with an ironical smile be it written, the Anglo-Catholic finally appeals.

The edition of the Homilies from which the excerpts below are quoted was published by the S.P.C.K. in 1864, three hundred and two years after they were first published in the reign of Elizabeth and therefore presumably representing the considered opinion of the large majority of English churchmen. In the general index, the first reference under Matrimony is headed 'not a sacrament', and that is the very page to which Bishop Forbes appeals to justify his contention that the Twenty-fifth Article does not repudiate the other five sacraments as sacraments.

Here is the relevant passage from *An Homily of Common Prayer and Sacraments*:

> Absolution is no such Sacrament as Baptism and the Communion are . . . neither it nor any other Sacrament be such. But in a general acception the name of a Sacrament may be attributed to any thing whereby an holy thing is signified. In which understanding of the word the ancient writers have given this name, not only to the other five commonly of late years taken and used for supplying the number of the seven Sacraments, but also to divers and sundry other ceremonies, as to oil, washing of feet, and such like; not meaning thereby to repute them as Sacraments in the same significance that the two forenamed Sacraments are. . . . And, although there are retained by the order of the Church of England, besides these two, certain other rites and ceremonies about the Institution of Ministers in the Church, Matrimony . . .; yet no man ought to take these for Sacraments in such signification and meaning as the Sacrament of Baptism and the Lord's Supper are, but either for godly states of life, necessary in Christ's Church, and therefore worthy to be set forth by public action and solemnity by the ministry of the Church, or else judged to be such ordinances as may make for the instruction, comfort, and edification of Christ's Church.

In other words these five 'minor' Sacraments of the Anglican reformers are not more than sacramentals. There is no word of that sanctifying and instrumental grace which the sacraments confer on the worthy recipient.

The last hope of discovering an unambiguous exposition of the Church of England's teaching about marriage lies in the *Homily of the State of Matrimony*. There is here no word of its being a sacrament, no hint of its indissolubility. The sermon would take a B.B.C. announcer over three-quarters of an hour to deliver, so it is not handicapped by want of time.

> Matrimony [the preacher begins] is instituted by God, to the intent that man and woman should live lawfully in a perpetual friendly fellowship, to bring forth fruit and avoid fornication: by which means a good conscience might be preserved on both parties in bridling the corrupt inclinations of the flesh within the limits of honesty.

An occasion to speak of the grace conferred by the sacrament of matrimony is not long in presenting itself:

> We see how wonderfully the devil deludeth and scorneth this state, how few matrimonies there be without chidings, brawlings, tauntings, repentings, bitter cursings, and fightings.

Mr A. P. Herbert could not have summed up the worse side of marriage better. What remedy does the preacher offer? Prayer. And prayer is but a sacramental. Not a word of what the Penny Roman Catholic Catechism calls " a special grace, to enable them to bear the difficulties of this state, to love and be faithful to one another, and to bring up their children in the fear of God," which " the Sacrament of Matrimony gives to those who receive it worthily."

Page after page of the homily maunders on almost entirely about the unpleasant side of marriage, and prayers will cure everything—a woman of being beaten by her husband and a husband of being chafed by " a wrathful woman, a drunkard, a beastly, without wit and reason."

It is difficult to be convinced by the proposition that the Church of England in the Marriage Service, the Catechism, the Homilies, or the XXXIX Articles plainly teaches that Matrimony is a Sacrament.

That the Church of England after recovery from the moral collapse which immediately succeeded the violent acts of the Reformation tried to reassert the sanctity of the matrimonial bond is unquestionable. We have a hint of what had been going on from the *Second Part of the Sermon against Adultery*.

> Of this vice [whoredom] cometh a great part of the divorces which nowadays be so commonly accustomed and used by men's private authority, to the great displeasure of God, and the breach of the most holy knot and bond of matrimony.

This may refer to the break up of marriages without regard to matrimonial obligations during that moral collapse after the fever of destruction; but it may as plausibly be a condemnation, in accord with the gradual recovery during the reign of Elizabeth, of the quasi-regular divorces that were at last stopped by the action of the Star Chamber in the Fuljambe case when the abuse had grown intolerable to public morality. Canon 106 suggests that the ecclesiastical courts had found it imperative to reassert and insist upon their authority.

However, in spite of the discouragement extended by the Book of Common Prayer to the sacramental view of matrimony and the ambiguities attached to the four canons on marriage the general feeling of the Church of England unmistakably hardened against the possibility of divorce, though of course separations from bed and board continued to be granted by the ecclesiastical courts. The case of Charles Blount, Earl of Devonshire, will serve to illustrate that feeling. Penelope, a sister of the Earl of Essex, was married against her will in 1580 at the age of twenty to the brutal Lord Rich, having for five years been the lover of Sir Philip Sidney. She is the Stella of the sonnets. This love affair was kept up after her marriage until Sidney himself married in 1583. Some years after Sidney's death in 1586 Lord Mountjoy, as Devonshire was then, became her lover, and she bore him three sons and two daughters besides the seven to her husband. So long as Penelope's brother Essex was alive Rich was *complaisant*, but not long after his death Rich obtained a separation *a mensa et thoro*. In spite of the promulgation of the Canons Mountjoy was determined to marry Penelope Rich, and finally he persuaded his chaplain William Laud to perform the rite on December 26th 1605. Laud afterwards repented and referred always in his Diary to " my cross about the Earl of Devon's marriage " which he believed for many years was a bar to his preferment. So long as Devonshire and Lady Rich were living in open adultery they were well received at Court, but their marriage caused great offence. Devonshire defended his second marriage in a pamphlet dedicated to James I, and Laud who had married him sought to confute his arguments. The poets took his part. Ford's great tragedy *The Broken Heart* was founded on the tale of Devonshire's love. Daniel wrote his funeral elegy. Nevertheless, the rest of the world was against him, and the heralds refused to impale his widow's arms with his.

We hear no more of divorce after this scandal until the year 1670 when Lord Roos obtained a Bill of Divorce from Parliament to enable him to marry again. It has suited Anglican apologists to pass over this critical occasion lightly * and reserve all their denunciations for the 1857 Act which

---

* *E.g.*, Report of the Joint Committees of the Convocations of Canterbury and York on *The Church and Marriage*, 1935 :
" The breach of the principle of the indissolubility of the marriage tie was first made by the State in 1857 (if private Acts of Parliament be ignored). ..."

for the first time made divorce feasible for the ordinary man ; but the 1857 Act is the child of the private Divorce Bill of 1670.

Lord Roos * had been granted a separation by the ecclesiastical courts and was able to prove against his wife that children he was bound to father were not his own. Consequently a Bill had been passed to declare them illegitimate. Charles II was anxious that the Bill enabling Lord Roos to remarry should pass, and used his influence actively, going so far indeed as to preside over the debate at the third reading in the House of Lords. After thus reviving a royal custom which had fallen into desuetude Charles took to attending debates regularly. He said ' it was as good as going to a play.' It was believed his interest in the Roos Bill was dictated by his own desire to obtain a divorce from Queen Catherine and remarry.

Gilbert Burnet had put forward a specious argument in favour of divorce for barrenness and a justification, under the Gospel, of polygamy. The future Bishop of Salisbury's view of marriage is typical of the new school of Latitudinarian divines just beginning to come into prominence

> Marriage is a Contract founded upon the Laws of Nature, its End being the Propagation of Mankind; and the Formality of doing it by Churchmen, is only a supervenient Benediction, or pompous solemnising of it; and therefore the nature of Marriage, and not any Forms used in the Celebration of it is to be considered.

The Duke of York on the other hand had opposed the Bill strongly. At this date he had not been received into the Catholic Church, and his hostile critics, who far exceed in number his charitable judges, have attributed his opposition to the Roos Bill to his fear lest if it passed his brother the King might avail himself of it as a precedent to obtain a divorce from Catherine, thus perhaps cheating himself out

---

* John Manners (b. 1638) who failed to establish his claim to the title of Lord Ross, was the third son and heir of John, 8th Earl of Rutland. He married Lady Anne Pierrepoint, d. of Henry, Marquis of Dorchester. In 1671 he married Lady Anne Bruce, daughter of Robert, Earl of Aylesbury, who died the following year. He married as his third wife six months later Catherine, d. of Baptist, Viscount Campden, by whom he had issue. George, Duke of Buckingham, established his claim to the De Roos barony, and Manners was summoned to the House of Lords as Lord Manners of Haddon, but succeeded to the Earldom of Rutland the same year. In 1703 as a reward for having helped Queen Anne to desert her father James II at the Revolution he was created Marquis of Granby and Duke of Rutland.

of the succession.   The answer to this is that the Bill was passed and Charles II did not avail himself of it to divorce his Queen.   It is more likely that the Duke of York's opposition was caused by his study of Catholic doctrine.

The Bill was hotly debated in the Lords, and was passed by a majority of two.   Eighteen bishops voted against it. Two voted for it.   Of these two whose votes were of such disastrous weight on this occasion, one was John Wilkins, the cultured Bishop of Chester, who had been warden of Wadham College, Oxford, and Master of Trinity College, Cambridge.   The other was John Cosin, the Bishop of Durham.   Now Cosin was from the point of view of the Anglo-Catholic the most eminent theologian, liturgiologist, and administrator the Church of England possessed in the year 1670, and his action in voting for this Bill is so inexplicable to his admirers of to-day that the desire to pass lightly over this occasion fraught with such grave consequences for orthodoxy is hardly to be wondered at.   Laud, another Anglo-Catholic hero, may have married his patron Devonshire to a lady whose husband had been granted separation, but Laud repented of it all his life.   Cosin did much more than Laud to wreck the sanctity of marriage and never expressed even mild regret.   It should be remembered that the passage of a Bill enabling the remarriage of a divorced party at this time necessarily involved that marriage's being celebrated in church.   There was no civil marriage yet.   It is true that thirteen of the bishops signed the protest of dissentients in the Journals of the House which was headed by the Duke of York; but it is difficult to believe that they felt strongly on the matter, and that Anglican prelates of that period were capable of profound conviction would soon be demonstrated when some preferred to be deprived of their sees rather than take the oath to William and Mary.*   The best of the English clergy became nonjurors.   Hardly one

---

* To quote Lecky (*England in the Eighteenth Century*):

" At the time of the Reformation the great body of the English clergy, rather than give up their preferments, oscillated to and fro between Protestantism and Catholicism at the command of successive sovereigns, and their conduct in 1702 was very similar.   With scarcely an exception they bowed silently before the law, and consented to take an oath which to every unsophisticated mind was an abnegation of the most cherished part of their teaching."

Thomas Ken, the saintly Bishop of Bath and Wells, was deprived of his see when the Whigs carried through their fiction of James II's abdication, and in old age refused Queen Anne's offer to restore him without taking the oath of abjuration.   *Si sic omnes !*

was left to refuse the Oath of Abjuration when Anne came to the Throne.

The Roos Bill remained a solitary measure until the case of Henry, a Protestant Duke of Norfolk. He married Lady Mary Mordaunt, daughter of Henry, Earl of Peterborough. In 1685 she was charged with having committed adultery with Sir John Germain, a soldier of fortune who was almost certainly the half-brother of William of Orange. The charge was brought again in 1690 and 1691, and in that and the following year Bills of Divorce were introduced in the House of Lords by the Duke and rejected. In 1692 he brought an action against Germain in the King's Bench claiming £50,000 damages for 'lascivious conversation' with his Duchess. The verdict was in his favour, but the jury awarded for damages and costs only a hundred marks. Germain was created a baronet in 1698. Finally in 1700 a third Bill for a Divorce was brought in and passed by the House of Lords. On September 15th 1701 a licence for marriage was granted by the Archbishop of Canterbury to 'Sir John Germain, of St James's, Westminster . . . and Lady Mary Mordaunt, of same, spinster,' and soon after they were married. Lady Mary died in 1705 and her effigy rests upon a marble tomb in Lowick Church. Sir John was given a marble tomb near his first wife by his second wife, the enchanting Lady Elizabeth Berkeley; but it is said that on his death-bed in 1718 Dr Clarke of St James, Westminster, "refused him the Sacrament," which if true, is a sad example of ecclesiastical illogicality, for his life with his second wife was happy and his repentance of early irregularities sincere.

The significance of the Norfolk divorce is immense. Not only does it confirm the precedent established by the Roos divorce, but it creates a fresh precedent whereby the guilty parties may be married by the licence of the Archbishop of Canterbury. Let it be pointed out now that no believer in the sacramental indissolubility of matrimony can accept any difference between the remarriage of the guilty parties in a divorce and the remarriage of the innocent party to another party not involved in that divorce. It illustrates the uncertainty of the doctrinal teaching of the Church of England that even to-day most reverend, right reverend, very reverend, venerable, and reverend clerics are still arguing this point because they will not face up to the meaning of the Latin word 'indissolubilis'. It is safe to assert that ninety per cent of the laity of the Church of England are convinced that the only ecclesiastical objection to the remarriage of divorced persons is when either of them has been a guilty party in a divorce suit. For this deplorable notion the clerical leaders of Anglicanism have none except themselves to thank.

Three Bills of Divorce were granted between 1700 and 1715. According to the *Encyclopædia Britannica,* " Between 1715 and 1775 there were sixty such Acts, in the next twenty-five years there were seventy-four, and between 1800 and 1850 there were ninety." *

The abuse by the Anglican clergy of their monopoly of marriage during the first half of the eighteenth century at last became so outrageous that in 1753 the Marriage Act was introduced by Lord Hardwicke to restore decency.

> A multitude of clergymen, usually prisoners for debt and almost always men of notoriously infamous lives [says Lecky] made it their business to celebrate clandestine marriages, in or near the Fleet. They performed the ceremony without licence or question . . . in public-houses, brothels, or garrets. . . Almost every tavern or brandy-shop in the neighbourhood had a Fleet parson in its pay. . . . Desertion, conjugal infidelity, bigamy, fictitious marriages . . . were the natural and frequent consequences. . . . It was proved before Parliament that on one occasion there had been 2,954 Fleet marriages in four months . . . one Fleet parson had married 173 couples in a single day.

Lord Hardwicke's Marriage Act provided that, with the exception of Quaker and Jewish marriages, no marriage should be valid in England unless celebrated by a priest according to the form of solemnisation in the Book of Common Prayer, that such a marriage could not be performed unless the banns had been published for three successive Sundays in the parish church, or unless a licence had been obtained. A special licence to celebrate a marriage elsewhere than in their parish church, and costing a considerable sum, could be obtained only from the Archbishop of Canterbury. All marriages which did not conform to these provisions were to be held null, and the penalty for celebrating such was transportation.

The Marriage Act of 1753, while it confirmed the marriage monopoly of the Established Church and was therefore supported by the Bishops, was yet an unmistakable abrogation by the State of control over what had hitherto been a purely

---

* The figures and dates vary in different accounts, but these can be accepted at any rate as a basis for accuracy.

ecclesiastical matter, and as such it paved the way for the Dissenters' Marriage Act of 1836, by the provisions of which marriage by notice to the Registrar of a district was legalised, as well as the publication of banns or licence, and marriages of Dissenters * might be solemnised in their own chapels ; or if they preferred it, they might enter into a civil contract before the Registrar.

To the failure of the Church of England in 1836 to take the opportunity to surrender its established privileges and come into line with other religious denominations may be ascribed the moral humiliations inflicted by the State upon it ever since, those moral humiliations from which it seemed that a strong, celibate, High Church Archbishop of Canterbury had in 1936 successfully rescued them, until in his broadcast he allowed exultation to master him and crowed, which was what neither of those two sainted predecessors of his in the See of Canterbury, Anselm and Thomas à Becket, would have made the mistake of doing. It was one of the greatest spiritual opportunities Almighty God ever granted to one of His prelates, and perhaps no prelate has failed more signally to take advantage of such a spiritual opportunity.

Let it clearly be understood that the Church of England's attitude toward matrimony is not being impugned for its acceptance of the laws and regulations of the temporal authority. The criticism is directed at the time-serving attitude of mind which is afraid to take advantage of such laws and regulations to safeguard spiritual authority.

In 1563 the Council of Trent promulgated a dogmatic decree (with twelve canons) on marriage as a sacrament and a reformatory decree (in ten chapters) which treated the various conditions requisite for contracting a valid marriage.

The decree *Tametsi* reads :

> Those who attempt to contract matrimony otherwise than in the presence of the parish priest or of another priest with leave of the parish priest or of the ordinary, and before two or three witnesses, the Holy Synod renders altogether incapable of such a contract, and declares such contracts null and void.

This decree does not run counter to the fundamental proposition *Matrimonium facit consensus*, in which is contained implicitly the doctrine that the persons contracting marriage are themselves the ministers of the sacrament. The priest

---

* *I.e.*, all not members of the Established Church.

only confers the blessing and approbation of the Church on such a contract; but it is the natural and expressed consent of the parties which confers on themselves the sacramental grace. It is necessary for the Church to do all that is possible to guard against the abuse of a sacrament, and the implication of this decree is that without these safeguards the true intention of the parties conferring upon one another the sacrament cannot be presumed. Hence the disciplinary caution.

This Tridentine decree was not promulgated everywhere. In countries like England, Scotland, and Denmark so predominantly Protestant it was never promulgated. Hence in such countries the canonical validity of a Catholic's marriage was not dependent on fulfilling the conditions of the Tridentine decree. Indeed it was not until the *Ne Temere* decree was published in 1908 that the rules of the Church were made binding on all Catholics throughout the world and in all countries except Germany. The *Ne Temere* decree does not conflict with the civil regulations for marriage contracts. A marriage between a Catholic and a non-Catholic is legally valid if it conforms to the laws of the State in which it is made. No mixed marriage is canonically valid unless it takes place in the presence of an accredited priest and two witnesses, and for this to be effected a dispensation is necessary from the bishop of the diocese who will demand certain conditions before granting it, one of which is the pledge that the offspring will all be brought up as Catholics.

The *Ne Temere* decree is a thorn to those who fear the growing influence of the Roman Catholic Church, but nobody with the elements of logic in his mind can object to it. Until the Church of England puts itself on a level with other denominations by accepting civil preliminaries, discussion about its attitude to the remarriage of divorced persons is idle, because such persons can argue that they have never received a clear and explicit statement of Anglican doctrine upon marriage, with the full weight of the Church of England's authority behind it. Discussion of what precisely constitutes that full weight of authority is not for these pages; but it may be pointed out that the suspension of Convocation by Parliament from 1717 until 1853 adds to the difficulty of finding out what was the Church of England's doctrine during that period. We have nothing to guide us about that authoritative doctrine except the utterances of the Bishops in the House of Lords. These prelates, being for the greater part of the period the fruit of an unashamed Erastianism, may mislead the earnest inquirer. Nevertheless, the passive assent of the whole body of clergy to such a tyranny of State over Church does not dispose the critic to believe in the fervour of such a body. He notes that with the loss of the nonjuring clergy and, a generation later, of the Methodists the Church of England had apparently lost the animation of faith, and when he learns that in the year 1800 there were only six communicants at St Paul's Cathedral on Easter Day he is not astonished. If the ambiguity of the Church of England's teaching about marriage were a temporary result of eighteenth-century decay it would be an agreeable duty to rejoice at the definiteness of to-day. Alas, the ambiguity has subsisted from the time that compromise was held to be truth. If the *Via Media* of the Anglican Church shall be judged by God the way of His truth it will not be because it is a way which corkscrews toward eternity between the roads on either side of it so that the pilgrim can walk with his right foot in Rome, his left foot in Geneva, and his eyes on Jerusalem, but because that *Via Media* has discovered for itself a line as straight as that which the judicious Hooker believed he had discovered in the sixteenth century.

If the surrender over divorce had been confined to the ruling of Cranmer and his fellows in the Northampton case that a marriage once dissolved by a separation *a mensa et thoro* was as though it had never been, a ruling which was given legal effect by a Parliamentary Bill later, it might confidently be laid down that the publication of the Canons of 1604 nullified that decision; but the acceptance of the Roos Bill in 1670 without active protest, and the confirmation of that acceptance by the acceptance of the Norfolk Bill in 1700, to the extent of granting a licence to the guilty parties to remarry, saddled the Church of England with precedents from which it will be difficult to free itself without a definite and authoritative dissociation of its doctrine and discipline from civil control. The achievement of that will entail a sacrifice of temporalities, and there is not much evidence at present of the Church of England's willingness to make such a sacrifice.

We can sympathise with the humiliating position in which the Established Church was placed by the suspension of Convocation for over a century and a quarter; but sympathy cannot be extended to admiration of a body of clergy that was content to tolerate such ignominious treatment at the hands of the civil authority.   It is not from such a supine body of clergy that we should expect a protest against the moral obliquity of the Royal Marriages Act.   And none was made.

The confident assertion by Mr Baldwin to King Edward VIII that morganatic marriage was unknown in this country may suitably be examined at this point before we continue our investigation of divorce.

The marriage of George IV as Prince of Wales to Mrs Fitzherbert offers one or two nice problems.

The Act of 1689 laid down:

> And whereas it hath been found by experience that it is inconsistent with the safety and welfare of this Protestant kingdom to be governed by a Popish Prince, or any King or Queen marrying a Papist, the said Lords Spiritual and Temporal, and Commons, do further pray that it may be enacted, that all and every person and persons that is, are, or shall be reconciled to, or shall hold communion with the See or Church of Rome, or shall profess the Popish religion, or *shall marry a Papist*, shall be excluded and be for ever incapable to inherit, possess or enjoy the Crown and Government of this realm, and Ireland, and the dominions thereto belonging, or any part of the same, or to have, use or exercise any regal power, authority or jurisdiction within the same; and in all and every such case or cases the people of these realms shall be and are hereby absolved of their allegiance; and the said Crown and Government should from time to time descend to, and be enjoyed by, such person or persons being Protestants, as should have inherited and enjoyed the same in case the said person or persons so reconciled, holding communion, or professing, or marrying aforesaid, were naturally dead.

Had the Prince of Wales in marrying Mrs Fitzherbert, who was a professing Catholic, become in the concluding words of that section 'naturally dead'?   It is arguable.

Lord Brougham said:

> It was in discussing the question ever contended, that the marriage being illegal, as having been contracted without Royal assent, which the Royal Marriage Act requires, there could be no forfeiture, the ceremony being a mere nullity; but all lawyers agree in that acts of various kinds, both by the laws of England and Scotland, are followed by forfeiture of the party's rights who commits the acts "as if he were naturally dead," and by the succession of the King's heir, the forfeiture being denounced in order to deter from even the attempt to do the thing forbidden, how ineffectual soever that thing might be in itself for any purpose save the incurring the penalty.   Indeed the case of bigamy is precisely of this description; the second wife has no rights whatever, her marriage is a nullity, but she and her pretended husband incur the penalty of felony.

That the Prince's friends were worried was shown by the willingness with which they categorically denied the marriage in Parliament. If the Duke of York had been ambitious or disloyal he might have made a bid for the throne with a prospect of success. Moreover, it may not be so certain as Brougham lays down that the marriage was null and void until the nullity declared by Parliament in the Royal Marriages Act had been pronounced by an Ecclesiastical Court.* The action taken in respect of the marriage of the Duke of Sussex to Lady Augusta Murray will give point to this doubt.

The marriage of the Prince of Wales to Mrs Fitzherbert was treated as non-existent by the civil authority, but only by an agreement to feign that it had never taken place. The attitude of the religious authority is another matter. That Mrs Fitzherbert's marriage was canonically valid at that date is unquestionable. If to-day a Mrs Fitzherbert were to go through a similar form of clandestine marriage with a non-Catholic the decree *Ne Temere* would render such a marriage canonically invalid because she would not have been married by an accredited priest. If the Tridentine decree had been promulgated in England Mrs Fitzherbert's marriage to the Prince of Wales would have been canonically invalid. But that decree had not been promulgated. Therefore when her husband desired her to return to him after he had been legally married to Princess Caroline, and she appealed to Rome, the Pope declared her freedom to do so provided she was satisfied that her husband was truly penitent.

This decision has put the Church of England upon a dilemma. If the marriage had been performed by a Roman Catholic priest the problem would have been delicate enough; but the marriage was performed by an English clergyman, and in order to sustain its canonical invalidity the Church of England would have to accept the superior force of the civil law. It might be argued that this had been recognised already by the acceptance of Lord Hardwicke's 1753 Act and that the Royal Marriages Act was equally binding. On the other hand it could be argued with equal force by upholders of the Church's right that the suspension of Convocation made every Marriage Act passed between 1717 and 1853 canonically not binding upon the conscience of the clergy inasmuch as such

---

* An Act of 1835 made the marriages of all those within the prohibited degrees absolutely void instead of being valid until annulled by the sentence of an Ecclesiastical Court.

Acts were a breach of the Reformation settlement, which laid down that no law affecting the doctrine and discipline of the Church could be made without the consent of the Sovereign as Supreme Governor, the four houses of the Convocations of Canterbury and York, and both houses of Parliament. Even such a process is more Erastian than many learned and devout Anglicans approve, but it is an irreducible minimum for any Church which is not content to be a branch of the State.

It is imaginable, nay, it is probable that in the year 1800 when the Papal decision about the validity of Mrs Fitzherbert's marriage was given a majority of the English clergy would have accepted its illegality under the civil law as rendering it canonically invalid. But it is certain that to-day almost all the English clergy would accept its validity, though still denying its legality. In order to sustain that position they would have to accept what can only be described as a morganatic marriage, and in fact is so described by the *Encyclopædia Britannica.*

No steps were taken to annul the marriage of the Prince of Wales; but as soon as George III heard of a younger son's marriage in Rome Heseltine, his proctor, instituted a suit for nullity of marriage against the Lady Augusta Murray, and on July 14th 1794 Sir William Wynne, the Dean of Arches, declared of the marriage in Rome, " or rather show and effigy of marriage, had, or solemnised, or pretended to be had and solemnised, there is not sufficient proof by witnesses that any such act, or rather show and effigy, was had." The second marriage at St George's, Hanover Square, was then annulled as a contravention of the Royal Marriages Act.

It was felt that somebody at St George's ought to be prosecuted, but this idea was given up. Lord Eldon wrote:

> It seemed singular that banns should be published where one of the parties was of the royal family, and that the clergyman publishing the banns should not be struck upon the reading of the name; it appeared, however, that in the parish there were many of the name (I think Augustus Frederick) by which he was called in the publication. Then, great blame was imputed to the rector for publishing the banns without enquiry as to the residence of the parties in the parish; so it was proposed to call upon the clergy of the church, St. George's, Hanover Square, to account for the marriage having taken place by banns, without the proper residence of the party in the parish, and without their knowing the parties. The rector first appeared: he said he had two most respectable curates, and he had always most

solemnly enjoined them not to marry parties without having first enquired about their residence.   The curates were then examined, and they said theirs was a most respectable parish clerk, who wore a gown, and they had always most solemnly given a like injunction to him.   The clerk was then called, and he declared no man in the parish had a more excellent careful wife than he had, and that he daily gave her most solemnly a like injunction.   She then made her appearance, and said that she must sometimes be about her own, and not about parish business; but that she had two female servants, as discreet as any in the parish, and she had always given them a like solemn injunction, when anybody brought a paper about publication of banns in her and her husband's absence, to make proper enquiries about the parties' residence.   All this put Lord Thurlow out of humour, and he then said to me angrily, " Sir, why have you not prosecuted, under the Act of Parliament, all the parties concerned in this abominable marriage ? "   To which I answered: " That it was a very difficult business to prosecute; that the Act, it was understood, had been drawn by Lord Mansfield, and *Mr Attorney-General Thurlow*, and Mr Solicitor-General Wedderburn, and unluckily they had made all parties present at the marriage guilty of felony; and as nobody could prove the marriage except a person who had been present at it, there could be no prosecution, because nobody present could be compelled to be a witness."—This put an end to the matter.

In 1831 when Sir Augustus D'Este filed his bill in Chancery to establish his right to succeed his father as Duke of Sussex eminent counsel like Lushington and Griffiths gave as their opinion that the Royal Marriages Act did not extend to marriages contracted out of Great Britain, and that the Roman marriage could have been sustained.   O'Connell was even more definite.   He declared that the status of Sir Augustus and his sister was that of a prince and princess of the blood royal in England, and that as regards the Kingdom of Ireland it was a true marriage.

That the first marriage of the Duke of Sussex if doubtful legally was valid canonically is indisputable, and one regrets that he did not test clerical ideas on marriage by inviting a clergyman to marry him to Lady Cecilia Buggin before his first wife was dead.   However, whatever the clergy might have done, the Duke himself had the decency to wait.

The contention that Queen Victoria bought Prince Albert's precedence after herself by appearing to recognise her royal uncle's marriage to Lady Cecilia—also celebrated in St George's, Hanover Square—by creating his wife Duchess of Inverness is not to be refuted.   The Duke of Sussex had asked for more.   He wanted a grant of an extra £6000 a year and the public recognition of Lady Cecilia as H.R.H. the Duchess of Sussex. This was refused, but the creation of 'Duchess of Inverness' was presumably not bestowed upon a lady living in open concubinage. Queen Victoria with all her qualities lacked either the gay impudence of Charles II or the brutal indifference to decency of George I and George II. The fact that the marriage was not formally annulled must be held to signify a quasi-recognition. The creation of the title 'Duchess of Inverness' and the withholding of 'Her Royal Highness' is exactly on a par with the creation of Countess Julia Hauke Princess of Battenberg or Countess Claudine Rhédey Countess Hohenstein and many more similar creations for the dignity of morganatic wives.

If after this any lingering doubt exist in the reader's mind of the possibility of morganatic marriage in this country, he is invited to consider the Duke of Cambridge's marriage to Louisa Fairbrother. True, in this case there was no creation of a title, but it is difficult to suppose that if the Duke had pressed for a title it would not have been conferred. Certainly the marriage was recognised by the Church as canonically valid, and even the use of 'Mrs Fitzgeorge' may be considered on a par with the bestowal of a title. Mrs Jordan was never Mrs Fitzclarence, though her eldest son was created Earl of Munster and the other nine were all Lord or Lady Something Fitzclarences, ranking as the younger sons and daughters of a marquess. In the *Encyclopædia Britannica*, in Debrett, and in the authorised life of the Duke by Canon Sheppard, the marriage is described as morganatic.

If we do not accept the marriages of Queen Victoria's uncle and first cousin as morganatic we are driven into allowing that in Great Britain there are marriages canonically valid but legally null and void which are not morganatic but a peculiar type unknown in any other country. If the Duke of Clarence had married Mrs Jordan we might have called such a marriage jordanatic, but he did not marry her. To call such marriages 'whorganatic' would insult the Church: to call them anything else is apparently a contempt of the law. But is it not simpler to believe that Mr Baldwin and the Cabinet lacked between them enough knowledge of history to be aware that Queen Victoria recognised morganatic marriage in the country of which she was the Sovereign ? That she was perfectly aware of what was and what was not a morganatic marriage was shown when she created the Duke of Teck a Royal Highness. Mr Baldwin and the Cabinet might perhaps have pleaded that the necessity of framing the Royal Marriages Act was evidence that morganatic marriage was not recognised in this country ; but in effect the marriage of the Duke of Windsor has been rendered morganatic, not by the exclusion of his future children from the throne, which was done before he married, but by the refusal of the style of Royal Highness to his wife.   Therefore, if morganatic marriage is not recognised in this country, the refusal of the rank of Royal Highness cannot be justified and is indeed an illegality. As for the attitude various dignitaries of the Church of England have taken up toward the Duke of Windsor's marriage, the best comment on that will be provided by resuming the survey which forms the title of this chapter.

The episcopal attitude toward marriage at the beginning of the nineteenth century is well illustrated by the speeches of the Bishops in the debates over Lord Auckland's Adultery Prevention Bill of 1800.   Noble lords both temporal and spiritual had been shocked by the steadily growing number of private Divorce Bills.   In 1771 the Duke of Atholl had brought in a Bill to prevent the subsequent marriage of the offending parties to which was added a clause prohibiting the adulteress, during a limited period from contracting any marriage whatsoever.   This Bill passed the Lords, but was rejected by the Commons.   In 1779 " a right reverend prelate of high respectability " * then Bishop of Llandaff, and in 1800 Bishop of Durham, introduced the same Bill again, and again it was rejected by the Commons.

Auckland's Bill of 1800 confined the prevention of marriage to the guilty parties and made adultery a misdemeanour liable to punishment by fine and imprisonment.   The opposition was led by the Duke of Clarence, who at this date was living with Mrs Jordan at Bushey.   His speeches were full of nice learning and rugged common sense, and were a great deal more humane than those of the right reverend prelates " whose minds were not more strongly impressed than his own with the idea that adultery was a pernicious crime, striking at the root of all domestic comfort and destructive of the best interests of society."   His Royal Highness pointed out, however, that crime was increased rather than diminished by

---

* Shute Barrington, a son of Lord Barrington. Hence the respectability. His brother Daines was Gilbert White's correspondent.

excessive severity in the punishment of it, and instanced the failure of the death penalty to prevent military desertion. If adultery had increased recently he attributed it to the effect of the war " which detained officers of the army and navy a long time from their wives."

Other noble lords pointed out that the increase of Bills of Divorce did not necessarily mean the increase of adultery, but was more probably to be attributed to the increase of wealth gained through the war, which had made divorce a luxury attainable by a wider circle. To this others added the increase of the population in proportion to which, it was claimed, divorce had not increased.

The Bishop of Durham could not understand why the royal duke should imagine that a divorced adulteress rightly punished by being prevented from marrying her paramour might be driven into prostitution. There was nothing in the Bill which prevented her marrying anybody else.

The Bishop of London " complimented the illustrious duke on the honourable and eloquent manner in which he had stated his reasons for objecting to the Bill, and rejoiced to hear from his royal highness that he was a firm advocate for the religious principles of the Church of England, and for the morality of the people." *

At this date there were already four little Fitzclarences, and a fifth was on the way, Elizabeth, who would marry the sixteenth Earl of Errol and become an ancestress of the Duke of Fife.

The Bishop of Rochester † was not prepared to demand the revival of the death penalty for adultery which had been imposed during the Commonwealth, but he suggested that this was the limit of any concession he would make toward penal weakness. One noble lord (the Earl of Carlisle) had characterised the ecclesiastical courts as Augean stables. He did not agree : " the proceedings in the ecclesiastical courts were as regular, and went with as much certainty to serve the purposes of substantial justice as those in the temporal courts." The same noble lord had taunted himself and his right reverend brethren on this bench, and even the noble and learned lord upon the woolsack and *his* brethren in West-

---

* This was not said ironically. See note on page 378.

† Dr Samuel Horsley was a man of some intellectual force and eloquence with a fine flexible bass voice. He had a high sense of his own importance and " his coach was always driven by four horses." He was heavily in debt at the time of his death in 1808, when he was " expecting Napoleon to set up as Messiah."

minister-hall, with lacking the necessary knowledge of the world to deal with a subject like adultery.   The right reverend prelate asserted on the contrary that " divines and canonists were the best persons qualified to judge what was deemed adultery."   He then hinted at an obstinate thought lingering in his mind, " that it had been a happy thing for the public if no bill of divorce had ever been passed."   However, " the manners of married women in foreign countries professing the Roman Catholic religion which allowed not of divorce for any cause " had expelled that thought from his mind.   The prohibition of divorce must encourage adultery, and that seemed to him a very strong argument in favour of divorce.   Then after quoting Juvenal, Tacitus, the *Reformatio Legum*, and even Cowper's *Task* at great length, the right reverend prelate finished a speech which had lasted well over an hour by appealing to the emotions of the noble lords to secure the punishment of the adulteress :

" My lords, once more I conjure you to remember, that justice, not compassion for the guilty, is the great principle of legislation.   Yet, my lords, your compassion may find worthy objects : turn, my lords, your merciful regards to the illustrious suppliants prostrate at this moment at your bar,— Conjugal fidelity, domestic happiness, public manners, the virtue of the sex !   These, my lords, are the suppliants now kneeling before you, and imploring the protection of your wisdom and your justice."

Lord Grenville supported the Bishop of Rochester in thinking that the " voluptuousness and dissipation " of Roman Catholic ladies who could not be divorced was a strong argument in favour of divorce,* but not of a divorce in which the " offending woman " could marry the " very person who had dishonourably seduced her," for " he differed widely from his noble friend who had spoken last [Lord Mulgrave] in the application of the word ' honour '; he could not allow that there was any such thing as an honourable seducer."

After this the Lords passed the Bill by a majority of eight votes.   Perhaps the Bishop of Rochester's expert knowledge of adultery was wanting ; or perhaps Sheridan's scathing wit was too much for the House of Commons : anyway there the Bill was rejected.†

* Justice demands a note that in spite of this ridiculous remark Grenville himself was a consistent supporter of Catholic Emancipation, and indeed sacrificed his political career by that support.

† It is perhaps unnecessary to add that at least one honourable member

There was a curious sequel to the defeat of the Adultery Prevention Bill the following year when, the House of Lords being in committee on a Divorce Bill to dissolve the marriage of George Taylor and enable him to marry again, the Marquis of Buckingham moved that a special clause should be inserted to prevent Mrs Taylor's marrying her paramour, who was a country clergyman in Devonshire with the pastoral name of Birdwood.   This revelation of " a rooted depraved mind, of deliberate and repeated acts of criminality, and a violation of an express commandment, to which the adulterer could be no stranger . . . was so atrocious," that several right reverend prelates were stirred to indignant eloquence, and perhaps because the future of a clergyman was at stake the whole debate took on a much more scriptural character than the discussion of the previous Bill.

The Bishop of Rochester hoped the clause would be passed " to prevent the scandal that must otherwise fall upon the Church . . . for though the evidence against the adulterer was clear enough for their lordships to act upon it, it might not be sufficient to justify the ecclesiastical court to pronounce sentence of degradation."

The Bishop of London thought the clause only a partial remedy, as it did not go to the punishment of the seducer. But that could be brought forward on a future occasion.   In the meantime this was a step in the right direction.   " My lords, the hydra of adultery cannot be subdued all at once; but we may cut off the many heads of the monster one by one, till at last it may become a lifeless trunk." *

The Bishop of Rochester returned to that uneasy doubt at the back of his mind lest after all the marriage contract might not be indissoluble, but explained that " this doctrine was called in question at the time of the Reformation, from an idea entertained of its being considered with the Popish doctrine of marriage being a sacrament."   That being so, he

---

attributed the alarming increase of adultery to the modern novel. So now we know what Jane Austen's influence was and understand why the Regent travelled always with a set of her works. When will people grasp that the novel is a piece of glass which reflects its period, often with distortion, but very seldom sets fire to it ?

* This ardent episcopal Hercules was Beilby Porteus, a favourite preacher of George III, whose chief claims to spiritual renown are a fulsome panegyric of George II (quoted by Thackeray) and his campaign against Sunday concerts with professional performers in private houses.

felt that the prohibition of after-marriage between the adulterer and the adulteress was a necessity.

The Bishop of London was unable to agree with his right reverend brother. He believed our Blessed Saviour meant to " give relief to the injured party."

The Duke of Clarence offered to support cheerfully any measure likely to prevent the crime of adultery, but declared " it was not by cruel laws against the women that the evil would be remedied."

And in the end the House agreed with his Royal Highness, so that Mr Taylor got his Bill and Mrs Taylor was left free to marry the Reverend William Birdwood, to the scandal of a Church with insufficient evidence to degrade him for an intrigue which had been proved to have been going on in the depths of Devonshire for four years.

Later in the same session a Divorce Bill was debated in the Lords which caused much perturbation of mind. This was nothing less than a request from Jane Campbell to dissolve her marriage with " Edward Addison, her now husband, and to enable her to marry again."

This innovation was apparently too much for the right reverend bench : the bishops must have grown too well used to denouncing the iniquity of the adulteress to be able to contemplate a woman's innocence with the requisite fervour of eloquence. It was left to the Duke of Clarence to move the rejection of the first enacting clause. He agreed that Mrs Addison's wrongs were so grave that if any woman ever did deserve being granted a divorce it was she. At the same time the noble lords must remember what a dangerous precedent would be set.

Lord Thurlow pointed out that this was an incestuous adultery in that it had taken place with Mrs Addison's sister. No reconciliation could legally take place between the husband and wife, and the guilty parties were debarred from marriage by the law of England. The strongest argument, however, in favour of granting Mrs Addison her divorce was that by the law of England all children were under the power and authority of their father . . . and their lordships must all agree, that such a father as Mr Addison was unfit to be entrusted with the education of an innocent and virtuous daughter.

Other noble lords agreed, and the Duke of Clarence was so much impressed by the arguments he had heard that he begged leave to withdraw his motion.

So Mrs Addison was the first of four women to obtain divorce before the passing of the 1857 Act.

In the same session there was debated in the Commons a Bill to prevent persons in Holy Orders from sitting in the House, provoked by the election of that radical cleric Mr Horne Tooke by the solitary voter of the borough of Old Sarum.

In the course of the debate Sir William Scott (later Lord Stowell), the leading ecclesiastical lawyer and canonist of the day and the vicar-general of the Archbishop of Canterbury, asserted that " at the period of the Reformation it was some time in doubt whether holy orders was or was not a sacrament; it was at length determined in the negative." But he went on to argue that " though it ceased to be a sacrament, it certainly did not become a mere civil contract, liable to be dissolved according to the interest, the inclination, or the caprice of an individual. No, it became a high and mysterious ordinance, by which a man . . . assumed a character which he could never after lay aside. . . . It appeared to him that holy orders were in many respects like marriage, which was also a sacrament, and ceased to be so at the Reformation ; but it did not then become a mere civil contract which might be put an end to by the consent of the parties."

In fact Sir William Scott showed in the course of his able speech a singular appreciation of Catholic sacramental doctrine in what reads like a half-hearted attempt to deny that matrimony and holy orders were sacraments.

No wonder Mr Horne Tooke was unconvinced. " The honourable and learned member, at the same time that he denied holy orders to be a sacrament in the Protestant Church, yet maintained the indelibility of the clerical character, by arguing, that if it was not quite a sacrament, it was at least half a sacrament, as it had, like matrimony, the outward and visible signs of one." Mr Horne Tooke had " heard of casuists splitting hairs, but this was the first instance he ever heard of a casuist splitting sacraments." The learned gentleman reminded him of the Divine who, wishing to investigate the mystery of the legion of devils that entered into a herd of swine, took the number of men in a Roman legion in the reign of Tiberius as a happy medium and next enquired in various eastern countries what was the number in the average herd of swine. " He then divided a Mesopotamian swinery by a Roman legion, and proved by the quotient that each hog was possessed by somewhat less than a devil and three-quarters. The name of the Divine was Dr Smallwell or Smallbridge or Smallbrock, but he was ever afterwards called Dr Split-devil."

Thus that irreverent reverend member for Old Sarum. But what a hash he would have made in the House of Lords of some of those right reverend prelates who could not or would not recognise that, except to casuists like Dr Split-devil, the remarriage of the guilty parties was not a whit greater or more obnoxious a violation of matrimony than the remarriage of the innocent party, or that if marriage was not a sacrament it could only be a civil contract. Alas, they were obsessed by the notion of compromise and punishment, and that obsession still endures. Procrustes suffered from a similar obsession. And in the end Theseus slew him.

The advantage which wealth gave in the matter of divorce by means of private Parliamentary Bills gradually impressed itself on the conscience of the nation. Royal commissions were held and motions were brought before Parliament, but legend relates that the final impetus to reform was given by Mr Justice Maule in sentencing a prisoner convicted of bigamy :

"Prisoner at the bar : You have been convicted of the offence of bigamy, that is to say, of marrying a woman while you had a wife still alive, although it is true she has deserted you and is living in adultery with another man. You have, therefore, committed a crime against the laws of your country, and you have also acted under a very serious misapprehension of the course which you ought to have pursued. You should have gone to the ecclesiastical court and there obtained against your wife a decree *a mensa et thoro*. You should then have brought an action in the courts of common law and recovered, as no doubt you would have recovered, damages against your wife's paramour. Armed with these decrees, you should have approached the legislature and obtained an act of parliament which would have rendered you free and legally competent to marry the person whom you have taken on yourself to marry with no such sanction. It is quite true that these proceedings would have cost you many hundreds of pounds, whereas you probably have not as many pence. But the law knows no distinction between rich and poor. The sentence of the court upon you, therefore, is that you be imprisoned for one day, which period has already been exceeded, as you have been in custody since the commencement of the assizes."

In 1857 Lord Palmerston's Government brought in the Matrimonial Causes Bill to effect:

1. The constitution of a lay court for the administration of all matters connected with divorce.

2. The transfer to that court with as little change as possible, of the powers exercised in matrimonial matters by (*a*) the House of Lords, (*b*) the Ecclesiastical Courts, (*c*) the Courts of Common Law.

In May 1857 the Bill was moved in the House of Lords by Lord Cranworth, the Lord Chancellor. Dr Sumner, the Archbishop of Canterbury, declared his intention of voting for the Second Reading, but reserved his right to oppose the final Reading unless it included a clause forbidding remarriage to the guilty parties in a suit for divorce. Dr Sumner * was still in the state of mind as conspicuous among prelates in the first year of the century as it is to-day.

The Duke of Norfolk speaking as a Catholic declared his absolute opposition to the Bill, and in a speech that was a model alike of pungent logic, grave eloquence and sound learning reminded right reverend prelates of the Church of England that their own homilies twice alluded to marriage as a sacrament. None of the right reverend prelates was sufficiently conversant with the homilies of his Church to argue with the noble Duke that the references in the homilies were rather less clear either in their implications or their statements than the noble duke somewhat too generously supposed.

The Bishop of St David's † answering the noble duke paid that generosity a tribute and expressed his appreciation of his " being ready to submit the doctrine of his own Church

---

* Dr Sumner opposed the attempt by Samuel Wilberforce, the Bishop of Oxford, to restore Convocation to its dignity after being prorogued since the year 1717. He and the Archbishop of York concurred with the Privy Council in the Gorham judgment which declared it was unnecessary for an Anglican clergyman to believe in baptismal regeneration.

† This was Connop Thirlwall, a man of wide culture whose history of Greece was overshadowed by Grote, but who welcomed the work of his friend and rival generously. They lie in the same tomb. He read Latin at three and Greek at four and his father published a collection of his work written at the age of eleven, copies of which the bishop destroyed when he came across them during the rest of his life.

to the same scriptural test which Protestants were in the habit of applying to the doctrines of theirs." In accepting those grounds he was still unable to agree with the noble duke's motion, " That the Bill be referred to a Select Committee, for the Purpose of taking Evidence and resolving as to whether the Permission for divorced Persons to marry again has any warrant in Holy Scripture." He did not believe that " our Blessed Lord intended to take upon himself the character of a temporal legislator." He thought that the Matrimonial Causes Bill was regrettable because it was likely to " familiarise the minds of the people of this country with divorce," but " it was too late to offer any opposition to the measure."

So the Bishop of St David's with the Archbishop of Canterbury and eleven other prelates voted against the Duke of Norfolk's clause, which was supported by four prelates, Bishop Wilberforce of Oxford * proving himself throughout these debates the only at once determined and skilful opponent of the Bill. Yet even he, a staunch High Churchman, never once in his long and closely argued speeches ventured to hint the Church of England taught that marriage was a sacrament.

The Bishop of Oxford moved to insert a proviso " that no clerk in holy orders of the Church of England should be liable to any censure, penalty, or punishment for refusing to perform the marriage service over any person or persons who, having been married and divorced, shall seek to be married again during the lifetime of the husband or wife from whom they have been divorced under the provisions of this Act."

He was supported by the Earl of Carnarvon, but he was opposed by the Bishops of Bangor † and London.‡ The latter went so far as to question the validity of Canon 107. He did not believe that by the law of the Church of England marriage was indissoluble. If that was true " any clergyman who had celebrated these marriages, rendered legal by Act of Parliament for the last 150 years, had been violating

---

* Samuel Wilberforce hardly needs a footnote. Of his fight Gladstone wrote to his wife : " The Bp of Oxford has done himself great honour, but I suppose at a further sacrifice of popularity and prospects."

† Christopher Bethell was now 84 years of age. He was accounted a High Churchman. He held the see of Bangor for thirty years, but his episcopal serviceableness was impaired by his being unable to speak Welsh, which was the only language of 195,000 out of his diocesan flock of 200,000.

‡ Dr A. G. Tait, who succeeded Dr Summer as Archbishop of Canterbury.

N

a higher law which he was bound in conscience to obey."

On this proviso, so vital, one might have supposed, to the moral and doctrinal health of the Church of England, only five prelates voted, three for and two against. The Bishop of London, as many a right reverend prelate before him, made the best of both worlds, by speaking against the proviso and abstaining from voting one way or the other. In the debates on Mr Herbert's Matrimonial Causes Bill of 1937 the present Archbishop of Canterbury would follow this epis-copal example by speaking, but not voting, against the Bill.

So did his predecessor of Canterbury in 1857. He, however, spoke in favour of the Bill, but did not vote for or against it at the Third Reading, for which five bishops voted, against which seven.

The Bishop of Exeter * besides voting against the Bill signed a protest in the Journals of the House against the remarriage of the guilty parties. The Bishops of Oxford and Salisbury † signed a protest against the remarriage of any divorced persons guilty or innocent. The other seventeen spiritual lords were mute either with vote or voice or pen.

An attempt was made a month later to introduce a Bill making it compulsory for the guilty parties in a divorce suit to be married at a registry-office; but this was rejected by the House of Lords. The Archbishop of Canterbury and five bishops voted for this Bill, unable to perceive that once the dissolubility of marriage was accepted the marriage of the guilty parties became a moral obligation, and that this Bill was, indeed, equivalent to eating one's wedding-cake and having it. It may be observed that Dr Hamilton of Salisbury who at this date was the only bishop in England that dared openly express his belief that marriage was a sacrament did not vote on what ecclesiastically speaking was an absurd and illogical Bill.

* Henry Phillpotts was an uncompromising bishop. He had fought the Marriage Registration Act of 1836 and accused the Whigs of " treachery aggra-vated by perjury." It was his action in refusing to induct Gorham which provoked the notorious judgment.

† Walter Kerr Hamilton was a man of saintly character, who from beginning his clerical life as an Evangelical became a leader of the Anglo-Catholic party. He was attacked for his doctrine by Lord Portman in the House of Lords, but defended himself without an attempt at compromise. A few more Hamiltons, and the episcopal bench would be a bench indeed, and not the fence into which the majority of its occupants have turned it.

The protagonist of the opposition to the Matrimonial Causes Bill in the House of Commons was Mr Gladstone. It is true that acting on the report of a Royal Commission of 1853 the Cabinet of which Mr Gladstone was a member had in 1854 introduced a Bill similar to the one now presented, and that in 1856 another Bill similar in scope had been presented and rejected; but in the interval Mr. Gladstone had changed his mind, or rather perhaps with the help of Bishop Wilberforce of Oxford he had made up his mind. Says Lord Morley in his biography:

> As soon as the Bill came down to the House of Commons Mr Gladstone hastened up to London in the dog-days. "*A companion in the railway carriage,*" he wrote to Mrs Gladstone, "*more genial than congenial, offered me his ' Times ' and then brandy. This was followed by a proposal to smoke, so that he had disabled me from objecting on personal grounds.*" Tobacco, brandy at odd hours, and the newspaper made a triple abomination at a single dose.

And what a fight Mr Gladstone made! It almost looked at one time as if sheer exhaustion would drive the House to adjourn in that hot dusty August. But Palmerston vowed the House should sit through September if necessary. He had entrusted the Bill to the Attorney-General, Sir Richard Bethell, and the Government meant business.

The boom of Mr Gladstone's big guns still sounds for us in letters to his wife:

11, Carlton House Terrace
July 31, 1857.

Parliamentary affairs are very black: the poor Church gets deeper and deeper into the mire. I am to speak to-night: it will do good. . . .

August 8.

We are fighting hard as you will see on the D.B. All this is preparatory to the great effort from exempting the Church from its scandal and the Clergy from its cruelty. . . .

August 12.

This is a blacker day . . . all we can do is to put shoulder to shoulder and fight the Bill to the last and this please God we will do. . . .

August 13.

> We are fighting more fiercely than ever. . . . I write in the interval before the evening sitting, having refreshed myself with a bath and being about to dine at the Club on my beloved mutton chops. . . .

Mr Gladstone must have assimilated those mutton chops to some purpose. The next day in a sitting of ten hours " including questions, explanations and interlocutory suggestions, Mr Gladstone made nine and twenty speeches, some of them of considerable length. Sometimes he was argumentative, frequently ingenious and critical, often personal, and not less often indignant at the alleged personality of others." Thus, according to Lord Morley, wrote " an unfriendly but not wholly unveracious chronicler."

Yet in all those speeches there was little but casuistry and self-confident scriptural exegesis. One good point *was* made when Gladstone was arguing that the sacramental aspect of marriage did not bear upon its indissolubility. He maintained that the Tridentine decree had made this clear from the point of view of Rome, and pointed out that the Orthodox Church of the East which recognised marriage as a sacrament nevertheless allowed divorce and remarriage on wide grounds. The argument from the Orthodox Church was certainly a palpable hit; but it is questionable whether a Roman theologian would accept the proposition that the indissolubility of marriage could be separated from its sacramental aspect.

Gladstone tried to maintain that the Matrimonial Causes Bill brought in a fundamentally new law about marriage, and in this argument he has been followed by many Anglicans since. His contention will not stand examination for a moment under the lamp of logic. Gladstone's argument was that the comparative rarity of private Divorce Bills to grant permission to be remarried in the parish church of the party in whose interest the Bill was passed did not violate the conscience of the Church of England as a whole. But even if we allow for the uncertainty of the marriage law and procedure in the sixteenth century it is impossible to accept the Roos Divorce Bill of 1670 as an exception or an irregularity, when we remember that it was repeated in the case of the Duke of Norfolk thirty years later and that the Archbishop of Canterbury's licence granted the guilty parties marriage. It could be maintained that the clergy were not strong enough to withstand the authority of the State, but no evidence that they ever made any serious attempt to do so in this matter has been adduced, or ever can be adduced may be added, for it is not to be found.

Those who argued that the 1857 Act was a change of judicial procedure but not a change of the law itself had on their side both history and logic. Catholics opposed the Bill as a novelty only in so far as it would obviously greatly increase the number of divorces; but Catholics would have opposed any private Divorce Bill had not their own disabilities deprived them of a hearing over so many years. It may be asked why Catholics should concern themselves with the divorces of those who are not Catholics, and it may seem an attempt at bigoted interference with a freedom they are themselves denied, until it is remembered that Catholics accept the sacramental validity of all other religious marriages. The *Ne Temere* decree is a disciplinary regulation promulgated for Catholics. Two Protestants married to one another are not remarried should they be received into the Roman Catholic Church. Hence the marriage of Protestants is not a matter which can be outside Catholic cognisance.

The terms in which the protest of the dissentient Catholic lords was entered in the Journals of the House express lucidly the Catholic point of view:

1. Because the Bill contains provisions authorising in certain cases divorce *a vinculo matrimonii* of Christian marriage, and is thus in direct opposition to what our Lord has declared both in His own words and in the unvarying teaching of His Church.

2. Because the harmony and stability of the family relations, upon which the well-being of the State is ultimately based, will be unsettled and impaired by the facilities which are offered for divorce.

So at the end of that hot August of the year of the Great Indian Mutiny the Matrimonial Causes Act was passed and came into force on January 1st 1858. One concession had been secured for the Anglican clergy: they were not to be penalised either for marrying or refusing to marry divorced persons, but should they refuse they were obliged to give

the use of their churches to any clergymen who were willing
to perform the service.

Let us quote from three leaders in *The Times* of July 31st,
August 4th, and August 5th 1857 which may be usefully
compared with some of that great journal's leaders of December 1936:

> July 31st:—The advocates of the Bill say that they want to extinguish
> the immense scandal of conducting minute and disagreeable investiga-
> tions in the great Council of the nation, and enacting a succession of
> *privilegia* hateful to the principles of this and every sound constitution.
> The opponents then, including, it is said, seven thousand clergymen,
> with the usual proportion of country gentlemen and lawyers, reply—
> "Oh, we know all that; we admit all that; we don't pretend that
> marriage is indissoluble; we don't pretend to understand what the
> Bible says about it; the readings are corrupt; nobody knows quite
> what they mean; but, if you pass this Bill, we intend to hold you
> answerable for all the divorces, dissolutions of marriage, adulteries,
> fornications, bigamies, polygamies, and matrimonial improprieties of
> all kinds that may take place, and probably abound, for the future."
> This is a very free and easy mode of proceeding on the part of the
> objectors, who think to wield the thunders of HEAVEN without burn-
> ing their own fingers. It is a sort of bush war. Our statesmen are
> obliged to act in the face of day, to take a position, and announce
> precisely what they think necessary for the public welfare and morality.
> Their opponents, being not statesmen, but divines, and divines of the
> very worst class—amateurs—feel no such responsibility. They are
> under no obligation to tell the nation what it ought to do. Being
> generally respectable men, with wives, families, and good positions,
> and few drawbacks to their earthly comforts, except that they have not
> quite enough money for their existing families, and being therefore
> under no temptation to superadd a second marriage, they do not want
> this Bill for themselves. With the unfortunates who may happen to
> want it they have nothing to do.
>
> August 4th:—Some of the opponents declared that the most
> objectionable part of the measure was the permission for remarriage
> accorded to the guilty party; but the objection, if it has any validity,
> applies equally to the wrongdoer and to the wronged. No human or
> Divine law prohibits the marriage of those who may previously have
> led questionable lives. The real meaning of the dissentients is, not
> that the divorced woman is unworthy of marriage, but that she is
> married already; and the same disability must necessarily attach to
> the injured husband. The pretended desecration of the wedding
> ceremony is a frivolous afterthought. None of the remonstrant
> clergy would hesitate to bestow the nuptial benediction on a seducer
> and on his repentant victim. It would be a monstrous abuse of
> power if the legislature were to compel a divorced woman to remain
> the mistress of her paramour.

August 5th:—If the Bill did really affect the clergy—if it really altered their position with regard to the marriage of divorced persons, it would be time to consider their claim to relief.   But the fact is that every year several couples of divorced persons are launched on society to be remarried by somebody or other.   They might fall to the lot of any clergyman, yet it so happens we never heard of any objection to perform the service, nor do we believe such an objection has yet been shown.   The clergy are only too desirous to marry as many as they can, without any enquiry at all, and taking the word of the people themselves that there is no obstacle to their union.   There are numerous Acts of Parliament securing to particular churches the marriages of large districts, like the old monopolies compelling people to take their corn to one particular mill, and the result is that in the metropolis, and in many large towns, scores of couples are married at once, all equally and utterly unknown to the officiating minister. The grievance, then, as far as we see, is not at all likely to be felt, even if each clergyman's chance of having such a marriage as that under question should be somewhat increased.   Were the grievance real, and were the clergy now called on to do what they might not have been called on to do before, there might be a clause for the benefit of those who have taken orders on a different understanding.   Of course, all who may henceforth become candidates for ordination will do so with their eyes open, and be prepared to obey the law.   The existing clergy, on the proof of a real grievance, might be permitted to make a formal protest before the first day of the operation of the new Act, and be allowed the benefit of that protest till, on further consideration, they saw reason to withdraw it.   There are things to be said for and against such a provision, but it would give no inconvenience, for there will always be clergymen ready to perform the ceremony, and it might deprive some wrongheads, or blunderheads, of a very foolish opportunity of making a disturbance.

The figures for divorce crept up slowly and steadily from 1858 when there were 326 divorces to 1898 when there were 750.

Allusion has been made in an earlier chapter to the campaign of Father William Black against the remarriage of divorced persons, which was warmly supported by Anglo-Catholics because by this date the belief that marriage was a sacrament was much more widely diffused in the Church of England, but also partly because the arguable violation of Canon 107 gave the Anglo-Catholics an opportunity to hit back at bishops who were interfering with various Anglo-Catholic practices in the way of alleged Romish doctrine and ritual.

This was the kind of thing that was being written :

To the Editor
The Church Times.

Another Uncanonical Marriage.

Sir,

May I call the attention of Churchmen to the fact that the Rev. ——,* vicar of ——, pretended to convey the Church's blessing on the marriage of Sir —— and Mrs —— at —— —— on the 5th inst. Mrs —— has a " canonical " husband still living.

The indulgence was granted by the Archbishop of Canterbury. When will Convocation put an end to this scandal ?

WILLIAM BLACK.

6, Gray's Inn Square, W.C
February 15th, 1898.

Marriage of Divorced Persons.

Sir,

Prebendary Webb-Peploe has, I observed, sent a petition to the Bishop of London stating that he is pained and scandalised at the ritual observances of some of his neighbours.

Now, a short time ago, Mr Webb-Peploe, in direct and open defiance of the command of our Lord, married in his Church, by the hands of his curate, an American clergyman who had divorced his wife for incompatibility of temper.

Surely, after this, Mr Webb-Peploe can hardly make a public appeal against what he considers irregularities of observances on the part of his fellow-Christians.

WILLIAM BLACK.

6, Gray's Inn Square,
March 8th, 1898.

On July 15th 1898 *The Church Times* said :

THE BISHOPS AND THE MARRIAGE LAW.

The report of the Bishops of the Southern Province on the burning subject of the remarriage of divorced persons cannot but be regarded with somewhat mixed feelings. At first a study of the report leads one to the conclusion that the Bishops have at last realised the demand for a stricter observance of the law of the Church, in regard to indissolubility of marriage, is based upon a genuine conviction, and moreover voices the feelings of a large number of persons whose opinions are worth weighing. This impression is, to a certain extent, justified; the report gives in detail an excellent summary of the attitude of the Church generally towards the sacrament of matrimony and proceeds to advise what, in the opinion of the Bishops should be done in those cases which imply a distinct breach of that principle of indissolubility to which they give their assent. It is here that their pronouncement

---

* The full names were given at the time, but are omitted here.

will, we believe, fail to convey the assurance and confidence which English Churchmen are anxious to feel in their Episcopal rulers. The report falls back upon the Lambeth recommendations of 1888, in so far as it does not pronounce definitely against the remarriage of both the parties to a divorce, but contents itself with urging the clergy to dissuade even the innocent party from proceeding to the complication of a fresh union. In spite of the fact that there are historical precedents which may be alleged in favour of such unions, it is disappointing in the extreme to find that after a further ten years' operation of the Divorce Acts, together with the consequent accumulation of evidence why the discipline of the Church should not be refined rather than relaxed, the Upper House of the Convocation of Canterbury should persistently ignore, by a deplorable silence, the indisputable law of the English Church. It is with the law of the English Church that they have to do, and to have omitted all reference to it is to desert those upholders of the ecclesiastical law to which in other respects, and rightly, the Bishops demand obedience. By such a pronouncement the Upper House of Convocation places itself in conflict with the Lower, the former becoming champion of laxity whereas the Lower is left to bear the burden of opposing the unrestrained desires of a society all too rapidly losing its hold on moral restraint. . . .

On February 17th 1899 *The Church Times* printed the following correspondence between Father Black and the Archbishop of Canterbury, who with his most reverend brother of York was presently going to preside over an enquiry into the legality of incense and processional lights in the services of the Church of England. The publication of this correspondence was no doubt intended to shake his authority and impugn his knowledge of ecclesiastical observance:

THE DIVORCE QUESTION.

The following correspondence has been sent to us for publication:—

> 6, *Gray's Inn Square,*
> *February 6th, 1899.*

To the Archbishop of Canterbury.

YOUR GRACE,
        It has been announced in the newspapers that —— is about to marry. . . . This gentleman divorced his canonical wife some time ago and she is still living.

Your Grace has hitherto purposely avoided publicly upholding the Prayer Book and Canon which declare marriage indissoluble, but I am not without hope that a sense of fitness may lead you to stand by this now, when you and the Archbishop of York have issued an invitation to us in *The Times* newspaper to regard you as our guardians.

I would ask you then to let it be known publicly beforehand that you forbid any clergyman in your Province to perform this marriage.

Failing such a pronouncement from Your Grace, you are well aware that this so-called marriage will be performed by some clergyman, to the great sin of all concerned, and the great scandal of the Church.

Your Grace may reply that you have no power to enforce such a direction. If that be so, still the moral weight of a declaration from you is all that is needed; and I would add that it will be specially welcome to Churchmen at this moment, for you will thus be supporting the Prayer Book: not in a matter determined by popular clamour, but in one opposed by a clamour so popular as to have found expression in an Act of Parliament—the Divorce Act of 1857.

Then again a public pronouncement by Your Grace will no doubt bring back the Bishop of —— [the diocese in which the lady lived] to his allegiance to the Prayer Book, or will at least leave him without any support from you in his endeavour to betray the doctrine of marriage therein laid down. He and the wrongdoers in his diocese may rely upon your Grace's silence, your public direction they will not disregard.

Your Grace will, I think, acknowledge that to urge you to this is not an impertinence on my part, if you will take into consideration some circumstances in your dealing with Church doctrines, which have, by chance, come to my notice, and which, I will, if you wish it, recall to your mind.

Meanwhile, I wish to point out, that the intended breach of the Church's rule has been publicly announced in the newspapers; that your Grace knows that clergy will be found to do this thing unless you intervene; that the people are in high station, and their evil example will be felt far and wide, and that the Bishop of the diocese has publicly spoken unfaithfully, and will no doubt, if left unchecked, betray the Church.

Your Grace's respectful and faithful

WILLIAM BLACK.

Lambeth Palace,
February 7th, 1899.

REVEREND SIR,

The Book of Common Prayer does not pronounce marriage indissoluble.

It declares those whom God hath joined together no man may put asunder.

Our Lord's exception in the case of adultery shows that a divorce in such a case is not man's doing but the Lord's.

Yours faithfully,

F. CANTUAR.

Rev. W. Black.

YOUR GRACE,

Let me thank you for your letter and beg to be allowed to point out that the Church of England (as witness her canons on marriage, the unbroken practice of her courts down to 1857 and with all respect to Your Grace, I must again say, the Marriage Service in the Prayer Book), has not believed our Blessed Lord's teaching to be what Your Grace supposes.   Otherwise she would have directly contravened His Law by her own.

And secondly, that your assertion about the Prayer Book is, it seems to me, contrary to the facts as brought out by the recent discussion in Convocation.

You will, accordingly, I trust, permit me to renew my appeal to you to uphold in this urgent and vital matter the law of the Church of England.   Also, Your Grace will, I hope, make no objection to my publishing this correspondence.

Your Grace's most respectfully and faithfully in Christ,
WILLIAM BLACK

Nor did Father Black confine himself to correspondence. On September 22nd 1899 *The Church Times* reported:

REMARRIAGE OF DIVORCED PERSONS.

Forbidding the Banns.

Some excitement was caused on Sunday at the Church of St Clement Danes, Strand, where during the morning service, the well-known preacher Father Black, made another protest against the remarriage of divorced persons.

Following the usual custom, the Reverend J. J. H. Septimus Pennington, the Rector, read out the banns of marriage of three or four couples after the second lesson.   Scarcely had he finished reading the first banns in which the woman was described as a " single woman " when a clergyman who turned out to be Father Black, rose and made the following protest :

" I hereby declare cause and just impediment to their marriage and forbid the banns of J— and L— on the grounds firstly that you have in the banns wrongly designated and described one of them, so rendering the pretended publication worthless; secondly that the woman has a canonical husband living and cannot therefore be married in church after the publication of the banns after an objection on these grounds has been raised."

The protest made, the Rector turning to Father Black said " I shall be pleased to see you in the vestry after the service," and the service proceeded as usual.

The present writer remembers Father Black well.   He was a good preacher, albeit his mouth was perhaps too tight for the richest and most emotional eloquence.   His chin was determined; his complexion fresh.   He did not confine his active efforts to forbidding oanns, but on two or three occasions protested at the actual wedding. The writer saw him hustled out of one fashionable church by indignant favour-bedecked ushers, and a more completely unperturbed 'brawler' was never beheld.

The first year of Edward VII's reign brought a big jump up in the number of petitions for divorces and in 1902 they were all but thirteen from a thousand. By 1910 the proportion of dissolved marriages was 1 in 377. By 1920 it was 1 in 123. The Duke of Clarence was right once upon a time when he fancied war upset matrimony. By 1932 the proportion was 1 in 79, and in that same year 5,773 judicial separation orders were made by Courts of Summary Jurisdiction. As early as 1912 a Royal Commission on Matrimonial Causes had recommended extension of the grounds for divorce, and it is right to note that the Archbishop of York (Dr Lang) was one of three signing a minority report.* As a general observation it may be noted, without suggesting any deductions, that celibate Anglican clergy have always been the strongest upholders of the strict interpretation of the Church of England's marriage laws.

With a feeling that another Matrimonial Causes Bill was not far off, the Church of England paid more and more attention to the necessity of finding a compromise that would salve all except the consciences of a few extremists. It was a tricky business, because there were many influential Anglican clergymen who hoped to achieve with one or other of the Orthodox Churches a reunion that went beyond the exchange of pious compliments and the joint participation in sentimentally impressive if sometimes slightly confused services. That desire made it impossible for such idealists to support the excommunication of divorced persons who had remarried in or out of church, for the Orthodox Churches enjoy a Byzantine laxity in the matter of divorce.

At last in 1935 a Joint Committee of the Convocations of Canterbury and York issued a Report on the Church, Marriage and Divorce which offers a fascinating panorama of the *Via Media*. The present writer might have hesitated to say as

---

* The other two were Sir Lewis Dibdin and Sir William Anson, the Warden of All Souls. Anson was the tutor of the Prince of Wales in Constitutional Law when he was up at Magdalen. One asks, with as little chance of an answer as to the question about what songs the Sirens sang, what instruction Sir William, his eyes twinkling and glittering as they always did, gave his royal pupil about royal marriages.

much without the encouragement of ' *Some Comments on the Report of the Joint Committee published on behalf of the Council of the Church Union*,' which provide criticism far more destructive from within than he would have ventured to apply from without.

Here are the crucial resolutions of the Joint Committee according to the Church Union *Comments* :

1. That this House affirms as our Lord's principle and standard of marriage a lifelong and indissoluble union for better or for worse of one man with one woman, to the exclusion of all others on either side.

2. That this House also affirms its belief that, as a consequence, in no circumstances can Christian men or women remarry during the lifetime of a wife or husband without a breach of the moral * principles by which the institution of marriage is governed according to Christ's teaching.

3. That in order to maintain the principle of a lifelong obligation clearly expressed in the Marriage Service—

(*a*) The Church should not allow the use of that Service in the case of anyone who has a partner still living; and

(*b*) Any person who has remarried contrary to the second of the above Resolutions ought not to be admitted to the Sacraments and privileges of the Church except † on such conditions as the Church may require.

4. That while affirming its adherence to the ancient tradition of the Western Church, as stated in the first and second of the above Resolutions, this House recognises that the actual discipline of particular Christian communions in this matter has varied widely from time to time and place to place, according to the needs or distresses of the moment; and holds that the Church of England is competent to enact such a discipline of its own in regard to marriage (as in other cases) as may from time to time appear most salutary and efficacious.

5. That accordingly, after due consideration of all the factors involved, this House maintains that the most salutary form of discipline applicable to the circumstances of the day, which can be adopted by the Church of England, is as follows:

Where under the present English law as to divorce and remarriage two persons have contracted a legal marriage during the lifetime of a former partner of one of them, the Bishop shall be informed of all the circumstances of the case, and if he be satisfied *that the parties have acted in all good conscience, and after mature reflection and* ‡ that for them to abide as husband

---

* The Upper House of Canterbury deleted the word " moral ".

† The Upper House of Canterbury substituted the words " on such conditions as the Church may require." for " as is provided in the two Resolutions which follow."

‡ The words italicised appear only in the Canterbury edition of the Resolutions.

and wife in a marriage so contracted is, in the circumstances, morally preferable to any other course, and that no other impediment stands in the way, he shall be free to give directions that they may be admitted to the Sacraments.

The Lower House of the Convocation of York made some trifling emendations which need not concern us.

The non-Anglican who has ploughed through this chapter may wonder after reading those resolutions if he is still reading about the same Church of England as has figured on previous pages.* It is usual for a Church to glorify its origins, but the Established Church of England is unique in regarding its origins as unhappily as a *nouveau riche*. There is something curiously unapostolic about Henry VIII and the Protector Somerset and even Thomas Cranmer. So we are not surprised to find that the *Report* skates rapidly over the thin ice of the past and suggests that " conditions which face the Church of England to-day " are all that matter. In one sense that may be true, but it will have to be borne in mind by those who are proposing to confront present conditions that they are still tying themselves down to confronting them with an equipment of doctrine and discipline provided by those earlier centuries they are so eager to forget.

The *Comments of the Church Union* point out that the resolutions of the *Report* while claiming that marriage is indissoluble do in fact claim no more than that marriage ought to be indissoluble. The *Comments* are convinced that marriage is a sacrament, and that the *Report* by refusing to recommend excommunication without exception to divorced persons who have remarried " is an implicit declaration that the mode of conduct is not sin—that it is at the least morally neutral, innocent, or permissible."

Such a position is the Roman Catholic position, and the Church Union while sensible of the advantages of reunion with the Orthodox Church of the East is extremely reluctant " to drive a new wedge between us and ' that great Latin Church of the West.' "

Here is the position of the Church Union :

* Yet between 1929 and 1936 five remarriages of divorced persons in the peerage were performed in three fashionable London churches. How many outside the peerage were performed during the same period may be guessed. Perhaps in spite of these resolutions the Church of England has not changed so much.

. . . the witness of the formularies of the Church of England, at least, shows that the doctrine of indissolubility (apart from which the sacramental and mystical character of marriage can hardly be in practice maintained) is a distinctive part of the historic Anglican position, as this was under the guidance of God's good providence permitted to crystallise and define itself, after the confusion of the Reformation period.   Given the position that the Prayer Book doctrine is the Scriptural and primitive Catholic doctrine—that is, the teaching of our Lord himself—it will follow that the preservation of this doctrine through the storms of the sixteenth century, and the non-enactment of the *Reformatio Legum Ecclesiasticarum,* which would have destroyed it, is just as much an instance of Divine over-ruling as the preservation of the threefold ministry and the episcopal succession, or of the ancient eucharistic Liturgy in a vernacular form. It was inevitable that the precise significance, both of the changes which the English Reformation introduced and (if we may so say) of those which it did *not* introduce—that is, of its leaving the essential outlines of the Faith, Order and Worship of the Church untouched— should take two or three centuries to be fully and consciously apprehended.   Before the distinction between the English and the Continental Reformations had been fully realised, and when it was still natural to think of all non-Roman Christians in the West in a vague general sense as constituting " the Reformed Churches," there would doubtless, be a consequent tendency to assume that the Church of England must be on the side of that revolt against the matrimonial doctrine and law of the ancient Western Church which was characteristic of Continental Protestantism; and it is therefore not surprising to find that it is possible to produce a *catena* of post-Reformation Anglican divines who favoured departure, to a greater or less extent, from the strict law of indissolubility; the most eminent of these was, perhaps, Cosin.   It is also possible to quote the late Dr William Bright and the revered and beloved Bishop Edward King in the same sense. . . . They are less sure guides to the understanding of the essential mind of Anglicanism on this point than Charles Gore.   Gore lived at a time when the English Church had had three and a half centuries in which to reflect upon the meaning of the position to which, owing to the Reformation changes, she found herself committed, and when her overseas expansion, amongst peoples of many races and political allegiances, had compelled the conscious articulation and formulation of Anglicanism as a substantive presentation of Catholic Christianity, not tied to these shores but claiming to exist everywhere and in its own right, and (if true at all) to be as true for Japanese and Hindus as for Englishmen; and he possessed the characteristic power of a great dogmatic theologian, that of grasping revealed truth as a majestic whole, which is what it is, and cannot be modified to suit the whims of men.

That may be accepted as a statement of the Anglo-Catholic position, and it will be observed that in the last part of the extract quoted it makes large, even exalted claims for the English Church. It is not within the scope of this work to investigate such claims with a critical eye, but it is vital to the comprehension of the chief event of which this book treats to make no mistake about the strength and extent of the ecclesiastical ambition in the face of which the Supreme Governor of the Church of England, most unexpectedly was to find himself, not a king but a pawn in the game.

Yet, with all this almost Hildebrandine assertion of spiritual domination, so far beyond anything that was imaginably conferred with the pallium of an Anselm or a Beckett, neither the Church Union nor the Houses of Convocation propose any practical steps to effect against the British Commonwealth of Nations what in the end was not even possible to effect against an exiled Duke of Windsor. " No one is compelled to be a Churchman," the *Report* declares tolerantly. " There are many Englishmen who do not profess to be Churchmen." That is true of all except one Englishman. The Sovereign upon the Throne is compelled to be a member of the Church of England. And that being the case it was necessary that the highest dignitary of the Church of England who prepared him for Confirmation should put before him at least what that particular high dignitary himself believed to be the doctrine of the Church of England about marriage. We know that at his Confirmation in 1910 the hymn ' Fight the good fight ' was sung, but we can feel perfectly sure that Dr Davidson gave no instruction about marriage to that young Prince which included even one of the recommendations of the Report of the Joint Committee of the Convocations. That being so, those nationals of the British Commonwealth outside the Church of England, be they Roman Catholics or Presbyterians, be they Baptists, Quakers or Seventh Day Adventists, be they indeed not Christians at all but Jews, Mohammedans, and Hindus have a right to demand of the Church of England that from henceforth it shall never again be possible to add the religious pressure of a privileged minority to whatever political pressure the exigencies of the future may inflict upon the King or Queen Regnant, until that privileged minority has declared beyond any possibility of evasion the doctrine it teaches and the discipline it proposes to enforce.

That the Church of England will display either unanimity in the exegesis of its present doctrine embodied in the Thirty-nine Articles or attain unanimity in the restatement of its creed is improbable, and indeed impossible until that Church cuts itself free from the State. Yet even the opportunity of securing independence in the carrying out of what after a long process of evolutionary religious opinion it now believes to be its marriage laws was rejected by the Majority Report of the Joint Committee when it refused to recommend the adoption of universal civil preliminaries and thus give the Church of England the freedom of solemnisation enjoyed by the Nonconformist Churches. Dr Pollock, the Bishop of Norwich, made out what an outsider would call a convincing case for such a step in his Minority Report:

> It is to be observed that before 1836 the Church of England enjoyed an almost complete monopoly of authority to perform a legally binding marriage ceremony.
>
> This privilege was, however, completely destroyed by the 1836 and subsequent Marriage Acts. By this legislation it became possible for persons to contract purely civil marriages or to become legally married by other religious rites than those of the Church of England. . . . But the Church of England, though losing the privilege of its previous monopoly, has remained subject to the obligations previously annexed to that privilege, viz., its responsibility for maintaining a system of ecclesiastical preliminaries and its real, if indefinite, obligation to marry persons presenting themselves who satisfy legal requirements.
>
> The reason for the proposal of civil preliminaries is that the Church of England should be rendered free to discriminate on religious grounds as to those whom it would or would not marry, as in the case of the Roman Catholic Church and the Free Churches. . . . A revision of marriage preliminaries would offer a satisfactory common ground for co-operation between the ecclesiastical and civil authorities. The Church would be in a stronger position if it took its part in some general review of the marriage law than if it had to go to Parliament solely on its own account.

If Dr Pollock's recommendation were adopted the Church of England could promulgate its equivalent of the *Ne Temere* decree and ensure its effect. The quarrels and quibbles about the remarriage of divorced persons or their excommunication would cease. Even the Supreme Governor might understand what he was governing.

Mr W. R. Rowley Elliston (St Edmundsbury and Ipswich) when arguing with Lord Hugh Cecil (London) at the autumn session of the 1937 Church Assembly that the Praemunire writ was not obsolete irradiated the topic with a rushlight of his own:

" In the reign of George III, when Parliament had dealt with the question of royal marriages and passed the Royal Marriages Act, that was the very penalty that Parliament chose for all those who should assist or be present at such illegal marriages, and only in the previous December that Royal Marriages Act had been an important factor in a great constitutional question."

We who by now know rather more about the Royal Marriages Act might laugh at Mr Elliston if his remark were not so disagreeably typical of the ignorance of many people much more influential than he was.

And it is difficult to preserve a decent gravity when we hear those bold members of the Church Assembly, descendants of the clergy and laity who had grovelled at the feet of Henry VIII at the threat of a Praemunire, so defiant of the Crown and the King's Bench at long last. The Dean of Chichester declared that it was " morally and spiritually intolerable for a dean and chapter to pray for the guidance of the Holy Spirit to elect a bishop whom they had been told to elect." Whereupon the Archdeacon of Ipswich suggested that, though the Statute of Praemunire might be an anachronism, the election of bishops by deans and chapters was as great an anachronism. Nevertheless the significance of Lord Hugh Cecil's motion should be noted. It is the thin edge of the wedge to achieve disestablishment without disendowment. Disendowment is the terror; how much a terror may be judged by the Majority Report of the Sub-Committee which refused to recommend universal civil preliminaries. It is signed by Dr Inskip the Bishop of Barking and Chancellor H. B. Vaisey, K.C.

Many arguments are used against the proposed change, among others that the Church of England as the Church at least nominally of the whole nation confers a social cachet by its marriage in church, that many people who are married in church thereby obtain their first introduction to a life of religious observance, that there might be " a disposition to let the civil authorities carry the whole matter through without troubling about the (supposedly) superfluous religious rite," and that " the Church has in its marriages an opportunity of reaching those who are not now, but may be made or become its faithful children."

But the vital argument is uttered at the end, a golden-mouthed argument:

" The financial aspect of the matter is not to be ignored, for at present a sum estimated at not less than £25,000 per annum is divided between Chancellors, diocesan registrars and surrogates in connection with the grant of licences. (This estimate does not include the larger fees payable for special or Archbishop's licences, which would disappear with the rest when the change took effect.) "

And then feeling perhaps that Mammon has been a little too conspicuous, Dr Inskip and Chancellor Vaisey return to God.

" If the matter were *res integra* the attractions of the contemplated system would be greater. But the Church finds itself in a position which affords opportunities of spiritual advantage, and ought not, it is thought, to surrender these."

One is at a loss whether to write ' *Amen* ' or ' *Verb. Sap.*' at the end of this exhalation of pious breath.

We will leave to Dr Inskip and Chancellor Vaisey the gold and the frankincense, and let Lord Russell of Killowen offer a little astringent myrrh.

The occasion was the Third Reading of Mr A. P. Herbert's Matrimonial Causes Bill of 1937 in the House of Lords on July 19th. Mr Herbert, with a father's fondness for his offspring, found Lord Russell's speech " offensive ". In its ruthless exposure of the hypocrisy (in a Pickwickian sense of course) of certain right reverend prelates, who only a few weeks previously had made the question of divorce the prime cause against King Edward VIII, during what Mr Herbert himself, with what may be considered a slightly exaggerated notion of the present dignity of the House of Commons, calls " the Constitutional crisis," perhaps Lord Russell's speech *was* offensive. He must be forgiven for he was not defending a compromise, but proclaiming his belief in an absolute truth :

" Those of us who adhere to the old faith are but a small minority in the country. We are only a tiny minority in either House of Parliament, while in this House only is Christianity represented as such. And it is for these reasons that we Catholics looked forward with anxiety and hope to hear what lead would be given in this House by the Lords Spiritual to the members of the Established Church who compose the great majority of the Christians in this country. I take leave to say that the disappointment has been general and has been grievous. The hungry sheep looked up and were not fed. The most reverend Primate, in his speech on the Second Reading, described the principal proposals of this Bill as being contrary to Christian principles. Yet he gives no vote against the Bill. On the contrary, he voted for the exclusion of the amended Clause I. These things are difficult to a plain man to understand. How it can be I know not, and the only conclusion which one can draw is that the sheep of his flock are of so many breeds that no diet is found which will agree with the constitutions of all. About this matter we Catholics, at all events, have no doubts, no hesitation, and no difficulty. We believe divorce to be an evil thing. We believe it to be contrary to the teachings of Christ, and we believe that the holy bond of matrimony, once validly established, can, and should, only be dissolved by death. For these reasons I will vote against this Bill, and I urge your Lordships to adopt a similar course."

After quoting an "offensive" speech like that, how is it possible to contemplate King Edward VIII's marriage with a woman who had divorced two husbands? The contemplation of such a possibility would certainly be out of the question if we could be sure that King Edward in all his life ever heard such words from any Anglican clergyman uttered with the authority of his Church behind them. Without the guidance of a tall lighthouse upon a rock, and with nothing before him but the ebb and flow of a doctrinal tide and the uncertain swell of a disciplinary sea, what blame can be imputed to him for supposing he was at liberty to steer his own barque on the course he believed was best and safest for himself? He was not to imagine that the validity of acts to which his predecessors had given their assent and against which history related no active protest by the Church was dubious. His royal heritage bound him fast to that Church, and now he was to discover the existence of acts to which as a constitutional monarch he must conform but which as supreme governor of the Church of England he must contemn. It is not surprising he found such an antithesis incomprehensible. King Edward's attitude toward divorce cannot be judged except on the evidence that was laid before him of his Church's teaching. Such evidence, it is contended, acquits him completely of any deliberate violation of a generally recognised and accepted law.

Put the Church of England's doctrine about marriage on one side for a moment, and let its Divines answer for their teaching on the great fundamental truths of the Christian faith.   There has recently been published the Report of the Commission on Christian Doctrine appointed by the Archbishops of Canterbury and York in 1922.

For fifteen years a body of prominent ecclesiastics and laymen have met for a week or two every year to produce a booklet of 242 pages stamped on the cover with a dark vignette of Lambeth that seems to rival the very Vatican itself in its suggestion of authority.   The book is called *Doctrine in the Church of England*, and is perhaps the most lucid exposition of ambiguous belief ever penned.   The pastoral theology possesses the exquisite optimistic insouciance of a Bo-Peep, and the dogmatic theology recalls Edwin Lear's

> There was an Old Lady of Prague,
> Whose language was horribly vague;
>   When they said, " Are these caps ? "
>   She answered " Perhaps ! "
> That oracular lady of Prague.

Here, for instance, is the Commission's ruling on immortality: " As between the affirmation of the doctrine known as *conditional immortality*, and the assertion of the *universal* immortality of mankind, the Commission as a whole does not feel itself called upon to make a pronouncement."

That comment on immortality is typical of the Commission's attitude towards the Virgin Birth, the Resurrection, the Ascension, and in fact to the whole body of Christian doctrine. To ask for bread and be offered a stone may be disappointing, but it is not less disappointing to ask for a rock and be offered potter's clay.   After so much accommodation over the great mysteries of the Christian creed we might expect an extreme rigidity over marriage to balance it; but that too remains as malleable as the commission's eschatology.   To be sure marriage is promoted to sacramental rank in the theological gazette as one of the small five, but lest that should offer too alarming a hint of definite doctrine the Commission concludes soothingly :

> The fuller consideration of the subject would involve questions which are not only doctrinal, but belong also to the fields of Ethics, of Moral Theology, and of Discipline; and the different aspects of the enquiry cannot be isolated from one another.   We believe that many points might be clarified, to the great benefit of the Church, by a Commission specially appointed for the purpose, and selected so as to

have competence in all the fields of enquiry that would be affected. We would urge that this task may be undertaken at an early date.

This clarification may have been effected in time for the next problem of royal matrimony. At present, *Lambeth locuta est : causa indefinita est.*

But the fog over Lambeth may be lifting.

The Archbishop of Canterbury in his broadcast of Sunday, December 13th 1936, proclaimed that " even more strange and sad " than the abdication was that King Edward VIII " should have sought his happiness in a manner inconsistent with Christian principles of marriage." No Anglican Primate since old Archbishop Warham died had delivered such an unequivocal affirmation of his belief in the indissolubility of matrimony, and that such an unequivocal doctrinal affirmation should have been at long last wrung from an Anglican Primate may be a sign that through those four centuries the Church of England had been waiting like the Sleeping Beauty for a Prince to wake her from the spell with which that bad Erastian fairy had bound her; or, as some might put it, that founded upon one divorce the Church of England has now been triumphantly refounded upon another.

CHAPTER XX

SUMMER 1936

THOSE who have had the patience to read through the pages in which an attempt has been made to present some of the problems which have faced the less remote ancestors of King Edward VIII in regard to their personal behaviour may feel that the ' burden ' of which he was to speak in that last broadcast was an unduly mild word to use for such a formidable weight of responsibility if henceforth it is ever going to be carried through by a true child of the age into which he has been born. Lip-service has been paid to that responsibility with such resonant participles as ' appalling '; but the pleas a politician like Lord Baldwin has made for the charity and imagination of his fellow-men in trying to appreciate the isolation of a Prime Minister's life should remind us in what an infinitely bleaker isolation the Sovereign will henceforth be

called upon to live if he or she is to embody successfully the
spirit of that preamble to the Statute of Westminster which
was drafted with apparently so faint a sense of the gravity of
the task.

That, granted time, royalty might succeed in evolving a
type of humanity capable of sustaining as a matter of course the
new conception of its status in the Western world is possible;
but it is questionable whether such a type could be evolved
without a return to a process of in-breeding more intensive
than during the two previous centuries, and it will not be easy
to persuade a conceivably more enlightened public opinion of
the future to tolerate this.   Meanwhile, and until the evolution of this perfect machine, the British Commonwealth must
be prepared to face the risk of a survival of humanity among
these monarchical symbols, and with that the further risk that
this humanity will occasionally insist on asserting itself.

In a letter from Lord Baldwin to the late Lord Oxford on
his retirement in 1926 the following sentence occurs:

" I don't think that anyone who has not been a Prime
Minister can realise the essential and ultimate loneliness of
that position; there is no veil between him and the human
heart (or no veil through which he cannot see) and in his less
happy moments he may feel himself to be the repository of
the sins and follies of the whole world."

Without pausing to argue with Lord Baldwin about the
clairvoyance of Prime Ministers, for which one might desire
better evidence than is obtainable from the sum total of their
actions during the last twenty years, it may be observed that
the post of Prime Minister is one that is considered the reward
of a political career, acceptance of which implies a man's belief
in his own fitness for it.   That it is an arduous and exacting
job nobody with the slightest imagination will hesitate to
believe.   Nevertheless it must have compensations in excess
of the night's repose granted to Longfellow's Village Blacksmith; the unwillingness Prime Ministers display to relinquish their post is otherwise inexplicable.   In justice to Lord
Baldwin we must admit that he never lost an opportunity to
assure an audience of his longing for rest from his labours,
like " the voices of the wandering wind which moan for rest,
and rest can never find."   The late Mr Ramsay MacDonald
was another political Philomel whose plaint of loneliness and
overwhelming responsibility was constant.   Yet both these
tormented souls must have enjoyed occasional relief from their

purgatory in the pleasure of self-romanticism. Neither ever
grew tired of contemplating the miracle of finding himself
Prime Minister and both kept throughout their tenure of office
the naïve pleasure of a young bride over her reflection in the
mirror, or of a schoolboy who sees upon the notice-board that he
has been given his cricket colours. Rudyard Kipling as a writer
had the same romantic conception of his position, but he was
more skilful than his cousin in hiding it from the public. The
accomplished professional who can retain the spirit of the
amateur is to be envied, and some of the compassion we might
have extended to figures like Lord Baldwin and Mr Ramsay
MacDonald was withheld because we had a feeling that so
much protestation of self-sacrifice disguised a hearty relish for
their job. There was indeed no justification for supposing
anything else unless we had been willing to credit them with the
excessive vanity of believing that they alone were capable of
steering the Ship of State and that therefore come snow, come
hail, come icebergs and fog and hidden shoals, they must obey
the call of duty.

That awed awareness of mundane fame as the Prime
Ministers of a mighty Empire which so much fascinated the
Shropshire lad in the heart of one, the Lossiemouth loon in
the heart of the other, was denied to King Edward by a descent
from Charlemagne. Beside Mr Baldwin, the burly, gifted,
earnest and romantic amateur, his Sovereign appeared like a
hard-bitten little wiry professional, and moreover at that a
professional to whom no other profession was open. He could
not go to the microphone and whisper an appeal for listeners
to trust him. The most he could venture to do was to affirm
that kingship had not changed him. He was still the same
man they used to know as Prince of Wales. That first broadcast of a king whom inheritance had loaded with a burden so
much heavier than the burden of any prime minister was a
matter-of-fact business after the soliloquies of a Baldwin or
the exhortations of a MacDonald, like the entrance of young
Fortinbras at the end of *Hamlet*. It was a simple announcement that the business of the Sovereign would be carried on,
with perhaps a hint, for those who cared to perceive it, that
in certain directions the business would be brought into line
with modern ideas.

"Though I now speak as King, I am still that same man
     better known to most of my listeners as Prince of Wales,"

It would be rash to impute to the King an intention of delivering a formal challenge with those words; he had probably been searching for the happy phrase which without injuring the dignity of his new position would bridge the first awkwardness of it and establish the old affectionate *rapport* between himself and his people. Yet, it was taken as a challenge. Indeed it was taken as something more: it was taken by the great Goliath of Philistine opinion encased in the brassy armour of privilege as the first stone from David's sling.

The first question asked was whether the new King would give up his friendship with Mrs Simpson, and it was soon made clear that the friendship would continue. The word friendship is not used as a euphemism: those who do not accept it in its primary meaning may as well close this book and read no more because no payment of devoted attention will help them to understand what it is all about. The most moving drama of personal relations which has ever been played before so vast an audience collapses into a melodramatic farce unless that friendship be granted what the French call ' whiteness '. To believe anything else is merely to advertise the believer's inexperience of men and women. That King Edward loved the woman who is now his wife before she became his wife we know from his own lips; but the simplest and the bravest tribute man ever paid to woman in such a nightmare of harsh circumstances since the first dim legends of human love was not paid by a liar. The strain of such an avowal upon the poor split creature we call a liar is beyond imagination. The ordeal of that last broadcast could have been faced only by a man conscious of his own integrity. No ordeal devised by the most ingenious mediæval judge could have rivalled the terror of that microphone to a man whose courage was not sustained by that consciousness of integrity when after the world flung that friendship into the gutter to trample on it he picked it up and before the whole world placed it on his heart.

The new reign began. It was noted that Mr and Mrs Simpson had been with the King at St James's to watch from a window the ceremony of proclamation. So the friendship was to continue. That seemed to imply a final acceptance of bachelorhood. It meant also presumably that the influence of Mrs Simpson would be predominant, and the fact having to be faced the French Secret Service concentrated on trying to discover what effect this influence was likely to have on the future of France.

When one nation's secret service starts intensive investigation it always sets off others. The British Secret Service had lately come to grief over Abyssinia and was in need of rehabilitation. They began to investigate. So no doubt did the Secret Services of Germany, Italy and Russia. The buzz grew. The future of King Edward was felt to be so closely interwoven with the future of Europe that there is some excuse for so much subterranean activity. In whatever direction one looked war-clouds were looming. The imagination fastened on Edward as the sun which could dissolve them. His personality was the surest safeguard of the peace of Europe. It was seeming vital to know what he intended to do.

The announcement of a revised Civil List at the end of April excited popular anticipation in Great Britain, and at the same time soothed informed opinion in Paris, because it contained provisions for the contingency of the King's marriage. Gossip set up every eligible princess and at least one religiously-speaking inelegible Infanta as the future Queen of England. Nobody stopped to consider that provision for the possibility of the King's marriage need not be taken as a sign of his definite intention to quit bachelorhood. There was, however, one serious result of this renewed speculation about his marriage, and that was a great deal of gossip about the King's friends, Mr and Mrs Simpson. Fantastic tales began to circulate, some of the most fantastic, it is to be feared, reaching the ears of one or two high ecclesiastical dignitaries, and therein festering. Inevitably the rise in the tide of scandal touched the feet of those who were walking along the edge.

The King decided to erect a breakwater.

Buckingham Palace.
May 27.

The King gave a dinner-party at St James's Palace this evening, to which the following had the honour to be invited: Commander the Lord Louis Mountbatten, R.N. and the Lady Louis Mountbatten, the Right Hon. Stanley Baldwin, M.P. and Mrs Baldwin, Col. the Lord Wigram and Lady Wigram, the Right Hon. A. Duff Cooper, M.P. and the Lady Diana Cooper, Lt.-Col. the Hon. Piers Legh and the Hon. Mrs Legh, Lady Cunard, Admiral of the Fleet Sir Ernle Chatfield and Lady Chatfield, Col. Charles Lindbergh and Mrs Lindbergh, and Mr and Mrs Ernest Simpson.

That informed the little world which was all that was concerned at present that Mr and Mrs Simpson were friends of the King, and by implication his desire that they should be spared further scandal.   Unfortunately the effect was exactly the reverse of what he might have hoped it would be, and presently the larger world considered this announcement in the *Court Circular* authority to comment on the situation. The lead was given by the American weekly *Time* : the rest of the American Press followed that lead.   No attempt was made by the Foreign Office to protect the King against such comment, a display of sinister indolence which caused astonishment in Paris.   The British Press remained silent, for which they were blessed by bishops, lauded by politicians, and fervidly congratulated by their own leader-writers.   Virtue has been carved out of necessity before 1936.   What paper would have ventured to distinguish between gossip and fact during that Spring and Summer ?   The British Press was afraid of publishing libels.   That was the predominant reason of the golden silence.   And it was a valid reason which required no tricking out with the bunting of self-righteousness.

Within a few weeks came a second announcement in the *Court Circular* :

> *Buckingham Palace,*
> *July 9.*
>
> The King gave a dinner-party at York House this evening, at which the Duke and Duchess of York were present.   The following had the honour of being invited.
>
> The Marquess and the Marchioness of Willingdon, the Lady Diana Cooper, the Earl and Countess of Stanhope, the Countess of Oxford and Asquith, Major the Hon. Alexander and Mrs Hardinge, the Right Hon. Winston Spencer-Churchill, the Right Hon. Sir Samuel Hoare, Bt., M.P. and the Lady Maude Hoare, the Right Hon. Sir Philip Sassoon, Bt., M.P., Captain the Right Hon. David Margesson, M.P., Sir Edward and Lady Peacock, Lady Colefax and Mrs Ernest Simpson.

By now it was known that a divorce suit was impending. And this was the moment when the King's Ministers ought to have faced up to the possibility of a royal marriage.

That nobody in a position to mould external circumstance nearer to the desire of the King's heart grasped this basic factor in the situation is a reflection on the imagination of his Ministers.   If Mr Baldwin had read a little more Propertius and a little less Cicero, a little more Stendhal and a great deal less Mary Webb, or even thoroughly mastered the *Hippolytus* of Euripides he might have been better equipped to handle

the problem he was set.   Mr Baldwin was no Melbourne:
he lacked his predecessor's experience of life or of literature.
Like an amiable bumble bee he had gone booming from
flower to flower of the classics, gathering here and there
a little honey for his own speeches but none for the great comb
of humanity.   Brought up against a state of affairs outside
the range of his experience, possibly even of his imagination,
he was baffled.   He was as much bewildered as a mastiff by
an open parasol moving across a lawn in the May breeze and
like the most courageous mastiff in such an emergency of the
untutored mind he fled from the inexplicable phenomenon.
And it was this retreat of Mr Baldwin from the problem in
July which allowed it to attain the vastness and complicacy it
did during that Micawber of a rest-cure his doctors advised, so
that when at last the bailiffs of decision were knocking at the
door of the State and nothing meanwhile had turned up the
Prime Minister was so much overwhelmed by the dimensions
of the muddle that his only consolation for failure to clear it
up would be an ability to assure himself and the country of
his conviction that where he had failed nobody could have
succeeded.

So blind were all the political leaders of the nation to the
contingencies that the myopia of Mr Baldwin must be forgiven.   Yet he had written ten years earlier to Lord Oxford
that there was no veil between him and the human heart through
which he could not see.   It was lucky for Mr Baldwin that
he did not become a professional clairvoyant : so rapid a decay
of his faculties would have threatened his livelihood.   The
kindly English exact less from their prime ministers than
from their palmists.

It should have been clear by the summer that King Edward's
intentions, as they used to say of Victorian suitors, were serious.
The theory that various highly placed officials conspired with
certain elements in the Government to ' frame ' him is attractive to cinematographic minds, but belief in such a conspiracy
involves crediting the principals with a length of foresight
beyond any extension we are entitled by experience to accord it.

The remark about the seriousness of the King's intentions
should not be taken to suggest that he had yet said a word
about the possibility of one day marrying Mrs Simpson.
And in that summer of 1936, for the King, presumably in
response to comments in the American Press, to sever all
social intercourse with a lady whose friendship had been the

most cherished privilege of his life would have seemed an admission to the world that she was his mistress and that frightened of the publicity he was running from it.

The quandary was one that might have made the most courageous and the most chivalrous of men collapse before it. Only supreme courage and perfect chivalry could have guided that King on the course he chose; and when the last red drop of blood has been drained from all the hearts that were beating while his own heart still beat, that courage and that chivalry will give to this time of ours an eternal warmth of life which will mercifully make it independent of its poetry.

Mr Winston Churchill was to say later that " it was not in October, but in August or earlier that the first serious advice should have been tendered to King Edward."

By serious advice Mr Churchill meant ministerial advice, which he himself was not competent to give, having been excluded from the Government as another of those dynamic forces that Mr Baldwin so much dreaded. Mr Baldwin himself was debarred by doctor's orders from confronting the situation. The Keeper of the King's conscience, Lord Hailsham, was also under doctor's orders. So was the Lord President of the Council. But there was Mr Neville Chamberlain: there was Sir Samuel Hoare: there was Sir John Simon: there was Sir Thomas Inskip: there was Mr Anthony Eden, that bright epiphytal orchid with his roots in the decaying bark of Mr Ramsay MacDonald and Mr Baldwin and his own fragrant blossoms in the air. And if none of the Cabinet Ministers was brave enough to give the King advice, there were the Archbishops of Canterbury and York. If at this date the Archbishops had the slightest suspicion that divorce proceedings between Mr and Mrs Simpson were pending and a further suspicion that in the event of Mrs Simpson's becoming free the King intended to marry her, it was surely their business to lay before the Supreme Governor of the Church of England the Report of the Joint Committees of the Convocations on the Church, Marriage, and Divorce. We must believe, if we are not to distrust the sincerity of the Archbishops' faith, that in the summer of 1936 they had no suspicion of the King's intention to marry Mrs Simpson, and we must also believe if we are not to distrust the rigidity of their Graces' moral views, that they accepted the friendship of the King and Mrs Simpson as a friendship to which they could extend primatial approbation. We must further believe that the Archbishop of Canterbury who admitted to that great audience of listeners on December 13th that throughout he had been in Mr Baldwin's confidence had reassured the Prime Minister and advised him to take his rest-cure in peace. That would acquit the Prime Minister of any suspected procrastination.

Reflection upon the inertia of the political and religious leaders of the State during that summer has made it easy to understand why so many people believed at the time and believe even more firmly to-day that already there was a conspiracy to give the new King enough rope to hang himself; but this theory must be discarded. We were told by Prince Edward that Mrs Simpson herself did everything she could to divert him from the course on which he was set. Press and politicians turned their backs on the situation that was developing, and prayed for a miracle to be worked by time. The notion a lot of old women of both sexes share with a few hard-boiled gold-diggers that Mrs Simpson was playing to become Queen of England is so ridiculous to anything except worldly ignorance or *demi-mondaine* knowingness as to be unworthy of argument. Then why did she not withdraw at this stage from an unhappy and untenable situation? The answer is surely a simple one. The King needed her. How much he needed her he was to tell literally the whole world in a single phrase five months hence. It is beyond the skill of the most anxious apologist to add one illuminating word to it—" the help and support of the woman I love."

On a brilliant summer's morning exactly a week after that second dinner-party the King rode with a Captain's Escort of the Blues and the Duke of York, Colonel of the Scots Guards, in attendance as personal A.D.C. to present new colours in Hyde Park to six battalions of the Foot Guards.

Standing at a reading-desk in the Royal pavilion, the newly consecrated colours resting upon the piled-up drums before him, the King said:

" Grenadiers, Coldstreamers, and Scots Guardsmen: It is with mingled feelings that I address you on this solemn occasion. I am glad, so soon after becoming Colonel-in-Chief of your respective regiments, to entrust new Colours to your charge. But, when I know that it was his late Majesty my father's wish in the closing months of his reign to give them to you himself, my heart is full of reverent remembrance of the great example which he set us all, and of gratitude for his constant interest in the Brigade of Guards during the eventful quarter of a century in which he held the position that I do to-day.

" These Colours recall great actions of the past and splendid feats of arms recorded for ever in British history. Almost everything changes as the centuries pass ; but the oldest regiments of the British Army, Guards and Line alike, embody a tradition of discipline and devotion, unbroken by the shocks of 250 years, unequalled in duration and not surpassed in fame by any other military units now surviving in the world. Your Colours not only represent a scroll of the past with all its glories, but to-day and for the future, they are emblems of all that stands for the honour of a soldier and the honour of your regiments as much in years of peace as on the field of war.

" Only a few of us on parade this morning have known the awful weight of war, with all its horrors, and yet its comrade-ships, during the world struggle of 20 years ago. With all my heart I hope, and indeed I pray, that never again will our age and generation be called upon to face such stern and terrible days. Humanity cries out for peace and the assurance of peace, and you will find in peace opportunities of duty and service as noble as any that bygone battlefields can show.

" Keep then, the message of these Colours ever before you, and the honour of your regiment and of your country will rest safe and sure in your hands."

" Every word," *The Times* commented, " indeed every reflection of the King's distinctive voice was carried clearly by microphones to the farthest limits of the great crowd watching the ceremony. Emotion was momentarily apparent as he touched on the great example of King George, and again in his words, ' Humanity cries out for peace and the assurance of peace.' "

Most of us who read that speech felt with a quickening of the pulses that this man meant passionately what he said and that nowhere in the world was there a leader born or made who was so likely to give humanity heart's ease from war. When we read those words we did not know he was planning to exert his personal influence on foreign politics, but if we had known it with what fervour we should have wished him God speed.

On the way back to Buckingham Palace as the King was riding behind the massed bands of the Guards past cheering crowds a man threw a loaded revolver which fell in the road-way beside his horse. The King looked round for a moment, but rode on as if nothing had happened. The incident occurred at almost the same spot on Constitution Hill where Edward Oxford had shot at Queen Victoria nearly a century before.

It was a pity that the loyal House of Commons did not keep some of its breath to cheer his Majesty when he stood in greater need of their cheers. However, loyalty to King Edward was still *à la mode* in July 1936, and honourable members were not worrying about their constituencies. So when at question time Sir John Simon, the Home Secretary, gave Mr Attlee, the leader of the Opposition in the House, a reassuring account of the efficiency of the police in dealing with the assailant the cheers were loud and long. At Bow Street the assailant proved to be a lame journalist called George Andrew McMahon who was suffering from a sense of in-justice and desired to call attention to it. He was one of too many broken by the machinery of modern government. He had been prosecuted and sentenced for a criminal libel on the police, and on appeal the sentence had been quashed only to leave the unfortunate man at the mercy of the petty revenges officialdom can so easily inflict. At Bow Street evidence was given that McMahon, after his arrest on July 16th, declared it had been his intention to make his protest against injustice by shooting himself in front of the King, but that at the last moment his nerve failed him and he had flung the revolver in the roadway.

On September 14th, the same day as the King returned to England after his holiday in the *Nahlin*, McMahon was brought up at the Central Criminal Court before Mr Justice Greaves-Lord. He then told a story of having been in touch since October 1935 with the Embassy of a foreign Power and in particular with a certain baron. Here he alleged he had been offered £150 to shoot the King in the interests of this foreign Power. He had been in touch with M.I.5, "the secret part of the War Office," and had kept them informed of the plot. McMahon was warned by his counsel, Mr St John Hutchinson, K.C., that a representative of M.I.5 had been subpoena'd who would be called to rebut his evidence if not true. However, no witness from M.I.5 appeared in the box, and the jury after a quarter of an hour found McMahon guilty of producing a revolver near the person of the King with intent to alarm his Majesty. The Judge expressed his agreement with the jury in not being misled by the story about the War Office and the foreign Power, and his satisfaction that McMahon had not intended to harm the King. He then sentenced him to twelve months' hard labour.

The Times in a leader of September 15th rebuked counsel for the defence for suggesting that as the authorities were aware of McMahon's eccentricity greater care should have been shown. The same leader moralised for a sentence or two on the existence of " monomaniacs " like McMahon, declared nobody in England would believe on McMahon's evidence that any foreign Power had hostile intentions toward his Majesty, and concluded with what in the light of after events reads like a sardonic warning : " Not even the King can be put beyond the reach of every conceivable danger."

Mr St John Hutchinson's observations may have been responsible for a rumour which ran after the McMahon trial that the whole business was deliberately arranged by the authorities to give them an excuse to insist on the King's paying better attention to his personal safety and discontinuing his habit of walking unattended about the streets with a despatch case under his arm. In discussing this piece of gossip most people passed over the much greater significance of the evidence that was led at the trial ; but one or two asked. why an alleged cock-and-bull story which cast suspicion on either the Italian or the German Embassy was allowed to be given in court if evidence was available to provide a sworn contradiction to McMahon's statements. Counsel for the defence warned his client that a representative of M.I.5 (Military Intelligence fifth section, not M.15 as it is printed in *The Times* report), was in court to contradict him if his story was not true. Then why was that representative not produced ? The court could have sat *in camera* if the representative's disguise had to be preserved. Every protection is accorded by the Law to men risking their lives, not to mention their reputations, in the deadly work of counter-espionage. How did the prosecution divine from the expressions on the faces of the jury that they would refuse to be misled by such a story ? How did even the learned Judge know that ?

That there is still a firm belief in America and on the Continent in a theory of a combination of powerful interests political, ecclesiastical, social and journalistic to drive King Edward from the Throne is not to be wondered at when we

o

are brought up against facts like the McMahon trial and what appears the sinister evasiveness of the authorities in regard to it.   No amount of propaganda against the Duke of Windsor will wash out this belief.   It is as useless as all the perfumes of Arabia.   The rest of the world stands aside and like the Doctor in *Macbeth* murmurs ' Foul whisperings abroad '. It will be so much wiser to drop it, for that very propaganda is being adduced in America as evidence of a guilty conscience. When in June 1937 Lady Astor, arriving in New York, declared ' Edward's position is tragic ' she was asked ' For Edward or for England ? ' *; but like a sibyl she retreated from exposition.   Yes, in view of the fact that presently the flesh of the Labour Party and the Communist Party was to be made to creep with cock-and-bull stories sedulously circulated about Mrs Simpson's Nazi sympathies, it was a most unfortunate coincidence that this tale of McMahon's was allowed so much publicity on the very day the King arrived back from the cruise of the *Nahlin*.

The effect that cruise had on the development of the situation is of outstanding importance.   Before it is examined the King's speech at the unveiling of the great Canadian War Memorial on the Vimy Ridge to the men with unknown graves may be read with profit :

" In the capital city of Canada, at the heart of the Dominion, there is a memorial chamber set apart as a perpetual reminder of the service and losses of Canada in the Great War.

" Nine years ago I had the privilege of dedicating the altar within it, where will lie for ever a book of remembrance, recording the names of more than 60,000 Canadians who gave their lives for the cause which Canada made her own.   Above the door of the Chamber is engraved : ' All's well, for over there among his peers a happy warrior sleeps.'

" These words reveal the inner meaning of what we do to-day.   They tell us that, beautiful and impressive as is the memorial at Ottawa, the Canadian people could not feel that it was complete.   It was ' Over there ' that the Canadian armies fought and died.   It is ' Over there ' that their final monument must stand.

" To-day, thousands of miles from the shores of Canada, we are assembled around the monument.   Yet we are not on alien soil !   One of our English poets wrote that where he lay would be ' For ever England '—that England for which he

* *Cards the Windsors Hold.*   Leeds.

died.   He spoke a parable; but here to-day that parable is
living truth.   The realisation of it will, I know, bring comfort
to many thousand Canadian men and women.   For this
glorious monument crowning the hill of Vimy is now, and for
all time, a part of Canada.   Though the mortal remains of
Canada's sons lie far from home, yet here where we now stand
in ancient Artois their immortal memory is hallowed, upon the
soil that is as surely Canada's as any acre within her nine
provinces.

" By a gesture which all can understand, the soldiers
especially, the laws of France have decreed that here Canada
shall stand for ever.   We raise this memorial to Canadian
warriors.   It is the inspired impression in stone, chiselled
by a skilful Canadian hand, of Canada's salute to her fallen
sons.   It marks the scene of feats of arms which history will
long remember and Canada can never forget.   And the
ground it covers is the gift of France to Canada.

" All the world over there are battlefields the names of which
are written indelibly on the pages of our troubled human
story.   It is one of the consolations which time brings that
deeds of valour done on those battlefields long survive the
quarrels which drove the opposing hosts to conflict.

" Vimy will be one such name.   Already the scars of war
have well nigh vanished from the fair landscape spread before
us.   Around us here to-day there is peace and the rebuilding
of hope.   And so also in dedicating this memorial to our fallen
comrades our thoughts turn rather to the splendour of their
sacrifice and to the consecration of our love for them, than to
the cannonade which beat upon its ridge a score of years ago.

" In that spirit, in the spirit of thankfulness for their
example, of reverence for their devotion, and of pride in their
comradeship I unveil this memorial to Canada's dead."

Once again the King's appeal for peace had a clearer note
than the rest.   His Ministers talked assiduously about their
longing for peace, but it was somehow ineffective.   With
them peace always seemed a serviceable topic, and they talked
about it dutifully as a chatty barber breaks the ice with a
platitude about the weather.   If war had come, one felt,
they would have regarded it as a thunderstorm against which
they had provided as many umbrellas as possible but for the
bursting of which they must be held blameless.

To hear the King speaking about peace was almost to restore
one's belief that peace really was going to be achieved.   The

very timbre of his voice had a tonic quality.   It was like a
light dry wine.   The writer was told that when in Canada
after the abdication a film was shown of this solemn occasion
it was too much for the emotion of the audiences and had to be
withdrawn.   He relates that tale in the hope it is true because
he will presently have a less agreeable tale to relate of Canada.

It was reported that M. Lebrun, the President of the
French Republic, took advantage of meeting the King at this
ceremony of the unveiling to express a hope that he would
give up the plan to spend his holiday on the Riviera.   The
outbreak of the civil war in Spain had alarmed the French
Government with fears of communist or fascist disorder at
home, and the responsibility of having the King as a guest on
French soil at this moment was too great.   Whether that talk
with M. Lebrun played a decisive part in the resolve the King
took soon after it to visit the countries of Eastern Europe is not
known.   What is certain is that he made up his mind to see
for himself what was happening in Europe.

At this point the dapper figure of Mr Anthony Eden crosses
upstage.

Immediately after the funeral of King George V, M.
Litvinov had been received in private audience by King
Edward VIII.   This favour was presumably accorded with the
idea of helping Mr Eden, who set such store on a *rapprochement*
with Russia.   The late King had never received in private
audience a representative of the Soviets.   In May 1936 the
ex-Emperor Haile Selassie reached England, and it was
announced by the B.B.C. that he would be received by the
King.   This was repeated in several newspapers next day.
That Mr Eden hoped King Edward would receive the fugitive
Emperor is the presumable explanation of that B.B.C. announcement.   Fortunately King Edward did not receive him.   It
might have led to war if he had.   Whatever the rights and
wrongs of the miserable Abyssinian business it is certain that
the British Government was as much responsible for it as the
Italian Government.   When the archives of the Foreign
Office during 1935 and 1936 are published posterity may be as
much astounded as we have lately been by the publication of
British Documents on the Origins of the War to read that in 1898
a secret treaty between Great Britain and Germany for the
partition of the Portuguese colonies in Africa was signed at
Mr Alfred Rothschild's house in London.*

* " In 1911 Grey wrote to Sir Edward Goschen : ' It is clear . . . that the

What looked like an attempt to force King Edward's hand by a semi-official announcement into receiving the ex-Emperor was regarded in some circles as an attempt by Mr Eden to save his political face. Whatever the reason there is no doubt that during the first six months of his reign many people believed that King Edward was growing increasingly alarmed alike at the trend and the administration of his Government's foreign policy.

The Italians were convinced that if Mr Eden's heart were opened 'Italy' would not be found graved inside of it as in the case of a similar operation on the poet Browning. He and the Duce appeared to disagree fundamentally about the future of Europe. On the other hand, Mr Eden had been warmly welcomed in Moscow and thence onward he and Stalin had appeared to agree if not fundamentally, for Mr Eden was not converted to communism, at any rate superficially about the future of Europe. How much Mr Eden's consistent anti-Italian policy was based on a reasoned conviction that British and Italian interests were too incompatible for friendship does not really matter. This policy nearly brought about war between the two countries. Many people believed two years ago and believe even more fervently to-day that war would be all to the advantage of this country. The Left would welcome it because for the Left foreign policy has become an expression of domestic opinion. For the Left it is not a question of the sea-way to India or the protection of British oil and cotton interests or the fear of Italian penetration of Brazil by cutting across to West Africa and using the Canaries as a mercantile base. For the Left it is a passionate desire to abase the figure of a Fascist tyrant. Now it is unusual for the Left to find itself spiritually approved by the great solid mass of the Centre; but the apparent political sympathies of the Pope and the Duce have given the Centre the same kind of uncomfortable feeling the Elizabethan Centre had about Philip of Spain. Signor Mussolini has no beard to singe, and for that matter very

---

Germans would like the division of the Portuguese colonies to take place as soon as possible. So should I. . . . And Portugal won't part with her colonies. . . .'

"In a minute to another document found in the 1912 file, Sir Eyre Crowe wrote of 'the deplorable impression which the transaction of 1898 will make not only in Portugal but all over the world, from the point of view of what Great Britain was capable of contemplating doing to her own ally. I think there is now general agreement that that transaction was not creditable to a country like England.'"

few hairs on top of his head, but what hairs remained Left and Centre are longing to singe.

At the moment Mr Eden is democracy's pet doll,* and if he can persuade Sir Archibald Sinclair to keep his popular front neat and clean there is a hope that with the help of the Labour Party we shall soon be fighting another war to keep the world safe for democracy.

That thanks to the foreign policy of Mr Eden and Mr Baldwin's fond surrender to it such a war might end in the obliteration of European democracy for a century was an alternative which preoccupied King Edward's attitude sufficiently to make him go and see what *was* happening in Eastern Europe. It was rumoured that ever since he ascended the Throne he had been showing an earnest desire to learn what likelihood there was of the Foreign Office's making a mess of matters.

When the French authorities heard of the cruise of the *Nahlin* there was no hostile criticism. They knew that Mr Eden's personality had failed to charm the capitals of Eastern Europe; they knew that England was arming against Italy; they were frightened lest a war against Italy without an Eastern Mediterranean friendly to Great Britain might give Italy an initial advantage which would tempt Germany to strike; the Spanish Civil War was opening up a new source of trouble. All that anxiety about the King's foreign sympathies was forgotten. Peace was what the French wanted, and King Edward VIII looked a better dove to back than Mr Eden. How far the obstinacy of Mr Eden may have undone the good that King Edward accomplished by those visits to Eastern capitals in the summer of 1936 the swift changes in the European situation make it absurd to speculate. It is more useful to note the good that was done. In the first place the very fact that the King was going to tour the Mediterranean in a yacht allayed public anxiety in that month of August which, until a greater war blots the fame of some other month, will always be associated in the imagination of Europe with war.

Mr Eden like an anxious jackdaw had been flying backwards and forwards for so long between London and Geneva that nobody could settle down. When it was known that the King's yacht had sailed with sealed orders and that the King's

---

* Since that was written the voice that breathed o'er Mr Eden seems to have changed its timbre, and his latest speech (June 11th 1938) suggests an inclination to return to the sepulchre-strewn desert of Tory Democracy.

Minister for War was accompanying him to whatever nepenthe
of rest he had chosen there was a sigh of relief from humbler
folk who were thinking about their own holiday nepenthes in
or out of Great Britain.   The *Nahlin* could not cast anchor off
Geneva at any rate.

That the danger of war's breaking out in August has not
been exaggerated is clear from the fact that Parliament on the
last day of July was not prorogued but merely adjourned and
liable to be summoned with five days' notice.   The more
deeply one reflects the greater appears the service King Edward
rendered to peace by that cruise of the *Nahlin*.   If the King
had sailed attended only by his Minister for War and his
Private Secretary, Sir Godfrey Thomas, it would have been
too obvious a diplomatic move.   By camouflaging it as
apparently nothing more than a well-deserved holiday he was
able to learn what he wanted to learn and by his personal
interest rouse the Eastern Mediterranean States to an enthusiasm which only somebody who had served out there
through many moments of crisis could appreciate.

The 1936 crisis in the Mediterranean was the result of
mishandling crisis after crisis from 1914 onwards, and in every
one of them the influence of Italy was underestimated by the
British Government, which seemed unable to grasp that if
Great Britain intended after the war to maintain her command of the Mediterranean of which the symbols were
Gibraltar and Malta she could do so only in three ways.   The
first would have been to guarantee France wholehearted and
practical support on the Rhine on condition that France placed
the whole of her naval strength in the Mediterranean.   This
was not done.   Consequently France for a long time paid more
attention to Brest than to Marseilles and during the years
after Versailles built an alarming flotilla of submarines the
impulse to build which could only have been dictated by her
fear of a perfidious *rapprochement* between Albion and Alle-
magne.   The second way would have been for Great Britain
to act in the closest co-operation with Italy.   This would have
involved leaving the French to stew in their own juice, turning
down Venizelos, encouraging Italy to take Corfu, and supporting Italy in breaking her word to Greece over the return of
Rhodes which had been occupied as an offensive measure during
the Turko–Italian war with assurances to Greece that the islands
of the Dodecanese were to be handed over as soon as peace with
Turkey was settled.   Further it would have involved support-

ing Italy's claim to Tunis where practically the whole of the European settlers were Italian, and, perhaps, denouncing the Anglo–French–Italian tripartite agreement of 1906 and declaring Abyssinia to be a joint Italo–British Protectorate. The third way was to support Venizelos in establishing Greek predominance in the Eastern Mediterranean, with all Britain's naval resources behind him and a close alliance. Efforts were made in 1916 by the British Legation at Athens to extract a policy from the Foreign Office, but the reply was that H.M.'s Government had no policy in the Eastern Mediterranean except to temper the sometimes inconvenient ardour of the French. When Mr Lloyd George came into power he was much more alive to the importance of adjusting the situation in the Eastern Mediterranean to British interests in the future. Unfortunately in April 1917 at the Conference of St Jean de Maurienne which took place in a train just outside an Alpine tunnel he made a verbal promise to the Italian representatives that they should have Smyrna and the hinterland after the war. However, that part of military opinion led by Sir Henry Wilson, which was becoming more influential all the time, declared that the best policy for Great Britain in the Mediterranean was to clear out of it altogether and restore the old trade route to India by the Cape and make arrangements with Portugal for the freedom of the Azores and Madeira. In the end, the Greeks were allowed to occupy Smyrna and given *carte blanche* to deal with Mustapha Kemal's marvellous reorganisation of the Turkish Army. The result was tragedy, and after the tragedy a complete confusion of the aims, the interests and the obligations of the various Powers set free by Germany and Austria's collapse and the Russian Revolution to make the Mediterranean the storm-centre it has been for three thousand years of history. Thence onward year by futile year the problem of the Mediterranean dragged on until exacerbated by the development of the Spanish and Abyssinian situations. To deal with this exacerbation Great Britain opposed a policy as soft as a jelly-fish stranded by the tide to which remained one tiny but irritating little sting in the personality of Mr Anthony Eden. Small wonder that King Edward VIII decided it was high time he found out for himself what kind of a disastrous state of affairs this exacerbation was likely to produce in the near future.

The first ruler he visited was the Prince Regent of Yugoslavia. Prince Paul had attended the funeral of King George in January and on the way home had taken the opportunity to discuss with various prominent statesmen of different countries in Paris the threatening future. Yugoslavia had applied sanctions to Italy at considerably greater cost to itself than the sanctions applied by enthusiastic leaguers like Norway. It was in consequence of this lost trade that Yugoslavia tried to make up for it by entering into a beneficial commercial arrangement with Germany, the result of which was that Yugoslavia failed to support Czechoslovakia in protesting against the German re-occupation of the Rhineland. Moreover, after giving a three-million pound order to Germany mostly for railway material, Yugoslavia restricted imports from Great Britain. Dr Schacht was at Belgrade in June when further discussions took place on commercial lines. This drawing together of Yugoslavia and Germany was likely in the event of war between Great Britain and Italy to make a benevolently neutral Yugoslavia out of the question and might possibly make Yugoslavia an open enemy of Great Britain in the event of Germany's practical support of Italy. It was at this critical moment that King Edward appeared on the scene to effect with his personality what Mr Eden had apparently proved incapable of effecting with his. Yet all that the British Press could do while watching a move of the profoundest importance to the peace of Europe was to sit growling over photographs of Mrs Simpson like dogs unable to chew up a bone themselves but determined that no other dog should chew it up.

After Yugoslavia came Greece where the situation was even more delicate. Years of political squabbling had made the only possible appeasement the return of King George II, and his return was supported by Great Britain because in the autumn of 1935 it was seeming essential for the British fleet to use the harbours of the Greek islands, Malta being considered too vulnerable to Italian aeroplanes. It was no doubt due to British prompting that King George was so firm in insisting upon an amnesty for the leaders of the late revolt. Opposition in Greece to that amnesty was overcome by death. In January Kondylis died and a new Government was formed under Demerdjis. In March Venizelos died in Paris and his body was taken direct to Crete. Even now the proposed lying-in-state in Athens might have let slip the dogs of civil war. In April Demerdjis died and a month later Tsaldaris, head of the Popular Party, died as suddenly as the three previous statesmen. This left General Metaxas at the head of the Government, and on August 4th Metaxas anticipated what he announced was to be a communist outbreak by obtaining King George's signature for a decree of martial law and the dissolution of the Chamber, thus making himself virtual dictator of Greece. Metaxas, who had been Assistant-Chief of the General Staff when war broke out, was a devoted pro-German and it was his brain that had been primarily responsible for all the troubles which befell King Constantine. His accession to power fore-shadowed a Greece no longer benevolently neutral in the event of a war between Great Britain and Italy. The ubiquitous Dr Schacht had carried through another big scheme of com-mercial barter between Greece and Germany, and no doubt this would presently be developed by restrictions on British imports similar to those already introduced by Yugoslavia. The effect of King Edward's visit to Athens was most helpful, and his inspection of the Greek fleet at Salamis impressive. At the back of this visit was an atmosphere of belief that war between England and Italy was ridiculous, and this was accepted as King Edward's convinced opinion. It was probably the feeling in Eastern Europe that Mr Eden wanted war with Italy and that King Edward did not which gave rise to tales of disagreement between him and the Foreign Office. These tales were lent colour by the failure to protect King Edward against the Press carnival in America. Such stories about the indignation of the Foreign Office should be disregarded. King Edward himself during the Dennis libel case was to make it clear that he did not go over the heads of his Ministers, one of whom was with him on this cruise.

In April of this year Turkey had sent a request to the League of Nations for a revision of the Straits Convention and the right to fortify the Dardanelles. The four Powers which were pledged to defend the Straits in accord with the decisions of the League Council were Great Britain, France, Italy and Japan. Japan was now out of the League altogether and although Italy remained in it she was as unruly as an Irish Member of the 'eighties. The League of Nations was so much gratified by this good-boy attitude of Turkey that sovereignty over the Straits and the right to remilitarise the zone was given back. So when King Edward arrived to visit the battlefields and graveyards of Gallipoli he found Turkish troops again in full occupation. After he had visited Anzac he telegraphed to the Governor-General of

Australia : " I send my best wishes to surviving members of
that corps, with the assurance that the last resting-places of
their fallen comrades are well and reverently cared for."

And as the *Nahlin* proceeded up the Straits King Edward
dropped a wreath in those waters where twenty-one years
before the cries from the sailors of the stricken *Goliath* were
borne to their comrades on Helles as they were swept past into
eternity. Over the port bow Achi Baba rising in this
September weather like a great tumulus of human bones and
dust : astern to starboard the lush water-meadows of Troy
wearing an almost English green : and on the starboard bow the
knoll whereon Xerxes sat enthroned almost two thousand five
hundred years before and wept because of all that mighty host
which crossed the bridge from Abydos not one would be alive
a hundred years hence. Then King Edward in those fateful
waters dropped not a golden goblet and a Persian short-sword
but a wreath. And perhaps as the *Nahlin* passed Aegospotam,
where Athens suffered that last fatal defeat which would cause
her walls to be razed to the sound of the Lacedaemonian flute-
players, King Edward may have thought not of Athens nor of
Troy but of all those thousands of Englishmen, Scotsmen,
Irishmen, Welshmen, Australians, New Zealanders, Indians,
Gurkhas, Jews, Frenchmen, Turks and Germans who had laid
down their lives here, and in that thought he may have renewed
within his breast the determination that no such charnel-house
should be created again if any effort of his own could prevent it.
Mr Bolitho, who was not at Anzac, thinks that " had there
been a violent national distress to inspire him, the King might
have acted differently . . . would not have spent so many
weeks of his brief reign on holiday . . . not to gather
experience which might have helped him to estimate the voices
which were prophesying war at the time, but to amuse himself
in the way his will and fancy guided him."

In Constantinople, King Edward met Mustapha Ataturk
and was given a great welcome. At this time there was an
acrimonious dispute going on between France and Turkey
over the granting of a constitution to Syria by France. It
might be absurd to suggest that this meeting between King
Edward and Ataturk played any important part in clearing up
a difficult situation, but it is not absurd to credit King Edward
with that three-million-pound contract for an iron and steel
plant which was signed with a British firm on December 2nd,
particularly when we find that the contract was secured almost

immediately after a visit to Turkey by Dr Schacht. It was a sign that Turkey did not intend to be fettered any longer by subordinating her markets to the economic influence of Germany. King Edward took such a liking to Ataturk that he invited him to visit him.in London. Constantinople was not the end of King Edward's attempt to discover for himself what was happening in Eastern Europe. On his way to Vienna in Ataturk's *train de luxe*, which he put at the King's disposal, King Edward stopped to visit Sofia and spent a few hours with King Boris, where no doubt he made himself finally conversant with the prospects and policy of the Balkan Pact. In Vienna the King visited President Miklas and Chancellor von Schuschnigg, and, after visiting Baron Eugene Rothschild, flew home to land at Heathrow aerodrome.

He had done the State some service. He had restored confidence in Great Britain after the fiasco of sanctions. He had flown around the Mediterranean like a halcyon, leaving in his trail high summer and a sort of peace. "The pity of it all," says Mr Bolitho, " was that photographs showed a happy king."

He was in fact the true professional who could turn work into play and play into work.

CHAPTER TWENTY-ONE

AUTUMN

The King was in Scotland by September 18th, and on September 23rd Mrs Simpson arrived at Balmoral with her friends Mr and Mrs Herman L. Rogers. A tale used with vicious effect against King Edward was that he had broken his engagement to open the new Royal Infirmary in Aberdeen, deputing the Duke and Duchess of York to perform the opening ceremony because he wished to meet Mrs Simpson at the station. It may be true that he drove into Aberdeen to meet Mrs Simpson and Mr and Mrs Rogers that day, but it is not true that he had promised to open the new infirmary. After this *canard* had been flying round the world for ten months, Lord Provost Watt made the following statement on July 23rd 1937:

" Months before the opening date I was in communication with the King through the Scottish Office and the reply I received was to the effect that owing to Court mourning the King had decided that he would not perform any such ceremony as the opening of the Royal Infirmary. He had already refused many invitations and he could not make any exception in the case of Aberdeen. At the same time he was so much interested in the Infirmary that he had deputed the Duke of York to act for him and carry out the ceremony. The point is that I had not to ask the Duke and Duchess of York. They were deputed by the King, and I was instructed to get in touch with the Duke's Comptroller in regard to the arrangements."

Besides many newspapers several books about the Abdication repeated the rumour in various forms. When the Duke of Windsor brought his libel action against Mr Geoffrey Dennis and Messrs. Heinemann it was stated in court:

"There follows a reference to the day in Aberdeen, with regard to which the author gives some particulars of the alleged misdeed. ' That Deeside engagement,' says the book, ' was of long standing, and the silver city had decked herself not frugally to greet him. At the last moment he deputed the Duke and Duchess to open the Infirmary and carry out all his programme.' The book then asserts that having at the last moment thrown over his engagement he drove to the station to meet the lady who is now his wife.

" What are the facts, for the matter is put beyond controversy by documents ? The opening of the Aberdeen Infirmary took place on September 23rd 1936. The authorities in Aberdeen had been informed in the previous June that, following precedent, the King had decided shortly after his accession that, during the whole period of Court mourning, he himself would not undertake any opening ceremonies. They were informed that as on these grounds other requests of this nature had been refused his Majesty could not make an exception in the case of the Aberdeen Royal Infirmary, but they were informed that the King had deputed the Duke of York to perform the opening ceremony as his Majesty's representative.

" The suggestion, therefore, that he threw over the authorities of Aberdeen at the last moment for a purely personal reason or that he failed to keep his word to them in any way whatsoever is demonstrably false."

There is no doubt that the circulation of this rumour did great harm to the King's name in Scotland. Lord Provost Watt told the *Scottish Daily Express* on July 24th 1937 that he had only just heard of the rumour from a friend in Edinburgh and now made haste to contradict it. Although we can congratulate the Lord Provost on his deafness to gossip, it would have been useful for the King if he had been less deaf, for in that case we should not have had to wait ten months for contradiction and Aberdonians, who dislike waste, would have been spared the waste of their own breath. Even more ridiculous than this Aberdeen tale were the tales circulated about the Balmoral visit, but such drivel is not worth the amount of printers' ink it would take to contradict it in detail; there is a limit to the consideration a sane man can extend to a horde of credulous nincompoops. To such minds the Loch Ness monster offers a more suitable pastime than the reputation of a King. Yet one " disgraceful " act of King Edward's must be recorded, which is that, after stalking one of the Balmoral stags, instead of shooting it he photographed it ! On the other hand when the King attended service in Crathie Church, the congregation were so fidgety during the sermon in their efforts to stalk the King that he had to take advantage of the shelter offered by a pillar. On the following Sunday, instead of driving in an open carriage to Crathie Church, he drove there in a closed car with the Duke and Duchess of York and the two little Princesses. Readers may care to sample the quality of the sermons that were being preached round about this date, and were afterwards published in a book that was presumably intended as current reading for King Edward's coronation.

The Very Rev. C. A. Alington, D.D., preached on August 21st, 1936:

" It is not loyal flattery, but the plainest truth to say that in the Sovereign who now fills his [King George's] place we see one likely to preserve and enrich this most noble tradition. The people of England know that in the heart of their King the distress of those who suffer takes the foremost place: whether the sufferings are due directly to the war or to its tragic consequences in unemployment, the sufferers know that their sad lot is ever present in his mind.

" It is hard for us not to think of him as Prince of Wales, and as we realise how much lustre he has brought to that ancient title, and how much love he has won for it, we find it easy to believe that he will bring new glory to that greater title which is his to-day. He will carry in his heart, we know, the motto of his former rank 'I serve ', and it may not be mere fancy to suggest that it has given him inspiration in the past. . . .

" Our hearts go out to-day to him who, in a sense, ascends for the first time ' the awful throne he has inherited ' : we know that it means for him the sacrifice of much which he holds dear : his freedom to live his own life, and that occasional freedom from all responsibility which, for most of us, gives its true relish to a holiday ; we know, or we could know if we would use our imagination, something of that loneliness which is inseparable from the greatest of all earthly positions : ' What infinite heart's ease must kings neglect, that private men enjoy ! ' And knowing these things, and knowing our King more intimately than any British sovereign has been known in history, our prayers for his life and happiness have, as we trust he knows, a personal note that is often lacking on occasions such as this. . . .

" When we cry ' God Save the King ! ' it is in very truth because we believe that he can do more to ' save ' the people than any living man, and that to do so is the desire which is nearest to his heart."

The Rev. R. J. Campbell, D.D., Chancellor of Chichester Cathedral, preached :

" . . . The man on whom the eyes of the world are turned at this hour is himself a democrat by taste and sympathy and constitutional position. He is an example in this respect to all the potentates of the earth—manly and self-respecting, dignified without haughtiness, simple and unpretentious in demeanour, never holding himself aloof from the common life, regarding himself not as the master, but as the tireless servant of the people—no wonder he is beloved for his personal qualities no less than he is revered as the occupant of the throne. . . ."

The Rev. Alfred Thomas, M.A., F.R.S.L., of St Barnabas, Newcastle-on-Tyne, preached :

" A socialist Member of Parliament, a former Lord Privy Seal in the Labour Ministry, has declared, evidently impressed by the simplicity of his life, that if King Edward VIII had to be elected by democratic ballot, he would win by a thousand to one against any possible candidate. . . .

" Compelled henceforward somewhat to sacrifice his personal freedom, it is certain that his subjects will regard with sympathy and appreciation whatever measures he takes to preserve his personality as a man, to prevent himself from becoming merely a royal machine or a Sovereign remote from his people, a prisoner in splendid isolation."

We may suppose these sympathetic clergymen were unaware of the gossip that was going round. There is no need to suspect expediency. In reading through the mass of material published about King Edward, one begins to fancy that a knowledge of the King's friends was far more widely diffused than it was. The present writer was in Edinburgh at the time of the Balmoral visit and not a single person he met in the Scottish capital had heard of Mrs Simpson by then.

This general ignorance is a testimony to that discretion of the British Press which was the better part of valour.

At this stage it may be remarked that the tone of the stories in the American Press has been misrepresented. They were often flippant and often silly, but a careful search among them reveals little scurrility. It is important to realise this fact because one of the chief complaints against King Edward was the appalling effect of these American papers on the Dominions. To the charge that his behaviour by inspiring such comment had lowered the prestige of the monarchy, extracts quoted earlier in this book from eighteenth- and nineteenth-century papers published and printed in Great Britain provide sufficient answer. We may as well be honest and admit that those without goodwill towards King Edward deliberately used the American Press as ammunition. A great deal of the comment in it was dignified and sensible.

On September 30th the *Court Circular* announced:

> *Balmoral Castle.* The King left the Castle this evening for London. The Duke and Duchess of Kent, Commander the Lord Louis Mountbatten, R.N., and the Lady Louis Mountbatten, Lieut.-Commander and Mrs Colin Buist, Mrs Ernest Simpson and Mr and Mrs Herman L. Rogers have also left.

Even out of this harmless departure some people managed to extract a grievance because instead of taking a special train the King was content with a special coach hitched on to the Aberdeen night express at Ballater.

On October 1st and 2nd the Conservative Party held its 63rd Annual Conference at Margate. In spite of the bracing air of Kent, Mr Baldwin's medical advisers considered his attendance imprudent. So we hear nothing of Mr Baldwin until a few days later in October when his medical advisers found it possible for him to attend the annual dinner of the 1922 Committee of the Conservative Party in a dining-room of the House of Commons, with Sir Hugh O'Neill, ex-Speaker of the Northern Ireland Parliament, in the chair.   There were 140 members present, practically all of them back-benchers, and it was expected that Mr Baldwin would take the opportunity of uttering a stern rebuke to a hint of mutiny from the lower deck of the party, so much grumbling about his captaincy had there been of late.   But the Captain was in another mood, a mood indeed with which we are well familiar, the mood of the old longshoreman spinning yarns about the past.   He told the lower deck about the terrible storms he had weathered in the Ship of State, about his gradual rise from midshipman to captain, and at the end most significantly proclaimed that his " MISTAKES HAD ALWAYS PRECEDED HIS MOST GLORIOUS TRIUMPHS."   Mr Baldwin concluded in a burst of eloquence : " We will stand shoulder to shoulder against Labour intellectuals, against dictatorships and totalitarian perils."   What dictatorships and totalitarian perils at this date was he hinting at for Great Britain ? *

The Annual Conference of the Conservative Party at Margate was followed by the Annual Conference of the Labour Party in Edinburgh on October 5th and 6th.   Some curiously fatuous speeches were made about rearmament.   Mr Herbert Morrison, for instance, advocated support for the Government's armament policy but opposition to its foreign policy. Sir Stafford Cripps was in favour of rearmament but only by the Labour Party.   Mr Bevin was in favour of trusting the Government not to abuse its power.   But the most perfect expression of fatuity was reserved to himself by the Leader of the Opposition.   Mr Attlee, in summing up the debate before the motion that the ' Labour Party should support the Government's rearmament policy ' was put to the Conference, stated that even " if the motion were carried there could still be no question of the Labour Party supporting the Government's rearmament policy " (*A. R.*).   After that it seemed hardly worth while going to the trouble of counting the cards, which showed 1,738,000 votes to 657,000 in favour of supporting rearmament. After this the Conference, by a larger majority, rejected the application of the Communist Party for affiliation with themselves and followed this up by rejecting even more

* This speech was reported in the *News Review* (Oct. 15th).

decisively the foundation of a United Front of all working-class parties.

On October 19th Mr Attlee wrote a letter to the Prime Minister calling upon him to summon Parliament four or five days earlier in order to discuss breaches of the Spanish non-intervention agreement. But the mind of Mr Baldwin at this date was preoccupied with a more delicate question of non-intervention and he could only promise Mr Attlee a debate on Spain for October 29th, when Parliament re-assembled. He might have added, but he forbore, that the foggy speeches of the Labour leaders at their Conference had made the prospect of their being able to clarify the international situation doubtful.

Mr Baldwin's claim at the dinner of the 1922 Committee that his mistakes had always preceded his most glorious triumphs need not be attributed to his sense of having made a profound mistake in not discussing the personal future of the King three months earlier, nor to any hope that in consequence he would quit public life in a blaze of glory by giving the most brilliant exhibition ever witnessed of locking the stable-door after the horse was stolen. It is easy to believe that the state of his health destroyed any confidence he might have had of being able to handle the situation earlier. That rest during August and September had been complete, and it may have been when it seemed advisable to attend that dinner of the 1922 Committee that, in his own words, he felt he could not in fairness to his work take a further holiday. To continue in his own words, he came, as it were, on half-time before the middle of October and, for the first time, since the beginning of August, was in a position to look into things. It is not quite clear from the historic speech Mr Baldwin made to the House of Commons on December 10th, whether, "owing to the kindness of his staff and the consideration of all his colleagues," he spent August and September in a condition of suspended animation that can only be described as cataleptic, and only when he stepped into his office on half-time found with astonishment that he had to wade through a sea of correspondence " from British subjects and American citizens of British origin in the United States of America, from some of the Dominions and from this country, all expressing perturbation and uneasiness at what was then appearing in the American Press." We should probably conclude that ' the kindness of his staff ' had influenced them to say nothing

of this ' vast volume of correspondence ' and that when Mr
Baldwin first opened the door of Downing Street he had to
force his way like a Nansen into his official residence through
a blizzard of letters.   Another theory suggests that he slept
like a babe in the wood during August and September and
woke to find himself covered with letters thoughtfully deposited
upon him by busy birdlike secretaries.   Yet against any
theory which involves taking for granted a cataleptic trance
is Mr Baldwin's admission in that speech of December 10th,
" I was aware also that there was, in the near future, a divorce
case coming on, the results of which made me realise that
possibly a difficult situation might arise later."   Such an
admission seems to imply that Mr Baldwin was not playing
Rip van Winkle during August and September but was sharply
aware of what was going on and only debarred from taking
action by his feeble physical condition.

The Prime Minister on being informed that the divorce
petition was due to be heard on October 27th made up
a mind recuperated by two months' absolute rest that he
must have a talk with the King.   By a happy accident
which the Archbishop of Canterbury could cite as an
example of the Divine guidance during those days of
moral stress, Mr Baldwin found himself staying in the
neighbourhood of Fort Belvedere in the middle of October,
and we can imagine him, perhaps a little restless in a strange
bed, listening to the Windsor chimes through that ' night
in the lonesome October of his most immemorial year,' tossing
and turning until he reached the conclusion " that it was
essential that someone should see his Majesty and warn him
of the difficult situation that might arise later if occasion was
given for a continuation of this kind of gossip and of criticism,
and the danger that might come if that gossip and that
criticism spread from the other side of the Atlantic to this
country."

During that vigil Mr Baldwin may have comforted himself
with the reflection that neither *The Times* nor any of Lord
Camrose's papers would hint at criticism of the King until
he was able to assure them that he had done all he could;
but there were other elements in the British Press of whose
loyal support he could feel less sure.   There were papers
which in the past had shown the basest ingratitude for the
services he had rendered the country since he helped to drive
Mr Lloyd George out of power in 1922, and he may have

wondered whether such papers might not abuse his delicate situation to his own detriment. It was late in the year to reach a resolve, but we can sympathise with his feeling " that in the circumstances there was only one man who could speak to the King and talk the matter over with him, and that man was the Prime Minister." And we can feel a warmth of admiration for Mr Baldwin when he decided he was doubly bound to do his duty, as he conceived it, to the country and his duty to the King not only as a counsellor, but as a friend, and that, to quote Poe again, he " brought a dread burden down here," without consulting any of his colleagues.

In so far as this first attempt by Mr Baldwin to get to grips with the contingency would commit neither himself nor the King to anything more than the expression by each of them of his personal opinion, the Prime Minister's action in not consulting his colleagues beforehand will be censured by nobody. Mr Baldwin, in his account of this first discussion, said that when he was staying in the neighbourhood of Fort Belvedere he ascertained that his Majesty was leaving his house on Sunday, October 18th, to entertain a small shooting-party at Sandringham and that he was leaving on the Sunday afternoon. One asks from whom he ascertained this. From the inaccuracy of his information it might be fancied he had called in the secret service to help, for on telephoning from his friend's house on the Sunday morning he found that the King had left earlier than was expected. One realises how necessary it was for Mr Baldwin to occupy the curiosity of the House of Commons on December 10th with the most trivial facts of the preliminary negotiations so that the attention of the House should be diverted from the outstanding fact that throughout this time it had never been consulted; and there is no doubt that this deliberately maundering presentation of the story was highly effective. Thus do writers of detective fiction encourage their readers to explore blind turnings. Only when we hear from an admirer that " the form of his speech was marked by classic simplicity " do we search for the value of such elaborate irrelevance. Presumably if Mr Baldwin had got into communication with the King's secretary earlier he would have been granted his audience on that Sunday afternoon.

" In those circumstances I communicated with him through his secretary, and stated that I desired to see him—this is the first and only occasion on which I was the one to ask for an interview—that I desired to see him, that the matter was urgent. I told him what it was. I expressed my willingness to come to Sandringham on Tuesday, the 20th, but I said that I thought it wiser, if his Majesty thought fit, to see me at Fort Belvedere, for I was anxious that no one at that time should know of my visit, and that at any rate our *first* talk should be in complete privacy."

Although Mr Baldwin was so careful to point out to the House that this was the first and only occasion on which he was the one who called for an interview, he must have anticipated there would be other interviews, and his anxiety to throw upon the King the entire responsibility for those other interviews is a characteristic piece of self-justification with which students of Mr Baldwin's oratory are familiar. No doubt it was effective at the time, but perusal of it in print at this date leaves an impression of indecorous garrulity.

According to the social gossip of the week, among other guests at the King's shooting-party was Sir Samuel Hoare, and the same columnist reported that " when on Tuesday the shooting-party moved off after the beaters, King Edward was missing. Early that morning he had called for his car, sent his apologies to his guests, and left Sandringham, returning in the evening." Mr Baldwin better informed than the social gossips told the House of Commons that his Majesty motored back on the Monday, October 19th, to Fort Belvedere and let Mr Baldwin know he would see him on the Tuesday morning.

Mr Baldwin told the King how anxious he was over the " effect of a continuance of the kind of criticism that at that time was proceeding in the American Press, the effect it would have in the Dominions, and particularly in Canada, where it was widespread, the effect it would have in this country." The King might have retorted that if Mr Baldwin had not been enjoying a complete rest during August and September he would presumably have suggested to the Foreign Office the advisability of taking some steps to keep this criticism within the bounds of decency. Where the King refrained, it is not the place of others to score a point, and it may be admitted that by the end of October Mr Baldwin could have said no less than he did. Mr Baldwin went on to affirm that his second anxiety was about the prestige of the Crown. His argument was that the Crown was the last link of Empire left and the guarantee in this country, so long as it existed in integrity, against many evils that had afflicted other countries. This feeling largely depended on the respect that had grown up in the last three generations for the monarchy, but it might not take so long, in the face of the kind of criticism to which it was being exposed, to lose that power far more rapidly than it had been built up, and once lost, Mr Baldwin doubted if anything could restore it.

We who have noted what alarming assaults upon its dignity the Crown has survived since the accession of George I may doubt whether the dynamic force of King Edward might not have given the Crown a prestige beyond any it has yet achieved. At the same time we must recognise that Mr Baldwin's distrust of dynamic forces is shared by a great number of his country-men, and we must recognise also that a politician so sensitive to electoral opinion and so nervous about his own prestige could hardly have argued otherwise. He told the King definitely that in his view no popularity in the long run would be weighed against the effect of such criticism. He told the King how much he for one had looked forward to his reign being a great reign in a new age and how much he hoped the country would be able to see its hopes realised. He then indicated that he wanted to talk over the matter with the King as a friend and see if he could help him. This friendly intention was recognised by his Majesty who told Mr Baldwin, not once but many times during those many hours they had together, and especially towards the end, " You and I must settle this matter together ; I will not have anyone interfering."

How far Mr Baldwin was an accessory to violating the Constitution by accepting, as in his explanation to the House of Commons of December 10th he seemed to accept with some complacency, the position of a grand vizier talking matters over with an autocratic sultan, constitutional historians of the future will decide. That at this first discussion Mr Baldwin was completely justified in the position he took of giving unofficial advice as a friend, even though in a parenthesis he did tell the House of Commons it was as Prime Minister, cannot be gainsaid ; but his method does expose him to the charge from cynics of having put the issue before the country in the way least calculated to serve the King. In that last broadcast of King Edward which began, " At long last I am able to say a few words of my own. I have never wanted to withhold anything, but until now it has not been constitutionally possible for me to speak," there is a definite suggestion that the King would have welcomed an opportunity to settle the whole business directly with the country, and Mr Baldwin who was so fearful of violating the Constitution by advising the King of his competence to speak directly to his people should have been equally fearful of allowing a great many people in the country to suspect that he with the connivance of his Cabinet had overridden the rights of Parliament. When the Prime Minister discovered the perfect ductility of that Parliament he had tamed by kindness, he may have regretted that he had confronted it with a *fait accompli*.

It was as a friend that Mr Baldwin " pointed out the danger of the divorce proceedings, that if a verdict was given in that case that left the matter in suspense for some time, that period of suspense might be dangerous, because then everyone would be talking, and when once the Press began, as it must begin some time in this country, a most difficult situation would arise . . ." and here we must break off to point out with a sense of stupefaction that the first person whose difficult situation Mr Baldwin was foreseeing was not the King's but *his own* . . . " a most difficult situation would arise for me, for him, and there might well be a danger which both he and I had seen all through this—I shall come to that later— and it was one of the reasons why he wanted to take this action quickly—that is, that there might be sides taken and factions grow up in this country in a matter where no faction ought ever to exist."

But surely at this stage of the discussion Mr Baldwin was supposed to be ignorant that there was any notion in the King's head of marrying Mrs Simpson after her divorce, and it is demanding too great a credulity from the public to believe that he or anybody else would have criticised the King's private life in such a way as to create faction, We must presume then that at his *first* interview the King told Mr Baldwin, if not as his Prime Minister at least as his friend, that it was his intention to marry Mrs Simpson after the decree *nisi* was declared absolute. This anxiety about the rise of faction is strange if, as Mr. Baldwin professed to believe, the vast majority of the people of Great Britain and the Dominions overseas would not tolerate the notion of such a marriage. Why then did Mr Baldwin conceal from the country the fact that he knew on October 20th the King intended to marry

Mrs Simpson if the divorce decree rendered it possible? That this possibility of the growth of factions was thoroughly thrashed out at this first meeting can be judged by Mr Baldwin's express statement that this aspect of the question was discussed for an hour, after which he went away glad that the ice had been broken because he knew that it had to be broken. At the end of the audience he begged his Majesty to consider all that he had said, but pressed him for no kind of answer: he merely asked him to consider everything he had said.

The failure of Mr Baldwin to let Parliament know without equivocation that he was aware of the King's intention to marry Mrs Simpson should the divorce be granted adds something to the mystery which surrounds that announcement of the King's intention published with so authoritative an air by Mr Hearst on the very day before the divorce proceedings at Ipswich. Here is the text of the announcement which appeared in the *New York Journal* on October 26th:

> Within a few days Mrs Ernest Simpson, of Baltimore, Md., U.S.A., will obtain her divorce decree in England, and some eight months thereafter she will be married to Edward VIII, King of England.
>
> King Edward's most intimate friends state with the utmost positiveness that he is very deeply and sincerely enamoured of Mrs Simpson, that his love is a righteous affection, and that almost immediately after the coronation he will take her as his consort.
>
> He believes that it would be an actual mistake for a King of England to marry into any of the royal houses of the continent of Europe, and so involve himself and his empire in the complications and disasters of these royal houses.
>
> He believes, further, that in this day and generation it is absurd to maintain the tradition of royal intermarriages, with all the physical as well as the political disabilities likely to result from that outgrown custom.
>
> His brother, the Duke of York, has been extremely happy and fortunate in his marriage to a lady of the people, a commoner, so-called.
>
> King Edward believes that the marriage he contemplates would be equally happy, and that it would help him to do what he wants to do—namely, reign in the interests of the people.
>
> Finally, he believes that the most important thing for the peace and welfare of the world is an intimate understanding and relationship between England and America, and that his marriage with this very gifted lady may help to bring about that beneficial co-operation between English-speaking nations.
>
> Primarily, however, the King's transcendent reason for marrying Mrs Simpson is that he ardently loves her, and does not see why a King should be denied the privilege of marrying the lady he loves.
>
> So, in all human probability, in June 1937, one month after the

ceremonies of the coronation, will follow the festivities of the marriage to the very charming and intelligent Mrs Ernest Simpson, of Baltimore, Maryland, U.S.A.

That this announcement was phrased with such dignity and restraint led many people to believe that it was directly inspired by the King. Mr Hearst was staying in Wales at the time and it was stated positively by Mr Frank Owen and Mr R. J. Thompson in their well-informed and brilliantly presented narrative of the events leading up to the Abdication *￼ that the announcement was written by Mr Hearst himself who received the news from King Edward at Fort Belvedere. Mr S. B. Leeds,† however, states positively on the authority of the Duchess of Windsor that the King did not give this information to Mr Hearst. He declared that she told him this twice, at Cannes and at the Château de Candé. The American paper *Time* said that the information was given by Sir Godfrey Thomas, the King's secretary; but this has been denied by Sir Godfrey Thomas. It certainly seemed to many, among whom may be included the present writer, that the King's anxiety to be perfectly frank with these people had forced the issue by a dignified announcement in an American paper which would compel the British Press to break their silence and enable him to ascertain public feeling, which, at present, was being tested only by scandalous gossip. Mr Leeds's book lights up this announcement from another angle. He says that many people believe " Mr Hearst got the story himself from some highly placed person close to the King, and anxious to wreck his purposes."

Whatever person or whatever motive inspired this announcement, from the moment it appeared in print there was no looking back for the King. The theory that if he had thrown over Mrs Simpson the country, with Mr Baldwin acting as a genial chef, would have killed and roasted the fatted calf for the returned prodigal might stand the guttering candles of sentiment; but it falls to pieces under the cold arc-lamps of common sense. To have thrown over Mrs Simpson after such an announcement would have implied a moral cowardice which simply was not in the King's character. Let the reader cast his mind back to that moment when Charles James Fox, *recking not at all of any danger to himself or his career*, perjured his very soul to defend his Prince by disowning before an

* *His Was the Kingdom.*
† *Cards the Windsors Hold.*

unfriendly House of Commons the marriage with Mrs Fitzherbert. Let the reader analyse his opinion of that Prince of Wales's moral cowardice and ask himself if he would have wished such a display from King Edward. Even if the people of Great Britain could have squared the repudiation with their sense of decency, which it is not easy to believe of the great majority, what a miserable king of shreds and patches he would have seemed to the rest of the world. If his country owes him no other gratitude it owes him gratitude for proving that the King of a nation of shopkeepers was not a shopkeeper himself. If that announcement was published *with* the knowledge of the King it is a proof that his own conscience was perfectly clear about Mrs Simpson's divorce. If it was published *without* his knowledge it can only have been a clumsy attempt to block the divorce at Ipswich on October 27th. The fact that Mr Justice Hawke granted the decree *nisi* is surely conclusive proof that there was no flaw in Mrs Simpson's petition. Any implication of the contrary involves as gross a contempt of Court as may be imagined, inasmuch as it would imply that Mr Justice Hawke had been previously approached and had consented to weigh down the scales of justice with a handful of royal sugar.

While the Ipswich divorce was perplexing editorial hearts in Great Britain with the problem of whether to mention it or not, a problem which was solved by reporting it in such a way that only an infinitesimal minority of the country realised the importance of the brief paragraphs, Mr John Alfred Kensit, whom we last heard of at the end of the nineteenth century as a callow youth accompanying his father and mother to brawling parties in ritualistic churches, took fright at hearing that the Coronation oath was to be altered. Apparently, Mr Kensit had smelt a wicked whiff of incense in the air soon after the death of George V, not let it be added from any thurible swung by the new King but from the thurible swung by his Grace the Lord Archbishop of Canterbury, of whose loyalty to the Protestant Reformed Religion established by law Mr Kensit had the gloomiest doubts. Indeed he went out of his way to give what amounted to a testimonial to King Edward by observing, " the present King has not apparently taken much interest in the Church so far, though when he was at Balmoral he went on both Sundays to the Presbyterian service at Crathie, which seems to show that he likes a simple, modest service."

On hearing that the Coronation oath was to be altered, Mr Kensit wrote to the Prime Minister asking whether the vital clause—the King's promise to retain the Protestant Reformed Religion established by law—was to be tampered with. Mr Baldwin's secretary wrote back that there was no proposal to alter the vital clause. This was not strictly true. The original oath to maintain the Protestant Reformed Religion was applied to the whole of the Empire, but when the Coronation Service was officially published early in 1937, it was found that the Royal obligation to retain the Protestant religion was confined to the United Kingdom, and this alteration was made without seeking authority from Parliament. People should understand that the terminology of the oath is far more repulsive to a High Church archbishop who may administer it than to any king who so far has been called upon to take it. One of the basic arguments of Anglicans for the true Catholicity of the Established Church is that nowhere from the first page to the last of the Book of Common Prayer is there any mention of the Protestant Reformed Religion. It was a preposterous declaration to exact from the King in regard to Eire or Canada, and hardly less preposterous for Australia. Nevertheless, fear of the electorate prevented the Government from frankly making the change by statutory law and tempted them to hand over the responsibility to the Archbishop of Canterbury. His Grace naturally welcomed this opportunity to eliminate the Dominions from the oath because, with the growth of strong Anglican sentiment in the years to come, it would serve as a good precedent for getting rid of the offensive phrase altogether, and burying once and for all that mouldering skeleton which lurks in the vestry-cupboard of the Establishment. This suspicion of the *bona fides* of the Anglican episcopate was vocal as far back as the engagement of Prince Albert to Queen Victoria, and that was long before the full force of the Oxford Movement had been felt. No greater insult can be offered to what is called a sound Anglican than to call him a Protestant, and it will be observed with what care throughout this book the present writer has avoided wounding susceptibilities upon that point. It must be remembered that in the eyes of High Churchmen the King's lack of respect for the comparatively novel attitude adopted by the prelates of the Establishment toward divorce constituted his chief offence. His own ideas about divorce accorded better with those held in Scotland since the middle of the sixteenth century, ideas which

Dr Lang had rejected when he was received into the English Church and were therefore peculiarly obnoxious to him.   This very Autumn Presbyterian dignitaries had made tentative approaches to be granted an active part in the Coronation and had been politely refused consideration by the Archbishop of Canterbury on the grounds that they lacked the necessary sacerdotal qualifications to assist at a sacramental ceremony. There is no desire to criticise the large claims being made by the Anglican Church under its present Primate; but it is essential for readers to understand that these large claims were being made, for that will provide an explanation of what has seemed to so many the arrogant clerical bitterness toward the ex-King.   From the point of view of rigid ecclesiasticism it may have been unfortunate that King Edward should have found the spiritual leadership of men like ' Dick ' Sheppard and ' Tubby ' Clayton more profitable to his soul's health. Yet as long as the Church of England follows the principle of the expanding suit-case, lay members cannot be expected to approve its expanding at one end and contracting at the other. If the King were compelled to believe the orthodox doctrine of the High Church party he could not even worship at Crathie church without injury to his soul's health.

On the whole for the avoidance of religious faction which, with all deference to Lord Baldwin, is just as harmful as political faction, it is wiser, so long as the King of Great Britain, Ireland and the British Dominions Overseas is compelled to be in communion with the Church of England as by law established, that he should hold straitly as Supreme Governor to the legality of his spiritual attitude.   Throughout his reign he did not either by intention or by act trespass against that legality.   The party at present predominant in the Anglican Church may be congratulated on the success with which it has succeeded in making all the publicists and correspondents of the world accept the proposition that the Church of England does not sanction the remarriage of divorced persons. In other circumstances such a success would have been a cause for the profoundest rejoicing among those non-Anglicans who believe in the sanctity of the marriage bond ; but common honesty forbids acceptation of a proposition which has never yet been formally laid down as the authoritative doctrine of that Church.   It compels a melancholy smile to have to add that, when in November 1937 Lord Hugh Cecil urged the Church Assembly to pass a motion calling for an Act of

Parliament to enforce the rule against the remarriage by an Anglican churchman of any person whose spouse by a former marriage was still alive, it was the Archbishop of Canterbury himself who suavely succeeded in getting the motion quashed.

Lord Hugh Cecil found the present position intolerable. " Many people were being driven out of their communion because it seemed to them that the Church of England had nothing to teach or to order : that it spoke with a double tongue and stammering lips, was a city of confusion. ' Can this be the Catholic Church,' they asked, ' to allow such a scandal in a moral issue ? ' . . . Whether or no Parliament acceded to the Church's request in this matter, at least the Church would have done its best to get it set right and the responsibility would lie with the State."

On the other hand, the Rev R. J. E. Boggis (Exeter) " was anxious that the Assembly should express its approval of the remarriage in Church of the innocent party to a divorce." So was Sir Frederick Cripps (Gloucester). So was the Archdeacon of Dudley. " They were not concerned about the canon law of 1604. What concerned them was the fact that in their own lifetime and in the lifetime of their fathers and grandfathers, the Church had again and again sanctioned the marriage of the innocent party." The Bishop of Truro " quoted recorded words of Archbishop Randall Davidson in support of his own contention that the innocent party to a divorce might be remarried in church." * The Dean of Hereford was in entire agreement with the Bishop of Truro.

The Archbishop of Canterbury felt that " such a measure as Lord Hugh Cecil desired . . . must involve a most painful clash between the Church and Parliament. He would always be ready to take such a risk if some great question of right were involved or some large principle were at issue.† But, in this case, so far as fundamental principles were concerned, it was rather on the other side, and rather than run a risk that might result in most unfortunate consequences ‡ it was better

---

* Yet Dr Frere, his immediate predecessor, would have been horrified by such a contention. The Anglican Episcopate supplies a remarkable disproof of Euclid's axiom that things which are equal to the same thing are equal to one another.

† Two Voices are there : one is of the See, one of the Radio ; each a mighty Voice.

‡ Several speakers had warned the Assembly that such a motion might provoke the issue of Disestablishment.

to leave the comparatively few clergymen who desired to continue to celebrate these marriages in their somewhat unenviable isolation."

So in the words of the *Church Times* of November 26th 1937:

" Lord Hugh Cecil's motion fell to the ground."

And now we must return to November 1936, on the 3rd of which Parliament assembled for a new session. The King wearing the uniform of an Admiral of the Fleet drove in his State Daimler car to open the new session. There was criticism at the time of his not riding in the gilded coach behind eight horses, but in view of what we know about his private anxiety a breath of imagination will blow away all that criticism. In any case the weather was bad. We may hope Mr Kensit's apprehensions were allayed when he read that " wearing a purple velvet robe and ermine cape, the King made his statutory declaration of the Protestant faith in clear and unhesitating tones."

> The King's Speech stated that the policy of the Government continued to be based on membership of the League of Nations, and that they would co-operate with other Governments in examining proposals for improving the League. They would also persist in their efforts to bring about a meeting between the Locarno Powers, and in their determination to support the agreement for non-intervention in Spain. Rearmament was declared to be essential, at any rate till international relations improved. The general trade and industrial outlook was stated to be still favourable, with prospects of further improvement. The legislative programme announced for the session included measures for maintaining an adequate mercantile marine, for the unification of coal royalties under national control, for curbing the Fascist and Communist menace to public order, for bringing up to date the Factory Act of 1901, for assisting the live-stock industry, for transferring to the Ministry of transport the chief trunk roads of the country, for readjusting Ministerial salaries, and for promoting physical culture among the younger generation. The Speech also contained the announcement that the King intended to visit India after his coronation (*A. R.*).

For the first time in English history the motion for the Address was moved by a woman—Miss Horsburgh, one of the members for Dundee. In the course of the debate which succeeded, Mr Churchill attacked the Government for the dilatory way in which it had handled air rearmament, and by a strange, indeed a tragic irony of phrase, he demanded a Parliamentary enquiry to find out the truth because otherwise

Parliament " would have committed an act of abdication of
duty without parallel in its history." In reply to this moral
impeachment Mr Baldwin made perhaps the most surprising
apology even of his richly apologetic career. He admitted
that the Government had been late in starting a defence
programme, but he pointed out to the House that

> in the years 1933 and 1934 when he and his friends began to grow
> very uneasy over what was happening in Europe, there was probably a
> stronger pacifist feeling running through the country, than at any
> time since the war as indicated by the election at Fulham in the
> autumn of 1933. As Leader of the Conservative Party he asked
> himself what chance there was in the next year or two of that feeling
> being so changed that the country would give a mandate for re-
> armament, and he came to the conclusion that if he had gone to the
> country and said that Germany was rearming and that therefore they
> must rearm, he would have lost the election. By waiting till the
> proper moment they got from the country a mandate, with a large
> majority, for doing a thing that twelve months before no one would
> have believed possible. It was in the nature of democracies to be a
> couple of years behind dictatorships in preparing for war, but when
> they did commence they could act with at least equal vigour (*A. R.*).

If we attach the most charitable interpretation to this
extraordinary sacrifice of Mankind to Party, the best that
could have been pleaded on behalf of such a confession of
opportunism is that if the Government had defied the omen
of the Fulham election and had been defeated at the polls
on asking for a mandate for rearmament those well-informed
about the situation in Europe could have been accused of
taking an unpatriotic risk ; but it did not seem to occur to
Mr Baldwin that if he and his friends, with far better opportunities of knowing the facts, were so uneasy over what was
happening in Europe the right course was to take the electorate fully into their confidence and abide by the result.
Instead they sat mumbling like rheumatic old women whose
twinges were warning them of a change in the weather, but
who were afraid to ask for warmer clothes lest they should be
turned out of the almshouse.

There was only one outstanding problem in international
politics in 1933 and that was the determination and ability of
Germany to rearm with sufficient rapidity and effect to become
once again a menace to the peace of the world. In pre-
Hitler days the Labour Party had tried to raise every obstacle
in the way of a cast-iron agreement between Great Britain and

France or between Great Britain and Italy, and although by 1936 Labour had become comparatively bellicose we have noted earlier in this chapter the fatuity of its attitude at the Edinburgh Conference. The Labour Party was indeed no more than a great wobbly blancmange streaked here and there with cochineal. In 1935 the wave of pacificism came up with a splash against the menacing fact of the German reoccupation of the Rhine territory, and this direct violation of the Versailles Treaty by Germany was followed by another cynical breach of it in the shape of the Anglo–German naval agreement of 1935, which not merely convinced France of the duplicity of British foreign policy but drove Mussolini into his desperate Abyssinian adventure, he being equally convinced that Great Britain meant to come to terms with Germany and override the rest of Europe.

We in Great Britain who were aware what little blood and iron there was in that National Government found it hard to understand why it should have been credited with such a doughty ambition; but we had to wait until November 1936 to be told by the leader of that Government that our foreign policy was built of ballot-boxes. And for consolation the country was to be assured that it was in the nature of a democracy to be a couple of years behind dictatorship in the maturity of its plans. Mr Baldwin might as usefully have observed that it was in the nature of an elephant to spend two years in gestation, of a rabbit to spend six weeks. Yet when democracy did begin, he boasted, it could act with at least equal vigour. At least equal vigour in preparation is not enough to overtake an inertia of two years. However, the country was under Mr Baldwin's spell. He had succeeded in giving constipation as bright an aureole of romance as the poets of the eighteen-thirties gave consumption. Moreover, any apprehensions of the Government's moral courage were completely tranquillised on November 10th when the Public Order Bill was read and the country heard that Sir Oswald Mosley was no longer to be allowed to wear a black shirt in public.

King Edward attended the great gathering of ex-service men at the Albert Hall on Armistice Day as he had always attended it when Prince of Wales. The first part of the proceedings were broadcast; but before the moment came for his Majesty to read Laurence Binyon's poem *For the Fallen* the transmission stopped. No doubt the explanation would be found in the claims of the programme; but that abrupt silence struck chill on the hearts of listeners who knew that trouble was ahead; and it is not surprising that later they should have suspected the B.B.C. of having anticipated thus early the obliteration which was to be devised later by others.

On the night of November 11th the King travelled down to Portland to inspect the Home Fleet. Commander Kenneth Edwards, R.N., wrote: *

The sailor is a queer blend of sentimentalist and cynic. The men of the Fleet realised that the King had had a gruelling day before his arrival at Portland. It had been Armistice Day, and he had been at the Cenotaph in the morning, at Westminster Abbey and at the Albert Hall at night, and had caught a midnight train to Portland which had landed him in a tempest at 4 a.m. They realised, as no landsman can ever realise, just how tiring it is to climb on board ship after ship and to inspect men, mess decks and weapons.

Three battleships, an aircraft-carrier and three cruisers: that was the tale of the first day, and there was a visit to shore establishments into the bargain. At night a dinner-party, then a concert, then an officers' "at home." Back to the Royal Yacht long after midnight, only to begin the round of inspections again early the next morning.

The extent of the programme and the manner in which the King carried it out went straight to the hearts of the men. Not for an instant in all that long round of inspections did his attention flag. He spotted badges, medal ribbons, faces. Every comment he made was seamanlike and to the point.

Wet through himself, he thought of the men who were wet and gave orders that they should be got under cover with the minimum of delay. Inspecting men under weeping skies, he disdained a waterproof because the men were fallen in without waterproofs.

At the lower-deck concert in the hangar of the aircraft-carrier *Courageous* he entered into the spirit of the men. In the interval he led the singing of "Tipperary" and other well-known tunes. And he said a few words to the men—words that struck home to every one of them for the simple reason that he spoke to sailors as a sailor—to men as a man. Small wonder that the cheers which rolled over the water as he left the Fleet held a spontaneity rare in those days of reserve.

It was a very successful visit. Yet there were two things which were wrong—one small, one big.

It was noticed by every man that, whereas the King would not wear a waterproof while inspecting men in the rain, Sir Samuel Hoare (now First Lord of the Admiralty), wore his. A small thing, but sailors take note of small things, and in this they saw the real difference between the Politician and the Monarch.

And then there was the Fleet Air Arm. The King knew what the

Navy thought about the present system of dual control, knew that efficiency could only be achieved by the Air Arm becoming the sole property of the Admiralty. Apparently he wished to find out just how far this feeling had bitten into the hearts of those officers who, by reason of their loyalty, are committed to striving to make an unworkable system efficient.

For this reason the King asked certain questions. They, and their answers, were illuminating. . . . He heard one officer remark that, unless the Admiralty had full control of the Fleet Air Arm for at least two years before a war, the Air Arm, which should be one of the greatest assets to a Navy, would be only an inefficient embarrassment to a naval commander.

The King went back to London. One may be sure that he remembered this blot of the Fleet Air Arm on the general efficiency and " happiness " of the Fleet. It was, perhaps, due to this that two or three days later it became known that the control of the Air Arm was eventually to be vested in the Admiralty.

Thus did King Edward bring to an end a bitter quarrel which had lasted for over twenty years. When the next war comes we shall be grateful to him.

On November 14th Mr Malcolm Stewart, the Commissioner for the Special Areas for England and Wales, resigned his post on the grounds of health. A report published by him a few days previously suggested that the real reason for his resignation was the steady obstruction of his plans. He even went so far as to criticise strongly the Iron and Steel Federation for having opposed the erection of new works in the town of Jarrow. Some two hundred of the inhabitants marched to lay their case before the Prime Minister, but he had refused to see them when they reached London at the beginning of November. Mr Baldwin in defending his action against Labour criticism said that " since the war the question of marches had been a difficult one which had faced all Governments," but nobody retorted that during the war in which Mr Baldwin's Government seemed likely to involve the country the question of marches might become even more acute.

Mr Malcolm Stewart's report published in November had actually been in the hands of the Government since July, but the King's speech had contained no more than a perfunctory reference to the special areas, and Mr Runciman had nothing better to say to the petition from Jarrow than that the town should wait for better times. The special areas " were already receiving all the consideration which they could reasonably expect, and accordingly the Government did not feel called upon to do more for them than to ask Parliament to renew the Bill making special provision for them which was due to expire in March." Some forty or so of the younger Conservatives, led by Viscount Wolmer, were so indignant at this attitude that they threatened to vote for the Opposition unless some attempt was made to deal with the problem of the special areas. So, when on November 17th the Special Areas Act came before the House for renewal, Mr Chamberlain promised before it expired " to bring forward an amending Act which should embody such of Mr Stewart's recommendations as the Government found acceptable." Note that date.

The account Mr Baldwin gave of his second interview with the King on November 16th at Buckingham Palace is less clear when studied in the printed word than it may have seemed to a hero-worshipping House of Commons at its delivery. Mr Baldwin was insistent that the King had sent for him on that occasion. He had meant to see his Majesty later in the week, but the King had sent for him first. In those circumstances it is surprising that Mr Baldwin did not give his Majesty an opportunity of explaining why he had sent for him. Yet Mr Baldwin felt it was his duty to *begin* the conversation and he spoke to his Master for a quarter of an hour or twenty minutes on the question of marriage. He broke off here to tell the House " again we must remember that the Cabinet had not been in this at all— I had reported to about four of my senior colleagues the conversation at Fort Belvedere."

We were told in our youth when robbing nests that no hen-bird could distinguish between three or four or five eggs, but surely Mr Baldwin could distinguish between three or four or five of his senior colleagues, or was his estimate of " about four " making allowance for their being married men ?

In case the House was by now muddled with the account of this November 16th visit, Mr Baldwin repeated the date : " I saw the King on Monday November 16th and began by giving him my view of a possible marriage." Mr Baldwin went on to tell the King that he did not think a particular marriage was one that would receive the approbation of the country. To the expression of that opinion we may readily agree Mr Baldwin was entitled. It was at this point no more than an expression of personal opinion. He was still interviewing the King in a private capacity, for apart from " about four " of his senior colleagues the rest of the Cabinet were in ignorance of these discussions. The next remark in the light of later knowledge of events is suggestive. It was to the effect that such a marriage would involve the lady's becoming Queen. Why was this said now? At this point there was no earthly reason for supposing it would involve anything else. Are we to believe that Mr Baldwin tried to implant in the mind of King Edward that the objection was not to Mrs Simpson as the King's wife but as the Queen? That is incredible, and if we pause to consider so disagreeable a possibility Mr Baldwin's will-o'-the-wisp narrative is alone to be blamed. He had gone out of his way at the beginning of it to remind the House that he had but little time to compose a speech for delivery, so he must tell what he had to tell truthfully, sincerely, and plainly, with no attempt to dress up or to adorn. Therefore any suspicion we may have acquired of Mr Baldwin's motive for suggesting to the King that his proposed wife must be Queen has been due to Mr Baldwin's lack of leisure to notice that in doing so he might seem to be suggesting an alternate. In his next sentence he stressed this difficulty of the lady's becoming Queen. " I did tell his Majesty once that I might be a remnant of the old Victorians but that my worst enemy would not say of me that I did not know what the reaction of the English people would be to any particular course of action, and I told him that in so far as that went, I was certain that would be impracticable."

This fine instinct Mr Baldwin possessed for the reaction of the electorate to any particular course of action had already caused the country some awkward moments and in fact at this very moment it was responsible for the country's being completely incapable of handling the rapidly growing seriousness of the European situation. Mr Baldwin then pointed out to his Majesty that the position of the King's wife was different from the position of the wife of any other citizen in the country; it was part of the price which the King had to pay. His wife became Queen; the Queen became the Queen of the country, and, therefore, in the choice of a Queen the voice of the people must be heard. In his speech to the House of Commons on December 10th Mr Baldwin covered up what may be the enunciation of a constitutional fallacy by quoting Laertes. We will leave Laertes until December 10th, and continue to observe Mr Baldwin in the rôle of Polonius. There is nowhere in the whole body of constitutional and common law, ecclesiastical canons, or even general use and custom the faintest shadow of authority for Mr Baldwin's assertion that in the choice of a Queen the voice of the people must be heard. Stay, there is one opportunity for the voice of the people and that is provided in the clause of the Act of Settlement that forbids the King to marry a Roman Catholic. That the King possesses the sole right, in the words of a constitutional authority like Dr Berriedale Keith, to determine for himself the desirability of marriage is as incontestable as his initiative in choice. Dr Keith qualifies this by observing, " the mere fact that the Sovereign may legally wed whom he will imposes upon him the task of fixing his affections on one whose selection will be widely welcomed by his people." It is well that Dr Keith uses the word ' task ', for it is indeed a task beyond any human being since Adam, whose choice was conveniently limited but not therefore more advantageous to the human race. Nevertheless we may readily agree with Dr Keith that " the Prime Minister in his confidential intercourse with his sovereign is not overstepping the limits of his authority " by touching on the attitude of the people in any suggested marriage. Where Mr Baldwin did overstep the mark was in saying to King Edward that the voice of the people must be heard.

So far Mr Baldwin seemed to have been granting an audience to the King, and it comes with almost a shock when we read, " then his Majesty said to me—I have his permission to state this—that he wanted to tell me something that he had long wanted to tell me. He said, ' I am going to marry Mrs Simpson and I am prepared to go.' I said, ' Sir, that is most grievous news, it is impossible for me to make any comment on it.'

Mr Baldwin's failure to comment may have been due to his realisation that this Royal ultimatum had carried matters beyond the atmosphere of friendly talks. What does perplex the student is why the King should have wanted to tell Mr Baldwin an intention of which, if we accept Mr Baldwin's account of his interview, he was already perfectly aware. Perhaps we are to understand from Mr Baldwin's unadorned eloquence that the news lay only in the latter part of the King's announcement, that is to say in his readiness to abdicate if, as Mr Baldwin had led him to suppose during the long previous audiences the King had had of him, opposition were created against his marriage to Mrs Simpson.

That night the King told Queen Mary of his intention, and the following day he told the Duke of York and the Duke of Gloucester. The Duke of Kent was told later in the week because he was out of London on Tuesday, November 17th. It may be assumed that but for the effect on the King of the visit to the distressed areas in Wales the Government would have been forced to tell the country within a week that it had notified the King of its refusal to accept Mrs Simpson as Queen and the King's determination to abdicate in consequence. It may also be assumed that the King's chivalry which throughout these days was *sans peur* and *sans reproche*, would have helped the Government in every way it could to present the case to the nation to the Government's best advantage.

King Edward travelled down to Wales during the night of November 17th, the night of the day on which as we have noted the younger Conservatives under Lord Wolmer were seriously perturbing the Government about their handling of the special areas. The King was accompanied by Sir Kingsley Wood, the Minister of Health, and Mr Ernest Brown, the Minister of Labour. Pontypridd, Merthyr, Dowlais, Dinais, Abertillery, Aberdare, Pontypool—mile after mile of desolation under that pale blue autumnal sky, and above the desolation the voices of thousands of Welshmen singing with fresh hope in their breasts. On the afternoon of the Midsummer Eve on which was born that royal figure, King for not yet a year but Prince of Wales for a quarter of a century, an explosion at the Albion Colliery near Pontypridd had killed 260 men and boys. How ominous a salute !

That night in the train the King dined with the new Chief Commissioner for the Special Areas, Sir George Gillett ; but he invited to dinner the late Commissioner, Mr Malcolm Stewart, whose report was lying so indigestibly upon the conscience of the Government. The King had done more than invite Mr Malcolm Stewart to dinner presumably to discuss with him the practical measures that might be taken to alleviate the distress of South Wales. Yes, the King had done more than that. Several times during the tour he had assured eager groups he was going to help them. To his Ministers he had said, " Something must be done." To the people of South Wales he had said, " Something will be done."

Those words of the King have been held against him as a deliberate attempt to win popular sympathy for what he knew was going to be a struggle between himself and the Government. Those words have been held against him as an example of his waywardness and caprice and irresponsibility. Mr Maxton, according to one account,* declared in the lobby of the House of Commons that the tour of Wales was " designed to overcome the vehement objections to a possible marriage from the ruling classes, especially their spokesman the Archbishop of Canterbury. Finding himself in difficulties with the aristocracy, the King was on a campaign to consolidate his personal popularity with the masses. He would win." Perhaps Mr Maxton was wrong. Perhaps, so far from being part of a campaign to consolidate his personal popularity with the masses, that tour of South Wales drove the King to reconsider his notification to Mr Baldwin that he was prepared to go, and set him to find a possible way out of what when Mr Baldwin left the presence on November 16th had seemed an insurmountable barrier to his remaining on the throne. It is certain that his Majesty began to make plans to urge the Government along the same lines as Lord Wolmer and his young Conservatives.

It is significant that the next visit proposed for the King by the Labour Ministry and the Ministry of Health was a visit to Staffordshire on December 9th and 10th. Staffordshire might be counted upon to counteract some of the effect of the South Wales desolation. It is equally significant that the King was not satisfied with the proposed Staffordshire visit, but was insisting on a visit to Tyneside, which the Government knew would be as embarrassing an experience for them as the visit to South Wales. Some of the papers were already contrasting the vigour of the King with the flaccidity of the Government, and not only the *Daily Mail* and the *Daily Express* which had always been exasperated by Mr Baldwin's leadership. The *News Chronicle*, the organ, let it be remembered, of Nonconformist opinion, had commented on the Welsh tour, " The King is above and outside politics. What he has done is in the sole interest of truth and public service. . . . The man in the street feels that Whitehall stands condemned." Disconcerting comment this from the last of the Roundheads !

* " The Woman I Love " (*News Review*).

Throughout that talk on November 16th Mr Baldwin had laid stress on the necessity that the King's choice of a wife should be made with the fullest realisation that the lady chosen would have to be Queen and therefore that in his choice the voice of the people must be heard.   It would seem from Mr Baldwin's account of the interview that the King accepted this pronouncement as final and definite by the fact of his having told Queen Mary that night of his determination to marry Mrs Simpson and abdicate, and of his having told the Duke of York and the Duke of Gloucester the following day.   He could not, however, embarrass the Government at that stage by cancelling the tour of South Wales, and therefore he ful-filled his engagement, to receive that fearful emotional shock from the spectacle of desolation presented to him.   It is not within the scope of this volume to argue where lay the blame for that desolation.   It rests with many another as yet un-determined sin of omission upon the soul of the National Government when it stands before the bar of the future for judgment.

The King himself was certainly so profoundly moved that he desired to do whatever lay in his power to help, and during the days immediately after this visit to Wales he sought for a way by which he might be able to help.   Free from self-deception to an extent one wishes could be said of some of his official advisers, he knew that one vital condition for making his royal collaboration effective over the long stretch of time that reform exacts was a tranquil emotional life.   He had no illusions about the ultimate effect on himself of the grand gesture of renunciation.   If you like, he could not quench that craving for private happiness ; but in calling it that let it be remembered that he had the courage and clarity of mind to recognise that it was impossible for him " to carry the heavy burden of responsibility and discharge his duties as King as he would wish to do without the help and support of the woman he loved."

So, in a last desperate effort to find a way out, he sent word to Mr Baldwin proposing a compromise.   One little sentence from Mr Baldwin's own speech confirms this.   Telling the House about that fateful week which began on November 16th, he said, " For the rest of the week, so far as I know, he was considering that point."

The compromise suggested to Mr Baldwin was that the King as Duke of Lancaster should marry Mrs Simpson.   She would then become Her Highness (not Her Royal Highness) the Duchess of Lancaster, ranking below the three Royal Duchesses. She would be the King's wife, not his Queen, and aristocratic prejudice was to be appeased by the complete absence of curtseys. There were, of course, rumours of this compromise running round London that week, but Mr S. B. Leeds received it in writing from Mr Herman Rogers at his villa in Cannes. And until it is officially contradicted we are entitled to accept it as an historical fact.

That this proposal was a source of grave alarm to one body of English opinion may be gathered from a leader in *The Times* of November 24th, written with the apparent intention of letting the King know that he would not be allowed to play any practical part in the reconstruction of the country's economic life :

> The King's Ministers are his Majesty's advisers, and to contrast his personal and representative concern for the well-being of a section of the people with the administrative slips of his advisers, is a constitutionally dangerous proceeding, and would threaten, if continued, to entangle the Throne in politics.

The day after this was published, on Wednesday, November 25th, the King sent for Mr Baldwin again and asked whether the proposition that Parliament should pass an Act enabling the lady to be the King's wife without the position of Queen had been put to his Prime Minister. Mr Baldwin replied that it had. The King asked him what he thought of it. Mr Baldwin told the King he had not considered it. His actual words according to himself were : " I can give you no considered opinion." Leaving on one side for a moment Mr Baldwin's peculiar method of performing his advisory duties either as a friend or as a prime minister, we shall note that the King in his anxiety to behave with the strictest constitutional correctness handed Mr Baldwin an extra weapon. There was no need whatever for Parliament to pass an Act enabling the lady to be the King's wife without the position of Queen. George IV had conclusively established that when he refused coronation to Queen Caroline. We are not arguing for the moment the advisability for the country of the course proposed by the King. That is a matter on which different people will have different opinions, and no amount of argument is ever likely to change those opinions. In his account of this interview Mr Baldwin said that if the King asked him his first reaction informally it was that Parliament would never pass such a Bill.   Such a remark can only be construed as a veiled threat that Mr Baldwin would use his full weight as Prime Minister to make the opposition to such a Bill an opposition of the Government. The only other explanation would be that Mr Baldwin was indulging in one of those boasts about his own clairvoyance. Having uttered this veiled threat, Mr Baldwin asked the King if he desired that he should examine the proposition formally. The King said he did so desire.   Mr Baldwin explained that it would mean putting the proposition before the whole Cabinet, and communicating with the Prime Ministers of all the Dominions and asked if that was his Majesty's wish.   The King told him that it was and Mr Baldwin said that he would do it.

And now comes a mystery.   In the House of Commons on December 10th Mr Baldwin was insistent that the first interview of October 20th was the first and only occasion on which it was he who asked for an interview.   Presumably, by making that statement, he was guarding himself against any suspicion of having forced the King's hand.   But why in that elaborately frank speech of December 10th did he omit to mention the interview at Buckingham Palace that was said to have taken place on Friday, November 27th?   Why did he proceed straight from the November 25th interview to the interview on December 2nd when the King asked him to go and see him, though again, in Mr Baldwin's words, he had intended asking for an interview later that week?   Can the explanation of Mr Baldwin's omitting any mention of that interview of November 27th be that this was an occasion on which he *did* ask to see the King, and that it was of all the interviews the one that was most crucial in the ultimate development of the situation?   Until the minutes of that Cabinet meeting held on Friday, November 27th, are made available to the historian—and it has already been pointed out that Cabinet Government has now made it impossible for history ever to feel sure that history is not being told what the vanity of dead bones wants it to believe—it would be pretentious to claim authentic knowledge of what took place.   Yet even the sides of a Cabinet have ears, and Fleet Street believed it did know what was the result of that Cabinet meeting on the Friday.   What Fleet Street believed was printed in *His Was the Kingdom*.   It was that, late on the evening of the Cabinet meeting which was supposed to be occupying itself with the question of non-intervention in

Spain, Mr Baldwin drove to Buckingham Palace, which he entered " through a little-used door and was taken through the long corridors to the King " for all the world like some plumed figure in the first chapter of a Dumas romance. This audience was not mentioned in the *Court Circular*, and in case suspicion should have been aroused " it was given out that Mr Baldwin was staying in town that night to attend a private dinner." To quote Mr Frank Owen and Mr R. J. Thompson further :

" Mr Baldwin had been asked to go to the King again and to say definitely that the Cabinet would give up office if the King insisted on his action. . . . The interview lasted, so it was said, two hours, and it was a frank one on both sides.

" The King had said that he was determined to go on with his project, that he had as much right as anyone to a private life. Mr Baldwin had replied that in that event the Cabinet had authorised him to say that they could not continue as the King's advisers. Then he took his leave without any definite reply from the King."

The importance of this story IF TRUE requires no underlining by the present writer. IF TRUE, it blows into dust the whole of Mr Baldwin's careful speech which he made to the House of Commons on December 10th, for it makes a complete mockery of those consultations with the Prime Ministers of the Dominions ; and when in the next chapter we examine Mr Baldwin's account of the interview on December 2nd, we shall understand why decency compelled him to admit what a great gentleman the King had been. If, on the other hand, the story which Fleet Street heard and which Mr Owen and Mr Thompson printed has no foundation in fact, a public service will have been done by reprinting it here and affording the Government an opportunity of denying it.

That Mr Baldwin and Mr Geoffrey Dawson, the Editor of *The Times*, were already communing with one another seems evident by the tone of the leaders at the end of this November. The rebuke to those who had praised the King's initiative in the matter of the distressed areas in Wales was followed next day by a comment on the appointment of a Governor-General to South Africa :

It is the position—the position of the King's deputy no less than that of the King himself—that must be kept high above public reproach and ridicule, and that is incomparably more important than the individual who fills it. . . . The King's deputy, like the King himself, should be invested with a certain detachment and dignity, which need not at all preclude his contact with all sorts and conditions of people, but which are not so easily put on as a change of clothes.

But the most serious warning was delivered on November 30th after the Cabinet's ultimatum. In a sonorous eulogy of Parliament *The Times* declared:

> The House of Commons has shown the power of democratic institutions to give a country steadiness and balance, and at the same time the capacity to act in difficult times. Given the continuance of this spirit—and it shows no sign of weakening—the House of Commons may well prove itself what the country has often required in similar times during its long history, but has seldom been given— namely, a Council of State which is able to demonstrate its solid strength in any crisis that may arise, whether foreign or domestic.

The bell had rung for the curtain to rise upon that tragic winter's tale.

CHAPTER XXII

WINTER

A TRAGIC poet of the future who shall turn to the events of 1936 will find omens as impressive as Shakespeare found for the death of Caesar.

> When beggars die there are no comets seen;
> The heavens themselves blaze forth the death of princes.

The destruction by fire of the Crystal Palace on the last day of that November was so portentous a coincidence that only the collapse of the Albert Memorial could have added significance to it. Yet the omen possessed the ambiguity which we have learned to associate with such manner of prognostication. That it was significant the superstitious agreed; it was when they tried to interpret the significance that opinion differed. Had the last remnants of Victorianism been consumed in that great pyre? Or was it a witness to Victorianism's endurance as the fires of Smithfield and Oxford to the Protestant Reformed Religion? Or was it necessary that this immense glasshouse of Britannia should vanish before the stones began to be thrown?

The combustion of this megahyaline monument without
beauty and without utility was announced by the B.B.C. with
so ludicrous a straining after elegiac solemnity that sane men
might have apprehended how near at this time the country
was to losing its sense of proportion.

In the Press accounts of the end of the Crystal Palace the
same hysteria was noticeable; but there was some excuse for
that. By Tuesday morning, December 1st, the whole of
Fleet Street knew that the story of the King's proposed
marriage and the attitude towards it of Mr Baldwin and his
Cabinet of echoes could not be kept out of the great London
dailies many hours longer. It has already become one of the
idle ' ifs ' of history to speculate whether if the British Press
had responded to King Edward's desire for frankness there
would ever have been a crisis; but it is certain that the way in
which that crisis was first postponed and then precipitated
brought the King the maximum of unnecessary pain and the
country the maximum of unnecessary anxiety.

A general belief has grown up that when Mr Baldwin made
himself responsible for the handling of the King the Editor of
The Times made himself responsible for the handling of the
people. It was common talk in Fleet Street that a leading
article delivering what amounted to an ultimatum to the King
was already in type at Printing House Square, and it was
presumed that this leading article was to be published at the
moment most serviceable to the plans of those who had resolved
that the King should not have his way. It was the actual
timing of the whole business which first put into people's heads
the notion that there had been a conspiracy to push the King
off the Throne. There was no conspiracy, though in certain
quarters there was ill will toward the King. Once the Government had agreed to oppose the King's marriage its main preoccupation was to make this opposition effective at the smallest
cost to its own prestige. Throughout, the King must be
presented as the prime mover in the matter with complete
freedom of choice. He was now, to put it crudely, to be given
enough rope to hang himself. The verdict was to be suicide,
whether *felo de se* or while temporarily of unsound mind; that
at one time the country seemed to be considering a verdict of
wilful murder against the Government promoted the alarm in
high circles which inspired those desperate efforts throughout
1937 to satisfy the country that the verdict was the right one.
It was not Mr Baldwin's handling of the emergency during

those difficult days that stirred the hearts of so many of his countrymen to the profoundest resentment of any political action since the days of Cromwell, but what seemed a remarkable failure to use his personal influence or his homely eloquence to protect the ex-King in whose abdication he had apparently acquiesced with such benefit to his own reputation. And indeed when people recovered from the excitement and were able to examine the sequence of events with a measure of judicial detachment there was much to rouse suspicion.

The great newspaper-proprietors and editors of Fleet Street appear now like women holding their breath at a scene in which a pistol may be fired and sighing with relief when the shot is heard off stage. Thus may be described the effect of that leader in the *Yorkshire Post*. We can acquit the *Yorkshire Post* of giving the signal. That was given by *The Times* on November 30th. The attack started on December 1st.

The excuse was the Bishop of Bradford's address to his Diocesan Conference on Tuesday, December 1st, an address which was primarily occupied by an assertion of the Anglo-Catholic position in the matter of the Coronation against the anti-sacramental utterances of the Bishop of Birmingham. In the course of this theological wrangle Dr Blunt took it upon himself to make the remarks which have already been quoted about the need of the King for grace. Until the Bishop decides to tell us on which side of the Atlantic he was speaking without confusion of mind or corrects his words if wrongly reported, it would be a waste of time to theorise whether he was acting in accord with any deliberate plan : whether, for instance, as certain newspapers stated, he was aware on November 17th, the day after that second interview with Mr Baldwin, that the King had declared his intention to abdicate if his decision to marry Mrs Simpson did not meet with official approval. Before we leave the Bishop of Bradford, a few sentences, the importance of which have been overlooked, should be extracted from his Diocesan Address :

> At the Coronation Service, the King holds an avowedly representa-
> tive position. His personal views and opinions are his own and, as an
> individual, he has the right of everybody to be keeper of his own
> private conscience. But in his public capacity at his Coronation he
> stands for the English people's idea of Kingship. It has been for
> centuries an essential part of that idea that the King needs the grace
> of God for his office. In the Coronation ceremony the nation
> definitely acknowledges that individual need. Whatever it may

mean, much or little, to the individual who is crowned, to the people as a whole it means their dedication of the English monarchy to the care of God, in whose rule and governance are the hearts of Kings. Secondly, and far more important than the King's personal feelings at his Coronation, are the feelings of the people of England towards it. Our part in the ceremony is to fill it with reality, by the sincerity of our belief in the power of God to overrule for good our national history, and by the sincerity with which we commend King and nation to His providence.

Those observations might have been used as an argument in favour of the King's proposed solution of the difficulty by making the lady he married his wife but not his Queen. The *Yorkshire Post* preferred to believe that Dr Blunt was not at all concerned with the spiritual obligations of the British nation but entirely with the King's domestic future.

Here is the leader, which is offered for contemplation as some ungainly piece of ordnance that survives a war is offered to a municipal park:

THE KING AND HIS PEOPLE

The Bishop of Bradford said yesterday that the benefit to be derived by the people from the King's Coronation would depend in the first instance on " the faith, prayer and self-dedication of the King himself." * Referring to the moral and spiritual side of that self-dedication, the Bishop said the King would abundantly need Divine grace if he were to do his duty faithfully, and he added: " We hope that he is aware of his need. Some of us wish that he gave more positive signs of that awareness."

Dr Blunt must have good reason for so pointed a remark. Most people, by this time, are aware that a great deal of rumour regarding the King has been published of late in the more sensational American newspapers. It is proper to treat with contempt mere gossip such as is frequently associated with the names of European royal persons. The Bishop of Bradford would certainly not have condescended to recognise it. But certain statements which have appeared in reputable United States journals, and even, we believe, in some Dominion newspapers, cannot be treated with quite so much indifference. They are too circumstantial and have plainly a foundation in fact. For this reason, an increasing number of responsible people is led to fear lest the King may not yet have perceived how complete in our day must be that self-dedication of which Dr Blunt spoke if the Coronation is to bring a blessing to all the peoples of the Empire, and is not, on the contrary, to prove a stumbling-block.

---

* The Bishop did not say this. It would start another theological wrangle to discuss what he did say ; but the excerpt quoted above will show the line he was taking. It was the benefit, under God, to the King himself not to the people to which Dr Blunt was referring.

When King Edward succeeded King George " the well-beloved," the nation acclaimed him with the glad conviction that he would indeed, as he himself promised, follow in his father's footsteps. Deep disappointment must necessarily result if instead of this continuity of example, there should develop a dispute between the King and his Ministers such as must almost inevitably raise a constitutional issue of the gravest character. There is no man or woman in any rank of life who has not some conception of the very high demands which are made on the King-Emperor, demands which many men might well shun. But the demands carry with them to-day the greatest opportunity, perhaps, that could be given to any one man. The King, by manifesting his own grave sense of responsibility, can do more than any other man to ensure that his subjects likewise will be of one mind to walk warily in very dangerous days.

Besides the *Yorkshire Post*, the *Yorkshire Observer* with its associated papers the *Nottingham Journal* and the *Birmingham Gazette* and the *Northern Echo* commented in similar strain ; so too did the *Birmingham Post* which declared " the private and public life of the King-Emperor inseparable."

All that was required in Printing House Square now was a garnishing paragraph of a couple of dozen lines, and that *Times* leader which was believed to have been kept on ice since November 17th was ready to serve. This leader of December 3rd did not suggest any divergence between the King and his Ministers about the Constitution. It merely alluded in general terms to the gossip which had been stirred up by American newspapers and reads like a digest of what Mr Baldwin said to the King on October 20th. The main point stressed was that the personality of the King as a man must be merged in the high office he held. The *Trimmer* Halifax was quoted from the seventeenth century : " Princes might rather expect to be lamented than to be envied, for being in a station that exposeth them, if they do not do more to answer Men's Expectations than human Nature will allow." This was doubly true in the twentieth century. Private inclination must give way to public duty. It was left to the *Daily Herald* to declare that " a Constitutional crisis of a grave character has developed as a consequence of serious differences between the King and Cabinet."

But before we analyse the state of mind to which the Labour Party had by this time been reduced after Mr Attlee's interview with Mr Baldwin, it will be necessary to ascertain what happened at the interview between Mr Baldwin and the King on December 2nd. Mr Baldwin told the House of Commons on

December 10th that the King asked him to go and see him on December 2nd, adding that he had intended asking for an audience later in the week, because such enquiries as he thought proper to make about legislation for enabling the lady to be the King's wife without the position of Queen he had not yet completed. We may pause to wonder whether that morning the King had read the Bishop of Bradford's Diocesan Address and whether he had not some reason to suppose that his Government was choosing its own time for publicity.

The Prime Minister considered himself in a position to inform the King on December 2nd that his enquiries had gone far enough to show that neither in the Dominions nor here was there any prospect that the legislation the King had suggested would be accepted. To quote Mr Baldwin at this point, " His Majesty asked me if I could answer his question. I gave him the reply that I was afraid it was impracticable for those reasons." What reasons ? * It would appear that what Mr Baldwin was trying to tell the House was that he had sounded overseas opinion with such persuasiveness that he felt sure he would receive a formal refusal to legislate and that he felt entitled to draw in advance on that refusal and put the King out of his agony at once. That Mr Baldwin was uneasy may be guessed by a certain confusion which at this moment mars the classic simplicity of that great speech. If on November 27th the Cabinet gave the King an ultimatum before the Dominions had been consulted, it would have been vitally necessary to prevent the House of Commons and the people of the British Commonwealth from realising that the Statute of Westminster had been violated by not affording the King an opportunity to communicate directly through his Governors-General with the Dominion Governments and so bluffing the Dominion premiers into refusing legislation for a step constitutional law did not require to be taken. We shall hear presently that Mr Lyons received a personal and secret cablegram from Mr Baldwin on November 28th on the subject of the marriage. The date should be noted. While it was

---

* Humpty Dumpty's poem is recalled by this answer :

> " I sent a message to the fish :
> I told them ' This is what I wish.'
> The little fishes of the sea,
> They sent an answer back to me.
> The little fishes' answer was :
> ' We cannot do it, Sir, because——' "

true that there was no precedent for the King's wife occupying
the position proposed for her, there was equally no precedent
for her not occupying it. Indeed the only precedent in
connection with the King's marriage was his constitutional
right to choose his own wife and refuse or grant her a Coronation at his own will. Presumably on December 2nd the
King still had a faint hope, due no doubt to his belief that he
had done the Dominions some service, that those Dominions
might support his request and induce the British Cabinet to
modify its attitude. And now listen to Mr Baldwin's Cice-
ronian exposition of what happened when he had to tell the
King that the Dominion Premiers had toed the line :

"I do want the House to realise this : His Majesty said he
was not surprised at that answer. He took my answer with
no question, and he never recurred to it again. I want the
House to realise—because if you can put yourself in his
Majesty's place, and you know what his Majesty's feelings are,
and you know how glad you would have been had this been
possible—that he behaved there as a great gentleman ; he said
no more about it. The matter was closed. I never heard
another word about it from him."

There was a superb rhetorical effrontery, an effrontery
which we miss from the classic orators but which no doubt was
familiar enough in the mouths of the Roman tribunes, in Mr
Baldwin's reminding the House of Commons how glad they
would have been to do something they had never been given
an opportunity of doing ; but what word shall we use for his
suggestion that even such a gutta-percha House of Commons
could put itself in his Majesty's place? We can hardly
believe this was intended to be the piece of insolent condescension it appears and are driven to suppose that Mr Baldwin
in telling the House of Commons that his Majesty had
behaved as a great gentleman by saying no more about it was
pleading with them to accept his account of the whole matter
and be great gentlemen too. "That decision," Mr Baldwin
continued, "was, of course, a formal decision." What decision? Was such a decision taken at a Cabinet meeting of
November 27th and conveyed to the King that night? Mr
Baldwin had just admitted that even on December 2nd his
enquiries were not complete. He was certainly destined for
knighthood if not by the laws of chivalry at any rate by the
moves of chess. "That decision was, of course, a formal
decision, and that was the only formal decision of any kind

taken by the Cabinet, until I come to the history of yesterday." The history of yesterday was the formal abdication
of which we have yet to read, but note the express admission at
this point that the Cabinet *had* taken a formal decision. The
details and date of it are owed to history. When he had
finished what Mr Baldwin, with a certain looseness of phraseology in view of the King's silence, calls " that conversation,"
he pointed out to the King that " the possible alternatives had
been narrowed, and that it really had brought him into the
position that he would be placed in a grievous situation between
two conflicting loyalties in his own heart—either complete abandonment of the project on which his heart was set, and remaining
as King, or doing as he intimated to me that he was prepared
to do, in the talk which I have reported, going, and later on
contracting that marriage, if it were possible. During the
last days, from that day until now, that has been the struggle
in which his Majesty has been engaged. We had many talks,
and always on the various aspects of this limited problem."

.The Prime Minister was by now on velvet. We must infer
from Mr Baldwin's own account of what happened that before
the visit to South Wales he had been compelled to suggest that
he and his Cabinet might resign if the King was determined to
make the lady he wished to marry Queen. This possibility the
King had anticipated by announcing that he was prepared to
abdicate as an alternative. It was grievous news to Mr
Baldwin because, although as a remnant of the old Victorians
he could feel sure of his attitude's being endorsed by a large
number of electors, he was not perfectly sure whether they
were a majority, so that, if the King should abdicate and be so
ungentlemanly as to tell the country why, it would almost
certainly involve the Government's going to the country and
asking for a renewal of the country's confidence. This they
might obtain, or they might not. It is one of the glories
of English political life that everything, even the country, is
sacrificed to party, which, without attempting a paradox, may
fairly be counted as one of the great elements that make for
stability in the Government of this country.

Then came the South Wales visit, and under the impulse
of that misery he had beheld the King gave a promise to the
people which he desired to carry out. He sent for Mr
Baldwin again and asked if he had considered the proposal
about the private marriage. That gave Mr Baldwin, or
rather his mouthpiece in *The Times* an opportunity of saying :
" What is demanded is statutory recognition of the fact that

she is not fitted to be Queen." There was now no longer any possibility of the lady the King desired to marry becoming Queen. By suggesting a private marriage the King himself had destroyed that possibility because the orthodox marriage could now be presented to the country as something the King had rendered impossible; and as his Majesty, much to Mr Baldwin's unctuous and exuberant gratitude, had not pressed the matter of the private marriage, Mr Baldwin might hope that the abdication could be accomplished without the risk of the National Government's losing any of its prestige.

A full meeting of the Cabinet was held on the morning of December 2nd, after which the Prime Minister had his hour's audience with the King at Buckingham Palace. He then drove to 10 Downing Street where he had a consultation of an hour and a half with Sir John Simon, at which presumably he told Sir John that the King would certainly abdicate but that he would abdicate like a great gentleman, thereby relieving Sir John of any further strain upon his knowledge of constitutional law. Sir John as a lawyer may have suggested that the strict legality of the whole proceeding was not quite as watertight as it ought to be in dealing with the Overseas Dominions, and Mr Baldwin decided to secure himself against any possible chance of the Labour Party's making political capital out of the situation by having a heart-to-heart talk with Mr Attlee. Mr Lloyd George, commenting on the negotiations over the American debt, remarked that, " a business transaction between Mr Mellon and Mr Baldwin was in the nature of a negotiation between a weasel and its quarry." If this be true, one must add that political negotiation between Mr Baldwin and Mr Attlee was in the nature of a negotiation between that quarry and a lettuce. We shall never know what arguments Mr Baldwin used to frighten Mr Attlee, for it is improbable that either of them will run the risk of immortal ridicule by giving away the secret. We may, however, guess that Mr Baldwin hinted that the King was in a mood to defy his advisers and that he extracted from Mr Attlee an assurance that such Stuart conduct would never be countenanced by the Labour Party. Unless we assume this, there is no explanation of the announcement in the *Daily Herald* of December 3rd that there was a grave crisis between the King and the Cabinet or Mr Harold Laski's text-book exposition on the leader page of the "constitutional position of the King in the British system." Mr Laski ignored the immemorial right of the

Sovereign to decide for himself about his marriage and notify the Privy Council *not* the Cabinet of his intention. He insisted that " it does not matter what the subject of the advice is ; it is always in the discretion of the Ministers to tender it. Nothing save the formation of a new Government able to secure a majority in the House of Commons can justify the King in refusing to do what his Ministers advise him to do." In other words, the Labour Party would support Mr Baldwin for fear of having to take office and find themselves in the position of being set to solve the problem of non-intervention in Spain. Actually, as we know, there was no danger of the King's provoking a crisis, and so all that history will discover from Mr Laski's article is that the Labour Party were pusillanimous and that there had been no need to betray their pusillanimity. They had as much chance of finding themselves in office as of finding themselves in Valhalla. The rabbit had eaten the lettuce.

Besides this conversation with Mr Attlee on December 2nd the Prime Minister had a conversation with Sir Archibald Sinclair. Gulliver was not going to neglect Lilliput. One must presume that Sir Archibald was as docile as Mr Attlee, for all that the leading organ of Liberal opinion, the *News Chronicle*, did suggest in an admirably reasoned article that the King should marry Mrs Simpson as Duke of Cornwall. It was in effect almost the same as the King's own enquiry about the possibility of marrying as Duke of Lancaster. One would fain believe that the small Liberal group in the House of Commons would have supported such a proposal, but it must probably be attributed to liberal opinion in a sense other than political.

On the morning of December 3rd in Parliament, members found that Colonel Josiah Wedgwood had put down the following motion :

" In the opinion of this House, the oath of allegiance which they have already taken to King Edward VIII is unaffected by any form of Coronation ceremony, or by the presence or absence therefrom, of any dignitary or personage whatsoever ; nor will they substitute any other for the King of England."

This motion coupled with the fact that the moral, but not constitutional crisis, had been precipitated by the Bishop of Bradford's address naturally fed the rumour that the Archbishop of Canterbury had threatened to refuse to crown the

King if he avowed his intention of marrying Mrs Simpson. There is no reason to suppose the Archbishop had threatened anything of the kind. He is far too able a man not to recognise the wisdom of allowing the laity a free hand without premature ecclesiastical interference which might prejudice the whole issue. That broadcast was but the momentary intoxication of a great spiritual victory. The Ark was dancing before David.

The effect of Mr Baldwin's tender nibbling at Mr Attlee's green heart was perceptible that afternoon in Parliament when the submissive leader of the Opposition rose to perform the duologue which most people supposed had been rehearsed the day before:

> *Mr Attlee*: " May I ask the Prime Minister the following question, of which I have given him private notice—namely, whether any constitutional difficulties have arisen, and whether he has a statement to make ? "
>
> *Mr Baldwin*: " I have no statement to make to-day, but while there does not at present exist any constitutional difficulty, the situation is of such a nature as to make it inexpedient that I should be questioned about it at this stage."
>
> *Mr Attlee*: " May I ask the right hon. gentleman whether, in view of the anxiety that these reports are causing in the minds of many people, he can assure the House that he will make a statement at the earliest possible time that a statement can be made ? "
>
> *Mr Baldwin*: " I can assure the right hon. gentleman that all that he says I have very much in mind."

At this stage the curtain should have come down amid applause; but the effect of the duologue was seriously damaged by Mr Winston Churchill's rising to ask his right honourable friend to give the House an assurance that no irrevocable step would be taken before a formal statement was made to Parliament. This was the last thing Mr Baldwin wanted to promise. And Mr Churchill was no lettuce. Indeed at that moment he must have presented himself to the rabbit as a most aggressive terrier. Mr Baldwin replied he had nothing to add to the statement he had just made, but he would consider and examine the question his right honourable friend had asked. With this the rabbit retreated into its burrow.

At six o'clock that evening the first item of news from the B.B.C. was that game of pat-ball between the Prime Minister and Mr Attlee, the latter serving. This was the first that thousands of people in remote parts of the country had heard of this world-shaking event and it was presented to them in a misleading form for which the Government must be held responsible.*   In London at the same time the pent-up secrecy of months exploded in the evening papers to burn with wilder and ever wilder rumours throughout the country.   This was the first taste the King was to receive of the response to his own behaviour as a great gentleman.   That evening Mr Baldwin visited Buckingham Palace again.   We do not know whether he made any excuses for the disgraceful way in which the King's Government had betrayed the King's confidence. What simile can one find for them ?   They were like showmen who had set fire to their tent and run away leaving a caged lion to the flames.   After Mr Baldwin quitted the Palace at 10.40 p.m. the King went to Marlborough House and saw Queen Mary and the Duke and Duchess of York.   Later, he drove to Fort Belvedere.   That night Mrs Simpson was driven to Newhaven to catch the Dieppe boat escorted by the King's Lord-in-Waiting, Lord Brownlow.   This Government of all the talents could not even guarantee her safety.

That evening there had been a great meeting in the Albert Hall at which Mr Winston Churchill, and Sir Walter Citrine head of the Trades Union Congress, had been present.   A voice in the audience had cried ' Long live the King !' and the volume of assenting cheers had been so vast that Mr Churchill had come away from that meeting confident that the King could be kept on the Throne.   It looked as if the Government would require something stronger than the bland assertion of a constitutional precedent now that other people seemed less inclined than the King to behave like great gentlemen.

Yet over in America Mr Hugh Walpole interviewed by a reporter made no mistake about the wind that would prevail at home.

" It is not because Mrs Simpson is an American," he affirmed, " that England would spurn her as a Queen.   It is because the Crown, that very sensitive ideal, would lose caste by unity with a woman twice divorced." †

At this point it is right to beg the reader to hold his attention amid the apparent confusion of People, Parliament and

* The writer cannot pledge his memory to the exact words used, but he can assert that the country was misled by this announcement, and that the form in which it was made prejudiced the whole issue, as no doubt it was intended it should.

† Reported in *Sydney Morning Herald*, December 4th.

Press to one fact, which is that the issue of King Edward's abdication was by now to all practical purposes decided, and that the whole preoccupation of the Government was how that abdication might be carried out at the cost of the fewest possible votes to that Government when next it invited the confidence of the electorate. Inasmuch as it was a ' National ' Government, party could breathe comfortably behind the mask of patriotism. Yet there was a dread lest King Edward should insist on refusing to abdicate at the ' psychological moment ' that suited the Government: one uses with relish and deliberation a phrase of such bastard English for such a Government. Incredible as it may seem the most anxious fear which beset these showmen was that the lion should burst from his cage before he had been burnt to death and leave them wondering whether the insurance companies would pay up on the tent. The measure of the Government's gratitude for the help they received from the King in this regard may be read in Mr Baldwin's speech to the House of Commons, and since it is human nature to resent the emotion of gratitude the measure of that resentment was discernible in the Archbishop of Canterbury's broadcast.

When Mr Churchill came away from that great meeting in the Albert Hall, the cheers of seven thousand people resounding in his ears, he was sincerely convinced that if the country were given time to consider the situation calmly and recover from the shock of the sudden explosion of the news, abdication could be avoided. It was perhaps unfortunate that the statement published by Mr Churchill to the Press on Saturday December 5th followed a request from King Edward to Mr Baldwin that he might consult Mr Churchill as a friend, because it allowed the release of a poison-breathing rumour that Mr Churchill, with the King's approval, was trying to launch a King's Party and take the helm himself. The average Member of Parliament's knowledge of history is rather less than that of a child in the fourth standard, and the two words ' King's Party ' evoked a nightmare of Judge Jefferies in a black shirt, Lord Strafford in a brown shirt, Charles I with his Vandyck beard replaced by a Charlie Chaplin moustache, Sir Oswald Mosley in a Ramillies wig, a whole Cabinet crop-eared, and a second battle of Worcester with Mr Baldwin as a very inadequate Cromwell, and Mr Churchill as an all too adequate Rupert. A few extreme Conservatives had their own historical nightmare in which Mr Harry Pollitt appeared

as Jack Cade and Mr Willie Gallacher as Wat Tyler in a kind
of fancy-dress ball for the funds of the Communist Party.
What these historians forgot was that the previous King's
Party, which broke the power of the Whig obligarchy, was led
by Lord North and coincided with what all patriotic members
of the National Government should have believed the opening
of the most glorious epoch of British history.   Readers of this
book may even feel that Edward VIII was a more reasonable
King on whom to found a party than George III.   As a
matter of cold fact these nightmares were a superfluous excitement, for King Edward VIII never considered for one moment
the possibility of such a Party.   Here is Mr Churchill's
statement which was circulated to the Press :

> I plead for time and patience.   The nation must realise the character
> of the constitutional issue.   There is no question of any conflict
> between the King and Parliament.   Parliament has not been con-
> sulted in any way, nor allowed to express any opinion.
>
> The question is whether the King is to abdicate upon the advice
> of the Ministry of the day.   No such advice has ever before been
> tendered to a Sovereign in Parliamentary times.
>
> This is not a case where differences have arisen between the
> Sovereign and his Ministers on any particular measure.   These could
> certainly be resolved by normal processes of Parliament or dissolution.
>
> In this case we are in presence of a wish expressed by the Sovereign
> to perform an act which in no circumstances can be accomplished for
> nearly five months, and may conceivably, for various reasons, never be
> accomplished at all.
>
> That, on such a hypothetical and supposititious basis the supreme
> sacrifice of abdication and potential exile of the Sovereign should be
> demanded, finds no support whatever in the British Constitution.   No
> Ministry has the authority to advise the abdication of the Sovereign.
> Only the most serious Parliamentary processes could even raise the
> issue in a decisive form
>
> The Cabinet has no right to prejudge such a question without
> having previously ascertained at the very least the will of Parliament.
> This could, perhaps, be obtained by messages from the Sovereign to
> Parliament, and by addresses of both Houses after due consideration of
> these messages.
>
> For the Sovereign to abdicate incontinently in the present circum-
> stances would inflict an injury upon the constitutional position of
> the monarchy which is measureless and cannot fail to be grievous to
> the institution itself, irrespective of the existing occupant of the
> Throne.
>
> Parliament would also fail entirely in its duty if it allowed such an
> event to occur as the signing of an abdication in response to the advice
> of Ministers without taking all precautions to make sure that these
> same processes may not be repeated with equal uncanny facility at no

distant date in unforeseen circumstances.   Clearly time is needed for searching constitutional debate.

The next question is—What has the King done ?   If it be true, as is alleged, that the King has proposed to his Ministers legislation which they are not prepared to introduce, the answer of Ministers should be not to call for abdication, but to refuse to act upon the King's request, which thereupon becomes inoperative.

If the King refuses to take the advice of his Ministers they are, of course, free to resign.   They have no right whatever to put pressure upon him to accept their advice by soliciting beforehand assurances from the Leader of the Opposition that he will not form an alternative Administration in the event of their resignation, and thus confronting the King with an ultimatum.   Again, there is cause for time and patience.

Why cannot time be granted ?   The fact that it is beyond the King's power to accomplish the purpose which Ministers oppose until the end of April surely strips the matter of constitutional urgency.

There may be some inconvenience, but that inconvenience stands on a different plane altogether from the grave constitutional issues I have set forth.

National and Imperial considerations alike require that before such a dread step as a demand for abdication is taken, not only should the constitutional position be newly defined by Parliament, but that every method should be exhausted which gives the hope of a happier solution.

Lastly, but surely not least, there is the human and personal aspect.

The King has been for many weeks under the greatest strain, moral and mental, that can fall upon a man.   Not only has he been inevitably subjected to the supreme stress of his public duty, but also to the agony of his own personal feelings.

Surely, if he asks for time to consider the advice of his Ministers, now that at length matters have been brought to this dire culmination, he should not be denied.

Howsoever this matter may turn, it is pregnant with calamity and inseparable from inconvenience.   But all the evil aspects will be aggravated beyond measure if the utmost chivalry and compassion is not shown, both by Ministers and by the British nation, towards a gifted and beloved King torn between private and public obligations of love and duty.

The Churches stand for charity.   They believe in the efficacy of prayer.   Surely their influence must not oppose a period of reflection. I plead, I pray, that time and tolerance will not be denied.

The King has no means of personal access to his Parliament or his people.   Between him and them stand in their office the Ministers of the Crown.   If they thought it their duty to engage all their power and influence against him, still he must remain silent.

All the more must they be careful not to be the judge in their own case, and to show a loyal and Christian patience even at some political embarrassment to themselves.

If an abdication were to be hastily extorted the outrage so committed would cast its shadow forward across many chapters of the history of the British Empire.

On December 3rd *The Times* quoted the *Trimmer* to rein-
force an argument for the King's behaviour. We shall now
quote Halifax against the Government:

> Our *Trimmer* believeth, that by the advantage of our Situation,
> there can hardly any such Disease come upon us, but that the King
> may have time enough left to consult with his Physicians in Parliament;
> pretences indeed may be made, but a real necessity so pressing, that no
> delay is to be admitted, is hardly to be imagined, and it will be neither
> easie to give an instance of any such thing for the time past, or to
> presume it will ever happen for the time to come.

It will be noticed that Mr Winston Churchill suggests that
the King was being advised by his Ministers to abdicate, and
though it may be true that such a phrase telescoped the
procedure and gave Mr Baldwin an opportunity to relieve
himself of responsibility and throw it back upon the King it is
impossible for logic to allow Mr Baldwin anything more than a
verbal distinction with no essential difference. Mr Baldwin
first notified the King that the lady he proposed to marry
would not be acceptable as Queen, in other words that if the
King persisted in trying to make her his Queen, Mr Baldwin
and his Government would resign. The King then told
Mr Baldwin that he intended to marry Mrs Simpson and that
he was prepared to abdicate rather than, as we may suppose,
compel a disapproving Government to resign. Mr Baldwin
went away to think over this announcement. The King then
asked Mr Baldwin if it were possible for him to marry the
lady not as King but as a private individual, with an Act of
Exclusion. Mr Baldwin replied that this would involve legislation and that he did not think the Cabinet would wish to put
this before Parliament or invite the Dominion Governments to
put it before their Parliaments. Two days later, at an alleged
interview which was not mentioned in his speech, he presumably
notified the King that the Cabinet would not agree to such legislation. On December 2nd he certainly notified the King that
enquiries in the Dominions showed that the Dominion Governments would not agree to such legislation. No Parliaments
anywhere were given an opportunity of discussing anything
except a *fait accompli* by Mr Baldwin, and we shall see presently
when we read the account of the Canberra debate how completely the British people were deceived as to the true facts of
Australian feeling at any rate. The King notified his Ministers
that he would abdicate rather than not marry Mrs Simpson.
The Prime Minister tendered him formal advice that the

Government would not legislate for a morganatic marriage. This threw upon the King the responsibility of making a party question of his private affairs. He might have split the country into what very shortly would have been two irreconcilable factions, and his failure to form a stable Government would certainly have been branded by future historians as unconstitutional behaviour, who if they should allow him to have preserved the letter of the Constitution would certainly accuse him of violating the spirit of it. Regarding these contingencies one must accept the fairness of Mr Churchill's contention that the King was in effect abdicating on the advice of his Ministers. Mr Baldwin's business when he rose to address the House on December 10th was to repudiate such a suggestion and dispel all grounds for it. In the emotional excitement of the moment and with the help of a wax-work Opposition he succeeded.

With the aid of ruthless propaganda, at the moment of writing these words less vicious but not yet stopped, the various interests that welcomed King Edward's abdication have bulldosed the public; but it is inevitable that sooner or later restoratives will be applied, and already an examination of the facts presented by Mr Baldwin, without any of the enlightenment that the future may hope for, leaves no doubt about the King's constitutional behaviour; but such an examination leaves a very grave doubt about the Government's constitutional behaviour, a doubt which we shall not rely on Mr Winston Churchill to voice but on his Majesty's Opposition in the Australian House of Representatives. Of that, anon.

To return to Mr Churchill's statement. What frightened politicians was that observation about the freedom of his Majesty's Ministers to resign and the assertion that they had no right to solicit beforehand assurances from the Leader of the Opposition that he would not form an alternative administration. It was denied that such assurances had been solicited or obtained. The meekness of Mr Attlee made his denial difficult to accept, but we must have a sturdy faith and not emulate the agnostic earnestness of certain Anglican theologians over the great mysteries of the Christian religion. We must assume that Mr Attlee's salaams from the front Opposition Bench were not an acknowledgment of any bargain between himself and Mr Baldwin but that like a country bumpkin in a dusky lane he had been frightened by a turnip's head with a Charlie Chaplin moustache and a tasselled smoking-cap, and that his own convincing pallor had frightened the rest of those diapason mouth-organs of democracy into a dribbling silence. Whatever else Mr Baldwin's renown may or may not be in history, he will never be accused of being unable to say ' bo ' to a goose. The writer had the pleasure of taunting one of the junior members of the Labour Party with the recreancy of his leaders, at which this young Rienzi declared that he and many another potential tribune had felt strongly that it was the duty of such a democratic body to withdraw and take no part in a dispute about such an anachronism as a king. However, they were quickly whipped into line, these revolutionary hacks. *Sic itur ad astra.*

Apart from the suggestion that his Majesty's Ministers were free to resign, the greater part of Mr Churchill's statement was taken up with a passionate plea for time and patience, and Mr Churchill is owed the justice of at least as much faith in his disinterestedness as Mr Baldwin in his own. He has always been too proud to preach his own disinterestedness, and his very pride has told against him with a nation which is so curiously susceptible to a well-staged modesty. That Mr Churchill would not have refused the King's invitation to form a Government may be true, but that he ever attempted to develop the situation toward that end is not true. He believed that time would solve the problem. He may even have believed—this is the merest speculation—that the King would change his mind about his resolve to marry. The King, however, had made up his mind. The King recognised that his mind being made up it would be doing wrong both to the brother he desired should succeed him and to his people to prolong unduly the state of suspense. Even that poor delay of a week was not due to him but to the Government's anxiety to get everything settled as comfortably as possible. It was to this end that he sacrificed his own feelings by allowing it to appear that he was still making up his mind. We know now to our relief that the makers of Coronation mugs reaped a double profit by selling as souvenirs all those they had already made for King Edward's Coronation and all those they would make for King George's ; but if one Coronation mug had remained unsold it was a Government pantry that should have bought it.

This is a suitable moment to remind readers that the succession had to be settled as well as the abdication. King Edward had always had a frank admiration for the Duke of York's character and abilities, and in taking the decision he did, after Mr Baldwin had made it perfectly clear to him that it was to be impossible for him to marry Mrs Simpson and remain King, with a working Government, that decision was strengthened by the knowledge that from no angle could a breath of criticism touch the Duke.   There is some doubt whether the Duke of York did not for a while hold out against succeeding and advocate the succession of Princess Elizabeth with a Regency ; but until the facts are published we are in the region of surmise, and all we have a right to say is that the Duke of York in painful and difficult circumstances did sacrifice all his personal feelings to serve his country and his brother.   This obedience to the call of duty has been so gratefully recognised by the country that loyal subjects of his present Majesty have a right to resent the campaign to defame the Duke of Windsor, not merely because it is directed against a Royal figure whom they esteem, but also because the dignity of his present Majesty is assailed by the notions such propaganda against his brother fosters.

The first fever of propaganda against the Duke of Windsor may have been due to a dread in certain Court and Government circles lest the new King's health might break down under the strain and lest his elder brother's return to the throne might become a fact with which they had to reckon.   No doubt there were many guilty consciences whose owners were aware that they had done all they could to exaggerate the state of affairs which was alluded to in the Archbishop's broadcast.   The instinct of such people was to build up as rapidly as possible such a legend about the ex-King as would make his restoration unimaginable in any circumstances.   It will always be a regret to many of us that King Edward VIII was not allowed an opportunity to display those qualities he had displayed as Prince of Wales ; but those who feel that regret will allay it with the reflection that the people of Great Britain were frightened of the experiment, and that therefore it would have been impossible for King Edward to display those qualities even if he had remained on the Throne.   His own decision to abdicate was a recognition of this fact, and the most devoted of his admirers are willing to bow before his far-sightedness and desire only to express their admiration for the courage and the sincerity with which he dared abide by his own judgment.   They are not content, however, to surrender another step of ground, and those who believe that the Duke of Windsor will gradually pass out of sight and out of mind as a discredited figure are warned that this will not happen. They are further warned that any revival of slander will cause severe discontent among the more vital part of the population. The country is already sufficiently divided on political issues to imperil gravely the effectiveness of its foreign policy, and should that foreign policy collapse a domestic crisis is inevitable. No Government has ever dealt such a blow to the prestige of the Throne as Mr Baldwin's Government in 1936. In the words of the Marquis of Salisbury, speaking in the House of Lords on December 10th of that year:

" I cannot help saying, my Lords, how profoundly I feel the formidable character to this country of an abdication. An abdication of a Sovereign is a momentous, almost a desperate act. He has a mandate from nobody to whom he can return his trust. He sits there by an authority which is outside the ordinary human methods of appointment, and his abdication is a wound in the body politic which is a disaster. It leaves it mutilated. No doubt his successor, whom we shall do our utmost to serve, will amply vindicate the traditions of his forefathers; yet we shall know for all time that there has happened in this country the abdication of a Sovereign."

Lord Salisbury had previously expressed his appreciation of the way Mr Baldwin and his colleagues had borne themselves and represented the nation in this crisis, but when Lord Salisbury spoke those words neither he nor anybody else had had time to study the damning facts of Mr Baldwin's exegesis. Much will depend on the ability of the present Government to avert war. Should that calamity befall it is certain that the abdication of King Edward will be regarded as one of the causes that brought it about, and the people of this country will ask in wrath why that abdication was forced upon him.* What was no doubt the honest belief of his advisers that marriage with the woman he loved would undermine monarchy will seem a pestilent superstition to a country in arms, and Mr Baldwin who sowed the wind with such stolid determination may live to see the reaping of a whirlwind.

On Friday, December 4th, there had been a good deal of talk about proposals and theories put forward by various papers that the King should marry privately, and the possibility of this had been given extra weight by a rumour that no less a person than Sir John Simon had advised such a course.

* Not by the Government directly, but indirectly by playing upon his generosity.

That afternoon in the House, Mr Attlee, whose dependence on time and time only during these anxious days gives him the air of a B.B.C. announcer, rose obediently to ask Mr Baldwin if he had any statement to make. Mr Baldwin replied:

" In view of the widely circulated suggestions as to certain possibilities in the event of the King's marriage, I think it advisable to make a statement.

" Suggestions have appeared in certain organs of the Press yesterday, and again to-day, that, if the King decided to marry, his wife need not become Queen. These ideas are without foundation. There is no such thing as what is called morganatic marriage known to our law.

" The Royal Marriages Act of 1772 has no application to the Sovereign himself. Its only effect is that the marriage of any other member of the Royal Family is null and void unless the Sovereign's consent, declared under the Great Seal, is first obtained. The Act, therefore, has nothing to do with the present case. The King himself requires no consent from any other authority to make his marriage legal.

" But, as I have said, the lady whom he marries, by the fact of her marriage to the King, necessarily becomes Queen. She herself therefore enjoys all the status, rights and privileges which both by positive law and by custom attach to that position, and with which we are familiar in the case of her late Majesty Queen Alexandra, and her Majesty Queen Mary, and her children would be in the direct succession to the Throne.

" The only way in which this result could be avoided would be by legislation dealing with a particular case. His Majesty's Government are not prepared to introduce such legislation.

" Moreover, the matters to be dealt with are of common concern to the Commonwealth as a whole, and such a change could not be effected without the assent of all the Dominions. I am satisfied, from enquiries I have made, that this assent would not be forthcoming.

" I have felt it right to make this statement before the House adjourns to-day in order to remove a widespread misunderstanding. At this moment I have no other statement to make."

Mr Baldwin was probably right in declaring that there was no such thing as morganatic marriage in our law, but it was begging the question. Morganatic marriage is a custom and does not depend so much on the law as upon the will of the prince who grants that marriage. If that prince is not a ruling monarch himself, it is the custom of the ruling monarch to whom that prince owes suzerainty to mark his approval of such a morganatic marriage by conferring a title on the wife. Such was done in the case of the Archduke Ferdinand. Such was done when Countess Claudine Rhédey was made Countess Hohenstein. Such was done when Prince Alexander of Hesse's wife was created Princess of Battenberg. Such was done, it must be maintained, when Queen Victoria created Lady Cecilia Buggin Duchess of Inverness, for there was certainly no law in Great Britain, common, canon, or heraldic, which could make the wife of H.R.H. the Duke of Sussex the Duchess of Inverness. It was indeed an exercise of the Royal prerogative, and there is no doubt whatever that if King Edward VIII had insisted he could have exercised the Royal prerogative with regard to his own marriage.

We may digress for a moment to note that *The Times* when commenting in a leader on Mr Baldwin's learned observations would not admit the word ' morganatic ' to the English vocabulary but printed it in inverted commas like a piece of American slang. It is useful to remind *The Times* that on March 13th 1904 its obituary of the Duke of Cambridge said, " H.R.H. married morganatically the late Miss Louisa Fairbrother, who was known as Mrs Fitzgeorge," and that in recording this fact no demand was made upon the inverted commas of Printing House Square. We must add to *autres temps autres moeurs*, *autres temps autres mots*. Perhaps after this excursion into the past of *The Times* readers will be less inclined to believe the assurance in that leader that " this is no crisis precipitated by a Government composed of Mrs Grundys or of snobs." There was no doubt *The Times* was alarmed by the proposed solution. It recognised the vital importance of taking advantage of the surprise and allowing public opinion no chance to deliberate; it was this anxiety which revealed the wish of those in touch with the editorial office that King Edward would abdicate. *The Times* was even prepared to hand out lollipops to the *Daily Herald* like an old gentleman to his best-behaved grandchild.

At the bottom of this article, with a headline all to himself, the report that Sir John Simon was at variance with his colleagues on the point at issue was declared to be without foundation. It was as well to make this contradiction. In the absence of the Lord Chancellor, Sir John Simon was the

Q

highest legal authority in the Government, almost deputy-keeper of the King's conscience, and if Mr Baldwin's jaunty exposition of English law were unsupported by counsel's opinion the consequences might be unpleasant. But for this contradiction we might have believed that Sir John Simon had reminded Mr Baldwin about the refusal of George IV to grant Queen Caroline a coronation, or even admittance to the Abbey when she drove up in her robes attended by Lord Hood. That did not sound as if ' positive law and custom ' exacted for that Queen all the ' status, rights and privileges attached to her position.' However, Mr Baldwin had been encouraged that morning by the hostile murmurs of the House when Mr Churchill repeated his question of the day before, asking for an assurance that no irrevocable step would be taken before a statement was made in the House. Mr Baldwin had nothing to add to what he said yesterday, and for this defiance of Parliament by a Prime Minister he was loudly cheered.

That evening, the Archbishop of Canterbury issued the following statement :

" At this moment of deep anxiety and bewilderment in the public mind I venture to express two earnest hopes.

" The first is that, during this critical week-end, and especially on Sunday, those who have a duty to speak to the people from the pulpit or otherwise will refrain from speaking directly on the matters which have arisen affecting the King himself and his subjects.

" Words spoken with imperfect knowledge of an extremely difficult situation can give no helpful guidance, and may only mislead or confuse public thought and feeling. Silence is fitting until the ultimate decisions are made known.

" Secondly, I hope, and indeed I take it for granted, that on Sunday prayers will be offered in all our churches, as surely they must be continually offered in the hearts of all Christian people, that God may in these momentous hours overrule the decision of the King and of his Government for the lasting good of the Realm and Empire."

How far the Anglican clergy generally obeyed his Grace's request does not appear from contemporary newspaper reports, but there was plenty of Puritan eloquence on tap, and by Monday Scotland and the provinces felt sure that the King's morals were sadly inferior to those of his great-grandmother. Much damage to the King's case was done by the papers of the Allied Press. It is fair to add that Lord Camrose and his brother had long been staunch supporters of Mr Baldwin and that their attitude during these December days was therefore consistent.   At the same time, the fact that Lord Rothermere's papers supported the King did not detract from the vigour with which Lord Camrose's papers pressed against him.   It must have been a wonderful moment in the office of the *Daily Telegraph* when its editor could feel for the first time since the reign of King Edward VII that its leaders were exerting an influence on public opinion, a moment which could have been grudged by nobody able to remember that proud poster ' Over half a million daily.   Largest circulation in the world.' The attitude of Lord Beaverbrook is less easy to understand. Most of the time his papers were strongly supporting the King; but sometimes they seemed to waver, and an outsider might have fancied that there were two parties with opposing views on the directorate.   There was no doubt, however, of Lord Craigavon's attitude.   To reporters waiting to inter-view him after his visit to the Prime Minister on Saturday evening the sagacious and broad-minded Premier of Northern Ireland had nothing to say but two words : ' Trust Baldwin.' They were as impressive as a tip from the owner of the Derby favourite on the eve of the race.

That week-end was fatal to the King's cause.   The shock to the country of the sudden revelation had made the issue purely a moral one for the present.   Constitutional decisions, legal niceties, and political expediencies were all submerged beneath a flood of village gossip.

With the provincial Press unanimously hostile to the King there was no chance to present the King's point of view accurately or justly.   Even if this had been possible, it would have taken too long to penetrate the prejudice.   Down in London crowds could jeer in Downing Street and be dispersed by the police for singing *God save the King*.   Down in London Cabinet Ministers could be frightened into their cars with pallid faces, but that did not help the King in the provinces. To the provinces the King was in love with another man's wife and most disgracefully he wanted to marry her.   That good man Mr Baldwin was doing his best to stop such a marriage.   Members of Parliament who went down to their constituencies that week-end returned to London determined not to lose a vote by being suspected of supporting such a state of affairs.   On Friday, there had been an appreciable number of Conservatives and a certain number of back-bench

Labour members with no hope of office in the future who had determined that Parliament should be asked to endorse the decisions of the Cabinet, but on Monday practically all these malcontents had been frightened by their constituents and were cheering as loudly for Mr Baldwin as the rest. Over that week-end the Government made diligent enquiries through various Ministries about the way the wind was blowing. The writer is not able to say how the country was divided among them for this census of opinion, but he can assert that Inverness-shire was canvassed by the Ministry of Health, and that various prominent residents in the county received confidential enquiries by telephone asking for their opinion about the reaction of the majority to the King's abdication. We may surmise that even the Milk Board helped in this grand assessment of popular feeling, and the secret service that week-end must have felt like boy-scouts at a jamboree.

That Monday afternoon, when the members of the House of Commons reassembled after their stethoscopic examination of the hearts of their constituencies, in the moving words of *The Times*, " all other sounds were swamped for a full minute by a full-throated cheer raised as Mr Baldwin entered." He might have been going in to bat for England, whose cricket team to the alleviation of public distress were engaged in making an unexpectedly stout resistance to the Australian bowling at Brisbane. When Mr Baldwin took his stand at the wicket Colonel Wedgwood rose to ask for a discussion of the motion placed by him on the order paper.

' No, sir,' Mr Baldwin replied sternly, as he drove that long-hop to the boundary.

Colonel Wedgwood attempted a supplementary question.

" Arising out of that answer, may I ask the right honourable gentleman whether he can at least give us an assurance that the fatal and final step of abdication or acceptance of abdication——" but the rest of his words were lost in a howl of disapproval from the democratic pack.

To quote *The Times*, " Mr Baldwin remained in his seat after answering, looking grave and somewhat worn, but certainly fresher than at any time since the present trying period began." The howling down of a loyalist like Colonel Wedgwood must have been as refreshing as a lemon-squash to a batsman who had been stonewalling all day for England.

At last the moment came for Mr Attlee to ask his question, which he did as punctually and politely as a footman bringing in the afternoon tea.

" May I ask the Prime Minister whether he has anything to add to the statement which he made on Friday ? "

Mr Baldwin expanded.

" Yes, sir.   I am glad to have the occasion of making a further statement on the position.

" In considering the whole matter it has always been, and remains, the earnest desire of the Government to afford to His Majesty the fullest opportunity of weighing a decision which involves so directly his own future happiness and the interests of all his subjects.

" At the same time they cannot but be aware that any considerable prolongation of the present state of suspense and uncertainty would involve risk of the gravest injury to national and imperial interests, and indeed no one is more insistent upon this aspect of the situation than his Majesty.

" In view of certain statements which had been made about the relations between the Government and the King, I should add that, with the exception of the question of morganatic marriage, no advice has been tendered by the Government to his Majesty, with whom all my conversations have been strictly personal and informal.

" These matters were not raised first by the Government, but by his Majesty himself, in conversation with me some weeks* ago, when he first informed me of his intention to marry Mrs Simpson whenever she would be free.

" The subject has been for some time in the King's mind, and as soon as his Majesty has arrived at a conclusion as to the course he desires to take, he will no doubt communicate it to his Governments in this country and the Dominions.

" It will then be for those Governments to decide what advice, if any, they would feel it their duty to tender to him in the light of his conclusion.

" I cannot conclude this statement without expressing— what the whole House feels—our deep and respectful sympathy with his Majesty at this time."

When the statement was finished " the House showed its plain reluctance to have any supplementary questions at all " ; but we are not surprised to read that " Mr Attlee changed its reluctance into approval as far as he was concerned " by saying :

" Everyone will agree with the sympathy expressed by the

---

* On October 20th in fact, not on November 16th as Mr Baldwin would presently inform that House of Commons on the security of whose ears willingly lent he was to pledge his credit with history.

Prime Minister in the last words of his statement. (*Cheers.*) I am assuming from his statement that his Majesty has not yet come to a decision on the advice tendered to him on a morganatic marriage,* and if this is so it is difficult to press the Prime Minister for a further explanation at the present time.

" But I would like him to bear in mind, and I am sure he does, that the House and the country is deeply anxious to receive the fullest information as soon as possible, as without that it is not possible to have any proper discussion on these issues."

Mr Baldwin gained even louder cheers by the following reply :

" I am obliged to the right hon. gentleman for the point he has put. I was not aware that he was going to put it, and I am grateful to him because I agree with every word of it. (*Cheers.*) I shall be only too glad at the suitable moment to give the House the fullest information of which I am capable. While I am willing to answer supplementary questions, as the House knows, I think that the whole House will agree with me that at this moment, when the situation is so grave and anxious, and while the King is considering these matters and has not yet made up his mind, I should feel great difficulty in answering supplementary questions, especially considering that those answers would have to be improvised." (*Cheers.*†)

Mr Baldwin expressly stated here that there was no collusion between him and Mr Attlee, which looks as if Mr Attlee's subordination had roused the suspicions even of that completely uncritical House of Commons ; but when Mr Churchill, " who had been leaning forward in his corner seat below the gangway with set and flushed face, rose to put a further question, the House turned impatient. As Mr Churchill uttered the first mystifying and familiar words of his now usual request that ' no irrevocable steps should be taken ' there were cries on all sides of ' no ' and ' sit down '." This *The Times* described as " the most striking rebuff of modern parliamentary history," and went on to regret that Mr Churchill did not attempt to move an adjournment so that the House would have been able to see for the first time the insignificant size of the section which was following him. Mr

---

* What *does* this mean ?

† Of sympathetic horror at the notion of truth standing naked on the floor of the House ? That might have evoked the loudest cry of " I spy strangers " a Speaker ever heard.

George Lambert asked to vociferous applause if the Prime
Minister was aware that in this House there was a deep personal
sympathy with him, whereupon Mr Baldwin, refreshed by this
National Liberal's affectionate lick, rose to tell Mr Churchill
that he did not know yet, and could not know yet, what the
King might decide or how he might decide to act.   It was
quite impossible for him to enter into hypothetical questions.
After this, Mr Gallacher, the only Communist member
in the House, wanted to know if the Prime Minister was
aware that this crisis expressed a deeper crisis in the economic
system.   This uncomfortably intelligent question reduced
the House to laughter.   Mr Thurtle, a back-bench Labour
member, followed with another intelligent question, " Might
I ask the Prime Minister whether the point at issue between
Parliament and King—(cries of ' Oh ! ')—that is, the question
of a morganatic marriage—whether the opinion of the House
may be ascertained on that particular point ? "   No answer
was vouchsafed, and Mr Bellenger, another Labour member,
rose to ask whether, in view of the serious dislocation which
was being caused to industry and trade, the Prime Minister
would endeavour to obtain an early reply from his Majesty.
From such a question may be judged the profound ignorance
in the House of what was really going on.   That day
at a luncheon of the Anglo–French Club, Mr Churchill
had tried to counter the innuendoes of the Goverment Press
by declaring that neither in the letter nor in the spirit
would the King ever be found to act contrary to the
British Constitution.   Quotations from *The Times* of a
century earlier have shown what an intemperate youth it
spent, but in those days *The Times* did not represent more
than party.   It was not yet the recognised mouthpiece of
culture and sobriety.   Through the years the great paper
steadily enhanced its renown until it was even able to survive
the purchase and publication of the forgeries about Parnell
and retain its dignity as the mirror of respectable opinion.
The tragedy of the campaign it led against King Edward,
with the gratefully received support of the *Daily Herald*
and the *Daily Telegraph*, was that in the conduct of that
campaign it did represent what one would have desired to
call respectable opinion, and if there still exists throughout
the world an ineradicable belief that the proposed marriage
of the King was a godsend to those who distrusted his in-

fluence upon the country and decided upon his elimination, the evidence to provide apparent support for that belief may be found in the pages of *The Times* during that drear-nighted December of 1936.

On December 8th, the day after what *The Times* called " Mr Churchill's bad day," two leaders were devoted to aspects of the Royal Marriage Crisis in one of which it alluded to the " abominable insinuation that the Government are pressing the King to abdicate because he was too sympathetic in South Wales." Most of its arguments, however, that Tuesday morning were directed against the proposal of morganatic marriage which by now was lightened of its quotation marks :

> It is contended again that there are precedents for a morganatic union of the kind contemplated. There are none. No British precedents exist and no Continental precedents apply. The analogy from them is both false and foolish. Some Continental monarchs have been constitutionally restricted to wives of certain rank or birth. The morganatic marriage was a means whereby they could choose a wife outside the permitted circle, but without conferring upon her the status of a Royal consort. In England this has never been necessary. THE KING OF ENGLAND—it needs to be repeated—is to-day, and throughout history has ever been, completely free in his choice of a wife, irrespective of rank and nationality, and is trammelled by no obligation to the Constitution or to his advisers. There has, as LORD ROTHERMERE says, been no suggestion at any time from any quarter that the lady for whom the morganatic exception is recommended should become Queen. Yet in law—apart from the fact that she is not legally free to remarry—there is nothing to bar her from becoming Consort and Queen in the full sense. The disqualification here is not, as on the Continent, one of law, but of fact. What is demanded is statutory recognition of the fact that she is not fitted to be Queen. The Prime Ministers of the Empire are to be asked to propose, and the Parliaments to accept and ratify, a permanent statutory apology for the status of the lady whom the KING desires to marry. The Constitution is to be amended in order that she may carry in solitary prominence the brand of unfitness for the Queen's Throne. Can anyone in possession of his faculties imagine any Prime Minister moving, or any Parliament undertaking to support, a proposition so invidious and so distressing ?
>
> This foolish and deplorable product of misguided ingenuity must be cleared away once for all, and delicate and difficult ground will be freed of at least one superfluous encumbrance.
>
> Nor are its intrinsic embarrassments and absurdities the only reason for condemning its resurrection at this stage. Those who purport to be advancing it in HIS MAJESTY's interest are doing so in the face of the considered and unanimous decision of the five Empire Governments. In the form of advocacy which they have chosen, it is an

unpleasantly significant recrudescence of the same movement—in the same quarter—which threatened not long ago to depict the SOVEREIGN as in conflict with his elected and Ministerial advisers. It is also an attempt to force upon the KING a decision which is his and his only, and which he may be trusted to make in his own time with full regard for the Constitution of which he is a custodian and for the hereditary trust, written and unwritten, that came into his hands from his father ten months ago.

In the other leader *The Times* ventured to rebuke Mr Bernard Shaw for " an article which offended in every detail not only against every canon of taste but against its own plea." We need not search beyond that sentence for the phrase with which to condemn the extract cited above. It is beyond credulity that Mr Geoffrey Dawson, who had had the advantage of the Archbishop of Canterbury's spiritual direction at Magdalen College, Oxford, in the very year of King Edward's birth, should not have enjoyed the privilege of many earnest consultations with Mr Baldwin during this anxious time. In that case Mr Dawson must have known that it was Mr Baldwin who anticipated any possible desire of King Edward to make Mrs Simpson his Queen by implying that should he persist in such an intention his Ministers would resign. The King accepted this advice and notified Mr Baldwin that it was his intention to marry Mrs Simpson and that he was prepared to go. The King realised that, from the moment there was any question about the advisability of his marriage, nay, probably from the very moment that his intentions were a topic in the American and European Press, he had no alternative except to withdraw unless he was prepared to face the world in a position repugnant alike to decency, to honour, and to royal pride. Yet after the South Wales visit, emotion roused by the deplorable condition of his own principality, which was due primarily to Mr Baldwin's mishandling of the coal strike and had been aggravated by months of official jealousy and inertia, drove him to search for a compromise by which he could remain on the Throne and carry out worthily his duties of kingship. That compromise was rejected, and to that rejection the Editor of *The Times* chose to append an insult which the lady herself could not answer and from which the King could not protect her.

In March 1931 Mr Baldwin had denounced the *Daily Mail* and the *Daily Express* for insulting Mrs Baldwin by failing to report a public appeal she had made for maternity services :

" What the proprietorship of these papers is aiming at is power, and power without responsibility—the prerogative of the harlot throughout the ages."

If so comparatively trivial a slight could once upon a time set in motion such a landslide of indignant language why was that chivalry slumbering now ?

It is opportune to turn for a while to that lady to whom *The Times* saw fit to offer that insult.   What was there against her ?   She had divorced her first husband without any suggestion against herself and she had obtained a decree *nisi* against her second husband without any suggestion against herself.   Had it been supposed that she hoped to marry a third husband who was not in a public position of extreme eminence nobody would have heard a word of criticism.   She would have been in the position of hundreds of other American women to-day.   It is impossible to apply the laws of the Catholic Church to men and women outside that Church.   It has been shown that the laws of the Anglican Church still admit of so many diverse interpretations that in the present state of confusion and inconsistency it is impossible to lay down any discipline which is generally acceptable to Anglicans or can be effectively enforced.   Publicity, not of her own seeking, gossip, not of her own feeding, had distorted her friendship with King Edward. She had realised like any woman of the world what, in such circumstances, would be the effect of King Edward's avowed intention to marry her.   She had done all she could to dissuade him from his intention.   For that we have the authority of the man who loved her.   It was Napoleon who said of love that the only victory over it was flight.   If it had been that kind of love, we may readily believe that she might have won a victory ; but it is less easy to run away when the other person may be hurt mortally by such a desertion ; and if King Edward was prepared to lose what he has lost to gain what he has gained, men and women the world over may be awed by such a display of moral courage, and may humbly ask themselves whether they would have been capable of it.   With the words of that last broadcast from Windsor still in his ears the present writer admits himself incapable of surrendering to the impertinence of discussing why these two loved one another.   Since time began poets have tried to tell their love and finally have spoken only for themselves.   The proof of love lies not in words but in deeds, and those simple words from Windsor were so heavily fraught with courageous action and indomitable purpose that all Shakespeare's art could not have touched them with a more serene finality.

When the stored-up secrecy of months suddenly burst into flames ninety-seven per cent of the population of this country heard for the first time of Mrs Simpson's existence, and in circumstances calculated to create an intense resentment against her. Thanks to the skilful timing of the disclosure, to the unanimous disapproval of what was accepted as the serious Press, and to the failure of the lighter Press to introduce her to the public without resisting the temptation to place a premium upon news value at the expense of good taste, it was inevitable that even her personal safety should be a source of grave concern, and prudence made it imperative for her to be out of England while the problem remained unresolved. Hence her departure on the night of December 3rd escorted by Lord Brownlow, driven by the King's chauffeur, and guarded by a detective-inspector. The pursuit across France by news-paper correspondents might have been shorn of some of its anxiety and unpleasantness if anybody had had the fore-thought to warn the French Sûreté in advance. One or two writers have permitted themselves to sneer at this cinemato-graphic flight from Dieppe to Cannes, but the failure to secure a more tranquil journey cannot be blamed on Mrs Simpson. A refuge had been offered by Mr and Mrs Herman Rogers at their villa in Cannes, and this refuge she reached late at night on Saturday December 5th. Some ill-informed criticism was directed against allowing herself to be photographed, but this was done in order to raise the siege of the Villa Lou Viei in exchange for a promise from newspapermen that they would let her alone afterwards. This was an act of simple courtesy by a grateful guest. It may be unnecessary to offer even the most unimaginative reader a hint that few women can have experienced such a weight of anxiety and such an intensity of nervous strain as Mrs Simpson must have suffered during those December days in Cannes; but it is not out of place to recall the complete dignity of a lady who in the words of *The Times* was carrying " in solitary prominence the brand of unfitness for the King's Throne." The bluest blood in Europe might have turned pale as watered milk under such an ordeal. A faint echo of it comes to us from an announcement Lord Brownlow made on Monday, December 7th, to a specially convened meeting of Press representatives in the Hôtel Majestic at Cannes :

" What I have to say to-night is divided into two sections,

separate and distinct. First, a denial; secondly, an official statement from Mrs Simpson, which she has signed. The denial is as follows:

" Mrs Simpson has given no interviews of any sort or kind or made any statements to the Press whatsoever other than the statement I now make on her behalf.

" The following is the official statement by Mrs Simpson:

" Mrs Simpson, throughout the last few weeks, has invariably wished to avoid any action or proposal which would hurt or damage his Majesty or the Throne.

" To-day her attitude is unchanged, and she is willing, if such action would solve the problem, to withdraw forthwith from a situation that has been rendered both unhappy and untenable."

This statement, which was surely a model of dignified and simple frankness, was contemptuously dismissed by *The Times* as a dramatic offer to which it was surprising so much importance had been attached.

No wonder some people began to ask if *The Times* was afraid the King might find a way out.

The background darkened.

> Quo ruitis, generosa domus ?   Male creditis hosti.
> Simplex nobilitas, perfida tela cave.
>
> Whither away, illustrious House ?   It is ill to trust the foe.
> Simple and noble heart, beware the treacherous blade.

The next sensation in the newspapers was the arrival in Cannes of Mr Theodore Goddard, Mrs Simpson's solicitor, and his clerk Mr Baron, accompanied by a Dr Kirkwood. That was on the evening of Wednesday, December 9th. Rumour ran wild for a few hours until it was discovered that Mr Goddard had never flown before and that Dr Kirkwood had accompanied him as a friend to look after his heart. The official reason given for the visit by Lord Brownlow was the need of settling some business about the closing of Mrs Simpson's London house. Nevertheless, preposterous stories were circulated, some of which have even found their way into books. Without claiming that the following item of news necessarily explains that visit, it is better worth attention than most rumours. It is taken from *The Week* of December 16th 936:

When, as the London *Spectator* said in effect, the venerable head of a great law firm is hoisted into an aeroplane with his medical attendant to fly through a storm in which ordinary aircraft will not venture, it is unlikely that he is merely going to see a lady about a house. Apparently, however, the only English newspaper to deduce from his visit that something might be stirring in the Divorce Court was the Communist *Daily Worker*, and they secured a scoop. On Tuesday of Abdication week, just before the Register was closed for the evening, an Intervener filed an application to show cause why the Simpson divorce should not be made absolute. For the rest of the week, the Register was, for some reason, closed, and so no other paper could check up on the story and perhaps for this reason did not mention it. The Intervener had now withdrawn, but on Wednesday before Abdication his action was of vital importance because if the Simpson divorce was not to be made absolute, the constitutional problem was automatically solved. Yet, except for the *Daily Worker* this, perhaps the most important happening in the crisis, was entirely ignored.

We shall hear more of this Intervener in the Spring and learn that he was merely a busybody making use of that medieval relic, the King's Proctor.

In a leader of Wednesday, December 9th, entitled " A Lull " *The Times* displayed so accurate a knowledge not merely of the line Mr Baldwin had taken but of the very dates on which grave advice was offered, that whether Mr Baldwin was was empowered to communicate the gist of Cabinet decisions and personal conversations with the King to the Editor of *The Times* or whether the Editor combined clairvoyance with ratiocination has become a problem which awaits solution.

The facts set out by Mr Baldwin are worth recalling in this interval because it is clear that they must have been stated with the KING's full approval and are therefore the final answer to the charge that there has been any breach between HIS MAJESTY and his Ministers. Last Friday afternoon, replying to the LEADER of the Opposition, the PRIME MINISTER made a preliminary statement, the purpose of which was to cut short a certain line of speculative suggestion, which had been advanced in the British Press and elsewhere, but which by British law, custom, and existing sentiment was bound to be sterile, and meanwhile if continued might poison the public atmosphere in which the KING was pondering his choice. A further statement on Monday afternoon gave the first authoritative account of what had passed between the KING and his Ministers. With one notable exception, all the conversations had been " strictly personal and informal "—conducted, that is to say, under conditions permitting HIS MAJESTY to seek counsel in complete frankness and confidence from an older man of great public experience.   In these circumstances several weeks ago the KING informed MR BALDWIN of his desire to marry MRS SIMPSON whenever she should be free—she being then, presumably, in the position she still occupies, that of a petitioner for divorce passing through the probationary period before a decree *nisi* is made absolute.   It is surely unnecessary to argue that MR BALDWIN is incapable of being influenced, in what he may have said to HIS MAJESTY, by any other consideration than desire both for the KING's personal happiness and for the continued performance of the manifold duties of the Crown—the two elements of the present problem.   He may be presumed to have discussed with complete openness every circumstance bearing on either aspect of the case; but nothing he may have said amounted to what in the technical constitutional sense is called " advice", or exerted any pressure on the KING.

At the end of these informal conversations HIS MAJESTY's intentions were formulated in a definite proposal.   He desired to marry MRS SIMPSON, but not to confer on her the rank of Queen Consort of England, which in the present state of law cannot be denied to the KING's wife.   His proposal therefore required a change in the law; and, if the KING requires a change in the law, he must ask his Ministers to move Parliament accordingly.   At this stage therefore HIS MAJESTY for the first time consulted MR BALDWIN as the Prime Minister instead of the confidential friend, and asked for constitutional " advice ". Would the PRIME MINISTER introduce the necessary legislation ? MR BALDWIN has not given the date of the request, but it is known to have been in the last days of November.   He immediately consulted the Cabinet,* which then for the first time had the question of the KING's marriage under formal consideration.   Further, the suggested Bill would have affected the succession to the Throne, and so would have been of the kind that, according to what the Statute of Westminster defines as the " established constitutional position," requires the assent of all the self-governing Dominions.   At the KING's desire MR BALDWIN accordingly went on to consult all the Prime Ministers of the self-governing Dominions, so that, when he delivered his reply to the KING's question, he was able to say that he spoke in unison with all the Governments of the Empire.   The reply was to the effect that the Governments were not in favour of the proposed creation of a hitherto unknown kind of marriage, and that none of the Imperial Parliaments was likely to approve of it.   That is the only constitutional advice that has been offered to HIS MAJESTY at any stage in the present crisis; and it was tendered at his own request.   The date was in the middle of last week, almost simultaneously with the incident which caused the whole matter to be exposed to public controversy.

It is strange that the whole matter should have been exposed to public controversy almost simultaneously with that visit to the King on December 2nd, but it is not the first time in

* This seems to support the statement about that Cabinet meeting on November 27th.

English history that the advisers of the Crown have been aware of an impending explosion and used it in the service of the State. The powder-barrels of Guy Fawkes were of great use in their day.

Meanwhile, we must take advantage of this lull to make some investigations into what was happening at this time in one of the Dominions. As soon as the news reached Australia, Sir Robert Garran, an ex-Solicitor-General for the Commonwealth, set out to instruct Australians upon the legal aspects of the King's marriage. On December 3rd he wrote from Canberra that the Royal Marriages Act of 1772

" may at first sight be thought not to refer to the marriage of the King himself, but the King is a descendant of George II, and thus clearly within the terms of the Act. . . . The King, to contract a valid marriage, must either procure the consent of one of his Ministers to the affixing of the Great Seal or else give twelve months' notice of his intention to the Privy Council. In the latter case, he can still not contract a valid marriage if both Houses of Parliament within the twelve months have passed resolutions of disapproval. . . . In the event of the King going through the ceremony of marriage without the consent of a Minister * not only would the marriage be null and void, but every person assisting at the marriage . . . would be liable to the penalties of Praemunire. What these penalties may be, seeing that the Praemunire Act has been repealed may be a matter for conjecture."

As conjectural indeed as Sir Robert Garran's exposition of the Royal Marriages Act. On December 4th he wrote :

" Formerly under the Common Law the office of King of England was hereditary. . . . Since the Bill of Rights it has always been recognised that the title to the Crown is derived from Act of Parliament."

On December 6th Sir Robert Garran tried to hedge over the Royal Marriages Act after Mr Baldwin had announced in the House of Commons that the Act did not apply to the King.

" Doubtless he did not make this statement without the advice of the Crown Law Officers whose opinions are entitled to the greatest respect."

* A Cabinet Minister of course, not a minister of the Gospel.

If the Crown Law Officers read this testimonial from Sir Robert Garran, they must have found it hard to keep their wigs on. However, Sir Robert was not prepared to admit his fallibility but blethered on :

" There is no judicial decision on the question and nothing but a judicial decision could settle it, but it would be disastrous if, the King being married without the consent of a Minister, there were a doubt as to the status of his wife as a married woman and as to legitimacy of his children."

The pen of the man who created the Chancellor in *Iolanthe* is required. What did good Sir Robert mean by the consent of a Minister ? Was he seriously inviting Australia to believe that Mr Malcolm MacDonald or Mr Hore-Belisha could have given the King a licence to marry without reference to the rest of the Cabinet ?

On December 7th Sir Robert wrote :

" One inference seems to be that the King has asked Mr Baldwin to introduce certain legislation, and that Mr Baldwin after consulting the Dominion Prime Ministers, has refused to do so. Another inference is that the legislation for which the King asked was for the purpose of enabling him to contract a morganatic marriage. . . . If that were all that had happened there would be no crisis . . . the further inference is justified that the King has announced his determination to marry without such legislation."

In view of the fact that this sapient effusion was published six days after Mr Baldwin was supposed to have found out all that it was possible to find out about Dominion opinion, we are justified in asking whether British opinion or Dominion opinion was misled.

By December 8th Sir Robert Garran's head had cleared slightly and he succeeded in producing a reasonably fair presentation of the case which was published the next day. For the next two days Sir Robert's attention was distracted from the legal position of the King by the necessity of having to enter into an argument with Mr Curtin, the leader of the Opposition in the Australian House of Representatives, who had declared himself uncompromisingly hostile to the business of rigging Australian opinion to save the face of the British Government.

We shall now turn to Mr Curtin and those stalwarts of the Federal Opposition who fought for their King as tenaciously at Canberra as Australians had fought for their King at Gallipoli.

On December 7th Mr Lyons, the Prime Minister, declared " that the whole of his Cabinet was solidly behind him in his action in informing the Baldwin Government that the Commonwealth Government supported the views of his Government."

Mr Curtin denied at Melbourne that he had agreed to support Mr Lyons. Mr Attlee had given a similar denial. We shall see presently the difference in the mettle of the two men. Meanwhile, the official Labour organ in Sydney accused Mr Lyons of having deliberately sent the Federal Parliament into recess while he consulted with Mr Baldwin to bring about the King's abdication, and Mr F. A. Brodie, President of the Constitutional Association of New South Wales, published the fact that the Executive of the Association had cabled Mr Baldwin as follows :

" Strongly urge full delay. Public opinion in Australia seriously divided. Widespread feeling exists that abdication would be major disaster.

" The Association feels that the most disturbing feature of the constitutional crisis is the haste which has marked the actions of the British Cabinet. The Association is distressed to think that there has not been time for all the elements in the situation to be carefully weighed.

" There can be no doubt that an abdication is a calamitous event, the far-reaching consequences of which should be carefully thought out.

" It is obvious that Dominion Parliaments cannot have had time to despatch an acquiescence in the actions of the Cabinet, which in the circumstances is more than formal.

" The Association feels that a matter involving the British Crown is one not only for Parliamentary action, but also for the millions whose future may be jeopardised by a hasty irrevocable step."

On December 8th it was necessary for the Federal Minister to warn all broadcasting stations in the Commonwealth : " That they must refrain from sending over the air anything that might be likely to influence Australian public opinion on the issue." Serious action was threatened for any disregard of this warning.

Below may be read some of the broadcast statements which impelled that suppression of free speech :

" It is certain that in this battle between autocracy and democracy, the King is on the side of democracy."

" Mr Baldwin is certainly not speaking for the mass of the people."

" Mrs Simpson will make the finest Queen England has known."

" Although we know that, in the interests of the Empire, it is better that the King should accept the advice of his Ministers, we do not think that this advice should go so far as to decide the selection of his wife."

On December 9th the Federal Parliament met. The following report of the sitting, which lasted less than half an hour, is taken from the *Sydney Morning Herald* of December 10th 1936:

The Prime Minister (Mr Lyons) announced, when the House met, that it was not the intention of the Government to submit any business to the House to-day nor to answer questions without notice.

Mr Lyons, having obtained leave to make a statement, then said: " Shortly after the Parliament rose the possibilities of a serious Constitutional problem relating to the suggested marriage of his Majesty the King became apparent. The position is still uncertain, though we all hope profoundly that a crisis may be averted. In the circumstances, it seemed wise to the Government to recall members, as we would desire to be in a position to consult Parliament without delay in relation to any action which proves necessary.

" As the matter stands, and pending his Gracious Majesty's decision, Parliamentary discussion could no nothing but harm. All I need say as to the particular issues involved is that the Commonwealth Government concurs in the decision of the Government of the United Kingdom not to legislate for something in the nature of a morganatic marriage.

" In a state of affairs so delicate, so fraught with possibilities of good or ill, for the future of all of us, a respectful and sympathetic silence in Parliament is the best contribution we can offer to a happy solution. (Hear, hear.) May God strengthen his Majesty and guide his decision aright."

On the motion for the adjournment, Mr Curtin said that Parliament had been called together so that the Government might consult with it on a matter of supreme moment to Australia and to the Empire. He thought that the consultations should have begun with full and unfettered intimation to Parliament of the extent of the communications which had passed between Mr Lyons and the British Government. All of the facts, as far as was possible at present, should be made available.

" The Opposition has strong views on this very difficult and delicate matter," Mr Curtin went on. " It says that there must be no coercion by Ministers of this Dominion, or any other dominion upon the King in the choosing of his wife. (Labour ' Hear, hear.')

" The King, on the other hand, must not ask Parliament for any special legislation to suit his convenience in the choosing of his wife. He must choose his wife from among those ladies of the land to whom he may be lawfully married, as the law stands at present. In respect of any matter involving legislation, the King must accept the advice of his Ministers of State.

" We would object to the King, or the Parliaments, in the King's choice of a wife, arranging to confer upon her a lesser status than that of Queen. He must not be permitted in any way to alter the status of the lady whom he would choose to be his wife. Because he is King, his wife must and should be the Queen.

" The King must be fully prepared to accept all the natural and logical consequences of his marriage. If there should be children, they must come into the first line of succession to the British Throne.

" THE OPPOSITION WILL LEAVE THE KING UNFETTERED IN THE CHOICE OF HIS WIFE. IT WILL NOT AGREE THAT HIS SELECTION SHOULD BE IMPAIRED BY ANY INFLUENCE OF ANY SORT. THE KING MUST ACCEPT ALL RESPONSIBILITY TO HIS OWN CONSCIENCE AND TO THE EMPIRE FOR HIS CHOICE."

" We will not interfere with him, but we will not convenience him," Mr Curtin added. " The Labour Party hopes that the King will remain on the Throne, and the party desires to remain, as it will remain, loyal to King Edward VIII." (Labour cheers.)

Mr Beasley (Lab., N.S.W.) rose to speak, but the Minister for Defence (Sir Archdale Parkhill) moved that the question for the adjournment be put.

There was an immediate outcry from the Opposition Benches, and division bells were run.

" God save the King," called Mr James (Lab., N.S.W.).

Mr Beasley: " This is a fine way to ask members to remain silent."

Mr Brennan (Lab., Vic.): " When do we meet again ? "

When the Speaker (Mr Bell) called for order, Mr James cried out: " Anyhow, you gagged me and would not let me mention the King's name."

The Speaker asked that more respect should be paid to the Chair.

Mr Beasley (angrily): " I would not have given leave for any statement in these conditions. You will never get leave again. You want to drive him out."

As the House was dividing, Mr Beasley called to Ministers: " His thoughts for the masses are too democratic."

Mr James: " This will show little Teddy that someone is with him in Australia."

The Minister for Health (Mr Hughes) was voting with the Government, and Mr James called: " Billy Hughes is gagged again."

Messrs. McCall (U.A.P., N.S.W.) and Holt (U.A.P., Vic.) voted with the Opposition against the gag, but the motion was agreed to by 40 votes to 23.

There were eight absentees from the House.

When the Speaker announced the result of the division, Mr James interjected: " You want to have an election to test the country on this issue."

Mr Lyons (warmly): " You were not so keen on an election a little time ago."

There were flashes from cameras in the Press gallery during the division, and somebody among the Opposition benches hummed " God save the King."

When the motion for the adjournment was put, there were loud cries of dissent from the Opposition, and the division bells were rung a second time.

Messrs. McCall and Holt remained with their own party for this division, and the motion was agreed to, on a party basis, by 42 votes to 21.

The House was adjourned until 2.30 to-morrow afternoon.

More muffled bars of " God save the King " were heard, and, as members dispersed, Mr James cried out: " This will back him up."

New South Wales members of the Opposition had prepared a number of questions which they had intended to ask the Prime Minister when the House met, but as Mr Lyons intimated it was not the intention of the Ministers to answer questions without notice they later placed their questions on the notice paper for to-morrow

The questions were as follows:

MR GANDER (LAB., N.S.W.), TO ASK THE PRIME MINISTER: " (1) WHETHER THE COMMONWEALTH GOVERNMENT WAS ASKED FOR A DECISION ON ANY POINT OF A CERTAIN MATTER; IF SO, WHAT WAS THAT DECISION ? (2) WHETHER THE GOVERNMENT WAS ASKED FOR ANY ADVICE ON A CERTAIN MATTER; IF SO, WHAT WAS THAT ADVICE, AND WAS IT TENDERED TO THE BRITISH PRIME MINISTER OR TO ANOTHER PERSON ? (3) WHETHER, IN THE EVENT OF CERTAIN ADVICE TENDERED BY THE BRITISH PRIME MINISTER ON A CERTAIN MATTER BEING REJECTED AND THE BRITISH PRIME MINISTER RESIGNING, WOULD THE COMMONWEALTH GOVERNMENT BE INVOLVED IN ANY WAY AS THE RESULT OF THE ACTION TAKEN BY THE BRITISH PRIME MINISTER ? "

MR BEASLEY (LAB., N.S.W.), TO ASK THE PRIME MINISTER: " WILL HE EXPLAIN BY WHAT AUTHORITY HE TENDERED CERTAIN ADVICE TO THE BRITISH PRIME MINISTER ON A CERTAIN MATTER WITHOUT FIRST CONSULTING PARLIAMENT ? "

MR JAMES (LAB., N.S.W.), TO ASK THE PRIME MINISTER: " IS THE PRIME MINISTER PREPARED TO JUSTIFY THE ACTION HE HAS TAKEN IN REGARD TO A CERTAIN MATTER BY ASKING THE PEOPLE FOR ITS VERDICT AT AN ELECTION ? "

MR GARDEN (LAB., N.S.W.), TO ASK THE PRIME MINISTER: " (1) IS THE PRESS STATEMENT THAT THE BRITISH HIGH COM-MISSIONER (SIR GEOFFREY WHISKARD) SAT WITH THE CABINET DURING ANY OF ITS RECENT DISCUSSIONS ON A CERTAIN MATTER TRUE ? (2) IF SO, WILL THE PRIME MINISTER EXPLAIN WHAT RIGHT

Sir Geoffrey Whiskard had to participate in any discussion by an Australian Cabinet? (3) Was the Government instructed by the British Government to admit Sir Geoffrey Whiskard to its discussions? (4) Is it true that proposed legislation relating to a certain matter was submitted to Sir Geoffrey Whiskard?"

Another question to the Prime Minister was placed on the notice paper by Mr Holt (U.A.P., Vic.) as follows: "Will he inform the House whether the Government has obtained the views of his Majesty the King upon the Constitutional crisis through his Majesty's personal representative in the Commonwealth, the Governor-General, and, if not, will he take early steps to do so?"

So this is how matters stood in Australia on the eve of the abdication and it requires no comment to appreciate the deadliness of the questions placed on the notice paper by members of the Federal Opposition. Questions when unanswered can become accusations, and these questions which, as we shall hear, were never answered accuse the British Government of making a mockery of the Statute of Westminster. It was fortunate for Mr Baldwin that he had such a stout ally in the Premier of Canada, Mr Mackenzie King.

In curious contrast to this scene at Canberra was a news item from Canada on the same page of the *Sydney Morning Herald*:

ALLEGIANCE TO THE KING

Kitchener (Ontario) Dec. 9. The City Council has decided to defer passing the resolution renewing the Council's allegiance to the King "until a more suitable time presents itself."

On December 10 those awkard questions put down by members of the Federal Opposition were deliberately refused any answer by the closure. The *Sydney Morning Herald* reported:

When the House met at 2.30 p.m. prayers were read, and the Prime Minister (Mr Lyons) immediately moved that the House should adjourn. He said that the Government did not intend to reply to any questions without notice to-day.

"In connection with the matter I mentioned yesterday in this chamber, I have no further information, but I expect to be able to make a definite statement to the House to-morrow," Mr Lyons added.

Mr Lyons's statement was followed by jeers from the Opposition, particularly from the New South Wales section. The closure was applied in both Houses.

In the Senate, Senator Collings was called to order, when he demanded the right of direct approach to the King.

The leader of the Opposition (Mr Curtin) speaking on the motion for the adjournment, said that this was the second day on which the Prime Minister had immediately moved the adjournment. Mr Lyons had made no informative statement other than that Parliament had been recalled to deal with a certain matter. Apparently that matter had not yet arisen.

" Obviously steps have been taken somewhere, and may have been taken by this Government," he said, " which may lead to a decisive and irrevocable decision, although this Parliament, having been called together, has not been asked to deliberate as to whether that decision is one the Parliament agrees with or opposes. I submit that the Australian Government cannot be blind to the statements in the newspapers, or cannot be deaf to the rumours now in circulation."

Mr Curtin said that the opinions which apparently other Dominions had expressed were reported in the newspapers, whereas from the Commonwealth there appeared to be no information about the matter at all. He (Mr Curtin) had asked the Prime Minister on the previous day to make available to the House and to the country the whole extent of the communications which had passed between himself and the Government of the United Kingdom.

There had been no response. Members did not know what advice the Government had given to the Prime Minister of England or to the King. The King, as far as the Commonwealth of Parliament was concerned, was the King of Australia.

" I further suggest that Parliament is being put in a position now by the course taken by the Prime Minister of being silenced on a matter of major importance to the Throne, to Australia's membership of the Commonwealth of Nations, and to the succession to the Throne," added Mr Curtin. " This Parliament is to be silenced apparently while discussions and negotiations are proceeding, and presumably while advice is being tendered to his Majesty under circumstances which make it impossible for him to intimate to this Parliament his personal wishes in the matter. The Opposition is very much dissatisfied with the whole situation. We feel there is a great distinction between reticence on a grave and delicate matter, and the discharge of that major responsibility that rests on the Government and the Parliament. The Prime Minister owes it to the Parliament to-day, to a greater extent than yesterday, to make known what advice he has tendered to his Majesty, and what his Majesty has had to say in response to that advice, and make known the origin of the difficulty."

Mr Curtin said that Mr Lyons owed it to Parliament to make known whether the present difficulty was the result of the representations made to his Majesty or the outcome of suggestions made by his Majesty to the United Kingdom Government. He (Mr Curtin) objected to the Parliament of this self-governing dominion, which had the right in every major matter directly to advise the King, being reduced to the status of having merely to legalise whatever action might be taken in another Parliament without reference to the

Commonwealth. If the adjournment motion had not been moved he would have asked leave to move that the following resolution should be presented through the Governor-General to the King:

"We, the members of the House of Representatives of the Commonwealth Parliament, desire to assure your Majesty of our loyalty and allegiance, and to express our earnest hope that your Majesty will not relinquish the Throne."

Mr Curtin said that the opposition desired the Government to tender that advice to the King. That was the wish of the Australian Labour movement. Since the course of action he had proposed was impossible, he now moved, as an amendment to the adjournment motion, that all the words after " that " should be omitted with a view to the insertion of the words of the motion he had just mentioned. These words, he said, represented a specific statement of the wishes of the Opposition. No other advice which the Commonwealth had given to the King should be acceptable to the Parliament.

Mr Makin (Lab., S.A.) seconded the amendment, but the Speaker (Mr Bell) ruled it out of order, as all amendments to motions for the adjournment are out of order.

The Speaker's action was followed by many interjections, particularly from the New South Wales Labour members.

Mr Beasley (Lab., N.S.W.) rose to speak, but for the second time in two days he was prevented from doing so.

Mr Thompson (U.C.P., N.S.W.) moved that the question be put.

Mr Beasley (heatedly): " You are a lot of cowards."

Mr Lane (U.A.P., N.S.W.): " You should have shown your loyalty earlier."

Mr Beasley: " You are a hypocrite."

At the Speaker's demand Mr Beasley withdrew his remark.

The division bells were now ringing and the House divided on Mr Thompson's motion.

" Let negotiations go on till he is dumped," called Mr James (Lab., N.S.W.)

Mr Beasley (to Government members): " You have not got an opinion of your own."

There were more interjections and the Speaker warned Mr James.

The motion for the closure was agreed on a party division by 39 votes to 22.

" TWENTY-TWO WITH THE KING," CRIED MR MULCAHY (LAB., N.S.W.).

The Opposition then demanded a division on the motion for the adjournment.

MR BEASLEY: " THIS IS SEDITION—PUTTING A MONARCH OFF HIS THRONE WITHOUT CONSULTING PARLIAMENT."

Mr Mulcahy: " What does all your lip loyalty count for now ? "

Mr James: " Why, even the Speaker will not allow us to express loyalty to his Majesty. He has gagged us."

To-day's sitting lasted 25 minutes.

The House adjourned until 10.30 a.m. to-morrow, the voting for adjournment being on the party lines, with 39 votes to 22.

If a perusal of that scene in the Australian House of Representatives floods the cheeks of the Labour Opposition in Great Britain with as shameful blush as it should, they will be a redder party than they ever have been or are ever likely to be.

Twelve hours later at two o'clock in the morning, Mr Lyons broadcast to Australia the news of the King's abdication.

It may be admitted that the strongest expression of Dominion disapproval of the way the British Government had handled the crisis was given in Australia, but it would be a grave wrong to the judgment of those overseas Dominions to suggest that there was any approach to unanimity of the kind that was reported to the people of Great Britain. Nothing is easier than by quoting extracts from the leaders of famous papers from South Africa, Canada, Australia and New Zealand to suggest such unanimity, but the Dominion papers quoted were usually the organs of Government opinion, and the British Government had taken steps to secure the favour of that opinion. The *Sydney Daily Telegraph* was not quoted when it said :

> Cable messages arriving from London seem to suggest that an altogether disproportionate importance is being placed on the views of the Dominions. So far as Australia is concerned, the people have had no chance to express their opinions, and it is impossible to say whether or not they support the attitude of the Federal Government.

Nor was the *Ottawa Citizen* quoted when it wrote :

> It is possible that some consequences [of King Edward's abdication] would be felt too by some high authorities in the land who are asserting themselves as keepers of the King's conscience.
>
> An inherent sense of fair play would surely demand that this solicitude for the national conscience as reflected in the King's life shall also manifest itself more in the awakening of a conscience with reference to the living conditions of millions of the British people.
>
> King Edward has been unwilling to conform by going through the hypocrisy of a State-inspired marriage. He has rather remained single until, at the age of forty-one, he has apparently come to the point of daring to claim the right to decide for himself.
>
> It may be taken as certain that his Majesty is starting a train of thought that will lead to a searching of the British conscience in other directions, perhaps on the living conditions of destitute people on the Clyde, in South Wales, in Durham under the shadow of Durham Cathedral, and on Tyneside under the shadow of St. Nicholas's.
>
> It is probable that his Majesty has already given offence to some vested interests in showing up the official neglect of people in distress —as he did very soon after coming to the Throne when he visited the slums of Glasgow on the day of the launching of the *Queen Mary*.

A brief item of news from South Africa on December 6th is worth noting.

" While General Hertzog was speaking at Smithfield, a bearded Dutch farmer shouted in Africaans : ' What's going to happen to our King ? ' "

General Hertzog replied :   " If your father or your mother did wrong, you would not refer to it publicly.   Let us show delicacy by not discussing this matter publicly."

The South African Premier, who is so often credited with extreme nationalist sentiments, is evidently becoming more British than the British.   His remark to the Dutch farmer suggests that the situation was prejudged by the South African Government.   Nevertheless, in spite of what was believed to be the stern attitude of the Dutch Reformed Church toward divorce, a moderator of it declared in an interview that the King had a right to his own private life. General Hertzog's delicacy about moral issues appears to have been excessive.

Native Indian opinion was entirely favourable to the King. The *Ceylon Times* expressed the opinion of India and Ceylon in a heading across seven columns, " THE PEOPLE ARE WITH HIM.   THE KING MUST NOT GO."

On December 10th *The Times*, which seemed so well read in the thoughts of Mr Baldwin that it could hardly have written another leader upon what was happening behind the scenes without spoiling Mr Baldwin's speech next day, tried its hand at an exhibition of reading the thoughts of the nation, by writing a leader on the letters it had received from correspondents, " ranging from strict theological orthodoxy to frank, worldly wisdom."   The specimen of strict theological orthodoxy contains the passage :

" If the King marries a divorcee without the sanction of the Church, of which he is Defender, how can he retain his holy office of kingship, having just impugned the regulations that he is supposed to enforce, or at least uphold ? "

That this balderdash, whether we regard its theology or its history, should have been awarded space in the first leader of *The Times* on the eve of the King's abdication indicates the lengths to which *The Times* was prepared to go, the depths to which it was prepared to sink, to perplex public opinion. When we are told that this letter was dated from a well-known public school, we are presumably to understand that it was written by a master, for we can hardly suppose that *The Times* was indulging in the gross frivolity of publishing the letter of a fourth-form boy.   If the Church of England recognises the indissolubility of marriage, it could not sanction that marriage even to a King as hopeful of its subservience as Henry VIII.   The King is not Defender of the Church of England.   Henry VIII was granted the title of Defender of the Faith by Pope Leo X for his defence of the Seven Sacraments against Luther.   This title was retained by his successors until with a perfect sense of proportion King Edward relinquished it in his Deed of Abdication.   We need not discuss this letter further.   The answer to the rest of its contentions will have to be read in Chapter XIX of this book.

Other letters of various degrees of fatuity are then quoted, and finally, " a letter in which the writer does not think it necessary to include the close reasoning with which others support that case."   This letter is so typical of the prevailing hysteria of thought and expression that it seems worth while to preserve it :

> " Our King is being asked to give up the woman he loves that the Empire may still be on solid ground.   In the war and at the onset thousands of men gave up the women they loved at once and much more than the King is asked to—some gave everything.   I cannot believe that the King we have always loved and looked up to *can* fail to do the same for the British Empire."

This good lady, and with her many other good ladies, forgot that the King was willing to give up everything at the onset of the war and was not allowed to proceed with his battalion to France ; but hysteria is sometimes cruel, often indecent, and always unjust.   To that unreasonable woman may be quoted a letter of Lord Esher's written to the Prince of Wales on March 5th 1916 :

> " I wonder if you remember our talks at Balmoral when you were so miserable at leaving the Navy.   If you do, you can realise that I understand and have understood all along exactly what you are going through and have gone through !
> " It is so difficult to judge exactly where one's duty lies, when one's inclinations are very strong.   This country, which may presently be going through very difficult times— I mean some years hence—will require leadership from you,

and if the Empire is to hold together, you, thanks to what
you are and what you have done and are doing, will provide
a rallying point that no one else can provide.

" I know this sort of blunt statement which looks like
flattery, but is not, vexes you.   But it is true, and therefore
for England you must sacrifice much, all your inclinations,
your companions, your secret wishes.   It is a big sacrifice
but a noble one ! "

That leadership for which Lord Esher pleaded the Prince
had given.   When he felt himself incapable of giving that
leadership without the help and support of the woman he
loved he had the courage to say so.   He was informed by his
Prime Minister that there was no way by which his country
could grant him that help and support and that, painful
though it was, his country was prepared to do without him.
It was a refusal which was all but impeccable : the only flaw in
it was that the country was neither invited nor allowed to
participate in it, for the promissory note which Mr Baldwin
drew upon public opinion was honoured by a ductile Parliament.

On that 9th of December when the Editor of *The Times*
was reading extracts from his correspondence, the royal
family gathered at Royal Lodge, the home of the Duke and
Duchess of York in Windsor Great Park, and the King who
had not left Fort Belvedere for six days, arrived at 4 o'clock,
just about the time when Mr Attlee was due to rise in the
House of Commons and ask Mr Baldwin if he had any
further information to give.   Mr Baldwin regretted he had
nothing to add to-day, but he hoped to make a statement
to-morrow.   Mr Attlee asked him to give the House a good
hope that in his statement to-morrow the Prime Minister
would realise the anxiety which was continually increasing so
long as the matter was not dealt with.   Mr Baldwin was able
to assure the right honourable gentleman and the House that
no one realised that more than he did.   Then Mr Bellenger
bounced up to ask whether the Prime Minister was aware that
grave financial inconvenience was being caused to many subjects
in this country by the delay in coming to a decision, and would
the Prime Minister kindly suggest to his Majesty the necessity
of coming to an early decision ?   This crude and vulgar enquiry
was too crude and too vulgar even for that House of Commons,
several members of which ejaculated ' Oh ! '   Mr Baldwin, who

had been so curt with Colonel Wedgwood for his loyal and gentlemanly behaviour, found himself incapable of snubbing the egregious Mr Bellenger. He had had so many duologues with Mr Attlee that he had acquired some of Mr Attlee's meekness, and deprecatingly assured Mr Bellenger that the grave financial inconvenience had not escaped him. He did not add that Santa Claus had not escaped him, for to-morrow Mr Baldwin was to play Santa Claus himself.

On Thursday, December 10th, the Speaker of the House of Commons took the Chair at 2.45 p.m. All the seats on the floor of the House were occupied: the Members' Gallery, the Peers' Gallery and the Strangers' Gallery were thronged. The seats of the Ambassadors showed not a single vacancy. In the whole House there was room only for a single person, and to this seat amid the cheers of the House Mr Baldwin proceeded at half-past three o'clock, interrupting for a minute or two by his entrance the fifty-one questions on the order paper which had to be disposed of before the King's message could be read, a message which has left fifty times fifty questions unanswered, many of which through the caution or generosity of the chief actors in this drama may remain riddles until Doomsday. At the end of questions Mr Baldwin left the Treasury Bench and walked to the Bar of the House. Turning to the Speaker, he announced amid a solemn silence:

"A message from his Majesty the King, signed by his Majesty's own hand."

After bowing to the Chair, Mr Baldwin stepped forward and handed the message to the Speaker who read it. The Speaker's hand trembled so much that the shuffle of the three foolscap sheets with the scarlet seal was audible.

"'After long and anxious consideration, I have determined to renounce the Throne to which I succeeded on the death of my Father, and I am now communicating this my final and irrevocable decision. Realising as I do the gravity of this step, I can only hope that I shall have the understanding of my people in the decision I have taken and the reasons which have led me to take it.

"'I will not enter now into my private feelings, but I would beg that it should be remembered that the burden which constantly rests upon the shoulders of a Sovereign is so heavy that it can only be borne in circumstances different from those in which I now find myself.

" ' I conceive that I am not overlooking the duty that rests on me to place in the forefront the public interest when I declare that I am conscious that I can no longer discharge this heavy task with efficiency or with satisfaction to myself. I have accordingly this morning executed an Instrument of Abdication in the terms following :

" ' " I, Edward VIII, of Great Britain, Ireland, and the British Dominions beyond the seas, King, Emperor of India, do hereby declare my irrevocable determination to renounce the Throne for myself and for my descendants and my desire that effect should be given to this Instrument of Abdication immediately.
" ' " In token whereof I have hereunto set my hand this 10th day of December 1936, in the presence of the witnesses whose signatures are subscribed.
" ' " (*signed*) EDWARD R.I.' "

" ' My execution of this Instrument has been witnessed by my three brothers, their Royal Highnesses the Duke of York, the Duke of Gloucester, and the Duke of Kent.
" ' I deeply appreciate the spirit which has actuated the appeals which have been made to me to take a different decision, and I have, before reaching my final determination, most fully pondered over them.   But my mind is made up. Moreover, further delay cannot but be most injurious to the peoples whom I have tried to serve as Prince of Wales and as King and whose future happiness and prosperity are the constant wish of my heart.
" ' I take my leave of them in the confident hope that the course which I have thought it right to follow is that which is best for the stability of the Throne and Empire and the happiness of my peoples.   I am deeply sensible of the consideration which they have always extended to me, both before and after my accession to the Throne, and which I know they will extend in full measure to my successor.
" ' I am most anxious that there should be no delay of any kind in giving effect to the Instrument which I have executed, and that all necessary steps should be taken immediately to secure that my lawful successor, my brother, his Royal Highness the Duke of York, should ascend the Throne.
" ' EDWARD R.I. ' "

When the Speaker finished, a sigh was heard from all over the House, one could wish to add of unanimous sorrow, but that we bitterly know from too many it was a sigh of relief that business would once again be as usual, that the Christmas shopping could be resumed, that the Stock Exchange could get back to its gambling, and that makers of Coronation mugs could attend to their estimates and promise delivery. As the sigh died away, Mr Baldwin rose to move the motion, " That his Majesty's most gracious message be now considered."

The most self-confident of statesmen might have shown signs of nervousness at the double task before him of presenting the King's story without unfairness to the King and always with ample justice to himself. Yet we are informed by those who heard his performance of oratorical jugglery that Mr Baldwin evinced no more signs of nervousness than a well-trained servant who opens the door for his master to pass out.

Here is the full text of the story offered to the world :

" No more grave message has ever been received by Parliament, and no more difficult, I may almost say repugnant, task has ever been imposed upon a Prime Minister. I would ask the House, which I know will not be without sympathy for me in my position to-day, to remember that in this last week I have had but little time in which to compose a speech for delivery to-day, so I must tell what I have to tell truthfully, sincerely, and plainly, with no attempt to dress up or to adorn.

[*As early in the speech as this we have evidence of the tense, emotional condition of the orator's audience, for on any less tremendous occasion his implication that every speech he had made with due notice of the need for it had been untrue, insincere, and equivocal, dressed up and adorned for effect, would have drawn from the House of Commons a Gargantuan peal of derisive laughter.*]

" I shall have little or nothing to say in the way of comment or criticism, or of praise or of blame. I think my best course to-day, and the one that the House would desire, is to tell them, so far as I can, what has passed between his Majesty and myself, and what led up to the present situation.

[*So far as I can? Is this modesty about the form or reluctance about the matter of his narrative?*]

" I should like to say at the start that his Majesty, as Prince of Wales, has honoured me for many years with a friendship which I value, and I know that he would agree with me in saying to you that it was not only a friendship but, between man and man, a friendship of affection. I would like to tell the House that when we said ' Good-bye ' on Tuesday night at Fort Belvedere we both knew, and felt, and said to each other that this friendship, so far from being impaired by the discussions of this last week, bound us more closely together than ever, and would last for life.

[*This refers to the dinner which the Prime Minister had with the King, the Duke of York and the Duke of Kent on December 8th. It would be highly improper to suggest that those remarks on friendship were merely an expression of sentimental theory, and we can only account for Mr Baldwin's later failure to demonstrate the enduring adamant of this friendship in defending the Duke of Windsor against his traducers by the fact that as Swinburne wrote, " His life is a watch or a vision between a sleep and a sleep," a sleep whence he had emerged to handle the King's matrimonial project and into which he sank back exhausted by his own skill.*]

" Now, Sir, the House will want to know how it was that I had my first interview with his Majesty. I may say that his Majesty has been most generous in allowing me to tell the House the pertinent parts of the discussions which took place between us. As the House is aware, I had been ordered in August and September a complete rest which, owing to the kindness of my colleagues, I was able to enjoy to the full.

[*He was luckier than Sir Samuel Hoare in the previous December.*]

" And when October came, although I had been ordered to take a rest in that month, I felt I could not in fairness to my work take a further holiday, and I came, as it were, on half-time, before the middle of October and, for the first time since the beginning of August, was in a position to look into things.

[*Evidently Mr Baldwin's illness had been much more severe than the country had appreciated. It was a pity bulletins were not issued.*]

" There were two things that disquieted me at that moment. There was coming to my office a vast volume of correspondence, mainly at that time from British subjects and American citizens of British origin in the United States of America, from some of the Dominions, and from this country, all expressing perturbation and uneasiness at what was then appearing in the American Press. I was aware also that there was, in the near future, a divorce case coming on, the results of which made me realise that possibly a difficult situation might arise later, and I felt that it was essential that someone should see his Majesty and warn him of the difficult situation that might arise later if occasion was given for a continuation of this kind of gossip and criticism, and the danger that might come if that gossip and that criticism spread from the other side of the Atlantic to this country.

[*Mr Baldwin ignored the fact that gossip had already reached this country and that no attempt had been made by his Government to protect the King against such gossip in other countries. It was a misfortune that Mr Baldwin's doctors apparently forbade even the briefest consultation with the Editor of 'The Times,' who might have been able to explain to the simple politician the complicated motives which regulate the actions of the British Press. A decision might then have been reached to treat the situation in a dignified and straightforward manner and by such handling compel the American and European Press to treat it with equal dignity and straightforwardness. It was the silence of the British Press which encouraged indiscretion abroad, and for the silence of the British Press the failure of H.M.'s Government to face the contingencies must bear the sole responsibility.*]

" I felt that in the circumstances there was only one man who could speak to him and talk the matter over with him, and that man was the Prime Minister. I felt deeply bound to do it by my duty, as I conceived it, to the country, and my duty to him not only as counsellor, but as a friend. I consulted, I am ashamed to say—and they have forgiven me—none of my colleagues.

[*When we remember the horror the average British Minister has of any action for which he can be called to account, it is surprising to learn that there was no more emotional expression of relief than a general handshake. Mr Baldwin standing alone like a Casabianca on the burning deck of the Ship of State should have evoked some of those quick-flowing Parliamentary tears.*]

" I happened to be staying in the neighbourhood of Fort Belvedere about the middle of October, and I ascertained that his Majesty was leaving his house on Sunday, October 18th, to entertain a small shooting-party at Sandringham, and that he was leaving on the Sunday afternoon. I telephoned from my friend's house on the Sunday morning, and found that he had left earlier than was expected. In those circumstances I communicated with him through his secretary, and stated that

I desired to see him—this is the first and only occasion on
which I was the one who asked for an interview—that I
desired to see him, that the matter was urgent. I told him
what it was. I expressed my willingness to come to Sandringham on Tuesday, the 20th, but I said that I thought it
wiser, if his Majesty thought fit, to see me at Fort Belvedere,
for I was anxious that no one at that time should know of my
visit, and that at any rate our first talk should be in complete
privacy. The reply came from his Majesty that he would
motor back on the Monday, 19th October, to Fort Belvedere
and he would see me on the Tuesday morning. And on the
Tuesday morning I saw him.

[*The ingenuity with which Mr Baldwin secured the attention
of the House to what in the circumstances were utterly trivial
details will be noted by students of rhetoric in the future as an
example of the way a clever performer will make his audience
strain their ears in listening to a gnat while the padded feet
of a heavily loaded camel recede conveniently away into the
distance.*]

" Sir, I may say, before I proceed to the details of the
conversation, that an adviser to the Crown can be of no
possible service to his master unless he tells him at all times
the truth as he sees it, whether that truth be welcome or not.
And let me say here, as I may say several times before I finish,
that during those talks, when I look back, there is nothing I
have not told his Majesty of which I felt he ought to be aware—
nothing. His Majesty's attitude all through has been—let me
put it in this way : Never has he shown any sign of offence, of
being hurt at anything I have said to him. The whole of our
discussions have been carried out, as I have said, with an
increase, if possible, of that mutual respect and regard in
which we stood.

[*As Mr Baldwin will reiterate these asseverations of mutual
respect and regard, the critic cannot be blamed for reiterating his
asseveration that from the moment the Duke of Windsor left the
shores of his native land any evidence for the public manifestation
of Mr Baldwin's respect and regard is wanting.*]

" I told his Majesty that I had two great anxieties—one the
effect of a continuance of this kind of criticism that at that time
was proceeding in the American Press, the effect it would have
in the Dominions, and particularly in Canada, where it was
widespread, the effect it would have in this country.

" That was the first anxiety. And then I reminded him of

R

what I had often told him and his brothers in years past. The British Monarchy is a unique institution.

[*This assertion evokes a conversation-piece at which the mind shudders. We now understand Mr Bolitho's remark about the Prince of Wales's impatience of elder statesmen.*]

" The Crown in this country through the centuries has been deprived of many of its prerogatives, but to-day, while that is true, it stands for far more than it ever has done in history. The importance of its integrity is, beyond all question, far greater than it has ever been, being as it is not only the last link of Empire that is left, but the guarantee in this country, so long as it exists in that integrity, against many evils that have affected and afflicted other countries. There is no man in this country, to whatever party he may belong, who would not subscribe to that.

[*This was an excess of optimism. In the debate next day on this very speech, of the eight members who discussed Mr Baldwin's motion no less than three refused to subscribe to this assertion.*]

" But while this feeling largely depends on the respect that has grown up in the last three generations for the Monarchy, it might not take so long, in face of the kind of criticism to which it was being exposed, to lose that power far more rapidly than it was built up, and once lost, I doubt if anything could restore it.

" That was the basis of my talk on that aspect, and I expressed my anxiety and desire that such criticism should not have cause to go on. I said that, in my view, no popularity in the long run would be weighed against the effect of such criticism. I told his Majesty that I for one had looked forward to his reign being a great reign in a new age—he has so many of the qualities necessary—and that I hoped we should be able to see our hopes realised. I told him I had come—naturally. I was his Prime Minister—but I wanted to talk it over with him as a friend to see if I could help him in this matter. Perhaps I am saying what I should not say here; I have not asked him whether I may say this, but I will say it because I do not think he would mind, and I think it illustrates the basis on which our talks proceeded. He said to me, not once, but many times during those many, many hours we have had together, and especially toward the end, ' You and I must settle this matter together; I will not have anyone interfering.'

[*It was suggested in another chapter that this decision reached by the King and his Prime Minister was not strictly constitutional, but on reconsidering the remark that was repeated without the King's permission the speculation occurs whether ' anyone ' may not have been the Archbishop of Canterbury and that the King desired that the matter should be settled without reference to ecclesiastical prejudice.*]

" I then pointed out the danger of the divorce proceedings, that if a verdict was given in that case that left the matter in suspense for some time, that period of suspense might be dangerous because then everyone would be talking, and when once the Press began, as it must begin sometime in this country, a most difficult situation would arise for me, for him, and there might well be a danger which both he and I had seen all through this—I shall come to that later—and it was one of the reasons why he wanted to take this action quickly—that is, that there might be sides taken and factions grow up in this country in a matter where no faction ought ever to exist.

" It was on that aspect of the question that we talked for an hour, and I went away glad that the ice had been broken, because I knew that it had to be broken. For some little time we had no further meetings. I begged his Majesty to consider all I had said. I said that I pressed him for no kind of answer, but would he consider everything I had said ? The next time I saw him was on Monday, November 16th. That was at Buckingham Palace. By that date the decree *nisi* had been pronounced in the divorce case. His Majesty had sent for me on that occasion. I had meant to see him later in the week, but he had sent for me first. I felt it my duty to begin the conversation, and I spoke to him for a quarter of an hour or twenty minutes on the question of marriage.

[*It is not clear why, after Mr Baldwin was so careful to point out to the House that on this occasion the King had sent for him, he should have taken it on himself to talk for twenty minutes about marriage before presumably he knew what the King wanted to talk to him about. Perhaps it was Mr Baldwin's anxiety to let the House know that he was technically exculpated from what ' The Times ' called the " abominable and malignant insinuations that pressure had been brought to bear upon the King by his Ministers."*]

" Again, we must remember that the Cabinet had not been in this at all. I had reported to about four of my senior colleagues the conversation at Fort Belvedere.

" I saw the King on Monday, November 16th, and I

began by giving him my view of a possible marriage. I told
him that I did not think that a particular marriage was one that
would receive the approbation of the country. That marriage would have involved the lady becoming Queen. I did
tell his Majesty once that I might be a remnant of the old
Victorians, but that my worst enemy would not say of me that
I did not know what the reaction of the English people would
be to any particular course of action, and I told him that so far
as they went, I was certain that they would be impracticable.
I cannot go further into the details, but that was the substance.
I pointed out to him that the position of the King's wife was
different from the position of the wife of any other citizen in
the country; it was part of the price which the King had to pay.
His wife becomes Queen: the Queen becomes the Queen of
the country; and, therefore, in the choice of a Queen the
voice of the people must be heard. It is the truth expressed
in those lines that may come to your minds:

> " ' His will is not his own;
> For he himself is subject to his birth,
> He may not, as unvalued persons do,
> Carve for himself; for on his choice depends
> The safety and the health of the whole State.'

*[Even for the reminder of this apt quotation Mr Baldwin
may have been indebted to ' The Times ', where on December
8th the fourth leader headed " Authors as Exhibits," a letter from
Lieut-Colonel Kidd of Camberley informed the Editor that he
had opened Shakespeare at random that morning and those very
lines had leapt to his eye. That, however, is of less importance than
to note that it was Mr Baldwin who as a remnant of the old
Victorians notified the King that he was convinced the people of
England—he did not claim to speak then except for England—
would not allow the lady he proposed to marry to be Queen. We
shall read presently that Mr Baldwin sent a secret and personal
cable to the Premier of Australia on November 28th informing him
" that the King had told him he intended to marry Mrs Simpson, but
that at the same time he appreciated that the idea of her becoming
Queen and her children succeeding to the Throne was out of the
question." Thus having prejudiced the Australian Premier's
mind against Mrs Simpson, he subsequently asked for an
opinion about the private marriage. Presumably the other
Dominions were informed to the same effect and the people of this
country have a right to resent the action of a Prime Minister who
tells one story to the Dominion Premiers and another story to the*

House of Commons. In any case, it was not Mr Baldwin's constitutional right to communicate the King's intention to the Dominion Premiers. That was the King's right speaking through the mouths of his Governor-Generals. The Statute of Westminster was evoked to justify the necessity for consulting the Dominions about the King's marriage, but the letter and the spirit of it were conveniently violated by a ductile and ignorant House of Commons at the behest of a Prime Minister who chose to forget that he was not the Prime Minister of the King of Australia, the King of Africa, the King of Canada, the King of New Zealand and the King of Ireland.]

"Then his Majesty said to me—I have his permission to state this—that he wanted to tell me something that he had long wanted to tell me. He said, ' I am going to marry Mrs Simpson, and I am prepared to go.' I said, ' Sir, that is most grievous news, and it is impossible for me to make any comment on it to-day.' He told the Queen that night; he told the Duke of York and the Duke of Gloucester the next day, and the Duke of Kent, who was out of London, either on the Wednesday or the Thursday; and for the rest of the week, so far as I know, he was considering that point.

" He sent for me again on Wednesday, November 25th. In the meantime a suggestion had been made to me that a possible compromise might be arranged to avoid those two possibilities that had been seen, first in the distance, and then approaching nearer and nearer. The compromise was that the King should marry, that Parliament should pass an Act enabling the lady to be the King's wife without the position of Queen; and when I saw his Majesty on November 25th he asked me whether that proposition had been put to me, and I said yes. He asked me what I thought of it. I told him that I had not considered it. I said, ' I can give you no considered opinion.' If he asked me my first reaction informally, my first reaction was that Parliament would never pass such a Bill. But I said that, if he desired it I would examine it formally. He said he did so desire. Then I said, ' It will mean my putting that formally before the whole Cabinet, and communicating with the Prime Ministers of all Dominions, and was that his wish ? ' He told me that it was. I said that I would do it.

" On December 2nd the King asked me to go and see him.

[The country is still waiting to know why if it took place that meeting on November 27th was ignored in this meticulous narrative ;

or why if it did not take place the assertion in print that it did was ignored.]

"Again I had intended asking for an audience later that week, because such enquiries as I thought proper to make I had not completed. The enquiries had gone far enough to show that neither in the Dominions nor here would there be any prospect of such legislation being accepted. His Majesty asked me if I could answer his question. I gave him the reply that I was afraid it was impracticable for those reasons. I do want the House to realise this : His Majesty said he was not surprised at that answer. He took my answer with no question, and he never recurred to it again. I want the House to realise—because if you can put yourself in his Majesty's place, and you know what his Majesty's feelings are, and you know how glad you would have been had this been possible—that he behaved there as a great gentleman : he said no more about it. The matter was closed. I never heard another word about it from him.

[And if the King kept silence like a great gentleman to avoid embarrassing Mr Baldwin, we can add that for the same reason, the mother of Parliaments held her tongue like a perfect lady.]

"That decision was, of course, a formal decision, and that was the only formal decision of any kind taken by the Cabinet until I come to the history of yesterday. When we had finished that conversation, I pointed out that the possible alternatives had been narrowed, and that it really had brought him into the position that he would be placed in a grievous position between two conflicting loyalties in his own heart— either complete abandonment of the project on which his heart was set, and remaining as King, or doing as he had intimated to me that he was prepared to do in the talk which I have reported, going, and later on contracting that marriage, if it were possible. During the last days, from that day until now, that has been the struggle in which his Majesty has been engaged. We had many talks, but always on the various aspects of this limited problem.

"The House must remember—it is difficult to realise—that his Majesty is not a boy, although he looks so young. We have all thought of him as our Prince, but he is a mature man, with wide and great experience of life and the world.

[A wide enough and great enough experience, one might have supposed, to choose a wife. It is a delicious tribute to Mr Baldwin's

*opinion of the House of Commons that he felt it was necessary to ex-
plain to the members that the King was not a boy.   We may sympathise with Mr Baldwin's anxiety about the level of intelligence
in that House of Commons, but we might hesitate to publish it to
the world.*]

" And he always had before him three, nay four, things,
which in these conversations at all hours, he repeated again
and again—That if he went, he would go with dignity.   He
would not allow a situation to arise in which he could not
do that.   He wanted to go with as little disturbance of his
Ministers and his people as possible.   He wished to go in
circumstances that would make the succession of his brother
as little difficult for his brother as possible ; and I may say that
any idea to him of what might be called a King's Party, was
abhorrent.   He stayed down at Fort Belvedere because he said
he was not coming up to London while these things were in
dispute, because of the cheering crowds.   I honour and respect
him for the way he behaved at that time.

[*So all those scarecrows which had frightened the robin-redbreasts
of Labour, the blue-tits of Conservatism, and that decrepit dodo,
the Liberal Party, had been a waste of ingenuity !   There never
was any likelihood of 'what might be called a King's Party'.   That
Dickens never met Mr Baldwin must be counted as the greatest
loss the Comic Muse has sustained.*]

" I have something here which, I think, will touch the
House.   It is a pencilled note, sent to me by his Majesty this
morning, and I have his authority for reading it.   It is just
scribbled in pencil :

" ' Duke of York.   He and the King have always been on
the best of terms as brothers, and the King is confident that
the Duke deserves and will receive the support of the whole
Empire.'

" I would say a word or two on the King's position.   The
King cannot speak for himself.   The King has told us that
he cannot, and does not see his way to carry, these almost
intolerable burdens of kingship without a woman at his side,
and we know that.

[*If Mr Baldwin and the House of Commons " representing "
the nation did know that, why could not they have been as
frank as the King whose frankness Mr Baldwin went on to
praise ?*]

" This crisis, if I may use the word,

[*It was rather late in the day to apologise for using a word which had been used by others the world over with the deadliest intention of prejudicing the King's case.*]
" has arisen now rather than later from that very frankness of his Majesty's character which is one of his many attractions. It would have been perfectly possible for his Majesty not to have told me at the date when he did, and not to have told me for some months to come.   But he realised the damage that might be done in the interval by gossip, rumour, and talk, and he made that declaration to me when he did, on purpose to avoid what he felt might be dangerous, not only here, but throughout the Empire, to the moral force of the Crown which we are all determined to sustain.

[*Note his Majesty's appreciation of the damage that could be done by gossip, rumour, and talk, and then recall how that frankness of his was betrayed.*]
" He told me his intentions, and he has never wavered from them.   I want the House to understand that.   He felt it his duty to take into his anxious consideration all the representations that his advisers might give him, and not until he had fully considered them did he make public his decision.   There has been no kind of conflict in this matter.   My efforts during these last days have been directed, as have the efforts of those most closely round him, in trying to help him make the choice which he has not made ; and we have failed.   The King has made his decision to take this moment to send his Gracious Message because of his confident hope that by that he will preserve the unity of this country, and of the whole Empire, and avoid those factious differences which might so easily have arisen.

[*We must pause a moment to savour the exquisite euphemism " trying to help him make the choice which he has not made" as a phrase to express those days of mental agony throughout which, in the words of one of his friends, the King stood like the rock of Gibraltar.*]
" It is impossible, unfortunately, to avoid talking to-day about one's self.   These last days have been days of great strain,

[*Trying to help the King make the choice which he has not made . . . but we have long been familiar with Mr Baldwin's capacity for self-commiseration.*]
" but it was a great comfort to me, and I hope it will be to the House, when I was assured before I left him on Tuesday night, by that intimate circle that was with him at the Fort that

evening, that I had left nothing undone that I could have done to move him from the decision at which he had arrived, and which he has communicated to us. While there is not a soul among us who will not regret this from the bottom of his heart, there is not a soul here to-day that wants to judge. We are not judges. He has announced his decision. He has told us what he wants us to do, and I think we must close our ranks, and do it.

[*It would have been a great comfort to the country if there had been less concern to close their ranks and more concern to close their mouths.*]

" At a later stage this evening I shall ask leave to bring in the necessary Bill so that it may be read the first time, printed, and made available in the Vote Office as soon as the House has ordered the Bill to be printed. The House will meet to-morrow at the usual time, 11 o'clock, when we shall take the second reading and the remaining stages of the Bill. It is very important that it should be passed into law to-morrow, and I shall put on the Order Paper to-morrow a motion to take Private Members' time, and to suspend the Four-o'clock Rule.

" I have only two other things to say. The House will forgive me for saying now something which I should have said a few minutes ago. I have told them of the circumstances under which I am speaking, and they have been very generous and sympathetic. Yesterday morning, when the Cabinet received the King's final and definite answer officially, they passed a Minute, and in accordance with it I sent a message to his Majesty, which he has been good enough to permit me to read to the House, with his reply:

" ' Mr Baldwin, with his humble duty to the King.

" ' This morning Mr Baldwin reported to the Cabinet his interview with your Majesty yesterday, and informed his colleagues that your Majesty then communicated to him informally your firm and definite intention to renounce the Throne.

" ' The Cabinet received this statement of your Majesty's intention with profound regret, and wished Mr Baldwin to convey to your Majesty immediately the unanimous feeling of your Majesty's servants.

" ' Ministers are reluctant to believe that your Majesty's resolve is irrevocable, and still venture to hope that before your Majesty pronounces any formal decision your Majesty may be pleased to reconsider an intention which must so deeply distress and so vitally affect all your Majesty's subjects.

" ' Mr Baldwin is at once communicating with the Dominion Prime Ministers for the purpose of letting them know that your Majesty has now made to him the informal intimation of your Majesty's intention.'

" His Majesty's reply was received last night:

" ' The King has received the Prime Minister's letter of the 9th December, 1936, informing him of the views of the Cabinet.

" ' His Majesty has given the matter his further consideration, but regrets that he is unable to alter his decision.'

" My last words on that subject are that I am convinced that where I have failed no one could have succeeded.

[*We are on familiar ground again. Mr Baldwin has always seemed convinced that he represents the ne plus ultra of human effort and human ability.*]

" His mind was made up, and those who know his Majesty best will know what that means.

[*This is a testimony to the King's stability of purpose. When he was gone it was called obstinacy. Diocletian probably considered the Christian martyrs obstinate.*]

" This House to-day is a theatre which is being watched by the whole world. Let us conduct ourselves with that dignity which his Majesty is showing in this hour of his trial. Whatever our regret at the contents of the message, let us fulfil his wish, do what he asks, and do it with speed. Let no word be spoken to-day that the utterer of that word may regret in days to come, let no word be spoken that causes pain to any soul, and let us not forget to-day the revered and beloved figure of Queen Mary, what all this time has meant to her, and think of her when we have to speak, if speak we must, during this debate. We have, after all, as the guardians of democracy [!] in this little island to see that we do our work to maintain the integrity [!] of that democracy, and of the monarch which, as I said at the beginning of my speech, is now the sole link of our whole Empire, and the guardian of our freedom. Let us look forward and remember our country [!] and the trust reposed by our country in this [!], the House of Commons, and let us rally behind the new King—(Hon. Members: ' Hear hear ') —stand behind him, and help him; and let us hope that,

whatever the country may have suffered by what we are passing
through, it may soon be repaired, and that we may take what
steps we can in trying to make this country a better country
for all the people to live in it."

[*A dangerous phrase that, when we remember a predecessor's
" Land fit for heroes to live in." It only remained, in a
Pickwickian sense, for Mr Baldwin to add that he had done his
best to make the world safe for hypocrisy and he doubted if any other
human being could have done as much.*]

The Prime Minister resumed his seat amid the loud cheers
of a House which supposed it was applauding not an actor
but a statesman.   Then Mr Attlee rose to ask the Speaker to
suspend the sitting till six o'clock.   That gave members an
hour and a half to chatter.   Mr Attlee himself, however, had
to retire into a Committee Room and let his followers know
what he was going to say.

It was a colourless speech, but unmarred by any lapse of
good taste.   Mr Attlee was followed by the Leader of the
little band of Opposition Liberals, who read the House a brief
lecture on the Statute of Westminster without appreciating
that it had been violated by Mr Baldwin's determination to
emulate Atlas and carry the whole Empire on his own
shoulders :

" Grief-stricken as we are to-day," said Sir Archibald
Sinclair, " it is our duty to face the future with clear eyes and
firm resolve.   Any prolongation of the crisis would be fraught
with peril."

It is difficult to understand what prolongation the Liberal
leader imagined, but Sir Archibald is a romantic figure and
may have been seeing himself in marble in that charming
Square of Thurso, for the hikers of posterity to gaze at.

The leader of the Opposition Liberals was followed by Mr
Winston Churchill.   His speech may be printed without
comment, beyond desiring a devoted attention to the sentence
printed in capitals :

" Nothing is more certain or more obvious than that
recrimination or controversy at this time would not only be
useless, but harmful and wrong.   What is done, is done.
What has been done, or left undone, belongs to history, and
to history, so far as I am concerned, it shall be left.   I will,
therefore, make two observations only.   The first is this : It
is clear from what we have been told this afternoon that there

was at no time any constitutional issue between the King and his Ministers, or between the King and Parliament. The supremacy of Parliament over the Crown; the duty of the Sovereign to act in accordance with the advice of his Ministers; neither of those was ever at any moment in question. Supporting my right hon. friend, the leader of the Liberal Party, I venture to say that no Sovereign has ever conformed more strictly or more faithfully to the letter and spirit of the Constitution than his present Majesty. IN FACT, HE HAS VOLUNTARILY MADE A SACRIFICE FOR THE PEACE AND STRENGTH OF HIS REALM, WHICH GO FAR BEYOND THE BOUNDS REQUIRED BY THE LAW AND CONSTITUTION. This is my first observation.

" My second is this: I have, throughout, pleaded for time; anyone can see how grave would have been the evils of protracted controversy. On the other hand it was, in my view, our duty to endure these evils, even at serious inconvenience, if there was any hope that time would bring a solution. Whether there was any hope or not is a mystery which, at the present time, it is impossible to resolve. Time was also important from another point of view. It was essential that there should be no room for aspersions, after the event, that the King had been hurried to his decision. I believe that, if this decision had been taken last week, it could not have been declared that it was an unhurried decision, so far as the King himself was concerned, but now I accept wholeheartedly what the Prime Minister has proved, namely, that the decision taken this week has been taken by his Majesty freely, voluntarily and spontaneously, in his own time and in his own way. As I have been looking at this matter, as is well known, from an angle different from that of most members, I thought it my duty to place this fact also upon record.

" That is all I have to say upon the disputable part of this matter, but I hope the House will bear with me for a minute or two, because it was my duty as Home Secretary, more than a quarter of a century ago, to stand beside his Majesty and proclaim his style and titles at his investiture as Prince of Wales amid the sunlit battlements of Caernarvon Castle, and ever since then he has honoured me here, and also in war-time, with his personal kindness and, I may even say, friendship. I should have been ashamed if, in my independent and unofficial position, I had not cast about for every lawful means, even the most forlorn, to keep him on the Throne of his fathers, to which he only recently succeeded amid the hopes and prayers of all. In this Prince there were discerned qualities of courage, of simplicity, of sympathy and, above all, of sincerity, qualities rare and precious which might have made his Reign glorious in the annals of this ancient Monarchy. It is the acme of tragedy that these very virtues should, in the private sphere, have led only to this melancholy and bitter conclusion. But, although to-day our hopes are withered, still I will assert that his personality will not go down uncherished to future ages, that it will be particularly remembered in the homes of his poorer subjects, and that they will ever wish from the bottoms of their hearts for his private peace and happiness, and for the happiness of those who are dear to him.

" I must say one word more, and I say it especially to those who here and out of doors—and do not underrate their numbers —who are most poignantly afflicted by what has occurred. Danger gathers upon our path. We cannot afford—we have no right—to look back. We must look forward ; we must obey the exhortation of the Prime Minister to look forward. The stronger the advocate of monarchical principle a man may be, the more zealously must he now endeavour to fortify the Throne, and to give his Majesty's successor that strength which can only come from the love of a united nation and Empire."

Mr Maxton who spoke next extended sympathy both to the King and the Prime Minister, but felt that the monarchical institution had now outlived its usefulness. The leader of the Independent Labour Party was followed by Colonel Josiah Wedgwood, who made a brief but moving speech, the dignity of which was beyond the appreciation of the House :

" I put a Motion on the Paper, and I do not regret it ; but after the sincere and admirable speech of the Prime Minister, that Motion is dead. I could have wished that the King had been allowed to live here married, happy, and King, but he has wished otherwise. A thousand years hence, perhaps, we shall be liberal enough to allow such a thing ; it is too early now. He has been very kind to me and to a great many people throughout this Empire personally known to him, and I think we may all wish him a happy life there, if not here. The right honourable Gentleman has made it perfectly clear that, in spite of what I wished, and many others wished, there were really only two alternatives—to continue lonely, disappointed, bitter, ruling the Empire, or else do what he has done, to throw up royalty and remain a man. We shall all commend him for that choice of the two, for nothing could have been worse than a kingdom ruled by a man with a grievance, partly hostile to every Minister who had put him in the dilemma—(Hon. Members : ' No ! ')—collecting round him false friends—(Hon. Members : ' No ! ')—collecting round him those who would use the King's feelings against the Ministry and against the Constitution. That would be an alternative which everyone must have seen ahead of us, the most dreadful alternative. To-morrow we shall take a new Oath of Allegiance. There will be no non-jurors this time, because it is by the King's wish that we take it. There will be no non-jurors below the Gangway, no non-jurors throughout the country. There will be, I would say, millions of people with aching hearts. They will carry on for England. They will take that oath because he wished it, and if they sometimes raise their glass to the King over the water, who shall blame them ? "

Colonel Wedgwood was followed by Mr William Gallacher, who, for a man of such large experience and such high nobility of character, made a singularly foolish speech, in the course of which he asserted that Mrs Simpson's social set was " closely identified with a certain foreign Government and the Ambassador of that foreign Government." Mr Gallacher, in effect, declared that one of the bogeys rigged up to frighten the House was a real bogey and that he for one had been frightened by it. The Communist member's credulity was a most unfortunate earnest of what may happen if his party should ever gain power; the substitute of old wives' tales for revealed religion will mark a retrogression in human thought for which no amount of common sense about economic theory will compensate. On the other hand, tribute must be paid to Mr Gallacher's perception that there was no issue between King and Parliament, and that Parliament had never been consulted from beginning to end.

Mr George Buchanan felt he should go a step further than Mr Maxton and protest that if the King " had not voluntarily stepped from the Throne, the same people in the House who had paid lip-service to him, would have poured out scorn, abuse, and filth." What Mr Buchanan did not foresee was that in spite of the King's abdication and withdrawal from the country to avoid any possibility of the growth of faction, the scorn, the abuse, and the filth would still be poured out.

The discussion was brought to a close by Captain Ian Fraser, who, blind himself, had devoted himself to the help of ex-service men and who recognised the work King Edward had done for them as a personal friend for a quarter of a century.

From the proceedings in the House of Lords an extract from the speech of the Lord Archbishop of Canterbury must be quoted in admiration of its grave eloquence, but also because it offers such an incomprehensible contrast to the words he would speak three days later :

" My Lords, it is most difficult to add anything to the moving words of mingled reticence which have fallen from the noble Lords who have spoken.   This is an occasion when our thoughts lie too deep for tears, certainly too deep for words. No such tragedy of a pathos so profound has ever been enacted on the stage of our national history.   I wonder whether in all history any renunciation has ever been made comparable with that which has been announced in the gracious message we have just received.   Of the motive which has compelled that renunciation we dare not speak.*   It takes us into the region of the inner mysteries of human life and human nature.   The heart knoweth its own bitterness, yet even we can understand in some measure the ordeal through which his Majesty has been passing and the cost of his renunciation.   We can only offer him the profound sympathy of our hearts and accept with infinite sorrow the decision he has made.

" Was there not, my Lords, something like a stab in our hearts when we heard the words in which his Majesty took leave of his subjects ?   Yet, with those inevitable feelings of sympathy and sorrow, there must needs arise also the remembrance of all that his Majesty has done in the past for this nation and Empire by the frankness and charm of his personality, by his most genuine care of the poor and suffering and the unemployed, by his gifts of speech in which he interpreted and directed the thought of his fellow-countrymen, by his embassies across the seas which kindled the loyalty of the whole Empire.   The thought of all these manifold services, of the rich promises so suddenly and unexpectedly bereft of

---

* This remark has been asserted to be a hint at black magic, but read in the context that is obviously a misinterpretation.   What must be asked is why three days later his Grace did dare to expatiate on the motive.

their full fruition, cannot take away from the affection and admiration which we have felt in the past and which we shall never be able to forget in the unknown future.　It can only add to the infinite and inexpressible pathos of the present."

At 11 o'clock of the morning of December 11th the House gathered for the second reading of the Abdication Bill, the text of which was as hereunder :

" Whereas his Majesty by his royal message of the tenth day of December in this present year has been pleased to declare that he is irrevocably determined to renounce the Throne for himself and his descendants and has for that purpose executed the instrument of abdication set out in the schedule to this Act, and has signified his desire that effect thereto should be given immediately ;

" And whereas following upon the communication to his Dominions of his Majesty's said declaration and desire, the Dominion of Canada, pursuant to the provisions of Section Four of the Statute of Westminster, 1931, has requested and consented to the enactment of this Act, and the Commonwealth of Australia, the Dominion of New Zealand, and the Union of South Africa have assented thereto :

" Be it therefore enacted by the King's most excellent Majesty, by and with the advice and consent of the Lords spiritual and temporal and Commons, in this present Parliament assembled and by the authority of the same, as follows :

" 1.　(1) Immediately upon the Royal Assent being signified to this Act the instrument of abdication executed by his present Majesty on the tenth day of December 1936, set out in the schedule to this Act shall have effect, and thereupon His Majesty shall cease to be King and there shall be a demise of the Crown and accordingly the members of the Royal Family then next in succession to the Throne shall succeed thereto and to all the rights, privileges and dignities thereunto belonging.

" (2) His Majesty, his issue, if any, and the descendants of that issue, shall not after his Majesty's abdication have any right, title or interest in or to the succession to the Throne, and Section One of the Act of Settlement shall be construed accordingly.

" (3) The Royal Marriages Act, 1772, shall not apply

to his Majesty after his abdication nor to the issue, if any, of
his Majesty's descendants of that issue.

" 2.   This Act may be cited as his Majesty's Declaration of Abdication Act, 1936."

The Prime Minister, on entering to move the Second
Reading, received what was now his regular round of cheers.
His speech was merely a formal explanation of the provisions
of the Bill.   Mr Attlee, in offering the support of his party,
seemed to feel that he had to utter some sentiments to appease
the sense of embarrassment under which by now his followers
must have been suffering.   He was anxious about the continuance of old-fashioned Court ceremonial, oblivious or
wilfully blind to the fact that King Edward had been equally
anxious about this.   He believed that the note of monarchy
should be simplicity, and again conveniently ignored the
simplicity of King Edward.   He declared that his party stood
for the disappearance of class barriers and were moving
towards equality.   In fact, he offered the House as his ideal
of a constitutional monarchy the very ideal for which " a
narrow and privileged class had succeeded in making it
impossible for King Edward to fulfil."

Mr Maxton then moved a Republican amendment to
which Sir John Simon voiced the opposition.   Considering
that this was the first occasion on which the Home Secretary
had spoken about a business in which in private consultations
with his colleagues he had played a most important part, it was
a pity that so distinguished a lawyer made no attempt to present
the legal aspects of the abdication.   But perhaps Sir John
Simon was too good a lawyer to run the risk of argument.
Nevertheless, jejune though Sir John Simon's speech was, it
was not too jejune to secure the defeat of the Republican
amendment by 403 votes to 5.

After a brief time in Committee, Mr Baldwin moved that
the Bill be read a third time.   He said :

" I rise once more to-day, and only for a very few moments.
I do not want this Bill to leave the House without making the
few observations which I propose to make.   This is the last
Bill that will be presented for the Royal Assent during the
present reign.   The Royal Assent given to this Bill will be
the last act of his present Majesty, and I should not like the
Bill to go to another place without putting on record what, I
feel sure, will be the feeling of this House and of the country

that, though we have this duty to perform to-day, and though we are performing it with unanimity, we can never be unconscious of, and we shall always remember with regard and affection [!], the whole-hearted and loyal service that his Majesty has given to this country as Prince of Wales, and during the short time he has been on the Throne.   Like many of his generation, he was flung into the War as a very young man, and he has served us well in trying to qualify himself for that office which he knew must be his if he lived.   For all that work I should like to put on record here to-day that we are grateful [!] and that we shall not forget [!].   There is no need on this Bill to say anything of the future [!].   It deals with the fate of him who is still King, and who will cease to be King in a few short hours.   I felt that I could hardly reconcile it with my conscience or my feelings if I let this Bill go to another place without saying just these few words.

"There is no need on this Bill to say anything of the future " [!].

Mr Baldwin was now demobilised, and the Third Reading was taken without a division.

In contrast to the proceedings in the House of Commons we may read the proceedings in the Federal House of Representatives at Canberra on Friday, December 11th 1936:

"' In presenting this message of abdication,' said Mr Lyons, ' I desire to set out briefly the history of this matter so far as it concerns the King and his advisers, and particularly the part taken in the discussion by the Government of the Commonwealth of Australia.

"'On November 28th I received from the Prime Minister of the United Kingdom a personal and secret cable informing me that he had had conversations with his Majesty the King about Mrs Simpson, and that his Majesty had stated his intention of marrying Mrs Simpson, but that at the same time his Majesty had said that he appreciated that the idea of her becoming Queen and her children succeeding to the Throne was out of the question, and that consequently he contemplated abdication and leaving the Duke of York to succeed on the Throne.

[*Why did not Mr Baldwin tell the House of Commons all this? According to his account it was he who on October 20th notified the King that the idea of Mrs Simpson's becoming Queen was out of the question. This was accepted by his Majesty on November 16th by his offer to abdicate. On November 25th his Majesty asked for a reply to his enquiry about the private marriage, with an Act of Exclusion. It was presumably not until after that alleged Cabinet meeting on November 27th, of which Mr Baldwin said nothing to the House of Commons, that he communicated the question to the Australian Premier about the private marriage. What the Federal Opposition wanted to know was the terms of the previous communications between Mr Baldwin and Mr Lyons. Did Mr Lyons ever notify Mr Baldwin that there would be difficulty in persuading Australian opinion to fall in with the British Government's refusal to accept Mrs Simpson as Queen? That feeling was strong on this point is clear from the earlier speeches of Mr Curtin.*

The longer one ponders over this statement by Mr Lyons the more disquieting it is to British opinion. The mystery demands clarification. The national honour is gravely affected by this discrepancy between the story told by Mr Baldwin and that told by Mr Lyons.]

" ' His Majesty had subsequently asked Mr Baldwin's views on a new proposal, namely that special legislative provision should be made for a marriage to Mrs Simpson, which would not make her Queen and would not entitle her issue to succeed to the Throne. Mr Baldwin informed me that he had advised his Majesty that he did not think there was any chance of such an arrangement receiving the approval of Parliament in Great Britain, also that the assent of the Dominions would be essential to the carrying out of such an arrangement. He invited my personal view.

" ' I then communicated with Mr Baldwin offering my personal view (since at that time the matter was highly secret and confidential) that the proposed marriage if it led to Mrs Simpson becoming Queen, would invoke widespread condemnation, and that the alternative proposal, or something in the nature of a specially sanctioned morganatic marriage, would run counter to the best popular conception of the Royal Family.

" ' Mr Baldwin suggested that I might convey to his Majesty the opinion of his Government in the Commonwealth of Australia. On December 5th I did so, informing his Majesty of the views of my Government, and in particular, stating that any proposal that Mrs Simpson should become consort and not Queen and that her issue should be barred from succession, would not be approved by my Government, nor on my advice could any Government be formed in the Commonwealth Parliament which would be prepared to sponser legislation sanctioning such a course.

" ' I have been glad to note that what I said on this occasion has since received the confirmation in this Parliament of the leader of the Opposition.

" ' On December 10th Mr Baldwin advised me that his Majesty's determination remained unalterably fixed, and that he had informed Mr Baldwin that it was his desire to abdicate. Mr Baldwin added that the Government was making a final appeal to his Majesty, but that they feared there was no hope of his Majesty changing his mind. Having received this information, I at once forwarded, through his Excellency the Governor-General, a message to his Majesty the King expressing the deep sympathy of my Government, sincerely regretting that his Majesty should feel it necessary to take such a step, and begging in the name of his Majesty's subjects in the Commonwealth of Australia that his Majesty would reconsider his decision and continue to reign over us.

" ' I cannot conclude this narrative without emphasising that his Majesty's decision to abdicate was in no sense advised by any of his Majesty's Governments, and was neither directly nor indirectly the outcome of any pressure exerted by them. . . .'

" After Mr Lyons had moved the resolution the leader of the Opposition (Mr Curtin) rose to speak :

" ' It would be idle to say that this is not a day of supreme importance to the people of Australia, and to the people of the British Empire. We are faced with the fact that King Edward VIII has abdicated the Throne. He has done so because of his desire to marry a lady, and because, in marrying her, he sought that the law in respect of the marriage of the King should be so altered that his wife would not be Queen of England, though in every way his mate and equal, and, further, that any children should not come into the first line of succession.

" ' It appears clear that the statement which the Prime Minister has just read to the House of the circumstances antecedent to the abdication represented the definite intention of his Majesty, and I quite agree that the course that he contemplated was one which this Parliament would not support. The Australian Labour movement would not agree, in any circumstances, to confer upon the wife of any man, even

if he be King, a status less than that which would be the right
of a wife as the wife of her husband.

[*Mr Curtin had previously indicated that the Federal Opposition would support his Majesty if he desired to make the lady he
married Queen. It was only when Mr Lyons, quoting Mr
Baldwin as his authority, said that the King himself did not wish
Mrs Simpson to become Queen that Mr Curtin fell into line.*]

" ' Therefore, as the King sought special legislation to suit
his convenience——'

" Mr Garden (Ind. Lab., N.S.W.) : ' Who said so ? '

" Mr Curtin continued : ' The Prime Minister has told us
and I accept unreservedly his statement. All through this
week we have asked for the facts, and to-day we have had them.'

" MR WARD (LAB., N.S.W.) : ' SOME OF THEM. YOUR
BELIEF IS NOT SHARED BY US.'

[*Nor by many millions throughout the Empire.*]

" Mr Curtin : ' I speak as the leader of the Opposition, and
of the Australian Labour movement and the judgment I made
in assessing the value or otherwise of the statements made to
me is the judgment 1 shall answer for anywhere and everywhere.'

" Mr Ward continued to interject and Mr Blackburn (Ind.
Lab., Vic.) was seen to remonstrate with him.

" Mr Curtin then said that he regretted very much that the
King should have relinquished the Throne. He had come
to the Throne after years of difficulty. He had made himself
probably the most conspicuous symbol of the unity of the
British people. He had travelled widely throughout every
part of the Dominions. He had known the people of the
Dominions better than any other British monarch. It appeared to him that there was nothing for Parliament to do
but to carry the resolution. . . . '

" Mr Beasley (Lab., N.S.W.) : ' I respectfully disagree
with the Leader of the Opposition that all of the facts have
been placed before the House.'

" Mr Rosevear (Lab., N.S.W.) : ' There is nothing in what
he said worth smothering up.'

" Mr Beasley said that Mr Baldwin had caused to be
circulated in the newspapers a statement that, if the King
refused his advice, he would resign, and that the leader of the
Labour Party in England would decline to form a Government.
That statement had been made for the express purpose of
bringing about the King's abdication.

" ' I will not be satisfied,' Mr Beasley went on, ' that all the facts have been made known until a complete file of the cablegrams and a report of all the telephone conversations between this Government and the British Government are tabled in the House or in the library.'

[*Nor many millions throughout the Empire.*]

" Mr A. G. Cameron (U.C.P., S.A.): ' Are you part of the official Opposition to-day ? '

" Mr Beasley: ' I am here respectfully to submit my observations on this matter, and not in any way to undermine or pass any adverse comment on my colleagues.   The issue does not end with this resolution.   The love and admiration felt for the gentleman who has abdicated is so widespread that it will never die in the hearts of the British people.'

" Mr Lane (U.A.P., N.S.W.): (satirically) ' You have always loved kings.'

" Mr Beasley went on to say there must have been some reason for Mr Baldwin's threatened resignation, and for the incorrect statement that the leader of the Labour Party in England would decline to form a Government.   No doubt Mr Baldwin desired to create the atmosphere necessary to bring about the abdication of the King.

[*A Daniel come to judgment !*]

" It appeared to him that Mr Lyons had sent a message of loyalty to the King only after he knew from England that the King intended to abdicate.

[*But a Daniel in the den of Mr Lyons.*]

" King Edward had apparently shown feelings too democratic for the Conservative forces.   He had emphasised the necessity for remedying the unfortunate circumstances of the mass of the English people.   There were more deep-seated reasons for his abdication than appeared on the surface.   Had he continued to reign he would have been a tremendous influence in the direction of social reform.

" ' We wish him every success in his future life, but we regret deeply the circumstances of his abdication,' Mr Beasley added. ' He was the most democratic King England ever knew.'

" The Attorney-General (Mr Menzies) quoted authorities to show that the succession to the British Throne in modern times depended essentially upon statute.   It seemed to follow inevitably that any alteration in the succession could not be brought about merely by a Royal Proclamation, or by a deed of abdication, but had to be achieved by the exercise of the power of Parliament. What was contained in a statute could only be modified by a statute.

" Explaining the reference in the resolution to the demise of the Sovereign, Mr Menzies said that Halsbury (second edition, volume VI, page 447) stated : ' The Sovereign is regarded legally as immortal, the maxim of law being that "the King never dies." The death of the Sovereign in his natural body is therefore termed legally his demise, meaning the transfer of the kingdom (*demissio*) to his successor.'

" Mr Menzies explained the Demise of the Crown Act, 1901, and said that the legislation introduced by the United Kingdom was expressly treating the abdication as if it were a demise of the Crown.

" The Commonwealth Parliament was being invited to express its assent to the British legislation by a resolution of both Houses because learned opinion was that the Commonwealth Parliament had no direct power to deal with the succession to the Throne.

[*Then what becomes of the preamble to the Statute of Westminster ?*]

" Mr Blackburn (Lab., Vic.) said that he did not accept the statement of Mr Lyons as a full and complete statement. THE LAWS OF ENGLAND AND SCOTLAND RECOGNISED DIVORCE. IT SEEMED TO HIM WRONG THAT IN A MATTER WHICH HE AND MOST PEOPLE REGARDED AS A PRIVATE ONE, THERE SHOULD HAVE BEEN INTERFERENCE BY PEOPLE THRUSTING THEIR ADVICE UPON THE KING. HE AGREED WITH MR LYONS THAT NO PARLIAMENT SHOULD COUNTENANCE A MORGANATIC MARRIAGE, BUT HE BELIEVED THAT THAT HAD BEEN PROPOSED ONLY BE-CAUSE OFFICIOUS PERSONS—AND HE DID NOT EXCEPT MR LYONS FROM THAT DESCRIPTION—HAD FORCED UPON THE KING GRATUITOUS ADVICE THAT THE MARRIAGE OF THE KING TO THE LADY OF HIS CHOICE WOULD NOT MEET WITH THE APPROVAL OF THE PEOPLE.

" Mr Ward (Lab., N.S.W.) said that it appeared that the decision of the King to abdicate had not been a voluntary one. Moralists said that the King should not have proposed marriage to a divorced woman, BUT THERE WAS NO MEMBER OF PARLIAMENT WHO HAD SAID ANYTHING ABOUT THE MORALITY OF THE WOMAN IN QUESTION.

" It had been said that the main objection to the King

selecting Mrs Simpson as his wife was because she had been divorced on two previous occasions.

"'I UNDERSTAND,' HE ADDED, 'SPEAKING FROM MEMORY, THAT THERE ARE SOME MEMBERS ON THE GOVERNMENT SIDE WHO HAVE ADOPTED THIS THEMSELVES. I AM NOT OBJECTING TO THAT—BUT THERE SHOULD NOT BE ONE LINE OF CONDUCT FOR THEM AND ANOTHER STANDARD FOR THE KING.'

" Mr Garden (Lab., N.S.W.) said that he realised that the King had given offence to a section of the Church because it was alleged he wanted to marry a woman who had been twice married. To attack the King, or the lady on whom his choice had fallen, for such a reason, was hypocrisy. EVERY MAN IN THE HOUSE HAD GIVEN TACIT APPROVAL TO DIVORCE LAWS BY NOT PROCLAIMING AGAINST THEM. THERE SHOULD BE A REFERENDUM ON EVERY QUESTION OF CONSTITUTIONAL REFORM.

" WHATEVER MIGHT BE DENIED TO THE KING IN EVERY OTHER PART OF THE EMPIRE SHOULD NOT BE DENIED TO HIM IN AUSTRALIA.

" Mr Holt (U.A.P., Vic.) said Mr Lyons had had the approval of his Government for the action he had taken, and he thought it could be said now that he had also the approval of the people in Australia.

" Mr Baker (Lab., Qld.) said that ' indecent haste ' had characterised the British Parliament and the Press.

" Mr. E. J. Harrison (U.A.P., N.S.W.) said that he wished to congratulate the leader of the Opposition on his restrained speech.

" The resolution was agreed to on the voices.

" The House was adjourned until a date and hour to be fixed."

[*And those searching questions tabled by various members of the Federal Opposition were apparently never answered by the Federal Government. The deduction requires no underlining.*]

BUCKINGHAM PALACE. *December* 11.

The Royal Assent was given at 1.52 p.m. to-day to his Majesty's Declaration of Abdication Bill.

145, PICCADILLY. *December* 11.

The Right Hon. Stanley Baldwin, M.P., Prime Minister and First Lord of the Treasury, had an audience of the King this afternoon.

These two curt announcements in the *Court Circular* lent such an air of ease to the whole complicated process that perhaps it is not surprising the nation sat back and admired itself in the mirror of its own complacency. Who but the English could have changed kings with less fuss than inferior nations could change trains?

As *The Times* proclaimed:

> The nation has treated a great issue worthily, its thought moving soberly and steadily, with reluctance but without sentimentality, with searching of heart but without tumult towards a firm conviction of the duty that might be laid upon it. This dignified judgment of a free people was given articulate expression yesterday in the practically unanimous passage of the Abdication Act through both Houses of Parliament in less than three hours . . . for some time the international esteem for Great Britain has been rising, as foreign policy, and the domestic basis of foreign policy, had been reconstructed on more resolute and confident lines . . . the British people, facing its ordeal under an unprecedented glare of foreign publicity, has earned the wonder and admiration of the world . . . not for the first time a sudden emergency has enabled the British nation to prove its native greatness.

There are depths of complacency which it would be sacrilegious to disturb; but one pebble must be thrown into this pool wherein Britannia watches entranced the reflection of her form, stripped of armour and naked as truth. That confident and resolute foreign policy was only to miss plunging the country into war because it was completely reversed by Mr Baldwin's successor. To the many debts of gratitude under which King Edward had laid the nation was to be added as his final gift the withdrawal of the last excuse Mr Baldwin could find for remaining indefinitely in power.

In the words of *The Times*, the Prime Minister could feel that " the episode had left him more firmly established in the hearts of M.P.'s than ever before, and they hope that in a few days from now it will be possible for him to begin a richly earned rest in Worcestershire."

> Abstulit clarum cita mors Achillen;
> Longa Tithonum minuit senectus.

> Untimely death carried off Achilles in his fame;
> A long old age reduced Tithonus to insignificance.

We turn with relief, weighted though that relief be with sorrow, to Prince Edward's farewell from Windsor. His broadcast at 10 o'clock that night of December 11th was listened to all over the world. No man since its creation had spoken to an audience one hundredth as large, and it may be

that no man ever will.   Theatres and cinemas included the
speech as part of their programmes, and in the great telephone
exchanges of London there was not a single call during those
seven poignant minutes.   From Iceland to Invercargill, from
China to Peru, in darkness and in daylight, by sea and by land,
the world listened.

" This is Windsor Castle.   His Royal Highness Prince
Edward."

Thus the voice of Sir John Reith, as gruff as the messenger
in *Richard III* who announces the death of Buckingham,
gruff and somewhat sinister as it breaks that mundane silence.
The sound of a door closing, and Prince Edward was alone
with the world.   It was his seventy-seventh broadcast.

" At long last I am able to say a few words of my own.

" I have never wanted to withold anything, but until now
it has not been constitutionally possible for me to speak.

" A few hours ago I discharged my last duty as King and
Emperor, and now that I have been succeeded by my
brother, the Duke of York, my first words must be to declare
my allegiance to him.   This I do with all my heart.

" You all know the reasons which have impelled me to
renounce the Throne, but I want you to understand that in
making up my mind I did not forget the country or the
Empire, which as Prince of Wales, and lately as King, I
have for twenty-five years tried to serve.

" But you must believe me when I tell you that I have
found it impossible to carry the heavy burden of responsibility, and to discharge my duties as King as I would wish
to do, without the help and support of the woman I love.

" And I want you to know that the decision I have made
has been mine, and mine alone.   This was a thing I had to
judge entirely for myself.   The other person most nearly
concerned has tried up to the last to persuade me to take a
different course.

" I have made this, the most serious decision of my life,
only upon the single thought of what would in the end be
best for all.

" This decision has been made less difficult to me by the
sure knowledge that my brother with his long training in
the public affairs of this country and with his fine qualities,
will be able to take my place forthwith, without interruption
or injury to the life and progress of the Empire.

"And he has one matchless blessing, enjoyed by so many of you, and not bestowed on me, a happy home with his wife and children.

"During these hard days I have been comforted by her Majesty, my mother, and my family, the Ministers of the Crown, and in particular Mr Baldwin, the Prime Minister, have always treated me with full consideration.

"There has never been any Constitutional differences between me and them, and between me and Parliament. Bred in the constitutional traditions of my father, I should never have allowed any such issue to arise.

"Ever since I was Prince of Wales, and later on when I occupied the Throne, I have been treated with the greatest kindness by all classes of people wherever I have lived or journeyed throughout the Empire. For that I am very grateful.

"I now quit altogether public affairs, and I lay down my burden. It may be some time before I return to my native land; but I shall always follow the fortunes of the British race and Empire with profound interest, and if at any time in the future I can be found of service to his Majesty in a private station, I shall not fail.

"And now we all have a new King. I wish him and you, his people, happiness and prosperity with all my heart. God bless you all. God save the King ! "

In an endeavour to utter that last "God Save the King" with all the fervour of his own loyalty the light, once buoyant voice broke. The B.B.C. had the decency to close down all the transmitters for the night; but that closing down was not a full atonement for daring to announce immediately after the announcement of the Abdication that prices on the Stock Exchange had rallied.*

* *The Gramophone, January* 1937 : "What a strange thing music is ! This platitudinous ejaculation was inspired by the Beethoven Quintet in C major, which has just been published by Columbia. It is a work with which I was not familiar and, whether or not my mind was preoccupied with other matters, it made no impression on me either the first time it was played or the second time. It was played a third time when I was trying to exclude from my mind, in order to concentrate on my own work, all thoughts about late events, and most of all a black rage which had come over me at hearing *immediately* after the news of the Abdication the prices of the Stock Exchange read by the six o'clock announcer out of their usual order. Was that the true anodyne for a nation's sorrow, a rise in the shares of some wretched motor-car company ? Had Elgar's *Land of Hope and Glory* been played as an overture to this eructation of bad taste ? Financial

The broadcast was heard by the present writer in a house which looks across eight miles of sea to that white beach of Eriskay whereon Prince Charles Edward had landed all but nine of two hundred years before to win back his father's kingdom and set foot for the first time in the country which had denied him nativity.   In such surroundings the murmur of the tide and the lisp of the December wind about the withered wintry grass added the last melancholy of a farewell sigh.   At that moment in some studio in Hollywood the scene-shifters stopped their work to listen and an English actress who was directing a picture told the writer that those men so well used to mock emotion were moved to tears.   At the same moment in London her sister, listening with a sophisticated crowd of Englishmen bearing up under the strain of being " let down ", found the broadcast superficial and undignified.   These three moods will serve to express the reaction of millions, but in justice to humanity, be it recorded that the first two moods represented the feelings of the vast majority.   The others were at the mercy of their neighbours' mood, and that mood often led by one member of the gathering, like a theatre audience, or a flock of sheep by a bell-wether.

The epilogue to this tragedy of a nation's failure to accept what a King had offered them was written by Queen Mary at Marlborough House and published next morning:

To the People of this Nation and Empire.

" I have been so deeply touched by the sympathy which has surrounded me at this time of anxiety that I must send a message of gratitude from the depth of my heart.

" The sympathy and affection which sustained me in my great sorrow less than a year ago have not failed me now, and are once again my strength and stay.

" I need not speak to you of the distress which fills a mother's heart when I think that my dear son has deemed it to be his duty to lay down his charge, and that the reign

---

anxiety is intelligible, but decency should have kept the Stock Exchange prices at such a tragic moment to their proper place in the lees of the news.

" I had cut off the wireless in a fury for some chamber music to be played, and was trying to get away from the present and back to the Greece of the fifth century B.C. about which I was writing when gradually I became aware of an exquisite melody that was washing away the sense of uncleanliness left by that conjunction of tragedy with commerce.   On asking what the music was I found that it was the second movement of this Beethoven Quintet in C major."

which had begun with so much hope and promise has so suddenly ended.

" I know that you will realise what it has cost him to come to this decision ; and that, remembering the years in which he tried so eagerly to serve and help his country and Empire, you will keep a grateful remembrance of him in your hearts.

" I commend to you his brother, summoned so un-expectedly and in circumstances so painful, to take his place. I ask you to give to him the same full measure of generous loyalty which you gave to my beloved husband, and which you would willingly have continued to give to his brother.

" With him I commend my dear daughter-in-law, who will be his Queen. May she receive the same unfailing affection and trust which you have given to me for six and twenty years. I know that you have already taken her children to your hearts.

" It is my earnest prayer that in spite of, nay through, this present trouble, the loyalty and unity of our land and Empire may by God's blessing be maintained and strengthened. May He bless and keep you always.

" MARY R."

If the curtain had been allowed to descend upon that moving and gracious appeal this book might never have been written, for a grateful remembrance of King Edward and a generous loyalty to King George would have prevented that detestable campaign—victualled by self-righteousness, guilty fears, petty revenge, bruised vanity, and distorted jealousy, and armed with scandal, slander, lie and innuendo—to wound a Prince's name, to slay a Prince's reputation, and even to expunge the very thought of him from the conscience of the nation.

Whatever might have been felt about the manner in which constitutional usage, Press opinion, religious prejudice, popular ignorance and political nervousness had been marshalled against that King in such a way as to render him practically incapable of doing anything in the end except losing the whole world to gain his soul, silence might have been main-tained if that soul gained had been granted its freedom. Yet, even as the greatest crime of the war was the peace, so the disgrace of the abdication was the aftermath. If, as was generally claimed, the real lesson of the crisis was the ability of the British nation to sustain such a crisis, not only without injury to itself but even to the enhancement of its prestige, if King George VI was the ideal King, if the result of so much agony of mind for the man who made the choice was to weld more strongly than ever the links of Empire, a measure of gratitude seemed owing to him who by his unselfish desire and perfect demeanour made such a consummation possible. Instead, he was reviled by some, derided by others, and misjudged by millions. Hardly one of those who had sped the parting guest stayed their tongues when he was out of sight. Who would not have been willing to grant Earl Baldwin of Bewdley, K.G., a recognition beyond any that even he himself might have hoped for, if he had had the courage—and it would not have taken the poorest tithe of his late master's courage—to come to the microphone and for five minutes use that tender voice with which he was wont to solicit the electorate's trust to beg fair play for the Duke of Windsor ?

It is bitter to recall that departure and reflect that, when Prince Edward left Windsor immediately after the broadcast in his car to take that Portsmouth road which sea-faring princes of his House in coach and chaise and carriage had so often taken before him, whatever leaden sorrow at parting with his mother, his family and his native land lay heavy upon him, he must have fancied that he had clearly explained to his people why he was going and felt that they would understand and approve. He drove in his car through the darkness of the countryside with his Cairn terrier beside him, utterly unconscious that, after those grave scenes in the Houses of Parliament where one after another men of state had risen to pronounce panegyrics upon the way he had sustained perhaps the most difficult ordeal of the mind any monarch has confronted, he had an even fiercer ordeal before him.

Those devoted to that Prince will always believe that he was treated unfairly throughout his reign ; but if justice had been accorded to him when his reign was over, they would have held their tongues. They would have read with a sigh that in Portsmouth he had to ask the way out of his own country, or, in other words, be directed to the ominously named Unicorn Gate of the Portsmouth Docks. They would have read how the destroyer *Fury* steamed away into that misty December night for Boulogne, knowing that it might be some time before he returned to his native land, but expecting that a year at most

would see him home again. They would have read of his
journey down to Castle Enzesfeld, wished him a happy
Christmas in Austria, and looked forward with the warmest
goodwill to his marriage. They would have read how when
he was received at the station in Vienna, he stopped to give
the photographers a chance to get some pictures of him,
those photographers who had had a very rough journey and
deserved some results. ' How like him ! ' his devoted adherents
would have murmured, and with a last sigh they would have
closed the paper.

And then on Sunday morning, December 13th, the Church
of England spoke.

The Bishop of Portsmouth, Dr Frank Partridge, preached
in his cathedral :

" Events have shown the soundness of the English temperament and its aversion from evil things. Almost univer
sally there was a shudder at the indecency and impropriety of
wild conduct [!] that knew no law [!], of which there had been
such plain signs [!]. English people would not stand it.
They hate Pharisaism [!] and cannot abide smugness [!].
They have a sense of propriety in great places and in great
affairs, and will not tolerate headlong slips into the abyss of
shamefulness.

" Only one other scene in history is comparable to that of
the previous Friday night at Portsmouth, and that was when
Napoleon [! !] stood upon the deck of the *Bellerophon*, a
British man-of-war, and looked back after Waterloo on the
fair land of France."

So Mr Baldwin already likened to Cromwell was to be Pitt
as well. This Dr Partridge was a Chaplain to the King. His
recreations are cricket and classical literature. Cricket should
have taught him fair play. Classical literature should have
provided him with warnings enough against human arrogance
and insolence.

Dr Hicks, the Bishop of Lincoln, older and wiser and with
a much richer experience of the world than Dr Partridge,
preached more truthfully and more charitably :

" The former King has done more than we could have
thought possible in investing his great surrender with dignity,
grace, and loyalty to his people, to the Constitution and to his
successor. . . . Would you and I have done differently in his
circumstances ? We dare not say."

In Gloucester Cathedral Dr Headlam was omniscient :

". . . The King, inspired by an unlawful passion, re-
nounced the greatest Throne the world has seen and the
most splendid position a man could hold.   Indiscretions so
great that they have been notorious throughout the civilised
world, cannot be held to belong merely to private life."

The Bishop of Manchester, Dr Warman, spoke with sympathy about King Edward, but reserved his higher flights of
eloquence for a panegyric on the behaviour of the *Manchester
Guardian*.

The Dean of Exeter, Dr S. C. Carpenter, expressed the
Church's relief at the passing of a scandal, in the danger of
which the Establishment would have gone down into the
abyss.   The Dean of Exeter was at least frank.

The Dean of Westminster, Dr Foxley-Norris, urged his
hearers to refrain from engaging in or listening to gossip and
to remember the debt which rich and poor alike owed to the
ability, work and devotion which Prince Edward showed as a
Prince and a Sovereign.

If the Archbishop of Canterbury had listened to the Dean of
Westminster's sermon that Sunday morning instead of ponti-
ficating that night in Broadcasting House, he might have
escaped the Bishop of Durham's acid observation to a
meeting of his clergy :

" I was always trained to believe that the Church of England
was an episcopal church governed by bishops, ruling in their
several dioceses.   Now I find it is coming to be some kind of
novel body governed by the British Broadcasting Corporation
and two Archbishops.   I do not like it."

On that fatal Sunday, December 13th, the Primate of All
England came to the microphone and said :

" During the last ten days we have seen strange things.

[*Such strange things that the scepticism evinced by Anglican
theologians in the report of the Commission on Christian Doctrine
appointed by the Archbishops of Canterbury and York might have
been modified, and one is surprised to read therein that " the
expectations of a single great Day of General Resurrection presents
great difficulties " or that " the notion of a Virgin Birth tends
to mar the completeness of the belief that in the Incarnation
God revealed himself at every point in and through human
nature."*]

" Very rarely in the long course of its history has the nation
passed through a week of such bewilderment, suspense,
anxiety.   Within twenty-four hours one King went and

another King came.   Yet there has been no confusion, no
strife, no clash of parties.   Truly it has been a wonderful proof
of the steadiness of the people in this country and throughout
the Empire.   It seems as if some strong tide of instinct rather
than of reasoned thought, flowing deep beneath the surface
eddies of excitement, has borne them through the rapids of the
crisis.   It is right to be proud of the way in which the nation
has stood the test.   Yet let there be no boasting in our pride.
Rather let it pass into humble and reverent thankfulness for
this renewed token of the guidance of the nation's life by the
overruling Providence of our God.

[*At what stage the expression of self-complacency becomes
boasting would be a nice problem of Christian behaviour for some
future Commission appointed by the Archbishops of Canterbury and
York.   We may no doubt acquit Dr Lang of any intention to boast
at the beginning of his broadcasting address, but a less felicitous
direction of his eloquence than that to which we are accustomed from
such an accomplished tongue suggested even to many of his own
children in God a note of elation in those opening words which was
unfortunate.   It may be added that the evidence for " the guidance
of the nation's life by the overruling Providence of our God " in
this particular matter was a great deal slighter than the evidence
for some of those great Christian mysteries which presented such
insurmountable stumbling-blocks to the faith of a few Anglican
theologians.*]

" What pathos, nay what tragedy, surrounds the central
figure of these swiftly moving scenes!   On the 11th day of
December, 248 years ago, King James II fled from Whitehall.

[*To avoid the clash of faction in the capital of his kingdom ;
to make it unnecessary for Lord Craven and his Guards to shoot
down the Dutch invaders marching along Whitehall.   It had
been wiser for Archbishop Lang to forbear from reminding his
hearers of that earlier triumph of Anglicanism.   Some of them
remembered that Archbishop Sancroft, though he had fought more
boldly with a King upon the Throne than ever Archbishop Lang,
could not accept King James's flight as an abdication and preferred
to surrender Lambeth itself rather than trim his conscience to
deny his King.   Archbishop Lang was more fortunate than his
predecessor in never having to face the remotest possibility of such
a strain upon his self-abnegation.   That being so, he should have
rejected the comparison as unworthy of a prelate, a scholar, or a
gentleman.*]

" By a strange coincidence, on the 11th day of December

last week King Edward VIII, after speaking his last words to his people, left Windsor Castle, the centre of all the splendid traditions of his ancestors and his Throne, and went out an exile.

[*But how imperfect a coincidence to recall, recalling as it did the treachery of those in high places, the lithe gyrations of opinion in menials and men of state, the base desertion of a King by his own daughters, the loss to the Church of England of all its holiest bishops and priests, and, though Mr Winston Churchill would not admit this, the self-accommodation of England's greatest soldier to his own ambition—a blot upon the escutcheon of the Churchills which was gloriously erased from it two hundred and forty-eight years later by himself. There is another observation to be made. Poetic licence might justify the use of a word like ' exile,' but it was highly injudicious for somebody in the position of the Archbishop of Canterbury to indulge in poetic licence before such a mixed audience. The first meaning of exile is penal banishment. Hundreds, if not thousands of his Grace's listeners, must have got into their heads a notion, which from their point of view later events seemed to confirm, that the Duke of Windsor had been pressed by the Government to leave the country. Well-informed opinion knew that this was not so, but well-informed opinion was submerged in that ocean of ill-informed opinion at the edge of which the Archbishop was paddling his archiepiscopal toes. It was, in fact, an indiscretion, and it is a grateful task to reassure public opinion that it was the Duke himself who desired to leave his native land for some time and thereby set the seal on his perfect demeanour throughout the crisis.*]

" In the darkness he left these shores.

[*Inasmuch as it was half an hour after midnight when the Duke reached Portsmouth, this statement was surely a pleonasm, unless it was a piece of melodramatic chiaroscuro applied by a partial brush.*]

" Seldom if ever has any Sovereign been welcomed by a more enthusiastic loyalty. From God he received a high and sacred trust. Yet by his own will he has abdicated—he has surrendered the trust.

[*The ascription to a prelate of a peculiar intimacy with the working of the Divine mind is a courtesy of common usage ; but such a courtesy has no support from dogmatic theology. If his Grace had stopped at ' abdication ' and not amplified that ' abdication ' with ' surrender,' his phraseology might have passed without criticism ; but we are permitted to speculate that an all-*

merciful and all-knowing God may have found in that surrender
the expression of a humility not found in the earthly judges of that
royal conduct.]
    " With characteristic frankness he has told us his motive.
It was a craving for private happiness. Strange and sad it
must be that for such a motive, however strongly it pressed
upon his heart, he should have disappointed hopes so high,
and abandoned a trust so great.
    [*The use of the word ' craving ' in this connection is a piece of*
rhetorical subtlety to suggest the unhealthiness of a moral narcotic.
Moreover, it is not true that King Edward abdicated even to
gratify a wish for private happiness. He abdicated because his
Prime Minister advised him that his proposed marriage was
incompatible with his people's craving for their private happiness.
He was not prepared to prolong his friendship with the woman
he loved in a manner that would have exposed her and himself to
scandal. He did not feel able to sustain worthily his high and
sacred trust without her help and support. When Mr Cosmo
Gordon Lang decided to leave the Church of Scotland and be
received into the Church of England, he was, from the point of view
of everybody except sincere Anglicans, gratifying his own craving
for private happiness. Surely we may ask from him as ready a
recognition of the sincerity of King Edward's motives as he would
justifiably expect us to accord to his own.]
    " Even more strange and sad it is that he should have
sought his happiness in a manner inconsistent with the
Christian principles of marriage,
    [*If this were even true of the King subjectively, and not merely*
objectively from the point of the Archbishop's personal belief, we
should have a right to retort that for centuries the Church of
England has sought its own convenience and pursued expediency in
a manner inconsistent with the Christian principles of marriage.
Roman Catholics and Anglo-Catholics could only have rejoiced at so
clear an affirmation of Dr Lang's own belief if he had followed it
up at the Church Assembly by showing his willingness to run the
risk even of a conflict between Church and State rather than allow
the present ambiguity of Anglican teaching about marriage to
continue.]
" and within a social circle whose standards and ways of
life are alien to all the best instincts and traditions of his
people. Let those who belong to this circle know that to-day
they stand rebuked by the judgment of the nation which had
loved King Edward. I have shrunk from saying these words.

But I have felt compelled for the sake of sincerity and truth to say them.

[*Enough has been written and said about this large accusation, and no more will be said now except that if the Archbishop's knowledge of the world had been equalled by his concern for sincerity and truth he would have abstained from this intemperate outburst. The shock of hearing so definite a pronouncement from the lips of an Archbishop gave his listeners an impression of courage, and that reputation for courage might have been confirmed if, when Lord Brownlow pointed out the slur on those like himself who were in the circle of the King's intimacy, the Archbishop instead of apologising to Lord Brownlow privately had apologised publicly over the radio.*]

" Yet for one who has known him since his childhood, who has felt his charm and admired his gifts, these words cannot be the last.   How can we forget the high hopes and promise of his youth ; his most genuine care for the poor, the suffering, the unemployed ; his years of eager service both at home and across the seas ?   It is the remembrance of these things that wrings from our heart the cry—' the pity of it, O, the pity of it ! '   To the infinite mercy and protecting care of God we commit him now wherever he may be.

[*These last words sounded in closer harmony with the moving words the Archbishop spoke in the House of Lords before the Duke of Windsor had left the country, but it was a failure of phrase to suggest by ' wherever he may be ' that the Duke was being blown across Europe like the fragments of a torn-up envelope.*]

" There are two other figures who will always stand out among the memories of these fateful days.   One is the ever-honoured and beloved Queen Mary.   She knows, for in her moving message she has told us so, that the respectful sympathy of the whole nation and Empire surrounds her.   During all the strain and tense anxiety, deep as her distress has been, her wonderful calmness, self-control, steadiness of judgment have never failed.   The thought of her reign by the side of her beloved husband for 25 years, of the sorrow which came to her when he passed from her sight, and of the fresh sorrow which within less than a year she has had to bear is a threefold cord which binds her fast to the hearts of her people.

" The other person who has earned our gratitude and admiration is the Prime Minister.   With great courage he took the whole burden on himself.   As one to whom throughout all these anxieties he has given his confidence I can personally testify that he has combined as perhaps he only could, the

Constitutional responsibility of a Minister, the human understanding of a man, and the faithfulness of a friend. History
will record that he was the pilot who by God's help steered the
Ship of State through difficult currents, through dangerous
rocks and shoals into the harbour where it now safely rests.

[*It was a pity that this eloquent and obviously sincere tribute
to the Prime Minister should have been uttered in conjunction
with an equally sincere but completely mistaken exposition of King
Edward's motives and behaviour.*]

" So much for the past, and now for the future. The
darkness of an anxious time is over. A new morning has
dawned. A new reign has begun. George VI is King.
You can readily imagine what it means to him to be summoned
so suddenly, so unexpectedly in circumstances so painful to
himself—for he was bound to his brother by ties of closest
affection—to face the immense responsibilities of Kingship.
Sympathy for him there must be, deep and real and personal.
But it passes into loyalty, a loyalty all the more eager, strong
and resolute because it rises from this heart of sympathy. It
is this wholehearted loyalty which with one heart and voice the
peoples of this Realm and Empire offer him to-day. He will
prove worthy of it.

" What I shall venture to say of him will be no mere
conventional eulogy. It will be said from the personal
knowledge I am sure he would allow me to say—of many
years of friendship.

" In manner and speech he is more quiet and reserved than
his brother. (And here may I add a parenthesis which may
not be unhelpful. When his people listen to him they will
note an occasional and momentary hesitation in his speech.
But he has brought it into full control, and to those who hear it
need cause no sort of embarrassment, for it causes none to him
who speaks.) He is frank, straightforward, unaffected. The
6000 boys from our public schools and from the homes of
working-folk whom for the last 15 years he has gathered in the
comradeship of a summer camp know that he has been himself
a boy among them.

" In varied fields of service—in the Navy, in the Air Force,
in association with all manner of public and charitable causes—
he has gained a wide experience. He has made the welfare of
industrial workers his special care and study. There is no
branch of industry where he is not at home. In this visits
with the Queen to Central Africa, to Australia and New

Zealand he has studied the peoples and the problems of the great Empire over which he is now called to rule. He has high ideals of life and duty, and he will pursue them with a quiet steadfastness of will. He inherits the name, he will follow the example of King George V, to whose memory let us offer now the homage of our undying affection and respect.

"No passage in the last message of the Duke of Windsor, as we must now learn to call our late King, was more touching than that in which he spoke of his brother's 'matchless blessing—a happy home with his wife and children.' King George will have at his side the gentle strength and quiet wisdom of a wife who has already endeared herself to all by her charm, her bright and eager kindliness of heart. As for her dear children, I will only say that they are as delightful and fascinating as she was in her own childhood as I remember it over thirty years ago. Truly it is good to think that among all the homes of the Empire—the homes from which all that is best within it springs—none can be more happy and united than the home of our King and Queen.

"A King has gone. God be with him. A King has come. God bless him, keep him, guide him now and ever.

"Only a few moments are left in which to say what I had most chiefly wished to say.

[How sad that unfulfilled pluperfect! It suggests that his Grace at the last moment changed the whole tone of his broadcast, and it was perhaps not surprising that the man in the street, bewildered by what he considered an unjustified and unjustifiable attack upon a Prince who was gone, should have supposed that much of the first part of this address was an impromptu, a sudden loss of self-control in fact. Others pretending to inside information declared that the effect of Queen Mary's message required an antidote. In high circles of Government and Court alike there was an unreasonable terror of the new King's ability to sustain the dignity of the Crown against what was known to be the overwhelming popularity of the Duke of Windsor. For this nervousness there was no sort of justification. The people of Great Britain were loyally determined to recognise the immense sacrifice which had been demanded of King George; Queen Mary had indicated with extreme appropriateness and infinite grace the right attitude. Such a lack of confidence in the common sense and decency of the general public belied all that adulation of the nation's behaviour during the ' crisis.' Nevertheless, plausible though the explanation of the antidote may have seemed at the time, a study

*of what remains of the Archbishop's address will supply a full
explanation of the terms in which it was framed.*]

"I must now reserve it for the message which I hope to
broadcast a fortnight hence on the last Sunday of the year. My
desire is then, if God will help me, to make to the nation a
somewhat solemn recall to religion. Who can doubt that in
all the events of these memorable days God has been speaking?

[*Only those, one may add, who had an uncomfortable feeling
that it might sometimes have been Mammon.*]

"It has been a time of shaking—a shaking, in possibility,
thank God, not in fact, of the very Throne itself; a shaking
of confidence, of seemingly assured hopes. Is there not a call
to us to see that 'those things which cannot be shaken may
remain'—faith in God, in His will, in His Kingdom? We
are all rallying to our new King. Will there not be a rally
also to the King of Kings?

"There is, I am persuaded, a real deep instinct of religion
in the heart of the people. But instinct, if it is to hold in times
of stress such as these in which we are living, must be made
strong by conviction and kindled by conscious faith. We
still call ourselves a Christian nation. But, if the title is to be
a reality and not a mere phrase, there must be a renewal in our
midst of definite and deliberate allegiance to Christ—to His
standards of life, to the principles of His Kingdom.

"We are now able to look forward with hope and joy to the
Coronation of our King. He himself and his Kingship will
then be solemnly consecrated to the service of the Most High
God. But the august ceremony will be bereft of a great
part of its true meaning unless it is accompanied by a new
consecration of his people to the same high service. So may
King and people alike acknowledge their allegiance to God
and dedicate themselves to seek first His Kingdom and His
Righteousness. 'Wherefore we receiving a kingdom which
cannot be moved, let us have grace whereby we may serve God
acceptably with reverence and godly fear.' "

In those final words may be found the inspiration of that
luckless broadcast. They must be read with the date mentioned at the beginning of it in mind. The moral crisis had
been precipitated—accidentally or deliberately awaits a final
and authoritative elucidation from the Bishop of Bradford—
by a prelate of the Church of England, and it was essential
that the Church of England should take advantage of what

looked like its most dazzling triumph since December 11th 1688, a triumph of which that party in the Church of England which aimed to assert its apostolicity and its catholicity was determined to take the fullest advantage.   Earlier in the autumn there had been those overtures to the Archbishop from other denominations to give their ministers and pastors an opportunity to share in the rites and ceremonies of the Coronation.   There had even been a proposal that the King's Communion should be omitted, and it was in attacking the Bishop of Birmingham's apparent support for such an innovation that most of the Bishop of Bradford's diocesan address had been taken up.   The Archbishop of Canterbury had been rigid in his refusal to allow any except Anglican prelates and clerics to participate.   It was the importance the Anglican clergy attached to their exclusive right to officiate at the Coronation which made them so jealous of any criticism that might be directed against the King's acknowledgment of their own sacerdotal claims, by the display from him of even as much indifference as that of the average Anglican to whom his Church represents something more like a social order than a divinely inspired institution.   Dr Lang from the time he became Bishop of Stepney had devoted the whole of his acute mind, the whole of his personal charm, the whole of his power of organisation to strengthening what sincere Anglicans called good churchmanship; to him King Edward's attitude towards ecclesiastical observances was a bitter mortification.

Some of this mortification found expression in that broadcast address, and bewildered those who did not understand the particular chagrin of the Primate.   It would have been a wise self-restraint not to speak thus even in the Cathedral of Canterbury.   From Broadcasting House such an address dealt a disastrous blow to religious feeling throughout the country and destroyed in advance any possible effect of the Archbishop's ' recall to religion ' a fortnight later.   ' The pity of it, O, the pity of it,' that the Primate did not recall his own speech in the House of Lords twenty-five years earlier when as Archbishop of York he reluctantly voted with the Government during the crisis of the Finance Bill.   " There were times when he that ruleth his spirit is better than he that taketh a city."

With those words taken from his own mouth his broadcast must stand rebuked.

And now let the sorry Christmas of 1936 draw closer to the spirit of that hallowed and gracious time.

From David Lloyd George, in Jamaica, to the Duke of Windsor, in Austria :

" Best Christmas greetings from an old Minister of the Crown who holds you in as high esteem as ever and regards you with deeper loyal affection, deplores the shabby and stupid treatment accorded to you, resents the mean and ungenerous attacks upon you, and regrets the loss sustained by the British Empire of a monarch who sympathised with the lowliest of his subjects."

CHAPTER XXIII

SPRING

IT was significant that the message from Mr Lloyd George came from Jamaica. Distance had detached him from the prevalent hysteria. The writer noted at the time that people in every walk of life who were compelled by their circumstances to make up their minds for themselves showed a strong majority in favour of the Duke of Windsor, and one may lay down as a general law for the trend of opinion that when people on the outskirts of a crowd are at odds with the mass in the centre their opinion is likely to prevail when the centre has boiled up suddenly, but likely to be overwhelmed when the mental agitation of the centre has come slowly to boiling point.

What told against the Duke of Windsor at the time was the suddenness with which the ' crisis ' had been generated. Tacitus has observed that truth thrives upon delay, falsity upon haste. In the brief time allowed there was no possibility of presenting the facts fairly even if conflicting interests had desired to present them fairly. Women who abused Mrs Simpson did not perceive that she had put women back on the map. Men who abused King Edward did not perceive that he had restored to humanity the true idea of kingship. Those who praised Mr Baldwin did not grasp that he had treated the Constitution as a managing director will sometimes treat the shareholders of a limited liability company. Those who talked glibly of the Church of England's attitude toward the remarriage of divorced persons were ignorant that this attitude had taken four centuries to crystallise and was even now not accepted with unanimity by members of that Church, clerical and lay. The best account of this orgy of self-complacent ill-informed sentimental egotism may be read in a book by Sir Philip Gibbs called *Ordeal in England*. There is no better journalist in the country than Sir Philip, which means that no man is more sensitive to the influence of the passing moment. It is an uncomfortable experience now to read the chapter he calls *The Crisis of the Crown* ; but it is as well to remind ourselves of the depths of stupidity to which Englishmen and Scotsmen can sink and one's discomfort is not assuaged by Sir Philip's apparent toleration of such stupidity.

> My soldier friend talked over the situation a little.
> " It may be for the best. The life at Fort Belvedere was not a shining example to the nation. No dignity. Jogging about to jazz tunes. Very strange people! Very odd behaviour! . . ."
> Astonishing man! He didn't seem to turn a hair at all this. . . . He was like many of those Brigadiers who had commanded during the war . . . steady eyes, and nerves like steel. . . .

And no doubt a cast-iron brain.

Then there were those young pilots of bombing machines in a mess of the Royal Air Force. " He has let us down," they shouted. And there was a dentist who " spoke with intense anger, ' We believed in him—and he's let us down.' "

Sir Philip Gibbs " heard that phrase a score of times, within forty-eight hours of the abdication." If he had found himself being jostled along in a flock of sheep there might have been a similar monotony of bleating to record.

And above this barnyard chorus of quacking, clucking, gobbling, bleating, mooing, neighing, and grunting the leaders of the Church of England fancied they heard a choir of angels. The Commission on Doctrine had " not felt called upon to discuss in detail the narratives of the Ascension," or in fact to say in so many words whether the members did or did not believe in it. The miracle of the Church of England's revival by the Abdication, the " physical features " of which did not have " to be interpreted symbolically," provided a more fruitful topic.

In January the Archbishop of York addressing the Convocation of the Northern Province put forward the startling proposition that the King was the incarnation of the Community. " He is not chiefly the first officer of the State." The meaning of the Coronation was the dedication of the King and his Consort to the service of the King of kings, and their consecration by Him through His Church to the service of their people.

We shall not at this stage of a long book pause to argue with Dr Temple about this novel dogma of the Community's incarnation in the King beyond observing that it might have puzzled the Council of Chalcedon in the year 451. It may be pointed out, however, that even the clouds of the mind have usually a silver lining, and of this theological nebula the silver lining is to be found in those three words " through His Church." The claim is made that the consecration of the King would be invalid except ' through His Church.' If by His Church we are to understand the Church of England, and presumably we are to understand that, the statement is controversial. Obviously such a challenge cannot be accepted here. All that readers are invited to note is that the Primate of England by that statement rallied to the support of the Primate of All England, and although not hitherto identified with High Church theory now surrendered to it. One speculates what a former Bishop of London would have replied to that little fat thirteen-year old son of his in June 1894 if he had asked his father whether the community was incarnate in Queen Victoria; but such a scene from the Fulham Palace of over forty years earlier is too fanciful. It is more useful to note what the late Canon ' Dick ' Sheppard had to say about the Archbishop of Canterbury's recall to religion a month after it was sounded, and let it be borne in mind that Canon Sheppard was Dean of Canterbury for the first two or three years of Dr Lang's occupation of the See.

Canon Sheppard writing in the *Sunday Express* of February 7th 1937 invited his readers to reflect whether " recall to religion " suggested to them " a nation imbued with a passion for righteousness, or merely a nation resolved on respectability."

And with that severe but perhaps just comment by a man as near to God's little poor man of Assisi as any the Church of England has yet inspired we must leave the bishops and the clergy. That they played a great part in stirring up the mud which was flung after the Duke of Windsor is undeniable; but clergymen are a credulous class, even if the report of the Commission on Christian Doctrine may suggest the contrary. We should remember their susceptibility to share-pushers, and the lack of worldly experience to check their belief in the

fantastic tales circulated about the Duke.   The Archbishop of
Canterbury himself was at the mercy of tittle-tattle.   So much
was obvious from his broadcast.   His judgment collapsed
under the strain.   He may have regretted that outburst by
now, and if that be so his fellow-Christians must pray
that Almighty God will grant him the courage to admit
his mistake.   Cranmer atoned for much by his demeanour in
the flames.   Dr Lang's immediate predecessor was spiritually
chastened by the remorse he felt for the destruction of Dolling's
work in that Portsmouth slum, and though Dr Davidson was
naturally fearful of finding himself in a minority he wiped out
that earlier folly by his courage during the General Strike.
Yet even if the Archbishop of Canterbury should not be
granted the grace to admit he made an error of judgment it
should still be easier to forgive his speech than Mr Baldwin's
silence.   Not a word did the Prime Minister utter in public
on behalf of that former King whose friendship he claimed,
whose magnanimity he had lauded, throughout that bleak
and bitter Spring of 1937.

Let us allow that Mr Baldwin approached the problem
of King Edward's marriage with perfect integrity.   Let us
believe that throughout these months he never once considered his own fame.   Let us in fact accept his own estimate
of his character and his philosophy, his means and his ends.
Let us recognise that he was faced with a task that required
tact and resolution.   Let us recognise equally the skill with
which he carried through that task.   Thanks to his handling
of the business the King's abdication was accomplished with
nothing more than a nine days' lag in the Christmas shopping
and some uncertainty on the Stock Exchange.   Mr Baldwin
as good as told a House of Commons on whose sympathy with
himself he was perhaps justifiably playing that it was King
Edward's behaviour that was to be thanked for the harmony
preserved.   He admitted that if the King had chosen he
could have married in due course and presented the Government
with a *fait accompli*, which it was certain could not have been
undone except at the cost of splitting the nation into two
factions.   He accepted Prince Edward's acknowledgement
that he had been treated with every consideration by his
Ministers.   When Prince Edward left the country Mr Baldwin
retired for that well-earned rest to Worcestershire.   There he
was accorded a volume of adulation to match the extravagance
of which we must scan the contemporary German Press or the

eulogies of their patrons by eighteenth-century poets. He remained at the head of the Government until after the Coronation. During that time he made it clear that the steady aggrandisement of the Prime Minister's power during his term of office was to reflect an attitude not beheld in an English Prime Minister since the eighteenth century.

If Mr Baldwin's Government had encroached on the Royal prerogative by offering a piece of Somaliland to Abyssinia without having obtained the consent of the Sovereign in advance, if in 1935 he had to all intent and purpose dissolved Parliament on his own initiative, if in a dozen ways he had undermined the Legislature and the Throne to strengthen the Executive and incorporate it in the person of the Prime Minister, he was most willing to show his appreciation of what *The Times* on November 30th had called " the power of democratic institutions to give a country steadiness and balance . . . and its [Parliament's] solid strength in any crisis that may arise, whether foreign or domestic." He added £37,000 a year to the salaries of Cabinet Ministers, secured their legal status which they did not possess before, and under criticism " emphasised the importance of placing men in high office in a position where they should be free from temptation—an example which he thought might with advantage be followed by other countries," though he said nothing about Marconi shares or Budget leakage in this country. The Prime Minister was to have £10,000 a year and a pension of £2,000 (which last Mr Baldwin himself would decline), and the Leader of the Opposition £2,000 a year while he was on the job. The day before Mr Baldwin retired he let the House of Commons know that the Government would introduce a motion raising members' salaries from £400 to £600, an increase which that obedient House less than a month later voted itself with only seventeen dissentients And Santa Claus had not finished yet.

When Mr Baldwin retired he shattered precedent by appearing to appoint his successor, the choice of whom when a Prime Minister resigns without a general election has always been the prerogative of the Sovereign. The appearance of constitutional etiquette was probably preserved; but there was a cynical lack of decency in the way Mr Baldwin allowed his nomination of Mr Chamberlain to be public knowledge weeks in advance. This was on top of another blow to the dignity of the Crown by the Regency Act which took away from the

King his discretion in the appointment of Counsellors of State to act for him during illness. We know of course that it was not the Prime Minister, but that it was King George who created him Earl Baldwin of Bewdley and gave him the Garter. However, if the Garter was a pleasant surprise for the stocking of Santa Claus himself, there were, in accord with custom, decorations for the reindeer of the secretariat and a viscounty for Sir J. J. C. Davidson, for whose exclusively political services a viscounty appeared an excessive reward. Nor was that the end. On June 21st Earl Baldwin of Bewdley, K.G., announced that an anonymous admirer " in appreciation of his services to the country " had placed £250,000 at his disposal for the creation of a fund to strengthen the ties of Empire. After pulling out this plum for the country Britannia's Jack Horner faded more or less from public life until the morning paper of the day on which these last pages have been written revealed that he had taken to making speeches again. On May 14th 1938, in Worcester he was presented with an illuminated address and some seventeenth-century tapestry : an appropriate gift that tapestry if it illustrated the year 1688. In his speech of thanks Lord Baldwin declared :

" I always hoped to be a blacksmith. It is a man's job, but as the fates would have it I found another kind of man's job that took just as much patience as that of a blacksmith, and dealt with material hardly less malleable."

Malleable, indeed, that House of Commons in December 1936 ! For this confession Lord Baldwin is owed " such thanks as fits a king's remembrance." But was not that sometime king owed such thanks as fitted a minister's re-membrance ? Without a king's chivalry and honesty and self-discipline that bright ladder up which Mr Baldwin climbed to his renown as saviour of the State would have dissolved like a ' dusky ladder of steep rain.'

Yet not a word did he utter in public on behalf of that former King whose friendship he claimed, whose magnanimity he had lauded, throughout that bleak and bitter Spring of 1937.

While Mr Baldwin was resting himself in Worcestershire a mysterious spirit inspired the gramophone companies not to publish the record of Prince Edward's last broadcast from Windsor. A record made in America from the broadcast as received there was sold on order at one of the great London stores. That was the first dirty piece of denigration nodded upon by officialdom. The excuse was that it was unfair to their present Majesties to allow the record to be circulated. Commands from the directorate were issued to the newspaper offices which throughout had worked against King Edward that the Duke of Windsor was never to be mentioned unless it was absolutely necessary and then always without prominence. No measures were taken to stop the lies that were buzzing like fat blowflies round what was hoped was a dead renown. The country succumbed to a hysteria of defamation.

Rather than bring blushes to the faces of readers who have recovered from and, it may be hoped, repented of that drunken debauch of calumny by reminding them of the nonsense they talked and listened to during those days it will be more serviceable to history to deal with print.

To *Maclean's Magazine* which has a circulation of a quarter of a million in Canada Mr Beverley Baxter, M.P., contributed for January 15th 1937 an article called *Why Edward Quit*. From this gall-bladder we will extract a few stones:

> It is with no desire to revive the torrent of gossip, conjecture and dispute about the tragedy of Edward VIII that I write this letter. I know what a deep personal hurt it has been to Canada, because he was more in tune with the tempo of Canadian life than with that of any other Dominion.

Therefore it was important to present the Duke of Windsor to Canada as henceforth for ever out of tune. Mr Baxter himself was a piece of Canadian raw material which had been shaped in England and was now being reimported to its native land.

> Yet I think I should set down the facts of this unhappy thing, since it was inevitable that, as a Member of Parliament and as a journalist, I should see the unfolding of that drama from its beginning to its incredible end. . . .
> I refuse to believe, with the sentimentalists, that this is a love affair of such depth that even the story of Tristan and Isolde loses some of its glamour in comparison.
> We should face the truth. King Edward did not abdicate the throne in order to marry Mrs Simpson. He abdicated because, in his own opinion, his actions rendered him unfit to occupy the throne of Britain any longer.

How far journalism of this kind is a breach of its privileges may be left to the House of Commons to decide ; but to resent as members did Dr Salter's accusation of drunkenness in 1926 and allow Mr Beverley Baxter by implication to present them as a set of cads argues an undue sensitiveness about the drink.   If this legislator had disclaimed what he wrote as an expression of Parliamentary opinion and made it clear that his point of view was that of a Canadian journalist it would still be questionable whether he was privileged to insult the Duke of Windsor like this, directly and by his remarks about his future wife ; but he doubled the offence by claiming authority ' as a Member of Parliament and as a journalist.'

> Napoleon on the *Bellerophon* was a less pathetic figure.   There were still thousands of F renchmen who would have died for the fallen Emperor.   Y et, four hours previously I had sat in a theatre where Edward's farewell broadcast was relayed, and not one cheer greeted the last words of the former King.

That theatrical audience was far too deeply moved to cheer.   Cheers are the facile expression of a Parliament's ductility.   There would have been plenty of Englishmen to lay down their lives for King Edward if the King's standard had been raised ; there may be even enough to kick Mr Beverley Baxter out of his Wood Green constituency at the next election.

> The implacable spirit of Cromwell had risen from the grave and entered the soul of a man named Baldwin.   The challenge of the King was not to the rights of Parliament but to the moral standards of the nation, and Parliament, as the nation's spokesman, closed its ranks as it did when the threat came from King Charles I.

The word ' implacable ' should be noted.   It is not an epithet the present writer would have ventured to apply to Mr Baldwin during this time ; but presumably it represents lobby opinion, and the possible appropriateness of it may be considered.

" Parliament as the nation's spokesman " is a fine flight of hyperbole, but if it be accepted we may be driven to deride that spokesman as a ventriloquist's dummy.   First Napoleon, then Cromwell, then Charles I !   Mr Baxter's mind is a pageant— or a penny wax-work show.

> The Archbishop of Canterbury, as head of the Established Church, informed his Majesty that he would not permit any of his priests to solemnise the marriage.

If the Archbishop of Canterbury made such a statement, which is most improbable, he had no power to do so. Mr Baxter has an exaggerated notion of what the Archbishop of Canterbury can do; but as the *Daily Sun-Times* (Owen Sound, Ontario) has claimed that the Archbishop of Canterbury is " God's vicegerent [*sic*] on earth," * Mr Baxter may be following orthodox Canadian opinion.

In the course of his next remarks which are unprintable, Mr Baxter picked up a slop-bowl holding the dregs of vulgar opinion at the moment and emptied the contents over the people of Canada, after which he had the insolence to observe:

> My own feelings are somewhat restrained by an acquaintanceship with the Simpsons going back a long time.

This restrained politician and journalist who at present is employed as editorial adviser by Allied Newspapers then proceeded to insult his former King and his former hostess in words he would not have dared to print in England. It is from no consideration for Mr Baxter's feelings that they are not reprinted in this book.

> Baldwin came to the House next day and announced the abdication. He did not make a political speech. He seemed to call us about the fireside like members of one family and tell us of the tragedy of the eldest son; the son from whom we had expected so much. . . .

---

* " Hanover, May 11. St James Anglican Church was filled to capacity on Sunday evening to hear Mr Wm. Perkins Bull, K.C., of Toronto, deliver his Coronation address. This well-known Canadian based his talk on the exemplary life of the man who in his opinion was the greatest man who ever lived, the Prophet Moses, and when he compared King George of Great Britain with that great Prophet and declared that the forthcoming Coronation procession would be second only to the world's greatest and most gorgeous procession, the burial of Moses, his listeners were thrilled with the spirit of loyalty and were proud that they were citizens of the great British Empire. . . .
" Evidently in heaven as on earth, processions express man's deepest emotions whether of grief or joy.
" It has been so since time began. In 2349 B.C., the animals went into the Ark two by two, and 12th July 1937 will find Orangemen walking in colorful array.
" Were a Moses available to-day, it occurs to me that the Children of Israel and the descendants of Ham would have vastly different stories to tell of processions in and out of Germany and Ethiopia.
" Our King and Moses have much in common. . . .
" His Majesty and Moses have in common the further fact that they play leading rôles in the two greatest processions known to history. Both religious ceremonies: the one conducted by the Almighty Himself; the other, in the hands of His Grace, the Archbishop of Canterbury, God's vicegerent on earth. . . ."

There was one fatal sentence in it [*i.e.* King Edward's broadcast]. The King said that if at any time in the future he could serve England he would do so. It sounded like a man who had deserted from the front line saying he would give a hand in the next war.

On this last dastardly insult a Member of Parliament may be left to his constituents, a journalist to his readers.

Mr Baxter's remarks were taken up in the Editorial of *Maclean's Magazine* which asked in heavy type :

WAS EDWARD UNWITTINGLY DUPED BY INTERNATIONAL SCHEMERS? WAS HIS INFATUATION USED AS A MEANS TO PRECIPITATE A CRISIS IN WHICH IT WAS HOPED THE BALDWIN GOVERNMENT WOULD BE UPSET AND FOREIGN POLICIES ALTERED ? NO OFFICIAL DOCUMENTS WILL EVER ANSWER THESE QUESTIONS. BUT SOME DAY THEY MAY BE ANSWERED.

Those questions can be answered now once for all by two sharp and contemptuous negatives.

What the Editor of *Maclean's Magazine*, in a pathetic attempt to impress his quarter of a million readers with his own inside information, kept as questions were stated as facts in a sinister little pamphlet published by the Periscope Publishing Company in Toronto, under the title of *International Espionage behind Edward's Abdication.*

The copy in the writer's possession is marked 6th edition, so that this wretched compilation of ignorance, fanaticism and malevolence has evidently had an extended vogue in Ontario. Here are some less vile excerpts :

. . . Only those in the highest councils of State KNOW what a hairbreadth escape we, Anglo-Saxondom, have so recently experienced (Dec. 1936). Nothing but a miracle explains why we are not in Jan. 1937 in the throes, first of all, of the most devastating revolution WITHIN THE COMMONWEALTH over the momentous constitutional question of King Edward's abdication, but also not in the throes of the most devilish war in which human life, wholesale, is being ripped in pieces. And here we are, going about as complacently as ever, (since 1918) blissfully unconscious of all that which had been deliberately planned for our nation to experience.

. . . It would amaze the reader if he knew the mind of Germany and Italy! He would no longer discount the reality of their fiendish designs and he would stand, petrified, if he knew how very near to realisation did those designs come ! He would be most ready to admit that failure of their maturity was not due to our preparedness or ability to muddle through, but to some mysterious miscalculation on the part of the perpetrators of these designs. They failed to take into consideration the fact that the Anglo-Saxon people really believe under the surface, the precepts of Christianity, though so delinquent in putting them into practice.   Further, our Race has ever turned to God for intervention at the time of a major crisis and in every instance has found deliverance.   This turning to God has taken the form of simple supplication nationally, as, for instance,on June 16th, 1918. The answer to that Day of Prayer came back within twenty-four hours, as revealed by the reverse change of direction in the course the Great War was taking. . . .

. . . Did God have something to do with the fact that the King's choice should have been, of all persons, a divorcee, so that ON THIS VERY ISSUE, PUBLIC OPINION would be caused to revolt rather than allow the Throne to become so detrimentally affected ?   Herein lay the all-determining factor.   ROME BLUNDERED AGAIN.

. . . From Rome, international Finance has been working ceaselessly for more than five years to gain access to Britain's State Secrets, for the avowed purpose of springing a constitutional crisis in which the Throne would be the centre of controversy.   If such a crisis could be created, then the Commonwealth, caught in the confusion and distress of an internal constitutional issue, would be most vulnerable to a smashing blow to be delivered by the combined navies and air forces of Italy, Germany and their Allies.   Broken, the Commonwealth could be sliced up as desired. . . .

. . . For more than three and a half years, certain State Secrets have been divulged by these foreign agents who were, therefore, at work during the closing years of the reign of King George V, and whose activities were not only causing grave concern to State authorities, but undoubtedly had much to do with the premature death of our former beloved monarch.   Not satisfied with having brought his life, his influence for good, and his own personal happiness to an untimely end, these same agents extended their vicious operations to involve the HEIR to the Throne. . . .

. . . The single accomplishment of Stanley Baldwin in having saved the Throne and the unity of the people in the recent crisis of the King's abdication, is but the latest of a long series of lesser (but none the less vital) achievements he has made.   His remarkable success was largely due to his SIMPLE HONESTY, CLEAR THINKING, WISDOM AND CAUTIOUS ACTION in everything to which he has put his hand. . .

This pamphlet, which imperatively demands a prosecution for criminal libel, is still being circulated in this country, but no steps have been taken to suppress it.   A Member of Parliament makes certain innuendoes.   On these innuendoes the editor of the paper in which they are printed asks rhetorical questions which support the innuendoes.   Finally the questions become statements of fact in a pamphlet.   In every case Lord Baldwin is put forward and extolled as the saviour of his country. What circulation would be allowed to a pamphlet asserting that Mr Baldwin had betrayed the King in the interests of his own self-glorification? None. Yet, much crueller and equally false allegations against the Duke and Duchess of Windsor have been tolerated by those in power. Throughout that sowing of tares Mr Baldwin himself remained rolled up as quiet as a woodlouse under a flower-pot. He should beware lest the verdict of history on him and the Archbishop of Canterbury may coincide with Alice's verdict upon the Walrus and the Carpenter:

"I like the Walrus best," said Alice, "because you see he was a *little* sorry for the poor oysters."
"He ate more than the Carpenter, though," said Tweedledee. "You see he held his handkerchief in front, so that the Carpenter couldn't see how many he took: contrariwise."
"That was mean!" Alice said indignantly. "Then I like the Carpenter best—if he didn't eat so many as the Walrus."
"But he ate as many as he could get," said Tweedledum.

The generosity with which Ministers of the Crown had voted themselves another £37,000 a year besides calling on the country to give life-pensions to all retired prime ministers, suggested that as much generosity might be displayed toward King Edward, but it was not forthcoming. Those fierce *sans culottes* in the Labour Party were determined to oppose a State Grant. That once so edible lettuce had become as prickly as a thistle. When one remembers the Duke of Windsor's twenty-five years of devoted service as Prince of Wales it is difficult to write with restraint of such a petty piece of self-assertiveness. The Labour members of that Parliament will live on to earn the contempt of history as the men who handed over the red flag to Mr Baldwin so that he could wave it like an old bucolic railway-guard intent on safety first.

On December 8th 1936 a Mr Francis Stephenson, a middle-aged lawyer's clerk, employed by Messrs. Thorp, Saunders and Thorp, a firm of London solicitors, had paid half a crown at the Somerset House Divorce Registry and served an affidavit on the King's Proctor "reporting that he had reasons to show why the Simpson divorce should not be made absolute, by reason of material facts not having been brought before the court, and/or by reason of the divorce having been obtained by collusion."

Four days later the Intervener told Mrs Simpson's solicitors that he had decided not to proceed further and that he was satisfied that he had no reason to intervene.

On January 19th 1937 Sir Boyd Merriman ordered that the King's Proctor should be asked to examine Mr Stephenson's intervention because " as long as its appearance remains on the records, a decree absolute cannot be pronounced."

Mr Stephenson had had nothing except a few nonsensical rumours with which to feed the King's Proctor and he soon retired into an obscurity from which it was a pity he ever emerged. The King's Proctor, however, had already been at work making investigations of his own in answer to a mass of wild letters. As an honourable man he could not lend himself to gratify the hopes of many people that he would be able to intervene successfully and jam the divorce. We shall never see his correspondence; we shall never hear an echo of the whispers that cold-hearted correct officials and highly placed clerics breathed in his ear. This much is certain : if it had been possible to upset that divorce, it would have been upset. It was impossible.

In February men and women of good will heard with joy that the Princess Royal accompanied by the Earl of Harewood had visited her brother in Austria. It was rumoured that the King's advisers had intervened to prevent the Duke of Kent's going on from the Dutch royal wedding to Enzesfeld and this had added to the growing tide of resentment against the Prime Minister. The rumour was repeated in print and no contradiction was offered at the time, nor has any been offered since.

On April 27th the decree *nisi* was pronounced and the Duke of Windsor was able to join Mrs Warfield at the Château de Candé where they were the guests of Mr and Mrs Charles Bedaux.

The immense interest in this reunion agitated the people at home over its effect on the Coronation, and indeed they had reason to be agitated when this kind of drivel was being published in Canada :

GET OUT THE FUNNY COSTUMES FOR CORONATION'S
BIG NIGHT

The evening of May 12th, Coronation Day, in Owen Sound, should be one to be long remembered. Armistice Day or the New Orleans Mardi Gras are the nearest approach one can think of.

The Empire has come through difficult times, the new King will be crowned, the ceremonies over, a new day has dawned, a new era has begun. So let us cast dull care away and be merry. Get out the funny costumes and the fantastic raiment. Let joy be unconfined. Let it be a veritable tintinabulation of happiness. Let the fat, the thin, the tall, the short and his brother and sister laugh and the world will laugh with him.

Let us be unpacified and unpasteurised as we swing into the parade at the park. Follow the band, and wind up at the city square; hold your girl's hand, in fact hold anybody's hand and we will salute not only Georgian Bay but the happy Georgian Era.

We will be seeing you Samantha! When? In the parade Wednesday night, and be sure and wear your funny suit.

We are going to have a time.

The funniest costume of all would have been Truth in a maple-leaf. " O God! O Montreal! " Samuel Butler once apostrophised in disgust.*

The policy of dark and deliberate silence about the Duke and Duchess of Windsor which was followed by the majority of newspapers was extended even to the *Annual Register*, of which the volume for 1937 contains not a single reference to the Duke and Duchess of Windsor. The wealth of material in the *Annual Register* has shrunk since the war, but it is still an indispensable publication. What will the historian of fifty years hence say about this volume for 1937, larded with the charitable bequests of Lord Nuffield and glistening with Lord Baldwin's honours, when he wishes to check the date of the marriage of the Duke of Windsor and finds that the victory of Mid-Day Sun in the Derby is the only event recorded in the Chronicle for the first three weeks of June? What will he say when he refers to the date on which the decree *nisi* was made absolute and discovers that the gift of 300 acres of woodland by the Graves Charitable Trust to the City of Sheffield has rendered April 27th 1937 a more significant date in history?

On May 18th the following announcement was handed to Press reporters by Mr Herman Rogers:

OFFICIAL ANNOUNCEMENT OF
THE DUKE OF WINDSOR'S MARRIAGE.

His Royal Highness the Duke of Windsor announces that his marriage to Mrs Wallis Warfield, daughter of the

* But we must not be too critical of Canada. The day after the abdication, the B.B.C. announced that the date of the Coronation would be the same as that fixed for King Edward's. " There will, however, be an important change," the announcer added. " As there is now a Queen, peeresses will wear coronets."

late Mr and Mrs Teakle Warfield, of Maryland, will take place at the Château de Candé, Monts, on Thursday, June 3.

Invitations to the wedding of the Duke of Windsor and Mrs Warfield will be confined to those who have been with them during the past months.

There will be no member of the royal family present.

The announcement that no member of the Royal Family would be present roused fresh indignation over the Duke's treatment, and that indignation was by now far more widely spread than during the nation's hysterical collapse immediately after the abdication. Sanity and decency were returning to the country. The subject is too delicate to be discussed at present, but of one thing we may feel sure : it was not the Royal Family which desired this sop to the Cerberus of Church, State, and Court. The date chosen for the wedding was the birthday of King George V, a happy thought. Yet, even this happy thought was held against the Duke of Windsor by those determined to " kill " him. It was not to be expected that the ecclesiastical authorities would encourage a religious ceremony. That would have demanded an illogicality beyond anything of which even they had so often shown themselves capable. However, the Reverend R. A. Jardine, Vicar of St Paul's, Darlington, hearing that the Duke desired a religious ceremony, volunteered to perform it, and his offer was accepted.

At this even the Bishop of Durham lost his temper. He was right in saying, " Mr Jardine has no authority whatever to officiate in any other diocese than Durham unless he has the sanction of the proper ecclesiastical authority," but when he went on to say, " If the marriage of the Duke of Windsor were taking place within the diocese of Durham, the Bishop of Durham would consider himself in duty bound to inhibit him," he was talking nonsense. Dr Hensley Henson could no more have inhibited Mr Jardine from marrying the Duke of Windsor in St Paul's, Darlington, provided the banns had been duly called, than he could have inhibited the Pope from preaching in St Peter's. And if the wedding had been performed without banns or special licence Dr Hensley Henson would have had to summon the aid of the civil arm to deal with his turbulent priest. The *Church Times* which in 1898 was so worried over the laxity of the bishops in upholding the marriage law of the Church was gratified by this display of " the principle of authority and jurisdiction."

Within an hour of Mr. Jardine's intentions being disclosed . . . the episcopal authorities did all that was possible to dissociate the Church from the proceedings. There is no process of law by which a clergyman wandering abroad may be prevented from saying prayers in a private house at the request of his host, and that, of course, is all that the pretended solemnisation with the rites of the Church amounted to. . . .

Although Roman Catholics believe that as between the present Archbishop of Canterbury and that Balliol undergraduate Mr Cosmo Gordon Lang who, 'made up as a doctor of divinity,' read the prologue at the first performance of the O.U.D.S. there is a difference merely in age, but none in his sacerdotal qualifications, no Roman Catholic would dream of describing a celebration of marriage by the Archbishop as a 'pretended solemnisation.' The *Church Times* must look up the Catholic doctrine of marriage to which it is so eager the Church of England should conform. There has been no *Ne Temere* decree from Lambeth.

But perhaps the *Church Times* would call this " one more striking example of the growing Roman Catholic opposition to democracy," for that is what, on December 11th 1936, it discovered was the inspiration of the attitude of the Catholic Press toward the abdication. Well, well, who would have thought that one day the Establishment would aspire to be scarlet ?

The film of the marriage ceremony was not exhibited. The campaign of obliteration continued. Without directly accusing Government spies it is worth recording that a letter from the private secretary acknowledging a telegram of wedding wishes, to the Duke and Duchess, dated June 9th 1937, and postmarked from Nötsch * on June 10th, was not delivered at its destination until September 8th. It looked as if a list had been made of those who wished well to a great gentleman and a great lady, and that by an accident this particular letter lingered three months in the wrong file. That sort of thing has happened before, and there were two kinds of gum on the flap of the envelope.

This very June Mr Laurence Housman's *Victoria Regina* which had been so long forbidden by the censor was produced at the Lyric Theatre thanks to an order wh'ch King Edward made shortly before the Crystal Palace was burnt that the prohibition to represent Queen Victoria on the stage

* The post-office for Schloss Wasserleonburg where the honeymoon was spent.

should lapse after the hundreth anniversary of her accession to the Throne.

When Mr Housman was called before the curtain on the first night, he said :

" I shall not make the speech I have been asked not to make. I shall content myself with saying, ' At last, at last! ' "

So fearful were those in power that the name of King Edward would be cheered in a London theatre !

An experiment was made in public calumny when Garter King of Arms at a lunch moaned about the hardship of the heraldic lot by telling his listeners that King Edward had insisted on the arrangements for the funeral of his father being carried through in eight days. The Duke had to issue the contradiction already recorded.

That bleak and bitter Spring was lingering. June has been a glorious month in the annals of England; but the June of 1937 disgraced them, even if Lord Baldwin was presented by an anonymous admirer with £250,000 to start a fund for strengthening the ties of Empire.

And we have not yet mentioned the nation's wedding-present to the Duke of Windsor in May. Mr Attlee and his *sans culottes* had let it be known they would oppose a grant from the Civil List in gratitude for a quarter of a century's devoted service to the State. So we knew that the wedding-present from the nation would not take the form of gold or silver. Nevertheless, we had not expected that the wedding-present would take the shape it did. The announcement of it was made in the *London Gazette* :

> The King has been pleased by Letters Patent under the Great Seal of the Realm bearing date the 27th day of May 1937, to declare that the Duke of Windsor shall, notwithstanding his Instrument of Abdication . . . be entitled to hold and enjoy for himself only the title style or attribute of Royal Highness so however that his wife and descendants if any shall not hold the said title style or attribute.

And to wrap up the wedding-present Mr Baldwin's earldom was announced on the same page.

This withdrawal from the Duke of Windsor's wife of the title style or attribute of Royal Highness was in effect to make his marriage morganatic, and as Lord Baldwin had declared morganatic marriage did not exist in this country something seemed to have gone wrong. When the Lady Elizabeth Bowes-Lyon married the Duke of York it was announced in the *London Gazette* that she would take the title style or attribute of Royal Highness " in accordance with the settled general rule that a wife takes the status of her husband." A similar announcement was made when the Lady Alice Montagu-Douglas-Scott married the Duke of Gloucester. No such announcement was made on behalf of the Viscount Lascelles when he married the Princess Mary, for the reason that it is not a settled general rule that a husband takes the status of his wife. The theory that by the Instrument of Abdication the title of Royal Highness was merged in the Crown and had to be granted afresh will not bear examination. Nothing could make the abdicated king less than H.R.H. Prince Edward. The grant was the Dukedom of Windsor. It would be far easier to make out a case for the Crown's resting in abeyance between their Royal Highnesses Princess Elizabeth and Princess Margaret Rose should (which God forfend) his present Majesty cease to reign. The confusion caused has been such that Burke and Debrett have issued mutually contradictory tables of precedence.

The trouble is that too many of the people involved in that unhappy business of December 1936 are the prey of the mawworm, self-righteousness. If the Duchess of Windsor was to be accorded the title of Royal Highness those queasy people feared lest public opinion, particularly in Australia, might suffer a reaction and ask why if the Duchess of Windsor could be her Royal Highness after the abdication she could not have been her Majesty without an abdication. Add to this itch to be right the anxious manners of our now largely *nouvelle noblesse*, whose women have so little confidence in their own dignity that they dread the effect on it of having to curtsey to the Duchess of Windsor. Add further the wilful blindness of the Establishment which is still trying to pretend that the Duke of Windsor's marriage differs in some mysterious way from many other Anglican marriages in which one of the parties has divorced a husband or wife. Add finally the hope of many guilty consciences that so long as the title of Royal Highness is denied to the Duchess of Windsor the Duke himself will not return to his native land. No more subtle decree to ensure perpetual banishment was ever penned than that announcement in the *London Gazette* of May 27th 1937. Not Venice nor Byzantium nor even Susa of the Medes and Persians devised a deadlier sentence.

And to gratify an implacable minority which does not represent a tenth of the Empire's population the Empire is to be denied the service of the Duke of Windsor in the thunderous future ahead. This malignity of vain and foolish men must cease. No more can be exacted from the Duke. Their Royal Highnesses must return. This is not to plead a favour, but to assert a right. The tide of reaction against the treatment with which the Duke has been betrayed is running more strongly all the time. Mr Chamberlain has lately revealed himself as a statesman. Let him allow his imagination more play. King Edward VIII, torn between two duties, chose to follow that which he believed himself best able to fulfil. The verdict of history is secure. He chose rightly. The moral influence of his choice has been immense, and by it he has restored self-respect to millions of his countrymen.

The grand corruption of our age is the inability of eminent human beings to preserve the integrity of their essential selves beneath the weighty trappings of the figures they present to the world. Perhaps it has been the grand corruption of every age, and remembering the Gospel we need not restrict that inability to eminence. The supreme lesson of the Divine Incarnation is the perfection of that awe-inspiring manhood of God, which is yet always within the comprehension of the feeblest of human creatures. To few Kings has been granted the gift of being intelligible human beings to the humblest of their subjects. King Edward was one of these few. Turn back the pages of this book and find therein his peer in that single regard. If he has made mistakes, they were common to fallible humanity: it has been the courage and sincerity with which he has accepted the sole responsibility for any mistakes he may have made that has given him uniqueness in the world of to-day. As a nation believed by the rest of the world to be mentally dishonest we cannot afford to disown such a witness to the honesty that we can achieve and show forth.

Lord Baldwin's speeches and actions, the Archbishop's sermons and conduct, accused them both of presenting to the world not themselves, but effigies of themselves. They may have believed that those effigies served a moral purpose, that in fact the effigies of the leader of the National Government and the leader of the National Church were something better than the essential Stanley Baldwin and the essential Cosmo Gordon Lang. They might plausibly insist that people want their leaders to be cast in the image of their own preconceptions of such leaders and that King Edward's indulgence of his own desire for truth was fatal to his beneficent sway as a monarch. He too should have wrought an effigy of himself for the world to admire. To be sure, such an effigy would have saved the myriad jealousies of foolish women who wondered why one apparently ordinary woman should win a King's love, the myriad vanities of petty men who enjoyed feeling that the greatest sovereign on earth was at their mercy. Yet the man was greater than the King.

Truth may come like death as a leveller; but on both judgment attends, and from that judgment what a golden legend shall be linked with the name of a king who weighed his crown against truth and found it lighter metal!

And with these words let the rattle of the loom be silent. There is much that might still be urged, much that might still be rebutted, much that might have been better said, and perhaps much that had been better left unsaid; but he who with the conviction in his soul of a great wrong done set out to weave this tapestry finds himself at last slashing madly at figures drawn with wool and driving his pen through an arras to prick rats, until from this war with pretence and figments he turns to eye reality in that human being he has followed from a warm and tranquil June evening in Richmond forty-four years ago, and eyeing it stays content, his faith renewed.

EXPLICIT

APPENDIX

THE PRINCE OF WALES AT OXFORD.

A Record and an Appreciation.

The appointment of the Prince of Wales to be aide-de-camp to Sir John French's Staff, which was referred to in " The Times " yesterday, was gazetted last night.

(By the President of Magdalen.)

The war cut short many things. Amongst them it cut short the Prince of Wales's Oxford time. He was to have returned for yet one more term, and added something further to his education, to his studies, to his sports, to his Oxford friendships and memories. It would have been very pleasant for Oxford and for his college and for himself. He would have mingled with yet a third generation of young Oxford Englishmen as happily as he had mingled with two.

But this was not to be. The Prince, and this is what he would have wished, has suffered the common lot of his compeers. Like two-thirds and more of the men with whom he was up, like ever so many " second year " men of 1914, he was swept off into the service of his country, and his second year of Oxford has proved his last. It is the more fortunate that he has given these two years uninterruptedly and to the full. Those who knew him well, who remember his advent and saw him often throughout his course, will agree that few undergraduates, taking things all round, could have got more, if so much, out of two fast-fleeting years. The Prince arrived, at a little over 18, well forward in the studies and training of the Navy—moral, physical, and intellectual—but naturally somewhat newer to, and less directly prepared for, university life and studies than the Public School boy.

" Par Inter Pares."

In a very few weeks, however, he began to find his feet and develop rapidly. From the first he took his own line, with equal modesty and firmness, determined in his own mind that he would be really *par inter pares*, that he would seek and accept no tribute except on his merits, that he would take as habitual and as assiduous trouble to avoid deference or preference as others take to cultivate it, desiring, as the old Roman poet put it, " that men should give, what he wanted, but that they should be free to deny ": *Quodque dari voluit, voluit sibi posse negari.* His natural dignity and charm, and, it should be added, the good sense and good feeling of his college companions, and of Oxford generally, that democratic aristocracy, enabled him to go far in this resolve without mishap or untoward result. Once having started upon it, he pursued this narrow, nice line with increased confidence, until it seemed the most easy and natural and unconscious thing in the world.

Some sacrifice had to be made. He saw very little of the seniors in the University, and was little seen by them, except by those with whom he came officially in contact. He did not want to spend any time at all, even a little, in being treated *en prince.* But all the more he made a wide acquaintance with a great variety of juniors. Neither his equerry, Major the Hon. William Cadogan, whose soldier's death will place Oxford in mourning, and in whom Magdalen College loses one who had become an intimate and personal friend, nor his tutor, Mr H. P. Hansell, stood in the way of this. Indeed, they only helped him to it. His rooms were more and more open to his friends and to his friends' friends. He went in turn to scores of rooms of other men.

GAMES AND SPORTS.

He played football, lawn tennis, golf, tennis, and squash rackets; he motored; he ran with the college boats, he ran a great deal with the beagles, he shot at various country houses round Oxford; he rode, for exercise, and to hounds. In this last accomplishment he started at a disadvantage; but by real perseverance and pluck soon made up for it and became quite proficient, though among one of the genuine losses involved by the loss of another winter at Oxford is the missing of yet further days with the Oxford hunts. He was withal a punctual and diligent member, in the ranks, of the O.T.C. He drilled, he marched, he went into camp like any other private.

As to his set studies, his time was short. It was not clear at the first that he would have the second year; the career for which he was to prepare was a unique one. Strict educational " economy " had to be practised. French, German, and English, especially the command of literary expression in his own language, were necessary for him. History, political economy, political science, and constitutional law were desirable.

Sir William Anson's Influence.

For this last study he was singularly fortunate in having at hand one of the first living authorities, and perhaps the first living teacher, in the late Sir William Anson. Young himself in mind and body to the last, a country gentleman and sportsman, as well as a great jurist and publicist, and singularly happy in his relations with undergraduates, Sir William Anson at once put the Prince at his ease, and there sprung up between them a friendship which grew and strengthened every term. Together, beginning with the British system, they went through the Constitutions of the world, if not from China to Peru, yet literally from Switzerland to Japan, the Prince reading and writing and taking notes, Sir William talking and expounding. His " hour with the Warden " was a pleasure to which he looked forward every week, and it was indeed a singular coincidence and piece of good fortune that the removal of this friend and teacher, sad and sudden as it was, did not occur until just before the end of the Prince's undergraduate time.

Lectures and Tutors.

Side by side with this, the Prince attended lectures on history, on political economy, and on political science. He also had many special hours of instruction with the University teachers of French and German, Mr Berthon, the University lecturer in French, and Professor Fiedler, the Professor of German. He further went for special tuition in history to Mr C. Grant Robertson and Mr A. L. F. Smith, the college tutors in that subject, and once every week he wrote an English essay for the president. Lectures he chiefly attended in the earlier part of his career. More and more as time went on he found that he preferred the Oxford system of private and individual tuition in which the pupil writes or prepares work and his work is criticised, and he is " catechised " orally by his tutor, to the system of the larger general lectures. He found that he learned more, and more quickly, under the first method, and, indeed, that is the usual experience of Oxford students, and is the *raison d'être* of the " Tutorial Classes " which have recently been added with such remarkable effect to the old extension lectures for working-men. It is interesting to find that Prince and working-man as pupils are at one on this point. He learned, as J. K. Stephen says in his poem, first " to write and then to read," and then, it may be added, to write again, for both arts go together. Like other writers, young and old, he soon found that he could write best about a subject for which he really cared, and also that when he cared for a subject he could make it more truly his own by writing about it.

It is interesting to notice how his command of all three languages proceeded together, and how he acquired a sense of literary style, as regards both arrangement and form, in both English and French, at much the same rate. His essays, which at first were conscientious reproductions and compilations, became more and more his own, both in thought and expression. In the end, though not yet 20 and only at the age when many sixth form boys are just beginning Oxford, he acquired a considerable mastery. Gifted with a good verbal memory, a freshness of view, and decided independence of character, his essays, if not exactly literary, became more and more interesting, and again and again were striking and eloquent, if only in their genuine sincerity and simple honesty.

THE PRINCE'S QUALITIES.

Bookish he will never be: not a " Beauclerk," still less a " British Solomon." Kings, perhaps fortunately, seldom are this last. That is not to be desired, but the Prince of Wales will not want for power of ready and forcible presentation, either in speech or writing. And all the time he was learning more and more every day of men, gauging character, watching its play, getting to know what Englishmen are like, both individually and still more in the mass.

Oxford might then have given him a little more. The cumulative influence of her studies and her life might have deepened still further, but she has given him essentially what she had to give. He leaves her, if young, already able to be, what England expects him to be, a force and a factor in national life. If the *rôle* of Princes in a constitutional country is to guide rather than to dominate, to persuade rather than to compel, to influence by the attraction of character and personality, and the example of the chivalry of modern days, and of duty, stedfastly and eagerly if unostentatiously pursued, he stands on the threshold of life to-day wanting neither in natural gifts nor in such preparation in its more modern form as it has been the privilege of England's ancient and historic schools and seminaries of " true religion and useful learning " from age to age to confer upon each succeeding generation of her sons.

The Times, Nov. 18th 1914.

T

AUTHORITIES

The Almanach de Gotha.
The Annual Register for all the period covered.
The Book of Common Prayer.
The Cambridge Modern History.
The Catholic Encyclopædia.
The Complete Peerage.
The Dictionary of National Biography.
The Encyclopædia Britannica.
The Gentleman's Magazine.
The Dictionary of Religion and Ethics.
The Illustrated London News.
Notes and Queries.
Parliamentary Debates.
The Parliamentary History.
The Times.
Who's Who.
Who Was Who.
And personal reminiscence throughout.

Actors by Gaslight or " Boz " in the Boxes.

Arbellot, S.	Edouard VIII, Roi Moderne. Paris, 1936.
Arthur, Sir George.	Seven Heirs Apparent, 1937.
Beaverbrook, Lord.	Politicians and the Press, 1926.
Belloc, Hilaire.	James the Second, 1928.
Benson, E. F.	Queen Victoria. New York, 1935.
Birch, Dr.	Life of Henry, Prince of Wales, 1760.

Blackfriars.
British Documents on the Origins of the War, 1938.

Buckingham and Chandos, Duke of.	Memoirs of Courts and Cabinets of George III, 1853.
Burges, J. Bland.	Selections from Letters and Correspondence, 1885.
Burke, Edmund.	Speeches, 1816.
Campbell, Lady Charlotte.	Diary Illustrative of the Times of George IV, 1838.
Carroll, Lewis.	Alice's Adventures in Wonderland.

Carroll, Lewis. Alice Through the Looking-Glass.

Cavendish, Charlotte. H.M. Queen Mary, 1930.

Ceylon Times.

Channon, Henry. The Ludwigs of Bavaria, 1933.

Childe-Pemberton, W. The Romance of Princess Amelia, 1910.

The Church and Marriage. The Report of the Joint Committee of the Convocations of Canterbury and York, 1935.

The Church and Marriage. Some Comments on the Report of the Joint Committee of Convocation on Marriage—published on behalf of the Church Union.

The Church Times.

Constitutions and Canons Ecclesiastical. Ed. J. V. Bullard.

Cooke, Sir C. Kinloch-. A Memoir of H.R.H. Princess Mary Adelaide, Duchess of Teck, 1900.

Cooke, Sir C. Kinloch-. Life of Queen Mary, 1911.

Corti, Count Egon. The Downfall of Three Dynasties, based on the letters and diaries of Prince Alexander of Hesse-Darmstadt, 1934.

Corti, Count Egon. Elizabeth, Empress of Austria, 1936.

Coxe, William. Memoirs of Sir R. Walpole 1798.

Cranmer, T., and Others. *Reformatio Legum Ecclesiasticarum*, 1571.

The Creevey Papers. Ed. Maxwell, 1903.

Creevey's Life and Times. Ed. John Gore, 1934.

The Croker Papers. Ed. Jennings, 1884.

Curties, Henry. A Forgotten Prince of Wales, 1912.

Daily Chronicle.
Daily Express.
Daily Herald.
Daily Mail.

Daily News.
Daily Sun-Times (Ontario).
D'Arblay, Madame. — Diary and Letters. Ed. Barrett, 1904.
Delany, Mrs. — Autobiography and Correspondence. Ed. Lady Llanover, 1865.
Dibdin, L., and Chadwyck-Healey. — English Church Law and Divorce, 1912.
Doctrine in the Church of England. The Report of the Commissions on Christian Doctrine Appointed by the Archbishops of Canterbury and York, 1922.
Dodington, Bubb. — Diary. Ed. Wyndham, 1828.
Dolling, R. R. — Ten Years in a Portsmouth Slum, 1896.

Dundee Advertiser.
Princess Elizabeth, Landgravine of Hesse-Homburg. — Letters. Ed. P. Yorke, 1898.
Esher, Lord. — Journals and Letters of Reginald, Viscount Esher. Ed. Maurice Brett, 1934–1938.

Etough, H. — MS. Letter to Dr Birch.
Farington, J. — Diary. Ed. J. Grieg, 1928.
Felbermann, L. — The House of Teck, 1904.
Fitzgerald, P. — The Life of George IV., 1881.
Fitzgerald, P. — Royal Dukes and Duchesses of the Family of George III, 1882.
Fitzgerald, P. — Life and Times of William IV.
Fitzmaurice, Lord. — Life of William, Earl of Shelburne, 1875.
Fitzroy, Sir A. — Memoirs. Hutchinson, 1925.
Fox, Charles James. — Early Part of the Reign of James the Second, 1886.
Fox, Charles James. — Memorials and Correspondence. Ed. Lord John Russell, 1882.
Frederica Sophia Wilhelmina, Princess Royal of Prussia, Margravine of Bayreuth. — Memoirs, 1828.

Fulford, Roger. George IV, 1935.

Fulford, Roger. Royal Dukes, 1933.

George III. Correspondence from 1760 to 1783. Ed. Fortescue.

Gibbs, Philip. Ordeal in England, England Speaks Again. 1937.

Gladstone, W. E. Gleanings of Past Years (1843–1878).

Gladstone, W. E. Letters to his Wife. Ed. Tilney-Bassett. Methuen, 1936.

Glueck-Rosenthal, L. Memoir of H.R.H. the Duke of Sussex, 1846.

Graham, Evelyn. Edward, P., a New and Intimate Life Story of H.R.H. The Prince of Wales, 1929.

The Gramophone. January, 1937.

Green, John. Mr. Baldwin.

The Grenville Papers.

Gretton, R. H. A Modern History of the English People, 1913.

Greville, C. F. Memoirs. Ed. Henry Reeve, 1888.

The Greville Diary. Ed. P. W. Wilson, 1927.

Gunther, John. Inside Europe. New York, 1938.

Hallam, Henry. Constitutional History of England.

Halifax, George Savile Marquis of. Works. Ed. Foxcroft, 1898.

Hamilton, General Sir Ian. Gallipoli Diary, 1920.

Hammond, J. le B. Charles James Fox, a political study, 1903.

Herbert, A. P. The Ayes Have it, 1937.

Hervey, John, Lord Some Materials towards Memoirs of the Reign of George II.

Historical Fragment. 1824.

Homilies and Canons of the Church of England. S.P.C.K. 1864.

Huish, R. Memoirs of Her late Royal Highness Charlotte Augusta, 1818.

Huish, R. — Memoirs of Caroline, Queen of Great Britain, 1821.

Huish, R. — The Public and Private Life of George III, 1821.

Ilchester, Countess of, and Lord Stavordale. — The Life and Letters of Lady Sarah Lennox, 1701.

The Isis.

Jennings, Ivor. — Cabinet Government.

Jerrold, Clare. — Early Court of Queen Victoria, 1912.

Jesse, J. Heneage. — Life and Reign of George III.

Jesse, J. Heneage. — Memoirs of the Court of England from the Revolution of 1688 to the Death of George II, 1843.

Junius. — Letters. Ed. J. M. Good, 1889.

Keith, A. Berriedale. — Privileges and Rights of the Crown, 1936.

Keith, A. Berriedale. — The King, the Constitution, the Empire and Foreign Affairs, 1937.

Keith, A. Berriedale. — The King and the Imperial Crown, the Powers and Duties of His Majesty, 1936.

Kipling, Rudyard. — Something of Myself, 1937.

Lecky, W. E. H. — History of England in the Eighteenth Century, 1892.

Lee, Sidney. — Queen Victoria, 1904.

Lee, Sidney. — King Edward VII, 1927.

Leeds, Stanton B. — Cards the Windsors Hold. New York, 1937.

Leslie, Shane. — George IV, 1926.

Lingard, John. — History of England, 1849.

Liverpool Times.

The Lockhart Papers. — Memoirs and Commentaries on the Affairs of Scotland from 1702 to 1715, by George Lockhart.

Lucas, R. J. — Lord North, 2nd Earl of Guilford, 1913.

Lucas, R. J. — Prince Francis of Teck, 1910.

Mackenzie, Compton.   Gallipoli Memories, 1929.

Mackenzie, Compton.   First Athenian Memories, 1931.

Mackinnon, A.   The Oxford Amateurs, 1910.

Macky, J.   Memoirs of the Secret Service. Ed. A. R., 1733.

Maclean's Magazine.   Jan. 15, 1937.

Magnus, Laurie.   Herbert Warren of Magdalen, 1932.

Maine, Basil.   Edward VIII, Duke of Windsor, 1937.

Malmesbury, James Harris, 1st Earl of.   Diaries, 1844.

Malortie, C. E. Von.   Beitraege zur Geschichte des Braunschweig-Lueneburgischen Hauses und Hofes, Hanover, 1860–1872.

Martin, Kingsley.   The Magic of Monarchy, 1937.

Melville, Lewis.   The First George, 1906.

Merris, V. R.   Eduard, Herzog von Windsor, Vienna, 1937.

Moore, Harras.   The Prince of Wales and his Bride, 1921.

Morley, John.   Life of William Ewart Gladstone, 1903.

News Chronicle.

New York Journal.

Nicolson, Hon. Harold.   Curzon: The Last Phase (1919–1925), 1934.

Nottingham Express.

The Observer.

Owen, Frank and Thompson, R. J.   His Was the Kingdom, 1937.

Ottawa Citizen.

Oxford.

Oxford and Asquith, Lord.   Memories and Reflections, 1928.

Papendiek, Mrs.   Court and Private Life in the Time of Queen Charlotte, 1887.

Parkhurst, Genevieve.   A King in the Making, 1925.

Paris-Soir.

Pendered, Mary L. — The Fair Quaker, 1910.

Public Advertiser.

Punch.

The Recall to Religion. — 1937.

Reynolds' News.

Roberts, E. Bechhofer. — Stanley Baldwin: Man or Miracle? 1936.

Rockingham, Marquis of. — Memoirs. Ed. Earl of Albemarle, 1852.

Ronaldshay, Lord. — Life of Lord Curzon, 1928.

Sanders, L. C. — Lord Melbourne's Papers, 1889.

Selwyn, George. — Letters (ed. Roscoe and Clergue), 1899.

Selwyn, George and his Contemporaries. — Letters. Ed. Jesse, 1843.

Sheppard, Canon Edgar. — George, Duke of Cambridge, a Memoir of his Private Life, 1906.

Sherwood, W. E. — Oxford Rowing, 1906.

Sitwell, Edith. — Victoria of England, 1936.

Society in London, 1885.

Somervell, D. C. — The Reign of King George V, 1936.

Sophie in London, 1786. — Being the Diary of Sophie von la Roche. Ed. Williams, 1933.

Strachey, G. Lytton. — Queen Victoria, 1921.

Sunday Express.

Sunday Dispatch.

Sunday Times.

Sydney Daily Telegraph.

Sydney Morning Herald.

Thackeray, W. M. — The Four Georges.

Trevelyan, Sir G. O. — The Early History of Charles James Fox, 1889.

Vehse, Eduard. — Geschichte der Höfe des Hauses Braunschweig in Deutschland und England.

Verney, Frank E. — H.R.H.—A Character Study of the Prince of Wales, 1926.

Vulliamy, C. E. — Royal George, A Study of George III, 1937.

Wakeman, H. O. — An Introduction to the History of the Church of England, 1914.

Walpole, Horace. — Letters. Ed. Toynbee, 1903.

Walpole, Horace. — Memoirs of the Reign of George II. Ed. Holland, 1857.

Walpole, Horace. — Journal of the Reign of George III. Ed. Doran, 1859.

Warren, T. H. — Christian Victor, the Story of a Young Soldier, 1903.

Wells, Warre Bradley. — Why Edward Went. New York, 1938.

The Week.

White, J. Lincoln. — The Abdication of Edward VIII, 1937.

Whyte, A. Gowans. — Stanley Baldwin, 1926.

Wilkins, W. H. — The Love of an Uncrowned Queen, Sophia Dorothea, Consort of George I, 1903.

Wilkins, W. H. — A Queen of Tears, Caroline Matilda, Queen of Denmark, 1904.

Wilkins, W. H. — Mrs Fitzherbert and George IV, 1905.

Wilson, E. H. — The Duchess of Windsor, 1937.

Worcester Herald.

Wraxall, Sir C. F. L. — Life and Times of Caroline Matilda, 1864.

Wraxall, Sir Nathaniel. — Historical and Posthumous Memoirs of his Own Time, 1884.

The Yellow Book.

Yorkshire Post.

Young, Sir George. — Poor Fred, the People's Prince, 1937.